INTERNATIONAL INTELLECTUAL PROPERTY: LAW AND POLICY

DOCUMENTARY SUPPLEMENT

INTERNATIONAL INTELLECTUAL PROPERTY: LAW AND POLICY
DOCUMENTARY SUPPLEMENT

Graeme B. Dinwoodie
Professor of Law
Chicago-Kent College of Law

William O. Hennessey
Professor of Law
Franklin Pierce Law Center

Shira Perlmutter
Vice President and Associate General Counsel,
Intellectual Property Policy, AOL Time Warner, Inc
Former Associate Register for Policy and International Affairs,
U.S. Copyright Office
Former Consultant on Copyright and Electronic Commerce,
World Intellectual Property Organization

:

ISBN: 0-8205-4526-0

This publication is designed to provide accurate and authoritative information in regard to the subject matter covered. It is sold with the understanding that the publisher is not engaged in rendering legal, accounting, or other professional services. If legal advice or other expert assistance is required, the services of a competent professional should be sought.

LexisNexis, the knowledge burst logo, and Michie are trademarks of Reed Elsevier Properties Inc, used under license. Matthew Bender is a registered trademark of Matthew Bender Properties Inc.

Editorial Offices
744 Broad Street, Newark, NJ 07102 (973) 820-2000
201 Mission St., San Francisco, CA 94105-1831 (415) 908-3200
www.lexisnexis.com
Pub. 3068

Preface

This supplement contains the leading treaties, directives and other documents pertinent to the study of international intellectual property law and policy. Many of these documents can be found online on the web sites of the World Intellectual Property Organization (www.wipo.int) the European Union (www.europa.eu.int) or the World Trade Organization (www.wto.org). As a general rule, we have included in this volume only agreements or laws that have been adopted or enacted (although not necessarily yet in force). There are countless additional proposed treaties, directives and resolutions on intellectual property; indeed, we have excerpted many of these proposals in our casebook. Links to these additional documents in their entirety, along with many other documents relevant to international intellectual property law and policy, can be found at www.kentlaw.edu/classes/gdinwood/iipl/sup_mat/index.html; this site is periodically updated to reflect the latest developments in this field. Continually updated lists of parties to the different multinational treaties administered by the World Intellectual Property Organization can be found at www.wipo.int/treaties/general/parties.html#1.

We are very grateful to Eric Moran and Sheng Wu for their assistance in compiling these materials.

G.B.D
W.O.H.
S.P.

TABLE OF CONTENTS

Page

v

E. Industrial Designs

F. Patent Law

G. Copyright and Related Rights

Page

A. INTERNATIONAL INSTITUTIONS

CONVENTION ESTABLISHING THE
WORLD INTELLECTUAL PROPERTY ORGANIZATION
Signed at Stockholm on July 14, 1967, as amended
on September 28, 1979

The Contracting Parties,

Desiring to contribute to better understanding and cooperation among States for their mutual benefit on the basis of respect for their sovereignty and equality,

Desiring, in order to encourage creative activity, to promote the protection of intellectual property throughout the world,

Desiring to modernize and render more efficient the administration of the Unions established in the fields of the protection of industrial property and the protection of literary and artistic works, while fully respecting the independence of each of the Unions,

Agree as follows:

Article 1
Establishment of the Organization

The World Intellectual Property Organization is hereby established.

Article 2
Definitions

For the purposes of this Convention:

  (i)   "Organization" shall mean the World Intellectual Property Organization (WIPO);

  (ii) "International Bureau" shall mean the International Bureau of Intellectual Property;

  (iii) "Paris Convention" shall mean the Convention for the Protection of Industrial Property signed on March 20, 1883, including any of its revisions;

  (iv) "Berne Convention" shall mean the Convention for the Protection of Literary and Artistic Works signed on September 9, 1886, including any of its revisions;

  (v)   "Paris Union" shall mean the International Union established by the Paris Convention;

  (vi) "Berne Union" shall mean the International Union established by the Berne Convention;

  (vii) "Unions" shall mean the Paris Union, the Special Unions and Agreements established in relation with that Union, the Berne Union, and any other international agreement designed to

1

promote the protection of intellectual property whose administration is assumed by the Organization according to Article 4(iii);

 (viii) "intellectual property" shall include the rights relating to:

- literary, artistic and scientific works,
- performances of performing artists, phonograms, and broadcasts,
- inventions in all fields of human endeavor,
- scientific discoveries,
- industrial designs,
- trademarks, service marks, and commercial names and designations,
- protection against unfair competition,

and all other rights resulting from intellectual activity in the industrial, scientific, literary or artistic fields.

Article 3
Objectives of the Organization

The objectives of the Organization are:

 (i) to promote the protection of intellectual property throughout the world through cooperation among States and, where appropriate, in collaboration with any other international organization,

 (ii) to ensure administrative cooperation among the Unions.

Article 4
Functions

In order to attain the objectives described in Article 3, the Organization, through its appropriate organs, and subject to the competence of each of the Unions:

 (i) shall promote the development of measures designed to facilitate the efficient protection of intellectual property throughout the world and to harmonize national legislation in this field;

 (ii) shall perform the administrative tasks of the Paris Union, the Special Unions established in relation with that Union, and the Berne Union;

 (iii) may agree to assume, or participate in, the administration of any other international agreement designed to promote the protection of intellectual property;

 (iv) shall encourage the conclusion of international agreements designed to promote the protection of intellectual property;

 (v) shall offer its cooperation to States requesting legal-technical assistance in the field of intellectual property;

 (vi) shall assemble and disseminate information concerning the protection of intellectual property, carry out and promote studies in this field, and publish the results of such studies;

(vii) shall maintain services facilitating the international protection of intellectual property and, where appropriate, provide for registration in this field and the publication of the data concerning the registrations;

(viii) shall take all other appropriate action.

Article 5
Membership

(1) Membership in the Organization shall be open to any State which is a member of any of the Unions as defined in Article 2(vii).

(2) Membership in the Organization shall be equally open to any State not a member of any of the Unions, provided that:

(i) it is a member of the United Nations, any of the Specialized Agencies brought into relationship with the United Nations, or the International Atomic Energy Agency, or is a party to the Statute of the International Court of Justice, or

(ii) it is invited by the General Assembly to become a party to this Convention.

Article 6
General Assembly

(1)

(a) There shall be a General Assembly consisting of the States party to this Convention which are members of any of the Unions.

(b) The Government of each State shall be represented by one delegate, who may be assisted by alternate delegates, advisors, and experts.

(c) The expenses of each delegation shall be borne by the Government which has appointed it.

(2) The General Assembly shall:

(i) appoint the Director General upon nomination by the Coordination Committee;

(ii) review and approve reports of the Director General concerning the Organization and give him all necessary instructions;

(iii) review and approve the reports and activities of the Coordination Committee and give instructions to such Committee;

(iv) adopt the biennial budget of expenses common to the Unions;

(v) approve the measures proposed by the Director General concerning the administration of the international agreements referred to in Article 4(iii);

(vi) adopt the financial regulations of the Organization;

(vii) determine the working languages of the Secretariat, taking into consideration the practice of the United Nations;

(viii) invite States referred to under Article 5(2)(ii) to become party to this Convention;

(ix)   determine which States not Members of the Organization and which intergovernmental and international non-governmental organizations shall be admitted to its meetings as observers;

(x)   exercise such other functions as are appropriate under this Convention.

(3)

(a) Each State, whether member of one or more Unions, shall have one vote in the General Assembly.

(b) One-half of the States members of the General Assembly shall constitute a quorum.

(c) Notwithstanding the provisions of subparagraph (b), if, in any session, the number of States represented is less than one-half but equal to or more than one-third of the States members of the General Assembly, the General Assembly may make decisions but, with the exception of decisions concerning its own procedure, all such decisions shall take effect only if the following conditions are fulfilled. The International Bureau shall communicate the said decisions to the States members of the General Assembly which were not represented and shall invite them to express in writing their vote or abstention within a period of three months from the date of the communication. If, at the expiration of this period, the number of States having thus expressed their vote or abstention attains the number of States which was lacking for attaining the quorum in the session itself, such decisions shall take effect provided that at the same time the required majority still obtains.

(d) Subject to the provisions of subparagraphs (e) and (f), the General Assembly shall make its decisions by a majority of two-thirds of the votes cast.

(e) The approval of measures concerning the administration of international agreements referred to in Article 4(iii) shall require a majority of three-fourths of the votes cast.

(f) The approval of an agreement with the United Nations under Articles 57 and 63 of the Charter of the United Nations shall require a majority of nine-tenths of the votes cast.

(g) For the appointment of the Director General (paragraph (2)(i)), the approval of measures proposed by the Director General concerning the administration of international agreements (paragraph (2)(v)), and the transfer of headquarters (Article 10), the required majority must be attained not only in the General Assembly but also in the Assembly of the Paris Union and the Assembly of the Berne Union.

(h) Abstentions shall not be considered as votes.

(i) A delegate may represent, and vote in the name of, one State only.

(4)

(a) The General Assembly shall meet once in every second calendar year in ordinary session, upon convocation by the Director General.

(b) The General Assembly shall meet in extraordinary session upon convocation by the Director General either at the request of the Coordination Committee or at the request of one-fourth of the States members of the General Assembly.

(c) Meetings shall be held at the headquarters of the Organization.

(5) States party to this Convention which are not members of any of the Unions shall be admitted to the meetings of the General Assembly as observers.

(6) The General Assembly shall adopt its own rules of procedure.

Article 7
Conference

(1)

(a) There shall be a Conference consisting of the States party to this Convention whether or not they are members of any of the Unions.

(b) The Government of each State shall be represented by one delegate, who may be assisted by alternate delegates, advisors, and experts.

(c) The expenses of each delegation shall be borne by the Government which has appointed it.

(2) The Conference shall:

(i)   discuss matters of general interest in the field of intellectual property and may adopt recommendations relating to such matters, having regard for the competence and autonomy of the Unions;

(ii) adopt the biennial budget of the Conference;

(iii) within the limits of the budget of the Conference, establish the biennial program of legal-technical assistance;

(iv) adopt amendments to this Convention as provided in Article 17;

(v)   determine which States not Members of the Organization and which intergovernmental and international non-governmental organizations shall be admitted to its meetings as observers;

(vi) exercise such other functions as are appropriate under this Convention.

(3)

(a) Each Member State shall have one vote in the Conference.

(b) One-third of the Member States shall constitute a quorum.

(c) Subject to the provisions of Article 17, the Conference shall make its decisions by a majority of two-thirds of the votes cast.

(d) The amounts of the contributions of States party to this Convention

not members of any of the Unions shall be fixed by a vote in which only the delegates of such States shall have the right to vote.

(e) Abstentions shall not be considered as votes.

(f) A delegate may represent, and vote in the name of, one State only.

(4)

(a) The Conference shall meet in ordinary session, upon convocation by the Director General, during the same period and at the same place as the General Assembly.

(b) The Conference shall meet in extraordinary session, upon convocation by the Director General, at the request of the majority of the Member States.

(5) The Conference shall adopt its own rules of procedure.

Article 8
Coordination Committee

(1)

(a) There shall be a Coordination Committee consisting of the States party to this Convention which are members of the Executive Committee of the Paris Union, or the Executive Committee of the Berne Union, or both. However, if either of these Executive Committees is composed of more than one-fourth of the number of the countries members of the Assembly which elected it, then such Executive Committee shall designate from among its members the States which will be members of the Coordination Committee, in such a way that their number shall not exceed the one-fourth referred to above, it being understood that the country on the territory of which the Organization has its headquarters shall not be included in the computation of the said one-fourth.

(b) The Government of each State member of the Coordination Committee shall be represented by one delegate, who may be assisted by alternate delegates, advisors, and experts.

(c) Whenever the Coordination Committee considers either matters of direct interest to the program or budget of the Conference and its agenda, or proposals for the amendment of this Convention which would affect the rights or obligations of States party to this Convention not members of any of the Unions, one-fourth of such States shall participate in the meetings of the Coordination Committee with the same rights as members of that Committee. The Conference shall, at each of its ordinary sessions, designate these States.

(d) The expenses of each delegation shall be borne by the Government which has appointed it.

(2) If the other Unions administered by the Organization wish to be represented as such in the Coordination Committee, their representatives must be appointed from among the States members of the Coordination Committee.

(3) The Coordination Committee shall:

(i) give advice to the organs of the Unions, the General Assembly, the Conference, and the Director General, on all administrative, financial and other matters of common interest either to two or more of the Unions, or to one or more of the Unions and the Organization, and in particular on the budget of expenses common to the Unions;

(ii) prepare the draft agenda of the General Assembly;

(iii) prepare the draft agenda and the draft program and budget of the Conference;

(iv) [deleted]

(v) when the term of office of the Director General is about to expire, or when there is a vacancy in the post of the Director General, nominate a candidate for appointment to such position by the General Assembly; if the General Assembly does not appoint its nominee, the Coordination Committee shall nominate another candidate; this procedure shall be repeated until the latest nominee is appointed by the General Assembly;

(vi) if the post of the Director General becomes vacant between two sessions of the General Assembly, appoint an Acting Director General for the term preceding the assuming of office by the new Director General;

(vii) perform such other functions as are allocated to it under this Convention.

(4)

(a) The Coordination Committee shall meet once every year in ordinary session, upon convocation by the Director General. It shall normally meet at the headquarters of the Organization.

(b) The Coordination Committee shall meet in extraordinary session, upon convocation by the Director General, either on his own initiative, or at the request of its Chairman or one-fourth of its members.

(5)

(a) Each State whether a member of one or both of the Executive Committees referred to in paragraph (1)(a), shall have one vote in the Coordination Committee.

(b) One-half of the members of the Coordination Committee shall constitute a quorum.

(c) A delegate may represent, and vote in the name of, one State only.

(6)

(a) The Coordination Committee shall express its opinions and make its decisions by a simple majority of the votes cast. Abstentions shall not be considered as votes.

(b) Even if a simple majority is obtained, any member of the Coordination Committee may, immediately after the vote, request that the votes be the subject of a special recount in the following manner: two separate lists shall be prepared, one containing the names of the States members of the Executive Committee of the Paris Union and the other the names of the States members of the Executive Committee of the Berne Union; the vote of each State shall be inscribed opposite its name in each list in which it appears. Should this special recount indicate that a simple majority has not been obtained in each of those lists, the proposal shall not be considered as carried.

(7) Any State Member of the Organization which is not a member of the Coordination Committee may be represented at the meetings of the Committee by observers having the right to take part in the debates but without the right to vote.

(8) The Coordination Committee shall establish its own rules of procedure.

Article 9
International Bureau

(1) The International Bureau shall be the Secretariat of the Organization.

(2) The International Bureau shall be directed by the Director General, assisted by two or more Deputy Directors General.

(3) The Director General shall be appointed for a fixed term, which shall be not less than six years. He shall be eligible for reappointment for fixed terms. The periods of the initial appointment and possible subsequent appointments, as well as all other conditions of the appointment, shall be fixed by the General Assembly.

(4)

(a) The Director General shall be the chief executive of the Organization.

(b) He shall represent the Organization.

(c) He shall report to, and conform to the instructions of, the General Assembly as to the internal and external affairs of the Organization.

(5) The Director General shall prepare the draft programs and budgets and periodical reports on activities. He shall transmit them to the Governments of the interested States and to the competent organs of the Unions and the Organization.

(6) The Director General and any staff member designated by him shall participate, without the right to vote, in all meetings of the General Assembly, the Conference, the Coordination Committee, and any other committee or working group. The Director General or a staff member designated by him shall be ex officio secretary of these bodies.

(7) The Director General shall appoint the staff necessary for the efficient performance of the tasks of the International Bureau. He shall appoint the Deputy Directors General after approval by the Coordination Committee. The conditions of employment shall be fixed by the staff regulations to be approved by the Coordination Committee on the proposal of the Director General. The paramount consideration in the employment of the staff and in the determination of the conditions of service shall be the necessity of

securing the highest standards of efficiency, competence, and integrity. Due regard shall be paid to the importance of recruiting the staff on as wide a geographical basis as possible.

(8) The nature of the responsibilities of the Director General and of the staff shall be exclusively international. In the discharge of their duties they shall not seek or receive instructions from any Government or from any authority external to the Organization. They shall refrain from any action which might prejudice their position as international officials. Each Member State undertakes to respect the exclusively international character of the responsibilities of the Director General and the staff, and not to seek to influence them in the discharge of their duties.

Article 10
Headquarters

(1) The headquarters of the Organization shall be at Geneva.

(2) Its transfer may be decided as provided for in Article 6(3)(d) and Article (6)(3)(g).

Article 11
Finances

(1) The Organization shall have two separate budgets: the budget of expenses common to the Unions, and the budget of the Conference.

(2)

(a) The budget of expenses common to the Unions shall include provision for expenses of interest to several Unions.

(b) This budget shall be financed from the following sources:

   (i)   contributions of the Unions, provided that the amount of the contribution of each Union shall be fixed by the Assembly of that Union, having regard to the interest the Union has in the common expenses;

   (ii) charges due for services performed by the International Bureau not in direct relation with any of the Unions or not received for services rendered by the International Bureau in the field of legal-technical assistance;

   (iii) sale of, or royalties on, the publications of the International Bureau not directly concerning any of the Unions;

   (iv) gifts, bequests, and subventions, given to the Organization, except those referred to in paragraph (3)(b)(iv);

   (v)   rents, interests, and other miscellaneous income, of the Organization.

(3)

(a) The budget of the Conference shall include provision for the expenses of holding sessions of the Conference and for the cost of the legal-technical assistance program.

(b) This budget shall be financed from the following sources:

    (i)   contributions of States party to this Convention not members of any of the Unions;

    (ii)   any sums made available to this budget by the Unions, provided that the amount of the sum made available by each Union shall be fixed by the Assembly of that Union and that each Union shall be free to abstain from contributing to the said budget;

    (iii) sums received for services rendered by the International Bureau in the field of legal-technical assistance;

    (iv) gifts, bequests, and subventions, given to the Organization for the purposes referred to in subparagraph (a).

(4)

(a) For the purpose of establishing its contribution towards the budget of the Conference, each State party to this Convention not member of any of the Unions shall belong to a class, and shall pay its annual contributions on the basis of a number of units fixed as follows:

Class A 10

Class B 3

Class C 1

(b) Each such State shall, concurrently with taking action as provided in Article 14(1), indicate the class to which it wishes to belong. Any such State may change class. If it chooses a lower class, the State must announce it to the Conference at one of its ordinary sessions. Any such change shall take effect at the beginning of the calendar year following the session.

(c) The annual contribution of each such State shall be an amount in the same proportion to the total sum to be contributed to the budget of the Conference by all such States as the number of its units is to the total of the units of all the said States.

(d) Contributions shall become due on the first of January of each year.

(e) If the budget is not adopted before the beginning of a new financial period the budget shall be at the same level as the budget of the previous year, in accordance with the financial regulations.

(5) Any State party to this Convention not member of any of the Unions which is in arrears in the payment of its financial contributions under the present Article, and any State party to this Convention member of any of the Unions which is in arrears in the payment of its contributions to any of the Unions, shall have no vote in any of the bodies of the Organization of which it is a member, if the amount of its arrears equals or exceeds the amount of the contributions due from it for the preceding two full years. However, any of these bodies may allow such a State to continue to exercise its vote in that body if, and as long as, it is satisfied that the delay in payment arises from exceptional and unavoidable circumstances.

(6) The amount of the fees and charges due for services rendered by the International Bureau in the field of legal-technical assistance shall be

established, and shall be reported to the Coordination Committee, by the Director General.

(7) The Organization, with the approval of the Coordination Committee, may receive gifts, bequests, and subventions, directly from Governments, public or private institutions, associations or private persons.

(8)

(a) The Organization shall have a working capital fund which shall be constituted by a single payment made by the Unions and by each State party to this Convention not member of any Union. If the fund becomes insufficient, it shall be increased.

(b) The amount of the single payment of each Union and its possible participation in any increase shall be decided by its Assembly.

(c) The amount of the single payment of each State party to this Convention not member of any Union and its part in any increase shall be a proportion of the contribution of that State for the year in which the fund is established or the increase decided. The proportion and the terms of payment shall be fixed by the Conference on the proposal of the Director General and after it has heard the advice of the Coordination Committee.

(9)

(a) In the headquarters agreement concluded with the State on the territory of which the Organization has its headquarters, it shall be provided that, whenever the working capital fund is insufficient, such State shall grant advances. The amount of these advances and the conditions on which they are granted shall be the subject of separate agreements, in each case, between such State and the Organization. As long as it remains under the obligation to grant advances, such State shall have an ex officio seat on the Coordination Committee.

(b) The State referred to in subparagraph (a) and the Organization shall each have the right to denounce the obligation to grant advances, by written notification. Denunciation shall take effect three years after the end of the year in which it has been notified.

(10) The auditing of the accounts shall be effected by one or more Member States, or by external auditors, as provided in the financial regulations. They shall be designated, with their agreement, by the General Assembly.

Article 12
Legal Capacity; Privileges and Immunities

(1) The Organization shall enjoy on the territory of each Member State, in conformity with the laws of that State, such legal capacity as may be necessary for the fulfillment of the Organization's objectives and for the exercise of its functions.

(2) The Organization shall conclude a headquarters agreement with the Swiss Confederation and with any other State in which the headquarters may subsequently be located.

(3) The Organization may conclude bilateral or multilateral agreements with the other Member States with a view to the enjoyment by the Organization, its officials, and representatives of all Member States, of such privileges and immunities as may be necessary for the fulfillment of its objectives and for the exercise of its functions.

(4) The Director General may negotiate and, after approval by the Coordination Committee, shall conclude and sign on behalf of the Organization the agreements referred to in paragraphs (2) and (3).

Article 13
Relations with Other Organizations

(1) The Organization shall, where appropriate, establish working relations and cooperate with other intergovernmental organizations. Any general agreement to such effect entered into with such organizations shall be concluded by the Director General after approval by the Coordination Committee.

(2) The Organization may, on matters within its competence, make suitable arrangements for consultation and cooperation with international non-governmental organizations and, with the consent of the Governments concerned, with national organizations, governmental or non-governmental. Such arrangements shall be made by the Director General after approval by the Coordination Committee.

Article 14
Becoming Party to the Convention

(1) States referred to in Article 5 may become party to this Convention and Member of the Organization by:

    (i)   signature without reservation as to ratification, or

    (ii)   signature subject to ratification followed by the deposit of an instrument of ratification, or

    (iii)   deposit of an instrument of accession.

(2) Notwithstanding any other provision of this Convention, a State party to the Paris Convention, the Berne Convention, or both Conventions, may become party to this Convention only if it concurrently ratifies or accedes to, or only after it has ratified or acceded to:

    —   either the Stockholm Act of the Paris Convention in its entirety or with only the limitation set forth in Article 20(1)(b)(i) thereof,

    —   or the Stockholm Act of the Berne Convention in its entirety or with only the limitation set forth in Article 28(1)(b)(i) thereof.

(3) Instruments of ratification or accession shall be deposited with the Director General.

Article 15
Entry into Force of the Convention

(1) This Convention shall enter into force three months after ten States members of the Paris Union and seven States members of the Berne Union have taken action as provided in Article 14(1), it being understood that, if a State is a member of both Unions, it will be counted in both groups. On that date, this Convention shall enter into force also in respect of States which, not being members of either of the two Unions, have taken action as provided in Article 14(1) three months or more prior to that date.

(2) In respect to any other State, this Convention shall enter into force three months after the date on which such State takes action as provided in Article 14(1).

Article 16
Reservations

No reservations to this Convention are permitted.

Article 17
Amendments

(1) Proposals for the amendment of this Convention may be initiated by any Member State, by the Coordination Committee, or by the Director General. Such proposals shall be communicated by the Director General to the Member States at least six months in advance of their consideration by the Conference.

(2) Amendments shall be adopted by the Conference. Whenever amendments would affect the rights and obligations of States party to this Convention not members of any of the Unions, such States shall also vote. On all other amendments proposed, only States party to this Convention members of any Union shall vote. Amendments shall be adopted by a simple majority of the votes cast, provided that the Conference shall vote only on such proposals for amendments as have previously been adopted by the Assembly of the Paris Union and the Assembly of the Berne Union according to the rules applicable in each of them regarding the adoption of amendments to the administrative provisions of their respective Conventions.

(3) Any amendment shall enter into force one month after written notifications of acceptance, effected in accordance with their respective constitutional processes, have been received by the Director General from three-fourths of the States Members of the Organization, entitled to vote on the proposal for amendment pursuant to paragraph (2), at the time the Conference adopted the amendment. Any amendments thus accepted shall bind all the States which are Members of the Organization at the time the amendment enters into force or which become Members at a subsequent date, provided that any amendment increasing the financial obligations of Member States shall bind only those States which have notified their acceptance of such amendment.

Article 18
Denunciation

(1) Any Member State may denounce this Convention by notification addressed to the Director General.

(2) Denunciation shall take effect six months after the day on which the Director General has received the notification.

Article 19
Notifications

The Director General shall notify the Governments of all Member States of:

 (i)   the date of entry into force of the Convention,

 (ii) signatures and deposits of instruments of ratification or accession,

 (iii) acceptances of an amendment to this Convention, and the date upon which the amendment enters into force,

 (iv) denunciations of this Convention.

Article 20
Final Provisions

(1)

 (a) This Convention shall be signed in a single copy in English, French, Russian and Spanish, all texts being equally authentic, and shall be deposited with the Government of Sweden.

 (b) This Convention shall remain open for signature at Stockholm until January 13, 1968.

(2) Official texts shall be established by the Director General, after consultation with the interested Governments, in German, Italian and Portuguese, and such other languages as the Conference may designate.

(3) The Director General shall transmit two duly certified copies of this Convention and of each amendment adopted by the Conference to the Governments of the States members of the Paris or Berne Unions, to the Government of any other State when it accedes to this Convention, and, on request, to the Government of any other State. The copies of the signed text of the Convention transmitted to the Governments shall be certified by the Government of Sweden.

(4) The Director General shall register this Convention with the Secretariat of the United Nations.

Article 21
Transitional Provisions

(1) Until the first Director General assumes office, references in this

Convention to the International Bureau or to the Director General shall be deemed to be references to the United International Bureaux for the Protection of Industrial, Literary and Artistic Property (also called the United International Bureaux for the Protection of Intellectual Property (BIRPI)), or its Director, respectively.

(2)

(a) States which are members of any of the Unions but which have not become party to this Convention may, for five years from the date of entry into force of this Convention, exercise, if they so desire, the same rights as if they had become party to this Convention. Any State desiring to exercise such rights shall give written notification to this effect to the Director General; this notification shall be effective on the date of its receipt. Such States shall be deemed to be members of the General Assembly and the Conference until the expiration of the said period.

(b) Upon expiration of this five-year period, such States shall have no right to vote in the General Assembly, the Conference, and the Coordination Committee.

(c) Upon becoming party to this Convention, such States shall regain such right to vote.

(3)

(a) As long as there are States members of the Paris or Berne Unions which have not become party to this Convention, the International Bureau and the Director General shall also function as the United International Bureaux for the Protection of Industrial, Literary and Artistic Property, and its Director, respectively.

(b) The staff in the employment of the said Bureaux on the date of entry into force of this Convention shall, during the transitional period referred to in subparagraph (a), be considered as also employed by the International Bureau.

(4)

(a) Once all the States members of the Paris Union have become Members of the Organization, the rights, obligations, and property, of the Bureau of that Union shall devolve on the International Bureau of the Organization.

(b) Once all the States members of the Berne Union have become Members of the Organization, the rights, obligations, and property, of the Bureau of that Union shall devolve on the International Bureau of the Organization.

AGREEMENT BETWEEN THE WORLD INTELLECTUAL PROPERTY ORGANIZATION AND THE WORLD TRADE ORGANIZATION
December 22, 1995, Geneva

Preamble

The World Intellectual Property Organization (WIPO) and the World Trade Organization (WTO),

Desiring to establish a mutually supportive relationship between them, and with a view to establishing appropriate arrangements for cooperation between them,

Agree as follows:

Article 1
Abbreviated Expressions

For the purposes of this Agreement:

(i)   "WIPO" means the World Intellectual Property Organization;

(ii)   "WTO" means the World Trade Organization;

(iii)   "International Bureau" means the International Bureau of WIPO;

(iv)   "WTO Member" means a party to the Agreement Establishing the World Trade Organization;

(v)   "the TRIPS Agreement" means the Agreement on Trade-Related Aspects of Intellectual Property Rights, Annex 1C to the Agreement Establishing the World Trade Organization;

(vi)   "Paris Convention" means the Paris Convention for the Protection of Industrial Property of March 20, 1883, as revised;

(vii)   "Paris Convention (1967)" means the Paris Convention for the Protection of Industrial Property of March 20, 1883, as revised at Stockholm on July 14, 1967;

(viii) "emblem" means, in the case of a WTO Member, any armorial bearing, flag and other State emblem of that WTO Member, or any official sign or hallmark indicating control and warranty adopted by it, and, in the case of an international intergovernmental organization, any armorial bearing, flag, other emblem, abbreviation or name of that organization.

Article 2
Laws and Regulations

(1) [Accessibility of Laws and Regulations in the WIPO Collection by WTO Members and Their Nationals] The International Bureau shall, on request, furnish to WTO Members and to nationals of WTO Members copies of laws and regulations, and copies of translations thereof, that exist in its collection, on the same terms as apply to the Member States of WIPO and to nationals

of the Member States of WIPO, respectively.

(2) [Accessibility of the Computerized Database] WTO Members and nationals of WTO Members shall have access, on the same terms as apply to the Member States of WIPO and to nationals of the Member States of WIPO, respectively, to any computerized database of the International Bureau containing laws and regulations. The WTO Secretariat shall have access, free of any charge by WIPO, to any such database.

(3) [Accessibility of Laws and Regulations in the WIPO Collection by the WTO Secretariat and the Council for TRIPS]

(a) Where, on the date of its initial notification of a law or regulation under Article 63.2 of the TRIPS Agreement, a WTO Member has already communicated that law or regulation, or a translation thereof, to the International Bureau and that WTO Member has sent to the WTO Secretariat a statement to that effect, and that law, regulation or translation actually exists in the collection of the International Bureau, the International Bureau shall, on request of the WTO Secretariat, give, free of charge, a copy of the said law, regulation or translation to the WTO Secretariat.

(b) Furthermore, if, for the purposes of carrying out its obligations under Article 68 of the TRIPS Agreement, such as monitoring the operation of the TRIPS Agreement or providing assistance in the context of dispute settlement procedures, the Council for TRIPS of the WTO requires a copy of a law or regulation, or a copy of a translation thereof, which had not previously been given to the WTO Secretariat under subparagraph (a), and which exists in the collection of the International Bureau, the International Bureau shall, upon request of either the Council for TRIPS or the WTO Secretariat, give to the WTO Secretariat, free of charge, the requested copy.

(c) The International Bureau shall, on request, furnish to the WTO Secretariat on the same terms as apply to Member States of WIPO any additional copies of the laws, regulations and translations given under subparagraph (a) or (b), as well as copies of any other laws and regulations, and copies of translations thereof, which exist in the collection of the International Bureau.

(d) The International Bureau shall not put any restriction on the use that the WTO Secretariat may make of the copies of laws, regulations and translations transmitted under subparagraph (a), (b) or (c).

(4) [Laws and Regulations Received by the WTO Secretariat from WTO Members]

(a) The WTO Secretariat shall transmit to the International Bureau, free of charge, a copy of the laws and regulations received by the WTO Secretariat from WTO Members under Article 63.2 of the TRIPS Agreement in the language or languages and in the form or forms in which they were received, and the International Bureau shall place such copies in its collection.

(b) The WTO Secretariat shall not put any restriction on the further use that the International Bureau may make of the copies of the laws and regulations transmitted under subparagraph (a).

(5) [Translation of Laws and Regulations] The International Bureau shall make available to developing country WTO Members which are not Member States of WIPO the same assistance for translation of laws and regulations for the purposes of Article 63.2 of the TRIPS Agreement as it makes available to Members of WIPO which are developing countries.

Article 3
Implementation of Article 6*ter* of the Paris Convention for the Purposes of the TRIPS Agreement

(1) [General]

(a) The procedures relating to communication of emblems and transmittal of objections under the TRIPS Agreement shall be administered by the International Bureau in accordance with the procedures applicable under Article 6*ter* of the Paris Convention (1967).

(b) The International Bureau shall not recommunicate to a State party to the Paris Convention which is a WTO Member an emblem which had already been communicated to it by the International Bureau under Article 6*ter* of the Paris Convention prior to January 1, 1996, or, where that State became a WTO Member after January 1, 1996, prior to the date on which it became a WTO Member, and the International Bureau shall not transmit any objection received from the said WTO Member concerning the said emblem if the objection is received by the International Bureau more than 12 months after receipt of the communication of the said emblem under Article 6*ter* of the Paris Convention by the said State.

(2) [Objections] Notwithstanding paragraph (1)(a), any objection received by the International Bureau from a WTO Member which concerns an emblem that had been communicated to the International Bureau by another WTO Member where at least one of the said WTO Members is not party to the Paris Convention, and any objection which concerns an emblem of an international intergovernmental organization and which is received by the International Bureau from a WTO Member not party to the Paris Convention or not bound under the Paris Convention to protect emblems of international intergovernmental organizations, shall be transmitted by the International Bureau to the WTO Member or international intergovernmental organization concerned regardless of the date on which the objection had been received by the International Bureau. The provisions of the preceding sentence shall not affect the time limit of 12 months for the lodging of an objection.

(3) [Information to Be Provided to the WTO Secretariat] The International Bureau shall provide to the WTO Secretariat information relating to any emblem communicated by a WTO Member to the International Bureau or communicated by the International Bureau to a WTO Member.

Article 4
Legal-Technical Assistance and Technical Cooperation

(1) [Availability of Legal-Technical Assistance and Technical Cooperation] The International Bureau shall make available to developing country WTO Members which are not Member States of WIPO the same legal-technical assistance relating to the TRIPS Agreement as it makes available to Member States of WIPO which are developing countries. The WTO Secretariat shall make available to Member States of WIPO which are developing countries and are not WTO Members the same technical cooperation relating to the TRIPS Agreement as it makes available to developing country WTO Members.

(2) [Cooperation Between the International Bureau and the WTO Secretariat] The International Bureau and the WTO Secretariat shall enhance cooperation in their legal-technical assistance and technical cooperation activities relating to the TRIPS Agreement for developing countries, so as to maximize the usefulness of those activities and ensure their mutually supportive nature.

(3) [Exchange of Information] For the purposes of paragraphs (1) and (2), the International Bureau and the WTO Secretariat shall keep in regular contact and exchange non-confidential information.

Article 5
Final Clauses

(1) [Entry into Force of this Agreement] This Agreement shall enter into force on January 1, 1996.

(2) [Amendment of this Agreement] This Agreement may be amended by common agreement of the parties to this Agreement.

(3) [Termination of this Agreement] If one of the parties to this Agreement gives the other party written notice to terminate this Agreement, this Agreement shall terminate one year after receipt of the notice by the other party, unless a longer period is specified in the notice or unless both parties agree on a longer or a shorter period.

MEMORANDUM OF UNDERSTANDING BETWEEN THE U.S. DEPARTMENT OF COMMERCE AND INTERNET CORPORATION FOR ASSIGNED NAMES AND NUMBERS

November 25, 1998

I. PARTIES

This document constitutes an agreement between the U.S. Department of Commerce (DOC or USG) and the Internet Corporation for Assigned Names and Numbers (ICANN), a not-for-profit corporation.

II. PURPOSE

A. Background

On July 1, 1997, as part of the Administration's Framework for Global Electronic Commerce, the President directed the Secretary of Commerce to privatize the management of the domain name system (DNS) in a manner that increases competition and facilitates international participation in its management.

On June 5, 1998, the DOC published its Statement of Policy, Management of Internet Names and Addresses, 63 Fed. Reg. 31741(1998) (Statement of Policy). The Statement of Policy addressed the privatization of the technical management of the DNS in a manner that allows for the development of robust competition in the management of Internet names and addresses. In the Statement of Policy, the DOC stated its intent to enter an agreement with a not-for-profit entity to establish a process to transition current U.S. Government management of the DNS to such an entity based on the principles of stability, competition, bottom-up coordination, and representation.

B. Purpose

Before making a transition to private sector DNS management, the DOC requires assurances that the private sector has the capability and resources to assume the important responsibilities related to the technical management of the DNS. To secure these assurances, the Parties will collaborate on this DNS Project (DNS Project). In the DNS Project, the Parties will jointly design, develop, and test the mechanisms, methods, and procedures that should be in place and the steps necessary to transition management responsibility for DNS functions now performed by, or on behalf of, the U.S. Government to a private-sector not-for-profit entity. Once testing is successfully completed, it is contemplated that management of the DNS will be transitioned to the mechanisms, methods, and procedures designed and developed in the DNS Project.

In the DNS Project, the parties will jointly design, develop, and test the mechanisms, methods, and procedures to carry out the following DNS management functions:

a. Establishment of policy for and direction of the allocation of IP number blocks;

b. Oversight of the operation of the authoritative root server system;

c. Oversight of the policy for determining the circumstances under which new top level domains would be added to the root system;

d. Coordination of the assignment of other Internet technical parameters as needed to maintain universal connectivity on the Internet; and

e. Other activities necessary to coordinate the specified DNS management functions, as agreed by the Parties.

The Parties will jointly design, develop, and test the mechanisms, methods, and procedures that will achieve the transition without disrupting the functional operation of the Internet. The Parties will also prepare a joint DNS Project Report that documents the conclusions of the design, development, and testing.

DOC has determined that this project can be done most effectively with the participation of ICANN. ICANN has a stated purpose to perform the described coordinating functions for Internet names and addresses and is the organization that best demonstrated that it can accommodate the broad and diverse interest groups that make up the Internet community.

C. The Principles

The Parties will abide by the following principles:

1. Stability

This Agreement promotes the stability of the Internet and allows the Parties to plan for a deliberate move from the existing structure to a private-sector structure without disruption to the functioning of the DNS. The Agreement calls for the design, development, and testing of a new management system that will not harm current functional operations.

2. Competition

This Agreement promotes the management of the DNS in a manner that will permit market mechanisms to support competition and consumer choice in the technical management of the DNS. This competition will lower costs, promote innovation, and enhance user choice and satisfaction.

3. Private, Bottom-Up Coordination

This Agreement is intended to result in the design, development, and testing of a private coordinating process that is flexible and able to move rapidly enough to meet the changing needs of the Internet and of Internet users. This Agreement is intended to foster the development of a private sector management system that, as far as possible, reflects a system of bottom-up management.

4. Representation.

This Agreement promotes the technical management of the DNS in a manner that reflects the global and functional diversity of Internet users and their needs. This Agreement is intended to promote the design, development, and testing of mechanisms to solicit public input, both domestic and international, into a private-sector decision making process. These mechanisms will promote the flexibility needed to adapt to changes in the composition of the Internet user community and their needs.

III. AUTHORITIES

A. DOC has authority to participate in the DNS Project with ICANN under the following authorities:

(1) 15 U.S.C. § 1525, the DOC's Joint Project Authority, which provides that the DOC may enter into joint projects with nonprofit, research, or public organizations on matters of mutual interest, the cost of which is equitably apportioned;

(2) 15 U.S.C. § 1512, the DOC's authority to foster, promote, and develop foreign and domestic commerce;

(3) 47 U.S.C. § 902, which specifically authorizes the National Telecommunications and Information Administration (NTIA) to coordinate the telecommunications activities of the Executive Branch and assist in the formulation of policies and standards for those activities including, but not limited to, considerations of interoperability, privacy, security, spectrum use, and emergency readiness;

(4) Presidential Memorandum on Electronic Commerce, 33 Weekly Comp. Presidential Documents 1006 (July 1, 1997), which directs the Secretary of Commerce to transition DNS management to the private sector; and

(5) Statement of Policy, Management of Internet Names and Addresses, (63 Fed. Reg. 31741(1998), which describes the manner in which the Department of Commerce will transition DNS management to the private sector.

B. ICANN has the authority to participate in the DNS Project, as evidenced in its Articles of Incorporation and Bylaws. Specifically, ICANN has stated that its business purpose is to:

(i) coordinate the assignment of Internet technical parameters as needed to maintain universal connectivity on the Internet;

(ii) perform and oversee functions related to the coordination of the Internet Protocol (IP) address space;

(iii) perform and oversee functions related to the coordination of the Internet domain name system, including the development of policies for determining the circumstances under which new top-level domains are added to the DNS root system;

(iv) oversee operation of the authoritative Internet DNS root server system; and

(v) engage in any other related lawful activity in furtherance of Items (i) through (iv).

IV. MUTUAL INTEREST OF THE PARTIES

Both DOC and ICANN have a mutual interest in a transition that ensures that future technical management of the DNS adheres to the principles of stability, competition, coordination, and representation as published in the

Statement of Policy. ICANN has declared its commitment to these principles in its Bylaws. This Agreement is essential for the DOC to ensure continuity and stability in the performance of technical management of the DNS now performed by, or on behalf of, the U.S. Government. Together, the Parties will collaborate on the DNS Project to achieve the transition without disruption.

V. RESPONSIBILITIES OF THE PARTIES

A. General.

1. The Parties agree to jointly participate in the DNS Project for the design, development, and testing of the mechanisms, methods and procedures that should be in place for the private sector to manage the functions delineated in the Statement of Policy in a transparent, non-arbitrary, and reasonable manner.

2. The Parties agree that the mechanisms, methods, and procedures developed under the DNS Project will ensure that private-sector technical management of the DNS shall not apply standards, policies, procedures or practices inequitably or single out any particular party for disparate treatment unless justified by substantial and reasonable cause and will ensure sufficient appeal procedures for adversely affected members of the Internet community.

3. Before the termination of this Agreement, the Parties will collaborate on a DNS Project Report that will document ICANN's test of the policies and procedures designed and developed pursuant to this Agreement.

4. The Parties agree to execute the following responsibilities in accordance with the Principles and Purpose of this Agreement as set forth in section II.

B. DOC.

The DOC agrees to perform the following activities and provide the following resources in support of the DNS Project:

1. Provide expertise and advice on existing DNS management functions.

2. Provide expertise and advice on methods and administrative procedures for conducting open, public proceedings concerning policies and procedures that address the technical management of the DNS.

3. Identify with ICANN the necessary software, databases, know-how, other equipment, and intellectual property necessary to design, develop, and test methods and procedures of the DNS Project.

4. Participate, as necessary, in the design, development, and testing of the methods and procedures of the DNS Project to ensure continuity including coordination between ICANN and Network Solutions, Inc.

5. Collaborate on a study on the design, development, and testing of a process for making the management of the root server system more robust and secure. This aspect of the DNS Project will address:

    a. Operational requirements of root name servers, including host hardware capacities, operating system and name server software versions, network connectivity, and physical environment.

b. Examination of the security aspects of the root name server system and review of the number, location, and distribution of root name servers considering the total system performance, robustness, and reliability.

c. Development of operational procedures for the root server system, including formalization of contractual relationships under which root servers throughout the world are operated.

6. Consult with the international community on aspects of the DNS Project.

7. Provide general oversight of activities conducted pursuant to this Agreement.

8. Maintain oversight of the technical management of DNS functions currently performed either directly, or subject to agreements with the U.S. Government, until such time as further agreement(s) are arranged as necessary, for the private sector to undertake management of specific DNS technical management functions.

C. <u>ICANN</u>. ICANN agrees to perform the following activities and provide the following resources in support of the DNS Project and further agrees to undertake the following activities pursuant to its procedures as set forth in [its] Articles of Incorporation [and By-Laws], as they may be revised from time to time in conformity with the DNS Project:

1. Provide expertise and advice on private sector functions related to technical management of the DNS such as the policy and direction of the allocation of IP number blocks and coordination of the assignment of other Internet technical parameters as needed to maintain universal connectivity on the Internet.

2. Collaborate on the design, development and testing of procedures by which members of the Internet community adversely affected by decisions that are in conflict with the bylaws of the organization can seek external review of such decisions by a neutral third party.

3. Collaborate on the design, development, and testing of a plan for introduction of competition in domain name registration services, including:

a. Development of procedures to designate third parties to participate in tests conducted pursuant to this Agreement.

b. Development of an accreditation procedure for registrars and procedures that subject registrars to consistent requirements designed to promote a stable and robustly competitive DNS, as set forth in the Statement of Policy.

c. Identification of the software, databases, know-how, intellectual property, and other equipment necessary to implement the plan for competition;

4. Collaborate on written technical procedures for operation of the primary root server including procedures that permit modifications, additions or deletions to the root zone file.

5. Collaborate on a study and process for making the management of the root server system more robust and secure. This aspect of the Project will address:

   a. Operational requirements of root name servers, including host hardware capacities, operating system and name server software versions, network connectivity, and physical environment.

   b. Examination of the security aspects of the root name server system and review of the number, location , and distribution of root name servers considering the total system performance; robustness, and reliability.

   c. Development of operational procedures for the root system, including formalization of contractual relationships under which root servers throughout the world are operated.

6. Collaborate on the design, development and testing of a process for affected parties to participate in the formulation of policies and procedures that address the technical management of the Internet. This process will include methods for soliciting, evaluating and responding to comments in the adoption of policies and procedures.

7. Collaborate on the development of additional policies and procedures designed to provide information to the public.

8. Collaborate on the design, development, and testing of appropriate membership mechanisms that foster accountability to and representation of the global and functional diversity of the Internet and its users, within the structure of private-sector DNS management organization.

9. Collaborate on the design, development and testing of a plan for creating a process that will consider the possible expansion of the number of gTLDs. The designed process should consider and take into account the following:

   a. The potential impact of new gTLDs on the Internet root server system and Internet stability.

   b. The creation and implementation of minimum criteria for new and existing gTLD registries.

   c. Potential consumer benefits/costs associated with establishing a competitive environment for gTLD registries.

   d. Recommendations regarding trademark/domain name policies set forth in the Statement of Policy; recommendations made by the World Intellectual Property Organization (WIPO) concerning: (i) the development of a uniform approach to resolving trademark/domain name disputes involving cyberpiracy; (ii) a process for protecting famous trademarks in the generic top level domains; (iii) the effects of adding new gTLDs and related dispute resolution procedures on trademark and intellectual property holders; and recommendations made by other independent organizations concerning trademark/domain name issues.

10.   Collaborate on other activities as appropriate to fulfill the purpose of this Agreement, as agreed by the Parties.

D. Prohibitions.

1.   ICANN shall not act as a domain name Registry or Registrar or IP Address Registry in competition with entities affected by the plan developed under this Agreement. Nothing, however, in this Agreement is intended to prevent ICANN or the USG from taking reasonable steps that are necessary to protect the operational stability of the Internet in the event of the financial failure of a Registry or Registrar or other emergency.

2.   Neither Party, either in the DNS Project or in any act related to the DNS Project, shall act unjustifiably or arbitrarily to injure particular persons or entities or particular categories of persons or entities.

3.   Both Parties shall act in a non-arbitrary and reasonable manner with respect to design, development, and testing of the DNS Project and any other activity related to the DNS Project.

VI. EQUITABLE APPORTIONMENT OF COSTS

The costs of this activity are equitably apportioned, and each party shall bear the costs of its own activities under this Agreement. This Agreement contemplates no transfer of funds between the Parties. [Each Party's estimated costs for the first six months of this Agreement were attached to the Memorandum]. The Parties shall review these estimated costs in light of actual expenditures at the completion of the first six month period and will ensure costs will be equitably apportioned.

VII. PERIOD OF AGREEMENT AND MODIFICATION/TERMINATION

This Agreement will become effective when signed by all parties. The Agreement will terminate on September 30, 2000, but may be amended at any time by mutual agreement of the parties. Either party may terminate this Agreement by providing one hundred twenty (120) days written notice to the other party. In the event this Agreement is terminated, each party shall be solely responsible for the payment of any expenses it has incurred. This Agreement is subject to the availability of funds.

B. INTERNATIONAL TRADE AGREEMENTS

AGREEMENT ON TRADE-RELATED ASPECTS OF INTELLECTUAL PROPERTY RIGHTS, INCLUDING TRADE IN COUNTERFEIT GOODS

Annex IC to the Agreement Establishing the World Trade Organization, April 15, 1994, Marrakesh, Morocco

PREAMBLE

Members,

Desiring to reduce distortions and impediments to international trade, and taking into account the need to promote effective and adequate protection of intellectual property rights, and to ensure that measures and procedures to enforce intellectual property rights do not themselves become barriers to legitimate trade;

Recognizing, to this end, the need for new rules and disciplines concerning:

(a) the applicability of the basic principles of GATT 1994 and of relevant international intellectual property agreements or conventions;

(b) the provision of adequate standards and principles concerning the availability, scope and use of trade-related intellectual property rights;

(c) the provision of effective and appropriate means for the enforcement of trade-related intellectual property rights, taking into account differences in national legal systems;

(d) the provision of effective and expeditious procedures for the multilateral prevention and settlement of disputes between governments; and

(e) transitional arrangements aiming at the fullest participation in the results of the negotiations;

Recognizing the need for a multilateral framework of principles, rules and disciplines dealing with international trade in counterfeit goods;

Recognizing that intellectual property rights are private rights;

Recognizing the underlying public policy objectives of national systems for the protection of intellectual property, including developmental and technological objectives;

Recognizing also the special needs of the least-developed country Members in respect of maximum flexibility in the domestic implementation of laws and regulations in order to enable them to create a sound and viable technological base;

Emphasizing the importance of reducing tensions by reaching strengthened commitments to resolve disputes on trade-related intellectual property issues through multilateral procedures;

Desiring to establish a mutually supportive relationship between the WTO and the World Intellectual Property Organization (referred to in this

Agreement as "WIPO") as well as other relevant international organizations;

Hereby agree as follows:

PART I
GENERAL PROVISIONS AND BASIC PRINCIPLES

Article 1
Nature and Scope of Obligations

1. Members shall give effect to the provisions of this Agreement. Members may, but shall not be obliged to, implement in their law more extensive protection than is required by this Agreement, provided that such protection does not contravene the provisions of this Agreement. Members shall be free to determine the appropriate method of implementing the provisions of this Agreement within their own legal system and practice.

2. For the purposes of this Agreement, the term "intellectual property" refers to all categories of intellectual property that are the subject of Sections 1 through 7 of Part II.

3. Members shall accord the treatment provided for in this Agreement to the nationals of other Members.[1] In respect of the relevant intellectual property right, the nationals of other Members shall be understood as those natural or legal persons that would meet the criteria for eligibility for protection provided for in the Paris Convention (1967), the Berne Convention (1971), the Rome Convention and the Treaty on Intellectual Property in Respect of Integrated Circuits, were all Members of the WTO members of those conventions.[2] Any Member availing itself of the possibilities provided in paragraph 3 of Article 5 or paragraph 2 of Article 6 of the Rome Convention shall make a notification as foreseen in those provisions to the Council for Trade-Related Aspects of Intellectual Property Rights (the "Council for TRIPS").

Article 2
Intellectual Property Conventions

1. In respect of Parts II, III and IV of this Agreement, Members shall comply with Articles 1 through 12, and Article 19, of the Paris Convention

---

1. When "nationals" are referred to in this Agreement, they shall be deemed, in the case of a separate customs territory Member of the WTO, to mean persons, natural or legal, who are domiciled or who have a real and effective industrial or commercial establishment in that customs territory.

2. In this Agreement, "Paris Convention" refers to the Paris Convention for the Protection of Industrial Property; "Paris Convention (1967)" refers to the Stockholm Act of this Convention of 14 July 1967. "Berne Convention" refers to the Berne Convention for the Protection of Literary and Artistic Works; "Berne Convention (1971)" refers to the Paris Act of this Convention of 24 July 1971. "Rome Convention" refers to the International Convention for the Protection of Performers, Producers of Phonograms and Broadcasting Organizations, adopted at Rome on 26 October 1961. "Treaty on Intellectual Property in Respect of Integrated Circuits" (IPIC Treaty) refers to the Treaty on Intellectual Property in Respect of Integrated Circuits, adopted at Washington on 26 May 1989. "WTO Agreement" refers to the Agreement Establishing the WTO.

(1967).

2.   Nothing in Parts I to IV of this Agreement shall derogate from existing obligations that Members may have to each other under the Paris Convention, the Berne Convention, the Rome Convention and the Treaty on Intellectual Property in Respect of Integrated Circuits.

Article 3
National Treatment

1.   Each Member shall accord to the nationals of other Members treatment no less favourable than that it accords to its own nationals with regard to the protection[3] of intellectual property, subject to the exceptions already provided in, respectively, the Paris Convention (1967), the Berne Convention (1971), the Rome Convention or the Treaty on Intellectual Property in Respect of Integrated Circuits. In respect of performers, producers of phonograms and broadcasting organizations, this obligation only applies in respect of the rights provided under this Agreement. Any Member availing itself of the possibilities provided in Article 6 of the Berne Convention (1971) or paragraph 1(b) of Article 16 of the Rome Convention shall make a notification as foreseen in those provisions to the Council for TRIPS.

2.   Members may avail themselves of the exceptions permitted under paragraph 1 in relation to judicial and administrative procedures, including the designation of an address for service or the appointment of an agent within the jurisdiction of a Member, only where such exceptions are necessary to secure compliance with laws and regulations which are not inconsistent with the provisions of this Agreement and where such practices are not applied in a manner which would constitute a disguised restriction on trade.

Article 4
Most-Favoured-Nation Treatment

With regard to the protection of intellectual property, any advantage, favour, privilege or immunity granted by a Member to the nationals of any other country shall be accorded immediately and unconditionally to the nationals of all other Members. Exempted from this obligation are any advantage, favour, privilege or immunity accorded by a Member:

(a) deriving from international agreements on judicial assistance or law enforcement of a general nature and not particularly confined to the protection of intellectual property;

(b) granted in accordance with the provisions of the Berne Convention (1971) or the Rome Convention authorizing that the treatment accorded be a function not of national treatment but of the treatment accorded

---

3. For the purposes of Articles 3 and 4, "protection" shall include matters affecting the availability, acquisition, scope, maintenance and enforcement of intellectual property rights as well as those matters affecting the use of intellectual property rights specifically addressed in this Agreement.

in another country;

(c) in respect of the rights of performers, producers of phonograms and broadcasting organizations not provided under this Agreement;

(d) deriving from international agreements related to the protection of intellectual property which entered into force prior to the entry into force of the WTO Agreement, provided that such agreements are notified to the Council for TRIPS and do not constitute an arbitrary or unjustifiable discrimination against nationals of other Members.

Article 5
Multilateral Agreements on Acquisition or Maintenance of Protection

The obligations under Articles 3 and 4 do not apply to procedures provided in multilateral agreements concluded under the auspices of WIPO relating to the acquisition or maintenance of intellectual property rights.

Article 6
Exhaustion

For the purposes of dispute settlement under this Agreement, subject to the provisions of Articles 3 and 4 nothing in this Agreement shall be used to address the issue of the exhaustion of intellectual property rights.

Article 7
Objectives

The protection and enforcement of intellectual property rights should contribute to the promotion of technological innovation and to the transfer and dissemination of technology, to the mutual advantage of producers and users of technological knowledge and in a manner conducive to social and economic welfare, and to a balance of rights and obligations.

Article 8
Principles

1. Members may, in formulating or amending their laws and regulations, adopt measures necessary to protect public health and nutrition, and to promote the public interest in sectors of vital importance to their socio-economic and technological development, provided that such measures are consistent with the provisions of this Agreement.

2. Appropriate measures, provided that they are consistent with the provisions of this Agreement, may be needed to prevent the abuse of intellectual property rights by right holders or the resort to practices which unreasonably restrain trade or adversely affect the international transfer of technology.

PART II
STANDARDS CONCERNING THE AVAILABILITY, SCOPE AND USE OF INTELLECTUAL PROPERTY RIGHTS

Section 1: Copyright and Related Rights

Article 9
Relation to the Berne Convention

1. Members shall comply with Articles 1 through 21 of the Berne Convention (1971) and the Appendix thereto. However, Members shall not have rights or obligations under this Agreement in respect of the rights conferred under Article 6*bis* of that Convention or of the rights derived therefrom.

2. Copyright protection shall extend to expressions and not to ideas, procedures, methods of operation or mathematical concepts as such.

Article 10
Computer Programs and Compilations of Data

1. Computer programs, whether in source or object code, shall be protected as literary works under the Berne Convention (1971).

2. Compilations of data or other material, whether in machine readable or other form, which by reason of the selection or arrangement of their contents constitute intellectual creations shall be protected as such. Such protection, which shall not extend to the data or material itself, shall be without prejudice to any copyright subsisting in the data or material itself.

Article 11
Rental Rights

In respect of at least computer programs and cinematographic works, a Member shall provide authors and their successors in title the right to authorize or to prohibit the commercial rental to the public of originals or copies of their copyright works. A Member shall be excepted from this obligation in respect of cinematographic works unless such rental has led to widespread copying of such works which is materially impairing the exclusive right of reproduction conferred in that Member on authors and their successors in title. In respect of computer programs, this obligation does not apply to rentals where the program itself is not the essential object of the rental.

Article 12
Term of Protection

Whenever the term of protection of a work, other than a photographic work or a work of applied art, is calculated on a basis other than the life of a natural person, such term shall be no less than 50 years from the end of the calendar year of authorized publication, or, failing such authorized publication within 50 years from the making of the work, 50 years from the end of the calendar year of making.

Article 13
Limitations and Exceptions

Members shall confine limitations or exceptions to exclusive rights to certain special cases which do not conflict with a normal exploitation of the work and do not unreasonably prejudice the legitimate interests of the right holder.

Article 14
Protection of Performers, Producers of Phonograms
(Sound Recordings) and Broadcasting Organizations

1. In respect of a fixation of their performance on a phonogram, performers shall have the possibility of preventing the following acts when undertaken without their authorization: the fixation of their unfixed performance and the reproduction of such fixation. Performers shall also have the possibility of preventing the following acts when undertaken without their authorization: the broadcasting by wireless means and the communication to the public of their live performance.

2. Producers of phonograms shall enjoy the right to authorize or prohibit the direct or indirect reproduction of their phonograms.

3. Broadcasting organizations shall have the right to prohibit the following acts when undertaken without their authorization: the fixation, the reproduction of fixations, and the rebroadcasting by wireless means of broadcasts, as well as the communication to the public of television broadcasts of the same. Where Members do not grant such rights to broadcasting organizations, they shall provide owners of copyright in the subject matter of broadcasts with the possibility of preventing the above acts, subject to the provisions of the Berne Convention (1971).

4. The provisions of Article 11 in respect of computer programs shall apply *mutatis mutandis* to producers of phonograms and any other right holders in phonograms as determined in a Member's law. If on 15 April 1994 a Member has in force a system of equitable remuneration of right holders in respect of the rental of phonograms, it may maintain such system provided that the commercial rental of phonograms is not giving rise to the material impairment of the exclusive rights of reproduction of right holders.

5. The term of the protection available under this Agreement to performers and producers of phonograms shall last at least until the end of a period of 50 years computed from the end of the calendar year in which the fixation was made or the performance took place. The term of protection granted pursuant to paragraph 3 shall last for at least 20 years from the end of the calendar year in which the broadcast took place.

6. Any Member may, in relation to the rights conferred under paragraphs

1, 2 and 3, provide for conditions, limitations, exceptions and reservations to the extent permitted by the Rome Convention. However, the provisions of Article 18 of the Berne Convention (1971) shall also apply, *mutatis mutandis*, to the rights of performers and producers of phonograms in phonograms.

Section 2: Trademarks

Article 15
Protectable Subject Matter

1. Any sign, or any combination of signs, capable of distinguishing the goods or services of one undertaking from those of other undertakings, shall be capable of constituting a trademark. Such signs, in particular words including personal names, letters, numerals, figurative elements and combinations of colours as well as any combination of such signs, shall be eligible for registration as trademarks. Where signs are not inherently capable of distinguishing the relevant goods or services, Members may make registrability depend on distinctiveness acquired through use. Members may require, as a condition of registration, that signs be visually perceptible.

2. Paragraph 1 shall not be understood to prevent a Member from denying registration of a trademark on other grounds, provided that they do not derogate from the provisions of the Paris Convention (1967).

3. Members may make registrability depend on use. However, actual use of a trademark shall not be a condition for filing an application for registration. An application shall not be refused solely on the ground that intended use has not taken place before the expiry of a period of three years from the date of application.

4. The nature of the goods or services to which a trademark is to be applied shall in no case form an obstacle to registration of the trademark.

5. Members shall publish each trademark either before it is registered or promptly after it is registered and shall afford a reasonable opportunity for petitions to cancel the registration. In addition, Members may afford an opportunity for the registration of a trademark to be opposed.

Article 16
Rights Conferred

1. The owner of a registered trademark shall have the exclusive right to prevent all third parties not having the owner's consent from using in the course of trade identical or similar signs for goods or services which are identical or similar to those in respect of which the trademark is registered where such use would result in a likelihood of confusion. In case of the use of an identical sign for identical goods or services, a likelihood of confusion shall be presumed. The rights described above shall not prejudice any existing prior rights, nor shall they affect the possibility of Members making rights available on the basis of use.

2. Article 6*bis* of the Paris Convention (1967) shall apply, *mutatis*

mutandis, to services. In determining whether a trademark is well-known, Members shall take account of the knowledge of the trademark in the relevant sector of the public, including knowledge in the Member concerned which has been obtained as a result of the promotion of the trademark.

3. Article 6*bis* of the Paris Convention (1967) shall apply, *mutatis mutandis*, to goods or services which are not similar to those in respect of which a trademark is registered, provided that use of that trademark in relation to those goods or services would indicate a connection between those goods or services and the owner of the registered trademark and provided that the interests of the owner of the registered trademark are likely to be damaged by such use.

Article 17
Exceptions

Members may provide limited exceptions to the rights conferred by a trademark, such as fair use of descriptive terms, provided that such exceptions take account of the legitimate interests of the owner of the trademark and of third parties.

Article 18
Term of Protection

Initial registration, and each renewal of registration, of a trademark shall be for a term of no less than seven years. The registration of a trademark shall be renewable indefinitely.

Article 19
Requirement of Use

1. If use is required to maintain a registration, the registration may be cancelled only after an uninterrupted period of at least three years of non-use, unless valid reasons based on the existence of obstacles to such use are shown by the trademark owner. Circumstances arising independently of the will of the owner of the trademark which constitute an obstacle to the use of the trademark, such as import restrictions on or other government requirements for goods or services protected by the trademark, shall be recognized as valid reasons for non-use.

2. When subject to the control of its owner, use of a trademark by another person shall be recognized as use of the trademark for the purpose of maintaining the registration.

Article 20
Other Requirements

The use of a trademark in the course of trade shall not be unjustifiably encumbered by special requirements, such as use with another trademark, use in a special form or use in a manner detrimental to its capability to distinguish the goods or services of one undertaking from those of other undertakings. This will not preclude a requirement prescribing the use of the trademark identifying the undertaking producing the goods or services along with, but without linking it to, the trademark distinguishing the specific goods or services in question of that undertaking.

Article 21
Licensing and Assignment

Members may determine conditions on the licensing and assignment of trademarks, it being understood that the compulsory licensing of trademarks shall not be permitted and that the owner of a registered trademark shall have the right to assign the trademark with or without the transfer of the business to which the trademark belongs.

Section 3: Geographical Indications

Article 22
Protection of Geographical Indications

1. Geographical indications are, for the purposes of this Agreement, indications which identify a good as originating in the territory of a Member, or a region or locality in that territory, where a given quality, reputation or other characteristic of the good is essentially attributable to its geographical origin.

2. In respect of geographical indications, Members shall provide the legal means for interested parties to prevent:

(a) the use of any means in the designation or presentation of a good that indicates or suggests that the good in question originates in a geographical area other than the true place of origin in a manner which misleads the public as to the geographical origin of the good;

(b) any use which constitutes an act of unfair competition within the meaning of Article 10*bis* of the Paris Convention (1967).

3. A Member shall, *ex officio* if its legislation so permits or at the request of an interested party, refuse or invalidate the registration of a trademark which contains or consists of a geographical indication with respect to goods not originating in the territory indicated, if use of the indication in the trademark for such goods in that Member is of such a nature as to mislead the public as to the true place of origin.

4. The protection under paragraphs 1, 2 and 3 shall be applicable against a geographical indication which, although literally true as to the territory, region or locality in which the goods originate, falsely represents to the public that the goods originate in another territory.

Article 23
Additional Protection for Geographical
Indications for Wines and Spirits

1. Each Member shall provide the legal means for interested parties to prevent use of a geographical indication identifying wines for wines not originating in the place indicated by the geographical indication in question or identifying spirits for spirits not originating in the place indicated by the geographical indication in question, even where the true origin of the goods is indicated or the geographical indication is used in translation or accompanied by expressions such as "kind", "type", "style", "imitation" or the like.[4]

2. The registration of a trademark for wines which contains or consists of a geographical indication identifying wines or for spirits which contains or consists of a geographical indication identifying spirits shall be refused or invalidated, *ex officio* if a Member's legislation so permits or at the request of an interested party, with respect to such wines or spirits not having this origin.

3. In the case of homonymous geographical indications for wines, protection shall be accorded to each indication, subject to the provisions of paragraph 4 of Article 22. Each Member shall determine the practical conditions under which the homonymous indications in question will be differentiated from each other, taking into account the need to ensure equitable treatment of the producers concerned and that consumers are not misled.

4. In order to facilitate the protection of geographical indications for wines, negotiations shall be undertaken in the Council for TRIPS concerning the establishment of a multilateral system of notification and registration of geographical indications for wines eligible for protection in those Members participating in the system.

Article 24
International Negotiations; Exceptions

1. Members agree to enter into negotiations aimed at increasing the protection of individual geographical indications under Article 23. The provisions of paragraphs 4 through 8 below shall not be used by a Member to refuse to conduct negotiations or to conclude bilateral or multilateral agreements. In the context of such negotiations, Members shall be willing to consider the continued applicability of these provisions to individual geographical indications whose use was the subject of such negotiations.

2. The Council for TRIPS shall keep under review the application of the provisions of this Section; the first such review shall take place within two years of the entry into force of the WTO Agreement. Any matter affecting

---

4. Notwithstanding the first sentence of Article 42, Members may, with respect to these obligations, instead provide for enforcement by administrative action.

the compliance with the obligations under these provisions may be drawn to the attention of the Council, which, at the request of a Member, shall consult with any Member or Members in respect of such matter in respect of which it has not been possible to find a satisfactory solution through bilateral or plurilateral consultations between the Members concerned. The Council shall take such action as may be agreed to facilitate the operation and further the objectives of this Section.

3. In implementing this Section, a Member shall not diminish the protection of geographical indications that existed in that Member immediately prior to the date of entry into force of the WTO Agreement.

4. Nothing in this Section shall require a Member to prevent continued and similar use of a particular geographical indication of another Member identifying wines or spirits in connection with goods or services by any of its nationals or domiciliaries who have used that geographical indication in a continuous manner with regard to the same or related goods or services in the territory of that Member either (a) for at least 10 years preceding 15 April 1994 or (b) in good faith preceding that date.

5. Where a trademark has been applied for or registered in good faith, or where rights to a trademark have been acquired through use in good faith either:

(a) before the date of application of these provisions in that Member as defined in Part VI; or

(b) before the geographical indication is protected in its country of origin;

measures adopted to implement this Section shall not prejudice eligibility for or the validity of the registration of a trademark, or the right to use a trademark, on the basis that such a trademark is identical with, or similar to, a geographical indication.

6. Nothing in this Section shall require a Member to apply its provisions in respect of a geographical indication of any other Member with respect to goods or services for which the relevant indication is identical with the term customary in common language as the common name for such goods or services in the territory of that Member. Nothing in this Section shall require a Member to apply its provisions in respect of a geographical indication of any other Member with respect to products of the vine for which the relevant indication is identical with the customary name of a grape variety existing in the territory of that Member as of the date of entry into force of the WTO Agreement.

7. A Member may provide that any request made under this Section in connection with the use or registration of a trademark must be presented within five years after the adverse use of the protected indication has become generally known in that Member or after the date of registration of the trademark in that Member provided that the trademark has been published by that date, if such date is earlier than the date on which the adverse use became generally known in that Member, provided that the geographical indication is not used or registered in bad faith.

8. The provisions of this Section shall in no way prejudice the right of any person to use, in the course of trade, that person's name or the name of that person's predecessor in business, except where such name is used in such a manner as to mislead the public.

9. There shall be no obligation under this Agreement to protect geographical indications which are not or cease to be protected in their country of origin, or which have fallen into disuse in that country.

Section 4: Industrial Designs

Article 25
Requirements for Protection

1. Members shall provide for the protection of independently created industrial designs that are new or original. Members may provide that designs are not new or original if they do not significantly differ from known designs or combinations of known design features. Members may provide that such protection shall not extend to designs dictated essentially by technical or functional considerations.

2. Each Member shall ensure that requirements for securing protection for textile designs, in particular in regard to any cost, examination or publication, do not unreasonably impair the opportunity to seek and obtain such protection. Members shall be free to meet this obligation through industrial design law or through copyright law.

Article 26
Protection

1. The owner of a protected industrial design shall have the right to prevent third parties not having the owner's consent from making, selling or importing articles bearing or embodying a design which is a copy, or substantially a copy, of the protected design, when such acts are undertaken for commercial purposes.

2. Members may provide limited exceptions to the protection of industrial designs, provided that such exceptions do not unreasonably conflict with the normal exploitation of protected industrial designs and do not unreasonably prejudice the legitimate interests of the owner of the protected design, taking account of the legitimate interests of third parties.

3. The duration of protection available shall amount to at least 10 years.

Section 5: Patents

Article 27
Patentable Subject Matter

1. Subject to the provisions of paragraphs 2 and 3, patents shall be available for any inventions, whether products or processes, in all fields of

technology, provided that they are new, involve an inventive step and are capable of industrial application.[5] Subject to paragraph 4 of Article 65, paragraph 8 of Article 70 and paragraph 3 of this Article, patents shall be available and patent rights enjoyable without discrimination as to the place of invention, the field of technology and whether products are imported or locally produced.

2. Members may exclude from patentability inventions, the prevention within their territory of the commercial exploitation of which is necessary to protect *ordre public* or morality, including to protect human, animal or plant life or health or to avoid serious prejudice to the environment, provided that such exclusion is not made merely because the exploitation is prohibited by their law.

3. Members may also exclude from patentability:

(a)   diagnostic, therapeutic and surgical methods for the treatment of humans or animals;

(b)   plants and animals other than micro-organisms, and essentially biological processes for the production of plants or animals other than non-biological and microbiological processes. However, Members shall provide for the protection of plant varieties either by patents or by an effective *sui generis* system or by any combination thereof. The provisions of this subparagraph shall be reviewed four years after the date of entry into force of the WTO Agreement.

Article 28
Rights Conferred

1.   A patent shall confer on its owner the following exclusive rights:

(a)   where the subject matter of a patent is a product, to prevent third parties not having the owner's consent from the acts of: making, using, offering for sale, selling, or importing[6] for these purposes that product;

(b)   where the subject matter of a patent is a process, to prevent third parties not having the owner's consent from the act of using the process, and from the acts of: using, offering for sale, selling, or importing for these purposes at least the product obtained directly by that process.

2.   Patent owners shall also have the right to assign, or transfer by succession, the patent and to conclude licensing contracts.

---

5. For the purposes of this Article, the terms "inventive step" and "capable of industrial application" may be deemed by a Member to be synonymous with the terms "non-obvious" and "useful" respectively.

6. This right, like all other rights conferred under this Agreement in respect of the use, sale, importation or other distribution of goods, is subject to the provisions of Article 6.

Article 29
Conditions on Patent Applicants

1. Members shall require that an applicant for a patent shall disclose the invention in a manner sufficiently clear and complete for the invention to be carried out by a person skilled in the art and may require the applicant to indicate the best mode for carrying out the invention known to the inventor at the filing date or, where priority is claimed, at the priority date of the application.

2. Members may require an applicant for a patent to provide information concerning the applicant's corresponding foreign applications and grants.

Article 30
Exceptions to Rights Conferred

Members may provide limited exceptions to the exclusive rights conferred by a patent, provided that such exceptions do not unreasonably conflict with a normal exploitation of the patent and do not unreasonably prejudice the legitimate interests of the patent owner, taking account of the legitimate interests of third parties.

Article 31
Other Use Without Authorization of the Right Holder

Where the law of a Member allows for other use[7] of the subject matter of a patent without the authorization of the right holder, including use by the government or third parties authorized by the government, the following provisions shall be respected:

(a)   authorization of such use shall be considered on its individual merits;

(b)   such use may only be permitted if, prior to such use, the proposed user has made efforts to obtain authorization from the right holder on reasonable commercial terms and conditions and that such efforts have not been successful within a reasonable period of time. This requirement may be waived by a Member in the case of a national emergency or other circumstances of extreme urgency or in cases of public non-commercial use. In situations of national emergency or other circumstances of extreme urgency, the right holder shall, nevertheless, be notified as soon as reasonably practicable. In the case of public non-commercial use, where the government or contractor, without making a patent search, knows or has demonstrable grounds to know that a valid patent is or will be used by or for the government, the right holder shall be informed promptly;

(c)   the scope and duration of such use shall be limited to the purpose for which it was authorized, and in the case of semi-conductor technology shall only be for public non-commercial use or to remedy a practice

---

7. "Other use" refers to use other than that allowed under Article 30.

determined after judicial or administrative process to be anti-competitive;

(d) such use shall be non-exclusive;

(e) such use shall be non-assignable, except with that part of the enterprise or goodwill which enjoys such use;

(f) any such use shall be authorized predominantly for the supply of the domestic market of the Member authorizing such use;

(g) authorization for such use shall be liable, subject to adequate protection of the legitimate interests of the persons so authorized, to be terminated if and when the circumstances which led to it cease to exist and are unlikely to recur. The competent authority shall have the authority to review, upon motivated request, the continued existence of these circumstances;

(h) the right holder shall be paid adequate remuneration in the circumstances of each case, taking into account the economic value of the authorization;

(i) the legal validity of any decision relating to the authorization of such use shall be subject to judicial review or other independent review by a distinct higher authority in that Member;

(j) any decision relating to the remuneration provided in respect of such use shall be subject to judicial review or other independent review by a distinct higher authority in that Member;

(k) Members are not obliged to apply the conditions set forth in subparagraphs (b) and (f) where such use is permitted to remedy a practice determined after judicial or administrative process to be anti-competitive. The need to correct anti-competitive practices may be taken into account in determining the amount of remuneration in such cases. Competent authorities shall have the authority to refuse termination of authorization if and when the conditions which led to such authorization are likely to recur;

(l) where such use is authorized to permit the exploitation of a patent ("the second patent") which cannot be exploited without infringing another patent ("the first patent"), the following additional conditions shall apply:

  (i) the invention claimed in the second patent shall involve an important technical advance of considerable economic significance in relation to the invention claimed in the first patent;

  (ii) the owner of the first patent shall be entitled to a cross-licence on reasonable terms to use the invention claimed in the second patent; and

  (iii) the use authorized in respect of the first patent shall be non-assignable except with the assignment of the second patent.

Article 32
Revocation/Forfeiture

An opportunity for judicial review of any decision to revoke or forfeit a patent shall be available.

Article 33
Term of Protection

The term of protection available shall not end before the expiration of a period of twenty years counted from the filing date.[8]

Article 34
Process Patents: Burden of Proof

1. For the purposes of civil proceedings in respect of the infringement of the rights of the owner referred to in paragraph 1(b) of Article 28, if the subject matter of a patent is a process for obtaining a product, the judicial authorities shall have the authority to order the defendant to prove that the process to obtain an identical product is different from the patented process. Therefore, Members shall provide, in at least one of the following circumstances, that any identical product when produced without the consent of the patent owner shall, in the absence of proof to the contrary, be deemed to have been obtained by the patented process:

(a) if the product obtained by the patented process is new;

(b) if there is a substantial likelihood that the identical product was made by the process and the owner of the patent has been unable through reasonable efforts to determine the process actually used.

2. Any Member shall be free to provide that the burden of proof indicated in paragraph 1 shall be on the alleged infringer only if the condition referred to in subparagraph (a) is fulfilled or only if the condition referred to in subparagraph (b) is fulfilled.

3. In the adduction of proof to the contrary, the legitimate interests of defendants in protecting their manufacturing and business secrets shall be taken into account.

Section 6: Layout-designs (Topographies) of Integrated Circuits

Article 35
Relation to the IPIC Treaty

Members agree to provide protection to the layout-designs (topographies) of integrated circuits (referred to in this Agreement as "layout-designs") in accordance with Articles 2 through 7 (other than paragraph 3 of Article 6),

---

8. It is understood that those Members which do not have a system of original grant may provide that the term of protection shall be computed from the filing date in the system of original grant.

Article 12 and paragraph 3 of Article 16 of the Treaty on Intellectual Property in Respect of Integrated Circuits and, in addition, to comply with the following provisions.

Article 36
Scope of the Protection

Subject to the provisions of paragraph 1 of Article 37, Members shall consider unlawful the following acts if performed without the authorization of the right holder:[9] importing, selling, or otherwise distributing for commercial purposes a protected layout-design, an integrated circuit in which a protected layout-design is incorporated, or an article incorporating such an integrated circuit only in so far as it continues to contain an unlawfully reproduced layout-design.

Article 37
Acts Not Requiring the Authorization of the Right Holder

1. Notwithstanding Article 36, no Member shall consider unlawful the performance of any of the acts referred to in that Article in respect of an integrated circuit incorporating an unlawfully reproduced layout-design or any article incorporating such an integrated circuit where the person performing or ordering such acts did not know and had no reasonable ground to know, when acquiring the integrated circuit or article incorporating such an integrated circuit, that it incorporated an unlawfully reproduced layout-design. Members shall provide that, after the time that such person has received sufficient notice that the layout-design was unlawfully reproduced, that person may perform any of the acts with respect to the stock on hand or ordered before such time, but shall be liable to pay to the right holder a sum equivalent to a reasonable royalty such as would be payable under a freely negotiated licence in respect of such a layout-design.

2. The conditions set out in subparagraphs (a) through (k) of Article 31 shall apply *mutatis mutandis* in the event of any non-voluntary licensing of a layout-design or of its use by or for the government without the authorization of the right holder.

Article 38
Term of Protection

1. In Members requiring registration as a condition of protection, the term of protection of layout-designs shall not end before the expiration of a period of 10 years counted from the date of filing an application for registration or from the first commercial exploitation wherever in the world it occurs.

2. In Members not requiring registration as a condition for protection,

---

9. The term "right holder" in this Section shall be understood as having the same meaning as the term "holder of the right" in the IPIC Treaty.

layout-designs shall be protected for a term of no less than 10 years from the date of the first commercial exploitation wherever in the world it occurs.

3. Notwithstanding paragraphs 1 and 2, a Member may provide that protection shall lapse 15 years after the creation of the layout-design.

Section 7: Protection of Undisclosed Information

Article 39

1. In the course of ensuring effective protection against unfair competition as provided in Article 10*bis* of the Paris Convention (1967), Members shall protect undisclosed information in accordance with paragraph 2 and data submitted to governments or governmental agencies in accordance with paragraph 3.

2. Natural and legal persons shall have the possibility of preventing information lawfully within their control from being disclosed to, acquired by, or used by others without their consent in a manner contrary to honest commercial practices[10] so long as such information:

(a) is secret in the sense that it is not, as a body or in the precise configuration and assembly of its components, generally known among or readily accessible to persons within the circles that normally deal with the kind of information in question;

(b) has commercial value because it is secret; and

(c) has been subject to reasonable steps under the circumstances, by the person lawfully in control of the information, to keep it secret.

3. Members, when requiring, as a condition of approving the marketing of pharmaceutical or of agricultural chemical products which utilize new chemical entities, the submission of undisclosed test or other data, the origination of which involves a considerable effort, shall protect such data against unfair commercial use. In addition, Members shall protect such data against disclosure, except where necessary to protect the public, or unless steps are taken to ensure that the data are protected against unfair commercial use.

Section 8: Control of Anti-competitive Practices in Contractual Licences

Article 40

1. Members agree that some licensing practices or conditions pertaining to intellectual property rights which restrain competition may have adverse

---

10. For the purpose of this provision, "a manner contrary to honest commercial practices" shall mean at least practices such as breach of contract, breach of confidence and inducement to breach, and includes the acquisition of undisclosed information by third parties who knew, or were grossly negligent in failing to know, that such practices were involved in the acquisition.

effects on trade and may impede the transfer and dissemination of technology.

2. Nothing in this Agreement shall prevent Members from specifying in their legislation licensing practices or conditions that may in particular cases constitute an abuse of intellectual property rights having an adverse effect on competition in the relevant market. As provided above, a Member may adopt, consistently with the other provisions of this Agreement, appropriate measures to prevent or control such practices, which may include for example exclusive grantback conditions, conditions preventing challenges to validity and coercive package licensing, in the light of the relevant laws and regulations of that Member.

3. Each Member shall enter, upon request, into consultations with any other Member which has cause to believe that an intellectual property right owner that is a national or domiciliary of the Member to which the request for consultations has been addressed is undertaking practices in violation of the requesting Member's laws and regulations on the subject matter of this Section, and which wishes to secure compliance with such legislation, without prejudice to any action under the law and to the full freedom of an ultimate decision of either Member. The Member addressed shall accord full and sympathetic consideration to, and shall afford adequate opportunity for, consultations with the requesting Member, and shall cooperate through supply of publicly available non-confidential information of relevance to the matter in question and of other information available to the Member, subject to domestic law and to the conclusion of mutually satisfactory agreements concerning the safeguarding of its confidentiality by the requesting Member.

4. A Member whose nationals or domiciliaries are subject to proceedings in another Member concerning alleged violation of that other Member's laws and regulations on the subject matter of this Section shall, upon request, be granted an opportunity for consultations by the other Member under the same conditions as those foreseen in paragraph 3.

PART III
ENFORCEMENT OF INTELLECTUAL PROPERTY RIGHTS

Section 1: General Obligations

Article 41

1. Members shall ensure that enforcement procedures as specified in this Part are available under their law so as to permit effective action against any act of infringement of intellectual property rights covered by this Agreement, including expeditious remedies to prevent infringements and remedies which constitute a deterrent to further infringements. These procedures shall be applied in such a manner as to avoid the creation of barriers to legitimate trade and to provide for safeguards against their abuse.

2. Procedures concerning the enforcement of intellectual property rights

shall be fair and equitable. They shall not be unnecessarily complicated or costly, or entail unreasonable time-limits or unwarranted delays.

3. Decisions on the merits of a case shall preferably be in writing and reasoned. They shall be made available at least to the parties to the proceeding without undue delay. Decisions on the merits of a case shall be based only on evidence in respect of which parties were offered the opportunity to be heard.

4. Parties to a proceeding shall have an opportunity for review by a judicial authority of final administrative decisions and, subject to jurisdictional provisions in a Member's law concerning the importance of a case, of at least the legal aspects of initial judicial decisions on the merits of a case. However, there shall be no obligation to provide an opportunity for review of acquittals in criminal cases.

5. It is understood that this Part does not create any obligation to put in place a judicial system for the enforcement of intellectual property rights distinct from that for the enforcement of law in general, nor does it affect the capacity of Members to enforce their law in general. Nothing in this Part creates any obligation with respect to the distribution of resources as between enforcement of intellectual property rights and the enforcement of law in general.

Section 2: Civil and Administrative Procedures and Remedies

Article 42
Fair and Equitable Procedures

Members shall make available to right holders[11] civil judicial procedures concerning the enforcement of any intellectual property right covered by this Agreement. Defendants shall have the right to written notice which is timely and contains sufficient detail, including the basis of the claims. Parties shall be allowed to be represented by independent legal counsel, and procedures shall not impose overly burdensome requirements concerning mandatory personal appearances. All parties to such procedures shall be duly entitled to substantiate their claims and to present all relevant evidence. The procedure shall provide a means to identify and protect confidential information, unless this would be contrary to existing constitutional requirements.

Article 43
Evidence

1. The judicial authorities shall have the authority, where a party has presented reasonably available evidence sufficient to support its claims and has specified evidence relevant to substantiation of its claims which lies in

---

11. For the purpose of this Part, the term "right holder" includes federations and associations having legal standing to assert such rights.

the control of the opposing party, to order that this evidence be produced by the opposing party, subject in appropriate cases to conditions which ensure the protection of confidential information.

2. In cases in which a party to a proceeding voluntarily and without good reason refuses access to, or otherwise does not provide necessary information within a reasonable period, or significantly impedes a procedure relating to an enforcement action, a Member may accord judicial authorities the authority to make preliminary and final determinations, affirmative or negative, on the basis of the information presented to them, including the complaint or the allegation presented by the party adversely affected by the denial of access to information, subject to providing the parties an opportunity to be heard on the allegations or evidence.

Article 44
Injunctions

1. The judicial authorities shall have the authority to order a party to desist from an infringement, *inter alia* to prevent the entry into the channels of commerce in their jurisdiction of imported goods that involve the infringement of an intellectual property right, immediately after customs clearance of such goods. Members are not obliged to accord such authority in respect of protected subject matter acquired or ordered by a person prior to knowing or having reasonable grounds to know that dealing in such subject matter would entail the infringement of an intellectual property right.

2. Notwithstanding the other provisions of this Part and provided that the provisions of Part II specifically addressing use by governments, or by third parties authorized by a government, without the authorization of the right holder are complied with, Members may limit the remedies available against such use to payment of remuneration in accordance with subparagraph (h) of Article 31. In other cases, the remedies under this Part shall apply or, where these remedies are inconsistent with a Member's law, declaratory judgments and adequate compensation shall be available.

Article 45
Damages

1. The judicial authorities shall have the authority to order the infringer to pay the right holder damages adequate to compensate for the injury the right holder has suffered because of an infringement of that person's intellectual property right by an infringer who knowingly, or with reasonable grounds to know, engaged in infringing activity.

2. The judicial authorities shall also have the authority to order the infringer to pay the right holder expenses, which may include appropriate attorney's fees. In appropriate cases, Members may authorize the judicial authorities to order recovery of profits and/or payment of pre-established damages even where the infringer did not knowingly, or with reasonable grounds to know, engage in infringing activity.

Article 46
Other Remedies

In order to create an effective deterrent to infringement, the judicial authorities shall have the authority to order that goods that they have found to be infringing be, without compensation of any sort, disposed of outside the channels of commerce in such a manner as to avoid any harm caused to the right holder, or, unless this would be contrary to existing constitutional requirements, destroyed. The judicial authorities shall also have the authority to order that materials and implements the predominant use of which has been in the creation of the infringing goods be, without compensation of any sort, disposed of outside the channels of commerce in such a manner as to minimize the risks of further infringements. In considering such requests, the need for proportionality between the seriousness of the infringement and the remedies ordered as well as the interests of third parties shall be taken into account. In regard to counterfeit trademark goods, the simple removal of the trademark unlawfully affixed shall not be sufficient, other than in exceptional cases, to permit release of the goods into the channels of commerce.

Article 47
Right of Information

Members may provide that the judicial authorities shall have the authority, unless this would be out of proportion to the seriousness of the infringement, to order the infringer to inform the right holder of the identity of third persons involved in the production and distribution of the infringing goods or services and of their channels of distribution.

Article 48
Indemnification of the Defendant

1. The judicial authorities shall have the authority to order a party at whose request measures were taken and who has abused enforcement procedures to provide to a party wrongfully enjoined or restrained adequate compensation for the injury suffered because of such abuse. The judicial authorities shall also have the authority to order the applicant to pay the defendant expenses, which may include appropriate attorney's fees.

2. In respect of the administration of any law pertaining to the protection or enforcement of intellectual property rights, Members shall only exempt both public authorities and officials from liability to appropriate remedial measures where actions are taken or intended in good faith in the course of the administration of that law.

Article 49
Administrative Procedures

To the extent that any civil remedy can be ordered as a result of administrative procedures on the merits of a case, such procedures shall conform to principles equivalent in substance to those set forth in this Section.

Section 3: Provisional Measures

Article 50

1. The judicial authorities shall have the authority to order prompt and effective provisional measures:

(a) to prevent an infringement of any intellectual property right from occurring, and in particular to prevent the entry into the channels of commerce in their jurisdiction of goods, including imported goods immediately after customs clearance;

(b) to preserve relevant evidence in regard to the alleged infringement.

2. The judicial authorities shall have the authority to adopt provisional measures *inaudita altera parte* where appropriate, in particular where any delay is likely to cause irreparable harm to the right holder, or where there is a demonstrable risk of evidence being destroyed.

3. The judicial authorities shall have the authority to require the applicant to provide any reasonably available evidence in order to satisfy themselves with a sufficient degree of certainty that the applicant is the right holder and that the applicant's right is being infringed or that such infringement is imminent, and to order the applicant to provide a security or equivalent assurance sufficient to protect the defendant and to prevent abuse.

4. Where provisional measures have been adopted *inaudita altera parte*, the parties affected shall be given notice, without delay after the execution of the measures at the latest. A review, including a right to be heard, shall take place upon request of the defendant with a view to deciding, within a reasonable period after the notification of the measures, whether these measures shall be modified, revoked or confirmed.

5. The applicant may be required to supply other information necessary for the identification of the goods concerned by the authority that will execute the provisional measures.

6. Without prejudice to paragraph 4, provisional measures taken on the basis of paragraphs 1 and 2 shall, upon request by the defendant, be revoked or otherwise cease to have effect, if proceedings leading to a decision on the merits of the case are not initiated within a reasonable period, to be determined by the judicial authority ordering the measures where a Member's law so permits or, in the absence of such a determination, not to exceed 20 working days or 31 calendar days, whichever is the longer.

7. Where the provisional measures are revoked or where they lapse due to any act or omission by the applicant, or where it is subsequently found that there has been no infringement or threat of infringement of an intellectual property right, the judicial authorities shall have the authority to order the applicant, upon request of the defendant, to provide the defendant appropriate compensation for any injury caused by these

measures.

8. To the extent that any provisional measure can be ordered as a result of administrative procedures, such procedures shall conform to principles equivalent in substance to those set forth in this Section.

Section 4: Special Requirements Related to Border Measures[12]

Article 51
Suspension of Release by Customs Authorities

Members shall, in conformity with the provisions set out below, adopt procedures[13] to enable a right holder, who has valid grounds for suspecting that the importation of counterfeit trademark or pirated copyright goods[14] may take place, to lodge an application in writing with competent authorities, administrative or judicial, for the suspension by the customs authorities of the release into free circulation of such goods. Members may enable such an application to be made in respect of goods which involve other infringements of intellectual property rights, provided that the requirements of this Section are met. Members may also provide for corresponding procedures concerning the suspension by the customs authorities of the release of infringing goods destined for exportation from their territories.

Article 52
Application

Any right holder initiating the procedures under Article 51 shall be required to provide adequate evidence to satisfy the competent authorities that, under the laws of the country of importation, there is *prima facie* an infringement of the right holder's intellectual property right and to supply a sufficiently detailed description of the goods to make them readily recognizable by the customs authorities. The competent authorities shall inform the applicant within a reasonable period whether they have accepted the application and, where determined by the competent authorities, the period for which the customs authorities will take action.

---

12. Where a Member has dismantled substantially all controls over movement of goods across its border with another Member with which it forms part of a customs union, it shall not be required to apply the provisions of this Section at that border.

13. It is understood that there shall be no obligation to apply such procedures to imports of goods put on the market in another country by or with the consent of the right holder, or to goods in transit.

14.For the purposes of this Agreement:
(a) "counterfeit trademark goods" shall mean any goods, including packaging, bearing without authorization a trademark which is identical to the trademark validly registered in respect of such goods, or which cannot be distinguished in its essential aspects from such a trademark, and which thereby infringes the rights of the owner of the trademark in question under the law of the country of importation;
(b) "pirated copyright goods" shall mean any goods which are copies made without the consent of the right holder or person duly authorized by the right holder in the country of production and which are made directly or indirectly from an article where the making of that copy would have constituted an infringement of a copyright or a related right under the law of the country of importation.

Article 53
Security or Equivalent Assurance

1. The competent authorities shall have the authority to require an applicant to provide a security or equivalent assurance sufficient to protect the defendant and the competent authorities and to prevent abuse. Such security or equivalent assurance shall not unreasonably deter recourse to these procedures.

2. Where pursuant to an application under this Section the release of goods involving industrial designs, patents, layout-designs or undisclosed information into free circulation has been suspended by customs authorities on the basis of a decision other than by a judicial or other independent authority, and the period provided for in Article 55 has expired without the granting of provisional relief by the duly empowered authority, and provided that all other conditions for importation have been complied with, the owner, importer, or consignee of such goods shall be entitled to their release on the posting of a security in an amount sufficient to protect the right holder for any infringement. Payment of such security shall not prejudice any other remedy available to the right holder, it being understood that the security shall be released if the right holder fails to pursue the right of action within a reasonable period of time.

Article 54
Notice of Suspension

The importer and the applicant shall be promptly notified of the suspension of the release of goods according to Article 51.

Article 55
Duration of Suspension

If, within a period not exceeding 10 working days after the applicant has been served notice of the suspension, the customs authorities have not been informed that proceedings leading to a decision on the merits of the case have been initiated by a party other than the defendant, or that the duly empowered authority has taken provisional measures prolonging the suspension of the release of the goods, the goods shall be released, provided that all other conditions for importation or exportation have been complied with; in appropriate cases, this time-limit may be extended by another 10 working days. If proceedings leading to a decision on the merits of the case have been initiated, a review, including a right to be heard, shall take place upon request of the defendant with a view to deciding, within a reasonable period, whether these measures shall be modified, revoked or confirmed. Notwithstanding the above, where the suspension of the release of goods is carried out or continued in accordance with a provisional judicial measure, the provisions of paragraph 6 of Article 50 shall apply.

Article 56
Indemnification of the Importer and of the Owner of the Goods

Relevant authorities shall have the authority to order the applicant to pay the importer, the consignee and the owner of the goods appropriate compensation for any injury caused to them through the wrongful detention of goods or through the detention of goods released pursuant to Article 55.

Article 57
Right of Inspection and Information

Without prejudice to the protection of confidential information, Members shall provide the competent authorities the authority to give the right holder sufficient opportunity to have any goods detained by the customs authorities inspected in order to substantiate the right holder's claims. The competent authorities shall also have authority to give the importer an equivalent opportunity to have any such goods inspected. Where a positive determination has been made on the merits of a case, Members may provide the competent authorities the authority to inform the right holder of the names and addresses of the consignor, the importer and the consignee and of the quantity of the goods in question.

Article 58
Ex Officio Action

Where Members require competent authorities to act upon their own initiative and to suspend the release of goods in respect of which they have acquired *prima facie* evidence that an intellectual property right is being infringed:

(a) the competent authorities may at any time seek from the right holder any information that may assist them to exercise these powers;

(b) the importer and the right holder shall be promptly notified of the suspension. Where the importer has lodged an appeal against the suspension with the competent authorities, the suspension shall be subject to the conditions, *mutatis mutandis*, set out at Article 55;

(c) Members shall only exempt both public authorities and officials from liability to appropriate remedial measures where actions are taken or intended in good faith.

Article 59
Remedies

Without prejudice to other rights of action open to the right holder and subject to the right of the defendant to seek review by a judicial authority, competent authorities shall have the authority to order the destruction or disposal of infringing goods in accordance with the principles set out in Article 46. In regard to counterfeit trademark goods, the authorities shall not allow the re-exportation of the infringing goods in an unaltered state or subject them to a different customs procedure, other than in exceptional circumstances.

Article 60
De Minimis Imports

Members may exclude from the application of the above provisions small quantities of goods of a non-commercial nature contained in travellers' personal luggage or sent in small consignments.

Section 5: Criminal Procedures

Article 61

Members shall provide for criminal procedures and penalties to be applied at least in cases of wilful trademark counterfeiting or copyright piracy on a commercial scale. Remedies available shall include imprisonment and/or monetary fines sufficient to provide a deterrent, consistently with the level of penalties applied for crimes of a corresponding gravity. In appropriate cases, remedies available shall also include the seizure, forfeiture and destruction of the infringing goods and of any materials and implements the predominant use of which has been in the commission of the offence. Members may provide for criminal procedures and penalties to be applied in other cases of infringement of intellectual property rights, in particular where they are committed wilfully and on a commercial scale.

PART IV
ACQUISITION AND MAINTENANCE OF INTELLECTUAL PROPERTY RIGHTS AND RELATED INTER-PARTES PROCEDURES

Article 62

1. Members may require, as a condition of the acquisition or maintenance of the intellectual property rights provided for under Sections 2 through 6 of Part II, compliance with reasonable procedures and formalities. Such procedures and formalities shall be consistent with the provisions of this Agreement.

2. Where the acquisition of an intellectual property right is subject to the right being granted or registered, Members shall ensure that the procedures for grant or registration, subject to compliance with the substantive conditions for acquisition of the right, permit the granting or registration of the right within a reasonable period of time so as to avoid unwarranted curtailment of the period of protection.

3. Article 4 of the Paris Convention (1967) shall apply *mutatis mutandis* to service marks.

4. Procedures concerning the acquisition or maintenance of intellectual

property rights and, where a Member's law provides for such procedures, administrative revocation and *inter partes* procedures such as opposition, revocation and cancellation, shall be governed by the general principles set out in paragraphs 2 and 3 of Article 41.

5. Final administrative decisions in any of the procedures referred to under paragraph 4 shall be subject to review by a judicial or quasi-judicial authority. However, there shall be no obligation to provide an opportunity for such review of decisions in cases of unsuccessful opposition or administrative revocation, provided that the grounds for such procedures can be the subject of invalidation procedures.

PART V
DISPUTE PREVENTION AND SETTLEMENT

Article 63
Transparency

1. Laws and regulations, and final judicial decisions and administrative rulings of general application, made effective by a Member pertaining to the subject matter of this Agreement (the availability, scope, acquisition, enforcement and prevention of the abuse of intellectual property rights) shall be published, or where such publication is not practicable made publicly available, in a national language, in such a manner as to enable governments and right holders to become acquainted with them. Agreements concerning the subject matter of this Agreement which are in force between the government or a governmental agency of a Member and the government or a governmental agency of another Member shall also be published.

2. Members shall notify the laws and regulations referred to in paragraph 1 to the Council for TRIPS in order to assist that Council in its review of the operation of this Agreement. The Council shall attempt to minimize the burden on Members in carrying out this obligation and may decide to waive the obligation to notify such laws and regulations directly to the Council if consultations with WIPO on the establishment of a common register containing these laws and regulations are successful. The Council shall also consider in this connection any action required regarding notifications pursuant to the obligations under this Agreement stemming from the provisions of Article 6*ter* of the Paris Convention (1967).

3. Each Member shall be prepared to supply, in response to a written request from another Member, information of the sort referred to in paragraph 1. A Member, having reason to believe that a specific judicial decision or administrative ruling or bilateral agreement in the area of intellectual property rights affects its rights under this Agreement, may also request in writing to be given access to or be informed in sufficient detail of such specific judicial decisions or administrative rulings or bilateral agreements.

4. Nothing in paragraphs 1, 2 and 3 shall require Members to disclose confidential information which would impede law enforcement or otherwise

be contrary to the public interest or would prejudice the legitimate commercial interests of particular enterprises, public or private.

Article 64
Dispute Settlement

1. The provisions of Articles XXII and XXIII of GATT 1994 as elaborated and applied by the Dispute Settlement Understanding shall apply to consultations and the settlement of disputes under this Agreement except as otherwise specifically provided herein.

2. Subparagraphs 1(b) and 1(c) of Article XXIII of GATT 1994 shall not apply to the settlement of disputes under this Agreement for a period of five years from the date of entry into force of the WTO Agreement.

3. During the time period referred to in paragraph 2, the Council for TRIPS shall examine the scope and modalities for complaints of the type provided for under subparagraphs 1(b) and 1(c) of Article XXIII of GATT 1994 made pursuant to this Agreement, and submit its recommendations to the Ministerial Conference for approval. Any decision of the Ministerial Conference to approve such recommendations or to extend the period in paragraph 2 shall be made only by consensus, and approved recommendations shall be effective for all Members without further formal acceptance process.

PART VI
TRANSITIONAL ARRANGEMENTS

Article 65
Transitional Arrangements

1. Subject to the provisions of paragraphs 2, 3 and 4, no Member shall be obliged to apply the provisions of this Agreement before the expiry of a general period of one year following the date of entry into force of the WTO Agreement.

2. A developing country Member is entitled to delay for a further period of four years the date of application, as defined in paragraph 1, of the provisions of this Agreement other than Articles 3, 4 and 5.

3. Any other Member which is in the process of transformation from a centrally-planned into a market, free-enterprise economy and which is undertaking structural reform of its intellectual property system and facing special problems in the preparation and implementation of intellectual property laws and regulations, may also benefit from a period of delay as foreseen in paragraph 2.

4. To the extent that a developing country Member is obliged by this Agreement to extend product patent protection to areas of technology not so protectable in its territory on the general date of application of this Agreement for that Member, as defined in paragraph 2, it may delay the

application of the provisions on product patents of Section 5 of Part II to such areas of technology for an additional period of five years.

5. A Member availing itself of a transitional period under paragraphs 1, 2, 3 or 4 shall ensure that any changes in its laws, regulations and practice made during that period do not result in a lesser degree of consistency with the provisions of this Agreement.

Article 66
Least-Developed Country Members

1. In view of the special needs and requirements of least-developed country Members, their economic, financial and administrative constraints, and their need for flexibility to create a viable technological base, such Members shall not be required to apply the provisions of this Agreement, other than Articles 3, 4 and 5, for a period of 10 years from the date of application as defined under paragraph 1 of Article 65. The Council for TRIPS shall, upon duly motivated request by a least-developed country Member, accord extensions of this period.

2. Developed country Members shall provide incentives to enterprises and institutions in their territories for the purpose of promoting and encouraging technology transfer to least-developed country Members in order to enable them to create a sound and viable technological base.

Article 67
Technical Cooperation

In order to facilitate the implementation of this Agreement, developed country Members shall provide, on request and on mutually agreed terms and conditions, technical and financial cooperation in favour of developing and least-developed country Members. Such cooperation shall include assistance in the preparation of laws and regulations on the protection and enforcement of intellectual property rights as well as on the prevention of their abuse, and shall include support regarding the establishment or reinforcement of domestic offices and agencies relevant to these matters, including the training of personnel.

PART VII
INSTITUTIONAL ARRANGEMENTS; FINAL PROVISIONS

Article 68
Council for Trade-Related Aspects of
Intellectual Property Rights

The Council for TRIPS shall monitor the operation of this Agreement and, in particular, Members' compliance with their obligations hereunder, and shall afford Members the opportunity of consulting on matters relating to the trade-related aspects of intellectual property rights. It shall carry out such other responsibilities as assigned to it by the Members, and it shall, in particular, provide any assistance requested by them in the context of dispute settlement procedures. In carrying out its functions, the Council for TRIPS may consult with and seek information from any source it deems appropriate. In consultation with WIPO, the Council shall seek to establish, within one year of its first meeting, appropriate arrangements for cooperation with bodies of that Organization.

Article 69
International Cooperation

Members agree to cooperate with each other with a view to eliminating international trade in goods infringing intellectual property rights. For this purpose, they shall establish and notify contact points in their administrations and be ready to exchange information on trade in infringing goods. They shall, in particular, promote the exchange of information and cooperation between customs authorities with regard to trade in counterfeit trademark goods and pirated copyright goods.

Article 70
Protection of Existing Subject Matter

1. This Agreement does not give rise to obligations in respect of acts which occurred before the date of application of the Agreement for the Member in question.

2. Except as otherwise provided for in this Agreement, this Agreement gives rise to obligations in respect of all subject matter existing at the date of application of this Agreement for the Member in question, and which is protected in that Member on the said date, or which meets or comes subsequently to meet the criteria for protection under the terms of this Agreement. In respect of this paragraph and paragraphs 3 and 4, copyright obligations with respect to existing works shall be solely determined under Article 18 of the Berne Convention (1971), and obligations with respect to the rights of producers of phonograms and performers in existing phonograms shall be determined solely under Article 18 of the Berne Convention (1971) as made applicable under paragraph 6 of Article 14 of this Agreement.

3. There shall be no obligation to restore protection to subject matter which on the date of application of this Agreement for the Member in question has fallen into the public domain.

4. In respect of any acts in respect of specific objects embodying protected subject matter which become infringing under the terms of legislation in conformity with this Agreement, and which were commenced, or in respect of which a significant investment was made, before the date of acceptance of the WTO Agreement by that Member, any Member may provide for a limitation of the remedies available to the right holder as to the continued performance of such acts after the date of application of this Agreement for that Member. In such cases the Member shall, however, at least provide for the payment of equitable remuneration.

5. A Member is not obliged to apply the provisions of Article 11 and of paragraph 4 of Article 14 with respect to originals or copies purchased prior to the date of application of this Agreement for that Member.

6. Members shall not be required to apply Article 31, or the requirement in paragraph 1 of Article 27 that patent rights shall be enjoyable without discrimination as to the field of technology, to use without the authorization of the right holder where authorization for such use was granted by the government before the date this Agreement became known.

7. In the case of intellectual property rights for which protection is conditional upon registration, applications for protection which are pending on the date of application of this Agreement for the Member in question shall be permitted to be amended to claim any enhanced protection provided under the provisions of this Agreement. Such amendments shall not include new matter.

8. Where a Member does not make available as of the date of entry into force of the WTO Agreement patent protection for pharmaceutical and agricultural chemical products commensurate with its obligations under Article 27, that Member shall:

(a) notwithstanding the provisions of Part VI, provide as from the date of entry into force of the WTO Agreement a means by which applications for patents for such inventions can be filed;

(b) apply to these applications, as of the date of application of this Agreement, the criteria for patentability as laid down in this Agreement as if those criteria were being applied on the date of filing in that Member or, where priority is available and claimed, the priority date of the application; and

(c) provide patent protection in accordance with this Agreement as from the grant of the patent and for the remainder of the patent term, counted from the filing date in accordance with Article 33 of this Agreement, for those of these applications that meet the criteria for protection referred to in subparagraph (b).

9. Where a product is the subject of a patent application in a Member in accordance with paragraph 8(a), exclusive marketing rights shall be granted, notwithstanding the provisions of Part VI, for a period of five years after obtaining marketing approval in that Member or until a product patent is granted or rejected in that Member, whichever period is shorter, provided that, subsequent to the entry into force of the WTO Agreement, a patent application has been filed and a patent granted for that product in another Member and marketing approval obtained in such other Member.

Article 71
Review and Amendment

1. The Council for TRIPS shall review the implementation of this Agreement after the expiration of the transitional period referred to in paragraph 2 of Article 65. The Council shall, having regard to the experience

gained in its implementation, review it two years after that date, and at identical intervals thereafter. The Council may also undertake reviews in the light of any relevant new developments which might warrant modification or amendment of this Agreement.

2. Amendments merely serving the purpose of adjusting to higher levels of protection of intellectual property rights achieved, and in force, in other multilateral agreements and accepted under those agreements by all Members of the WTO may be referred to the Ministerial Conference for action in accordance with paragraph 6 of Article X of the WTO Agreement on the basis of a consensus proposal from the Council for TRIPS.

Article 72
Reservations

Reservations may not be entered in respect of any of the provisions of this Agreement without the consent of the other Members.

Article 73
Security Exceptions

Nothing in this Agreement shall be construed:

(a) to require a Member to furnish any information the disclosure of which it considers contrary to its essential security interests; or

(b) to prevent a Member from taking any action which it considers necessary for the protection of its essential security interests;

  (i) relating to fissionable materials or the materials from which they are derived;

  (ii) relating to the traffic in arms, ammunition and implements of war and to such traffic in other goods and materials as is carried on directly or indirectly for the purpose of supplying a military establishment;

  (iii) taken in time of war or other emergency in international relations; or

(c) to prevent a Member from taking any action in pursuance of its obligations under the United Nations Charter for the maintenance of international peace and security.

UNDERSTANDING ON RULES AND PROCEDURES GOVERNING THE SETTLEMENT OF DISPUTES
Annex 2 to the Agreement Establishing the World Trade Organization, April 15, 1994, Marrakesh, Morocco

Members hereby *agree* as follows:

Article 1
Coverage and Application

1.   The rules and procedures of this Understanding shall apply to disputes brought pursuant to the consultation and dispute settlement provisions of the agreements listed in Appendix 1 to this Understanding (referred to in this Understanding as the "covered agreements"). The rules and procedures of this Understanding shall also apply to consultations and the settlement of disputes between Members concerning their rights and obligations under the provisions of the Agreement Establishing the World Trade Organization (referred to in this Understanding as the "WTO Agreement") and of this Understanding taken in isolation or in combination with any other covered agreement.

2.   The rules and procedures of this Understanding shall apply subject to such special or additional rules and procedures on dispute settlement contained in the covered agreements as are identified in Appendix 2 to this Understanding. To the extent that there is a difference between the rules and procedures of this Understanding and the special or additional rules and procedures set forth in Appendix 2, the special or additional rules and procedures in Appendix 2 shall prevail. In disputes involving rules and procedures under more than one covered agreement, if there is a conflict between special or additional rules and procedures of such agreements under review, and where the parties to the dispute cannot agree on rules and procedures within 20 days of the establishment of the panel, the Chairman of the Dispute Settlement Body provided for in paragraph 1 of Article 2 (referred to in this Understanding as the "DSB"), in consultation with the parties to the dispute, shall determine the rules and procedures to be followed within 10 days after a request by either Member. The Chairman shall be guided by the principle that special or additional rules and procedures should be used where possible, and the rules and procedures set out in this Understanding should be used to the extent necessary to avoid conflict.

Article 2
Administration

1.   The Dispute Settlement Body is hereby established to administer these rules and procedures and, except as otherwise provided in a covered agreement, the consultation and dispute settlement provisions of the covered

agreements. Accordingly, the DSB shall have the authority to establish panels, adopt panel and Appellate Body reports, maintain surveillance of implementation of rulings and recommendations, and authorize suspension of concessions and other obligations under the covered agreements. With respect to disputes arising under a covered agreement which is a Plurilateral Trade Agreement, the term "Member" as used herein shall refer only to those Members that are parties to the relevant Plurilateral Trade Agreement. Where the DSB administers the dispute settlement provisions of a Plurilateral Trade Agreement, only those Members that are parties to that Agreement may participate in decisions or actions taken by the DSB with respect to that dispute.

2. The DSB shall inform the relevant WTO Councils and Committees of any developments in disputes related to provisions of the respective covered agreements.

3. The DSB shall meet as often as necessary to carry out its functions within the time-frames provided in this Understanding.

4. Where the rules and procedures of this Understanding provide for the DSB to take a decision, it shall do so by consensus.[1]

Article 3
General Provisions

1. Members affirm their adherence to the principles for the management of disputes heretofore applied under Articles XXII and XXIII of GATT 1947, and the rules and procedures as further elaborated and modified herein.

2. The dispute settlement system of the WTO is a central element in providing security and predictability to the multilateral trading system. The Members recognize that it serves to preserve the rights and obligations of Members under the covered agreements, and to clarify the existing provisions of those agreements in accordance with customary rules of interpretation of public international law. Recommendations and rulings of the DSB cannot add to or diminish the rights and obligations provided in the covered agreements.

3. The prompt settlement of situations in which a Member considers that any benefits accruing to it directly or indirectly under the covered agreements are being impaired by measures taken by another Member is essential to the effective functioning of the WTO and the maintenance of a proper balance between the rights and obligations of Members.

4. Recommendations or rulings made by the DSB shall be aimed at achieving a satisfactory settlement of the matter in accordance with the rights and obligations under this Understanding and under the covered agreements.

---

1. The DSB shall be deemed to have decided by consensus on a matter submitted for its consideration, if no Member, present at the meeting of the DSB when the decision is taken, formally objects to the proposed decision.

5. All solutions to matters formally raised under the consultation and dispute settlement provisions of the covered agreements, including arbitration awards, shall be consistent with those agreements and shall not nullify or impair benefits accruing to any Member under those agreements, nor impede the attainment of any objective of those agreements.

6. Mutually agreed solutions to matters formally raised under the consultation and dispute settlement provisions of the covered agreements shall be notified to the DSB and the relevant Councils and Committees, where any Member may raise any point relating thereto.

7. Before bringing a case, a Member shall exercise its judgement as to whether action under these procedures would be fruitful. The aim of the dispute settlement mechanism is to secure a positive solution to a dispute. A solution mutually acceptable to the parties to a dispute and consistent with the covered agreements is clearly to be preferred. In the absence of a mutually agreed solution, the first objective of the dispute settlement mechanism is usually to secure the withdrawal of the measures concerned if these are found to be inconsistent with the provisions of any of the covered agreements. The provision of compensation should be resorted to only if the immediate withdrawal of the measure is impracticable and as a temporary measure pending the withdrawal of the measure which is inconsistent with a covered agreement. The last resort which this Understanding provides to the Member invoking the dispute settlement procedures is the possibility of suspending the application of concessions or other obligations under the covered agreements on a discriminatory basis vis-à-vis the other Member, subject to authorization by the DSB of such measures.

8. In cases where there is an infringement of the obligations assumed under a covered agreement, the action is considered *prima facie* to constitute a case of nullification or impairment. This means that there is normally a presumption that a breach of the rules has an adverse impact on other Members parties to that covered agreement, and in such cases, it shall be up to the Member against whom the complaint has been brought to rebut the charge.

9. The provisions of this Understanding are without prejudice to the rights of Members to seek authoritative interpretation of provisions of a covered agreement through decision-making under the WTO Agreement or a covered agreement which is a Plurilateral Trade Agreement.

10. It is understood that requests for conciliation and the use of the dispute settlement procedures should not be intended or considered as contentious acts and that, if a dispute arises, all Members will engage in these procedures in good faith in an effort to resolve the dispute. It is also understood that complaints and counter-complaints in regard to distinct matters should not be linked.

11. This Understanding shall be applied only with respect to new requests for consultations under the consultation provisions of the covered agreements made on or after the date of entry into force of the WTO Agreement. With respect to disputes for which the request for consultations was made under

GATT 1947 or under any other predecessor agreement to the covered agreements before the date of entry into force of the WTO Agreement, the relevant dispute settlement rules and procedures in effect immediately prior to the date of entry into force of the WTO Agreement shall continue to apply.[2]

12.   Notwithstanding paragraph 11, if a complaint based on any of the covered agreements is brought by a developing country Member against a developed country Member, the complaining party shall have the right to invoke, as an alternative to the provisions contained in Articles 4, 5, 6 and 12 of this Understanding, the corresponding provisions of the Decision of 5 April 1966 (BISD 14S/18), except that where the Panel considers that the time-frame provided for in paragraph 7 of that Decision is insufficient to provide its report and with the agreement of the complaining party, that time-frame may be extended. To the extent that there is a difference between the rules and procedures of Articles 4, 5, 6 and 12 and the corresponding rules and procedures of the Decision, the latter shall prevail.

Article 4
Consultations

1. Members affirm their resolve to strengthen and improve the effectiveness of the consultation procedures employed by Members.

2.   Each Member undertakes to accord sympathetic consideration to and afford adequate opportunity for consultation regarding any representations made by another Member concerning measures affecting the operation of any covered agreement taken within the territory of the former.[3]

3. If a request for consultations is made pursuant to a covered agreement, the Member to which the request is made shall, unless otherwise mutually agreed, reply to the request within 10 days after the date of its receipt and shall enter into consultations in good faith within a period of no more than 30 days after the date of receipt of the request, with a view to reaching a mutually satisfactory solution. If the Member does not respond within 10 days after the date of receipt of the request, or does not enter into consultations within a period of no more than 30 days, or a period otherwise mutually agreed, after the date of receipt of the request, then the Member that requested the holding of consultations may proceed directly to request the establishment of a panel.

4.   All such requests for consultations shall be notified to the DSB and the relevant Councils and Committees by the Member which requests consultations. Any request for consultations shall be submitted in writing and shall give the reasons for the request, including identification of the measures at issue and an indication of the legal basis for the complaint.

---

2. This paragraph shall also be applied to disputes on which panel reports have not been adopted or fully implemented.

3. Where the provisions of any other covered agreement concerning measures taken by regional or local governments or authorities within the territory of a Member contain provisions different from the provisions of this paragraph, the provisions of such other covered agreement shall prevail.

5. In the course of consultations in accordance with the provisions of a covered agreement, before resorting to further action under this Understanding, Members should attempt to obtain satisfactory adjustment of the matter.

6. Consultations shall be confidential, and without prejudice to the rights of any Member in any further proceedings.

7. If the consultations fail to settle a dispute within 60 days after the date of receipt of the request for consultations, the complaining party may request the establishment of a panel. The complaining party may request a panel during the 60-day period if the consulting parties jointly consider that consultations have failed to settle the dispute.

8. In cases of urgency, including those which concern perishable goods, Members shall enter into consultations within a period of no more than 10 days after the date of receipt of the request. If the consultations have failed to settle the dispute within a period of 20 days after the date of receipt of the request, the complaining party may request the establishment of a panel.

9. In cases of urgency, including those which concern perishable goods, the parties to the dispute, panels and the Appellate Body shall make every effort to accelerate the proceedings to the greatest extent possible.

10. During consultations Members should give special attention to the particular problems and interests of developing country Members.

11. Whenever a Member other than the consulting Members considers that it has a substantial trade interest in consultations being held pursuant to paragraph 1 of Article XXII of GATT 1994, paragraph 1 of Article XXII of GATS, or the corresponding provisions in other covered agreements,[4] such Member may notify the consulting Members and the DSB, within 10 days after the date of the circulation of the request for consultations under said Article, of its desire to be joined in the consultations. Such Member shall be joined in the consultations, provided that the Member to which the request for consultations was addressed agrees that the claim of substantial interest is well-founded. In that event they shall so inform the DSB. If the request to be joined in the consultations is not accepted, the applicant Member shall be free to request consultations under paragraph 1 of Article XXII or paragraph 1 of Article XXIII of GATT 1994, paragraph 1 of Article XXII or paragraph 1 of Article XXIII of GATS, or the corresponding provisions in other covered agreements.

---

4. The corresponding consultation provisions in the covered agreements are listed hereunder: Agreement on Agriculture, Article 19; Agreement on the Application of Sanitary and Phytosanitary Measures, paragraph 1 of Article 11; Agreement on Textiles and Clothing, paragraph 4 of Article 8; Agreement on Technical Barriers to Trade, paragraph 1 of Article 14; Agreement on Trade-Related Investment Measures, Article 8; Agreement on Implementation of Article VI of GATT 1994, paragraph 2 of Article 17; Agreement on Implementation of Article VII of GATT 1994, paragraph 2 of Article 19; Agreement on Preshipment Inspection, Article 7; Agreement on Rules of Origin, Article 7; Agreement on Import Licensing Procedures, Article 6; Agreement on Subsidies and Countervailing Measures, Article 30; Agreement on Safeguards, Article 14; Agreement on Trade-Related Aspects of Intellectual Property Rights, Article 64.1; and any corresponding consultation provisions in Plurilateral Trade Agreements as determined by the competent bodies of each Agreement and as notified to the DSB.

Article 5
Good Offices, Conciliation and Mediation

1. Good offices, conciliation and mediation are procedures that are undertaken voluntarily if the parties to the dispute so agree.

2. Proceedings involving good offices, conciliation and mediation, and in particular positions taken by the parties to the dispute during these proceedings, shall be confidential, and without prejudice to the rights of either party in any further proceedings under these procedures.

3. Good offices, conciliation or mediation may be requested at any time by any party to a dispute. They may begin at any time and be terminated at any time. Once procedures for good offices, conciliation or mediation are terminated, a complaining party may then proceed with a request for the establishment of a panel.

4. When good offices, conciliation or mediation are entered into within 60 days after the date of receipt of a request for consultations, the complaining party must allow a period of 60 days after the date of receipt of the request for consultations before requesting the establishment of a panel. The complaining party may request the establishment of a panel during the 60-day period if the parties to the dispute jointly consider that the good offices, conciliation or mediation process has failed to settle the dispute.

5. If the parties to a dispute agree, procedures for good offices, conciliation or mediation may continue while the panel process proceeds.

6. The Director-General may, acting in an *ex officio* capacity, offer good offices, conciliation or mediation with the view to assisting Members to settle a dispute.

Article 6
Establishment of Panels

1. If the complaining party so requests, a panel shall be established at the latest at the DSB meeting following that at which the request first appears as an item on the DSB's agenda, unless at that meeting the DSB decides by consensus not to establish a panel.[5]

2. The request for the establishment of a panel shall be made in writing. It shall indicate whether consultations were held, identify the specific measures at issue and provide a brief summary of the legal basis of the complaint sufficient to present the problem clearly. In case the applicant requests the establishment of a panel with other than standard terms of reference, the written request shall include the proposed text of special terms of reference.

---

5. If the complaining party so requests, a meeting of the DSB shall be convened for this purpose within 15 days of the request, provided that at least 10 days' advance notice of the meeting is given.

Article 7
Terms of Reference of Panels

1. Panels shall have the following terms of reference unless the parties to the dispute agree otherwise within 20 days from the establishment of the panel:

> "To examine, in the light of the relevant provisions in (name of the covered agreement(s) cited by the parties to the dispute), the matter referred to the DSB by (name of party) in document . . . and to make such findings as will assist the DSB in making the recommendations or in giving the rulings provided for in that/those agreement(s)."

2. Panels shall address the relevant provisions in any covered agreement or agreements cited by the parties to the dispute.

3. In establishing a panel, the DSB may authorize its Chairman to draw up the terms of reference of the panel in consultation with the parties to the dispute, subject to the provisions of paragraph 1. The terms of reference thus drawn up shall be circulated to all Members. If other than standard terms of reference are agreed upon, any Member may raise any point relating thereto in the DSB.

Article 8
Composition of Panels

1. Panels shall be composed of well-qualified governmental and/or non-governmental individuals, including persons who have served on or presented a case to a panel, served as a representative of a Member or of a contracting party to GATT 1947 or as a representative to the Council or Committee of any covered agreement or its predecessor agreement, or in the Secretariat, taught or published on international trade law or policy, or served as a senior trade policy official of a Member.

2. Panel members should be selected with a view to ensuring the independence of the members, a sufficiently diverse background and a wide spectrum of experience.

3. Citizens of Members whose governments[6] are parties to the dispute or third parties as defined in paragraph 2 of Article 10 shall not serve on a panel concerned with that dispute, unless the parties to the dispute agree otherwise.

4. To assist in the selection of panelists, the Secretariat shall maintain an indicative list of governmental and non-governmental individuals possessing the qualifications outlined in paragraph 1, from which panelists may be drawn as appropriate. That list shall include the roster of non-governmental panelists established on 30 November 1984 (BISD 31S/9), and other rosters and indicative lists established under any of the covered agreements, and shall retain the names of persons on those rosters and indicative lists at the

---

6. In the case where customs unions or common markets are parties to a dispute, this provision applies to citizens of all member countries of the customs unions or common markets.

time of entry into force of the WTO Agreement. Members may periodically suggest names of governmental and non-governmental individuals for inclusion on the indicative list, providing relevant information on their knowledge of international trade and of the sectors or subject matter of the covered agreements, and those names shall be added to the list upon approval by the DSB. For each of the individuals on the list, the list shall indicate specific areas of experience or expertise of the individuals in the sectors or subject matter of the covered agreements.

5. Panels shall be composed of three panelists unless the parties to the dispute agree, within 10 days from the establishment of the panel, to a panel composed of five panelists. Members shall be informed promptly of the composition of the panel.

6. The Secretariat shall propose nominations for the panel to the parties to the dispute. The parties to the dispute shall not oppose nominations except for compelling reasons.

7. If there is no agreement on the panelists within 20 days after the date of the establishment of a panel, at the request of either party, the Director-General, in consultation with the Chairman of the DSB and the Chairman of the relevant Council or Committee, shall determine the composition of the panel by appointing the panelists whom the Director-General considers most appropriate in accordance with any relevant special or additional rules or procedures of the covered agreement or covered agreements which are at issue in the dispute, after consulting with the parties to the dispute. The Chairman of the DSB shall inform the Members of the composition of the panel thus formed no later than 10 days after the date the Chairman receives such a request.

8. Members shall undertake, as a general rule, to permit their officials to serve as panelists.

9. Panelists shall serve in their individual capacities and not as government representatives, nor as representatives of any organization. Members shall therefore not give them instructions nor seek to influence them as individuals with regard to matters before a panel.

10. When a dispute is between a developing country Member and a developed country Member the panel shall, if the developing country Member so requests, include at least one panelist from a developing country Member.

11. Panelists' expenses, including travel and subsistence allowance, shall be met from the WTO budget in accordance with criteria to be adopted by the General Council, based on recommendations of the Committee on Budget, Finance and Administration.

Article 9
Procedures for Multiple Complaints

1. Where more than one Member requests the establishment of a panel related to the same matter, a single panel may be established to examine these complaints taking into account the rights of all Members concerned. A

single panel should be established to examine such complaints whenever feasible.

2.   The single panel shall organize its examination and present its findings to the DSB in such a manner that the rights which the parties to the dispute would have enjoyed had separate panels examined the complaints are in no way impaired. If one of the parties to the dispute so requests, the panel shall submit separate reports on the dispute concerned. The written submissions by each of the complainants shall be made available to the other complainants, and each complainant shall have the right to be present when any one of the other complainants presents its views to the panel.

3.   If more than one panel is established to examine the complaints related to the same matter, to the greatest extent possible the same persons shall serve as panelists on each of the separate panels and the timetable for the panel process in such disputes shall be harmonized.

Article 10
Third Parties

1.   The interests of the parties to a dispute and those of other Members under a covered agreement at issue in the dispute shall be fully taken into account during the panel process.

2.   Any Member having a substantial interest in a matter before a panel and having notified its interest to the DSB (referred to in this Understanding as a "third party") shall have an opportunity to be heard by the panel and to make written submissions to the panel. These submissions shall also be given to the parties to the dispute and shall be reflected in the panel report.

3.   Third parties shall receive the submissions of the parties to the dispute to the first meeting of the panel.

4.   If a third party considers that a measure already the subject of a panel proceeding nullifies or impairs benefits accruing to it under any covered agreement, that Member may have recourse to normal dispute settlement procedures under this Understanding. Such a dispute shall be referred to the original panel wherever possible.

Article 11
Function of Panels

The function of panels is to assist the DSB in discharging its responsibilities under this Understanding and the covered agreements. Accordingly, a panel should make an objective assessment of the matter before it, including an objective assessment of the facts of the case and the applicability of and conformity with the relevant covered agreements, and make such other findings as will assist the DSB in making the recommendations or in giving the rulings provided for in the covered agreements. Panels should consult regularly with the parties to the dispute and give them adequate opportunity to develop a mutually satisfactory solution.

Article 12
Panel Procedures

1. Panels shall follow the Working Procedures in Appendix 3 unless the panel decides otherwise after consulting the parties to the dispute.

2. Panel procedures should provide sufficient flexibility so as to ensure high-quality panel reports, while not unduly delaying the panel process.

3. After consulting the parties to the dispute, the panelists shall, as soon as practicable and whenever possible within one week after the composition and terms of reference of the panel have been agreed upon, fix the timetable for the panel process, taking into account the provisions of paragraph 9 of Article 4, if relevant.

4. In determining the timetable for the panel process, the panel shall provide sufficient time for the parties to the dispute to prepare their submissions.

5. Panels should set precise deadlines for written submissions by the parties and the parties should respect those deadlines.

6. Each party to the dispute shall deposit its written submissions with the Secretariat for immediate transmission to the panel and to the other party or parties to the dispute. The complaining party shall submit its first submission in advance of the responding party's first submission unless the panel decides, in fixing the timetable referred to in paragraph 3 and after consultations with the parties to the dispute, that the parties should submit their first submissions simultaneously. When there are sequential arrangements for the deposit of first submissions, the panel shall establish a firm time-period for receipt of the responding party's submission. Any subsequent written submissions shall be submitted simultaneously.

7. Where the parties to the dispute have failed to develop a mutually satisfactory solution, the panel shall submit its findings in the form of a written report to the DSB. In such cases, the report of a panel shall set out the findings of fact, the applicability of relevant provisions and the basic rationale behind any findings and recommendations that it makes. Where a settlement of the matter among the parties to the dispute has been found, the report of the panel shall be confined to a brief description of the case and to reporting that a solution has been reached.

8. In order to make the procedures more efficient, the period in which the panel shall conduct its examination, from the date that the composition and terms of reference of the panel have been agreed upon until the date the final report is issued to the parties to the dispute, shall, as a general rule, not exceed six months. In cases of urgency, including those relating to perishable goods, the panel shall aim to issue its report to the parties to the dispute within three months.

9. When the panel considers that it cannot issue its report within six months, or within three months in cases of urgency, it shall inform the DSB in writing of the reasons for the delay together with an estimate of the period

within which it will issue its report. In no case should the period from the establishment of the panel to the circulation of the report to the Members exceed nine months.

10.   In the context of consultations involving a measure taken by a developing country Member, the parties may agree to extend the periods established in paragraphs 7 and 8 of Article 4. If, after the relevant period has elapsed, the consulting parties cannot agree that the consultations have concluded, the Chairman of the DSB shall decide, after consultation with the parties, whether to extend the relevant period and, if so, for how long. In addition, in examining a complaint against a developing country Member, the panel shall accord sufficient time for the developing country Member to prepare and present its argumentation. The provisions of paragraph 1 of Article 20 and paragraph 4 of Article 21 are not affected by any action pursuant to this paragraph.

11.   Where one or more of the parties is a developing country Member, the panel's report shall explicitly indicate the form in which account has been taken of relevant provisions on differential and more-favourable treatment for developing country Members that form part of the covered agreements which have been raised by the developing country Member in the course of the dispute settlement procedures.

12.   The panel may suspend its work at any time at the request of the complaining party for a period not to exceed 12 months. In the event of such a suspension, the time-frames set out in paragraphs 8 and 9 of this Article, paragraph 1 of Article 20, and paragraph 4 of Article 21 shall be extended by the amount of time that the work was suspended. If the work of the panel has been suspended for more than 12 months, the authority for establishment of the panel shall lapse.

Article 13
Right to Seek Information

1.   Each panel shall have the right to seek information and technical advice from any individual or body which it deems appropriate. However, before a panel seeks such information or advice from any individual or body within the jurisdiction of a Member it shall inform the authorities of that Member. A Member should respond promptly and fully to any request by a panel for such information as the panel considers necessary and appropriate. Confidential information which is provided shall not be revealed without formal authorization from the individual, body, or authorities of the Member providing the information.

2.   Panels may seek information from any relevant source and may consult experts to obtain their opinion on certain aspects of the matter. With respect to a factual issue concerning a scientific or other technical matter raised by a party to a dispute, a panel may request an advisory report in writing from an expert review group. Rules for the establishment of such a group and its procedures are set forth in Appendix 4.

Article 14
Confidentiality

1. Panel deliberations shall be confidential.

2. The reports of panels shall be drafted without the presence of the parties to the dispute in the light of the information provided and the statements made.

3. Opinions expressed in the panel report by individual panelists shall be anonymous.

Article 15
Interim Review Stage

1. Following the consideration of rebuttal submissions and oral arguments, the panel shall issue the descriptive (factual and argument) sections of its draft report to the parties to the dispute. Within a period of time set by the panel, the parties shall submit their comments in writing.

2. Following the expiration of the set period of time for receipt of comments from the parties to the dispute, the panel shall issue an interim report to the parties, including both the descriptive sections and the panel's findings and conclusions. Within a period of time set by the panel, a party may submit a written request for the panel to review precise aspects of the interim report prior to circulation of the final report to the Members. At the request of a party, the panel shall hold a further meeting with the parties on the issues identified in the written comments. If no comments are received from any party within the comment period, the interim report shall be considered the final panel report and circulated promptly to the Members.

3. The findings of the final panel report shall include a discussion of the arguments made at the interim review stage. The interim review stage shall be conducted within the time-period set out in paragraph 8 of Article 12.

Article 16
Adoption of Panel Reports

1. In order to provide sufficient time for the Members to consider panel reports, the reports shall not be considered for adoption by the DSB until 20 days after the date they have been circulated to the Members.

2. Members having objections to a panel report shall give written reasons to explain their objections for circulation at least 10 days prior to the DSB meeting at which the panel report will be considered.

3. The parties to a dispute shall have the right to participate fully in the consideration of the panel report by the DSB, and their views shall be fully recorded.

4. Within 60 days after the date of circulation of a panel report to the

Members, the report shall be adopted at a DSB meeting[7] unless a party to the dispute formally notifies the DSB of its decision to appeal or the DSB decides by consensus not to adopt the report. If a party has notified its decision to appeal, the report by the panel shall not be considered for adoption by the DSB until after completion of the appeal. This adoption procedure is without prejudice to the right of Members to express their views on a panel report.

Article 17
Appellate Review

Standing Appellate Body

1. A standing Appellate Body shall be established by the DSB. The Appellate Body shall hear appeals from panel cases. It shall be composed of seven persons, three of whom shall serve on any one case. Persons serving on the Appellate Body shall serve in rotation. Such rotation shall be determined in the working procedures of the Appellate Body.

2. The DSB shall appoint persons to serve on the Appellate Body for a four-year term, and each person may be reappointed once. However, the terms of three of the seven persons appointed immediately after the entry into force of the WTO Agreement shall expire at the end of two years, to be determined by lot. Vacancies shall be filled as they arise. A person appointed to replace a person whose term of office has not expired shall hold office for the remainder of the predecessor's term.

3. The Appellate Body shall comprise persons of recognized authority, with demonstrated expertise in law, international trade and the subject matter of the covered agreements generally. They shall be unaffiliated with any government. The Appellate Body membership shall be broadly representative of membership in the WTO. All persons serving on the Appellate Body shall be available at all times and on short notice, and shall stay abreast of dispute settlement activities and other relevant activities of the WTO. They shall not participate in the consideration of any disputes that would create a direct or indirect conflict of interest.

4. Only parties to the dispute, not third parties, may appeal a panel report. Third parties which have notified the DSB of a substantial interest in the matter pursuant to paragraph 2 of Article 10 may make written submissions to, and be given an opportunity to be heard by, the Appellate Body.

5. As a general rule, the proceedings shall not exceed 60 days from the date a party to the dispute formally notifies its decision to appeal to the date the Appellate Body circulates its report. In fixing its timetable the Appellate Body shall take into account the provisions of paragraph 9 of Article 4, if relevant. When the Appellate Body considers that it cannot provide its report

---

7. If a meeting of the DSB is not scheduled within this period at a time that enables the requirements of paragraphs 1 and 4 of Article 16 to be met, a meeting of the DSB shall be held for this purpose.

within 60 days, it shall inform the DSB in writing of the reasons for the delay together with an estimate of the period within which it will submit its report. In no case shall the proceedings exceed 90 days.

6. An appeal shall be limited to issues of law covered in the panel report and legal interpretations developed by the panel.

7. The Appellate Body shall be provided with appropriate administrative and legal support as it requires.

8. The expenses of persons serving on the Appellate Body, including travel and subsistence allowance, shall be met from the WTO budget in accordance with criteria to be adopted by the General Council, based on recommendations of the Committee on Budget, Finance and Administration.

Procedures for Appellate Review

9. Working procedures shall be drawn up by the Appellate Body in consultation with the Chairman of the DSB and the Director-General, and communicated to the Members for their information.

10. The proceedings of the Appellate Body shall be confidential. The reports of the Appellate Body shall be drafted without the presence of the parties to the dispute and in the light of the information provided and the statements made.

11. Opinions expressed in the Appellate Body report by individuals serving on the Appellate Body shall be anonymous.

12. The Appellate Body shall address each of the issues raised in accordance with paragraph 6 during the appellate proceeding.

13. The Appellate Body may uphold, modify or reverse the legal findings and conclusions of the panel.

Adoption of Appellate Body Reports

14. An Appellate Body report shall be adopted by the DSB and unconditionally accepted by the parties to the dispute unless the DSB decides by consensus not to adopt the Appellate Body report within 30 days following its circulation to the Members.[8] This adoption procedure is without prejudice to the right of Members to express their views on an Appellate Body report.

Article 18
Communications with the Panel or Appellate Body

1. There shall be no *ex parte* communications with the panel or Appellate Body concerning matters under consideration by the panel or Appellate Body.

2. Written submissions to the panel or the Appellate Body shall be treated as confidential, but shall be made available to the parties to the dispute. Nothing in this Understanding shall preclude a party to a dispute from disclosing statements of its own positions to the public. Members shall treat

---

8. If a meeting of the DSB is not scheduled during this period, such a meeting of the DSB shall be held for this purpose.

as confidential information submitted by another Member to the panel or the Appellate Body which that Member has designated as confidential. A party to a dispute shall also, upon request of a Member, provide a non-confidential summary of the information contained in its written submissions that could be disclosed to the public.

Article 19
Panel and Appellate Body Recommendations

1. Where a panel or the Appellate Body concludes that a measure is inconsistent with a covered agreement, it shall recommend that the Member concerned[9] bring the measure into conformity with that agreement.[10] In addition to its recommendations, the panel or Appellate Body may suggest ways in which the Member concerned could implement the recommendations.

2. In accordance with paragraph 2 of Article 3, in their findings and recommendations, the panel and Appellate Body cannot add to or diminish the rights and obligations provided in the covered agreements.

Article 20
Time-frame for DSB Decisions

Unless otherwise agreed to by the parties to the dispute, the period from the date of establishment of the panel by the DSB until the date the DSB considers the panel or appellate report for adoption shall as a general rule not exceed nine months where the panel report is not appealed or 12 months where the report is appealed. Where either the panel or the Appellate Body has acted, pursuant to paragraph 9 of Article 12 or paragraph 5 of Article 17, to extend the time for providing its report, the additional time taken shall be added to the above periods.

Article 21
Surveillance of Implementation of
Recommendations and Rulings

1. Prompt compliance with recommendations or rulings of the DSB is essential in order to ensure effective resolution of disputes to the benefit of all Members.

2. Particular attention should be paid to matters affecting the interests of developing country Members with respect to measures which have been subject to dispute settlement.

---

9. The "Member concerned" is the party to the dispute to which the panel or Appellate Body recommendations are directed.

10. With respect to recommendations in cases not involving a violation of GATT 1994 or any other covered agreement, see Article 26.

3.   At a DSB meeting held within 30 days[11] after the date of adoption of the panel or Appellate Body report, the Member concerned shall inform the DSB of its intentions in respect of implementation of the recommendations and rulings of the DSB. If it is impracticable to comply immediately with the recommendations and rulings, the Member concerned shall have a reasonable period of time in which to do so. The reasonable period of time shall be:

(a) the period of time proposed by the Member concerned, provided that such period is approved by the DSB; or, in the absence of such approval,

(b) a period of time mutually agreed by the parties to the dispute within 45 days after the date of adoption of the recommendations and rulings; or, in the absence of such agreement,

(c) a period of time determined through binding arbitration within 90 days after the date of adoption of the recommendations and rulings.[12] In such arbitration, a guideline for the arbitrator[13] should be that the reasonable period of time to implement panel or Appellate Body recommendations should not exceed 15 months from the date of adoption of a panel or Appellate Body report. However, that time may be shorter or longer, depending upon the particular circumstances.

4.   Except where the panel or the Appellate Body has extended, pursuant to paragraph 9 of Article 12 or paragraph 5 of Article 17, the time of providing its report, the period from the date of establishment of the panel by the DSB until the date of determination of the reasonable period of time shall not exceed 15 months unless the parties to the dispute agree otherwise. Where either the panel or the Appellate Body has acted to extend the time of providing its report, the additional time taken shall be added to the 15-month period; provided that unless the parties to the dispute agree that there are exceptional circumstances, the total time shall not exceed 18 months.

5.   Where there is disagreement as to the existence or consistency with a covered agreement of measures taken to comply with the recommendations and rulings such dispute shall be decided through recourse to these dispute settlement procedures, including wherever possible resort to the original panel. The panel shall circulate its report within 90 days after the date of referral of the matter to it. When the panel considers that it cannot provide its report within this time frame, it shall inform the DSB in writing of the reasons for the delay together with an estimate of the period within which it will submit its report.

6.   The DSB shall keep under surveillance the implementation of adopted recommendations or rulings. The issue of implementation of the

---

11. If a meeting of the DSB is not scheduled during this period, such a meeting of the DSB shall be held for this purpose.

12. If the parties cannot agree on an arbitrator within ten days after referring the matter to arbitration, the arbitrator shall be appointed by the Director-General within ten days, after consulting the parties.

13. The expression "arbitrator" shall be interpreted as referring either to an individual or a group.

recommendations or rulings may be raised at the DSB by any Member at any time following their adoption. Unless the DSB decides otherwise, the issue of implementation of the recommendations or rulings shall be placed on the agenda of the DSB meeting after six months following the date of establishment of the reasonable period of time pursuant to paragraph 3 and shall remain on the DSB's agenda until the issue is resolved. At least 10 days prior to each such DSB meeting, the Member concerned shall provide the DSB with a status report in writing of its progress in the implementation of the recommendations or rulings.

7. If the matter is one which has been raised by a developing country Member, the DSB shall consider what further action it might take which would be appropriate to the circumstances.

8. If the case is one brought by a developing country Member, in considering what appropriate action might be taken, the DSB shall take into account not only the trade coverage of measures complained of, but also their impact on the economy of developing country Members concerned.

Article 22
Compensation and the Suspension of Concessions

1. Compensation and the suspension of concessions or other obligations are temporary measures available in the event that the recommendations and rulings are not implemented within a reasonable period of time. However, neither compensation nor the suspension of concessions or other obligations is preferred to full implementation of a recommendation to bring a measure into conformity with the covered agreements. Compensation is voluntary and, if granted, shall be consistent with the covered agreements.

2. If the Member concerned fails to bring the measure found to be inconsistent with a covered agreement into compliance therewith or otherwise comply with the recommendations and rulings within the reasonable period of time determined pursuant to paragraph 3 of Article 21, such Member shall, if so requested, and no later than the expiry of the reasonable period of time, enter into negotiations with any party having invoked the dispute settlement procedures, with a view to developing mutually acceptable compensation. If no satisfactory compensation has been agreed within 20 days after the date of expiry of the reasonable period of time, any party having invoked the dispute settlement procedures may request authorization from the DSB to suspend the application to the Member concerned of concessions or other obligations under the covered agreements.

3. In considering what concessions or other obligations to suspend, the complaining party shall apply the following principles and procedures:

    (a)   the general principle is that the complaining party should first seek to suspend concessions or other obligations with respect to the same sector(s) as that in which the panel or Appellate Body has found a violation or other nullification or impairment;

(b)   if that party considers that it is not practicable or effective to suspend concessions or other obligations with respect to the same sector(s), it may seek to suspend concessions or other obligations in other sectors under the same agreement;

(c)   if that party considers that it is not practicable or effective to suspend concessions or other obligations with respect to other sectors under the same agreement, and that the circumstances are serious enough, it may seek to suspend concessions or other obligations under another covered agreement;

(d) in applying the above principles, that party shall take into account:

  (i)   the trade in the sector or under the agreement under which the panel or Appellate Body has found a violation or other nullification or impairment, and the importance of such trade to that party;

  (ii) the broader economic elements related to the nullification or impairment and the broader economic consequences of the suspension of concessions or other obligations;

(e) if that party decides to request authorization to suspend concessions or other obligations pursuant to subparagraphs (b) or (c), it shall state the reasons therefor in its request. At the same time as the request is forwarded to the DSB, it also shall be forwarded to the relevant Councils and also, in the case of a request pursuant to subparagraph (b), the relevant sectoral bodies;

(f) for purposes of this paragraph, "sector" means:

  (i)   with respect to goods, all goods;

  (ii) with respect to services, a principal sector as identified in the current "Services Sectoral Classification List" which identifies such sectors;[14]

  (iii) with respect to trade-related intellectual property rights, each of the categories of intellectual property rights covered in Section 1, or Section 2, or Section 3, or Section 4, or Section 5, or Section 6, or Section 7 of Part II, or the obligations under Part III, or Part IV of the Agreement on TRIPS;

(g) for purposes of this paragraph, "agreement" means:

  (i)   with respect to goods, the agreements listed in Annex 1A of the WTO Agreement, taken as a whole as well as the Plurilateral Trade Agreements in so far as the relevant parties to the dispute are parties to these agreements;

  (ii) with respect to services, the GATS;

  (iii) with respect to intellectual property rights, the Agreement on TRIPS.

4. The level of the suspension of concessions or other obligations authorized by the DSB shall be equivalent to the level of the nullification or impairment.

---

14. The list in document MTN.GNS/W/120 identifies eleven sectors.

5. The DSB shall not authorize suspension of concessions or other obligations if a covered agreement prohibits such suspension.

6. When the situation described in paragraph 2 occurs, the DSB, upon request, shall grant authorization to suspend concessions or other obligations within 30 days of the expiry of the reasonable period of time unless the DSB decides by consensus to reject the request. However, if the Member concerned objects to the level of suspension proposed, or claims that the principles and procedures set forth in paragraph 3 have not been followed where a complaining party has requested authorization to suspend concessions or other obligations pursuant to paragraph 3(b) or (c), the matter shall be referred to arbitration. Such arbitration shall be carried out by the original panel, if members are available, or by an arbitrator[15] appointed by the Director-General and shall be completed within 60 days after the date of expiry of the reasonable period of time. Concessions or other obligations shall not be suspended during the course of the arbitration.

7. The arbitrator[16] acting pursuant to paragraph 6 shall not examine the nature of the concessions or other obligations to be suspended but shall determine whether the level of such suspension is equivalent to the level of nullification or impairment. The arbitrator may also determine if the proposed suspension of concessions or other obligations is allowed under the covered agreement. However, if the matter referred to arbitration includes a claim that the principles and procedures set forth in paragraph 3 have not been followed, the arbitrator shall examine that claim. In the event the arbitrator determines that those principles and procedures have not been followed, the complaining party shall apply them consistent with paragraph 3. The parties shall accept the arbitrator's decision as final and the parties concerned shall not seek a second arbitration. The DSB shall be informed promptly of the decision of the arbitrator and shall upon request, grant authorization to suspend concessions or other obligations where the request is consistent with the decision of the arbitrator, unless the DSB decides by consensus to reject the request.

8. The suspension of concessions or other obligations shall be temporary and shall only be applied until such time as the measure found to be inconsistent with a covered agreement has been removed, or the Member that must implement recommendations or rulings provides a solution to the nullification or impairment of benefits, or a mutually satisfactory solution is reached. In accordance with paragraph 6 of Article 21, the DSB shall continue to keep under surveillance the implementation of adopted recommendations or rulings, including those cases where compensation has been provided or concessions or other obligations have been suspended but the recommendations to bring a measure into conformity with the covered agreements have not been implemented.

---

15. The expression"arbitrator" shall be interpreted as referring either to an individual or a group.

16. The expression "arbitrator" shall be interpreted as referring either to an individual or a group or to the members of the original panel when serving in the capacity of arbitrator.

9. The dispute settlement provisions of the covered agreements may be invoked in respect of measures affecting their observance taken by regional or local governments or authorities within the territory of a Member. When the DSB has ruled that a provision of a covered agreement has not been observed, the responsible Member shall take such reasonable measures as may be available to it to ensure its observance. The provisions of the covered agreements and this Understanding relating to compensation and suspension of concessions or other obligations apply in cases where it has not been possible to secure such observance.[17]

Article 23
Strengthening of the Multilateral System

1. When Members seek the redress of a violation of obligations or other nullification or impairment of benefits under the covered agreements or an impediment to the attainment of any objective of the covered agreements, they shall have recourse to, and abide by, the rules and procedures of this Understanding.

2. In such cases, Members shall:

(a) not make a determination to the effect that a violation has occurred, that benefits have been nullified or impaired or that the attainment of any objective of the covered agreements has been impeded, except through recourse to dispute settlement in accordance with the rules and procedures of this Understanding, and shall make any such determination consistent with the findings contained in the panel or Appellate Body report adopted by the DSB or an arbitration award rendered under this Understanding;

(b) follow the procedures set forth in Article 21 to determine the reasonable period of time for the Member concerned to implement the recommendations and rulings; and

(c) follow the procedures set forth in Article 22 to determine the level of suspension of concessions or other obligations and obtain DSB authorization in accordance with those procedures before suspending concessions or other obligations under the covered agreements in response to the failure of the Member concerned to implement the recommendations and rulings within that reasonable period of time.

Article 24
Special Procedures Involving Least-Developed
Country Members

1. At all stages of the determination of the causes of a dispute and of dispute settlement procedures involving a least-developed country Member,

---

17. Where the provisions of any covered agreement concerning measures taken by regional or local governments or authorities within the territory of a Member contain provisions different from the provisions of this paragraph, the provisions of such covered agreement shall prevail.

particular consideration shall be given to the special situation of least-developed country Members. In this regard, Members shall exercise due restraint in raising matters under these procedures involving a least-developed country Member. If nullification or impairment is found to result from a measure taken by a least-developed country Member, complaining parties shall exercise due restraint in asking for compensation or seeking authorization to suspend the application of concessions or other obligations pursuant to these procedures.

2. In dispute settlement cases involving a least-developed country Member, where a satisfactory solution has not been found in the course of consultations the Director-General or the Chairman of the DSB shall, upon request by a least-developed country Member offer their good offices, conciliation and mediation with a view to assisting the parties to settle the dispute, before a request for a panel is made. The Director-General or the Chairman of the DSB, in providing the above assistance, may consult any source which either deems appropriate.

Article 25
Arbitration

1. Expeditious arbitration within the WTO as an alternative means of dispute settlement can facilitate the solution of certain disputes that concern issues that are clearly defined by both parties.

2. Except as otherwise provided in this Understanding, resort to arbitration shall be subject to mutual agreement of the parties which shall agree on the procedures to be followed. Agreements to resort to arbitration shall be notified to all Members sufficiently in advance of the actual commencement of the arbitration process.

3. Other Members may become party to an arbitration proceeding only upon the agreement of the parties which have agreed to have recourse to arbitration. The parties to the proceeding shall agree to abide by the arbitration award. Arbitration awards shall be notified to the DSB and the Council or Committee of any relevant agreement where any Member may raise any point relating thereto.

4. Articles 21 and 22 of this Understanding shall apply *mutatis mutandis* to arbitration awards.

Article 26

1. *Non-Violation Complaints of the Type Described in Paragraph 1(b) of Article XXIII of GATT 1994*

Where the provisions of paragraph 1(b) of Article XXIII of GATT 1994 are applicable to a covered agreement, a panel or the Appellate Body may only make rulings and recommendations where a party to the dispute considers that any benefit accruing to it directly or indirectly under the relevant covered agreement is being nullified or impaired or the attainment of any objective of that Agreement is being impeded as a result of the application by a Member of any measure, whether or not it conflicts with the provisions of that Agreement. Where and to the extent that such party considers and a panel or the Appellate Body determines that a case concerns a measure that does not conflict with the provisions of a covered agreement to which the provisions of paragraph 1(b) of Article XXIII of GATT 1994 are applicable, the procedures in this Understanding shall apply, subject to the following:

(a) the complaining party shall present a detailed justification in support of any complaint relating to a measure which does not conflict with the relevant covered agreement;

(b) where a measure has been found to nullify or impair benefits under, or impede the attainment of objectives, of the relevant covered agreement without violation thereof, there is no obligation to withdraw the measure. However, in such cases, the panel or the Appellate Body shall recommend that the Member concerned make a mutually satisfactory adjustment;

(c) notwithstanding the provisions of Article 21, the arbitration provided for in paragraph 3 of Article 21, upon request of either party, may include a determination of the level of benefits which have been nullified or impaired, and may also suggest ways and means of reaching a mutually satisfactory adjustment; such suggestions shall not be binding upon the parties to the dispute;

(d) notwithstanding the provisions of paragraph 1 of Article 22, compensation may be part of a mutually satisfactory adjustment as final settlement of the dispute.

2. *Complaints of the Type Described in Paragraph 1(c) of Article XXIII of GATT 1994*

Where the provisions of paragraph 1(c) of Article XXIII of GATT 1994 are applicable to a covered agreement, a panel may only make rulings and recommendations where a party considers that any benefit accruing to it directly or indirectly under the relevant covered agreement is being nullified or impaired or the attainment of any objective of that Agreement is being impeded as a result of the existence of any situation other than those to which the provisions of paragraphs 1(a) and 1(b) of Article XXIII of GATT 1994 are applicable. Where and to the extent that such party considers and a panel determines that the matter is covered by this paragraph, the procedures of this Understanding shall apply only up to and including the point in the proceedings where the panel report has been circulated to the Members. The dispute settlement rules and procedures contained in the Decision of 12 April 1989 (BISD 36S/61-67) shall apply to consideration for adoption, and surveillance and implementation of recommendations and rulings. The following shall also apply:

(a) the complaining party shall present a detailed justification in support of any argument made with respect to issues covered under this paragraph;

(b) in cases involving matters covered by this paragraph, if a panel finds that cases also involve dispute settlement matters other than those covered by this paragraph, the panel shall circulate a report to the DSB addressing any such matters and a separate report on matters falling under this paragraph.

Article 27
Responsibilities of the Secretariat

1. The Secretariat shall have the responsibility of assisting panels, especially on the legal, historical and procedural aspects of the matters dealt with, and of providing secretarial and technical support.

2. While the Secretariat assists Members in respect of dispute settlement at their request, there may also be a need to provide additional legal advice and assistance in respect of dispute settlement to developing country Members. To this end, the Secretariat shall make available a qualified legal expert from the WTO technical cooperation services to any developing country Member which so requests. This expert shall assist the developing country Member in a manner ensuring the continued impartiality of the Secretariat.

3. The Secretariat shall conduct special training courses for interested Members concerning these dispute settlement procedures and practices so as to enable Members' experts to be better informed in this regard.

APPENDIX 1
AGREEMENTS COVERED BY THE UNDERSTANDING

(A)   Agreement Establishing the World Trade Organization

(B)   Multilateral Trade Agreements

   Annex 1A: Multilateral Agreements on Trade in Goods

   Annex 1B: General Agreement on Trade in Services

   Annex 1C: Agreement on Trade-Related Aspects of Intellectual Property Rights

   Annex 2:   Understanding on Rules and Procedures Governing the Settlement of Disputes

(C)   Plurilateral Trade Agreements

   Annex 4:   Agreement on Trade in Civil Aircraft

   Agreement on Government Procurement

   International Dairy Agreement

   International Bovine Meat Agreement

The applicability of this Understanding to the Plurilateral Trade Agreements shall be subject to the adoption of a decision by the parties to each agreement setting out the terms for the application of the Understanding to the individual agreement, including any special or additional rules or procedures for inclusion in Appendix 2, as notified to the DSB.

. . . .

APPENDIX 3
WORKING PROCEDURES

1.   In its proceedings the panel shall follow the relevant provisions of this Understanding. In addition, the following working procedures shall apply.

2.   The panel shall meet in closed session. The parties to the dispute, and interested parties, shall be present at the meetings only when invited by the panel to appear before it.

3.   The deliberations of the panel and the documents submitted to it shall be kept confidential. Nothing in this Understanding shall preclude a party to a dispute from disclosing statements of its own positions to the public. Members shall treat as confidential information submitted by another Member to the panel which that Member has designated as confidential. Where a party to a dispute submits a confidential version of its written submissions to the panel, it shall also, upon request of a Member, provide a non-confidential summary of the information contained in its submissions that could be disclosed to the public.

4.   Before the first substantive meeting of the panel with the parties, the parties to the dispute shall transmit to the panel written submissions in which they present the facts of the case and their arguments.

5.   At its first substantive meeting with the parties, the panel shall ask the party which has brought the complaint to present its case. Subsequently, and still at the same meeting, the party against which the complaint has been brought shall be asked to present its point of view.

6.   All third parties which have notified their interest in the dispute to the DSB shall be invited in writing to present their views during a session of the first substantive meeting of the panel set aside for that purpose. All such third parties may be present during the entirety of this session.

7.   Formal rebuttals shall be made at a second substantive meeting of the panel. The party complained against shall have the right to take the floor first to be followed by the complaining party. The parties shall submit, prior to that meeting, written rebuttals to the panel.

8.   The panel may at any time put questions to the parties and ask them for explanations either in the course of a meeting with the parties or in writing.

9.   The parties to the dispute and any third party invited to present its views in accordance with Article 10 shall make available to the panel a written version of their oral statements.

10.   In the interest of full transparency, the presentations, rebuttals and statements referred to in paragraphs 5 to 9 shall be made in the presence of the parties. Moreover, each party's written submissions, including any comments on the descriptive part of the report and responses to questions put by the panel, shall be made available to the other party or parties.

11.   Any additional procedures specific to the panel.

12.   Proposed timetable for panel work:

(a)   Receipt of first written submissions of the parties:

  (1) complaining Party: 3-6 weeks

  (2) Party complained against: 2-3 weeks

(b)   Date, time and place of first substantive meeting with the parties; third party session: 1-2 weeks

(c)   Receipt of written rebuttals of the parties: 2-3 weeks

(d)   Date, time and place of second substantive meeting with the parties: 1-2 weeks

(e)   Issuance of descriptive part of the report to the parties: 2-4 weeks

(f)   Receipt of comments by the parties on the descriptive part of the report: 2 weeks

(g)   Issuance of the interim report, including the findings and conclusions, to the parties: 2-4 weeks

(h)   Deadline for party to request review of part(s) of report: 1 week

(i)   Period of review by panel, including possible additional meeting with parties: 2 weeks

(j)   Issuance of final report to parties to dispute: 2 weeks

(k)   Circulation of the final report to the Members: 3 weeks

The above calendar may be changed in the light of unforeseen developments. Additional meetings with the parties shall be scheduled if required.

APPENDIX 4
EXPERT REVIEW GROUPS

The following rules and procedures shall apply to expert review groups established in accordance with the provisions of paragraph 2 of Article 13.

1. Expert review groups are under the panel's authority. Their terms of reference and detailed working procedures shall be decided by the panel, and they shall report to the panel.

2. Participation in expert review groups shall be restricted to persons of professional standing and experience in the field in question.

3. Citizens of parties to the dispute shall not serve on an expert review group without the joint agreement of the parties to the dispute, except in exceptional circumstances when the panel considers that the need for specialized scientific expertise cannot be fulfilled otherwise. Government officials of parties to the dispute shall not serve on an expert review group. Members of expert review groups shall serve in their individual capacities and not as government representatives, nor as representatives of any organization. Governments or organizations shall therefore not give them instructions with regard to matters before an expert review group.

4. Expert review groups may consult and seek information and technical advice from any source they deem appropriate. Before an expert review group seeks such information or advice from a source within the jurisdiction of a Member, it shall inform the government of that Member. Any Member shall respond promptly and fully to any request by an expert review group for such information as the expert review group considers necessary and appropriate.

5. The parties to a dispute shall have access to all relevant information provided to an expert review group, unless it is of a confidential nature. Confidential information provided to the expert review group shall not be released without formal authorization from the government, organization or person providing the information. Where such information is requested from the expert review group but release of such information by the expert review group is not authorized, a non-confidential summary of the information will be provided by the government, organization or person supplying the information.

6. The expert review group shall submit a draft report to the parties to the dispute with a view to obtaining their comments, and taking them into account, as appropriate, in the final report, which shall also be issued to the parties to the dispute when it is submitted to the panel. The final report of the expert review group shall be advisory only.

NORTH AMERICAN FREE TRADE AGREEMENT

between the Government of Canada, the Government of the United
Mexican States, and the Government of the United States of America
Done at Washington on December 8 and 17, 1992,
at Ottawa on December 11 and 17, 1992 and
at Mexico City on December 14 and 17, 1992

PART SIX
INTELLECTUAL PROPERTY

Chapter Seventeen
Intellectual Property

Article 1701: Nature and Scope of Obligations

1. Each Party shall provide in its territory to the nationals of another
Party adequate and effective protection and enforcement of intellectual
property rights, while ensuring that measures to enforce intellectual
property rights do not themselves become barriers to legitimate trade.

2. To provide adequate and effective protection and enforcement of
intellectual property rights, each Party shall, at a minimum, give effect to
this Chapter and to the substantive provisions of:

(a)   the *Geneva Convention for the Protection of Producers of Phonograms
Against Unauthorized Duplication of their Phonograms*, 1971 (Geneva
Convention);

(b)   the *Berne Convention for the Protection of Literary and Artistic Works*,
1971 (Berne Convention);

(c)   the *Paris Convention for the Protection of Industrial Property*, 1967
(Paris Convention); and

(d)   the *International Convention for the Protection of New Varieties of
Plants*, 1978 (UPOV Convention), or the *International Convention for
the Protection of New Varieties of Plants*, 1991 (UPOV Convention).

If a Party has not acceded to the specified text of any such Conventions on or
before the date of entry into force of this Agreement, it shall make every
effort to accede.

3. Annex 1701.3 applies to the Parties specified in that Annex.

Article 1702: More Extensive Protection

A Party may implement in its domestic law more extensive protection of
intellectual property rights than is required under this Agreement, provided
that such protection is not inconsistent with this Agreement.

Article 1703: National Treatment

1. Each Party shall accord to nationals of another Party treatment no less

favorable than that it accords to its own nationals with regard to the protection and enforcement of all intellectual property rights. In respect of sound recordings, each Party shall provide such treatment to producers and performers of another Party, except that a Party may limit rights of performers of another Party in respect of secondary uses of sound recordings to those rights its nationals are accorded in the territory of such other Party.

2.   No Party may, as a condition of according national treatment under this Article, require right holders to comply with any formalities or conditions in order to acquire rights in respect of copyright and related rights.

3.   A Party may derogate from paragraph 1 in relation to its judicial and administrative procedures for the protection or enforcement of intellectual property rights, including any procedure requiring a national of another Party to designate for service of process an address in the Party's territory or to appoint an agent in the Party's territory, if the derogation is consistent with the relevant Convention listed in Article 1701(2), provided that such derogation:

(a)   is necessary to secure compliance with measures that are not inconsistent with this Chapter; and

(b)   is not applied in a manner that would constitute a disguised restriction on trade.

4.   No Party shall have any obligation under this Article with respect to procedures provided in multilateral agreements concluded under the auspices of the World Intellectual Property Organization relating to the acquisition or maintenance of intellectual property rights.

Article 1704: Control of Abusive or Anticompetitive Practices or Conditions

Nothing in this Chapter shall prevent a Party from specifying in its domestic law licensing practices or conditions that may in particular cases constitute an abuse of intellectual property rights having an adverse effect on competition in the relevant market. A Party may adopt or maintain, consistent with the other provisions of this Agreement, appropriate measures to prevent or control such practices or conditions.

Article 1705: Copyright

1.   Each Party shall protect the works covered by Article 2 of the Berne Convention, including any other works that embody original expression within the meaning of that Convention. In particular:

(a)   all types of computer programs are literary works within the meaning of the Berne Convention and each Party shall protect them as such; and

(b)   compilations of data or other material, whether in machine readable or other form, which by reason of the selection or arrangement of their contents constitute intellectual creations, shall be protected as such.

The protection a Party provides under subparagraph (b) shall not extend to the data or material itself, or prejudice any copyright subsisting in that data or material.

2. Each Party shall provide to authors and their successors in interest those rights enumerated in the Berne Convention in respect of works covered by paragraph 1, including the right to authorize or prohibit:

(a)   the importation into the Party's territory of copies of the work made without the right holder's authorization;

(b)   the first public distribution of the original and each copy of the work by sale, rental or otherwise;

(c)   the communication of a work to the public; and

(d)   the commercial rental of the original or a copy of a computer program.

Subparagraph (d) shall not apply where the copy of the computer program is not itself an essential object of the rental. Each Party shall provide that putting the original or a copy of a computer program on the market with the right holder's consent shall not exhaust the rental right.

3. Each Party shall provide that for copyright and related rights:

(a)   any person acquiring or holding economic rights may freely and separately transfer such rights by contract for purposes of their exploitation and enjoyment by the transferee; and

(b)   any person acquiring or holding such economic rights by virtue of a contract, including contracts of employment underlying the creation of works and sound recordings, shall be able to exercise those rights in its own name and enjoy fully the benefits derived from those rights.

4. Each Party shall provide that, where the term of protection of a work, other than a photographic work or a work of applied art, is to be calculated on a basis other than the life of a natural person, the term shall be not less than 50 years from the end of the calendar year of the first authorized publication of the work or, failing such authorized publication within 50 years from the making of the work, 50 years from the end of the calendar year of making.

5. Each Party shall confine limitations or exceptions to the rights provided for in this Article to certain special cases that do not conflict with a normal exploitation of the work and do not unreasonably prejudice the legitimate interests of the right holder.

6. No Party may grant translation and reproduction licenses permitted under the Appendix to the Berne Convention where legitimate needs in that Party's territory for copies or translations of the work could be met by the right holder's voluntary actions but for obstacles created by the Party's measures.

7. Annex 1705.7 applies to the Parties specified in that Annex.

Article 1706: Sound Recordings

1. Each Party shall provide to the producer of a sound recording the right

to authorize or prohibit:

(a)   the direct or indirect reproduction of the sound recording;

(b)   the importation into the Party's territory of copies of the sound recording made without the producer's authorization;

(c)   the first public distribution of the original and each copy of the sound recording by sale, rental or otherwise; and

(d)   the commercial rental of the original or a copy of the sound recording, except where expressly otherwise provided in a contract between the producer of the sound recording and the authors of the works fixed therein.

Each Party shall provide that putting the original or a copy of a sound recording on the market with the right holder's consent shall not exhaust the rental right.

2.   Each Party shall provide a term of protection for sound recordings of at least 50 years from the end of the calendar year in which the fixation was made.

3.   Each Party shall confine limitations or exceptions to the rights provided for in this Article to certain special cases that do not conflict with a normal exploitation of the sound recording and do not unreasonably prejudice the legitimate interests of the right holder.

Article 1707: Protection of Encrypted Program-Carrying Satellite Signals

Within one year from the date of entry into force of this Agreement, each Party shall make it:

(a)   a criminal offense to manufacture, import, sell, lease or otherwise make available a device or system that is primarily of assistance in decoding an encrypted program-carrying satellite signal without the authorization of the lawful distributor of such signal; and

(b)   a civil offense to receive, in connection with commercial activities, or further distribute, an encrypted program-carrying satellite signal that has been decoded without the authorization of the lawful distributor of the signal or to engage in any activity prohibited under subparagraph (a).

Each Party shall provide that any civil offense established under subparagraph (b) shall be actionable by any person that holds an interest in the content of such signal.

Article 1708: Trademarks

1.   For purposes of this Agreement, a trademark consists of any sign, or any combination of signs, capable of distinguishing the goods or services of one person from those of another, including personal names, designs, letters, numerals, colors, figurative elements, or the shape of goods or of their packaging. Trademarks shall include service marks and collective marks,

and may include certification marks. A Party may require, as a condition for registration, that a sign be visually perceptible.

2. Each Party shall provide to the owner of a registered trademark the right to prevent all persons not having the owner's consent from using in commerce identical or similar signs for goods or services that are identical or similar to those goods or services in respect of which the owner's trademark is registered, where such use would result in a likelihood of confusion. In the case of the use of an identical sign for identical goods or services, a likelihood of confusion shall be presumed. The rights described above shall not prejudice any prior rights, nor shall they affect the possibility of a Party making rights available on the basis of use.

3. A Party may make registrability depend on use. However, actual use of a trademark shall not be a condition for filing an application for registration. No Party may refuse an application solely on the ground that intended use has not taken place before the expiry of a period of three years from the date of application for registration.

4. Each Party shall provide a system for the registration of trademarks, which shall include:

(a) examination of applications;

(b) notice to be given to an applicant of the reasons for the refusal to register a trademark;

(c) a reasonable opportunity for the applicant to respond to the notice;

(d) publication of each trademark either before or promptly after it is registered; and

(e) a reasonable opportunity for interested persons to petition to cancel the registration of a trademark.

A Party may provide for a reasonable opportunity for interested persons to oppose the registration of a trademark.

5. The nature of the goods or services to which a trademark is to be applied shall in no case form an obstacle to the registration of the trademark.

6. Article 6bis of the Paris Convention shall apply, with such modifications as may be necessary, to services. In determining whether a trademark is well known, account shall be taken of the knowledge of the trademark in the relevant sector of the public, including knowledge in the Party's territory obtained as a result of the promotion of the trademark. No Party may require that the reputation of the trademark extend beyond the sector of the public that normally deals with the relevant goods or services.

7. Each Party shall provide that the initial registration of a trademark be for a term of at least 10 years and that the registration be indefinitely renewable for terms of not less than 10 years when conditions for renewal have been met.

8. Each Party shall require the use of a trademark to maintain a registration. The registration may be canceled for the reason of non-use only after an uninterrupted period of at least two years of non-use, unless valid

reasons based on the existence of obstacles to such use are shown by the trademark owner. Each Party shall recognize, as valid reasons for non-use, circumstances arising independently of the will of the trademark owner that constitute an obstacle to the use of the trademark, such as import restrictions on, or other government requirements for, goods or services identified by the trademark.

9.   Each Party shall recognize use of a trademark by a person other than the trademark owner, where such use is subject to the owner's control, as use of the trademark for purposes of maintaining the registration.

10.   No Party may encumber the use of a trademark in commerce by special requirements, such as a use that reduces the trademark's function as an indication of source or a use with another trademark.

11.   A Party may determine conditions on the licensing and assignment of trademarks, it being understood that the compulsory licensing of trademarks shall not be permitted and that the owner of a registered trademark shall have the right to assign its trademark with or without the transfer of the business to which the trademark belongs.

12.   A Party may provide limited exceptions to the rights conferred by a trademark, such as fair use of descriptive terms, provided that such exceptions take into account the legitimate interests of the trademark owner and of other persons.

13.   Each Party shall prohibit the registration as a trademark of words, at least in English, French or Spanish, that generically designate goods or services or types of goods or services to which the trademark applies.

14.   Each Party shall refuse to register trademarks that consist of or comprise immoral, deceptive or scandalous matter, or matter that may disparage or falsely suggest a connection with persons, living or dead, institutions, beliefs or any Party's national symbols, or bring them into contempt or disrepute.

Article 1709: Patents

1.   Subject to paragraphs 2 and 3, each Party shall make patents available for any inventions, whether products or processes, in all fields of technology, provided that such inventions are new, result from an inventive step and are capable of industrial application. For purposes of this Article, a Party may deem the terms "inventive step" and "capable of industrial application" to be synonymous with the terms "non-obvious" and "useful", respectively.

2.   A Party may exclude from patentability inventions if preventing in its territory the commercial exploitation of the inventions is necessary to protect *ordre public* or morality, including to protect human, animal or plant life or health or to avoid serious prejudice to nature or the environment, provided that the exclusion is not based solely on the ground that the Party prohibits commercial exploitation in its territory of the subject matter of the patent.

3.   A Party may also exclude from patentability:

(a)   diagnostic, therapeutic and surgical methods for the treatment of humans or animals;

(b)   plants and animals other than microorganisms; and

(c)   essentially biological processes for the production of plants or animals, other than non-biological and microbiological processes for such production.

Notwithstanding subparagraph (b), each Party shall provide for the protection of plant varieties through patents, an effective scheme of *sui generis* protection, or both.

4. If a Party has not made available product patent protection for pharmaceutical or agricultural chemicals commensurate with paragraph 1:

(a)   as of January 1, 1992, for subject matter that relates to naturally occurring substances prepared or produced by, or significantly derived from, microbiological processes and intended for food or medicine, and

(b)   as of July 1, 1991, for any other subject matter,

that Party shall provide to the inventor of any such product or its assignee the means to obtain product patent protection for such product for the unexpired term of the patent for such product granted in another Party, as long as the product has not been marketed in the Party providing protection under this paragraph and the person seeking such protection makes a timely request.

5. Each Party shall provide that:

(a)   where the subject matter of a patent is a product, the patent shall confer on the patent owner the right to prevent other persons from making, using or selling the subject matter of the patent, without the patent owner's consent; and

(b)   where the subject matter of a patent is a process, the patent shall confer on the patent owner the right to prevent other persons from using that process and from using, selling, or importing at least the product obtained directly by that process, without the patent owner's consent.

6. A Party may provide limited exceptions to the exclusive rights conferred by a patent, provided that such exceptions do not unreasonably conflict with a normal exploitation of the patent and do not unreasonably prejudice the legitimate interests of the patent owner, taking into account the legitimate interests of other persons.

7. Subject to paragraphs 2 and 3, patents shall be available and patent rights enjoyable without discrimination as to the field of technology, the territory of the Party where the invention was made and whether products are imported or locally produced.

8. A Party may revoke a patent only when:

(a)   grounds exist that would have justified a refusal to grant the patent; or

(b)   the grant of a compulsory license has not remedied the lack of exploitation of the patent.

9. Each Party shall permit patent owners to assign and transfer by succession their patents, and to conclude licensing contracts.

10. Where the law of a Party allows for use of the subject matter of a patent, other than that use allowed under paragraph 6, without the authorization of the right holder, including use by the government or other persons authorized by the government, the Party shall respect the following provisions:

(a) authorization of such use shall be considered on its individual merits;

(b) such use may only be permitted if, prior to such use, the proposed user has made efforts to obtain authorization from the right holder on reasonable commercial terms and conditions and such efforts have not been successful within a reasonable period of time. The requirement to make such efforts may be waived by a Party in the case of a national emergency or other circumstances of extreme urgency or in cases of public non-commercial use. In situations of national emergency or other circumstances of extreme urgency, the right holder shall, nevertheless, be notified as soon as reasonably practicable. In the case of public non-commercial use, where the government or contractor, without making a patent search, knows or has demonstrable grounds to know that a valid patent is or will be used by or for the government, the right holder shall be informed promptly;

(c) the scope and duration of such use shall be limited to the purpose for which it was authorized;

(d) such use shall be non-exclusive;

(e) such use shall be non-assignable, except with that part of the enterprise or goodwill that enjoys such use;

(f) any such use shall be authorized predominantly for the supply of the Party's domestic market;

(g) authorization for such use shall be liable, subject to adequate protection of the legitimate interests of the persons so authorized, to be terminated if and when the circumstances that led to it cease to exist and are unlikely to recur. The competent authority shall have the authority to review, on motivated request, the continued existence of these circumstances;

(h) the right holder shall be paid adequate remuneration in the circumstances of each case, taking into account the economic value of the authorization;

(i) the legal validity of any decision relating to the authorization shall be subject to judicial or other independent review by a distinct higher authority;

(j) any decision relating to the remuneration provided in respect of such use shall be subject to judicial or other independent review by a distinct higher authority;

(k) the Party shall not be obliged to apply the conditions set out in subparagraphs (b) and (f) where such use is permitted to remedy a practice determined after judicial or administrative process to be anticompetitive. The need to correct anticompetitive practices may be taken into account in determining the amount of remuneration in such cases. Competent authorities shall have the authority to refuse termination of authorization if and when the conditions that led to such authorization are likely to recur;

(l)   the Party shall not authorize the use of the subject matter of a patent to permit the exploitation of another patent except as a remedy for an adjudicated violation of domestic laws regarding anticompetitive practices.

11.   Where the subject matter of a patent is a process for obtaining a product, each Party shall, in any infringement proceeding, place on the defendant the burden of establishing that the allegedly infringing product was made by a process other than the patented process in one of the following situations:

(a)   the product obtained by the patented process is new; or

(b)   a substantial likelihood exists that the allegedly infringing product was made by the process and the patent owner has been unable through reasonable efforts to determine the process actually used.

In the gathering and evaluation of evidence, the legitimate interests of the defendant in protecting its trade secrets shall be taken into account.

12.   Each Party shall provide a term of protection for patents of at least 20 years from the date of filing or 17 years from the date of grant. A Party may extend the term of patent protection, in appropriate cases, to compensate for delays caused by regulatory approval processes.

Article 1710: Layout Designs of Semiconductor Integrated Circuits

1.   Each Party shall protect layout designs (topographies) of integrated circuits ("layout designs") in accordance with Articles 2 through 7, 12 and 16(3), other than Article 6(3), of the *Treaty on Intellectual Property in Respect of Integrated Circuits* as opened for signature on May 26, 1989.

2.   Subject to paragraph 3, each Party shall make it unlawful for any person without the right holder's authorization to import, sell or otherwise distribute for commercial purposes any of the following:

(a)   a protected layout design;

(b)   an integrated circuit in which a protected layout design is incorporated; or

(c)   an article incorporating such an integrated circuit, only insofar as it continues to contain an unlawfully reproduced layout design.

3.   No Party may make unlawful any of the acts referred to in paragraph 2 performed in respect of an integrated circuit that incorporates an unlawfully reproduced layout design, or any article that incorporates such an

integrated circuit, where the person performing those acts or ordering those acts to be done did not know and had no reasonable ground to know, when it acquired the integrated circuit or article incorporating such an integrated circuit, that it incorporated an unlawfully reproduced layout design.

4. Each Party shall provide that, after the person referred to in paragraph 3 has received sufficient notice that the layout design was unlawfully reproduced, such person may perform any of the acts with respect to the stock on hand or ordered before such notice, but shall be liable to pay the right holder for doing so an amount equivalent to a reasonable royalty such as would be payable under a freely negotiated license in respect of such a layout design.

5. No Party may permit the compulsory licensing of layout designs of integrated circuits.

6. Any Party that requires registration as a condition for protection of a layout design shall provide that the term of protection shall not end before the expiration of a period of 10 years counted from the date of:

(a)   filing of the application for registration; or

(b)   the first commercial exploitation of the layout design, wherever in the world it occurs.

7. Where a Party does not require registration as a condition for protection of a layout design, the Party shall provide a term of protection of not less than 10 years from the date of the first commercial exploitation of the layout design, wherever in the world it occurs.

8. Notwithstanding paragraphs 6 and 7, a Party may provide that the protection shall lapse 15 years after the creation of the layout design.

9. Annex 1710.9 applies to the Parties specified in that Annex.

Article 1711: Trade Secrets

1. Each Party shall provide the legal means for any person to prevent trade secrets from being disclosed to, acquired by, or used by others without the consent of the person lawfully in control of the information in a manner contrary to honest commercial practices, in so far as:

(a)   the information is secret in the sense that it is not, as a body or in the precise configuration and assembly of its components, generally known among or readily accessible to persons that normally deal with the kind of information in question;

(b)   the information has actual or potential commercial value because it is secret; and

(c)   the person lawfully in control of the information has taken reasonable steps under the circumstances to keep it secret.

2. A Party may require that to qualify for protection a trade secret must be evidenced in documents, electronic or magnetic means, optical discs, microfilms, films or other similar instruments.

3. No Party may limit the duration of protection for trade secrets, so long

as the conditions in paragraph 1 exist.

4. No Party may discourage or impede the voluntary licensing of trade secrets by imposing excessive or discriminatory conditions on such licenses or conditions that dilute the value of the trade secrets.

5. If a Party requires, as a condition for approving the marketing of pharmaceutical or agricultural chemical products that utilize new chemical entities, the submission of undisclosed test or other data necessary to determine whether the use of such products is safe and effective, the Party shall protect against disclosure of the data of persons making such submissions, where the origination of such data involves considerable effort, except where the disclosure is necessary to protect the public or unless steps are taken to ensure that the data is protected against unfair commercial use.

6. Each Party shall provide that for data subject to paragraph 5 that are submitted to the Party after the date of entry into force of this Agreement, no person other than the person that submitted them may, without the latter's permission, rely on such data in support of an application for product approval during a reasonable period of time after their submission. For this purpose, a reasonable period shall normally mean not less than five years from the date on which the Party granted approval to the person that produced the data for approval to market its product, taking account of the nature of the data and the person's efforts and expenditures in producing them. Subject to this provision, there shall be no limitation on any Party to implement abbreviated approval procedures for such products on the basis of bioequivalence and bioavailability studies.

7. Where a Party relies on a marketing approval granted by another Party, the reasonable period of exclusive use of the data submitted in connection with obtaining the approval relied on shall begin with the date of the first marketing approval relied on.

Article 1712: Geographical Indications

1. Each Party shall provide, in respect of geographical indications, the legal means for interested persons to prevent:

(a)   the use of any means in the designation or presentation of a good that indicates or suggests that the good in question originates in a territory, region or locality other than the true place of origin, in a manner that misleads the public as to the geographical origin of the good;

(b)   any use that constitutes an act of unfair competition within the meaning of Article 10*bis* of the Paris Convention.

2. Each Party shall, on its own initiative if its domestic law so permits or at the request of an interested person, refuse to register, or invalidate the registration of, a trademark containing or consisting of a geographical indication with respect to goods that do not originate in the indicated territory, region or locality, if use of the indication in the trademark for such goods is of such a nature as to mislead the public as to the geographical

origin of the good.

3. Each Party shall also apply paragraphs 1 and 2 to a geographical indication that, although correctly indicating the territory, region or locality in which the goods originate, falsely represents to the public that the goods originate in another territory, region or locality.

4. Nothing in this Article shall be construed to require a Party to prevent continued and similar use of a particular geographical indication of another Party in connection with goods or services by any of its nationals or domiciliaries who have used that geographical indication in a continuous manner with regard to the same or related goods or services in that Party's territory, either:

    (a)   for at least 10 years, or

    (b)   in good faith,

before the date of signature of this Agreement.

5. Where a trademark has been applied for or registered in good faith, or where rights to a trademark have been acquired through use in good faith, either:

    (a)   before the date of application of these provisions in that Party, or

    (b)   before the geographical indication is protected in its Party of origin,

no Party may adopt any measure to implement this Article that prejudices eligibility for, or the validity of, the registration of a trademark, or the right to use a trademark, on the basis that such a trademark is identical with, or similar to, a geographical indication.

6. No Party shall be required to apply this Article to a geographical indication if it is identical to the customary term in common language in that Party's territory for the goods or services to which the indication applies.

7. A Party may provide that any request made under this Article in connection with the use or registration of a trademark must be presented within five years after the adverse use of the protected indication has become generally known in that Party or after the date of registration of the trademark in that Party, provided that the trademark has been published by that date, if such date is earlier than the date on which the adverse use became generally known in that Party, provided that the geographical indication is not used or registered in bad faith.

8. No Party shall adopt any measure implementing this Article that would prejudice any person's right to use, in the course of trade, its name or the name of its predecessor in business, except where such name forms all or part of a valid trademark in existence before the geographical indication became protected and with which there is a likelihood of confusion, or such name is used in such a manner as to mislead the public.

9. Nothing in this Chapter shall be construed to require a Party to protect a geographical indication that is not protected, or has fallen into disuse, in the Party of origin.

Article 1713: Industrial Designs

1. Each Party shall provide for the protection of independently created industrial designs that are new or original. A Party may provide that:

(a) designs are not new or original if they do not significantly differ from known designs or combinations of known design features; and

(b) such protection shall not extend to designs dictated essentially by technical or functional considerations.

2. Each Party shall ensure that the requirements for securing protection for textile designs, in particular in regard to any cost, examination or publication, do not unreasonably impair a person's opportunity to seek and obtain such protection. A Party may comply with this obligation through industrial design law or copyright law.

3. Each Party shall provide the owner of a protected industrial design the right to prevent other persons not having the owner's consent from making or selling articles bearing or embodying a design that is a copy, or substantially a copy, of the protected design, when such acts are undertaken for commercial purposes.

4. A Party may provide limited exceptions to the protection of industrial designs, provided that such exceptions do not unreasonably conflict with the normal exploitation of protected industrial designs and do not unreasonably prejudice the legitimate interests of the owner of the protected design, taking into account the legitimate interests of other persons.

5. Each Party shall provide a term of protection for industrial designs of at least 10 years.

Article 1714: Enforcement of Intellectual Property Rights: General Provisions

1. Each Party shall ensure that enforcement procedures, as specified in this Article and Articles 1715 through 1718, are available under its domestic law so as to permit effective action to be taken against any act of infringement of intellectual property rights covered by this Chapter, including expeditious remedies to prevent infringements and remedies to deter further infringements. Such enforcement procedures shall be applied so as to avoid the creation of barriers to legitimate trade and to provide for safeguards against abuse of the procedures.

2. Each Party shall ensure that its procedures for the enforcement of intellectual property rights are fair and equitable, are not unnecessarily complicated or costly, and do not entail unreasonable time limits or unwarranted delays.

3. Each Party shall provide that decisions on the merits of a case in judicial and administrative enforcement proceedings shall:

(a) preferably be in writing and preferably state the reasons on which the decisions are based;

(b) be made available at least to the parties in a proceeding without undue delay; and

(c) be based only on evidence in respect of which such parties were offered the opportunity to be heard.

4. Each Party shall ensure that parties in a proceeding have an opportunity to have final administrative decisions reviewed by a judicial authority of that Party and, subject to jurisdictional provisions in its domestic laws concerning the importance of a case, to have reviewed at least the legal aspects of initial judicial decisions on the merits of a case. Notwithstanding the above, no Party shall be required to provide for judicial review of acquittals in criminal cases.

5. Nothing in this Article or Articles 1715 through 1718 shall be construed to require a Party to establish a judicial system for the enforcement of intellectual property rights distinct from that Party's system for the enforcement of laws in general.

6. For the purposes of Articles 1715 through 1718, the term "right holder" includes federations and associations having legal standing to assert such rights.

Article 1715: Specific Procedural and Remedial Aspects of Civil and Administrative Procedures

1. Each Party shall make available to right holders civil judicial procedures for the enforcement of any intellectual property right provided in this Chapter. Each Party shall provide that:

(a) defendants have the right to written notice that is timely and contains sufficient detail, including the basis of the claims;

(b) parties in a proceeding are allowed to be represented by independent legal counsel;

(c) the procedures do not include imposition of overly burdensome requirements concerning mandatory personal appearances;

(d) all parties in a proceeding are duly entitled to substantiate their claims and to present relevant evidence; and

(e) the procedures include a means to identify and protect confidential information.

2. Each Party shall provide that its judicial authorities shall have the authority:

(a) where a party in a proceeding has presented reasonably available evidence sufficient to support its claims and has specified evidence relevant to the substantiation of its claims that is within the control of the opposing party, to order the opposing party to produce such evidence, subject in appropriate cases to conditions that ensure the protection of confidential information;

(b) where a party in a proceeding voluntarily and without good reason refuses access to, or otherwise does not provide relevant evidence under that party's control within a reasonable period, or significantly impedes a proceeding relating to an enforcement action, to make preliminary and final determinations, affirmative or negative, on the basis of the evidence presented, including the complaint or the allegation presented by the party adversely affected by the denial of access to evidence, subject to providing the parties an opportunity to be heard on the allegations or evidence;

(c) to order a party in a proceeding to desist from an infringement, including to prevent the entry into the channels of commerce in their jurisdiction of imported goods that involve the infringement of an intellectual property right, which order shall be enforceable at least immediately after customs clearance of such goods;

(d) to order the infringer of an intellectual property right to pay the right holder damages adequate to compensate for the injury the right holder has suffered because of the infringement where the infringer knew or had reasonable grounds to know that it was engaged in an infringing activity;

(e) to order an infringer of an intellectual property right to pay the right holder's expenses, which may include appropriate attorney's fees; and

(f) to order a party in a proceeding at whose request measures were taken and who has abused enforcement procedures to provide adequate compensation to any party wrongfully enjoined or restrained in the proceeding for the injury suffered because of such abuse and to pay that party's expenses, which may include appropriate attorney's fees.

3.   With respect to the authority referred to in subparagraph 2(c), no Party shall be obliged to provide such authority in respect of protected subject matter that is acquired or ordered by a person before that person knew or had reasonable grounds to know that dealing in that subject matter would entail the infringement of an intellectual property right.

4.   With respect to the authority referred to in subparagraph 2(d), a Party may, at least with respect to copyrighted works and sound recordings, authorize the judicial authorities to order recovery of profits or payment of pre-established damages, or both, even where the infringer did not know or had no reasonable grounds to know that it was engaged in an infringing activity.

5.   Each Party shall provide that, in order to create an effective deterrent to infringement, its judicial authorities shall have the authority to order that:

(a) goods that they have found to be infringing be, without compensation of any sort, disposed of outside the channels of commerce in such a manner as to avoid any injury caused to the right holder or, unless this would be contrary to existing constitutional requirements, destroyed; and

(b) materials and implements the predominant use of which has been in the creation of the infringing goods be, without compensation of any sort, disposed of outside the channels of commerce in such a manner as to minimize the risks of further infringements.

In considering whether to issue such an order, judicial authorities shall take into account the need for proportionality between the seriousness of the infringement and the remedies ordered as well as the interests of other persons. In regard to counterfeit goods, the simple removal of the trademark unlawfully affixed shall not be sufficient, other than in exceptional cases, to permit release of the goods into the channels of commerce.

6. In respect of the administration of any law pertaining to the protection or enforcement of intellectual property rights, each Party shall only exempt both public authorities and officials from liability to appropriate remedial measures where actions are taken or intended in good faith in the course of the administration of such laws.

7. Notwithstanding the other provisions of Articles 1714 through 1718, where a Party is sued with respect to an infringement of an intellectual property right as a result of its use of that right or use on its behalf, that Party may limit the remedies available against it to the payment to the right holder of adequate remuneration in the circumstances of each case, taking into account the economic value of the use.

8. Each Party shall provide that, where a civil remedy can be ordered as a result of administrative procedures on the merits of a case, such procedures shall conform to principles equivalent in substance to those set out in this Article.

Article 1716: Provisional Measures

1. Each Party shall provide that its judicial authorities shall have the authority to order prompt and effective provisional measures:

(a) to prevent an infringement of any intellectual property right, and in particular to prevent the entry into the channels of commerce in their jurisdiction of allegedly infringing goods, including measures to prevent the entry of imported goods at least immediately after customs clearance; and

(b) to preserve relevant evidence in regard to the alleged infringement.

2. Each Party shall provide that its judicial authorities shall have the authority to require any applicant for provisional measures to provide to the judicial authorities any evidence reasonably available to that applicant that the judicial authorities consider necessary to enable them to determine with a sufficient degree of certainty whether:

(a) the applicant is the right holder;

(b) the applicant's right is being infringed or such infringement is imminent; and

(c) any delay in the issuance of such measures is likely to cause irreparable harm to the right holder, or there is a demonstrable risk of evidence being destroyed.

Each Party shall provide that its judicial authorities shall have the authority to require the applicant to provide a security or equivalent assurance sufficient to protect the interests of the defendant and to prevent abuse.

3. Each Party shall provide that its judicial authorities shall have the authority to require an applicant for provisional measures to provide other information necessary for the identification of the relevant goods by the authority that will execute the provisional measures.

4. Each Party shall provide that its judicial authorities shall have the authority to order provisional measures on an *ex parte* basis, in particular where any delay is likely to cause irreparable harm to the right holder, or where there is a demonstrable risk of evidence being destroyed.

5. Each Party shall provide that where provisional measures are adopted by that Party's judicial authorities on an *ex parte* basis:

(a)   a person affected shall be given notice of those measures without delay but in any event no later than immediately after the execution of the measures;

(b)   a defendant shall, on request, have those measures reviewed by that Party's judicial authorities for the purpose of deciding, within a reasonable period after notice of those measures is given, whether the measures shall be modified, revoked or confirmed, and shall be given an opportunity to be heard in the review proceedings.

6. Without prejudice to paragraph 5, each Party shall provide that, on the request of the defendant, the Party's judicial authorities shall revoke or otherwise cease to apply the provisional measures taken on the basis of paragraphs 1 and 4 if proceedings leading to a decision on the merits are not initiated:

(a)   within a reasonable period as determined by the judicial authority ordering the measures where the Party's domestic law so permits; or

(b)   in the absence of such a determination, within a period of no more than 20 working days or 31 calendar days, whichever is longer.

7. Each Party shall provide that, where the provisional measures are revoked or where they lapse due to any act or omission by the applicant, or where the judicial authorities subsequently find that there has been no infringement or threat of infringement of an intellectual property right, the judicial authorities shall have the authority to order the applicant, on request of the defendant, to provide the defendant appropriate compensation for any injury caused by these measures.

8. Each Party shall provide that, where a provisional measure can be ordered as a result of administrative procedures, such procedures shall conform to principles equivalent in substance to those set out in this Article.

Article 1717: Criminal Procedures and Penalties

1. Each Party shall provide criminal procedures and penalties to be applied at least in cases of willful trademark counterfeiting or copyright piracy on a commercial scale. Each Party shall provide that penalties

available include imprisonment or monetary fines, or both, sufficient to provide a deterrent, consistent with the level of penalties applied for crimes of a corresponding gravity.

2. Each Party shall provide that, in appropriate cases, its judicial authorities may order the seizure, forfeiture and destruction of infringing goods and of any materials and implements the predominant use of which has been in the commission of the offense.

3. A Party may provide criminal procedures and penalties to be applied in cases of infringement of intellectual property rights, other than those in paragraph 1, where they are committed wilfully and on a commercial scale.

Article 1718: Enforcement of Intellectual Property Rights at the Border

1. Each Party shall, in conformity with this Article, adopt procedures to enable a right holder, who has valid grounds for suspecting that the importation of counterfeit trademark goods or pirated copyright goods may take place, to lodge an application in writing with its competent authorities, whether administrative or judicial, for the suspension by the customs administration of the release of such goods into free circulation. No Party shall be obligated to apply such procedures to goods in transit. A Party may permit such an application to be made in respect of goods that involve other infringements of intellectual property rights, provided that the requirements of this Article are met. A Party may also provide for corresponding procedures concerning the suspension by the customs administration of the release of infringing goods destined for exportation from its territory.

2. Each Party shall require any applicant who initiates procedures under paragraph 1 to provide adequate evidence:

(a)   to satisfy that Party's competent authorities that, under the domestic laws of the country of importation, there is *prima facie* an infringement of its intellectual property right; and

(b)   to supply a sufficiently detailed description of the goods to make them readily recognizable by the customs administration.

The competent authorities shall inform the applicant within a reasonable period whether they have accepted the application and, if so, the period for which the customs administration will take action.

3. Each Party shall provide that its competent authorities shall have the authority to require an applicant under paragraph 1 to provide a security or equivalent assurance sufficient to protect the defendant and the competent authorities and to prevent abuse. Such security or equivalent assurance shall not unreasonably deter recourse to these procedures.

4. Each Party shall provide that, where pursuant to an application under procedures adopted pursuant to this Article, its customs administration suspends the release of goods involving industrial designs, patents, integrated circuits or trade secrets into free circulation on the basis of a decision other than by a judicial or other independent authority, and the

period provided for in paragraphs 6 through 8 has expired without the granting of provisional relief by the duly empowered authority, and provided that all other conditions for importation have been complied with, the owner, importer or consignee of such goods shall be entitled to their release on the posting of a security in an amount sufficient to protect the right holder against any infringement. Payment of such security shall not prejudice any other remedy available to the right holder, it being understood that the security shall be released if the right holder fails to pursue its right of action within a reasonable period of time.

5.   Each Party shall provide that its customs administration shall promptly notify the importer and the applicant when the customs administration suspends the release of goods pursuant to paragraph 1.

6.   Each Party shall provide that its customs administration shall release goods from suspension if within a period not exceeding 10 working days after the applicant under paragraph 1 has been served notice of the suspension the customs administration has not been informed that:

(a)   a party other than the defendant has initiated proceedings leading to a decision on the merits of the case, or

(b)   a competent authority has taken provisional measures prolonging the suspension,

provided that all other conditions for importation or exportation have been met. Each Party shall provide that, in appropriate cases, the customs administration may extend the suspension by another 10 working days.

7.   Each Party shall provide that if proceedings leading to a decision on the merits of the case have been initiated, a review, including a right to be heard, shall take place on request of the defendant with a view to deciding, within a reasonable period, whether these measures shall be modified, revoked or confirmed.

8.   Notwithstanding paragraphs 6 and 7, where the suspension of the release of goods is carried out or continued in accordance with a provisional judicial measure, Article 1716(6) shall apply.

9.   Each Party shall provide that its competent authorities shall have the authority to order the applicant under paragraph 1 to pay the importer, the consignee and the owner of the goods appropriate compensation for any injury caused to them through the wrongful detention of goods or through the detention of goods released pursuant to paragraph 6.

10. Without prejudice to the protection of confidential information, each Party shall provide that its competent authorities shall have the authority to give the right holder sufficient opportunity to have any goods detained by the customs administration inspected in order to substantiate the right holder's claims. Each Party shall also provide that its competent authorities have the authority to give the importer an equivalent opportunity to have any such goods inspected. Where the competent authorities have made a positive determination on the merits of a case, a Party may provide the competent authorities the authority to inform the right holder of the names

and addresses of the consignor, the importer and the consignee, and of the quantity of the goods in question.

11. Where a Party requires its competent authorities to act on their own initiative and to suspend the release of goods in respect of which they have acquired prima facie evidence that an intellectual property right is being infringed:

(a) the competent authorities may at any time seek from the right holder any information that may assist them to exercise these powers;

(b) the importer and the right holder shall be promptly notified of the suspension by the Party's competent authorities, and where the importer lodges an appeal against the suspension with competent authorities, the suspension shall be subject to the conditions, with such modifications as may be necessary, set out in paragraphs 6 through 8; and

(c) the Party shall only exempt both public authorities and officials from liability to appropriate remedial measures where actions are taken or intended in good faith.

12. Without prejudice to other rights of action open to the right holder and subject to the defendant's right to seek judicial review, each Party shall provide that its competent authorities shall have the authority to order the destruction or disposal of infringing goods in accordance with the principles set out in Article 1715(5). In regard to counterfeit goods, the authorities shall not allow the re exportation of the infringing goods in an unaltered state or subject them to a different customs procedure, other than in exceptional circumstances.

13. A Party may exclude from the application of paragraphs 1 through 12 small quantities of goods of a non-commercial nature contained in travellers' personal luggage or sent in small consignments that are not repetitive.

14. Annex 1718.14 applies to the Parties specified in that Annex.

Article 1719: Cooperation and Technical Assistance

1. The Parties shall provide each other on mutually agreed terms with technical assistance and shall promote cooperation between their competent authorities. Such cooperation shall include the training of personnel.

2. The Parties shall cooperate with a view to eliminating trade in goods that infringe intellectual property rights. For this purpose, each Party shall establish and notify the other Parties by January 1, 1994 of contact points in its federal government and shall exchange information concerning trade in infringing goods.

Article 1720: Protection of Existing Subject Matter

1. Except as required under Article 1705(7), this Agreement does not give rise to obligations in respect of acts that occurred before the date of application of the relevant provisions of this Agreement for the Party in

question.

2.   Except as otherwise provided for in this Agreement, each Party shall apply this Agreement to all subject matter existing on the date of application of the relevant provisions of this Agreement for the Party in question and that is protected in a Party on such date, or that meets or subsequently meets the criteria for protection under the terms of this Chapter. In respect of this paragraph and paragraphs 3 and 4, a Party's obligations with respect to existing works shall be solely determined under Article 18 of the Berne Convention and with respect to the rights of producers of sound recordings in existing sound recordings shall be determined solely under Article 18 of that Convention, as made applicable under this Agreement.

3.   Except as required under Article 1705(7), and notwithstanding the first sentence of paragraph 2, no Party may be required to restore protection to subject matter that, on the date of application of the relevant provisions of this Agreement for the Party in question, has fallen into the public domain in its territory.

4.   In respect of any acts relating to specific objects embodying protected subject matter that become infringing under the terms of laws in conformity with this Agreement, and that were begun or in respect of which a significant investment was made, before the date of entry into force of this Agreement for that Party, any Party may provide for a limitation of the remedies available to the right holder as to the continued performance of such acts after the date of application of this Agreement for that Party. In such cases, the Party shall, however, at least provide for payment of equitable remuneration.

5.   No Party shall be obliged to apply Article 1705(2)(d) or 1706(1)(d) with respect to originals or copies purchased prior to the date of application of the relevant provisions of this Agreement for that Party.

6.   No Party shall be required to apply Article 1709(10), or the requirement in Article 1709(7) that patent rights shall be enjoyable without discrimination as to the field of technology, to use without the authorization of the right holder where authorization for such use was granted by the government before the text of the Draft Final Act Embodying the Results of the Uruguay Round of Multilateral Trade Negotiations became known.

7.   In the case of intellectual property rights for which protection is conditional on registration, applications for protection that are pending on the date of application of the relevant provisions of this Agreement for the Party in question shall be permitted to be amended to claim any enhanced protection provided under this Agreement. Such amendments shall not include new matter.

Article 1721: Definitions

1.   For purposes of this Chapter:

confidential information includes trade secrets, privileged information and other materials exempted from disclosure under the Party's domestic law.

2. For purposes of this Agreement:

encrypted program-carrying satellite signal means a program-carrying satellite signal that is transmitted in a form whereby the aural or visual characteristics, or both, are modified or altered for the purpose of preventing the unauthorized reception, by persons without the authorized equipment that is designed to eliminate the effects of such modification or alteration, of a program carried in that signal;

geographical indication means any indication that identifies a good as originating in the territory of a Party, or a region or locality in that territory, where a particular quality, reputation or other characteristic of the good is essentially attributable to its geographical origin;

in a manner contrary to honest commercial practices means at least practices such as breach of contract, breach of confidence and inducement to breach, and includes the acquisition of undisclosed information by other persons who knew, or were grossly negligent in failing to know, that such practices were involved in the acquisition;

intellectual property rights refers to copyright and related rights, trademark rights, patent rights, rights in layout designs of semiconductor integrated circuits, trade secret rights, plant breeders' rights, rights in geographical indications and industrial design rights;

nationals of another Party means, in respect of the relevant intellectual property right, persons who would meet the criteria for eligibility for protection provided for in the Paris Convention (1967), the Berne Convention (1971), the Geneva Convention (1971), the International Convention for the Protection of Performers, Producers of Phonograms and Broadcasting Organizations (1961), the UPOV Convention (1978), the UPOV Convention (1991) or the *Treaty on Intellectual Property in Respect of Integrated Circuits*, as if each Party were a party to those Conventions, and with respect to intellectual property rights that are not the subject of these Conventions, "nationals of another Party" shall be understood to be at least individuals who are citizens or permanent residents of that Party and also includes any other natural person referred to in Annex 201.1 (Country Specific Definitions);

public includes, with respect to rights of communication and performance of works provided for under Articles 11, 11*bis*(1) and 14(1)(ii) of the Berne Convention, with respect to dramatic, dramatico-musical, musical and cinematographic works, at least, any aggregation of individuals intended to be the object of, and capable of perceiving, communications or performances of works, regardless of whether they can do so at the same or different times or in the same or different places, provided that such an aggregation is larger than a family and its immediate circle of acquaintances or is not a group comprising a limited number of individuals having similarly close ties that has not been formed for the principal purpose of receiving such performances and communications of works; and

secondary uses of sound recordings means the use directly for broadcasting or for any other public communication of a sound recording.

Annex 1701.3
Intellectual Property Conventions

1. Mexico shall:

(a)   make every effort to comply with the substantive provisions of the 1978 or 1991 UPOV Convention as soon as possible and shall do so no later than two years after the date of signature of this Agreement; and

(b)   accept from the date of entry into force of this Agreement applications from plant breeders for varieties in all plant genera and species and grant protection, in accordance with such substantive provisions, promptly after complying with subparagraph (a).

2.   Notwithstanding Article 1701(2)(b), this Agreement confers no rights and imposes no obligations on the United States with respect to Article 6*bis* of the Berne Convention, or the rights derived from that Article.

Annex 1705.7
Copyright

The United States shall provide protection to motion pictures produced in another Party's territory that have been declared to be in the public domain pursuant to 17 U.S.C. section 405. This obligation shall apply to the extent that it is consistent with the Constitution of the United States, and is subject to budgetary considerations.

Annex 1710.9
Layout Designs

Mexico shall make every effort to implement the requirements of Article 1710 as soon as possible, and shall do so no later than four years after the date of entry into force of this Agreement.

Annex 1718.14
Enforcement of Intellectual Property Rights

Mexico shall make every effort to comply with the requirements of Article 1718 as soon as possible and shall do so no later than three years after the date of signature of this Agreement.

C. TRADEMARK AND UNFAIR COMPETITION LAW

PARIS CONVENTION FOR THE PROTECTION OF INDUSTRIAL PROPERTY

of March 20, 1883, as revised at Brussels on December 14, 1900, at Washington on June 2, 1911, at The Hague on November 6, 1925, at London on June 2, 1934, at Lisbon on October 31, 1958, and at Stockholm on, July 14, 1967, and as amended on October 2, 1979

Article 1
[Establishment of the Union; Scope of Industrial Property][*]

(1) The countries to which this Convention applies constitute a Union for the protection of industrial property.

(2) The protection of industrial property has as its object patents, utility models, industrial designs, trademarks, service marks, trade names, indications of source or appellations of origin, and the repression of unfair competition.

(3) Industrial property shall be understood in the broadest sense and shall apply not only to industry and commerce proper, but likewise to agricultural and extractive industries and to all manufactured or natural products, for example, wines, grain, tobacco leaf, fruit, cattle, minerals, mineral waters, beer, flowers, and flour.

(4) Patents shall include the various kinds of industrial patents recognized by the laws of the countries of the Union, such as patents of importation, patents of improvement, patents and certificates of addition, etc.

Article 2
[National Treatment for Nationals of Countries of the Union]

(1) Nationals of any country of the Union shall, as regards the protection of industrial property, enjoy in all the other countries of the Union the advantages that their respective laws now grant, or may hereafter grant, to nationals; all without prejudice to the rights specially provided for by this Convention. Consequently, they shall have the same protection as the latter, and the same legal remedy against any infringement of their rights, provided that the conditions and formalities imposed upon nationals are complied with.

(2) However, no requirement as to domicile or establishment in the country where protection is claimed may be imposed upon nationals of countries of the Union for the enjoyment of any industrial property rights.

(3) The provisions of the laws of each of the countries of the Union relating

---

* Articles have been given titles by WIPO to facilitate their identification. There are no titles in the signed (French) text.

to judicial and administrative procedure and to jurisdiction, and to the designation of an address for service or the appointment of an agent, which may be required by the laws on industrial property are expressly reserved.

Article 3
[Same Treatment for Certain Categories of Persons as for Nationals of Countries of the Union]

Nationals of countries outside the Union who are domiciled or who have real and effective industrial or commercial establishments in the territory of one of the countries of the Union shall be treated in the same manner as nationals of the countries of the Union.

Article 4
[A to I: *Patents, Utility Models, Industrial Designs, Marks, Inventors' Certificates:* Right of Priority
G: *Patents:* Division of the Application]

A.—

(1)   Any person who has duly filed an application for a patent, or for the registration of a utility model, or of an industrial design, or of a trademark, in one of the countries of the Union, or his successor in title, shall enjoy, for the purpose of filing in the other countries, a right of priority during the periods hereinafter fixed.

(2)   Any filing that is equivalent to a regular national filing under the domestic legislation of any country of the Union or under bilateral or multilateral treaties concluded between countries of the Union shall be recognized as giving rise to the right of priority.

(3)   By a regular national filing is meant any filing that is adequate to establish the date on which the application was filed in the country concerned, whatever may be the subsequent fate of the application.

B.— Consequently, any subsequent filing in any of the other countries of the Union before the expiration of the periods referred to above shall not be invalidated by reason of any acts accomplished in the interval, in particular, another filing, the publication or exploitation of the invention, the putting on sale of copies of the design, or the use of the mark, and such acts cannot give rise to any third-party right or any right of personal possession. Rights acquired by third parties before the date of the first application that serves as the basis for the right of priority are reserved in accordance with the domestic legislation of each country of the Union

C.—

(1)   The periods of priority referred to above shall be twelve months for patents and utility models, and six months for industrial designs and trademarks.

(2)   These periods shall start from the date of filing of the first application; the day of filing shall not be included in the period.

(3)   If the last day of the period is an official holiday, or a day when the Office is not open for the filing of applications in the country where protection is claimed, the period shall be extended until the first following working day.

(4)   A subsequent application concerning the same subject as a previous first application within the meaning of paragraph (2), above, filed in the same country of the Union. shall be considered as the first application, of which the filing date shall be the starting point of the period of priority, if, at the time of filing the subsequent application, the said previous application has been withdrawn, abandoned, or refused, without having been laid open to public inspection and without leaving any rights outstanding, and if it has not yet served as a basis for claiming a right of priority. The previous application may not thereafter serve as a basis for claiming a right of priority.

D.—

(1)   Any person desiring to take advantage of the priority of a previous filing shall be required to make a declaration indicating the date of such filing and the country in which it was made. Each country shall determine the latest date on which such declaration must be made.

(2)   These particulars shall be mentioned in the publications issued by the competent authority, and in particular in the patents and the specifications relating thereto.

(3)   The countries of the Union may require any person making a declaration of priority to produce a copy of the application (description, drawings, etc.) previously filed. The copy, certified as correct by the authority which received such application, shall not require any authentication, and may in any case be filed, without fee, at any time within three months of the filing of the subsequent application. They may require it to be accompanied by a certificate from the same authority showing the date of filing, and by a translation.

(4)   No other formalities may be required for the declaration of priority at the time of filing the application. Each country of the Union shall determine the consequences of failure to comply with the formalities prescribed by this Article, but such consequences shall in no case go beyond the loss of the right of priority.

(5)   Subsequently, further proof may be required. Any person who avails himself of the priority of a previous application shall be required to specify the number of that application; this number shall be published as provided for by paragraph (2), above.

E.—

(1)   Where an industrial design is filed in a country by virtue of a right of priority based on the filing of a utility model, the period of priority shall be the same as that fixed for industrial designs

(2)   Furthermore, it is permissible to file a utility model in a country by virtue of a right of priority based on the filing of a patent application,

and vice versa.

F.— No country of the Union may refuse a priority or a patent application on the ground that the applicant claims multiple priorities, even if they originate in different countries, or on the ground that an application claiming one or more priorities contains one or more elements that were not included in the application or applications whose priority is claimed, provided that, in both cases, there is unity of invention within the meaning of the law of the country. With respect to the elements not included in the application or applications whose priority is claimed, the filing of the subsequent application shall give rise to a right of priority tinder ordinary conditions.

G.—

(1) If the examination reveals that an application for a patent contains more than one invention, the applicant may divide the application into a certain number of divisional applications and preserve as the date of each the date of the initial application and the benefit of the right of priority, if any.

(2) The applicant may also, on his own initiative, divide a patent application and preserve as the date of each divisional application the date of the initial application and the benefit of the right of priority, if any. Each country of the Union shall have the right to determine the conditions under which such division shall be authorized.

H.— Priority may not be refused on the ground that certain elements of the invention for which priority is claimed do not appear among the claims formulated in the application in the country of origin, provided that the application documents as a whole specifically disclose such elements.

I.—

(1) Applications for inventors' certificates filed in a country in which applicants have the right to apply at their own option either for a patent or for an inventor's certificate shall give rise to the right of priority provided for by this Article, under the same conditions and with the same effects as applications for patents.

(2) In a country in which applicants have the right to apply at their own option either for a patent or for an inventor's certificate, an applicant for an inventor's certificate shall, in accordance with the provisions of this Article relating to patent applications, enjoy a right of priority based on an application for a patent, a utility model, or an inventor's certificate.

Article 4*bis*
[*Patents:* Independence of Patents Obtained for the Same Invention in Different Countries]

(1) Patents applied for in the various countries of the Union by nationals of countries of the Union shall be independent of patents obtained for the same invention in other countries, whether members of the Union or not.

(2) The foregoing provision is to be understood in an unrestricted sense, in particular, in the sense that patents applied for during the period of priority

are independent, both as regards the grounds for nullity and forfeiture, and as regards their normal duration.

(3) The provision shall apply to all patents existing at the time when it comes into effect.

(4) Similarly, it shall apply, in the case of the accession of new countries, to patents in existence on either side at the time of accession.

(5) Patents obtained with the benefit of priority shall, in the various countries of the Union, have a duration equal to that which they would have, had they been applied for or granted without the benefit of priority.

Article 4*ter*
[*Patents:* Mention of the Inventor in the Patent]

The inventor shall have the right to be mentioned as such in the patent.

Article 4*quater*
[*Patents:* Patentability in Case of Restrictions of Sale by Law]

The grant of a patent shall not be refused and a patent shall not be invalidated on the ground that the sale of the patented product or of a product obtained by means of a patented process is subject to restrictions or limitations resulting from the domestic law.

Article 5
[A. *Patents:* Importation of Articles; Failure to Work or Insufficient Working; Compulsory Licenses
B. *Industrial Designs:* Failure to Work; Importation of Articles
C. *Marks:* Failure to Use; Different Forms; Use by Co-proprietors
D. *Patents, Utility Models, Marks, Industrial Designs:* Marking]

A.—

(1)   Importation by the patentee into the country where the patent has been granted of articles manufactured in any of the countries of the Union shall not entail forfeiture of the patent.

(2)   Each country of the Union shall have the right to take legislative measures providing for the grant of compulsory licenses to prevent the abuses which might result from the exercise of the exclusive rights conferred by the patent, for example, failure to work.

(3)   Forfeiture of the patent shall not be provided for except in cases where the grant of compulsory licenses would not have been sufficient to prevent the said abuses. No proceedings for the forfeiture or revocation of a patent may be instituted before the expiration of two years from the grant of the first compulsory license.

(4)   A compulsory license may not be applied for on the ground of failure to work or insufficient working before the expiration of a period of four years from the date of filing of the patent application or three years from the date of the grant of the patent, whichever period expires

last; it shall be refused if the patentee justifies his inaction by legitimate reasons. Such a compulsory license shall be non-exclusive and shall not be transferable, even in the form of the grant of a sub-license, except with that part of the enterprise or goodwill which exploits such license.

(5) The foregoing provisions shall be applicable, *mutatis mutandis*, to utility models.

B.— The protection of industrial designs shall not, under any circumstance, be subject to any forfeiture, either by reason of failure to work or by reason of the importation of articles corresponding to those which are protected.

C.—

(1) If, in any country, use of the registered mark is compulsory, the registration may be cancelled only after a reasonable period, and then only if the person concerned does not justify his inaction.

(2) Use of a trademark by the proprietor in a form differing in elements which do not alter the distinctive character of the mark in the form in which it was registered in one of the countries of the Union shall not entail invalidation of the registration and shall not diminish the protection granted to the mark.

(3) Concurrent use of the same mark on identical or similar goods by industrial or commercial establishments considered as co-proprietors of the mark according to the provisions of the domestic law of the country where protection is claimed shall not prevent registration or diminish in any way the protection granted to the said mark in any country of the Union, provided that such use does not result in misleading the public and is not contrary to the public interest.

D.— No indication or mention of the patent, of the utility model, of the registration of the trademark, or of the deposit of the industrial design, shall be required upon the goods as a condition of recognition of the right to protection.

Article 5*bis*
[*All Industrial Property Rights:* Period of Grace for the Payment of Fees for the Maintenance of Rights; *Patents:* Restoration]

(1) A period of grace of not less than six months shall be allowed for the payment of the fees prescribed for the maintenance of industrial property rights, subject, if the domestic legislation so provides, to the payment of a surcharge.

(2) The countries of the Union shall have the right to provide for the restoration of patents which have lapsed by reason of non-payment of fees.

Article 5*ter*
[*Patents:* Patented Devices Forming Part of Vessels, Aircraft, or Land Vehicles]

In any country of the Union the following shall not be considered as infringements of the rights of a patentee:

1. the use on board vessels of other countries of the Union of devices forming the subject of his patent in the body of the vessel, in the machinery, tackle, gear and other accessories, when such vessels temporarily or accidentally enter the waters of the said country, provided that such devices are used there exclusively for the needs of the vessel;

2. the use of devices forming the subject of the patent in the construction or operation of aircraft or land vehicles of other countries of the Union, or of accessories of such aircraft or land vehicles, when those aircraft or land vehicles temporarily or accidentally enter the said country.

Article 5*quater*
[*Patents:* Importation of Products Manufactured by a Process Patented in the Importing Country]

When a product is imported into a country of the Union where there exists a patent protecting a process of manufacture of the said product, the patentee shall have all the rights, with regard to the imported product, that are accorded to him by the legislation of the country of importation, on the basis of the process patent, with respect to products manufactured in that country.

Article 5*quinquies*
[Industrial Designs]

Industrial designs shall be protected in all the countries of the Union.

Article 6
[*Marks:* Conditions of Registration; Independence of Protection of Same Mark in Different Countries]

(1) The conditions for the filing and registration of trademarks shall be determined in each country of the Union by its domestic legislation.

(2) However, an application for the registration of a mark filed by a national of a country of the Union in any country of the Union may not be refused, nor may a registration be invalidated, on the ground that filing, registration, or renewal, has not been effected in the country of origin.

(3) A mark duly registered in a country of the Union shall be regarded as independent of marks registered in the other countries of the Union, including the country of origin.

Article 6*bis*
[*Marks:* Well-Known Marks]

(1) The countries of the Union undertake, ex officio if their legislation so permits, or at the request of an interested party, to refuse or to cancel the registration, and to prohibit the use, of a trademark which constitutes a reproduction, an imitation, or a translation, liable to create confusion, of a mark considered by the competent authority of the country of registration or use to be well known in that country as being already the mark of a person entitled to the benefits of this Convention and used for identical or similar goods. These provisions shall also apply when the essential part of the mark constitutes a reproduction of any such well-known mark or an imitation liable to create confusion therewith.

(2) A period of at least five years from the date of registration shall be allowed for requesting the cancellation of such a mark. The countries of the Union may provide for a period within which the prohibition of use must be requested.

(3) No time limit shall be fixed for requesting the cancellation or the prohibition of the use of marks registered or used in bad faith.

Article 6*ter*
[*Marks:* Prohibitions Concerning State Emblems, Official Hallmarks, and Emblems of Intergovernmental Organizations]

(1)

(a) The countries of the Union agree to refuse or to invalidate the registration, and to prohibit by appropriate measures the use, without authorization by the competent authorities, either as trademarks or as elements of trademarks, of armorial bearings, flags, and other State emblems, of the countries of the Union, official signs and hallmarks indicating control and warranty adopted by them, and any imitation from a heraldic point of view.

(b) The provisions of subparagraph (a), above, shall apply equally to armorial bearings, flags, other emblems, abbreviations, and names, of international intergovernmental organizations of which one or more countries of the Union are members, with the exception of armorial bearings, flags, other emblems, abbreviations, and names, that are already the subject of international agreements in force, intended to ensure their protection.

(c) No country of the Union shall be required to apply the provisions of subparagraph (b), above, to the prejudice of the owners of rights acquired in good faith before the entry into force, in that country, of this Convention. The countries of the Union shall not be required to apply the said provisions when the use or registration referred to in subparagraph (a), above, is not of such a nature as to suggest to the public that a connection exists between the organization concerned and the armorial bearings, flags, emblems, abbreviations, and names, or if such use or registration is probably not of such a nature as to mislead the public as to the existence of a connection between the user and the organization.

(2) Prohibition of the use of official signs and hallmarks indicating control and warranty shall apply solely in cases where the marks in which they are incorporated are intended to be used on goods of the same or a similar kind.

(3)

(a) For the application of these provisions, the countries of the Union agree to communicate reciprocally, through the intermediary of the International Bureau, the list of State emblems, and official signs and hallmarks indicating control and warranty, which they desire, or may hereafter desire, to place wholly or within certain limits tinder the protection of this Article, and all subsequent modifications of such list. Each country of the Union shall in due course make available to the public the lists so communicated. Nevertheless such communication is not obligatory in respect of flags of States.

(b) The provisions of paragraph (1)(b) of this Article shall apply only to such armorial bearings, flags, other emblems, abbreviations, and names, of international intergovernmental organizations as the latter have communicated to the countries of the Union through the intermediary of the International Bureau.

(4) Any country of the Union may, within a period of twelve months from the receipt of the notification, transmit its objections, if any, through the intermediary of the International Bureau, to the country or international intergovernmental organization concerned.

(5) In the case of State flags, the measures prescribed by paragraph (1), above, shall apply solely to marks registered after November 6, 1925.

(6) In the case of State emblems other than flags, and of official signs and hallmarks of the countries of the Union, and in the case of armorial bearings, flags, other emblems. abbreviations, and names, of international intergovernmental organizations, these provisions shall apply only to marks registered more than two months after receipt of the communication provided for in paragraph (3), above.

(7) In cases of bad faith, the countries shall have the right to cancel even those marks incorporating State emblems, signs, and hallmarks, which were registered before November 6, 1925.

(8) Nationals of any country who are authorized to make use of the State emblems, signs, and hallmarks, of their country may use them even if they are similar to those of another country.

(9) The countries of the Union undertake to prohibit the unauthorized use in trade of the State armorial bearings of the other countries of the Union, when the use is of such a nature as to be misleading as to the origin of the goods.

(10) The above provisions shall not prevent the countries from exercising the right given in Article 6*quinquies*(B)(3), to refuse or to invalidate the registration of marks incorporating, without authorization, armorial bearings, flags, other State emblems, or official signs and hallmarks adopted

by a country of the Union, as well as the distinctive signs of international intergovernmental organizations referred to in paragraph (1), above.

Article 6*quater*
[*Marks:* Assignment of Marks]

(1) When, in accordance with the law of a country of the Union, the assignment of a mark is valid only if it takes place at the same time as the transfer of the business or goodwill to which the mark belongs, it shall suffice for the recognition of such validity that the portion of the business or goodwill located in that country be transferred to the assignee, together with the exclusive right to manufacture in the said country, or to sell therein, the goods bearing the mark assigned.

(2) The foregoing provision does not impose upon the countries of the Union any obligation to regard as valid the assignment of any mark the use of which by the assignee would, in fact, be of such a nature as to mislead the public, particularly as regards the origin, nature, or essential qualities, of the goods to which the mark is applied.

Article 6*quinquies*
[*Marks:* Protection of Marks Registered in One Country of the Union in the Other Countries of the Union]

A.—

(1) Every trademark duly registered in the country of origin shall be accepted for filing and protected as is in the other countries of the Union, subject to the reservations indicated in this Article. Such countries may, before proceeding to final registration, require the production of a certificate of registration in the country of origin, issued by the competent authority. No authentication shall be required for this certificate.

(2) Shall be considered the country of origin the country of the Union where the applicant has a real and effective industrial or commercial establishment, or, if he has no such establishment within the Union, the country of the Union where he has his domicile, or, if he has no domicile within the Union but is a national of a country of the Union, the country of which he is a national.

B.— Trademarks covered by this Article may be neither denied registration nor invalidated except in the following cases:

1. when they are of such a nature as to infringe rights acquired by third parties in the country where protection is claimed;
2. when they are devoid of any distinctive character, or consist exclusively of signs or indications which may serve, in trade, to designate the kind, quality, quantity, intended purpose, value, place of origin, of the goods, or the time of production, or have become customary in the current language or in the bona fide and established practices of the trade of the country where protection is claimed;

3. when they are contrary to morality or public order and, in particular, of such a nature as to deceive the public. lt is understood that a mark may not be considered contrary to public order for the sole reason that it does not conform to a provision of the legislation on marks, except if such provision itself relates to public order.

This provision is subject, however, to the application of Article 10*bis*.

C.—

(1)   In determining whether a mark is eligible for protection, all the factual circumstances must be taken into consideration, particularly the length of time the mark has been in use.

(2)   No trademark shall be refused in the other countries of the Union for the sole reason that it differs from the mark protected in the country of origin only in respect of elements that do not alter its distinctive character and do not affect its identity in the form in which it has been registered in the said country of origin.

D.— No person may benefit from the provisions of this Article if the mark for which he claims protection is not registered in the country of origin.

E.— However, in no case shall the renewal of the registration of the mark in the country of origin involve an obligation to renew the registration in the other countries of the Union in which the mark has been registered.

F.— The benefit of priority shall remain unaffected for applications for the registration of marks filed within the period fixed by Article 4, even if registration in the country of origin is effected after the expiration of such period.

Article 6*sexies*
[*Marks:* Service Marks]

The countries of the Union undertake to protect service marks. They shall not be required to provide for the registration of such marks.

Article 6*septies*
[*Marks:* Registration in the Name of the Agent or Representative of the Proprietor Without the Latter's Authorization]

(1) If the agent or representative of the person who is the proprietor of a mark in one of the countries of the Union applies, without such proprietor's authorization, for the registration of the mark in his own name, in one or more countries of the Union, the proprietor shall be entitled to oppose the registration applied for or demand its cancellation or, if the law of the country so allows, the assignment in his favor of the said registration, unless such agent or representative justifies his action.

(2) The proprietor of the mark shall, subject to the provisions of paragraph (1), above, be entitled to oppose the use of his mark by his agent or representative if he has not authorized such use.

(3) Domestic legislation may provide an equitable time limit within which

the proprietor of a mark must exercise the rights provided for in this Article.

Article 7
[*Marks:* Nature of the Goods to which the Mark is Applied]

The nature of the goods to which a trademark is to be applied shall in no case form an obstacle to the registration of the mark.

Article 7*bis*
[*Marks:* Collective Marks]

(1) The countries of the Union undertake to accept for filing and to protect collective marks belonging to associations the existence of which is not contrary to the law of the country of origin, even if such associations do not possess an industrial or commercial establishment.

(2) Each country shall be the judge of the particular conditions under which a collective mark shall be protected and may refuse protection if the mark is contrary to the public interest.

(3) Nevertheless, the protection of these marks shall not be refused to any association the existence of which is not contrary to the law of the country of origin, on the ground that such association is not established in the country where protection is sought or is not constituted according to the law of the latter country.

Article 8
[Trade Names]

A trade name shall be protected in all the countries of the Union without the obligation of filing or registration, whether or not it forms part of a trademark.

Article 9
[*Marks, Trade Names:* Seizure, on Importation, etc., of Goods Unlawfully Bearing a Mark or Trade Name]

(1) All goods unlawfully bearing a trademark or trade name shall be seized on importation into those countries of the Union where such mark or trade name is entitled to legal protection.

(2) Seizure shall likewise be effected in the country where the unlawful affixation occurred or in the country into which the goods were imported.

(3) Seizure shall take place at the request of the public prosecutor, or any other competent authority, or any interested party, whether a natural person or a legal entity, in conformity with the domestic legislation of each country.

(4) The authorities shall not be bound to effect seizure of goods in transit.

(5) If the legislation of a country does not permit seizure on importation, seizure shall be replaced by prohibition of importation or by seizure inside the country.

(6) If the legislation of a country permits neither seizure on importation nor prohibition of importation nor seizure inside the country, then, until such time as the legislation is modified accordingly, these measures shall be replaced by the actions and remedies available in such cases to nationals under the law of such country.

Article 10
[*False Indications:* Seizure, on Importation, etc., of Goods Bearing False Indications as to their Source or the Identity of the Producer]

(1) The provisions of the preceding Article shall apply in cases of direct or indirect use of a false indication of the source of the good or the identity of the producer, manufacturer, or merchant.

(2) Any producer, manufacturer, or merchant, whether a natural person or a legal entity, engaged in the production or manufacture of or trade in such goods and established either in the locality falsely indicated as the source, or in the region where such locality is situated, or in the country falsely indicated, or in the country where the false indication of source is used, shall in any case he deemed an interested party.

Article 10*bis*
[Unfair Competition]

(1) The countries of the Union are bound to assure to nationals of such countries effective protection against unfair competition.

(2) Any act of competition contrary to honest practices in industrial or commercial matters constitutes an act of unfair competition.

(3) The following in particular shall be prohibited:

1. all acts of such a nature as to create confusion by any means whatever with the establishment, the goods, or the industrial or commercial activities, of a competitor;

2. false allegations in the course of trade of such a nature as to discredit the establishment, the goods, or the industrial or commercial activities, of a competitor;

3. indications or allegations the use of which in the course of trade is liable to mislead the public as to the nature, the manufacturing process, the characteristics, the suitability for their purpose, or the quantity, of the goods.

Article 10*ter*
[*Marks, Trade Names, False Indications, Unfair Competition:* Remedies, Right to Sue]

(1) The countries of the Union undertake to assure to nationals of the other countries of the Union appropriate legal remedies effectively to repress all the acts referred to in Articles 9, 10, and 10*bis*.

(2) They undertake, further, to provide measures to permit federations and associations representing interested industrialists, producers, or merchants, provided that the existence of such federations and associations is not contrary to the laws of their countries, to take action in the courts or before the administrative authorities, with a view to the repression of the acts referred to in Articles 9, 10, and 10*bis*, in so far as the law of the country in which protection is claimed allows such action by federations and associations of that country.

Article 11
[*Inventions, Utility Models, Industrial Designs, Marks:* Temporary Protection at Certain International Exhibitions]

(1) The countries of the Union shall, in conformity with their domestic legislation, grant temporary protection to patentable inventions, utility models, industrial designs, and trademarks, in respect of goods exhibited at official or officially recognized international exhibitions held in the territory of any of them.

(2) Such temporary protection shall not extend the periods provided by Article 4. If, later, the right of priority is invoked, the authorities of any country may provide that the period shall start from the date of introduction of the goods into the exhibition.

(3) Each country may require, as proof of the identity of the article exhibited and of the date of its introduction, such documentary evidence as it considers necessary.

Article 12
[Special National Industrial Property Services]

(1) Each country of the Union undertakes to establish a special industrial property service and a central office for the communication to the public of patents, utility models, industrial designs, and trademarks.

(2) This service shall publish an official periodical journal. It shall publish regularly:

(a) the names of the proprietors of patents granted, with a brief designation of the inventions patented;

(b) the reproductions of registered trademarks.

Article 13
[Assembly of the Union]

(1)

(a) The Union shall have an Assembly consisting of those countries of the Union which are bound by Articles 13 to 17.

(b) The Government of each country shall be represented by one delegate, who may be assisted by alternate delegates, advisors, and experts.

(c) The expenses of each delegation shall be borne by the Government which has appointed it.

(2)

(a) The Assembly shall:

(i) deal with all matters concerning the maintenance and development of the Union and the implementation of this Convention;

(ii) give directions concerning the preparation for conferences of revision to the International Bureau of Intellectual Property (hereinafter designated as "the International Bureau") referred to in the Convention establishing the World Intellectual Property Organization (hereinafter designated as "the Organization"), due account being taken of any comments made by those countries of the Union which are not hound by Articles 13 to 17;

(iii) review and approve the reports and activities of the Director General of the Organization concerning the Union, and give him all necessary instructions concerning matters within the competence of the Union;

(iv) elect the members of the Executive Committee of the Assembly;

(v) review and approve the reports and activities of its Executive Committee, and give instructions to such Committee;

(vi) determine the program and adopt the biennial budget of the Union, and approve its final accounts;

(vii) adopt the financial regulations of the Union;

(viii) establish such committees of experts and working groups as it deems appropriate to achieve the objectives of the Union;

(ix) determine which countries not members of the Union and which intergovernmental and international nongovernmental organizations shall be admitted to its meetings as observers;

(x) adopt amendments to Articles 13 to 17;

(xi) take any other appropriate action designed to further the objectives of the Union;

(xii) perform such other functions as are appropriate under this Convention;

(xiii) subject to its acceptance, exercise such rights as are given to it in the Convention establishing the Organization.

(b) With respect to matters which are of interest also to other Unions administered by the Organization, the Assembly shall make its decisions after having heard the advice of the Coordination Committee of the Organization.

(3)

(a) Subject to the provisions of subparagraph (b), a delegate may represent one country only.

(b) Countries of the Union grouped under the terms of a special agreement in a common office possessing for each of them the character of a special national service of industrial property as referred to in Article 12 may be jointly represented during discussions by one of their number.

(4)

(a) Each country member of the Assembly shall have one vote.

(b) One-half of the countries members of the Assembly shall constitute a quorum.

(c) Notwithstanding the provisions of subparagraph (b), if, in any session, the number of countries represented is less than one-half but equal to or more than one-third of the countries members of the Assembly, the Assembly may make decisions but, with the exception of decisions concerning its own procedure, all such decisions shall take effect only if the conditions, set forth hereinafter are fulfilled. The International Bureau shall communicate the said decisions to the countries members of the Assembly which were not represented and shall invite them to express in writing their vote or abstention within a period of three months from the date of the communication. If, at the expiration of this period, the number of countries having thus expressed their vote or abstention attains the number of countries which was lacking for attaining the quorum in the session itself, such decisions shall take effect provided that at the same time the required majority still obtains.

(d) Subject to the provisions of Article 17(2), the decisions of the Assembly shall require two-thirds of the votes cast.

(e) Abstentions shall not be considered as votes.

(5)

(a) Subject to the provisions of subparagraph (b), a delegate may vote in the name of one country only.

(b) The countries of the Union referred to in paragraph (3)(b) shall, as a general rule, endeavor to send their own delegations to the sessions of the Assembly. If, however, for exceptional reasons, any such country cannot send its own delegation, it may give to the delegation of another such country the power to vote in its name, provided that each delegation may vote by proxy for one country only. Such power to vote shall be granted in a document signed by the Head of State or the competent Minister.

(6) Countries of the Union not members of the Assembly shall be admitted to the meetings of the latter as observers.

(7)

(a) The Assembly shall meet once in every second calendar year in ordinary session upon convocation by the Director General and, in the absence of exceptional circumstances, during the same period and at the same place as the General Assembly of the Organization.

(b) The Assembly shall meet in extraordinary session upon convocation by the Director General, at the request of the Executive Committee or at the request of one-fourth of the countries members of the Assembly.

(8) The Assembly shall adopt its own rules of procedure.

Article 14
[Executive Committee]

(1) The Assembly shall have an Executive Committee.

(2)

(a) The Executive Committee shall consist of countries elected by the Assembly from among countries members of the Assembly. Furthermore, the country on whose territory the Organization has its headquarters shall, subject to the provisions of Article 16(7)(b), have an ex officio seat on the Committee.

(b) The Government of each country member of the Executive Committee shall be represented by one delegate, who may be assisted by alternate delegates, advisors, and experts.

(c) The expenses of each delegation shall be borne by the Government which has appointed it.

(3) The number of countries members of the Executive Committee shall correspond to one-fourth of the number of countries members of the Assembly. In establishing the number of seats to be filled, remainders after division by four shall be disregarded.

(4) In electing the members of the Executive Committee, the Assembly shall have due regard to an equitable geographical distribution and to the need for countries party to the Special Agreements established in relation with the Union to be among the countries constituting the Executive Committee.

(5)

(a) Each member of the Executive Committee shall serve from the close of the session of the Assembly which elected it to the close of the next ordinary session of the Assembly.

(b) Members of the Executive Committee may be re-elected, but only up to a maximum of two-thirds of such members.

(c) The Assembly shall establish the details of the rules governing the election and possible re-election of the members of the Executive Committee.

(6)

(a) The Executive Committee shall:

(i)   prepare the draft agenda of the Assembly;

(ii)   submit proposals to the Assembly in respect of the draft program and biennial budget of the Union prepared by the Director General;

(iii) *[deleted]*

(iv)   submit, with appropriate comments, to the Assembly the periodical reports of the Director General and the yearly audit reports on the accounts;

(v) take all necessary measures to ensure the execution of the program of the Union by the Director General, in accordance with the decisions of the Assembly and having regard to circumstances arising between two ordinary sessions of the Assembly;

(vi) perform such other functions as are allocated to it tinder this Convention.

(b) With respect to matters which are of interest also to other Unions administered by the Organization, the Executive Committee shall make its decisions after having heard the advice of the Coordination Committee of the Organization.

(7)

(a) The Executive Committee shall meet once a year in ordinary session upon convocation by the Director General, preferably during the same period and at the same place as the Coordination Committee of the Organization.

(b) The Executive Committee shall meet in extraordinary session upon convocation by the Director General, either on his own initiative, or at the request of its Chairman or one-fourth of its members.

(8)

(a) Each country member of the Executive Committee shall have one vote.

(b) One-half of the members of the Executive Committee shall constitute a quorum.

(c) Decisions shall be made by a simple majority of the votes cast.

(d) Abstentions shall not be considered as votes.

(e) A delegate may represent, and vote in the name of, one country only.

(9) Countries of the Union not members of the Executive Committee shall be admitted to its meetings as observers.

(10) The Executive Committee shall adopt its own rules of procedure.

Article 15
[International Bureau]

(1)

(a) Administrative tasks concerning the Union shall be performed by the International Bureau, which is a continuation of the Bureau of the Union united with the Bureau of the Union established by the International Convention for the Protection of Literary and Artistic Works.

(b) In particular, the International Bureau shall provide the secretariat of the various organs of the Union.

(c) The Director General of the Organization shall be the chief executive of the Union and shall represent the Union.

(2) The International Bureau shall assemble and publish information concerning the protection of industrial property. Each country of the Union shall promptly communicate to the International Bureau all new laws and official texts concerning the protection of industrial property. Furthermore, it shall furnish the International Bureau with all the publications of its industrial property service of direct concern to the protection of industrial property which the International Bureau may find useful in its work.

(3) The International Bureau shall publish a monthly periodical.

(4) The International Bureau shall, on request, furnish any country of the Union with information on matters concerning the protection of industrial property.

(5) The International Bureau shall conduct Studies, and shall provide services, designed to facilitate the protection of industrial property.

(6) The Director General and any staff member designated by him shall participate, without the right to vote, in all meetings of the Assembly, the Executive Committee, and any other committee of experts or working group. The Director General, or a staff member designated by him, shall be ex officio secretary of these bodies.

(7)

(a) The International Bureau shall, in accordance with the directions of the Assembly and in cooperation with the Executive Committee, make the preparations for the conferences of revision of the provisions of the Convention other than Articles 13 to 17.

(b) The International Bureau may consult with intergovernmental and international non-governmental organizations concerning preparations for conferences of revision.

(c) The Director General and persons designated by him shall take part, without the right to vote, in the discussions at these conferences.

(8) The International Bureau shall carry out any other tasks assigned to it.

Article 16
[Finances]

(1)

(a) The Union shall have a budget.

(b) The budget of the Union shall include the income and expenses proper to the Union, its contribution to the budget of expenses common to the Unions, and, where applicable, the sum made available to the budget of the Conference of the Organization.

(c) Expenses not attributable exclusively to the Union but also to one or more other Unions administered by the Organization shall be considered as expenses common to the Unions. The share of the Union in such common expenses shall be in proportion to the interest the Union has in them.

(2) The budget of the Union shall be established with due regard to the

requirements of coordination with the budgets of the other Unions administered by the Organization.

(3) The budget of the Union shall be financed from the following sources:

(i) contributions of the countries of the Union;

(ii) fees and charges due for services rendered by the International Bureau in relation to the Union;

(iii) sale of, or royalties on, the publications of the International Bureau concerning the Union;

(iv) gifts, bequests, and subventions;

(v) rents, interests, and other miscellaneous income.

(4)

(a) For the purpose of establishing its contribution towards the budget, each country of the Union shall belong to a class, and shall pay its annual contributions on the basis of a number of units fixed as follows:

Class I 25

Class II 20

Class III 15

Class IV 10

Class V 5

Class VI 3

Class VII 1

(b) Unless it has already done so, each country shall indicate, concurrently with depositing its instrument of ratification or accession, the class to which it wishes to belong. Any country may change class. If it chooses a lower class, the country must announce such change to the Assembly at one of its ordinary sessions. Any such change shall take effect at the beginning of the calendar year following the said session.

(c) The annual contribution of each country shall be an amount in the same proportion to the total sum to be contributed to the budget of the Union by all countries as the number of its units is to the total of the units of all contributing countries.

(d) Contributions shall become due on the first of January of each year.

(e) A country which is in arrears in the payment of its contributions may not exercise its right to vote in any of the organs of the Union of which it is a member if the amount of its arrears equals or exceeds the amount of the contributions due from it for the preceding two full years. However, any organ of the Union may allow such a country to continue to exercise its right to vote in that organ if, and as long as, it is satisfied that the delay in payment is due to exceptional and unavoidable circumstances.

(f) If the budget is not adopted before the beginning of a new financial period, it shall be at the same level as the budget of the previous year, as provided in the financial regulations.

(5) The amount of the fees and charges due for services rendered by the International Bureau in relation to the Union shall be established, and shall be reported to the Assembly and the Executive Committee, by the Director General.

(6)

(a) The Union shall have a working capital fund which shall be constituted by a single payment made by each country of the Union. If the fund becomes insufficient, the Assembly shall decide to increase it.

(b) The amount of the initial payment of each country to the said fund or of its participation in the increase thereof shall be a proportion of the contribution of that country for the year in which the fund is established or the decision to increase it is made.

(c) The proportion and the terms of payment shall be fixed by the Assembly on the proposal of the Director General and after it has heard the advice of the Coordination Committee of the Organization.

(7)

(a) In the headquarters agreement concluded with the country on the territory of which the Organization has its headquarters, it shall be provided that, whenever the working capital fund is insufficient, such country shall grant advances. The amount of these advances and the conditions on which they are granted shall be the subject of separate agreements, in each case, between such country and the Organization. As long as it remains under the obligation to grant advances, such country shall have an ex officio seat on the Executive Committee.

(b) The country referred to in subparagraph (a) and the Organization shall each have the right to denounce the obligation to grant advances, by written notification. Denunciation shall take effect three years after the end of the year in which it has been notified.

(8) The auditing of the accounts shall be effected by one or more of the countries of the Union or by external auditors, as provided in the financial regulations. They shall be designated, with their agreement, by the Assembly.

Article 17
[Amendment of Articles 13 to 17]

(1) Proposals for the amendment of Articles 13, 14, 15, 16, and the present Article, may be initiated by any country member of the Assembly, by the Executive Committee, or by the Director General. Such proposals shall be communicated by the Director General to the member countries of the Assembly at least six months in advance of their consideration by the Assembly.

(2) Amendments to the Articles referred to in paragraph (1) shall be adopted by the Assembly. Adoption shall require three-fourths of the votes cast, provided that any amendment to Article 13, and to the present paragraph, shall require four-fifths of the votes cast.

(3) Any amendment to the Articles referred to in paragraph (1) shall enter into force one month after written notifications of acceptance, effected in accordance with their respective constitutional processes, have been received by the Director General from three-fourths of the countries members of the Assembly at the time it adopted the amendment. Any amendment to the said Articles thus accepted shall bind all the countries which are members of the Assembly at the time the amendment enters into force, or which become members thereof at a subsequent date, provided that any amendment increasing the financial obligations of countries of the Union shall bind only those countries which have notified their acceptance of such amendment.

Article 18
[Revision of Articles 1 to 12 and 18 to 30]

(1) This Convention shall be submitted to revision with a view to the introduction of amendments designed to improve the system of the Union.

(2) For that purpose, conferences shall be held successively in one of the countries of the Union among the delegates of the said countries.

(3) Amendments to Articles 13 to 17 are governed by the provisions of Article 17.

Article 19
[Special Agreements]

It is understood that the countries of the Union reserve the right to make separately between themselves special agreements for the protection of industrial property, in so far as these agreements do not contravene the provisions of this Convention.

Article 20
[Ratification or Accession by Countries of the Union; Entry Into Force]

(1)

(a) Any country of the Union which has signed this Act may ratify it, and, if it has not signed it, may accede to it. Instruments of ratification and accession shall be deposited with the Director General.

(b) Any country of the Union may declare in its instrument of ratification or accession that its ratification or accession shall not apply:

(i)   to Articles 1 to 12, or

(ii)   to Articles 13 to 17.

(c) Any country of the Union which, in accordance with subparagraph (b), has excluded from the effects of its ratification or accession one of the two groups of Articles referred to in that subparagraph may at any later time declare that it extends the effects of its ratification or accession to that group of Articles. Such declaration shall be deposited with the Director General.

(2)

(a) Articles 1 to 12 shall enter into force, with respect to the first ten countries of the Union which have deposited instruments of ratification or accession without making the declaration permitted under paragraph (1)(b)(i), three months after the deposit of the tenth such instrument of ratification or accession.

(b) Articles 13 to 17 shall enter into force, with respect to the first ten countries of the Union which have deposited instruments of ratification or accession without making the declaration permitted under paragraph (1)(b)(ii), three months after the deposit of the tenth such instrument of ratification or accession.

(c) Subject to the initial entry into force, pursuant to the provisions of subparagraphs (a) and (b), of each of the two groups of Articles referred to in paragraph (1)(b)(i) and (1)(b)(ii), and subject to the provisions of paragraph (1)(b), Articles 1 to 17 shall, with respect to any country of the Union, other than those referred to in subparagraphs (a) and (b), which deposits an instrument of ratification or accession or any country of the Union which deposits a declaration pursuant to paragraph (1)(c), enter into force three months after the date of notification by the Director General of such deposit, unless a subsequent date has been indicated in the instrument or declaration deposited. In the latter case, this Act shall enter into force with respect to that country on the date thus indicated.

(3) With respect to any country of the Union which deposits an instrument of ratification or accession, Articles 18 to 30 shall enter into force on the earlier of the dates on which any of the groups of Articles referred to in paragraph (1)(b) enters into force with respect to that country pursuant to paragraph (2)(a), (2)(b), or (2)(c).

Article 21
[Accession by Countries Outside the Union; Entry Into Force]

(1) Any country outside the Union may accede to this Act and thereby become a member of the Union. Instruments of accession shall be deposited with the Director General.

(2)

(a) With respect to any country outside the Union which deposits its instrument of accession one month or more before the date of entry into force of any provisions of the present Act, this Act shall enter into force, unless a subsequent date has been indicated in the instrument of accession, on the date upon which provisions first enter into force pursuant to Article 20(2)(a) or 20(2)(b); provided that:

    (i)   if Articles 1 to 12 do not enter into force on that date, such country shall, during the interim period before the entry into force of such provisions, and in substitution therefor, be bound by Articles 1 to 12 of the Lisbon Act.

    (ii)   if Articles 13 to 17 do not enter into force on that date, such country shall, during the interim period before the entry into force of such provisions, and in substitution therefor, be bound by Articles 13 and 14(3), 14(4), and 14(5), of the Lisbon Act.

If a country indicates a subsequent date in its instrument of accession, this Act shall enter into force with respect to that country on the date thus indicated.

(b) With respect to any country outside the Union which deposits its instrument of accession on a date which is subsequent to, or precedes by less than one month, the entry into force of one group of Articles of the present Act, this Act shall, subject to the proviso of subparagraph (a), enter into force three months after the date on which its accession has been notified by the Director General, unless a subsequent date has been indicated in the instrument of accession. In the latter case, this Act shall enter into force with respect to that country on the date thus indicated.

(3) With respect to any country outside the Union which deposits its instrument of accession after the date of entry into force of the present Act in its entirety, or less than one month before such date, this Act shall enter into force three months after the date on which its accession has been notified by the Director General, unless a subsequent date has been indicated in the instrument of accession. In the latter case, this Act shall enter into force with respect to that country on the date thus indicated.

Article 22
[Consequences of Ratification or Accession]

Subject to the possibilities of exceptions provided for in Articles 20(1)(b) and 28(2), ratification or accession shall automatically entail acceptance of all the clauses and admission to all the advantages of this Act.

Article 23
[Accession to Earlier Acts]

After the entry into force of this Act in its entirety, a country may not accede to earlier Act of this Convention.

Article 24
[Territories]

(1) Any country may declare in its instrument of ratification or accession, or may inform the Director General by written notification any time thereafter, that this Convention shall be applicable to all or part of those territories, designated in the declaration or notification, for the external relations of which it is responsible.

(2) Any country which has made such a declaration or given such a notification may, at any time, notify the Director General that this Convention shall cease to be applicable to all or part of such territories.

(3)

(a) Any declaration made under paragraph (1) shall take effect on the same date as the ratification or accession in the instrument of which it was included, and any notification given under such paragraph shall take effect three months after its notification by the Director General.

(b) Any notification given tinder paragraph (2) shall take effect twelve months after its receipt by the Director General.

Article 25
[Implementation of the Convention on the Domestic Level]

(1) Any country party to this Convention undertakes to adopt, in accordance with its constitution, the measures necessary to ensure the application of this Convention.

(2) lt is understood that, at the time a country deposits its instrument of ratification or accession, it will be in a position under its domestic law to give effect to the provisions of this Convention.

Article 26
[Denunciation]

(1) This Convention shall remain in force without limitation as to time.

(2) Any country may denounce this Act by notification addressed to the Director General. Such denunciation shall constitute also denunciation of all earlier Acts and shall affect only the country making it, the Convention remaining in full force and effect as regards the other countries of the Union.

(3) Denunciation shall take effect one year after the day on which the Director General has received the notification.

(4) The right of denunciation provided by this Article shall not be exercised by any country before the expiration of five years from the date upon which it becomes a member of the Union.

Article 27
[Application of Earlier Acts]

(1) The present Act shall, as regards the relations between the countries to which it applies, and to the extent that it applies, replace the Convention of Paris of March 20, 1883 and the subsequent Acts of revision.

(2)

(a) As regards the countries to which the present Act does not apply, or does not apply in its entirety, but to which the Lisbon Act of October 31, 1958, applies, the latter shall remain in force in its entirety or to the extent that the present Act does not replace it by virtue of paragraph (1).

(b) Similarly, as regards the countries to which neither the present Act, nor portions thereof, nor the Lisbon Act applies, the London Act of June 2, 1934, shall remain in force in its entirety or to the extent that the present Act does not replace it by virtue of paragraph (1).

(c) Similarly, as regards the countries to which neither the present Act, nor portions thereof, nor the Lisbon Act, nor the London Act applies, the Hague Act of November 6, 1925, shall remain in force in its entirety or to the extent that the present Act does not replace it by virtue of paragraph (1).

(3) Countries outside the Union which become party to this Act shall apply it with respect to any country of the Union not party to this Act or which, although party to this Act, has made a declaration pursuant to Article 20(1)(b)(i). Such countries recognize that the said country of the Union may apply, in its relations with them, the provisions of the most recent Act to which it is party.

Article 28
[Disputes]

(1) Any dispute between two or more countries of the Union concerning the interpretation or application of this Convention, not settled by negotiation, may, by any one of the countries concerned, he brought before the International Court of Justice by application in conformity with the Statute of the Court, unless the countries concerned agree on some other method of settlement. The country bringing the dispute before the Court shall inform the International Bureau; the International Bureau shall bring the matter to the attention of the other countries of the Union.

(2) Each country may, at the time it signs this Act or deposits its instrument of ratification or accession, declare that it does not consider itself hound by the provisions of paragraph (1). With regard to any dispute between such country and any other country of the Union, the provisions of paragraph (1) shall not apply.

(3) Any country having made a declaration in accordance with the provisions of paragraph (2) may, at any time, withdraw its declaration by notification addressed to the Director General.

Article 29
[Signature, Languages, Depositary Functions]

(1)

(a) This Act shall be signed in a single copy in the French language and shall be deposited with the Government of Sweden.

(b) Official texts shall be established by the Director General, after consultation with the interested Governments, in the English, German, Italian, Portuguese, Russian and Spanish languages, and such other languages as the Assembly may designate.

(c) In case of differences of opinion on the interpretation of the various texts, the French text shall prevail.

(2) This Act shall remain open for signature at Stockholm until January 13, 1968.

(3) The Director General shall transmit two copies, certified by the

Government of Sweden, of the signed text of this Act to the Governments of all countries of the Union and, on request, to the Government of any other country.

(4) The Director General shall register this Act with the Secretariat of the United Nations.

(5) The Director General shall notify the Governments of all countries of the Union of signatures, deposits of instruments of ratification or accession and any declarations included in such instruments or made pursuant to Article 20(1)(c), entry into force of any provisions of this Act, notifications of denunciation, and notifications pursuant to Article 24.

Article 30
[Transitional Provisions]

(1) Until the first Director General assumes office, references in this Act to the International Bureau of the Organization or to the Director General shall be deemed to be references to the Bureau of the Union or its Director, respectively.

(2) Countries of the Union not hound by Articles 13 to 17 may, until five years after the entry into force of the Convention establishing the Organization, exercise, if they so desire. The rights provided under Articles 13 to 17 of this Act as if they were hound by those Articles. Any country desiring to exercise such rights shall give written notification to that effect to the Director General; such notification shall be effective from the date of its receipt. Such countries shall be deemed to be members of the Assembly until the expiration of the said period.

(3) As long as all the countries of the Union have not become Members of the Organization, the International Bureau of the Organization shall also function as the Bureau of the Union, and the Director General as the Director of the said Bureau.

(4) Once all the countries of the Union have become Members of the Organization, the rights, obligations, and property, of the Bureau of the Union shall devolve on the International Bureau of the Organization.

MADRID AGREEMENT
CONCERNING THE INTERNATIONAL REGISTRATION OF MARKS

of April 14, 1891, as revised at Brussels on December 14, 1900, at
Washington on June 2, 1911, at The Hague on November 6, 1925, at
London on June 2, 1934, at Nice on June 15, 1957, and at Stockholm on
July 14, 1967, and as amended on September 28, 1979

Article 1
[Establishment of a Special Union. Filing of Marks at International Bureau. Definition of Country of Origin]*

(1) The countries to which this Agreement applies constitute a Special
Union for the international registration of marks.

(2) Nationals of any of the contracting countries may, in all the other
countries party to this Agreement, secure protection for their marks
applicable to goods or services, registered in the country of origin, by filing
the said marks at the International Bureau of Intellectual Property
(hereinafter designated as "the International Bureau") referred to in the
Convention Establishing the World Intellectual Property Organization
(hereinafter designated as "the Organization"), through the intermediary of
the Office of the said country of origin.

(3) Shall be considered the country of origin the country of the Special
Union where the applicant has a real and effective industrial or commercial
establishment; if he has no such establishment in a country of the Special
Union, the country of the Special Union where he has his domicile; if he has
no domicile within the Special Union but is a national of a country of the
Special Union, the country of which he is a national.

Article 2
[Reference to Article 3 of Paris Convention (Same Treatment for Certain Categories of Persons as for Nationals of Countries of the Union)]

Nationals of countries not having acceded to this Agreement who, within
the territory of the Special Union constituted by the said Agreement, satisfy
the conditions specified in Article 3 of the Paris Convention for the Protection
of Industrial Property shall be treated in the same manner as nationals of
the contracting countries.

Article 3
[Contents of Application for International Registration]

(1) Every application for international registration must be presented on

---

* Articles have been given titles by WIPO to facilitate their identification. There are no titles in the signed
(French) text.

the form prescribed by the Regulations; the Office of the country of origin of the mark shall certify that the particulars appearing in such application correspond to the particulars in the national register, and shall mention the dates and numbers of the filing and registration of the mark in the country of origin and also the date of the application for international registration.

(2) The applicant must indicate the goods or services in respect of which protection of the mark is claimed and also, if possible, the corresponding class or classes according to the classification established by the Nice Agreement Concerning the International Classification of Goods and Services for the Purposes of the Registration of Marks. If the applicant does not give such indication, the International Bureau shall classify the goods or services in the appropriate classes of the said Classification. The indication of classes given by the applicant shall be subject to control by the International Bureau, which shall exercise the said control in association with the national Office. In the event of disagreement between the national Office and the International Bureau, the opinion of the latter shall prevail.

(3) If the applicant claims color as a distinctive feature of his mark, he shall be required:

1. to state the fact, and to file with his application a notice specifying the color or the combination of colors claimed;

2. to append to his application copies in color of the said mark, which shall be attached to the notification given by the International Bureau. The number of such copies shall be fixed by the Regulations.

(4) The International Bureau shall register immediately the marks filed in accordance with Article 1. The registration shall bear the date of the application for international registration in the country of origin, provided that the application has been received by the International Bureau within a period of two months from that date. If the application has not been received within that period, the International Bureau shall record it as at the date on which it received the said application. The International Bureau shall notify such registration without delay to the Offices concerned. Registered marks shall be published in a periodical journal issued by the International Bureau, on the basis of the particulars contained in the application for registration. In the case of marks comprising a figurative element of a special form of writing, the Regulations shall determine whether a printing block must be supplied by the applicant.

(5) With a view to the publicity to be given in the contracting countries to registered marks, each Office shall receive from the International Bureau a number of copies of the said publication free of charge and a number of copies at a reduced price, in proportion to the number of units mentioned in Article 16(4)(a) of the Paris Convention for the Protection of Industrial Property, under the conditions fixed by the Regulations. Such publicity shall be deemed in all the contracting countries to be sufficient, and no other publicity may be required of the applicant.

Article 3*bis*
[Territorial Limitation]

(1) Any contracting country may, at any time, notify the Director General of the Organization (hereinafter designated as "the Director General") in writing that the protection resulting from the international registration shall extend to that country only at the express request of the proprietor of the mark.

(2) Such notification shall not take effect until six months after the date of the communication thereof by the Director General to the other contracting countries.

Article 3*ter*
[Request for (Territorial Extension)]

(1) Any request for extension of the protection resulting from the international registration to a country which has availed itself of the right provided for in Article 3*bis* must be specially mentioned in the application referred to in Article 3(1).

(2) Any request for territorial extension made subsequently to the international registration must be presented through the intermediary of the Office of the country of origin on a form prescribed by the Regulations. It shall be immediately registered by the International Bureau, which shall notify it without delay to the Office or Offices concerned. It shall be published in the periodical journal issued by the International Bureau. Such territorial extension shall be effective from the date on which it has been recorded in the International Register; it shall cease to be valid on the expiration of the international registration of the mark to which it relates.

Article 4
[Effects of International Registration]

(1) From the date of the registration so effected at the International Bureau in accordance with the provisions of Articles 3 and 3*ter*, the protection of the mark in each of the contracting countries concerned shall be the same as if the mark had been filed therein direct. The indication of classes of goods or services provided for in Article 3 shall not bind the contracting countries with regard to the determination of the scope of the protection of the mark.

(2) Every mark which has been the subject of an international registration shall enjoy the right of priority provided for by Article 4 of the Paris Convention for the Protection of Industrial Property, without requiring compliance with the formalities prescribed in Section (4)D of that Article.

Article 4*bis*
[Substitution of International Registration for Earlier National Registrations]

(1) When a mark already filed in one or more of the contracting countries

is later registered by the International Bureau in the name of the same proprietor or his successor in title, the international registration shall be deemed to have replaced the earlier national registrations, without prejudice to any rights acquired by reason of such earlier registrations.

(2) The national Office shall, upon request, be required to take note in its registers of the international registration.

Article 5
[Refusal by National Offices]

(1) In countries where the legislation so authorizes, Offices notified by the International Bureau of the registration of a mark or of a request for extension of protection made in accordance with Article 3ter shall have the right to declare that protection cannot be granted to such mark in their territory. Any such refusal can be based only on the grounds which would apply, under the Paris Convention for the Protection of Industrial Property, in the case of a mark filed for national registration. However, protection may not be refused, even partially, by reason only that national legislation would not permit registration except in a limited number of classes or for a limited number of goods or services.

(2) Offices wishing to exercise such right must give notice of their refusal to the International Bureau, together with a statement of all grounds, within the period prescribed by their domestic law and, at the latest, before the expiration of one year from the date of the international registration of the mark or of the request for extension of protection made in accordance with Article 3ter.

(3) The International Bureau shall, without delay, transmit to the Office of the country of origin and to the proprietor of the mark, or to his agent if an agent has been mentioned to the Bureau by the said Office, one of the copies of the declaration of refusal so notified. The interested party shall have the same remedies as if the mark had been filed by him direct in the country where protection is refused.

(4) The grounds for refusing a mark shall be communicated by the International Bureau to any interested party who may so request.

(5) Offices which, within the aforesaid maximum period of one year, have not communicated to the International Bureau any provisional or final decision of refusal with regard to the registration of a mark or a request for extension of protection shall lose the benefit of the right provided for in paragraph (1) of this Article with respect to the mark in question.

(6) Invalidation of an international mark may not be pronounced by the competent authorities without the proprietor of the mark having, in good time, been afforded the opportunity of defending his rights. Invalidation shall be notified to the International Bureau.

Article 5*bis*
[Documentary Evidence of Legitimacy of Use of Certain Elements of Mark]

Documentary evidence of the legitimacy of the use of certain elements incorporated in a mark, such as armorial bearings, escutcheons, portraits, honorary distinctions, titles, trade names, names of persons other than the name of the applicant, or other like inscriptions, which might be required by the Offices of the contracting countries shall be exempt from any legalization or certification other than that of the Office of the country of origin.

Article 5*ter*
[Copies of Entries in International Register. Searches for Anticipation. Extracts from International Register]

(1) The International Bureau shall issue to any person applying therefor, subject to a fee fixed by the Regulations, a copy of the entries in the Register relating to a specific mark.

(2) The International Bureau may also, upon payment, undertake searches for anticipation among international marks.

(3) Extracts from the International Register requested with a view to their production in one of the contracting countries shall be exempt from all legalization.

Article 6
[Period of Validity of International Registration. Independence of International Registration. Termination of Protection in Country of Origin]

(1) Registration of a mark at the International Bureau is effected for twenty years, with the possibility of renewal under the conditions specified in Article 7.

(2) Upon expiration of a period of five years from the date of the international registration, such registration shall become independent of the national mark registered earlier in the country of origin, subject to the following provisions.

(3) The protection resulting from the international registration, whether or not it has been the subject of a transfer, may no longer be invoked, in whole or in part, if, within five years from the date of the international registration, the national mark, registered earlier in the country of origin in accordance with Article 1, no longer enjoys, in whole or in part, legal protection in that country. This provision shall also apply when legal protection has later ceased as the result of an action begun before the expiration of the period of five years.

(4) In the case of voluntary or ex officio cancellation, the Office of the country of origin shall request the cancellation of the mark at the International Bureau, and the latter shall effect the cancellation. In the case of judicial action, the said Office shall send to the International Bureau, ex

officio or at the request of the plaintiff, a copy of the complaint or any other documentary evidence that an action has begun, and also of the final decision of the court; the Bureau shall enter notice thereof in the International Register.

Article 7
[Renewal of International Registration]

(1) Any registration may be renewed for a period of twenty years from the expiration of the preceding period, by payment only of the basic fee and, where necessary, of the supplementary and complementary fees provided for in Article 8(2).

(2) Renewal may not include any change in relation to the previous registration in its latest form.

(3) The first renewal effected under the provisions of the Nice Act of June 15, 1957, or of this Act, shall include an indication of the classes of the International Classification to which the registration relates.

(4) Six months before the expiration of the term of protection, the International Bureau shall, by sending an unofficial notice, remind the proprietor of the mark and his agent of the exact date of expiration.

(5) Subject to the payment of a surcharge fixed by the Regulations, a period of grace of six months shall be granted for renewal of the international registration.

Article 8
[National Fee. International Fee. Division of Excess Receipts, Supplementary Fees, and Complementary Fees]

(1) The Office of the country of origin may fix, at its own discretion, and collect, for its own benefit, a national fee which it may require from the proprietor of the mark in respect of which international registration or renewal is applied for.

(2) Registration of a mark at the International Bureau shall be subject to the advance payment of an international fee which shall include:

    (a) a basic fee;

    (b) a supplementary fee for each class of the International Classification, beyond three, into which the goods or services to which the mark is applied will fall;

    (c) a complementary fee for any request for extension of protection under Article 3*ter*.

(3) However, the supplementary fee specified in paragraph (2)(b) may, without prejudice to the date of registration, be paid within a period fixed by the Regulations if the number of classes of goods or services has been fixed or disputed by the International Bureau. If, upon expiration of the said period, the supplementary fee has not been paid or the list of goods or services has not been reduced to the required extent by the applicant, the

application for international registration shall be deemed to have been abandoned.

(4) The annual returns from the various receipts from international registration, with the exception of those provided for under paragraph (2)(b) and (2)(c), shall be divided equally among the countries party to this Act by the International Bureau, after deduction of the expenses and charges necessitated by the implementation of the said Act. If, at the time this Act enters into force, a country has not yet ratified or acceded to the said Act, it shall be entitled, until the date on which its ratification or accession becomes effective, to a share of the excess receipts calculated on the basis of that earlier Act which is applicable to it.

(5) The amounts derived from the supplementary fees provided for in paragraph (2)(b) shall be divided at the expiration of each year among the countries party to this Act or to the Nice Act of June 15, 1957, in proportion to the number of marks for which protection has been applied for in each of them during that year, this number being multiplied in the case of countries which make a preliminary examination, by a coefficient which shall be determined by the Regulations. If, at the time this Act enters into force, a country has not yet ratified or acceded to the said Act, it shall be entitled, until the date on which its ratification or accession becomes effective, to a share of the amounts calculated on the basis of the Nice Act.

(6) The amounts derived from the complementary fees provided for in paragraph (2)(c) shall be divided according to the requirements of paragraph (5) among the countries availing themselves of the right provided for in Article 3*bis*. If, at the time this Act enters into force, a country has not yet ratified or acceded to the said Act, it shall be entitled, until the date on which its ratification or accession becomes effective, to a share of the amounts calculated on the basis of the Nice Act.

Article 8*bis*
[Renunciation in Respect of One or More Countries]

The person in whose name the international registration stands may at any time renounce protection in one or more of the contracting countries by means of a declaration filed with the Office of his own country, for communication to the International Bureau, which shall notify accordingly the countries in respect of which renunciation has been made. Renunciation shall not be subject to any fee.

Article 9
[Changes in National Registers also Affecting International Registration. Reduction of List of Goods and Services Mentioned in International Registration. Additions to that List. Substitutions in that List]

(1) The Office of the country of the person in whose name the international registration stands shall likewise notify the International Bureau of all

annulments, cancellations, renunciations, transfers, and other changes made in the entry of the mark in the national register, if such changes also effect the international registration.

(2) The Bureau shall record those changes in the International Register, shall notify them in turn to the Offices of the contracting countries, and shall publish them in its journal.

(3) A similar procedure shall be followed when the person in whose name the international registration stands requests a reduction of the list of goods or services to which the registration applies.

(4) Such transactions may be subject to a fee, which shall be fixed by the Regulations.

(5) The subsequent addition of new goods or services to the said list can be obtained only by filing a new application as prescribed in Article 3.

(6) The substitution of one of the goods or services for another shall be treated as an addition.

Article 9bis
[Transfer of International Mark Entailing Change in Country of Proprietor]

(1) When a mark registered in the International Register is transferred to a person established in a contracting country other than the country of the person in whose name the international registration stands, the transfer shall be notified to the International Bureau by the Office of the latter country. The International Bureau shall record the transfer, shall notify the other Offices thereof, and shall publish it in its journal. If the transfer has been effected before the expiration of a period of five years from the international registration, the International Bureau shall seek the consent of the Office of the country of the new proprietor, and shall publish, if possible, the date and registration number of the mark in the country of the new proprietor.

(2) No transfer of a mark registered in the International Register for the benefit of a person who is not entitled to file an international mark shall be recorded.

(3) When it has not been possible to record a transfer in the International Register, either because the country of the new proprietor has refused its consent or because the said transfer has been made for the benefit of a person who is not entitled to apply for international registration, the Office of the country of the former proprietor shall have the right to demand that the International Bureau cancel the mark in its Register.

Article 9ter
[Assignment of International Mark for Part Only of Registered Goods or Services or for Certain Contracting Countries. Reference to Article 6quater of Paris Convention (Assignment of Mark)]

(1) If the assignment of an international mark for part only of the registered goods or services is notified to the International Bureau, the Bureau shall record it in its Register. Each of the contracting countries shall have the right to refuse to recognize the validity of such assignment if the goods or services included in the part so assigned are similar to those in respect of which the mark remains registered for the benefit of the assignor.

(2) The International Bureau shall likewise record the assignment of an international mark in respect of one or several of the contracting countries only.

(3) If, in the above cases, a change occurs in the country of the proprietor, the Office of the country to which the new proprietor belongs shall, if the international mark has been transferred before the expiration of a period of five years from the international registration, give its consent as required by Article 9*bis*.

(4) The provisions of the foregoing paragraphs shall apply subject to Article 6*quater* of the Paris Convention for the Protection of Industrial Property.

Article 9*quater*
[Common Office for Several Contracting Countries. Request by Several Contracting Countries to be Treated as a Single Country]

(1) If several countries of the Special Union agree to effect the unification of their domestic legislations on marks, they may notify the Director General:

- (a) that a common Office shall be substituted for the national Office of each of them, and

- (b) that the whole of their respective territories shall be deemed to be a single country for the purposes of the application of all or part of the provisions preceding this Article.

(2) Such notification shall not take effect until six months after the date of the communication thereof by the Director General to the other contracting countries.

Article 10
[Assembly of the Special Union]

(1)(a) The Special Union shall have an Assembly consisting of those countries which have ratified or acceded to this Act.

(b) The Government of each country shall be represented by one delegate, who may be assisted by alternate delegates, advisors, and experts.

(c) The expenses of each delegation shall be borne by the Government which has appointed it, except for the travel expenses and the subsistence allowance of one delegate for each member country, which shall be paid from funds of the Special Union.

(2)(a) The Assembly shall:

- (i) deal with all matters concerning the maintenance and development of the Special Union and the implementation of this

Agreement;

(ii)   give directions to the International Bureau concerning the preparation for conferences of revision, due account being taken of any comments made by those countries of the Special Union which have not ratified or acceded to this Act;

(iii)   modify the Regulations, including the fixation of the amounts of the fees referred to in Article 8(2) and other fees relating to international registration;

(iv)   review and approve the reports and activities of the Director General concerning the Special Union, and give him all necessary instructions concerning matters within the competence of the Special Union;

(v)   determine the program and adopt the biennial budget of the Special Union, and approve its final accounts;

(vi)   adopt the financial regulations of the Special Union;

(vii) establish such committees of experts and working groups as it may deem necessary to achieve the objectives of the Special Union;

(viii) determine which countries not members of the Special Union and which intergovernmental and international non-governmental organizations shall be admitted to its meetings as observers;

(ix)   adopt amendments to Articles 10 to 13;

(x)   take any other appropriate action designed to further the objectives of the Special Union;

(xi)   perform such other functions as are appropriate under this Agreement.

(b) With respect to matters which are of interest also to other Unions administered by the Organization, the Assembly shall make its decisions after having heard the advice of the Coordination Committee of the Organization.

(3)(a) Each country member of the Assembly shall have one vote.

(b) One half of the countries members of the Assembly shall constitute a quorum.

(c) Notwithstanding the provisions of subparagraph (b), if, in any session, the number of countries represented is less than one half but equal to or more than one third of the countries members of the Assembly, the Assembly may make decisions but, with the exception of decisions concerning its own procedure, all such decisions shall take effect only if the conditions set forth hereinafter are fulfilled. The International Bureau shall communicate the said decisions to the countries members of the Assembly which were not represented and shall invite them to express in writing their vote or abstention within a period of three months from the date of the communication. If, at the expiration of this period, the number of countries having thus expressed their vote or abstention attains the number of countries which was lacking for attaining the quorum in the session itself, such decisions shall take effect provided that at the same time the required majority still obtains.

(d) Subject to the provisions of Article 13(2), the decisions of the Assembly shall require two thirds of the votes cast.

(e) Abstentions shall not be considered as votes.

(f) A delegate may represent, and vote in the name of, one country only.

(g) Countries of the Special Union not members of the Assembly shall be admitted to the meetings of the latter as observers.

(4)(a) The Assembly shall meet once in every second calendar year in ordinary session upon convocation by the Director General and, in the absence of exceptional circumstances, during the same period and at the same place as the General Assembly of the Organization.

(b) The Assembly shall meet in extraordinary session upon convocation by the Director General, at the request of one fourth of the countries members of the Assembly.

(c) The agenda of each session shall be prepared by the Director General.

(5) The Assembly shall adopt its own rules of procedure.

Article 11
[International Bureau]

(1)(a) International registration and related duties, as well as all other administrative tasks concerning the Special Union, shall be performed by the International Bureau.

(b) In particular, the International Bureau shall prepare the meetings and provide the secretariat of the Assembly and of such committees of experts and working groups as may have been established by the Assembly.

(c) The Director General shall be the chief executive of the Special Union and shall represent the Special Union.

(2) The Director General and any staff member designated by him shall participate, without the right to vote, in all meetings of the Assembly and of such committees of experts or working groups as may have been established by the Assembly. The Director General, or a staff member designated by him, shall be ex officio secretary of those bodies.

(3)(a) The International Bureau shall, in accordance with the directions of the Assembly, make the preparations for the conferences of revision of the provisions of the Agreement other than Articles 10 to 13.

(b) The International Bureau may consult with intergovernmental and international non-governmental organizations concerning preparations for conferences of revision.

(c) The Director General and persons designated by him shall take part, without the right to vote, in the discussions at those conferences.

(4) The International Bureau shall carry out any other tasks assigned to it.

Article 12
[Finances]

(1)(a) The Special Union shall have a budget.

(b) The budget of the Special Union shall include the income and expenses proper to the Special Union, its contribution to the budget of expenses common to the Unions, and, where applicable, the sum made available to the budget of the Conference of the Organization.

(c) Expenses not attributable exclusively to the Special Union but also to one or more other Unions administered by the Organization shall be considered as expenses common to the Unions. The share of the Special Union in such common expenses shall be in proportion to the interest the Special Union has in them.

(2) The budget of the Special Union shall be established with due regard to the requirements of coordination with the budgets of the other Unions administered by the Organization.

(3) The budget of the Special Union shall be financed from the following sources:

(i)   international registration fees and other fees and charges due for other services rendered by the International Bureau in relation to the Special Union;

(ii)   sale of, or royalties on, the publications of the International Bureau concerning the Special Union;

(iii)   gifts, bequests, and subventions;

(iv)   rents, interests, and other miscellaneous income.

(4)(a) The amounts of the fees referred to in Article 8(2) and other fees relating to international registration shall be fixed by the Assembly on the proposal of the Director General.

(b) The amounts of such fees shall be so fixed that the revenues of the Special Union from fees, other than the supplementary and complementary fees referred to in Article 8(2)(b) and 8(2)(c), and other sources shall be at least sufficient to cover the expenses of the International Bureau concerning the Special Union.

(c) If the budget is not adopted before the beginning of a new financial period, it shall be at the same level as the budget of the previous year, as provided in the financial regulations.

(5) Subject to the provisions of paragraph (4)(a), the amount of fees and charges due for other services rendered by the International Bureau in relation to the Special Union shall be established, and shall be reported to the Assembly, by the Director General.

(6)(a) The Special Union shall have a working capital fund which shall be constituted by a single payment made by each country of the Special Union. If the fund becomes insufficient, the Assembly shall decide to increase it.

(b) The amount of the initial payment of each country to the said fund or of its participation in the increase thereof shall be a proportion of the contribution of that country as a member of the Paris Union for the Protection of Industrial Property to the budget of the said Union for the year in which the fund is established or the decision to increase it is made.

(c) The proportion and the terms of payment shall be fixed by the Assembly on the proposal of the Director General and after it has heard the advice of the Coordination Committee of the Organization.

(d) As long as the Assembly authorizes the use of the reserve fund of the Special Union as a working capital fund, the Assembly may suspend the application of the provisions of subparagraphs (a), (b), and (c).

(7)(a) In the headquarters agreement concluded with the country on the territory of which the Organization has its headquarters, it shall be provided that, whenever the working capital fund is insufficient, such country shall grant advances. The amount of those advances and the conditions on which they are granted shall be the subject of separate agreements, in each case, between such country and the Organization.

(b) The country referred to in subparagraph (a) and the Organization shall each have the right to denounce the obligation to grant advances, by written notification. Denunciation shall take effect three years after the end of the year in which it has been notified.

(8) The auditing of the accounts shall be effected by one or more of the countries of the Special Union or by external auditors, as provided in the financial regulations. They shall be designated, with their agreement, by the Assembly.

Article 13
[Amendment of Articles 10 to 13]

(1) Proposals for the amendment of Articles 10, 11, 12, and the present Article, may be initiated by any country member of the Assembly, or by the Director General. Such proposals shall be communicated by the Director General to the member countries of the Assembly at least six months in advance of their consideration by the Assembly.

(2) Amendments to the Articles referred to in paragraph (1) shall be adopted by the Assembly. Adoption shall require three fourths of the votes cast, provided that any amendment to Article 10, and to the present paragraph, shall require four fifths of the votes cast.

(3) Any amendments to the Articles referred to in paragraph (1) shall enter into force one month after written notifications of acceptance, effected in accordance with their respective constitutional processes, have been received by the Director General from three fourths of the countries members of the Assembly at the time it adopted the amendment. Any amendment to the said Articles thus accepted shall bind all the countries which are members of the Assembly at the time the amendment enters into force, or which become members thereof at a subsequent date.

Article 14
[Ratification and Accession. Entry into Force. Accession to Earlier Acts. Reference to Article 24 of Paris Convention (Territories)]

(1) Any country of the Special Union which has signed this Act may ratify it, and, if it has not signed it, may accede to it.

(2)(a) Any country outside the Special Union which is party to the Paris Convention for the Protection of Industrial Property may accede to this Act and thereby become a member of the Special Union.

(b) As soon as the International Bureau is informed that such a country has acceded to this Act, it shall address to the Office of that country, in accordance with Article 3, a collective notification of the marks which, at that time, enjoy international protection.

(c) Such notification shall, of itself, ensure to the said marks the benefits of the foregoing provisions in the territory of the said country, and shall mark the commencement of the period of one year during which the Office concerned may make the declaration provided for in Article 5.

(d) However, any such country may, in acceding to this Act, declare that, except in the case of international marks which have already been the subject in that country of an earlier identical national registration still in force, and which shall be immediately recognized upon the request of the interested parties, application of this Act shall be limited to marks registered from the date on which its accession enters into force.

(e) Such declaration shall dispense the International Bureau from making the collective notification referred to above. The International Bureau shall notify only those marks in respect of which it receives, within a period of one year from the accession of the new country, a request, with the necessary particulars, to take advantage of the exception provided for in subparagraph (d).

(f) The International Bureau shall not make the collective notification to such countries as declare, in acceding to this Act, that they are availing themselves of the right provided for in Article 3bis. The said countries may also declare at the same time that the application of this Act shall be limited to marks registered from the day on which their accessions enter into force; however, such limitation shall not affect international marks which have already been the subject of an earlier identical national registration in those countries, and which could give rise to requests for extension of protection made and notified in accordance with Articles 3ter and 8(2)(c).

(g) Registrations of marks which have been the subject of one of the notifications provided for in this paragraph shall be regarded as replacing registrations effected direct in the new contracting country before the date of entry into force of its accession.

(3) Instruments of ratification and accession shall be deposited with the Director General.

(4)(a) With respect to the first five countries which have deposited their instruments of ratification or accession, this Act shall enter into force three months after the deposit of the fifth such instrument.

(b) With respect to any other country, this Act shall enter into force three months after the date on which its ratification or accession has been notified by the Director General, unless a subsequent date has been indicated in the instrument of ratification or accession. In the latter case, this Act shall enter into force with respect to that country on the date thus indicated.

(5) Ratification or accession shall automatically entail acceptance of all the clauses and admission to all the advantages of this Act.

(6) After the entry into force of this Act, a country may accede to the Nice Act of June 15, 1957, only in conjunction with ratification of, or accession to, this Act. Accession to Acts earlier than the Nice Act shall not be permitted, not even in conjunction with ratification of, or accession to, this Act.

(7) The provisions of Article 24 of the Paris Convention for the Protection of Industrial Property shall apply to this Agreement.

Article 15
[Denunciation]

(1) This Agreement shall remain in force without limitation as to time.

(2) Any country may denounce this Act by notification addressed to the Director General. Such denunciation shall constitute also denunciation of all earlier Acts and shall affect only the country making it, the Agreement remaining in full force and effect as regards the other countries of the Special Union.

(3) Denunciation shall take effect one year after the day on which the Director General has received the notification.

(4) The right of denunciation provided for by this Article shall not be exercised by any country before the expiration of five years from the date upon which it becomes a member of the Special Union.

(5) International marks registered up to the date on which denunciation becomes effective, and not refused within the period of one year provided for in Article 5, shall continue, throughout the period of international protection, to enjoy the same protection as if they had been filed direct in the denouncing country.

Article 16
[Application of Earlier Acts]

(1)(a) This Act shall, as regards the relations between the countries of the Special Union by which it has been ratified or acceded to, replace, as from the day on which it enters into force with respect to them, the Madrid Agreement of 1891, in its texts earlier than this Act.

(b) However, any country of the Special Union which has ratified or acceded to this Act shall remain bound by the earlier texts which it has not previously denounced by virtue of Article 12(4) of the Nice Act of June 15, 1957, as regards its relations with countries which have not ratified or acceded to this Act.

(2) Countries outside the Special Union which become party to this Act shall apply it to international registrations effected at the International Bureau through the intermediary of the national Office of any country of the Special Union not party to this Act, provided that such registrations satisfy, with respect to the said countries, the requirements of this Act. With regard to international registrations effected at the International Bureau through the intermediary of the national Offices of the said countries outside the Special Union which become party to this Act, such countries recognize that the aforesaid country of the Special Union may demand compliance with the requirements of the most recent Act to which it is party.

Article 17
[Signature, Languages, Depositary Functions]

(1)(a) This Act shall be signed in a single copy in the French language and shall be deposited with the Government of Sweden.

(b) Official texts shall be established by the Director General, after consultation with the interested Governments, in such other languages as the Assembly may designate.

(2) This Act shall remain open for signature at Stockholm until January 13, 1968.

(3) The Director General shall transmit two copies, certified by the Government of Sweden, of the signed text of this Act to the Governments of all countries of the Special Union and, on request, to the Government of any other country.

(4) The Director General shall register this Act with the Secretariat of the United Nations.

(5) The Director General shall notify the Governments of all countries of the Special Union of signatures, deposits of instruments of ratification or accession and any declarations included in such instruments, entry into force of any provisions of this Act, notifications of denunciation, and notifications pursuant to Articles 3*bis*, 9*quater*, 13, 14(7), and 15(2).

Article 18
[Transitional Provisions]

(1) Until the first Director General assumes office, references in this Act to the International Bureau of the Organization or to the Director General shall be construed as references to the Bureau of the Union established by the Paris Convention for the Protection of Industrial Property or its Director, respectively.

(2) Countries of the Special Union not having ratified or acceded to this Act may, until five years after the entry into force of the Convention establishing the Organization, exercise, if they so desire, the rights provided for under Articles 10 to 13 of this Act as if they were bound by those Articles. Any

country desiring to exercise such rights shall give written notification to that effect to the Director General; such notification shall be effective from the date of its receipt. Such countries shall be deemed to be members of the Assembly until the expiration of the said period.

PROTOCOL RELATING TO THE MADRID AGREEMENT CONCERNING THE INTERNATIONAL REGISTRATION OF MARKS
Adopted at Madrid on June 27, 1989

Article 1
Membership in the Madrid Union

The States party to this Protocol (hereinafter referred to as "the Contracting States"), even where they are not party to the Madrid Agreement Concerning the International Registration of Marks as revised at Stockholm in 1967 and as amended in 1979 (hereinafter referred to as "the Madrid (Stockholm) Agreement"), and the organizations referred to in Article 14(1)(b) which are party to this Protocol (hereinafter referred to as "the Contracting Organizations") shall be members of the same Union of which countries party to the Madrid (Stockholm) Agreement are members. Any reference in this Protocol to "Contracting Parties" shall be construed as a reference to both Contracting States and Contracting Organizations.

Article 2
Securing Protection Through International Registration

(1) Where an application for the registration of a mark has been filed with the Office of a Contracting Party, or where a mark has been registered in the register of the Office of a Contracting Party, the person in whose name that application (hereinafter referred to as "the basic application") or that registration (hereinafter referred to as "the basic registration") stands may, subject to the provisions of this Protocol, secure protection for his mark in the territory of the Contracting Parties, by obtaining the registration of that mark in the register of the International Bureau of the World Intellectual Property Organization (hereinafter referred to as "the international registration," "the International Register," "the International Bureau" and "the Organization," respectively), provided that,

(i) where the basic application has been filed with the Office of a Contracting State or where the basic registration has been made by such an Office, the person in whose name that application or registration stands is a national of that Contracting State, or is domiciled, or has a real and effective industrial or commercial establishment, in the said Contracting State,

(ii) where the basic application has been filed with the Office of a Contracting Organization or where the basic registration has been made by such an Office, the person in whose name that application or registration stands is a national of a State member of that Contracting Organization, or is domiciled, or has a real and effective industrial or commercial establishment, in the territory of the said Contracting Organization.

(2) The application for international registration (hereinafter referred to as "the international application") shall be filed with the International

Bureau through the intermediary of the Office with which the basic application was filed or by which the basic registration was made (hereinafter referred to as "the Office of origin"), as the case may be.

(3) Any reference in this Protocol to an "Office" or an "Office of a Contracting Party" shall be construed as a reference to the office that is in charge, on behalf of a Contracting Party, of the registration of marks, and any reference in this Protocol to "marks" shall be construed as a reference to trademarks and service marks.

(4) For the purposes of this Protocol, "territory of a Contracting Party" means, where the Contracting Party is a State, the territory of that State and, where the Contracting Party is an intergovernmental organization, the territory in which the constituting treaty of that intergovernmental organization applies.

Article 3
International Application

(1) Every international application under this Protocol shall be presented on the form prescribed by the Regulations. The Office of origin shall certify that the particulars appearing in the international application correspond to the particulars appearing, at the time of the certification, in the basic application or basic registration, as the case may be. Furthermore, the said Office shall indicate,

(i) in the case of a basic application, the date and number of that application,

(ii) in the case of a basic registration, the date and number of that registration as well as the date and number of the application from which the basic registration resulted.

The Office of origin shall also indicate the date of the international application.

(2) The applicant must indicate the goods and services in respect of which protection of the mark is claimed and also, if possible, the corresponding class or classes according to the classification established by the Nice Agreement Concerning the International Classification of Goods and Services for the Purposes of the Registration of Marks. If the applicant does not give such indication, the International Bureau shall classify the goods and services in the appropriate classes of the said classification. The indication of classes given by the applicant shall be subject to control by the International Bureau, which shall exercise the said control in association with the Office of origin. In the event of disagreement between the said Office and the International Bureau, the opinion of the latter shall prevail.

(3) If the applicant claims color as a distinctive feature of his mark, he shall be required

(i) to state the fact, and to file with his international application a notice specifying the color or the combination of colors claimed;

(ii) to append to his international application copies in color of the said mark, which shall be attached to the notifications given by the International Bureau; the number of such copies shall be fixed by the Regulations.

(4) The International Bureau shall register immediately the marks filed in accordance with Article 2. The international registration shall bear the date on which the international application was received in the Office of origin, provided that the international application has been received by the International Bureau within a period of two months from that date. If the international application has not been received within that period, the international registration shall bear the date on which the said international application was received by the International Bureau. The International Bureau shall notify the international registration without delay to the Offices concerned. Marks registered in the International Register shall be published in a periodical gazette issued by the International Bureau, on the basis of the particulars contained in the international application.

(5) With a view to the publicity to be given to marks registered in the International Register, each Office shall receive from the International Bureau a number of copies of the said gazette free of charge and a number of copies at a reduced price, under the conditions fixed by the Assembly referred to in Article 10 (hereinafter referred to as "the Assembly"). Such publicity shall be deemed to be sufficient for the purposes of all the Contracting Parties, and no other publicity may be required of the holder of the international registration.

Article 3*bis*
Territorial Effect

The protection resulting from the international registration shall extend to any Contracting Party only at the request of the person who files the international application or who is the holder of the international registration. However, no such request can be made with respect to the Contracting Party whose Office is the Office of origin.

Article 3*ter*
Request for "Territorial Extension"

(1) Any request for extension of the protection resulting from the international registration to any Contracting Party shall be specially mentioned in the international application.

(2) A request for territorial extension may also be made subsequently to the international registration. Any such request shall be presented on the form prescribed by the Regulations. It shall be immediately recorded by the International Bureau, which shall notify such recordal without delay to the Office or Offices concerned. Such recordal shall be published in the periodical gazette of the International Bureau. Such territorial extension shall be effective from the date on which it has been recorded in the International Register; it shall cease to be valid on the expiry of the international registration to which it relates.

Article 4
Effects of International Registration

(1)

(a) From the date of the registration or recordal effected in accordance with the provisions of Articles 3 and 3*ter*, the protection of the mark in each of the Contracting Parties concerned shall be the same as if the mark had been deposited direct with the Office of that Contracting Party. If no refusal has been notified to the International Bureau in accordance with Article 5(1) and 5(2) or if a refusal notified in accordance with the said Article has been withdrawn subsequently, the protection of the mark in the Contracting Party concerned shall, as from the said date, be the same as if the mark had been registered by the Office of that Contracting Party.

(b) The indication of classes of goods and services provided for in Article 3 shall not bind the Contracting Parties with regard to the determination of the scope of the protection of the mark.

(2) Every international registration shall enjoy the right of priority provided for by Article 4 of the Paris Convention for the Protection of Industrial Property, without it being necessary to comply with the formalities prescribed in Section 4.D of the Article.

Article 4*bis*
Replacement of a National or Regional Registration by an International Registration

(1) Where a mark that is the subject of a national or regional registration in the Office of a Contracting Party is also the subject of an international registration and both registrations stand in the name of the same person, the international registration is deemed to replace the national or regional registration, without prejudice to any rights acquired by virtue of the latter, provided that

(i)   the protection resulting from the international registration extends to the said Contracting Party under Article 3*ter*(1) or 3*ter*(2),

(ii) all the goods and services listed in the national or regional registration are also listed in the international registration in respect of the said Contracting Party,

(iii) such extension takes effect after the date of the national or regional registration.

(2) The Office referred to in paragraph (1) shall, upon request, be required to take note in its register of the international registration.

Article 5
Refusal and Invalidation of Effects of International Registration in Respect of Certain Contracting Parties

(1) Where the applicable legislation so authorizes, any Office of a

Contracting Party which has been notified by the International Bureau of an extension to that Contracting Party, under Article 3ter(1) or 3ter(2), of the protection resulting from the international registration shall have the right to declare in a notification of refusal that protection cannot be granted in the said Contracting Party to the mark which is the subject of such extension. Any such refusal can be based only on the grounds which would apply, under the Paris Convention for the Protection of Industrial Property, in the case of a mark deposited direct with the Office which notifies the refusal. However, protection may not be refused, even partially, by reason only that the applicable legislation would permit registration only in a limited number of classes or for a limited number of goods or services.

(2)

(a) Any Office wishing to exercise such right shall notify its refusal to the International Bureau, together with a statement of all grounds, within the period prescribed by the law applicable to that Office and at the latest, subject to subparagraphs (b) and (c), before the expiry of one year from the date on which the notification of the extension referred to in paragraph (1) has been sent to that Office by the International Bureau.

(b) Notwithstanding subparagraph (a), any Contracting Party may declare that, for international registrations made under this Protocol, the time limit of one year referred to in subparagraph (a) is replaced by 18 months.

(c) Such declaration may also specify that, when a refusal of protection may result from an opposition to the granting of protection, such refusal may be notified by the Office of the said Contracting Party to the International Bureau after the expiry of the 18-month time limit. Such an Office may, with respect to any given international registration, notify a refusal of protection after the expiry of the 18-month time limit, but only if

(i)   it has, before the expiry of the 18-month time limit, informed the International Bureau of the possibility that oppositions may be filed after the expiry of the 18-month time limit, and

(ii)   the notification of the refusal based on an opposition is made within a time limit of not more than seven months from the date on which the opposition period begins; if the opposition period expires before this time limit of seven months, the notification must be made within a time limit of one month from the expiry of the opposition period.

(d) Any declaration under subparagraphs (b) or (c) may be made in the instruments referred to in Article 14(2), and the effective date of the declaration shall be the same as the date of entry into force of this Protocol with respect to the State or intergovernmental organization having made the declaration. Any such declaration may also be made later, in which case the declaration shall have effect three months after its receipt by the Director General of the Organization (hereinafter referred to as "the Director General"), or at any later date indicated in the declaration, in respect of any international registration whose date is the same as or is later than the effective date of the declaration.

(e) Upon the expiry of a period of ten years from the entry into force of this Protocol, the Assembly shall examine the operation of the system established by subparagraphs (a) to (d). Thereafter, the provisions of the said subparagraphs may be modified by a unanimous decision of the Assembly.

(3) The International Bureau shall, without delay, transmit one of the copies of the notification of refusal to the holder of the international registration. The said holder shall have the same remedies as if the mark had been deposited by him direct with the Office which has notified its refusal. Where the International Bureau has received information under paragraph (2)(c)(i), it shall, without delay, transmit the said information to the holder of the international registration.

(4) The grounds for refusing a mark shall be communicated by the International Bureau to any interested party who may so request.

(5) Any Office which has not notified, with respect to a given international registration, any provisional or final refusal to the International Bureau in accordance with paragraphs (1) and (2) shall, with respect to that international registration, lose the benefit of the right provided for in paragraph (1).

(6) Invalidation, by the competent authorities of a Contracting Party, of the effects, in the territory of that Contracting Party, of an international registration may not be pronounced without the holder of such international registration having, in good time, been afforded the opportunity of defending his rights. Invalidation shall be notified to the International Bureau.

Article 5*bis*
Documentary Evidence of Legitimacy of Use of Certain Elements of the Mark

Documentary evidence of the legitimacy of the use of certain elements incorporated in a mark, such as armorial bearings, escutcheons, portraits, honorary distinctions, titles, trade names, names of persons other than the name of the applicant, or other like inscriptions, which might be required by the Offices of the Contracting Parties shall be exempt from any legalization as well as from any certification other than that of the Office of origin.

Article 5*ter*
Copies of Entries in International Register; Searches for Anticipations; Extracts from International Register

(1) The International Bureau shall issue to any person applying therefor, upon the payment of a fee fixed by the Regulations, a copy of the entries in the International Register concerning a specific mark.

(2) The International Bureau may also, upon payment, undertake searches for anticipations among marks that are the subject of international registrations.

(3) Extracts from the International Register requested with a view to their

production in one of the Contracting Parties shall be exempt from any legalization.

Article 6
Period of Validity of International Registration; Dependence and Independence of International Registration

(1) Registration of a mark at the International Bureau is effected for ten years, with the possibility of renewal under the conditions specified in Article 7.

(2) Upon expiry of a period of five years from the date of the international registration, such registration shall become independent of the basic application or the registration resulting therefrom, or of the basic registration, as the case may be, subject to the following provisions.

(3) The protection resulting from the international registration, whether or not it has been the subject of a transfer, may no longer be invoked if, before the expiry of five years from the date of the international registration, the basic application or the registration resulting therefrom, or the basic registration, as the case may be, has been withdrawn, has lapsed, has been renounced or has been the subject of a final decision of rejection, revocation, cancellation or invalidation, in respect of all or some of the goods and services listed in the international registration. The same applies if

(i)   an appeal against a decision refusing the effects of the basic application,

(ii)   an action requesting the withdrawal of the basic application or the revocation, cancellation or invalidation of the registration resulting from the basic application or of the basic registration, or

(iii) an opposition to the basic application

results, after the expiry of the five-year period, in a final decision of rejection, revocation, cancellation or invalidation, or ordering the withdrawal, of the basic application, or the registration resulting therefrom, or the basic registration, as the case may be, provided that such appeal, action or opposition had begun before the expiry of the said period. The same also applies if the basic application is withdrawn, or the registration resulting from the basic application or the basic registration is renounced, after the expiry of the five-year period, provided that, at the time of the withdrawal or renunciation, the said application or registration was the subject of a proceeding referred to in item (i), (ii) or (iii) and that such proceeding had begun before the expiry of the said period.

(4) The Office of origin shall, as prescribed in the Regulations, notify the International Bureau of the facts and decisions relevant under paragraph (3), and the International Bureau shall, as prescribed in the Regulations, notify the interested parties and effect any publication accordingly. The Office of origin shall, where applicable, request the International Bureau to cancel, to the extent applicable, the international registration, and the International Bureau shall proceed accordingly.

Article 7
Renewal of International Registration

(1) Any international registration may be renewed for a period of ten years from the expiry of the preceding period, by the mere payment of the basic fee and, subject to Article 8(7), of the supplementary and complementary fees provided for in Article 8(2).

(2) Renewal may not bring about any change in the international registration in its latest form.

(3) Six months before the expiry of the term of protection, the International Bureau shall, by sending an unofficial notice, remind the holder of the international registration and his representative, if any, of the exact date of expiry.

(4) Subject to the payment of a surcharge fixed by the Regulations, a period of grace of six months shall be allowed for renewal of the international registration.

Article 8
Fees for International Application and Registration

(1) The Office of origin may fix, at its own discretion, and collect, for its own benefit, a fee which it may require from the applicant for international registration or from the holder of the international registration in connection with the filing of the international application or the renewal of the international registration.

(2) Registration of a mark at the International Bureau shall be subject to the advance payment of an international fee which shall, subject to the provisions of paragraph (7)(a), include,

    (i)   a basic fee;

    (ii)   a supplementary fee for each class of the International Classification, beyond three, into which the goods or services to which the mark is applied will fall;

    (iii)   a complementary fee for any request for extension of protection under Article 3*ter*.

(3) However, the supplementary fee specified in paragraph (2)(ii) may, without prejudice to the date of the international registration, be paid within the period fixed by the Regulations if the number of classes of goods or services has been fixed or disputed by the International Bureau. If, upon expiry of the said period, the supplementary fee has not been paid or the list of goods or services has not been reduced to the required extent by the applicant, the international application shall be deemed to have been abandoned.

(4) The annual product of the various receipts from international registration, with the exception of the receipts derived from the fees mentioned in paragraph (2)(ii) and (2)(iii), shall be divided equally among the Contracting Parties by the International Bureau, after deduction of the expenses and charges necessitated by the implementation of this Protocol.

(5) The amounts derived from the supplementary fees provided for in paragraph (2)(ii) shall be divided, at the expiry of each year, among the interested Contracting Parties in proportion to the number of marks for which protection has been applied for in each of them during that year, this number being multiplied, in the case of Contracting Parties which make an examination, by a coefficient which shall be determined by the Regulations.

(6) The amounts derived from the complementary fees provided for in paragraph (2)(iii) shall be divided according to the same rules as those provided for in paragraph (5).

(7)

(a) Any Contracting Party may declare that, in connection with each international registration in which it is mentioned under Article 3*ter*, and in connection with the renewal of any such international registration, it wants to receive, instead of a share in the revenue produced by the supplementary and complementary fees, a fee (hereinafter referred to as "the individual fee") whose amount shall be indicated in the declaration, and can be changed in further declarations, but may not be higher than the equivalent of the amount which the said Contracting Party's Office would be entitled to receive from an applicant for a ten-year registration, or from the holder of a registration for a ten-year renewal of that registration, of the mark in the register of the said Office, the said amount being diminished by the savings resulting from the international procedure. Where such an individual fee is payable,

(i)   no supplementary fees referred to in paragraph (2)(ii) shall be payable if only Contracting Parties which have made a declaration under this subparagraph are mentioned under Article 3*ter*, and

(ii)   no complementary fee referred to in paragraph (2)(iii) shall be payable in respect of any Contracting Party which has made a declaration under this subparagraph.

(b) Any declaration under subparagraph (a) may be made in the instruments referred to in Article 14(2), and the effective date of the declaration shall be the same as the date of entry into force of this Protocol with respect to the State or intergovernmental organization having made the declaration. Any such declaration may also be made later, in which case the declaration shall have effect three months after its receipt by the Director General, or at any later date indicated in the declaration, in respect of any international registration whose date is the same as or is later than the effective date of the declaration.

Article 9
Recordal of Change in the Ownership of an International Registration

At the request of the person in whose name the international registration stands, or at the request of an interested Office made ex officio or at the request of an interested person, the International Bureau shall record in the International Register any change in the ownership of that registration, in respect of all or some of the Contracting Parties in whose territories the said registration has effect and in respect of all or some of the goods and services listed in the registration, provided that the new holder is a person who, under Article 2(1), is entitled to file international applications.

Article 9*bis*
Recordal of Certain Matters Concerning an International Registration

The International Bureau shall record in the International Register

(i)   any change in the name or address of the holder of the international registration,

(ii)   the appointment of a representative of the holder of the international registration and any other relevant fact concerning such representative,

(iii)   any limitation, in respect of all or some of the Contracting Parties, of the goods and services listed in the international registration,

(iv)   any renunciation, cancellation or invalidation of the international registration in respect of all or some of the Contracting Parties,

(v)   any other relevant fact, identified in the Regulations, concerning the rights in a mark that is the subject of an international registration.

Article 9*ter*
Fees for Certain Recordals

Any recordal under Article 9 or under Article 9*bis* may be subject to the payment of a fee.

Article 9*quater*
Common Office of Several Contracting States

(1) If several Contracting States agree to effect the unification of their domestic legislations on marks, they may notify the Director General

(i)   that a common Office shall be substituted for the national Office of each of them, and

(ii)   that the whole of their respective territories shall be deemed to be a single State for the purposes of the application of all or part of the provisions preceding this Article as well as the provisions of Articles 9*quinquies* and 9*sexies*.

(2) Such notification shall not take effect until three months after the date of the communication thereof by the Director General to the other Contracting Parties.

Article 9*quinquies*
Transformation of an International Registration into National or Regional Applications

Where, in the event that the international registration is cancelled at the request of the Office of origin under Article 6(4), in respect of all or some of the goods and services listed in the said registration, the person who was the holder of the international registration files an application for the registration of the same mark with the Office of any of the Contracting Parties in the territory of which the international registration had effect, that application shall be treated as if it had been filed on the date of the international registration according to Article 3(4) or on the date of recordal of the territorial extension according to Article 3*ter*(2) and, if the international registration enjoyed priority, shall enjoy the same priority, provided that

(i)   such application is filed within three months from the date on which the international registration was cancelled,

(ii)   the goods and services listed in the application are in fact covered by the list of goods and services contained in the international registration in respect of the Contracting Party concerned, and

(iii)   such application complies with all the requirements of the applicable law, including the requirements concerning fees.

Article 9*sexies*
Safeguard of the Madrid (Stockholm) Agreement

(1) Where, with regard to a given international application or a given international registration, the Office of origin is the Office of a State that is party to both this Protocol and the Madrid (Stockholm) Agreement, the provisions of this Protocol shall have no effect in the territory of any other State that is also party to both this Protocol and the Madrid (Stockholm) Agreement.

(2) The Assembly may, by a three-fourths majority, repeal paragraph (1), or restrict the scope of paragraph (1), after the expiry of a period of ten years from the entry into force of this Protocol, but not before the expiry of a period of five years from the date on which the majority of the countries party to the Madrid (Stockholm) Agreement have become party to this Protocol. In the vote of the Assembly, only those States which are party to both the said Agreement and this Protocol shall have the right to participate.

Article 10
Assembly

(1)

(a) The Contracting Parties shall be members of the same Assembly as the countries party to the Madrid (Stockholm) Agreement.

(b) Each Contracting Party shall be represented in that Assembly by one delegate, who may be assisted by alternate delegates, advisors, and experts.

(c) The expenses of each delegation shall be borne by the Contracting Party which has appointed it, except for the travel expenses and the subsistence allowance of one delegate for each Contracting Party, which shall be paid from the funds of the Union.

(2) The Assembly shall, in addition to the functions which it has under the Madrid (Stockholm) Agreement, also

(i)   deal with all matters concerning the implementation of this Protocol;

(ii) give directions to the International Bureau concerning the preparation for conferences of revision of this Protocol, due account being taken of any comments made by those countries of the Union which are not party to this Protocol;

(iii) adopt and modify the provisions of the Regulations concerning the implementation of this Protocol;

(iv) perform such other functions as are appropriate under this Protocol.

(3)

(a) Each Contracting Party shall have one vote in the Assembly. On matters concerning only countries that are party to the Madrid (Stockholm) Agreement, Contracting Parties that are not party to the said Agreement shall not have the right to vote, whereas, on matters concerning only Contracting Parties, only the latter shall have the right to vote.

(b) One-half of the members of the Assembly which have the right to vote on a given matter shall constitute the quorum for the purposes of the vote on that matter.

(c) Notwithstanding the provisions of subparagraph (b), if, in any session, the number of the members of the Assembly having the right to vote on a given matter which are represented is less than one-half but equal to or more than one-third of the members of the Assembly having the right to vote on that matter, the Assembly may make decisions but, with the exception of decisions concerning its own procedure, all such decisions shall take effect only if the conditions set forth hereinafter are fulfilled. The International Bureau shall communicate the said decisions to the members of the Assembly having the right to vote on the said matter which were not represented and shall invite them to express in writing their vote or abstention within a period of three months from the date of the communication. If, at the expiry of this period, the number of such members having thus expressed their vote or abstention attains the number of the members which was lacking for attaining the quorum in the session itself, such decisions shall take effect provided that at the same time the required majority still obtains.

(d) Subject to the provisions of Articles 5(2)(e), 9sexies(2), 12 and 13(2), the decisions of the Assembly shall require two-thirds of the votes cast.

(e) Abstentions shall not be considered as votes.

(f) A delegate may represent, and vote in the name of, one member of the Assembly only.

(4) In addition to meeting in ordinary sessions and extraordinary sessions as provided for by the Madrid (Stockholm) Agreement, the Assembly shall meet in extraordinary session upon convocation by the Director General, at

the request of one-fourth of the members of the Assembly having the right to vote on the matters proposed to be included in the agenda of the session. The agenda of such an extraordinary session shall be prepared by the Director General.

Article 11
International Bureau

(1) International registration and related duties, as well as all other administrative tasks, under or concerning this Protocol, shall be performed by the International Bureau.

(2)

(a) The International Bureau shall, in accordance with the directions of the Assembly, make the preparations for the conferences of revision of this Protocol.

(b) The International Bureau may consult with intergovernmental and international non-governmental organizations concerning preparations for such conferences of revision.

(c) The Director General and persons designated by him shall take part, without the right to vote, in the discussions at such conferences of revision.

(3) The International Bureau shall carry out any other tasks assigned to it in relation to this Protocol.

Article 12
Finances

As far as Contracting Parties are concerned, the finances of the Union shall be governed by the same provisions as those contained in Article 12 of the Madrid (Stockholm) Agreement, provided that any reference to Article 8 of the said Agreement shall be deemed to be a reference to Article 8 of this Protocol. Furthermore, for the purposes of Article 12(6)(b) of the said Agreement, Contracting Organizations shall, subject to a unanimous decision to the contrary by the Assembly, be considered to belong to contribution class I (one) under the Paris Convention for the Protection of Industrial Property.

Article 13
Amendment of Certain Articles of the Protocol

(1) Proposals for the amendment of Articles 10, 11, 12, and the present Article, may be initiated by any Contracting Party, or by the Director General. Such proposals shall be communicated by the Director General to the Contracting Parties at least six months in advance of their consideration by the Assembly.

(2) Amendments to the Articles referred to in paragraph (1) shall be adopted by the Assembly. Adoption shall require three-fourths of the votes cast, provided that any amendment to Article 10, and to the present paragraph, shall require four-fifths of the votes cast.

(3) Any amendment to the Articles referred to in paragraph (1) shall enter into force one month after written notifications of acceptance, effected in accordance with their respective constitutional processes, have been received by the Director General from three-fourths of those States and intergovernmental organizations which, at the time the amendment was adopted, were members of the Assembly and had the right to vote on the amendment. Any amendment to the said Articles thus accepted shall bind all the States and intergovernmental organizations which are Contracting Parties at the time the amendment enters into force, or which become Contracting Parties at a subsequent date.

Article 14
Becoming Party to the Protocol; Entry into Force

(1)

(a) Any State that is a party to the Paris Convention for the Protection of Industrial Property may become party to this Protocol.

(b) Furthermore, any intergovernmental organization may also become party to this Protocol where the following conditions are fulfilled:

(i) at least one of the member States of that organization is a party to the Paris Convention for the Protection of Industrial Property;

(ii) that organization has a regional Office for the purposes of registering marks with effect in the territory of the organization, provided that such Office is not the subject of a notification under Article 9*quater*.

(2) Any State or organization referred to in paragraph (1) may sign this Protocol. Any such State or organization may, if it has signed this Protocol, deposit an instrument of ratification, acceptance or approval of this Protocol or, if it has not signed this Protocol, deposit an instrument of accession to this Protocol.

(3) The instruments referred to in paragraph (2) shall be deposited with the Director General.

(4)

(a) This Protocol shall enter into force three months after four instruments of ratification, acceptance, approval or accession have been deposited, provided that at least one of those instruments has been deposited by a country party to the Madrid (Stockholm) Agreement and at least one other of those instruments has been deposited by a State not party to the Madrid (Stockholm) Agreement or by any of the organizations referred to in paragraph (1)(b).

(b) With respect to any other State or organization referred to in paragraph (1), this Protocol shall enter into force three months after the date on which its ratification, acceptance, approval or accession has been notified by the Director General.

(5) Any State or organization referred to in paragraph (1) may, when depositing its instrument of ratification, acceptance or approval of, or

accession to, this Protocol, declare that the protection resulting from any international registration effected under this Protocol before the date of entry into force of this Protocol with respect to it cannot be extended to it.

Article 15
Denunciation

(1) This Protocol shall remain in force without limitation as to time.

(2) Any Contracting Party may denounce this Protocol by notification addressed to the Director General.

(3) Denunciation shall take effect one year after the day on which the Director General has received the notification.

(4) The right of denunciation provided for by this Article shall not be exercised by any Contracting Party before the expiry of five years from the date upon which this Protocol entered into force with respect to that Contracting Party.

(5)

(a) Where a mark is the subject of an international registration having effect in the denouncing State or intergovernmental organization at the date on which the denunciation becomes effective, the holder of such registration may file an application for the registration of the same mark with the Office of the denouncing State or intergovernmental organization, which shall be treated as if it had been filed on the date of the international registration according to Article 3(4) or on the date of recordal of the territorial extension according to Article 3ter(2) and, if the international registration enjoyed priority, enjoy the same priority, provided that

  (i)   such application is filed within two years from the date on which the denunciation became effective,

  (ii)   the goods and services listed in the application are in fact covered by the list of goods and services contained in the international registration in respect of the denouncing State or intergovernmental organization, and

  (iii)   such application complies with all the requirements of the applicable law, including the requirements concerning fees.

(b) The provisions of subparagraph (a) shall also apply in respect of any mark that is the subject of an international registration having effect in Contracting Parties other than the denouncing State or intergovernmental organization at the date on which denunciation becomes effective and whose holder, because of the denunciation, is no longer entitled to file international applications under Article 2(1).

Article 16
Signature; Languages; Depositary Functions

(1)

(a) This Protocol shall be signed in a single copy in the English, French and Spanish languages, and shall be deposited with the Director General when it ceases to be open for signature at Madrid. The texts in the three languages shall be equally authentic.

(b) Official texts of this Protocol shall be established by the Director General, after consultation with the interested governments and organizations, in the Arabic, Chinese, German, Italian, Japanese, Portuguese and Russian languages, and in such other languages as the Assembly may designate.

(2) This Protocol shall remain open for signature at Madrid until December 31, 1989.

(3) The Director General shall transmit two copies, certified by the Government of Spain, of the signed texts of this Protocol to all States and intergovernmental organizations that may become party to this Protocol.

(4) The Director General shall register this Protocol with the Secretariat of the United Nations.

(5) The Director General shall notify all States and international organizations that may become or are party to this Protocol of signatures, deposits of instruments of ratification, acceptance, approval or accession, the entry into force of this Protocol and any amendment thereto, any notification of denunciation and any declaration provided for in this Protocol.

TRADEMARK LAW TREATY
adopted at Geneva on October 27, 1994

Article 1
Abbreviated Expressions
For the purposes of this Treaty, unless expressly stated otherwise:

(i) "Office" means the agency entrusted by a Contracting Party with the registration of marks;

(ii) "registration" means the registration of a mark by an Office;

(iii) "application" means an application for registration;

(iv) references to a "person" shall be construed as references to both a natural person and a legal entity;

(v) "holder" means the person whom the register of marks shows as the holder of the registration;

(vi) "register of marks" means the collection of data maintained by an Office, which includes the contents of all registrations and all data recorded in respect of all registrations, irrespective of the medium in which such data are stored;

(vii) "Paris Convention" means the Paris Convention for the Protection of Industrial Property, signed at Paris on March 20, 1883, as revised and amended;

(viii) "Nice Classification" means the classification established by the Nice Agreement Concerning the International Classification of Goods and Services for the Purposes of the Registration of Marks, signed at Nice on June 15, 1957, as revised and amended;

(ix) "Contracting Party" means any State or intergovernmental organization party to this Treaty;

(x) references to an "instrument of ratification" shall be construed as including references to instruments of acceptance and approval;

(xi) "Organization" means the World Intellectual Property Organization;

(xii) "Director General" means the Director General of the Organization;

(xiii) "Regulations" means the Regulations under this Treaty that are referred to in Article 17.

Article 2
Marks to Which the Treaty Applies
(1) [*Nature of Marks*]

(*a*) This Treaty shall apply to marks consisting of visible signs, provided that only those Contracting Parties which accept for registration three-dimensional marks shall be obliged to apply this Treaty to such marks.

(*b*) This Treaty shall not apply to hologram marks and to marks not consisting of visible signs, in particular, sound marks and olfactory marks.

(2) [*Kinds of Marks*]

(a) This Treaty shall apply to marks relating to goods (trademarks) or services (service marks) or both goods and services.

(b) This Treaty shall not apply to collective marks, certification marks and guarantee marks.

Article 3
Application

(1) [*Indications or Elements Contained in or Accompanying an Application; Fee*]

(a) Any Contracting Party may require that an application contain some or all of the following indications or elements:

(i) a request for registration;

(ii) the name and address of the applicant;

(iii) the name of a State of which the applicant is a national if he is the national of any State, the name of a State in which the applicant has his domicile, if any, and the name of a State in which the applicant has a real and effective industrial or commercial establishment, if any;

(iv) where the applicant is a legal entity, the legal nature of that legal entity and the State, and, where applicable, the territorial unit within that State, under the law of which the said legal entity has been organized;

(v) where the applicant has a representative, the name and address of that representative;

(vi) where an address for service is required under Article 4(2)(b), such address;

(vii) where the applicant wishes to take advantage of the priority of an earlier application, a declaration claiming the priority of that earlier application, together with indications and evidence in support of the declaration of priority that may be required pursuant to Article 4 of the Paris Convention;

(viii) where the applicant wishes to take advantage of any protection resulting from the display of goods and/or services in an exhibition, a declaration to that effect, together with indications in support of that declaration, as required by the law of the Contracting Party;

(ix) where the Office of the Contracting Party uses characters (letters and numbers) that it considers as being standard and where the applicant wishes that the mark be registered and published in standard characters, a statement to that effect;

(x) where the applicant wishes to claim color as a distinctive feature of the mark, a statement to that effect as well as the name or names of the color or colors claimed and an indication, in respect of each color, of the principal parts of the mark which are in that color;

(xi) where the mark is a three-dimensional mark, a statement to that effect;

(xii) one or more reproductions of the mark;

(xiii) a transliteration of the mark or of certain parts of the mark;

(xiv) a translation of the mark or of certain parts of the mark;

(xv) the names of the goods and/or services for which the registration is sought, grouped according to the classes of the Nice Classification, each group preceded by the number of the class of that Classification to which that group of goods or services belongs and presented in the order of the classes of the said Classification;

(xvi) a signature by the person specified in paragraph (4);

(xvii) a declaration of intention to use the mark, as required by the law of the Contracting Party.

(b) The applicant may file, instead of or in addition to the declaration of intention to use the mark referred to in subparagraph *(a)*(xvii), a declaration of actual use of the mark and evidence to that effect, as required by the law of the Contracting Party.

(c) Any Contracting Party may require that, in respect of the application, fees be paid to the Office.

(2) [*Presentation*] As regards the requirements concerning the presentation of the application, no Contracting Party shall refuse the application,

(i) where the application is presented in writing on paper, if it is presented, subject to paragraph (3), on a form corresponding to the application Form provided for in the Regulations,

(ii) where the Contracting Party allows the transmittal of communications to the Office by telefacsimile and the application is so transmitted, if the paper copy resulting from such transmittal corresponds, subject to paragraph (3), to the application Form referred to in item (i).

(3) [*Language*] Any Contracting Party may require that the application be in the language, or in one of the languages, admitted by the Office. Where the Office admits more than one language, the applicant may be required to comply with any other language requirement applicable with respect to the Office, provided that the application may not be required to be in more than one language.

(4) [*Signature*]

(a) The signature referred to in paragraph (1)*(a)*(xvi) may be the signature of the applicant or the signature of his representative.

(b) Notwithstanding subparagraph *(a)*, any Contracting Party may require that the declarations referred to in paragraph (1)*(a)*(xvii) and (1)*(b)* be signed by the applicant himself even if he has a representative.

(5) [*Single Application for Goods and/or Services in Several Classes*] One and the same application may relate to several goods and/or services, irrespective of whether they belong to one class or to several classes of the Nice Classification.

(6) [*Actual Use*] Any Contracting Party may require that, where a declaration of intention to use has been filed under paragraph (1)*(a)*(xvii), the

applicant furnish to the Office within a time limit fixed in its law, subject to the minimum time limit prescribed in the Regulations, evidence of the actual use of the mark, as required by the said law.

(7) [*Prohibition of Other Requirements*] No Contracting Party may demand that requirements other than those referred to in paragraphs (1) to (4) and (6) be complied with in respect of the application. In particular, the following may not be required in respect of the application throughout its pendency:

(i)   the furnishing of any certificate of, or extract from, a register of commerce;

(ii)   an indication of the applicant's carrying on of an industrial or commercial activity, as well as the furnishing of evidence to that effect;

(iii) an indication of the applicant's carrying on of an activity corresponding to the goods and/or services listed in the application, as well as the furnishing of evidence to that effect;

(iv) the furnishing of evidence to the effect that the mark has been registered in the register of marks of another Contracting Party or of a State party to the Paris Convention which is not a Contracting Party, except where the applicant claims the application of Article 6quinquies of the Paris Convention.

(8) [*Evidence*] Any Contracting Party may require that evidence be furnished to the Office in the course of the examination of the application where the Office may reasonably doubt the veracity of any indication or element contained in the application.

Article 4
Representation; Address for Service

(1) [*Representatives Admitted to Practice*] Any Contracting Party may require that any person appointed as representative for the purposes of any procedure before the Office be a representative admitted to practice before the Office.

(2) [*Mandatory Representation; Address for Service*]

(a) Any Contracting Party may require that, for the purposes of any procedure before the Office, any person who has neither a domicile nor a real and effective industrial or commercial establishment on its territory be represented by a representative.

(b) Any Contracting Party may, to the extent that it does not require representation in accordance with subparagraph (a), require that, for the purposes of any procedure before the Office, any person who has neither a domicile nor a real and effective industrial or commercial establishment on its territory have an address for service on that territory.

(3) [*Power of Attorney*]

(a) Whenever a Contracting Party allows or requires an applicant, a holder or any other interested person to be represented by a representative before the Office, it may require that the representative be appointed in a separate communication (hereinafter referred to as "power of attorney") indicating the name of, and signed by, the applicant, the holder or the other person, as the case may be.

(b) The power of attorney may relate to one or more applications and/or registrations identified in the power of attorney or, subject to any exception indicated by the appointing person, to all existing and future applications and/or registrations of that person.

(c) The power of attorney may limit the powers of the representative to certain acts. Any Contracting Party may require that any power of attorney under which the representative has the right to withdraw an application or to surrender a registration contain an express indication to that effect.

(d) Where a communication is submitted to the Office by a person who refers to himself in the communication as a representative but where the Office is, at the time of the receipt of the communication, not in possession of the required power of attorney, the Contracting Party may require that the power of attorney be submitted to the Office within the time limit fixed by the Contracting Party, subject to the minimum time limit prescribed in the Regulations. Any Contracting Party may provide that, where the power of attorney has not been submitted to the Office within the time limit fixed by the Contracting Party, the communication by the said person shall have no effect.

(e) As regards the requirements concerning the presentation and contents of the power of attorney, no Contracting Party shall refuse the effects of the power of attorney,

    (i)   where the power of attorney is presented in writing on paper, if it is presented, subject to paragraph (4), on a form corresponding to the power of attorney Form provided for in the Regulations,

    (ii)   where the Contracting Party allows the transmittal of communications to the Office by telefacsimile and the power of attorney is so transmitted, if the paper copy resulting from such transmittal corresponds, subject to paragraph (4), to the power of attorney Form referred to in item (i).

(4) *[Language]* Any Contracting Party may require that the power of attorney be in the language, or in one of the languages, admitted by the Office.

(5) *[Reference to Power of Attorney]* Any Contracting Party may require that any communication made to the Office by a representative for the purposes of a procedure before the Office contain a reference to the power of attorney on the basis of which the representative acts.

(6) *[Prohibition of Other Requirements]* No Contracting Party may demand that requirements other than those referred to in paragraphs (3) to (5) be complied with in respect of the matters dealt with in those paragraphs.

(7) *[Evidence]* Any Contracting Party may require that evidence be furnished to the Office where the Office may reasonably doubt the veracity of any indication contained in any communication referred to in paragraphs (2) to (5).

Article 5
Filing Date

(1) [*Permitted Requirements*]

(a) Subject to subparagraph (b) and paragraph (2), a Contracting Party shall accord as the filing date of an application the date on which the Office received the following indications and elements in the language required under Article 3(3):

(i) an express or implicit indication that the registration of a mark is sought;

(ii) indications allowing the identity of the applicant to be established;

(iii) indications sufficient to contact the applicant or his representative, if any, by mail;

(iv) a sufficiently clear reproduction of the mark whose registration is sought;

(v) the list of the goods and/or services for which the registration is sought;

(vi) where Article 3(1)(a)(xvii) or 3(1)(b) applies, the declaration referred to in Article 3(1)(a)(xvii) or the declaration and evidence referred to in Article 3(1)(b), respectively, as required by the law of the Contracting Party, those declarations being, if so required by the said law, signed by the applicant himself even if he has a representative.

(b) Any Contracting Party may accord as the filing date of the application the date on which the Office received only some, rather than all, of the indications and elements referred to in subparagraph (a) or received them in a language other than the language required under Article 3(3).

(2) [*Permitted Additional Requirement*]

(a) A Contracting Party may provide that no filing date shall be accorded until the required fees are paid.

(b) A Contracting Party may apply the requirement referred to in subparagraph (a) only if it applied such requirement at the time of becoming party to this Treaty.

(3) [*Corrections and Time Limits*] The modalities of, and time limits for, corrections under paragraphs (1) and (2) shall be fixed in the Regulations.

(4) [*Prohibition of Other Requirements*] No Contracting Party may demand that requirements other than those referred to in paragraphs (1) and (2) be complied with in respect of the filing date.

Article 6
Single Registration for Goods and/or
Services in Several Classes

Where goods and/or services belonging to several classes of the Nice Classification have been included in one and the same application, such an application shall result in one and the same registration.

Article 7
Division of Application and Registration

(1) [*Division of Application*]

(a) Any application listing several goods and/or services (hereinafter referred to as "initial application") may,

(i)   at least until the decision by the Office on the registration of the mark,

(ii)   during any opposition proceedings against the decision of the Office to register the mark,

(iii) during any appeal proceedings against the decision on the registration of the mark, be divided by the applicant or at his request into two or more applications (hereinafter referred to as "divisional applications") by distributing among the latter the goods and/or services listed in the initial application. The divisional applications shall preserve the filing date of the initial application and the benefit of the right of priority, if any.

(b) Any Contracting Party shall, subject to subparagraph (a), be free to establish requirements for the division of an application, including the payment of fees.

(2) [*Division of Registration*] Paragraph (1) shall apply, *mutatis mutandis*, with respect to a division of a registration. Such a division shall be permitted

(i)   during any proceedings in which the validity of the registration is challenged before the Office by a third party,

(ii)   during any appeal proceedings against a decision taken by the Office during the former proceedings, provided that a Contracting Party may exclude the possibility of the division of registrations if its law allows third parties to oppose the registration of a mark before the mark is registered.

Article 8
Signature

(1) [*Communication on Paper*] Where a communication to the Office of a Contracting Party is on paper and a signature is required, that Contracting Party

(i)   shall, subject to item (iii), accept a handwritten signature,

(ii)   shall be free to allow, instead of a handwritten signature, the use of other forms of signature, such as a printed or stamped signature, or the use of a seal,

(iii) may, where the natural person who signs the communication is its national and such person's address is in its territory, require that a seal be used instead of a handwritten signature,

(iv)   may, where a seal is used, require that the seal be accompanied by an indication in letters of the name of the natural person whose seal is used.

(2) [*Communication by Telefacsimile*]

(a) Where a Contracting Party allows the transmittal of communications to the Office by telefacsimile, it shall consider the communication signed if, on the printout produced by the telefacsimile, the reproduction of the signature, or the reproduction of the seal together with, where required under paragraph (1)(iv), the indication in letters of the name of the natural person whose seal is used, appears.

(b) The Contracting Party referred to in subparagraph *(a)* may require that the paper whose reproduction was transmitted by telefacsimile be filed with the Office within a certain period, subject to the minimum period prescribed in the Regulations.

(3) [*Communication by Electronic Means*] Where a Contracting Party allows the transmittal of communications to the Office by electronic means, it shall consider the communication signed if the latter identifies the sender of the communication by electronic means as prescribed by the Contracting Party.

(4) [*Prohibition of Requirement of Certification*] No Contracting Party may require the attestation, notarization, authentication, legalization or other certification of any signature or other means of self-identification referred to in the preceding paragraphs, except, if the law of the Contracting Party so provides, where the signature concerns the surrender of a registration.

Article 9
Classification of Goods and/or Services

(1) [*Indications of Goods and/or Services*] Each registration and any publication effected by an Office which concerns an application or registration and which indicates goods and/or services shall indicate the goods and/or services by their names, grouped according to the classes of the Nice Classification, and each group shall be preceded by the number of the class of that Classification to which that group of goods or services belongs and shall be presented in the order of the classes of the said Classification.

(2) [*Goods or Services in the Same Class or in Different Classes*]

(a) Goods or services may not be considered as being similar to each other on the ground that, in any registration or publication by the Office, they appear in the same class of the Nice Classification.

(b) Goods or services may not be considered as being dissimilar from each other on the ground that, in any registration or publication by the Office, they appear in different classes of the Nice Classification.

Article 10
Changes in Names or Addresses

(1) [*Changes in the Name or Address of the Holder*]

(a) Where there is no change in the person of the holder but there is a change in his name and/or address, each Contracting Party shall accept that a request for the recordal of the change by the Office in its register of marks

be made in a communication signed by the holder or his representative and indicating the registration number of the registration concerned and the change to be recorded. As regards the requirements concerning the presentation of the request, no Contracting Party shall refuse the request,

(i)   where the request is presented in writing on paper, if it is presented, subject to subparagraph *(c)*, on a form corresponding to the request Form provided for in the Regulations,

(ii) where the Contracting Party allows the transmittal of communications to the Office by telefacsimile and the request is so transmitted, if the paper copy resulting from such transmittal corresponds, subject to subparagraph *(c)*, to the request Form referred to in item (i).

(b) Any Contracting Party may require that the request indicate

(i)   the name and address of the holder;

(ii)   where the holder has a representative, the name and address of that representative;

(iii) where the holder has an address for service, such address.

(c) Any Contracting Party may require that the request be in the language, or in one of the languages, admitted by the Office.

(d) Any Contracting Party may require that, in respect of the request, a fee be paid to the Office.

(e) A single request shall be sufficient even where the change relates to more than one registration, provided that the registration numbers of all registrations concerned are indicated in the request.

(2) [*Change in the Name or Address of the Applicant*] Paragraph (1) shall apply, *mutatis mutandis*, where the change concerns an application or applications, or both an application or applications and a registration or registrations, provided that, where the application number of any application concerned has not yet been issued or is not known to the applicant or his representative, the request otherwise identifies that application as prescribed in the Regulations.

(3) [*Change in the Name or Address of the Representative or in the Address for Service*] Paragraph (1) shall apply, *mutatis mutandis*, to any change in the name or address of the representative, if any, and to any change relating to the address for service, if any.

(4) [*Prohibition of Other Requirements*] No Contracting Party may demand that requirements other than those referred to in paragraphs (1) to (3) be complied with in respect of the request referred to in this Article. In particular, the furnishing of any certificate concerning the change may not be required.

(5) [*Evidence*] Any Contracting Party may require that evidence be furnished to the Office where the Office may reasonably doubt the veracity of any indication contained in the request.

Article 11
Change in Ownership

(1) [*Change in the Ownership of a Registration*]

(*a*) Where there is a change in the person of the holder, each Contracting Party shall accept that a request for the recordal of the change by the Office in its register of marks be made in a communication signed by the holder or his representative, or by the person who acquired the ownership (hereinafter referred to as "new owner") or his representative, and indicating the registration number of the registration concerned and the change to be recorded. As regards the requirements concerning the presentation of the request, no Contracting Party shall refuse the request,

(i) where the request is presented in writing on paper, if it is presented, subject to paragraph (2)(*a*), on a form corresponding to the request Form provided for in the Regulations,

(ii) where the Contracting Party allows the transmittal of communications to the Office by telefacsimile and the request is so transmitted, if the paper copy resulting from such transmittal corresponds, subject to paragraph (2)(*a*), to the request Form referred to in item (i).

(*b*) Where the change in ownership results from a contract, any Contracting Party may require that the request indicate that fact and be accompanied, at the option of the requesting party, by one of the following:

(i) a copy of the contract, which copy may be required to be certified, by a notary public or any other competent public authority, as being in conformity with the original contract;

(ii) an extract of the contract showing the change in ownership, which extract may be required to be certified, by a notary public or any other competent public authority, as being a true extract of the contract;

(iii) an uncertified certificate of transfer drawn up in the form and with the content as prescribed in the Regulations and signed by both the holder and the new owner;

(iv) an uncertified transfer document drawn up in the form and with the content as prescribed in the Regulations and signed by both the holder and the new owner.

(*c*) Where the change in ownership results from a merger, any Contracting Party may require that the request indicate that fact and be accompanied by a copy of a document, which document originates from the competent authority and evidences the merger, such as a copy of an extract from a register of commerce, and that that copy be certified by the authority which issued the document or by a notary public or any other competent public authority, as being in conformity with the original document.

(*d*) Where there is a change in the person of one or more but not all of several co-holders and such change in ownership results from a contract or a merger, any Contracting Party may require that any co-holder in respect of which there is no change in ownership give his express consent to the change in ownership in a document signed by him.

(e) Where the change in ownership does not result from a contract or a merger but from another ground, for example, from operation of law or a court decision, any Contracting Party may require that the request indicate that fact and be accompanied by a copy of a document evidencing the change and that that copy be certified as being in conformity with the original document by the authority which issued the document or by a notary public or any other competent public authority.

(f) Any Contracting Party may require that the request indicate

(i)   the name and address of the holder;

(ii)   the name and address of the new owner;

(iii)   the name of a State of which the new owner is a national if he is the national of any State, the name of a State in which the new owner has his domicile, if any, and the name of a State in which the new owner has a real and effective industrial or commercial establishment, if any;

(iv)   where the new owner is a legal entity, the legal nature of that legal entity and the State, and, where applicable, the territorial unit within that State, under the law of which the said legal entity has been organized;

(v)   where the holder has a representative, the name and address of that representative;

(vi)   where the holder has an address for service, such address;

(vii)   where the new owner has a representative, the name and address of that representative;

(viii) where the new owner is required to have an address for service under Article 4(2)*(b)*, such address.

(g) Any Contracting Party may require that, in respect of the request, a fee be paid to the Office.

(h) A single request shall be sufficient even where the change relates to more than one registration, provided that the holder and the new owner are the same for each registration and that the registration numbers of all registrations concerned are indicated in the request.

(i) Where the change of ownership does not affect all the goods and/or services listed in the holder's registration, and the applicable law allows the recording of such change, the Office shall create a separate registration referring to the goods and/or services in respect of which the ownership has changed.

(2) [*Language; Translation*]

(a) Any Contracting Party may require that the request, the certificate of transfer or the transfer document referred to in paragraph (1) be in the language, or in one of the languages, admitted by the Office.

(b) Any Contracting Party may require that, if the documents referred to in paragraph (1)*(b)*(i) and (1)*(b)*(ii), (1)*(c)* and (1)*(e)* are not in the language, or in one of the languages, admitted by the Office, the request be accompanied by a translation or a certified translation of the required document in the language, or in one of the languages, admitted by the Office.

(3) *[Change in the Ownership of an Application]* Paragraphs (1) and (2) shall apply, *mutatis mutandis*, where the change in ownership concerns an application or applications, or both an application or applications and a registration or registrations, provided that, where the application number of any application concerned has not yet been issued or is not known to the applicant or his representative, the request otherwise identifies that application as prescribed in the Regulations.

(4) *[Prohibition of Other Requirements]* No Contracting Party may demand that requirements other than those referred to in paragraphs (1) to (3) be complied with in respect of the request referred to in this Article. In particular, the following may not be required:

(i)   subject to paragraph (1)*(c)*, the furnishing of any certificate of, or extract from, a register of commerce;

(ii)   an indication of the new owner's carrying on of an industrial or commercial activity, as well as the furnishing of evidence to that effect;

(iii)   an indication of the new owner's carrying on of an activity corresponding to the goods and/or services affected by the change in ownership, as well as the furnishing of evidence to either effect;

(iv)   an indication that the holder transferred, entirely or in part, his business or the relevant goodwill to the new owner, as well as the furnishing of evidence to either effect.

(5) *[Evidence]* Any Contracting Party may require that evidence, or further evidence where paragraph (1)*(c)* or (1)*(e)* applies, be furnished to the Office where that Office may reasonably doubt the veracity of any indication contained in the request or in any document referred to in the present Article.

Article 12
Correction of a Mistake

(1) *[Correction of a Mistake in Respect of a Registration]*

(a) Each Contracting Party shall accept that the request for the correction of a mistake which was made in the application or other request communicated to the Office and which mistake is reflected in its register of marks and/or any publication by the Office be made in a communication signed by the holder or his representative and indicating the registration number of the registration concerned, the mistake to be corrected and the correction to be entered. As regards the requirements concerning the presentation of the request, no Contracting Party shall refuse the request,

(i)   where the request is presented in writing on paper, if it is presented, subject to subparagraph *(c)*, on a form corresponding to the request Form provided for in the Regulations,

(ii)   where the Contracting Party allows the transmittal of communications to the Office by telefacsimile and the request is so transmitted, if the paper copy resulting from such transmittal corresponds, subject to subparagraph *(c)*, to the request Form referred to in item (i).

(b) Any Contracting Party may require that the request indicate

(i)   the name and address of the holder;

(ii)   where the holder has a representative, the name and address of that representative;

(iii)   where the holder has an address for service, such address.

(c) Any Contracting Party may require that the request be in the language, or in one of the languages, admitted by the Office.

(d) Any Contracting Party may require that, in respect of the request, a fee be paid to the Office.

(e) A single request shall be sufficient even where the correction relates to more than one registration of the same person, provided that the mistake and the requested correction are the same for each registration and that the registration numbers of all registrations concerned are indicated in the request.

(2) [*Correction of a Mistake in Respect of an Application*] Paragraph (1) shall apply, *mutatis mutandis*, where the mistake concerns an application or applications, or both an application or applications and a registration or registrations, provided that, where the application number of any application concerned has not yet been issued or is not known to the applicant or his representative, the request otherwise identifies that application as prescribed in the Regulations.

(3) [*Prohibition of Other Requirements*] No Contracting Party may demand that requirements other than those referred to in paragraphs (1) and (2) be complied with in respect of the request referred to in this Article.

(4) [*Evidence*] Any Contracting Party may require that evidence be furnished to the Office where the Office may reasonably doubt that the alleged mistake is in fact a mistake.

(5) [*Mistakes Made by the Office*] The Office of a Contracting Party shall correct its own mistakes, ex officio or upon request, for no fee.

(6) [*Uncorrectable Mistakes*] No Contracting Party shall be obliged to apply paragraphs (1), (2) and (5) to any mistake which cannot be corrected under its law.

Article 13
Duration and Renewal of Registration

(1) [*Indications or Elements Contained in or Accompanying a Request for Renewal; Fee*]

(a) Any Contracting Party may require that the renewal of a registration be subject to the filing of a request and that such request contain some or all of the following indications:

(i)   an indication that renewal is sought;

(ii)   the name and address of the holder;

(iii)   the registration number of the registration concerned;

(iv)   at the option of the Contracting Party, the filing date of the application which resulted in the registration concerned or the registration date of the registration concerned;

(v)   where the holder has a representative, the name and address of that representative;

(vi)   where the holder has an address for service, such address;

(vii)   where the Contracting Party allows the renewal of a registration to be made for some only of the goods and/or services which are recorded in the register of marks and such a renewal is requested, the names of the recorded goods and/or services for which the renewal is requested or the names of the recorded goods and/or services for which the renewal is not requested, grouped according to the classes of the Nice Classification, each group preceded by the number of the class of that Classification to which that group of goods or services belongs and presented in the order of the classes of the said Classification;

(viii) where a Contracting Party allows a request for renewal to be filed by a person other than the holder or his representative and the request is filed by such a person, the name and address of that person;

(ix)   a signature by the holder or his representative or, where item (viii) applies, a signature by the person referred to in that item.

(b) Any Contracting Party may require that, in respect of the request for renewal, a fee be paid to the Office. Once the fee has been paid in respect of the initial period of the registration or of any renewal period, no further payment may be required for the maintenance of the registration in respect of that period. Fees associated with the furnishing of a declaration and/or evidence of use shall not be regarded, for the purposes of this subparagraph, as payments required for the maintenance of the registration and shall not be affected by this subparagraph.

(c) Any Contracting Party may require that the request for renewal be presented, and the corresponding fee referred to in subparagraph *(b)* be paid, to the Office within the period fixed by the law of the Contracting Party, subject to the minimum periods prescribed in the Regulations.

(2) [*Presentation*] As regards the requirements concerning the presentation of the request for renewal, no Contracting Party shall refuse the request,

(i)   where the request is presented in writing on paper, if it is presented, subject to paragraph (3), on a form corresponding to the request Form provided for in the Regulations,

(ii)   where the Contracting Party allows the transmittal of communications to the Office by telefacsimile and the request is so transmitted, if the paper copy resulting from such transmittal corresponds, subject to paragraph (3), to the request Form referred to in item (i).

(3) [*Language*] Any Contracting Party may require that the request for renewal be in the language, or in one of the languages, admitted by the Office.

(4) [*Prohibition of Other Requirements*] No Contracting Party may demand

that requirements other than those referred to in paragraphs (1) to (3) be complied with in respect of the request for renewal. In particular, the following may not be required:

(i)   any reproduction or other identification of the mark;

(ii)   the furnishing of evidence to the effect that the mark has been registered, or that its registration has been renewed, in the register of marks of any other Contracting Party;

(iii) the furnishing of a declaration and/or evidence concerning use of the mark.

(5) [*Evidence*]   Any Contracting Party may require that evidence be furnished to the Office in the course of the examination of the request for renewal where the Office may reasonably doubt the veracity of any indication or element contained in the request for renewal.

(6) [*Prohibition of Substantive Examination*]   No Office of a Contracting Party may, for the purposes of effecting the renewal, examine the registration as to substance.

(7) [*Duration*] The duration of the initial period of the registration, and the duration of each renewal period, shall be 10 years.

Article 14
Observations in Case of Intended Refusal
An application or a request under Articles 10 to 13 may not be refused totally or in part by an Office without giving the applicant or the requesting party, as the case may be, an opportunity to make observations on the intended refusal within a reasonable time limit.

Article 15
Obligation to Comply with the Paris Convention
Any Contracting Party shall comply with the provisions of the Paris Convention which concern marks.

Article 16
Service Marks
Any Contracting Party shall register service marks and apply to such marks the provisions of the Paris Convention which concern trademarks.

Article 17
Regulations
(1) [*Content*]

(a) The Regulations annexed to this Treaty provide rules concerning

(i) matters which this Treaty expressly provides to be "prescribed in the Regulations";

(ii) any details useful in the implementation of the provisions of this

Treaty;

(iii) any administrative requirements, matters or procedures.

(b) The Regulations also contain Model International Forms.

(2) [Conflict Between the Treaty and the Regulations] In the case of conflict between the provisions of this Treaty and those of the Regulations, the former shall prevail.

Article 18
Revision; Protocols

(1) [Revision] This Treaty may be revised by a diplomatic conference.

(2) [Protocols] For the purposes of further developing the harmonization of laws on marks, protocols may be adopted by a diplomatic conference insofar as those protocols do not contravene the provisions of this Treaty.

Article 19
Becoming Party to the Treaty

(1) [Eligibility]   The following entities may sign and, subject to paragraphs (2) and (3) and Article 20(1) and 20(3), become party to this Treaty:

(i) any State member of the Organization in respect of which marks may be registered with its own Office;

(ii) any intergovernmental organization which maintains an Office in which marks may be registered with effect in the territory in which the constituting treaty of the intergovernmental organization applies, in all its member States or in those of its member States which are designated for such purpose in the relevant application, provided that all the member States of the intergovernmental organization are members of the Organization;

(iii) any State member of the Organization in respect of which marks may be registered only through the Office of another specified State that is a member of the Organization;

(iv) any State member of the Organization in respect of which marks may be registered only through the Office maintained by an intergovernmental organization of which that State is a member;

(v) any State member of the Organization in respect of which marks may be registered only through an Office common to a group of States members of the Organization.

(2) [Ratification or Accession] Any entity referred to in paragraph (1) may deposit

(i) an instrument of ratification, if it has signed this Treaty,

(ii) an instrument of accession, if it has not signed this Treaty.

(3) [Effective Date of Deposit]

(a) Subject to subparagraph (b), the effective date of the deposit of an instrument of ratification or accession shall be,

(i) in the case of a State referred to in paragraph (1)(i), the date on which the instrument of that State is deposited;

(ii) in the case of an intergovernmental organization, the date on which the instrument of that intergovernmental organization is deposited;

(iii) in the case of a State referred to in paragraph (1)(iii), the date on which the following condition is fulfilled: the instrument of that State has been deposited and the instrument of the other, specified State has been deposited;

(iv) in the case of a State referred to in paragraph (1)(iv), the date applicable under (ii), above;

(v) in the case of a State member of a group of States referred to in paragraph (1)(v), the date on which the instruments of all the States members of the group have been deposited.

(b) Any instrument of ratification or accession (referred to in this subparagraph as "instrument") of a State may be accompanied by a declaration making it a condition to its being considered as deposited that the instrument of one other State or one intergovernmental organization, or the instruments of two other States, or the instruments of one other State and one intergovernmental organization, specified by name and eligible to become party to this Treaty, is or are also deposited. The instrument containing such a declaration shall be considered to have been deposited on the day on which the condition indicated in the declaration is fulfilled. However, when the deposit of any instrument specified in the declaration is, itself, accompanied by a declaration of the said kind, that instrument shall be considered as deposited on the day on which the condition specified in the latter declaration is fulfilled.

(c) Any declaration made under paragraph *(b)* may be withdrawn, in its entirety or in part, at any time. Any such withdrawal shall become effective on the date on which the notification of withdrawal is received by the Director General.

Article 20
Effective Date of Ratifications and Accessions

(1) [*Instruments to Be Taken Into Consideration*] For the purposes of this Article, only instruments of ratification or accession that are deposited by entities referred to in Article 19(1) and that have an effective date according to Article 19(3) shall be taken into consideration.

(2) [*Entry Into Force of the Treaty*] This Treaty shall enter into force three months after five States have deposited their instruments of ratification or accession.

(3) [*Entry Into Force of Ratifications and Accessions Subsequent to the Entry Into Force of the Treaty*] Any entity not covered by paragraph (2) shall become bound by this Treaty three months after the date on which it has deposited its instrument of ratification or accession.

Article 21
Reservations

(1) [*Special Kinds of Marks*] Any State or intergovernmental organization may declare through a reservation that, notwithstanding Article 2(1)*(a)* and 2(2)*(a)*, any of the provisions of Articles 3(1) and 3(2), 5, 7, 11 and 13 shall not apply to associated marks, defensive marks or derivative marks. Such reservation shall specify those of the aforementioned provisions to which the reservation relates.

(2) [*Modalities*] Any reservation under paragraph (1) shall be made in a declaration accompanying the instrument of ratification of, or accession to, this Treaty of the State or intergovernmental organization making the reservation.

(3) [*Withdrawal*] Any reservation under paragraph (1) may be withdrawn at any time.

(4) [*Prohibition of Other Reservations*] No reservation to this Treaty other than the reservation allowed under paragraph (1) shall be permitted.

Article 22
Transitional Provisions

(1) [*Single Application for Goods and Services in Several Classes; Division of Application*]

(a) Any State or intergovernmental organization may declare that, notwithstanding Article 3(5), an application may be filed with the Office only in respect of goods or services which belong to one class of the Nice Classification.

(b) Any State or intergovernmental organization may declare that, notwithstanding Article 6, where goods and/or services belonging to several classes of the Nice Classification have been included in one and the same application, such application shall result in two or more registrations in the register of marks, provided that each and every such registration shall bear a reference to all other such registrations resulting from the said application.

(c) Any State or intergovernmental organization that has made a declaration under subparagraph *(a)* may declare that, notwithstanding Article 7(1), no application may be divided.

(2) [*Single Power of Attorney for More Than One Application and/or Registration*] Any State or intergovernmental organization may declare that, notwithstanding Article 4(3)*(b)*, a power of attorney may only relate to one application or one registration.

(3) [*Prohibition of Requirement of Certification of Signature of Power of Attorney and of Signature of Application*] Any State or intergovernmental organization may declare that, notwithstanding Article 8(4), the signature of a power of attorney or the signature by the applicant of an application may be required to be the subject of an attestation, notarization, authentication, legalization or other certification.

(4) [*Single Request for More Than One Application and/or Registration in Respect of a Change in Name and/or Address, a Change in Ownership or a Correction of a Mistake*] Any State or intergovernmental organization may declare that, notwithstanding Article 10(1)*(e)*, 10(2) and 10(3), Article 11(1)*(h)* and 11(3) and Article 12(1)*(e)* and 12(2), a request for the recordal of a change in name and/or address, a request for the recordal of a change in ownership and a request for the correction of a mistake may only relate to one application or one registration.

(5) [*Furnishing, on the Occasion of Renewal, of Declaration and/or Evidence Concerning Use*] Any State or intergovernmental organization may declare that, notwithstanding Article 13(4)(iii), it will require, on the occasion of renewal, the furnishing of a declaration and/or of evidence concerning use of the mark.

(6) [*Substantive Examination on the Occasion of Renewal*] Any State or intergovernmental organization may declare that, notwithstanding Article 13(6), the Office may, on the occasion of the first renewal of a registration covering services, examine such registration as to substance, provided that such examination shall be limited to the elimination of multiple registrations based on applications filed during a period of six months following the entry into force of the law of such State or organization that introduced, before the entry into force of this Treaty, the possibility of registering service marks.

(7) [*Common Provisions*]

(a) A State or an intergovernmental organization may make a declaration under paragraphs (1) to (6) only if, at the time of depositing its instrument of ratification of, or accession to, this Treaty, the continued application of its law would, without such a declaration, be contrary to the relevant provisions of this Treaty.

(b) Any declaration under paragraphs (1) to (6) shall accompany the instrument of ratification of, or accession to, this Treaty of the State or intergovernmental organization making the declaration.

(c) Any declaration made under paragraphs (1) to (6) may be withdrawn at any time.

(8) [*Loss of Effect of Declaration*]

(a) Subject to subparagraph *(c)*, any declaration made under paragraphs (1) to (6) by a State regarded as a developing country in conformity with the established practice of the General Assembly of the United Nations, or by an intergovernmental organization each member of which is such a State, shall lose its effect at the end of a period of eight years from the date of entry into force of this Treaty.

(b) Subject to subparagraph *(c)*, any declaration made under paragraphs (1) to (6) by a State other than a State referred to in subparagraph *(a)*, or by an intergovernmental organization other than an intergovernmental organization referred to in subparagraph *(a)*, shall lose its effect at the end of a period of six years from the date of entry into force

of this Treaty.

(c) Where a declaration made under paragraphs (1) to (6) has not been withdrawn under paragraph (7)(c), or has not lost its effect under subparagraph (a) or (b), before October 28, 2004, it shall lose its effect on October 28, 2004.

(9) [*Becoming Party to the Treaty*] Until December 31, 1999, any State which, on the date of the adoption of this Treaty, is a member of the International (Paris) Union for the Protection of Industrial Property without being a member of the Organization may, notwithstanding Article 19(1)(i), become a party to this Treaty if marks may be registered with its own Office.

Article 23
Denunciation of the Treaty

(1) [*Notification*] Any Contracting Party may denounce this Treaty by notification addressed to the Director General.

(2) [*Effective Date*] Denunciation shall take effect one year from the date on which the Director General has received the notification. It shall not affect the application of this Treaty to any application pending or any mark registered in respect of the denouncing Contracting Party at the time of the expiration of the said one-year period, provided that the denouncing Contracting Party may, after the expiration of the said one-year period, discontinue applying this Treaty to any registration as from the date on which that registration is due for renewal.

Article 24
Languages of the Treaty; Signature

(1) [*Original Texts; Official Texts*]

(a) This Treaty shall be signed in a single original in the English, Arabic, Chinese, French, Russian and Spanish languages, all texts being equally authentic.

(b) At the request of a Contracting Party, an official text in a language not referred to in subparagraph (a) that is an official language of that Contracting Party shall be established by the Director General after consultation with the said Contracting Party and any other interested Contracting Party.

(2) [*Time Limit for Signature*] This Treaty shall remain open for signature at the headquarters of the Organization for one year after its adoption.

Article 25
Depositary

The Director General shall be the depositary of this Treaty.

NICE AGREEMENT CONCERNING THE INTERNATIONAL CLASSIFICATION OF GOODS AND SERVICES FOR THE PURPOSES OF THE REGISTRATION OF MARKS
of June 15, 1957, as revised at Stockholm on July 14, 1967,
and at Geneva on May 13, 1977, and amended on
September 28, 1979

Article 1
Establishment of a Special Union;
Adoption of an International Classification;
Definition and Languages of the Classification

(1) The countries to which this Agreement applies constitute a Special Union and adopt a common classification of goods and services for the purposes of the registration of marks (hereinafter designated as "the Classification").

(2) The Classification consists of:

(i)   a list of classes, together with, as the case may be, explanatory notes;

(ii)   an alphabetical list of goods and services (herein-after designated as "the alphabetical list") with an indication of the class into which each of the goods or services falls.

(3) The Classification comprises:

(i)   the classification published in 1971 by the International Bureau of Intellectual Property (hereinafter designated as "the International Bureau") referred to in the Convention Establishing the World Intellectual Property Organization, it being understood, however, that the explanatory notes to the list of classes included in that publication shall be regarded as provisional and as recommendations until such time as explanatory notes to the list of classes are established by the Committee of Experts referred to in Article 3;

(ii)   the amendments and additions which have entered into force, pursuant to Article 4(1) of the Nice Agreement of June 15, 1957, and of the Stockholm Act of July 14, 1967, of that Agreement, prior to the entry into force of the present Act;

(iii)   any changes to be made in accordance with Article 3 of this Act and which enter into force pursuant to Article 4(1) of this Act.

(4) The Classification shall be in the English and French languages, both texts being equally authentic.

(5)

(a) The classification referred to in paragraph (3)(i), together with those amendments and additions referred to in paragraph (3)(ii) which have entered into force prior to the date this Act is opened for signature, is contained in one authentic copy, in the French language, deposited with the Director General of the World Intellectual Property Organization (hereinafter designated respectively "the Director General" and "the Organization"). Those amendments and additions referred to in paragraph (3)(ii) which enter into force after the date this Act is opened for signature shall also be deposited in one authentic copy, in the French language, with the Director General.

(b) The English version of the texts referred to in subparagraph (a) shall be established by the Committee of Experts referred to in Article 3 promptly after the entry into force of this Act. Its authentic copy shall be deposited with the Director General.

(c) The changes referred to in paragraph (3)(iii) shall be deposited in one authentic copy, in the English and French languages, with the Director General.

(6) Official texts of the Classification, in Arabic, German, Italian, Portuguese, Russian, Spanish and in such other languages as the Assembly referred to in Article 5 may designate, shall be established by the Director General, after consultation with the interested Governments and either on the basis of a translation submitted by those Governments or by any other means which do not entail financial implications for the budget of the Special Union or for the Organization.

(7) The alphabetical list shall mention, opposite each indication of goods or services, a serial number that is specific to the language in which the said list is established, together with:

(i)   in the case of the alphabetical list established in English, the serial number mentioned in respect of the same indication in the alphabetical list established in French, and vice versa;

(ii)   in the case of any alphabetical list established pursuant to paragraph (6), the serial number mentioned in respect of the same indication in the alphabetical list established in English or in the alphabetical list established in French.

Article 2
Legal Effect and Use of the Classification

(1) Subject to the requirements prescribed by this Agreement, the effect of the Classification shall be that attributed to it by each country of the Special Union. In particular, the Classification shall not bind the countries of the Special Union in respect of either the evaluation of the extent of the protection afforded to any given mark or the recognition of service marks.

(2) Each of the countries of the Special Union reserves the right to use the Classification either as a principal or as a subsidiary system.

(3) The competent Office of the countries of the Special Union shall include in the official documents and publications relating to registrations of marks the numbers of the classes of the Classification to which the goods or services for which the mark is registered belong.

(4) The fact that a term is included in the alphabetical list in no way affects any rights which might subsist in such a term.

Article 3
Committee of Experts

(1) A Committee of Experts shall be set up in which each country of the Special Union shall be represented.

(2)

(a) The Director General may, and, if requested by the Committee of Experts, shall, invite countries outside the Special Union which are members of the Organization or party to the Paris Convention for the Protection of Industrial Property to be represented by observers at meetings of the Committee of Experts.

(b) The Director General shall invite intergovernmental organizations specialized in the field of marks, of which at least one of the member countries is a country of the Special Union, to be represented by observers at meetings of the Committee of Experts.

(c) The Director General may, and if requested by the Committee of Experts, shall, invite representatives of other intergovernmental organizations and international non-governmental organizations to participate in discussions of interest to them.

(3) The Committee of Experts shall:

(i)   decide on changes in the Classification;

(ii)   address recommendations to the countries of the Special Union for the purpose of facilitating the use of the Classification and promoting its uniform application;

(iii) take all other measures which, without entailing financial implications for the budget of the Special Union or for the Organization, contribute towards facilitating the application of the Classification by developing countries;

(iv)   have the right to establish subcommittees and working groups.

(4) The Committee of Experts shall adopt its own rules of procedure. The latter shall provide for the possibility of participation in meetings of the subcommittees and working groups of the Committee of Experts by those intergovernmental organizations referred to in paragraph (2)(b) which can make a substantial contribution to the development of the Classification.

(5) Proposals for changes in the Classification may be made by the competent Office of any country of the Special Union, the International Bureau, any intergovernmental organization represented in the Committee of Experts pursuant to paragraph (2)(b) and any country or organization specially invited by the Committee of Experts to submit such proposals. The proposals shall be communicated to the International Bureau, which shall submit them to the members of the Committee of Experts and to the observers not later than two months before the session of the Committee of Experts at which the said proposals are to be considered.

(6) Each country of the Special Union shall have one vote.

(7)

(a) Subject to subparagraph (b), the decisions of the Committee of Experts shall require a simple majority of the countries of the Special Union represented and voting.

(b) Decisions concerning the adoption of amendments to the Classification shall require a majority of four-fifths of the countries of the Special Union represented and voting. "Amendment" shall mean any transfer of goods or services from one class to another or the creation of any new class.

(c) The rules of procedure referred to in paragraph (4) shall provide that, except in special cases, amendments to the Classification shall be adopted at the end of specified periods; the length of each period shall be determined by the Committee of Experts.

(8) Abstentions shall not be considered as votes.

Article 4
Notification, Entry Into Force and Publication of Changes

(1) Changes decided upon by the Committee of Experts and recommendations of the Committee of Experts shall be notified to the competent Offices of the countries of the Special Union by the International Bureau. Amendments shall enter into force six months after the date of dispatch of the notification. Any other change shall enter into force on a date to be specified by the Committee of Experts at the time the change is adopted.

(2) The International Bureau shall incorporate in the Classification the changes which have entered into force. Announcements of those changes shall be published in such periodicals as may be designated by the Assembly referred to in Article 5.

Article 5
Assembly of the Special Union

(1)

(a) The Special Union shall have an Assembly consisting of those countries which have ratified or acceded to this Act.

(b) The Government of each country shall be represented by one delegate, who may be assisted by alternate delegates, advisors, and experts.

(c) The expenses of each delegation shall be borne by the Government which has appointed it.

(2)

(a) Subject to the provisions of Articles 3 and 4, the Assembly shall:

    (i)   deal with all matters concerning the maintenance and development of the Special Union and the implementation of this Agreement;

    (ii)   give directions to the International Bureau concerning the preparation for conferences of revision, due account being taken of any comments made by those countries of the Special Union which have not ratified or acceded to this Act;

(iii) review and approve the reports and activities of the Director General of the Organization (hereinafter designated as "the Director General") concerning the Special Union, and give him all necessary instructions concerning matters within the competence of the Special Union;

(iv) determine the program and adopt the biennial budget of the Special Union, and approve its final accounts;

(v) adopt the financial regulations of the Special Union;

(vi) establish, in addition to the Committee of Experts referred to in Article 3, such other committees of experts and working groups as it may deem necessary to achieve the objectives of the Special Union;

(vii) determine which countries not members of the Special Union and which intergovernmental and international non-governmental organizations shall be admitted to its meetings as observers;

(viii) adopt amendments to Articles 5 to 8;

(ix) take any other appropriate action designed to further the objectives of the Special Union;

(x) perform such other functions as are appropriate under this Agreement.

(b) With respect to matters which are of interest also to other Unions administered by the Organization, the Assembly shall make its decisions after having heard the advice of the Coordination Committee of the Organization.

(3)

(a) Each country member of the Assembly shall have one vote.

(b) One-half of the countries members of the Assembly shall constitute a quorum.

(c) Notwithstanding the provisions of subparagraph (b), if, in any session, the number of countries represented is less than one-half but equal to or more than one-third of the countries members of the Assembly, the Assembly may make decisions but, with the exception of decisions concerning its own procedure, all such decisions shall take effect only if the conditions set forth hereinafter are fulfilled. The International Bureau shall communicate the said decisions to the countries members of the Assembly which were not represented and shall invite them to express in writing their vote or abstention within a period of three months from the date of the communication. If, at the expiration of this period, the number of countries having thus expressed their vote or abstention attains the number of countries which was lacking for attaining the quorum in the session itself, such decisions shall take effect provided that at the same time the required majority still obtains.

(d) Subject to the provisions of Article 8(2), the decisions of the Assembly shall require two-thirds of the votes cast.

(e) Abstentions shall not be considered as votes.

(f) A delegate may represent, and vote in the name of, one country only.

(g) Countries of the Special Union not members of the Assembly shall be admitted to the meetings of the latter as observers.

(4)

(a) The Assembly shall meet once in every second calendar year in ordinary session upon convocation by the Director General and, in the absence of exceptional circumstances, during the same period and at the same place as the General Assembly of the Organization.

(b) The Assembly shall meet in extraordinary session upon convocation by the Director General, at the request of one-fourth of the countries members of the Assembly.

(c) The agenda of each session shall be prepared by the Director General.

(5) The Assembly shall adopt its own rules of procedure.

Article 6
International Bureau

(1)

(a) Administrative tasks concerning the Special Union shall be performed by the International Bureau.

(b) In particular, the International Bureau shall prepare the meetings and provide the secretariat of the Assembly, the Committee of Experts, and such other committees of experts and working groups as may have been established by the Assembly or the Committee of Experts.

(c) The Director General shall be the chief executive of the Special Union and shall represent the Special Union.

(2) The Director General and any staff member designated by him shall participate, without the right to vote, in all meetings of the Assembly, the Committee of Experts, and such other committees of experts or working groups as may have been established by the Assembly or the Committee of Experts. The Director General, or a staff member designated by him, shall be ex officio secretary of those bodies.

(3)

(a) The International Bureau shall, in accordance with the directions of the Assembly, make the preparations for the conferences of revision of the provisions of the Agreement other than Articles 5 to 8.

(b) The International Bureau may consult with intergovernmental and international non-governmental organizations concerning preparations for conferences of revision.

(c) The Director General and persons designated by him shall take part, without the right to vote, in the discussions at those conferences.

(4) The International Bureau shall carry out any other tasks assigned to it.

Article 7
Finances

(1)

(a) The Special Union shall have a budget.

(b) The budget of the Special Union shall include the income and expenses proper to the Special Union, its contribution to the budget of expenses common to the Unions, and, where applicable, the sum made available to the budget of the Conference of the Organization.

(c) Expenses not attributable exclusively to the Special Union but also to one or more other Unions administered by the Organization shall be considered as expenses common to the Unions. The share of the Special Union in such common expenses shall be in proportion to the interest the Special Union has in them.

(2) The budget of the Special Union shall be established with due regard to the requirements of coordination with the budgets of the other Unions administered by the Organization.

(3) The budget of the Special Union shall be financed from the following sources:

    (i)   contributions of the countries of the Special Union;

    (ii)   fees and charges due for services rendered by the International Bureau in relation to the Special Union;

    (iii)   sale of, or royalties on, the publications of the International Bureau concerning the Special Union;

    (iv)   gifts, bequests, and subventions;

    (v)   rents, interests, and other miscellaneous income.

(4)

(a) For the purpose of establishing its contribution referred to in paragraph (3)(i), each country of the Special Union shall belong to the same class as it belongs to in the Paris Union for the Protection of Industrial Property, and shall pay its annual contributions on the basis of the same number of units as is fixed for that class in that Union.

(b) The annual contribution of each country of the Special Union shall be an amount in the same proportion to the total sum to be contributed to the budget of the Special Union by all countries as the number of its units is to the total of the units of all contributing countries.

(c) Contributions shall become due on the first of January of each year.

(d) A country which is in arrears in the payment of its contributions may not exercise its right to vote in any organ of the Special Union if the amount of its arrears equals or exceeds the amount of the contributions due from it for the preceding two full years. However, any organ of the Special Union may allow such a country to continue to exercise its right to vote in that

organ if, and as long as, it is satisfied that the delay in payment is due to exceptional and unavoidable circumstances.

(e) If the budget is not adopted before the beginning of a new financial period, it shall be at the same level as the budget of the previous year, as provided in the financial regulations.

(5) The amount of the fees and charges due for services rendered by the International Bureau in relation to the Special Union shall be established, and shall be reported to the Assembly, by the Director General.

(6)

(a) The Special Union shall have a working capital fund which shall be constituted by a single payment made by each country of the Special Union. If the fund becomes insufficient, the Assembly shall decide to increase it.

(b) The amount of the initial payment of each country to the said fund or of its participation in the increase thereof shall be a proportion of the contribution of that country for the year in which the fund is established or the decision to increase it is made.

(c) The proportion and the terms of payment shall be fixed by the Assembly on the proposal of the Director General and after it has heard the advice of the Coordination Committee of the Organization.

(7)

(a) In the headquarters agreement concluded with the country on the territory of which the Organization has its headquarters, it shall be provided that, whenever the working capital fund is insufficient, such country shall grant advances. The amount of those advances and the conditions on which they are granted shall be the subject of separate agreements, in each case, between such country and the Organization.

(b) The country referred to in subparagraph (a) and the Organization shall each have the right to denounce the obligation to grant advances, by written notification. Denunciation shall take effect three years after the end of the year in which it has been notified.

(8) The auditing of the accounts shall be effected by one or more of the countries of the Special Union or by external auditors, as provided in the financial regulations. They shall be designated, with their agreement, by the Assembly.

Article 8
Amendment of Articles 5 to 8

(1) Proposals for the amendment of Articles 5, 6, 7, and the present Article, may be initiated by any country member of the Assembly, or by the Director General. Such proposals shall be communicated by the Director General to the member countries of the Assembly at least six months in advance of their consideration by the Assembly.

(2) Amendments to the Articles referred to in paragraph (1) shall be adopted by the Assembly. Adoption shall require three-fourths of the votes

cast, provided that any amendment to Article 5, and to the present paragraph, shall require four-fifths of the votes cast.

(3) Any amendment to the Articles referred to in paragraph (1) shall enter into force one month after written notifications of acceptance, effected in accordance with their respective constitutional processes, have been received by the Director General from three-fourths of the countries members of the Assembly at the time it adopted the amendment. Any amendment to the said Articles thus accepted shall bind all the countries which are members of the Assembly at the time the amendment enters into force, or which become members thereof at a subsequent date, provided that any amendment increasing the financial obligations of countries of the Special Union shall bind only those countries which have notified their acceptance of such amendment.

Article 9
Ratification and Accession; Entry Into Force

(1) Any country of the Special Union which has signed this Act may ratify it, and, if it has not signed it, may accede to it.

(2) Any country outside the Special Union which is party to the Paris Convention for the Protection of Industrial Property may accede to this Act and thereby become a country of the Special Union.

(3) Instruments of ratification and accession shall be deposited with the Director General.

(4)

(a) This Act shall enter into force three months after both of the following conditions are fulfilled:

   (i)   six or more countries have deposited their instruments of ratification or accession;

   (ii)   at least three of the said countries are countries which, on the date this Act is opened for signature, are countries of the Special Union.

(b) The entry into force referred to in subparagraph (a) shall apply to those countries which, at least three months before the said entry into force, have deposited instruments of ratification or accession.

(c) With respect to any country not covered by subparagraph (b), this Act shall enter into force three months after the date on which its ratification or accession was notified by the Director General, unless a subsequent date has been indicated in the instrument of ratification or accession. In the latter case, this Act shall enter into force with respect to that country on the date thus indicated.

(5) Ratification or accession shall automatically entail acceptance of all the clauses and admission to all the advantages of this Act.

(6) After the entry into force of this Act, no country may ratify or accede to an earlier Act of this Agreement.

Article 10
Duration

This Agreement shall have the same duration as the Paris Convention for the Protection of Industrial Property.

Article 11
Revision

(1) This Agreement may be revised from time to time by a conference of the countries of the Special Union.

(2) The convocation of any revision conference shall be decided upon by the Assembly.

(3) Articles 5 to 8 may be amended either by a revision conference or according to Article 8.

Article 12
Denunciation

(1) Any country may denounce this Act by notification addressed to the Director General. Such denunciation shall constitute also denunciation of the earlier Act or Acts of this Agreement which the country denouncing this Act may have ratified or acceded to, and shall affect only the country making it, the Agreement remaining in full force and effect as regards the other countries of the Special Union.

(2) Denunciation shall take effect one year after the day on which the Director General has received the notification.

(3) The right of denunciation provided by this Article shall not be exercised by any country before the expiration of five years from the date upon which it becomes a country of the Special Union.

Article 13
Reference to Article 24 of the Paris Convention

The provisions of Article 24 of the Stockholm Act of 1967 of the Paris Convention for the Protection of Industrial Property shall apply to this Agreement, provided that, if those provisions are amended in the future, the latest amendment shall apply to this Agreement with respect to those countries of the Special Union which are bound by such amendment.

Article 14
Signature; Languages; Depositary Functions; Notifications

(1)

(a) This Act shall be signed in a single original in the English and French languages, both texts being equally authentic, and shall be deposited with the Director General.

(b) Official texts of this Act shall be established by the Director General, after consultation with the interested Governments and within two months from the date of signature of this Act, in the two other languages, Russian and Spanish, in which, together with the languages referred to in subparagraph (a), authentic texts of the Convention Establishing the World Intellectual Property Organization were signed.

(c) Official texts of this Act shall be established by the Director General, after consultation with the interested Governments, in the Arabic, German, Italian and Portuguese languages, and such other languages as the Assembly may designate.

(2) This Act shall remain open for signature until December 31, 1977.

(3)

(a) The Director General shall transmit two copies, certified by him, of the signed text of this Act to the Governments of all countries of the Special Union and, on request, to the Government of any other country.

(b) The Director General shall transmit two copies, certified by him, of any amendment to this Act to the Governments of all countries of the Special Union and, on request, to the Government of any other country.

(4) The Director General shall register this Act with the Secretariat of the United Nations.

(5) The Director General shall notify the Governments of all countries party to the Paris Convention for the Protection of Industrial Property of:

  (i)   signatures under paragraph (1);

  (ii)   deposits of instruments of ratification or accession under Article 9(3);

  (iii) the date of entry into force of this Act under Article 9(4)(a);

  (iv)   acceptances of amendments to this Act under Article 8(3);

  (v)   the dates on which such amendments enter into force;

  (vi)   denunciations received under Article 12.

EC TRADEMARK REGULATION
Council Regulation (EC) No 40/94 of 20 December 1993 on the Community trade mark, as amended by Council Regulation (EC) No 3288/94 of 22 December 1994

THE COUNCIL OF THE EUROPEAN UNION,

Having regard to the Treaty establishing the European Community, and in particular Article 235 thereof,

Having regard to the proposal from the Commission,

Having regard to the opinion of the European Parliament,

Having regard to the opinion of the Economic and Social Committee,

Whereas it is desirable to promote throughout the Community a harmonious development of economic activities and a continuous and balanced expansion by completing an internal market which functions properly and offers conditions which are similar to those obtaining in a national market; whereas in order to create a market of this kind and make it increasingly a single market, not only must be barriers to free movement of goods and services be removed and arrangements be instituted which ensure that competition is not distorted, but, in addition, legal conditions must be created which enable undertakings to adapt their activities to the scale of the Community, whether in manufacturing and distributing goods or in providing services; whereas for those purposes, trade marks enabling the products and services of undertakings to be distinguished by identical means throughout the entire Community, regardless of frontiers, should feature amongst the legal instruments which undertakings have at their disposal;

Whereas action by the Community would appear to be necessary for the purpose of attaining the Community's said objectives; whereas such action involves the creation of Community arrangements for trade marks whereby undertakings can by means of one procedural system obtain Community trade marks to which uniform protection is given and which produce their effects throughout the entire area of the Community; whereas the principle of the unitary character of the Community trade mark thus stated will apply unless otherwise provided for in this Regulation;

Whereas the barrier of territoriality of the rights conferred on proprietors of trade marks by the laws of the Member States cannot be removed by approximation of laws; whereas in order to open up unrestricted economic activity in the whole of the common market for the benefit of undertakings, trade marks need to be created which are governed by a uniform Community law directly applicable in all Member States;

Whereas since the Treaty has not provided the specific powers to establish such a legal instrument, Article 235 of the Treaty should be applied;

Whereas the Community law relating to trade marks nevertheless does not replace the laws of the Member States on trade marks; whereas it would not in fact appear to be justified to require undertakings to apply for registration of their trade marks as Community trade marks; whereas national trade marks continue to be necessary for those undertakings which do not want protection of their trade marks at Community level;

Whereas the rights in a Community trade mark may not be obtained otherwise than by registration, and registration is to be refused in particular if the trade mark is not distinctive, if it is unlawful or if it conflicts with earlier rights;

Whereas the protection afforded by a Community trade mark, the function of which is in particular to guarantee the trade mark as an indication of origin, is absolute in the case of identity between the mark and the sign and the goods or services; whereas the protection applies also in cases of similarity between the mark and the sign and the goods or services;

Whereas an interpretation should be given of the concept of similarity in relation to the likelihood of confusion; whereas the likelihood of confusion, the appreciation of which depends on numerous elements and, in particular, on the recognition of the trade mark on the market, the association which can be made with the used or registered sign, the degree of similarity between the trade mark and the sign and between the goods or services identified, constitutes the specific condition for such protection;

Whereas it follows from the principle of free flow of goods that the proprietor of a Community trade mark must not be entitled to prohibit its use by a third party in relation to goods which have been put into circulation in the Community, under the trade mark, by him or with his consent, save where there exist legitimate reasons for the proprietor to oppose further commercialization of the goods;

Whereas there is no justification for protecting Community trade marks or, as against them, any trade mark which has been registered before them, except where the trade marks are actually used;

Whereas a Community trade mark is to be regarded as an object of property which exists separately from the undertakings whose goods or services are designated by it; whereas accordingly, it must be capable of being transferred, subject to the overriding need to prevent the public being misled as a result of the transfer. It must also be capable of being charged as security in favour of a third party and of being the subject matter of licences;

Whereas administrative measures are necessary at Community level for implementing in relation to every trade mark the trade mark law created by this Regulation; whereas it is therefore essential, while retaining the Community's existing institutional structure and balance of powers, to establish an Office for Harmonization in the Internal Market (trade marks and designs) which is independent in relation to technical matters and has legal, administrative and financial autonomy; whereas to this end it is necessary and appropriate that it should be a body of the Community having legal personality and exercising the implementing powers which are conferred on it by this Regulation, and that it should operate within the framework of Community law without detracting from the competencies exercised by the Community institutions;

Whereas it is necessary to ensure that parties who are affected by decisions made by the Office are protected by the law in a manner which is suited to the special character of trade mark law; whereas to that end provision is made for an appeal to lie from decisions of the examiners and of the various divisions of the Office; whereas if the department whose decision is contested does not rectify its decision it is to remit the appeal to a Board of Appeal of the Office, which is to decide on it; whereas decisions of the Boards of Appeal are, in turn, amenable to actions before the Court of Justice of the European Communities, which has jurisdiction to annul or to alter the contested decision;

Whereas under Council Decision 88/591/ECSC, EEC, Euratom of 24 October 1988 establishing a Court of First Instance of the European Communities, as amended by Decision 93/350/Euratom, ECSC, EEC of 8 June 1993, that Court shall exercise at the first instance the jurisdiction conferred on the Court of Justice by the Treaties establishing the Communities with particular regard to appeals lodged under the second subparagraph of Article 173 of the EC Treaty and by the acts adopted in implementation thereof, save as otherwise provided in an act setting up a body governed by Community law; whereas the jurisdiction which this Regulation confers on the Court of Justice to cancel and reform decisions of the appeal courts shall accordingly be exercised at the first instance by the Court in accordance with the above Decision;

Whereas in order to strengthen the protection of Community trade marks the Member States should designate, having regard to their own national system, as limited a number as possible of national courts of first and second instance having jurisdiction in matters of infringement and validity of Community trade marks;

Whereas decisions regarding the validity and infringement of Community trade marks must have effect and cover the entire area of the Community, as this is the only way of preventing inconsistent decisions on the part of the courts and the Office and of ensuring that the unitary character of Community trade marks is not undermined; whereas the rules contained in the Brussels Convention of Jurisdiction and the Enforcement of Judgments in Civil and Commercial Matters will apply to all actions at law relating to Community trade marks, save where this Regulation derogates from those rules;

Whereas contradictory judgments should be avoided in actions which involve the same acts and the same parties and which are brought on the basis of a Community trade mark and parallel national trade marks; whereas for this purpose, when the actions are brought in the same Member State, the way in which this is to be achieved is a matter for national procedural rules, which are not prejudiced by this Regulation, whilst when the actions are brought in different Member States, provisions modelled on the rules on lis pendens and related actions of the abovementioned Brussels Convention appear appropriate;

Whereas in order to guarantee the full autonomy and independence of the

Office, it is considered necessary to grant it an autonomous budget whose revenue comes principally from fees paid by the users of the system; whereas however, the Community budgetary procedure remains applicable as far as any subsidies chargeable to general budget of the European Communities are concerned; whereas moreover, the auditing of accounts should be undertaken by the Court of Auditors;

Whereas implementing measures are required for the Regulation's application, particularly as regards the adoption and amendment of fees regulations and an Implementing Regulation; whereas such measures should be adopted by the Commission, assisted by a Committee composed of representatives of the Member States, in accordance with the procedural rules laid down in Article 2, procedure III(b), of Council Decision 87/373/EEC of 13 July 1987 laying down the procedures for the exercise of implementing powers conferred on the Commission,

HAS ADOPTED THIS REGULATION:

TITLE I
GENERAL PROVISIONS

Article 1
Community trade mark

1. A trade mark for goods or services which is registered in accordance with the conditions contained in this Regulation and in the manner herein provided is hereinafter referred to as a Community trade mark.

2. A Community trade mark shall have a unitary character. It shall have equal effect throughout the Community: it shall not be registered, transferred or surrendered or be the subject of a decision revoking the rights of the proprietor or declaring it invalid, nor shall its use be prohibited, save in respect of the whole Community. This principle shall apply unless otherwise provided in this Regulation.

Article 2
Office

An Office for Harmonization in the Internal Market (trade marks and designs), hereinafter referred to as the Office, is hereby established.

Article 3
Capacity to act

For the purpose of implementing this Regulation, companies or firms and other legal bodies shall be regarded as legal persons if, under the terms of the law governing them, they have the capacity in their own name to have rights and obligations of all kinds, to make contracts or accomplish other legal acts and to sue and be sued.

TITLE II
THE LAW RELATING TO TRADE MARKS

SECTION 1
DEFINITION OF A COMMUNITY TRADE MARK OBTAINING A COMMUNITY TRADE MARK

Article 4
Signs of which a Community trade mark may consist

A Community trade mark may consist of any signs capable of being represented graphically, particularly words, including personal names, designs, letters, numerals, the shape of goods or of their packaging, provided that such signs are capable of distinguishing the goods or services of one undertaking from those of other undertakings.

Article 5
Persons who can be proprietors of Community trade marks

1. The following natural or legal persons, including authorities established under public law, may be proprietors of Community trade marks:

(a) nationals of the Member States; or

(b) nationals of other States which are parties to the Paris Convention for the protection of industrial property, hereinafter referred to as the Paris Convention, or to the Agreement establishing the World Trade Organization; or

(c) nationals of States which are not parties to the Paris Convention who are domiciled or have their seat or who have real and effective industrial or commercial establishments within the territory of the Community or of a State which is party to the Paris Convention; or

(d) nationals, other than those referred to under subparagraph (c), of any State which is not party to the Paris Convention or to the Agreement establishing the World Trade Organization; and which, according to published findings, accords to nationals of all the Member States the same protection for trade marks as it accords to its own nationals and, if nationals of the Member States are required to prove registration in the country of origin, recognizes the registration of Community trade marks as such proof.

2. With respect to the application of paragraph 1, stateless persons as defined by Article 1 of the Convention relating to the Status of Stateless Persons signed at New York on 28 September 1954, and refugees as defined by Article 1 of the Convention relating to the Status of Refugees signed at Geneva on 28 July 1951 and modified by the Protocol relating to the Status of Refugees signed at New York on 31 January 1967, shall be regarded as nationals of the country in which they have their habitual residence.

3. Persons who are nationals of a State covered by paragraph 1(d) must prove that the trade mark for which an application for a Community trade

mark has been submitted is registered in the State of origin, unless, according to published findings, the trade marks of nationals of the Member States are registered in the State of origin in question without proof of prior registration as a Community trade mark or as a national trade mark in a Member State.

Article 6
Means whereby a Community trade mark is obtained

A Community trade mark shall be obtained by registration.

Article 7
Absolute grounds for refusal

1. The following shall not be registered:

(a) signs which do not conform to the requirements of Article 4;

(b) trade marks which are devoid of any distinctive character;

(c) trade marks which consist exclusively of signs or indications which may serve, in trade, to designate the kind, quality, quantity, intended purpose, value, geographical origin or the time of production of the goods or of rendering of the service, or other characteristics of the goods or service;

(d) trade marks which consist exclusively of signs or indications which have become customary in the current language or in the bona fide and established practices of the trade;

(e) signs which consist exclusively of:

(i)   the shape which results from the nature of the goods themselves; or

(ii)   the shape of goods which is necessary to obtain a technical result; or

(iii)   the shape which gives substantial value to the goods;

(f) trade marks which are contrary to public policy or to accepted principles of morality;

(g) trade marks which are of such a nature as to deceive the public, for instance as to the nature, quality or geographical origin of the goods or service;

(h) trade marks which have not been authorized by the competent authorities and are to be refused pursuant to Article 6ter of the Paris Convention;

(i)   trade marks which include badges, emblems or escutcheons other than those covered by Article 6ter of the Paris Convention and which are of particular public interest, unless the consent of the appropriate authorities to their registration has been given.

(j) trade marks for wines which contain or consist of a geographical indication identifying wines or for spirits which contain or consist of a geographical indication identifying spirits with respect to such wines or spirits not having that origin.

2. Paragraph 1 shall apply notwithstanding that the grounds of non-registrability obtain in only part of the Community.

3. Paragraph 1 (b), (c) and (d) shall not apply if the trade mark has become distinctive in relation to the goods or services for which registration is requested in consequence of the use which has been made of it.

Article 8
Relative grounds for refusal

1. Upon opposition by the proprietor of an earlier trade mark, the trade mark applied for shall not be registered:

(a) if it is identical with the earlier trade mark and the goods or services for which registration is applied for are identical with the goods or services for which the earlier trade mark is protected;

(b) if because of its identity with or similarity to the earlier trade mark and the identity or similarity of the goods or services covered by the trade marks there exists a likelihood of confusion on the part of the public in the territory in which the earlier trade mark is protected; the likelihood of confusion includes the likelihood of association with the earlier trade mark.

2. For the purposes of paragraph 1, "Earlier trade marks" means:

(a) trade marks of the following kinds with a date of application for registration which is earlier than the date of application for registration of the Community trade mark, taking account, where appropriate, of the priorities claimed in respect of those trade marks:

(i)   Community trade marks;

(ii)   trade marks registered in a Member State, or, in the case of Belgium, the Netherlands or Luxembourg, at the Benelux Trade Mark Office;

(iii) trade marks registered under international arrangements which have effect in a Member State;

(b) applications for the trade marks referred to in subparagraph (a), subject to their registration;

(c) trade marks which, on the date of application for registration of the Community trade mark, or, where appropriate, of the priority claimed in respect of the application for registration of the Community trade mark, are well known in a Member State, in the sense in which the words well known are used in Article 6*bis* of the Paris Convention.

3. Upon opposition by the proprietor of the trade mark, a trade mark shall not be registered where an agent or representative of the proprietor of the trade mark applies for registration thereof in his own name without the proprietor's consent, unless the agent or representative justifies his action.

4. Upon opposition by the proprietor of a non-registered trade mark or of

another sign used in the course of trade of more than mere local significance, the trade mark applied for shall not be registered where and to the extent that, pursuant to the law of the Member State governing that sign:

(a) rights to that sign were acquired prior to the date of application for registration of the Community trade mark, or the date of the priority claimed for the application for registration of the Community trade mark;

(b) that sign confers on its proprietor the right to prohibit the use of a subsequent trade mark.

5. Furthermore, upon opposition by the proprietor of an earlier trade mark within the meaning of paragraph 2, the trade mark applied for shall not be registered where it is identical with or similar to the earlier trade mark and is to be registered for goods or services which are not similar to those for which the earlier trade mark is registered, where in the case of an earlier Community trade mark the trade mark has a reputation in the Community and, in the case of an earlier national trade mark, the trade mark has a reputation in the Member State concerned and where the use without due cause of the trade mark applied for would take unfair advantage of, or be detrimental to, the distinctive character or the repute of the earlier trade mark.

SECTION 2
EFFECTS OF COMMUNITY TRADE MARKS

Article 9
Rights conferred by a Community trade mark

1. A Community trade mark shall confer on the proprietor exclusive rights therein. The proprietor shall be entitled to prevent all third parties not having his consent from using in the course of trade:

(a) any sign which is identical with the Community trade mark in relation to goods or services which are identical with those for which the Community trade mark is registered;

(b) any sign where, because of its identity with or similarity to the Community trade mark and the identity or similarity of the goods or services covered by the Community trade mark and the sign, there exists a likelihood of confusion on the part of the public; the likelihood of confusion includes the likelihood of association between the sign and the trade mark;

(c) any sign which is identical with or similar to the Community trade mark in relation to goods or services which are not similar to those for which the Community trade mark is registered, where the latter has a reputation in the Community and where use of that sign without due cause takes unfair advantage of, or is detrimental to, the distinctive character or the repute of the Community trade mark.

2. The following, *inter alia*, may be prohibited under paragraph 1:

(a) affixing the sign to the goods or to the packaging thereof;

(b) offering the goods, putting them on the market or stocking them for these purposes under that sign, or offering or supplying services thereunder;

(c) importing or exporting the goods under that sign;

(d) using the sign on business papers and in advertising.

3. The rights conferred by a Community trade mark shall prevail against third parties from the date of publication of registration of the trade mark. Reasonable compensation may, however, be claimed in respect of matters arising after the date of publication of a Community trade mark application, which matters would, after publication of the registration of the trade mark, be prohibited by virtue of that publication. The court seized of the case may not decide upon the merits of the case until the registration has been published.

Article 10
Reproduction of Community trade marks in dictionaries

If the reproduction of a Community trade mark in a dictionary, encyclopaedia or similar reference work gives the impression that it constitutes the generic name of the goods or services for which the trade mark is registered, the publisher of the work shall, at the request of the proprietor of the Community trade mark, ensure that the reproduction of the trade mark at the latest in the next edition of the publication is accompanied by an indication that it is a registered trade mark.

Article 11
Prohibition on the use of a Community trade mark registered in the name of an agent or representative

Where a Community trade mark is registered in the name of the agent or representative of a person who is the proprietor of that trade mark, without the proprietor's authorization, the latter shall be entitled to oppose the use of his mark by his agent or representative if he has not authorized such use, unless the agent or representative justifies his action.

Article 12
Limitation of the effects of a Community trade mark

A Community trade mark shall not entitle the proprietor to prohibit a third party from using in the course of trade:

(a) his own name or address;

(b) indications concerning the kind, quality, quantity, intended purpose, value, geographical origin, the time of production of the goods or of rendering of the service, or other characteristics of the goods or service;

(c) the trade mark where it is necessary to indicate the intended purpose of a product or service, in particular as accessories or spare parts, provided he uses them in accordance with honest practices in industrial or commercial matters.

Article 13
Exhaustion of the rights conferred by a Community trade mark

1. A Community trade mark shall not entitle the proprietor to prohibit its use in relation to goods which have been put on the market in the Community under that trade mark by the proprietor or with his consent.

2. Paragraph 1 shall not apply where there exist legitimate reasons for the proprietor to oppose further commercialization of the goods, especially where the condition of the goods is changed or impaired after they have been put on the market.

Article 14
Complementary application of national law relating to infringement

1. The effects of Community trade marks shall be governed solely by the provisions of this Regulation. In other respects, infringement of a Community trade mark shall be governed by the national law relating to infringement of a national trade mark in accordance with the provisions of Title X.

2. This Regulation shall not prevent actions concerning a Community trade mark being brought under the law of Member States relating in particular to civil liability and unfair competition.

3. The rules of procedure to be applied shall be determined in accordance with the provisions of Title X.

SECTION 3
USE OF COMMUNITY TRADE MARKS

Article 15
Use of Community trade marks

1. If, within a period of five years following registration, the proprietor has not put the Community trade mark to genuine use in the Community in connection with the goods or services in respect of which it is registered, or if such use has been suspended during an uninterrupted period of five years, the Community trade mark shall be subject to the sanctions provided for in this Regulation, unless there are proper reasons for non-use.

2. The following shall also constitute use within the meaning of paragraph 1:

(a) use of the Community trade mark in a form differing in elements which do not alter the distinctive character of the mark in the form in which it was registered;

(b) affixing of the Community trade mark to goods or to the packaging thereof in the Community solely for export purposes.

3. Use of the Community trade mark with the consent of the proprietor shall be deemed to constitute use by the proprietor.

SECTION 4
COMMUNITY TRADE MARKS AS OBJECTS OF PROPERTY

Article 16
Dealing with Community trade marks as national trade marks

1. Unless Articles 17 to 24 provide otherwise, a Community trade mark as an object of property shall be dealt with in its entirety, and for the whole area of the Community, as a national trade mark registered in the Member State in which, according to the Register of Community trade marks:

(a) the proprietor has his seat or his domicile on the relevant date; or

(b) where subparagraph (a) does not apply, the proprietor has an establishment on the relevant date.

2. In cases which are not provided for by paragraph 1, the Member State referred to in that paragraph shall be the Member State in which the seat of the Office is situated.

3. If two or more persons are mentioned in the Register of Community trade marks as joint proprietors, paragraph 1 shall apply to the joint proprietor first mentioned; failing this, it shall apply to the subsequent joint proprietors in the order in which they are mentioned. Where paragraph 1 does not apply to any of the joint proprietors, paragraph 2 shall apply.

Article 17
Transfer

1. A Community trade mark may be transferred, separately from any transfer of the undertaking, in respect of some or all of the goods or services for which it is registered.

2. A transfer of the whole of the undertaking shall include the transfer of the Community trade mark except where, in accordance with the law governing the transfer, there is agreement to the contrary or circumstances clearly dictate otherwise. This provision shall apply to the contractual obligation to transfer the undertaking.

3. Without prejudice to paragraph 2, an assignment of the Community trade mark shall be made in writing and shall require the signature of the parties to the contract, except when it is a result of a judgment; otherwise it shall be void.

4. Where it is clear from the transfer documents that because of the transfer the Community trade mark is likely to mislead the public concerning the nature, quality or geographical origin of the goods or services in respect of which it is registered, the Office shall not register the transfer unless the successor agrees to limit registration of the Community trade mark to goods or services in respect of which it is not likely to mislead.

5. On request of one of the parties a transfer shall be entered in the Register and published.

6. As long as the transfer has not been entered in the Register, the successor in title may not invoke the rights arising from the registration of the Community trade mark.

7. Where there are time limits to be observed *vis-à-vis* the Office, the successor in title may make the corresponding statements to the Office once the request for registration of the transfer has been received by the Office.

8. All documents which require notification to the proprietor of the Community trade mark in accordance with Article 77 shall be addressed to the person registered as proprietor.

Article 18
Transfer of a trade mark registered in the name of an agent

Where a Community trade mark is registered in the name of the agent or representative of a person who is the proprietor of that trade mark, without the proprietor's authorization, the latter shall be entitled to demand the assignment in his favour of the said registration, unless such agent or representative justifies his action.

Article 19
Rights in rem

1. A Community trade mark may, independently of the undertaking, be given as security or be the subject of rights in rem.

2. On request of one of the parties, rights mentioned in paragraph 1 shall be entered in the Register and published.

Article 20
Levy of execution

1. A Community trade mark may be levied in execution.

2. As regards the procedure for levy of execution in respect of a Community trade mark, the courts and authorities of the Member States determined in accordance with Article 16 shall have exclusive jurisdiction.

3. On request of one the parties, levy of execution shall be entered in the Register and published.

Article 21
Bankruptcy or like proceedings

1. Until such time as common rules for the Member States in this field enter into force, the only Member State in which a Community trade mark may be involved in bankruptcy or like proceedings shall be that in which such proceedings are first brought within the meaning of national law or of conventions applicable in this field.

2. Where a Community trade mark is involved in bankruptcy or like proceedings, on request of the competent national authority an entry to this effect shall be made in the Register and published.

Article 22
Licensing

1. A Community trade mark may be licensed for some or all of the goods or services for which it is registered and for the whole or part of the Community. A licence may be exclusive or non-exclusive.

2. The proprietor of a Community trade mark may invoke the rights conferred by that trade mark against a licensee who contravenes any provision in his licensing contract with regard to its duration, the form covered by the registration in which the trade mark may be used, the scope of the goods or services for which the licence is granted, the territory in which the trade mark may be affixed, or the quality of the goods manufactured or of the services provided by the licensee.

3. Without prejudice to the provisions of the licensing contract, the licensee may bring proceedings for infringement of a Community trade mark only if its proprietor consents thereto. However, the holder of an exclusive licence may bring such proceedings if the proprietor of the trade mark, after formal notice, does not himself bring infringement proceedings within an appropriate period.

4. A licensee shall, for the purpose of obtaining compensation for damage suffered by him, be entitled to intervene in infringement proceedings brought by the proprietor of the Community trade mark.

5. On request of one of the parties the grant or transfer of a licence in respect of a Community trade mark shall be entered in the Register and published.

Article 23
Effects vis-à-vis third parties

1. Legal acts referred to in Article 17, 19 and 22 concerning a Community trade mark shall only have effects *vis-à-vis* third parties in all the Member States after entry in the Register. Nevertheless, such an act, before it is so entered, shall have effect *vis-à-vis* third parties who have acquired rights in the trade mark after the date of that act but who knew of the act at the date on which the rights were acquired.

2. Paragraph 1 shall not apply in the case of a person who acquires the Community trade mark or a right concerning the Community trade mark by way of transfer of the whole of the undertaking or by any other universal succession.

3. The effects *vis-à-vis* third parties of the legal acts referred to in Article 20 shall be governed by the law of the Member State determined in accordance with Article 16.

4. Until such time as common rules for the Member States in the field of bankruptcy enter into force, the effects *vis-à-vis* third parties of bankruptcy or like proceedings shall be governed by the law of the Member State in which such proceedings are first brought within the meaning of national law or of conventions applicable in this field.

Article 24
The application for a Community trade mark as an object of property

Articles 16 to 23 shall apply to applications for Community trade marks.

TITLE III
APPLICATION FOR COMMUNITY TRADE MARKS

SECTION 1
FILING OF APPLICATIONS AND THE CONDITIONS WHICH GOVERN THEM

Article 25
Filing of applications

1. An application for a Community trade mark shall be filed, at the choice of the applicant,

(a) at the Office; or

(b) at the central industrial property office of a Member State or at the Benelux Trade Mark Office. An application filed in this way shall have the same effect as if it had been filed on the same date at the Office.

2. Where the application is filed at the central industrial property office of a Member State or at the Benelux Trade Mark Office, that office shall take all steps to forward the application to the Office within two weeks after filing. It may charge the applicant a fee which shall not exceed the administrative costs of receiving and forwarding the application.

3. Applications referred to in paragraph 2 which reach the Office more than one month after filing shall be deemed withdrawn.

4. Ten years after the entry into force of this Regulation, the Commission shall draw up a report on the operation of the system of filing applications for Community trade marks, together with any proposals for modifying this system.

Article 26
Conditions with which applications must comply

1. An application for a Community trade mark shall contain:

(a) a request for the registration of a Community trade mark;

(b) information identifying the applicant;

(c) a list of the goods or services in respect of which the registration is requested;

(d) a representation of the trade mark.

2. The application for a Community trade mark shall be subject to the payment of the application fee and, when appropriate, of one or more class fees.

3. An application for a Community trade mark must comply with the conditions laid down in the implementing Regulation referred to in Article 140.

Article 27
Date of filing

The date of filing of a Community trade mark application shall be the date on which documents containing the information specified in Article 26(1) are filed with the Office by the applicant or, if the application has been filed with the central office of a Member State or with the Benelux Trade Mark Office, with that office, subject to payment of the application fee within a period of one month of filing the abovementioned documents.

Article 28
Classification

Goods and services in respect of which Community trade marks are applied for shall be classified in conformity with the system of classification specified in the Implementing Regulation.

SECTION 2
PRIORITY

Article 29
Right of priority

1. A person who has duly filed an application for a trade mark in or for any State party to the Paris Convention or to the Agreement establishing the World Trade Organization, or his successors in title, shall enjoy, for the purpose of filing a Community trade mark application for the same trade mark in respect of goods or services which are identical with or contained within those for which the application has been filed, a right of priority during a period of six months from the date of filing of the first application.

2. Every filing that is equivalent to a regular national filing under the national law of the State where it was made or under bilateral or multilateral agreements shall be recognized as giving rise to a right of priority.

3. By a regular national filing is meant any filing that is sufficient to establish the date on which the application was filed, whatever may be the outcome of the application.

4. A subsequent application for a trade mark which was the subject of a previous first application in respect of the same goods or services, and which is filed in or in respect of the same State shall be considered as the first application for the purposes of determining priority, provided that, at the date of filing of the subsequent application, the previous application has been withdrawn, abandoned or refused, without being open to public inspection and without leaving any rights outstanding, and has not served as a basis for claiming a right of priority. The previous application may not thereafter serve as a basis for claiming a right of priority.

5. If the first filing has been made in a State which is not a party to the Paris Convention or to the Agreement establishing the World Trade Organization, paragraphs 1 to 4 shall apply only in so far as that State, according to published findings, grants, on the basis of a first filing made at the Office and subject to conditions equivalent to those laid down in this Regulation, a right of priority having equivalent effect.

Article 30
Claiming priority

An applicant desiring to take advantage of the priority of a previous application shall file a declaration of priority and a copy of the previous application. If the language of the latter is not one of the languages of the Office, the applicant shall file a translation of the previous application in one of those languages.

Article 31
Effect of priority right

The right of priority shall have the effect that the date of priority shall count as the date of filing of the Community trade mark application for the purposes of establishing which rights take precedence.

Article 32
Equivalence of Community filing with national filing

A Community trade mark application which has been accorded a date of filing shall, in the Member States, be equivalent to a regular national filing, where appropriate with the priority claimed for the Community trade mark application.

SECTION 3
EXHIBITION PRIORITY

Article 33
Exhibition priority

1. If an applicant for a Community trade mark has displayed goods or services under the mark applied for, at an official or officially recognized

international exhibition falling within the terms of the Convention on International Exhibitions signed at Paris on 22 November 1928 and last revised on 30 November 1972, he may, if he files the application within a period of six months from the date of the first display of the goods or services under the mark applied for, claim a right of priority from that date within the meaning of Article 31.

2. An applicant who wishes to claim priority pursuant to paragraph 1 must file evidence of the display of goods or services under the mark applied for under the conditions laid down in the Implementing Regulation.

3. An exhibition priority granted in a Member State or in a third country does not extend the period of priority laid down in Article 29.

SECTION 4
CLAIMING THE SENIORITY OF A NATIONAL TRADE MARK

Article 34
Claiming the seniority of a national trade mark

1. The proprietor of an earlier trade mark registered in a Member State, including a trade mark registered in the Benelux countries, or registered under international arrangements having effect in a Member State, who applies for an identical trade mark for registration as a Community trade mark for goods or services which are identical with or contained within those for which the earlier trade mark has been registered, may claim for the Community trade mark the seniority of the earlier trade mark in respect of the Member State in or for which it is registered.

2. Seniority shall have the sole effect under this Regulation that, where the proprietor of the Community trade mark surrenders the earlier trade mark or allows it to lapse, he shall be deemed to continue to have the same rights as he would have had if the earlier trade mark had continued to be registered.

3. The seniority claimed for the Community trade mark shall lapse if the earlier trade mark the seniority of which is claimed is declared to have been revoked or to be invalid or if it is surrendered prior to the registration of the Community trade mark.

Article 35
Claiming seniority after registration of the
Community trade mark

1. The proprietor of a Community trade mark who is the proprietor of an earlier identical trade mark registered in a Member State, including a trade mark registered in the Benelux countries, or of a trade mark registered under international arrangements having effect in a Member State, for identical goods or services, may claim the seniority of the earlier trade mark in respect of the Member State in or for which it is registered.

2. Article 34 (2) and (3) shall apply.

TITLE IV
REGISTRATION PROCEDURE

SECTION 1
EXAMINATION OF APPLICATIONS

Article 36
Examination of the conditions of filing

1. The Office shall examine whether:

(a) the Community trade mark application satisfies the requirements for the accordance of a date of filing in accordance with Article 27;

(b) the Community trade mark application complies with the conditions laid down in the Implementing Regulation;

(c) where appropriate, the class fees have been paid within the prescribed period.

2. Where the Community trade mark application does not satisfy the requirements referred to in paragraph 1, the Office shall request the applicant to remedy the deficiencies or the default on payment within the prescribed period.

3. If the deficiencies or the default on payment established pursuant to paragraph 1(a) are not remedied within this period, the application shall not be dealt with as a Community trade mark application. If the applicant complies with the Office's request, the Office shall accord as the date of filing of the application the date on which the deficiencies or the default on payment established are remedied.

4. If the deficiencies established pursuant to paragraph 1(b) are not remedied within the prescribed period, the Office shall refuse the application.

5. If the default on payment established pursuant to paragraph 1(c) is not remedied within the prescribed period, the application shall be deemed to be withdrawn unless it is clear which categories of goods or services the amount paid is intended to cover.

6. Failure to satisfy the requirements concerning the claim to priority shall result in loss of the right of priority for the application.

7. Failure to satisfy the requirements concerning the claiming of seniority of a national trade mark shall result in loss of that right for the application.

Article 37
Examination of the conditions relating to the entitlement of the proprietor

1. Where, pursuant to Article 5, the applicant may not be the proprietor of a Community trade mark, the application shall be refused.

2. The application may not be refused before the applicant has been given the opportunity to withdraw his application or submit his observations.

Article 38
Examination as to absolute grounds for refusal

1. Where, under Article 7, a trade mark is ineligible for registration in respect of some or all of the goods or services covered by the Community trade mark application, the application shall be refused as regards those goods or services.

2. Where the trade mark contains an element which is not distinctive, and where the inclusion of said element in the trade mark could give rise to doubts as to the scope of protection of the trade mark, the Office may request, as a condition for registration of said trade mark, that the applicant state that he disclaims any exclusive right to such element. Any disclaimer shall be published together with the application or the registration of the Community trade mark, as the case may be.

3. The application shall not be refused before the applicant has been allowed the opportunity of withdrawing or amending the application or of submitting his observations.

SECTION 2
SEARCH

Article 39
Search

1. Once the Office has accorded a date of filing to a Community trade mark application and has established that the applicant satisfies the conditions referred to in Article 5, it shall draw up a Community search report citing those earlier Community trade marks or Community trade mark applications discovered which may be invoked under Article 8 against the registration of the Community trade mark applied for.

2. As soon as a Community trade mark application has been accorded a date of filing, the Office shall transmit a copy thereof to the central industrial property office of each Member State which has informed the Office of its decision to operate a search in its own register of trade marks in respect of Community trade mark applications.

3. Each of the central industrial property offices referred to in paragraph 2 shall communicate to the Office within three months as from the date on which it received the Community trade mark application a search report which shall either cite those earlier national trade marks or trade mark applications discovered which may be invoked under Article 8 against the registration of the Community trade mark applied for, or state that the search has revealed no such rights.

4. An amount shall be paid by the Office to each central industrial property office for each search report provided by that office in accordance with paragraph 3. The amount, which shall be the same for each office, shall be fixed by the Budget Committee by means of a decision adopted by a majority of three-quarters of the representatives of the Member States.

5. The Office shall transmit without delay to the applicant for the Community trade mark the Community search report and the national search reports received within the time limit laid down in paragraph 3.

6. Upon publication of the Community trade mark application, which may not take place before the expiry of a period of one month as from the date on which the Office transmits the search reports to the applicant, the Office shall inform the proprietors of any earlier Community trade marks or Community trade mark applications cited in the Community search report of the publication of the Community trade mark application.

7. The Commission shall, five years after the opening of the Office for the filing of applications, submit to the Council a report on the operation of the system of searching resulting from this Article, including the payments made to Member States under paragraph 4, and, if necessary, appropriate proposals for amending this Regulation with a view to adapting the system of searching on the basis of the experience gained and bearing in mind developments in searching techniques.

SECTION 3
PUBLICATION OF THE APPLICATION

Article 40
Publication of the application

1. If the conditions which the application for a Community trade mark must satisfy have been fulfilled and if the period referred to in Article 39(6) has expired, the application shall be published to the extent that it has not been refused pursuant to Articles 37 and 38.

2. Where, after publication, the application is refused under Articles 37 and 38, the decision that it has been refused shall be published upon becoming final.

SECTION 4
OBSERVATIONS BY THIRD PARTIES AND OPPOSITION

Article 41
Observations by third parties

1. Following the publication of the Community trade mark application, any natural or legal person and any group or body representing manufacturers, producers, suppliers of services, traders or consumers may submit to the Office written observations, explaining on which grounds under Article 7, in particular, the trade mark shall not be registered ex officio. They shall not be parties to the proceedings before the Office.

2. The observations referred to in paragraph 1 shall be communicated to the applicant who may comment on them.

Article 42
Opposition

1. Within a period of three months following the publication of a Community trade mark application, notice of opposition to registration of the trade mark may be given on the grounds that it may not be registered under Article 8:

   (a) by the proprietors of earlier trade marks referred to in Article 8(2) as well as licensees authorized by the proprietors of those trade marks, in respect of Article 8 (1) and (5);

   (b) by the proprietors of trade marks referred to in Article 8(3);

   (c) by the proprietors of earlier marks or signs referred to in Article 8(4) and by persons authorized under the relevant national law to exercise these rights.

2. Notice of opposition to registration of the trade mark may also be given, subject to the conditions laid down in paragraph 1, in the event of the publication of an amended application in accordance with the second sentence of Article 44(2).

3. Opposition must be expressed in writing and must specify the grounds on which it is made. It shall not be treated as duly entered until the opposition fee has been paid. Within a period fixed by the Office, the opponent may submit in support of his case facts, evidence and arguments.

Article 43
Examination of opposition

1. In the examination of the opposition the Office shall invite the parties, as often as necessary, to file observations, within a period set them by the Office, on communications from the other parties or issued by itself.

2. If the applicant so requests, the proprietor of an earlier Community trade mark who has given notice of opposition shall furnish proof that, during the period of five years preceding the date of publication of the Community trade mark application, the earlier Community trade mark has been put to genuine use in the Community in connection with the goods or services in respect of which it is registered and which he cites as justification for his opposition, or that there are proper reasons for non-use, provided the earlier Community trade mark has at that date been registered for not less than five years. In the absence of proof to this effect, the opposition shall be rejected. If the earlier Community trade mark has been used in relation to part only of the goods or services for which it is registered it shall, for the purposes of the examination of the opposition, be deemed to be registered in respect only of that part of the goods or services.

3. Paragraph 2 shall apply to earlier national trade marks referred to in Article 8(2)(a), by substituting use in the Member State in which the earlier national trade mark is protected for use in the Community.

4. The Office may, if it thinks fit, invite the parties to make a friendly settlement.

5. If examination of the opposition reveals that the trade mark may not be registered in respect of some or all of the goods or services for which the Community trade mark application has been made, the application shall be refused in respect of those goods or services. Otherwise the opposition shall be rejected.

6. The decision refusing the application shall be published upon becoming final.

SECTION 5
WITHDRAWAL, RESTRICTION AND AMENDMENT
OF THE APPLICATION

Article 44
Withdrawal, restriction and amendment of the application

1. The applicant may at any time withdraw his Community trade mark application or restrict the list of goods or services contained therein. Where the application has already been published, the withdrawal or restriction shall also be published.

2. In other respects, a Community trade mark application may be amended, upon request of the applicant, only by correcting the name and address of the applicant, errors of wording or of copying, or obvious mistakes, provided that such correction does not substantially change the trade mark or extend the list of goods or services. Where the amendments affect the representation of the trade mark or the list of goods or services and are made after publication of the application, the trade mark application shall be published as amended.

SECTION 6
REGISTRATION

Article 45
Registration

Where an application meets the requirements of this Regulation and where no notice of opposition has been given within the period referred to in Article 42(1) or where opposition has been rejected by a definitive decision, the trade mark shall be registered as a Community trade mark, provided that the registration fee has been paid within the period prescribed. If the fee is not paid within this period the application shall be deemed to be withdrawn.

TITLE V
DURATION, RENEWAL AND ALTERATION OF
COMMUNITY TRADE MARKS

Article 46
Duration of registration

Community trade marks shall be registered for a period of ten years from the date of filing of the application. Registration may be renewed in accordance with Article 47 for further periods of 10 years.

Article 47
Renewal

1. Registration of the Community trade mark shall be renewed at the request of the proprietor of the trade mark or any person expressly authorized by him, provided that the fees have been paid.

2. The Office shall inform the proprietor of the Community trade mark, and any person having a registered right in respect of the Community trade mark, of the expiry of the registration in good time before the said expiry. Failure to give such information shall not involve the responsibility of the Office.

3. The request for renewal shall be submitted within a period of six months ending on the last day of the month in which protection ends. The fees shall also be paid within this period. Failing this, the request may be submitted and the fees paid within a further period of six months following the day referred to in the first sentence, provided that an additional fee is paid within this further period.

4. Where the request is submitted or the fees paid in respect of only some of the goods or services for which the Community trade mark is registered, registration shall be renewed for those goods or services only.

5. Renewal shall take effect from the day following the date on which the existing registration expires. The renewal shall be registered.

Article 48
Alteration

1. The Community trade mark shall not be altered in the register during the period of registration or on renewal thereof.

2. Nevertheless, where the Community trade mark includes the name and address of the proprietor, any alteration thereof not substantially affecting the identity of the trade mark as originally registered may be registered at the request of the proprietor.

3. The publication of the registration of the alteration shall contain a representation of the Community trade mark as altered. Third parties whose rights may be affected by the alteration may challenge the registration thereof within a period of three months following publication.

TITLE VI
SURRENDER, REVOCATION AND INVALIDITY

SECTION 1
SURRENDER

Article 49
Surrender

1. A Community trade mark may be surrendered in respect of some or all of the goods or services for which it is registered.

2. The surrender shall be declared to the Office in writing by the proprietor of the trade mark. It shall not have effect until it has been entered in the Register.

3. Surrender shall be entered only with the agreement of the proprietor of a right entered in the Register. If a licence has been registered, surrender shall only be entered in the Register if the proprietor of the trade mark proves that he has informed the licensee of his intention to surrender; this entry shall be made on expiry of the period prescribed by the Implementing Regulation.

SECTION 2
GROUNDS FOR REVOCATION

Article 50
Grounds for revocation

1. The rights of the proprietor of the Community trade mark shall be declared to be revoked on application to the Office or on the basis of a counterclaim in infringement proceedings:

(a) if, within a continuous period of five years, the trade mark has not been put to genuine use in the Community in connection with the goods or services in respect of which it is registered, and there are no proper reasons for non-use; however, no person may claim that the proprietor's rights in a Community trade mark should be revoked where, during the interval between expiry of the five-year period and filing of the application or counterclaim, genuine use of the trade mark has been started or resumed; the commencement or resumption of use within a period of three months preceding the filing of the application or counterclaim which began at the earliest on expiry of the continuous period of five years of non-use shall, however, be disregarded where preparations for the commencement or resumption occur only after the proprietor becomes aware that the application or counterclaim may be filed;

(b) if, in consequence of acts or inactivity of the proprietor, the trade mark has become the common name in the trade for a product or service in respect of which it is registered;

(c) if, in consequence of the use made of it by the proprietor of the trade mark or with his consent in respect of the goods or services for which it is registered, the trade mark is liable to mislead the public, particularly as to the nature, quality or geographical origin of those goods or services;

(d) if the proprietor of the trade mark no longer satisfies the conditions laid down by Article 5.

2. Where the grounds for revocation of rights exist in respect of only some of the goods or services for which the Community trade mark is registered, the rights of the proprietor shall be declared to be revoked in respect of those goods or services only.

SECTION 3
GROUNDS FOR INVALIDITY

Article 51
Absolute grounds for invalidity

1. A Community trade mark shall be declared invalid on application to the Office or on the basis of a counterclaim in infringement proceedings,

(a) where the Community trade mark has been registered in breach of the provisions of Article 5 or of Article 7;

(b) where the applicant was acting in bad faith when he filed the application for the trade mark.

2. Where the Community trade mark has been registered in breach of the provisions of Article 7(1) (b), (c) or (d), it may nevertheless not be declared invalid if, in consequence of the use which has been made of it, it has after registration acquired a distinctive character in relation to the goods or services for which it is registered.

3. Where the ground for invalidity exists in respect of only some of the goods or services for which the Community trade mark is registered, the trade mark shall be declared invalid as regards those goods or services only.

Article 52
Relative grounds for invalidity

1. A Community trade mark shall be declared invalid on application to the Office or on the basis of a counterclaim in infringement proceedings:

(a) where there is an earlier trade mark as referred to in Article 8(2) and the conditions set out in paragraph 1 or 5 of that Article are fulfilled;

(b) where there is a trade mark as referred to in Article 8(3) and the conditions set out in that paragraph are fulfilled;

(c) where there is an earlier right as referred to in Article 8(4) and the conditions set out in that paragraph are fulfilled.

2. A Community trade mark shall also be declared invalid on application to the Office or on the basis of a counterclaim in infringement proceedings where the use of such trade mark may be prohibited pursuant to the national law governing the protection of any other earlier right an in particular:

(a) a right to a name;

(b) a right of personal portrayal;

(c) a copyright;

(d) an industrial property right.

3. A Community trade mark may not be declared invalid where the proprietor of a right referred to in paragraphs 1 or 2 consents expressly to the registration of the Community trade mark before submission of the application for a declaration of invalidity or the counterclaim.

4. Where the proprietor of one of the rights referred to in paragraphs 1 or 2 has previously applied for a declaration that a Community trade mark is invalid or made a counterclaim in infringement proceedings, he may not submit a new application for a declaration of invalidity or lodge a counterclaim on the basis of another of the said rights which he could have invoked in support of his first application or counterclaim.

5. Article 51(3) shall apply.

Article 53
Limitation in consequence of acquiescence

1. Where the proprietor of a Community trade mark has acquiesced, for a period of five successive years, in the use of a later Community trade mark in the Community while being aware of such use, he shall no longer be entitled on the basis of the earlier trade mark either to apply for a declaration that the later trade mark is invalid or to oppose the use of the later trade mark in respect of the goods or services for which the later trade mark has been used, unless registration of the later Community trade mark was applied for in bad faith.

2. Where the proprietor of an earlier national trade mark as referred to in Article 8(2) or of another earlier sign referred to in Article 8(4) has acquiesced, for a period of five successive years, in the use of a later Community trade mark in the Member State in which the earlier trade mark or the other earlier sign is protected while being aware of such use, he shall no longer be entitled on the basis of the earlier trade mark or of the other earlier sign either to apply for a declaration that the later trade mark is invalid or to oppose the use of the later trade mark in respect of the goods or services for which the later trade mark has been used, unless registration of the later Community trade mark was applied for in bad faith.

3. In the cases referred to in paragraphs 1 and 2, the proprietor of a later Community trade mark shall not be entitled to oppose the use of the earlier right, even though that right may no longer be invoked against the later Community trade mark.

SECTION 4
CONSEQUENCES OF REVOCATION AND INVALIDITY

Article 54
Consequences of revocation and invalidity

1. The Community trade mark shall be deemed not to have had, as from the date of the application for revocation or of the counterclaim, the effects

specified in this Regulation, to the extent that the rights of the proprietor have been revoked. An earlier date, on which one of the grounds for revocation occurred, may be fixed in the decision at the request of one of the parties.

2. The Community trade mark shall be deemed not to have had, as from the outset, the effects specified in this Regulation, to the extent that the trade mark has been declared invalid.

3. Subject to the national provisions relating either to claims for compensation for damage caused by negligence or lack of good faith on the part of the proprietor of the trade mark, or to unjust enrichment, the retroactive effect of revocation or invalidity of the trade mark shall not affect:

(a) any decision on infringement which has acquired the authority of a final decision and been enforced prior to the revocation or invalidity decision;

(b) any contract concluded prior to the revocation or invalidity decision, in so far as it has been performed before that decision; however, repayment, to an extent justified by the circumstances, of sums paid under the relevant contract, may be claimed on grounds of equity.

SECTION 5
PROCEEDINGS IN THE OFFICE IN RELATION TO REVOCATION OR INVALIDITY

Article 55
Application for revocation or for a declaration of invalidity

1. An application for revocation of the rights of the proprietor of a Community trade mark or for a declaration that the trade mark is invalid may be submitted to the Office:

(a) where Articles 50 and 51 apply, by any natural or legal person and any group or body set up for the purpose of representing the interests of manufacturers, producers, suppliers of services, traders or consumers, which under the terms of the law governing it has the capacity in its own name to sue and be sued;

(b) where Article 52(1) applies, by the persons referred to in Article 42(1);

(c) where Article 52(2) applies, by the owners of the earlier rights referred to in that provision or by the persons who are entitled under the law of the Member State concerned to exercise the rights in question.

2. The application shall be filed in a written reasoned statement. It shall not be deemed to have been filed until the fee has been paid.

3. An application for revocation or for a declaration of invalidity shall be inadmissible if an application relating to the same subject matter and cause of action, and involving the same parties, has been adjudicated on by a court in a Member State and has acquired the authority of a final decision.

Article 56

Examination of the application

1. In the examination of the application for revocation of rights or for a declaration of invalidity, the Office shall invite the parties, as often as necessary, to file observations, within a period to be fixed by the Office, on communications from the other parties or issued by itself.

2. If the proprietor of the Community trade mark so requests, the proprietor of an earlier Community trade mark, being a party to the invalidity proceedings, shall furnish proof that, during the period of five years preceding the date of the application for a declaration of invalidity, the earlier Community trade mark has been put to genuine use in the Community in connection with the goods or services in respect of which it is registered and which he cites as justification for his application, or that there are proper reasons for non-use, provided the earlier Community trade mark has at that date been registered for non-use, provided the earlier Community trade mark has at that date been registered for not less than five years. If, at the date on which the Community trade mark application was published, the earlier Community trade mark had been registered for not less than five years, the proprietor of the earlier Community trade mark shall furnish proof that, in addition, the conditions contained in Article 43(2) were satisfied at that date. In the absence of proof to this effect the application for a declaration of invalidity shall be rejected. If the earlier Community trade mark has been used in relation to part only of the goods or services for which it is registered it shall, for the purpose of the examination of the application for a declaration of invalidity, be deemed to be registered in respect only of that part of the goods or services.

3. Paragraph 2 shall apply to earlier national trade marks referred to in Article 8(2)(a), by substituting use the examination of the application for a declaration of invalidity, be deemed to be registered in respect only of that part of the goods or services.

4. The Office may, if it thinks fit, invite the parties to make a friendly settlement.

5. If the examination of the application for revocation of rights or for a declaration of invalidity reveals that the trade mark should not have been registered in respect of some or all of the goods or services for which it is registered, the rights of the proprietor of the Community trade mark shall be revoked or it shall be declared invalid in respect of those goods or services. Otherwise the application for revocation of rights or for a declaration of invalidity shall be rejected.

6. The decision revoking the rights of the proprietor of the Community trade mark or declaring it invalid shall be entered in the Register upon becoming final.

TITLE VII
APPEALS

Article 57

Decisions subject to appeal

1. An appeal shall lie from decisions of the examiners, Opposition Divisions, Administration of Trade Marks and Legal Division and Cancellation Divisions. It shall have suspensive effect.

2. A decision which does not terminate proceedings as regards one of the parties can only be appealed together with the final decision, unless the decision allows separate appeal.

Article 58
Persons entitled to appeal and to be parties to appeal proceedings

Any party to proceedings adversely affected by a decision may appeal. Any other parties to the proceedings shall be parties to the appeal proceedings as of right.

Article 59
Time limit and form of appeal

Notice of appeal must be filed in writing at the Office within two months after the date of notification of the decision appealed from. The notice shall be deemed to have been filed only when the fee for appeal has been paid. Within four months after the date of notification of the decision, a written statement setting out the grounds of appeal must be filed.

Article 60
Interlocutory revision

1. If the department whose decision is contested considers the appeal to be admissible and well founded, it shall rectify its decision. This shall not apply where the appellant is opposed by another party to the proceedings.

2. If the decision is not rectified within one month after receipt of the statement of grounds, the appeal shall be remitted to the Board of Appeal without delay, and without comment as to its merit.

Article 61
Examination of appeals

1. If the appeal is admissible, the Board of Appeal shall examine whether the appeal is allowable.

2. In the examination of the appeal, the Board of Appeal shall invite the parties, as often as necessary, to file observations, within a period to be fixed by the Board of Appeal, on communications from the other parties or issued by itself.

Article 62
Decisions in respect of appeals

1. Following the examination as to the allowability of the appeal, the Board of Appeal shall decide on the appeal. The Board of Appeal may either exercise any power within the competence of the department which was responsible for the decision appealed or remit the case to that department for further prosecution.

2. If the Board of Appeal remits the case for further prosecution to the department whose decision was appealed, that department shall be bound by the ratio decidendi of the Board of Appeal, in so far as the facts are the same.

3. The decisions of the Boards of Appeal shall take effect only as from the date of expiration of the period referred to in Article 63(5) or, if an action has been brought before the Court of Justice within that period, as from the date of rejection of such action.

Article 63
Actions before the Court of Justice

1. Actions may be brought before the Court of Justice against decisions of the Boards of Appeal on appeals.

2. The action may be brought on grounds of lack of competence, infringement of an essential procedural requirement, infringement of the Treaty, of this Regulation or of any rule of law relating to their application or misuse of power.

3. The Court of Justice has jurisdiction to annul or to alter the contested decision.

4. The action shall be open to any party to proceedings before the Board of Appeal adversely affected by its decision.

5. The action shall be brought before the Court of Justice within two months of the date of notification of the decision of the Board of Appeal.

6. The Office shall be required to take the necessary measures to comply with the judgment of the Court of Justice.

TITLE VIII
COMMUNITY COLLECTIVE MARKS

Article 64
Community collective marks

1. A Community collective mark shall be a Community trade mark which is described as such when the mark is applied for and is capable of distinguishing the goods or services of the members of the association which is the proprietor of the mark from those of other undertakings. Associations of manufacturers, producers, suppliers of services, or traders which, under the terms of the law governing them, have the capacity in their own name to have rights and obligations of all kinds, to make contracts or accomplish other legal acts and to sue and be sued, as well as legal persons governed by public law, may apply for Community collective marks.

2. In derogation from Article 7(1)(c), signs or indications which may serve, in trade, to designate the geographical origin of the goods or services may constitute Community collective marks within the meaning of paragraph 1. A collective mark shall not entitle the proprietor to prohibit a third party from using in the course of trade such signs or indications, provided he uses them in accordance with honest practices in industrial or commercial matters; in particular, such a mark may not be invoked against a third party who is entitled to use a geographical name.

3. The provisions of this Regulation shall apply to Community collective marks, unless Articles 65 to 72 provide otherwise.

Article 65
Regulations governing use of the mark

1. An applicant for a Community collective mark must submit regulations governing its use within the period prescribed.

2. The regulations governing use shall specify the persons authorized to use the mark, the conditions of membership of the association and, where they exist, the conditions of use of the mark including sanctions. The regulations governing use of a mark referred to in Article 64(2) must authorize any person whose goods or services originate in the geographical area concerned to become a member of the association which is the proprietor of the mark.

Article 66
Refusal of the application

1. In addition to the grounds for refusal of a Community trade mark application provided for in Articles 36 and 38, an application for a Community collective mark shall be refused where the provisions of Article 64 or 65 are not satisfied, or where the regulations governing use are contrary to public policy or to accepted principles of morality.

2. An application for a Community collective mark shall also be refused if the public is liable to be misled as regards the character or the significance of the mark, in particular if it is likely to be taken to be something other than a collective mark.

3. An application shall not be refused if the applicant, as a result of amendment of the regulations governing use, meets the requirements of paragraphs 1 and 2.

Article 67
Observations by third parties

Apart from the cases mentioned in Article 41, any person, group or body referred to in that Article may submit to the Office written observations based on the particular grounds on which the application for a Community collective mark should be refused under the terms of Article 66.

Article 68
Use of marks

Use of a Community collective mark by any person who has authority to use it shall satisfy the requirements of this Regulation, provided that the other conditions which this Regulation imposes with regard to the use of Community trade marks are fulfilled.

Article 69
Amendment of the regulations governing use of the mark

1. The proprietor of a Community collective mark must submit to the Office any amended regulations governing use.

2. The amendment shall not be mentioned in the Register if the amended regulations do not satisfy the requirements of Article 65 or involve one of the grounds for refusal referred to in Article 66.

3. Article 67 shall apply to amended regulations governing use.

4. For the purposes of applying this Regulation, amendments to the regulations governing use shall take effect only from the date of entry of the mention of the amendment in the Register.

Article 70
Persons who are entitled to bring an action for infringement

1. The provisions of Article 22 (3) and (4) concerning the rights of licensees shall apply to every person who has authority to use a Community collective mark.

2. The proprietor of a Community collective mark shall be entitled to claim compensation on behalf of persons who have authority to use the mark where they have sustained damage in consequence of unauthorized use of the mark.

Article 71
Grounds for revocation

Apart from the grounds for revocation provided for in Article 50, the rights of the proprietor of a Community collective mark shall be revoked on application to the Office or on the basis of a counterclaim in infringement proceedings, if:

(a) the proprietor does not take reasonable steps to prevent the mark being used in a manner incompatible with the conditions of use, where these exist, laid down in the regulations governing use, amendments to which have, where appropriate, been mentioned in the Register;

(b) the manner in which the mark has been used by the proprietor has caused it to become liable to mislead the public in the manner referred to in Article 66(2);

(c) an amendment to the regulations governing use of the mark has been mentioned in the Register in breach of the provisions of Article 69(2), unless the proprietor of the mark, by further amending the regulations governing use, complies with the requirements of those provisions.

Article 72
Grounds for invalidity

Apart from the grounds for invalidity provided for in Articles 51 and 52, a Community collective mark which is registered in breach of the provisions of Article 66 shall be declared invalid on application to the Office or on the basis of a counterclaim in infringement proceedings, unless the proprietor of the mark, by amending the regulations governing use, complies with the requirements of those provisions.

TITLE IX
PROCEDURE

SECTION 1
GENERAL PROVISIONS

Article 73
Statement of reasons on which decisions are based

Decisions of the Office shall state the reasons on which they are based. They shall be based only on reasons or evidence on which the parties concerned have had on opportunity to present their comments.

Article 74
Examination of the facts by the Office of its own motion

1. In proceedings before it the Office shall examine the facts of its own motion; however, in proceedings relating to relative grounds for refusal of registration, the Office shall be restricted in this examination to the facts, evidence and arguments provided by the parties and the relief sought.

2. The Office may disregard facts or evidence which are not submitted in due time by the parties concerned.

Article 75
Oral proceedings

1. If the Office considers that oral proceedings would be expedient they shall be held either at the instance of the Office or at the request of any party to the proceedings.

2. Oral proceedings before the examiners, the Opposition Division and the Administration of Trade Marks and Legal Division shall not be public.

3. Oral proceedings, including delivery of the decision, shall be public before the Cancellation Division and the Boards of Appeal, in so far as the department before which the proceedings are taking place does not decide otherwise in cases where admission of the public could have serious and

unjustified disadvantages, in particular for a party to the proceedings.

Article 76
Taking of evidence

1. In any proceedings before the Office, the means of giving or obtaining evidence shall include the following:

(a) hearing the parties;

(b) requests for information;

(c) the production of documents and items of evidence;

(d) hearing witnesses;

(e) opinions by experts;

(f) statements in writing sworn or affirmed or having a similar effect under the law of the State in which the statement is drawn up.

2. The relevant department may commission one of its members to examine the evidence adduced.

3. If the Office considers it necessary for a party, witness or expert to give evidence orally, it shall issue a summons to the person concerned to appear before it.

4. The parties shall be informed of the hearing of a witness or expert before the Office. They shall have the right to be present and to put questions to the witness or expert.

Article 77
Notification

The Office shall, as a matter of course, notify those concerned of decisions and summonses and of any notice or other communication from which a time limit is reckoned, or of which those concerned must be notified under other provisions of this Regulation or of the Implementing Regulation, or of which notification has been ordered by the President of the Office.

Article 78
Restitutio in integrum

1. The applicant for or proprietor of a Community trade mark or any other party to proceedings before the Office who, in spite of all due care required by the circumstances having been taken, was unable to observe a time limit *vis-à-vis* the Office shall, upon application, have his rights re-established if the non-observance in question has the direct consequence, by virtue of the provisions of this Regulation, of causing the loss of any right or means of redress.

2. The application must be filed in writing within two months from the removal of the cause of non-compliance with the time limit. The omitted act must be completed within this period. The application shall only be admissible within the year immediately following the expiry of the

unobserved time limit. In the case of non-submission of the request for renewal of registration or of non-payment of a renewal fee, the further period of six months provided in Article 47(3), third sentence, shall be deducted from the period of one year.

3. The application must state the grounds on which it is based and must set out the facts on which it relies. It shall not be deemed to be filed until the fee for re-establishment of rights has been paid.

4. The department competent to decide on the omitted act shall decide upon the application.

5. The provisions of this Article shall not be applicable to the time limits referred to in paragraph 2 of this Article, Articles 29(1) and 42(1).

6. Where the applicant for or proprietor of a Community trade mark has his rights re-established, he may not invoke his rights *vis-à-vis* a third party who, in good faith, has put goods on the market or supplied services under a sign which is identical with or similar to the Community trade mark in the course of the period between the loss of rights in the application or in the Community trade mark and publication of the mention of re-establishment of those rights.

7. A third party who may avail himself of the provisions of paragraph 6 may bring third party proceedings against the decision re-establishing the rights of the applicant for or proprietor of a Community trade mark within a period of two months as from the date of publication of the mention of re-establishment of those rights.

8. Nothing in this Article shall limit the right of a Member State to grant *restitutio in integrum* in respect of time limits provided for in this Regulation and to be observed vis-à-vis the authorities of such State.

Article 79
Reference to general principles

In the absence of procedural provisions in this Regulation, the Implementing Regulation, the fees regulations or the rules of procedure of the Boards of Appeal, the Office shall take into account the principles of procedural law generally recognized in the Member States.

Article 80
Termination of financial obligations

1. Rights of the Office to the payment of a fee shall be extinguished after four years from the end of the calendar year in which the fee fell due.

2. Rights against the Office for the refunding of fees or sums of money paid in excess of a fee shall be extinguished after four years from the end of the calendar year in which the right arose.

3. The period laid down in paragraphs 1 and 2 shall be interrupted in the case covered by paragraph 1 by a request for payment of the fee and in the case covered by paragraph 2 by a reasoned claim in writing. On interruption

it shall begin again immediately and shall end at the latest six years after the end of the year in which it originally began, unless, in the meantime, judicial proceedings to enforce the right have begun; in this case the period shall end at the earliest one year after the judgement has acquired the authority of a final decision.

SECTION 2
COSTS

Article 81
Costs

1. The losing party in opposition proceedings, proceedings for revocation, proceedings for a declaration of invalidity or appeal proceedings shall bear the fees incurred by the other party as well as all costs, without prejudice to Article 115(6), incurred by him essential to the proceedings, including travel and subsistence and the remuneration of an agent, adviser or advocate, within the limits of the scales set for each category of costs under the conditions laid down in the Implementing Regulation.

2. However, where each party succeeds on some and fails on other heads, or if reasons of equity so dictate, the Opposition Division, Cancellation Division or Board of Appeal shall decide a different apportionment of costs.

3. The party who terminates the proceedings by withdrawing the Community trade mark application, the opposition, the application for revocation of rights, the application for a declaration of invalidity or the appeal, or by not renewing registration of the Community trade mark or by surrendering the Community trade mark, shall bear the fees and the costs incurred by the other party as stipulated in paragraphs 1 and 2.

4. Where a case does not proceed to judgment the costs shall be at the discretion of the Opposition Division, Cancellation Division or Board of Appeal.

5. Where the parties conclude before the Opposition Division, Cancellation Division or Board of Appeal a settlement of costs differing from that provided for in the preceding paragraphs, the department concerned shall take note of that agreement.

6. On request the registry of the Opposition Division or Cancellation Division or Board of Appeal shall fix the amount of the costs to be paid pursuant to the preceding paragraphs. The amount so determined may be reviewed by a decision of the Opposition Division or Cancellation Division or Board of Appeal on a request filed within the prescribed period.

Article 82
Enforcement of decisions fixing the amount of costs

1. Any final decision of the Office fixing the amount of costs shall be enforceable.

2. Enforcement shall be governed by the rules of civil procedure in force in

the State in the territory of which it is carried out. The order for its enforcement shall be appended to the decision, without other formality than verification of the authenticity of the decision, by the national authority which the Government of each Member State shall designate for this purpose and shall make known to the Office and to the Court of Justice.

3. When these formalities have been completed on application by the party concerned, the latter may proceed to enforcement in accordance with the national law, by bringing the matter directly before the competent authority.

4. Enforcement may be suspended only by a decision of the Court of Justice. However, the courts of the country concerned shall have jurisdiction over complaints that enforcement is being carried out in an irregular manner.

SECTION 3
INFORMATION OF THE PUBLIC AND OF THE OFFICIAL AUTHORITIES OF THE MEMBER STATES

Article 83
Register of Community trade marks

The Office shall keep a register to the known as the Register of Community trade marks, which shall contain those particulars the registration or inclusion of which is provided for by this Regulation or by the Implementing Regulation. The Register shall be open to public inspection.

Article 84
Inspection of files

1. The files relating to Community trade mark applications which have not yet been published shall not be made available for inspection without the consent of the applicant.

2. Any person who can prove that the applicant for a Community trade mark has stated that after the trade mark has been registered he will invoke the rights under it against him may obtain inspection of the files prior to the publication of that application and without the consent of the applicant.

3. Subsequent to the publication of the Community trade mark application, the files relating to such application and the resulting trade mark may be inspected on request.

4. However, where the files are inspected pursuant to paragraph 2 or 3, certain documents in the file may be withheld from inspection in accordance with the provisions of the Implementing Regulation.

Article 85
Periodical publications

The Office shall periodically publish:

(a) a Community Trade Marks Bulletin containing entries made in the Register of Community trade marks as well as other particulars the publication of which is prescribed by this Regulation or by the Implementing Regulation;

(b) an Official Journal containing notices and information of a general character issued by the President of the Office, as well as any other information relevant to this Regulation or its implementation.

Article 86
Administrative cooperation

Unless otherwise provided in this Regulation or in national laws, the Office and the courts or authorities of the Member States shall on request give assistance to each other by communicating information or opening files for inspection. Where the Office lays files open to inspection by courts, Public Prosecutors Offices or central industrial property offices, the inspection shall not be subject to the restrictions laid down in Article 84.

Article 87
Exchange of publications

1. The Office and the central industrial property offices of the Member States shall despatch to each other on request and for their own use one or more copies of their respective publications free of charge.

2. The Office may conclude agreements relating to the exchange or supply of publications.

SECTION 4
REPRESENTATION

Article 88
General principles of representation

1. Subject to the provisions of paragraph 2, no person shall be compelled to be represented before the Office.

2. Without prejudice to paragraph 3, second sentence, natural or legal persons not having either their domicile or their principal place of business or a real and effective industrial or commercial establishment in the Community must be represented before the Office in accordance with Article 89(1) in all proceedings established by this Regulation, other than in filing an application for a Community trade mark; the Implementing Regulation may permit other exceptions.

3. Natural or legal persons having their domicile or principal place of business or a real and effective industrial or commercial establishment in the Community may be represented before the Office by an employee, who must file with it a signed authorization for insertion on the files, the details of which are set out in the Implementing Regulation. An employee of a legal person to which this paragraph applies may also represent other legal persons which have economic connections with the first legal person, even if

those other legal persons have neither their domicile nor their principal place of business nor a real and effective industrial or commercial establishment within the Community.

Article 89
Professional representatives

1. Representation of natural or legal persons before the Office may only be undertaken by;

(a) any legal practitioner qualified in one of the Member States and having his place of business within the Community, to the extent that he is entitled, within the said State, to act as a representative in trade mark matters; or

(b) professional representatives whose names appear on the list maintained for this purpose by the Office.

Representatives acting before the Office must file with it a signed authorization for insertion on the files, the details of which are set out in the Implementing Regulation.

2. Any natural person who fulfils the following conditions may be entered on the list of professional representatives:

(a) he must be a national of one of the Member States;

(b) he must have his place of business or employment in the Community;

(c) he must be entitled to represent natural or legal persons in trade mark matters before the central industrial property office of the Member State in which he has his place of business or employment. Where, in that State, the entitlement is not conditional upon the requirement of special professional qualifications, per sons applying to be entered on the list who act in trade mark matters before the central industrial property office of the said State must have habitually so acted for at least five years. However, persons whose professional qualification to represent natural or legal persons in trade mark matters before the central industrial property office of one of the Member States is officially recognized in accordance with the regulations laid down by such State shall not be subject to the condition of having exercised the profession.

3. Entry shall be effected upon request, accompanied by a certificate furnished by the central industrial property office of the Member State concerned, which must indicate that the conditions laid down in paragraph 2 are fulfilled.

4. The President of the Office may grant exemption from:

(a) the requirement of paragraph 2(c), second sentence, if the applicant furnishes proof that he has acquired the requisite qualification in another way;

(b) the requirement of paragraph 2(a) in special circumstances.

5. The conditions under which a person may be removed from the list of

professional representatives shall be laid down in the Implementing Regulation.

TITLE X
JURISDICTION AND PROCEDURE IN LEGAL ACTIONS RELATING TO COMMUNITY TRADE MARKS

SECTION 1
APPLICATION OF THE CONVENTION ON JURISDICTION AND ENFORCEMENT

Article 90
Application of the Convention on Jurisdiction and Enforcement

1. Unless otherwise specified in this Regulation, the Convention on Jurisdiction and the Enforcement of Judgments in Civil and Commercial Matters, signed in Brussels on 27 September 1968, as amended by the Conventions on the Accession to that Convention of the States acceding to the European Communities, the whole of which Convention and of which Conventions of Accession are hereinafter referred to as the Convention on Jurisdiction and Enforcement, shall apply to proceedings relating to Community trade marks and applications for Community trade marks, as well as to proceedings relating to simultaneous and successive actions on the basis of Community trade marks and national trade marks.

2. In the case of proceedings in respect of the actions and claims referred to in Article 92:

(a) Articles 2, 4, 5 (1), (3), (4) and (5) and Article 24 of the Convention on Jurisdiction and Enforcement shall not apply;

(b) Articles 17 and 18 of that Convention shall apply subject to the limitations in Article 93(4) of this Regulation;

(c) the provisions of Title II of that Convention which are applicable to persons domiciled in a Member State shall also be applicable to persons who do not have a domicile in any Member State but have an establishment therein.

SECTION 2
DISPUTES CONCERNING THE INFRINGEMENT AND VALIDITY OF COMMUNITY TRADE MARKS

Article 91
Community trade mark courts

1. The Member States shall designate in their territories as limited a number as possible of national courts and tribunals of first and second instance, hereinafter referred to as Community trade mark courts, which shall perform the functions assigned to them by this Regulation.

2. Each Member State shall communicate to the Commission within three years of the entry into force of this Regulation a list of Community trade mark courts indicating their names and their territorial jurisdiction.

3. Any change made after communication of the list referred to in paragraph 2 in the number, names or territorial jurisdiction of the courts shall be notified without delay by the Member State concerned to the Commission.

4. The information referred to in paragraphs 2 and 3 shall be notified by the Commission to the Member States and published in the Official Journal of the European Communities.

5. As long as a Member State has not communicated the list as stipulated in paragraph 2, jurisdiction for any proceedings resulting from an action or application covered by Article 92, and for which the courts of that State have jurisdiction under Article 93, shall lie with that court of the State in question which would have jurisdiction *ratione loci* and *ratione materiae* in the case of proceedings relating to a national trade mark registered in that State.

Article 92
Jurisdiction over infringement and validity

The Community trade mark courts shall have exclusive jurisdiction:

(a) for all infringement actions and if they are permitted under national law actions in respect of threatened infringement relating to Community trade marks;

(b) for actions for declaration of non-infringement, if they are permitted under national law;

(c) for all actions brought as a result of acts referred to in Article 9(3), second sentence;

(d) for counterclaims for revocation or for a declaration of invalidity of the Community trade mark pursuant to Article 96.

Article 93
International jurisdiction

1. Subject to the provisions of this Regulation as well as to any provisions of the Convention on Jurisdiction and Enforcement applicable by virtue of Article 90, proceedings in respect of the actions and claims referred to in Article 92 shall be brought in the courts of the Member State in which the defendant is domiciled or, if he is not domiciled in any of the Member States, in which he has an establishment.

2. If the defendant is neither domiciled nor has an establishment in any of the Member States, such proceedings shall be brought in the courts of the Member State in which the plaintiff is domiciled or, if he is not domiciled in any of the Member States, in which he has an establishment.

3. If neither the defendant nor the plaintiff is so domiciled or has such an establishment, such proceedings shall be brought in the courts of the Member

State where the Office has its seat.

4. Notwithstanding the provisions of paragraphs 1, 2 and 3:

(a) Article 17 of the Convention on Jurisdiction and Enforcement shall apply if the parties agree that a different Community trade mark court shall have jurisdiction;

(b) Article 18 of that Convention shall apply if the defendant enters an appearance before a different Community trade mark court.

5. Proceedings in respect of the actions and claims referred to in Article 92, with the exception of actions for a declaration of non-infringement of a Community trade mark, may also be brought in the courts of the Member State in which the act of infringement has been committed or threatened, or in which an act within the meaning of Article 9(3), second sentence, has been committed.

Article 94
Extent of jurisdiction

1. A Community trade mark court whose jurisdiction is based on Article 93 (1) to (4) shall have jurisdiction in respect of:

– acts of infringement committed or threatened within the territory of any of the Member States,

– acts within the meaning of Article 9(3), second sentence, committed within the territory of any of the Member States.

2. A Community trade mark court whose jurisdiction is based on Article 93(5) shall have jurisdiction only in respect of acts committed or threatened within the territory of the Member State in which that court is situated.

Article 95
Presumption of validity—Defence as to the merits

1. The Community trade mark courts shall treat the Community trade mark as valid unless its validity is put in issue by the defendant with a counterclaim for revocation or for a declaration of invalidity.

2. The validity of a Community trade mark may not be put in issue in an action for a declaration of non-infringement.

3. In the actions referred to in Article 92 (a) and (c) a plea relating to revocation or invalidity of the Community trade mark submitted otherwise than by way of a counterclaim shall be admissible in so far as the defendant claims that the rights of the proprietor of the Community trade mark could be revoked for lack of use or that Community trade mark could be declared invalid on account of an earlier right of the defendant.

Article 96
Counterclaims

1. A counterclaim for revocation or for a declaration of invalidity may only

be based on the grounds for revocation or invalidity mentioned in this Regulation.

2. A Community trade mark court shall reject a counterclaim for revocation or for a declaration of invalidity if a decision taken by the Office relating to the same subject matter and cause of action and involving the same parties has already become final.

3. If the counterclaim is brought in a legal action to which the proprietor of the trade mark is not already a party, he shall be informed thereof and may be joined as a party to the action in accordance with the conditions set out in national law.

4. The Community trade mark court with which a counterclaim for revocation or for a declaration of invalidity of the Community trade mark has been filed shall inform the Office of the date on which the counterclaim was filed. The latter shall record this fact in the Register of Community trade marks.

5. Article 56 (3), (4), (5) and (6) shall apply.

6. Where a Community trade mark court has given a judgment which has become final on a counterclaim for revocation or for invalidity of a Community trade mark, a copy of the judgment shall be sent to the Office. Any party may request information about such transmission. The Office shall mention the judgment in the Register of Community trade marks in accordance with the provisions of the Implementing Regulation.

7. The Community trade mark court hearing a counterclaim for revocation or for a declaration of invalidity may stay the proceedings on application by the proprietor of the Community trade mark and after hearing the other parties and may request the defendant to submit an application for revocation or for a declaration of invalidity to the Office within a time limit which it shall determine. If the application is not made within the time limit, the proceedings shall continue; the counterclaim shall be deemed withdrawn. Article 100(3) shall apply.

Article 97
Applicable law

1. The Community trade mark courts shall apply the provisions of this Regulation.

2. On all matters not covered by this Regulation a Community trade mark court shall apply its national law, including its private international law.

3. Unless otherwise provided in this Regulation, a Community trade mark court shall apply the rules of procedure governing the same type of action relating to a national trade mark in the Member State where it has its seat.

Article 98
Sanctions

1. Where a Community trade mark court finds that the defendant has

infringed or threatened to infringe a Community trade mark, it shall, unless there are special reasons for not doing so, issue an order prohibiting the defendant from proceeding with the acts which infringed or would infringe the Community trade mark. It shall also take such measures in accordance with its national law as are aimed at ensuring that this prohibition is complied with.

2. In all other respects the Community trade mark court shall apply the law of the Member State to which the acts of infringement or threatened infringement were committed, including the private international law.

Article 99
Provisional and protective measures

1. Application may be made to the courts of a Member State, including Community trade mark courts, for such provisional, including protective, measures in respect of a Community trade mark or Community trade mark application as may be available under the law of that State in respect of a national trade mark, even if, under this Regulation, a Community trade mark court of another Member State has jurisdiction as to the substance of the matter.

2. A Community trade mark court whose jurisdiction is based on Article 93 (1), (2), (3) or (4) shall have jurisdiction to grant provisional and protective measures which, subject to any necessary procedure for recognition and enforcement pursuant to Title III of the Convention on Jurisdiction and Enforcement, are applicable in the territory of any Member State. No other court shall have such jurisdiction.

Article 100
Specific rules on related actions

1. A Community trade mark court hearing an action referred to in Article 92, other than an action for a declaration of non-infringement shall, unless there are special grounds for continuing the hearing, of its own motion after hearing the parties or at the request of one of the parties and after hearing the other parties, stay the proceedings where the validity of the Community trade mark is already in issue before another Community trade mark court on account of a counterclaim or where an application for revocation or for a declaration of invalidity has already been filed at the Office.

2. The Office, when hearing an application for revocation or for a declaration of invalidity shall, unless there are special grounds for continuing the hearing, of its own motion after hearing the parties or at the request of one of the parties and after hearing the other parties, stay the proceedings where the validity of the Community trade mark is already in issue on account of a counterclaim before a Community trade mark court. However, if one of the parties to the proceedings before the Community trade mark court so requests, the court may, after hearing the other parties to these proceedings, stay the proceedings. The Office shall in this instance continue

the proceedings pending before it.

3. Where the Community trade mark court stays the proceedings it may order provisional and protective measures for the duration of the stay.

Article 101
Jurisdiction of Community trade mark courts of second instance–Further appeal

1. An appeal to the Community trade mark courts of second instance shall lie from judgments of the Community trade mark courts of first instance in respect of proceedings arising from the actions and claims referred to in Article 92.

2. The conditions under which an appeal may be lodged with a Community trade mark court of second instance shall be determined by the national law of the Member State in which that court is located.

3. The national rules concerning further appeal shall be applicable in respect of judgments of Community trade mark courts of second instance.

SECTION 3
OTHER DISPUTES CONCERNING COMMUNITY TRADE MARKS

Article 102
Supplementary provisions on the jurisdiction of national courts other than Community trade mark courts

1. Within the Member State whose courts have jurisdiction under Article 90(1) those courts shall have jurisdiction for actions other than those referred to in Article 92, which would have jurisdiction *ratione loci* and *ratione materiae* in the case of actions relating to a national trade mark registered in that State.

2. Actions relating to a Community trade mark, other than those referred to in Article 92, for which no court has jurisdiction under Article 90(1) and paragraph 1 of this Article may be heard before the courts of the Member State in which the Office has its seat.

Article 103
Obligation of the national court

A national court which is dealing with an action relating to a Community trade mark, other than the action referred to in Article 92, shall treat the trade mark as valid.

SECTION 4
TRANSITIONAL PROVISION

Article 104

Transitional provision relating to the application of the Convention on Jurisdiction and Enforcement

The provisions of the Convention on Jurisdiction and Enforcement which are rendered applicable by the preceding Articles shall have effect in respect of any Member State solely in the text of the Convention which is in force in respect of that State at any given time.

TITLE XI
EFFECTS ON THE LAWS OF THE MEMBER STATES

SECTION 1
CIVIL ACTIONS ON THE BASIS OF MORE THAN ONE TRADE MARK

Article 105
Simultaneous and successive civil actions on the basis of Community trade marks and national trade marks

1. Where actions for infringement involving the same cause of action and between the same parties are brought in the courts of different Member States, one seized on the basis of a Community trade mark and the other seized on the basis of a national trade mark:

(a) the court other than the court first seized shall of its own motion decline jurisdiction in favour of that court where the trade marks concerned are identical and valid for identical goods or services. The court which would be required to decline jurisdiction may stay its proceedings if the jurisdiction of the other court is contested;

(b) the court other than the court first seized may stay its proceedings where the trade marks concerned are identical and valid for similar goods or services and where the trade marks concerned are similar and valid for identical or similar goods or services.

2. The court hearing an action for infringement on the basis of a Community trade mark shall reject the action if a final judgment on the merits has been given on the same cause of action and between the same parties on the basis of an identical national trade mark valid for identical goods or services.

3. The court hearing an action for infringement on the basis of a national trade mark shall reject the action if a final judgment on the merits has been given on the same cause of action and between the same parties on the basis of an identical Community trade mark valid for identical goods or services.

4. Paragraphs 1, 2 and 3 shall not apply in respect of provisional, including protective, measures.

SECTION 2
APPLICATION OF NATIONAL LAWS FOR THE PURPOSE OF PROHIBITING THE USE OF COMMUNITY TRADE MARKS

Article 106
Prohibition of use of Community trade marks

1. This Regulation shall, unless otherwise provided for, not affect the right existing under the laws of the Member States to invoke claims for infringement of earlier rights within the meaning of Article 8 or Article 52(2) in relation to the use of a later Community trade mark. Claims for infringement of earlier rights within the meaning of Article 8 (2) and (4) may, however, no longer be invoked if the proprietor of the earlier right may no longer apply for a declaration that the Community trade mark is invalid in accordance with Article 53(2).

2. This Regulation shall, unless otherwise provided for, not affect the right to bring proceedings under the civil, administrative or criminal law of a Member Sate or under provisions of Community law for the purpose of prohibiting the use of a Community trade mark to the extent that the use of a national trade mark may be prohibited under the law of that Member State or under Community law.

Article 107
Prior rights applicable to particular localities

1. The proprietor of an earlier right which only applies to a particular locality may oppose the use of the Community trade mark in the territory where his right is protected in so far as the law of the Member State concerned so permits.

2. Paragraph 1 shall cease to apply if the proprietor of the earlier right has acquiesced in the use of the Community trade mark in the territory where his right is protected for a period of five successive years, being aware of such use, unless the Community trade mark was applied for in bad faith.

3. The proprietor of the Community trade mark shall not be entitled to oppose use of the right referred to in paragraph 1 even though that right may no longer be invoked against the Community trade mark.

SECTION 3
CONVERSION INTO A NATIONAL TRADE MARK APPLICATION

Article 108
Request for the application of national procedure

1. The applicant for or proprietor of a Community trade mark may request the conversion of his Community trade mark application or Community trade mark into a national trade mark application

(a) to the extent that the Community trade mark application is refused, withdrawn, or deemed to be withdrawn;

(b) to the extent that the Community trade mark ceases to have effect.

2. Conversion shall not take place:

(a) where the rights of the proprietor of the Community trade mark have been revoked on the grounds of non-use, unless in the Member State for which conversion is requested the Community trade mark has been put to use which would be considered to be genuine use under the laws of that Member State;

(b) for the purpose of protection in a Member State in which, in accordance with the decision of the Office or of the national court, grounds for refusal of registration or grounds for revocation or invalidity apply to the Community trade mark application or Community trade mark.

3. The national trade mark application resulting from the conversion of a Community trade mark application or a Community trade mark shall enjoy in respect of the Member State concerned the date of filing or the date of priority of that application or trade mark and, where appropriate, the seniority of a trade mark of that State claimed under Article 34 or 35.

4. Where:

– the Community trade mark application is deemed to be withdrawn or is refused by a decision of the Office which has become final,

– the Community trade mark ceases to have effect as a result of a decision of the Office which has become final or as a result of registration of surrender of the Community trade mark,

the Office shall notify to the applicant or proprietor a communication fixing a period of three months from the date of that communication in which a request for conversion may be filed.

5. Where the Community trade mark application is withdrawn or the Community trade mark ceases to have effect as a result of failure to renew the registration, the request for conversion shall be filed within three months after the date on which the Community trade mark application is withdrawn or on which the registration of the Community trade mark expires.

6. Where the Community trade mark ceases to have effect as a result of a decision of a national court, the request for conversion shall be filed within three months after the date on which that decision acquired the authority of a final decision.

7. The effect referred to in Article 32 shall lapse if the request is not filed in due time.

Article 109
Submission, publication and transmission of the request for conversion

1. A request for conversion shall be filed with the Office and shall specify the Member States in which application of the procedure for registration of a national trade mark is desired. The request shall not be deemed to be filed until the conversion fee has been paid.

2. If the Community trade mark application has been published, receipt

of any such request shall be recorded in the Register of Community trade marks and the request for conversion shall be published.

3. The Office shall check whether conversion may be requested in accordance with Article 108(1), whether the request has been filed within the period laid down in Article 108 (4), (5) or (6), as the case may be, and whether the conversion fee has been paid. If these conditions are fulfilled, the Office shall transmit the request to the central industrial property offices of the States specified therein. At the request of the central industrial property office of a State concerned, the Office shall give it any information enabling that office to decide as to the admissibility of the request.

Article 110
Formal requirements for conversion

1. Any central industrial property office to which the request is transmitted shall decide as to its admissibility.

2. A Community trade mark application or a Community trade mark transmitted in accordance with Article 109 shall not be subjected to formal requirements of national law which are different from or additional to those provided for in this Regulation or in the Implementing Regulation.

3. Any central industrial property office to which the request is transmitted may require that the applicant shall, within not less than two months:

(a) pay the national application fee;

(b) file a translation in one of the official languages of the State in question of the request and of the documents accompanying it;

(c) indicate an address for service in the State in question;

(d) supply a representation of the trade mark in the number of copies specified by the State in question.

TITLE XII
THE OFFICE

SECTION 1
GENERAL PROVISIONS

Article 111
Legal status

1. The Office shall be a body of the Community. It shall have legal personality.

2. In each of the Member States the Office shall enjoy the most extensive legal capacity accorded to legal persons under their laws; it may, in particular, acquire or dispose of movable and immovable property and may be a party to legal proceedings.

3. The Office shall be represented by its President.

Article 112
Staff

1. The Staff Regulations of officials of the European Communities, the Conditions of Employment of other servants of the European Communities, and the rules adopted by agreement between the Institutions of the European Communities for giving effect to those Staff Regulations and Conditions of Employment shall apply to the staff of the Office, without prejudice to the application of Article 131 to the members of the Boards of Appeal.

2. Without prejudice to Article 120, the powers conferred on each Institution by the Staff Regulations and by the Conditions of Employment of other servants shall be exercised by the Office in respect of its staff.

Article 113
Privileges and immunities

The Protocol on the Privileges and Immunities of the European Communities shall apply to the Office.

Article 114
Liability

1. The contractual liability of the Office shall be governed by the law applicable to the contract in question.

2. The Court of Justice shall be competent to give judgment pursuant to any arbitration clause contained in a contract concluded by the Office.

3. In the case of non-contractual liability, the Office shall, in accordance with the general principles common to the laws of the Member States, make good any damage caused by its departments or by its servants in the performance of their duties.

4. The Court of Justice shall have jurisdiction in disputes relating to compensation for the damage referred to in paragraph 3.

5. The personal liability of its servants towards the Office shall be governed by the provisions laid down in their Staff Regulations or in the Conditions of Employment applicable to them.

Article 115
Languages

1. The application for a Community trade mark shall be filed in one of the official languages of the European Community.

2. The languages of the Office shall be English, French, German, Italian and Spanish.

3. The applicant must indicate a second language which shall be a language of the Office the use of which he accepts as a possible language of proceedings for opposition, revocation or invalidity proceedings.

If the application was filed in a language which is not one of the languages of the Office, the Office shall arrange to have the application, as described in Article 26(1), translated into the language indicated by the applicant.

4. Where the applicant for a Community trade mark is the sole party to proceedings before the Office, the language of proceedings shall be the language used for filing the application for a Community trade mark. If the application was made in a language other than the languages of the Office, the Office may send written communications to the applicant in the second language indicated by the applicant in his application.

5. The notice of opposition and an application for revocation or invalidity shall be filed in one of the languages of the Office.

6. If the language chosen, in accordance with paragraph 5, for the notice of opposition or the application for revocation or invalidity is the language of the application for a trade mark or the second language indicated when the application was filed, that language shall be the language of the proceedings.

If the language chosen, in accordance with paragraph 5, for the notice of opposition or the application for revocation or invalidity is neither the language of the application for a trade mark nor the second language indicated when the application was filed, the opposing party or the party seeking revocation or invalidity shall be required to produce, at his own expense, a translation of his application either into the language of the application for a trade mark, provided that it is a language of the Office, or into the second language indicated when the application was filed. The translation shall be produced within the period prescribed in the implementing regulation. The language into which the application has been translated shall then become the language of the proceedings.

7. Parties to opposition, revocation, invalidity or appeal proceedings may agree that a different official language of the European Community is to be the language of the proceedings.

Article 116
Publication; entries in the Register

1. An application for a Community trade mark, as described in Article 26(1), and all other information the publication of which is prescribed by this Regulation or the implementing regulation, shall be published in all the official languages of the European Community.

2. All entries in the Register of Community trade marks shall be made in all the official languages of the European Community.

3. In cases of doubt, the text in the language of the Office in which the application for the Community trade mark was filed shall be authentic. If the application was filed in an official language of the European Community other than one of the languages of the Office, the text in the second language indicated by the applicant shall be authentic.

Article 117

The translation services required for the functioning of the Office shall be provided by the Translation Centre of the Bodies of the Union once this begins operation.

Article 118
Control of legality

1. The Commission shall check the legality of those acts of the President of the Office in respect of which Community law does not provide for any check on legality by another body and of acts of the Budget Committee attached to the Office pursuant to Article 133.

2. It shall require that any unlawful acts as referred to in paragraph 1 be altered or annulled.

3. Member States and any person directly and personally involved may refer to the Commission any act as referred to in paragraph 1, whether express or implied, for the Commission to examine the legality of that act. Referral shall be made to the Commission within 15 days of the day on which the party concerned first became aware of the act in question. The Commission shall take a decision within one month. If no decision has been taken within this period, the case shall be deemed to have been dismissed.

SECTION 2
MANAGEMENT OF THE OFFICE

Article 119
Powers of the President

1. The Office shall be managed by the President.

2. To this end the President shall have in particular the following functions and powers:

(a) he shall take all necessary steps, including the adoption of internal administrative instructions and the publication of notices, to ensure the functioning of the Office;

(b) he may place before the Commission any proposal to amend this Regulation, the Implementing Regulation, the rules of procedure of the Boards of Appeal, the fees regulations and any other rules applying to Community trade marks after consulting the Administrative Board and, in the case of the fees regulations and the budgetary provisions of this Regulation, the Budget Committee;

(c) he shall draw up the estimates of the revenue and expenditure of the Office and shall implement the budget;

(d) he shall submit a management report to the Commission, the European Parliament and the Administrative Board each year;

(e) he shall exercise in respect of the staff the powers laid down in Article 112(2);

(f) he may delegate his powers.

3. The President shall be assisted by one or more Vice-Presidents. If the President is absent or indisposed, the Vice-President or one of the Vice-Presidents shall take his place in accordance with the procedure laid down by the Administrative Board.

Article 120
Appointment of senior officials

1. The President of the Office shall be appointed by the Council from a list of at most three candidates, which shall be prepared by the Administrative Board. Power to dismiss the President shall lie with the Council, acting on a proposal from the Administrative Board.

2. The term of office of the President shall not exceed five years. This term of office shall be renewable.

3. The Vice-President or Vice-Presidents of the Office shall be appointed or dismissed as in paragraph 1, after consultation of the President.

4. The Council shall exercise disciplinary authority over the officials referred to in paragraphs 1 and 3 of this Article.

SECTION 3
ADMINISTRATIVE BOARD

Article 121
Creation and powers

1. An Administrative Board is hereby set up, attached to the Office. Without prejudice to the powers attributed to the Budget Committee in Section 5 budget and financial control the Administrative Board shall have the powers defined below.

2. The Administrative Board shall draw up the lists of candidates provided for in Article 120.

3. It shall fix the date for the first filing of Community trade mark applications, pursuant to Article 143(3).

4. It shall advise the President on matters for which the Office is responsible.

5. It shall be consulted before adoption of the guidelines for examination in the Office and in the other cases provided for in this Regulation.

6. It may deliver opinions and requests for information to the President and to the Commission where it considers that this is necessary.

Article 122
Composition

1. The Administrative Board shall be composed of one representative of each Member State and one representative of the Commission and their alternates.

2. The members of the Administrative Board may, subject to the provisions of its rules of procedure, be assisted by advisers or experts.

Article 123
Chairmanship

1. The Administrative Board shall elect a chairman and a deputy chairman from among its members. The deputy chairman shall ex officio replace the chairman in the event of his being prevented from attending to his duties.

2. The duration of the terms of office of the chairman and the deputy chairman shall be three years. The terms of office shall be renewable.

Article 124
Meetings

1. Meetings of the Administrative Board shall be convened by its chairman.

2. The President of the Office shall take part in the deliberations, unless the Administrative Board decides otherwise.

3. The Administrative Board shall hold an ordinary meeting once a year; in addition, it shall meet on the initiative of its chairman or at the request of the Commission or of one-third of the Member States.

4. The Administrative Board shall adopt rules of procedure.

5. The Administrative Board shall take its decisions by a simple majority of the representatives of the Member States. However, a majority of three-quarters of the representatives of the Member States shall be required for the decisions which the Administrative Board is empowered to take under Article 120 (1) and (3). In both cases each Member State shall have one vote.

6. The Administrative Board may invite observers to attend its meetings.

7. The Secretariat for the Administrative Board shall be provided by the Office.

SECTION 4
IMPLEMENTATION OF PROCEDURES

Article 125
Competence

For taking decisions in connection with the procedures laid down in this Regulation, the following shall be competent:

(a) Examiners;

(b) Opposition Divisions;

(c) an Administration of Trade Marks and Legal Division;

(d) Cancellation Divisions;

(e) Boards of Appeal.

Article 126
Examiners

An examiner shall be responsible for taking decisions on behalf of the Office in relation to an application for registration of a Community trade mark, including the matters referred to in Articles 36, 37, 38 and 66, except in so far as an Opposition Division is responsible.

Article 127
Opposition Divisions

1. An Opposition Division shall be responsible for taking decisions on an opposition to an application to register a Community trade mark.

2. An Opposition Division shall consist of three members. At least one of the members must be legally qualified.

Article 128
Administration of Trade Marks and Legal Division

1. The Administration of Trade Marks and Legal Division shall be responsible for those decisions required by this Regulation which do not fall within the competence of an examiner, an Opposition Division or a Cancellation Division. It shall in particular be responsible for decisions in respect of entries in the Register of Community trade marks.

2. It shall also be responsible for keeping the list of professional representatives which is referred to in Article 89.

3. A decision of the Division shall be taken by one member.

Article 129
Cancellation Divisions

1. A Cancellation Division shall be responsible for taking decisions in relation to an application for the revocation or declaration of invalidity of a Community trade mark.

2. A Cancellation Division shall consist of three members. At least one of the members must be legally qualified.

Article 130
Boards of Appeal

1. The Boards of Appeal shall be responsible for deciding on appeals from decisions of the examiners, Opposition Divisions, Administration of Trade Marks and Legal Division and Cancellation Divisions.

2. A Board of Appeal shall consist of three members. At least two of the members must be legally qualified.

Article 131
Independence of the members of the Boards of Appeal

1. The members, including the chairmen, of the Boards of Appeal shall be appointed, in accordance with the procedure laid down in Article 120, for the appointment of the President of the Office, for a term of five years. They may not be removed from office during this term, unless there are serious grounds for such removal and the Court of Justice, on application by the body which appointed them, takes a decision to this effect. Their term of office shall be renewable.

2. The members of the Boards of Appeal shall be independent. In their decisions they shall not be bound by any instructions.

3. The members of the Boards of Appeal may not be examiners or members of the Opposition Divisions, Administration of Trade Marks and Legal Division or Cancellation Divisions.

Article 132
Exclusion and objection

1. Examiners and members of the Divisions set up within the Office or of the Boards of Appeal may not take part in any proceedings if they have any personal interest therein, or if they have previously been involved as representatives of one of the parties. Two of the three members of an Opposition Division shall not have taken part in examining the application. Members of the Cancellation Divisions may not take part in any proceedings if they have participated in the final decision on the case in the proceedings for registration or opposition proceedings. Members of the Boards of Appeal may not take part in appeal proceedings if they participated in the decision under appeal.

2. If, for one of the reasons mentioned in paragraph 1 or for any other reason, a member of a Division or of a Board of Appeal considers that he should not take part in any proceedings, he shall inform the Division or Board accordingly.

3. Examiners and members of the Divisions or of a Board of Appeal may be objected to by any party for one of the reasons mentioned in paragraph 1, or if suspected of partiality. An objection shall not be admissible if, while being aware of a reason for objection, the party has taken a procedural step. No objection may be based upon the nationality of examiners or members.

4. The Divisions and the Boards of Appeal shall decide as to the action to be taken in the cases specified in paragraphs 2 and 3 without the participation of the member concerned. For the purposes of taking this decision the member who withdraws or has been objected to shall be replaced in the Division or Board of Appeal by his alternate.

SECTION 5
BUDGET AND FINANCIAL CONTROL

Article 133
Budget Committee

1. A Budget Committee is hereby set up, attached to the Office. The Budget Committee shall have the powers assigned to it in this Section and in Article 39(4).

2. Articles 121(6), 122, 123 and 124 (1) to (4), (6) and (7) shall apply to the Budget Committee *mutatis mutandis*.

3. The Budget Committee shall take its decisions by a simple majority of the representatives of the Member States. However, a majority of three-quarters of the representatives of the Member States shall be required for the decisions which the Budget Committee is empowered to take under Articles 39(4), 135(3) and 138. In both cases each Member State shall have one vote.

Article 134
Budget

1. Estimates of all the Office's revenue and expenditure shall be prepared for each financial year and shall be shown in the Office's budget, and each financial year shall correspond with the calendar year.

2. The revenue and expenditure shown in the budget shall be in balance.

3. Revenue shall comprise, without prejudice to other types of income, total fees payable under the fees regulations, and, to the extent necessary, a subsidy entered against a specific Heading of the general budget of the European Communities, Commission Section.

Article 135
Preparation of the budget

1. The President shall draw up each year an estimate of the Office's revenue and expenditure for the following year and shall send it to the Budget Committee not later than 31 March in each year, together with a list of posts.

2. Should the budget estimates provide for a Community subsidy, the Budget Committee shall immediately forward the estimate to the Commission, which shall forward it to the budget authority of the Communities. The Commission may attach an opinion on the estimate along with an alternative estimate.

3. The Budget Committee shall adopt the budget, which shall include the Office's list of posts. Should the budget estimates contain a subsidy from the general budget of the Communities, the Office's budget shall, if necessary, be adjusted.

Article 136
Financial control

Control of commitment and payment of all expenditure and control of the existence and recovery of all revenue of the Office shall be carried out by the Financial Controller appointed by the Budget Committee.

Article 137
Auditing of accounts

1. Not later than 31 March in each year the President shall transmit to the Commission, the European Parliament, the Budget Committee and the Court of Auditors accounts of the Office's total revenue and expenditure for the preceding financial year. The Court of Auditors shall examine them in accordance with Article 188c of the Treaty.

2. The Budget Committee shall give a discharge to the President of the Office in respect of the implementation of the budget.

Article 138
Financial provisions

The Budget Committee shall, after consulting the Court of Auditors of the European Communities and the Commission, adopt internal financial provisions specifying, in particular, the procedure for establishing and implementing the Office's budget. As far as is compatible with the particular nature of the Office, the financial provisions shall be based on the financial regulations adopted for other bodies set up by the Community.

Article 139
Fees regulations

1. The fees regulations shall determine in particular the amounts of the fees and the ways in which they are to be paid.

2. The amounts of the fees shall be fixed at such a level as to ensure that the revenue in respect thereof is in principle sufficient for the budget of the Office to be balanced.

3. The fees regulations shall be adopted and amended in accordance with the procedure laid down in Article 141.

TITLE XIII
FINAL PROVISIONS

Article 140
Community implementing provisions

1. The rules implementing this Regulation shall be adopted in an Implementing Regulation.

2. In addition to the fees provided for in the preceding Articles, fees shall be charged, in accordance with the detailed rules of application laid down in the Implementing Regulation, in the cases listed below:

1. alteration of the representation of a Community trade mark;
2. late payment of the registration fee;
3. issue of a copy of the certificate of registration;

4. registration of the transfer of a Community trade mark;

5. registration of a licence or another right in respect of a Community trade mark;

6. registration of a licence or another right in respect of an application for a Community trade mark;

7. cancellation of the registration of a licence or another right;

8. alteration of a registered Community trade mark;

9. issue of an extract from the Register;

10. inspection of the files;

11. issue of copies of file documents;

12. issue of certified copies of the application;

13. communication of information in a file;

14. review of the determination of the procedural costs to be refunded.

3. The Implementing Regulation and the rules of procedure of the Boards of Appeal shall be adopted and amended in accordance with the procedure laid down in Article 141.

Article 141
Establishment of a committee and procedure for the adoption of implementing regulations

1. The Commission shall be assisted by a Committee on Fees, Implementation Rules and the Procedure of the Boards of Appeal of the Office for Harmonization in the Internal Market (trade marks and designs), which shall be composed of representatives of the Member States and chaired by a representative of the Commission.

2. The representative of the Commission shall submit to the Committee a draft of the measures to be taken. The Committee shall deliver its opinion on the draft within a time limit which the chairman may lay down according to the urgency of the matter. The opinion shall be delivered by the majority laid down in Article 148(2) of the Treaty in the case of decisions which the Council is required to adopt on a proposal from the Commission. The votes of the representatives of the Member States within the Committee shall be weighted in the manner set out in that Article. The chairman shall not vote.

The Commission shall adopt the measures envisaged if they are in accordance with the opinion of the Committee.

If the measures envisaged are not in accordance with the opinion of the Committee, or if no opinion is delivered, the Commission shall, without delay, submit to the Council a proposal relating to the measures to be taken. The Council shall act by a qualified majority.

If, on the expiry of a period of three months from the date of referral to the Council, the Council has not acted, the proposed measures shall be adopted by the Commission, save where the Council has decided against the measures by a simple majority.

Article 142
Compatibility with other Community legal provisions

This Regulation shall not affect Council Regulation (EEC) No 2081/92 on the protection of geographical indications and designations of origin for agricultural products and foodstuffs of 14 July 1992, and in particular Article 14 thereof.

Article 143
Entry into force

1. This Regulation shall enter into force on the 60th day following that of its publication in the Official Journal of the European Communities.

2. The Member States shall within three years following entry into force of this Regulation take the necessary measures for the purpose of implementing Articles 91 and 110 hereof and shall forthwith inform the Commission of those measures.

3. Applications for Community trade marks may be filed at the Office from the date fixed by the Administrative Board on the recommendation of the President of the Office.

4. Applications for Community trade marks filed within three months before the date referred to in paragraph 3 shall be deemed to have been filed on that date.

This Regulation shall be binding in its entirety and directly applicable in all Member States.

Done at Brussels, 20 December 1993.

EC TRADEMARK DIRECTIVE

First Council Directive of 21 December 1988 to approximate the laws of the Member States relating to trade marks (89/104/EEC)

THE COUNCIL OF THE EUROPEAN COMMUNITIES,

Having regard to the Treaty establishing the European Economic Community, and in particular Article 100a thereof,

Having regard to the proposal from the Commission,

In cooperation with the European Parliament,

Having regard to the opinion of the Economic and Social Committee,

Whereas the trade mark laws at present applicable in the Member States contain disparities which may impede the free movement of goods and freedom to provide services and may distort competition within the common market; whereas it is therefore necessary, in view of the establishment and functioning of the internal market, to approximate the laws of Member States;

Whereas it is important not to disregard the solutions and advantages which the Community trade mark system may afford to undertakings wishing to acquire trade marks;

Whereas it does not appear to be necessary at present to undertake full-scale approximation of the trade mark laws of the Member States and it will be sufficient if approximation is limited to those national provisions of law which most directly affect the functioning of the internal market;

Whereas the Directive does not deprive the Member States of the right to continue to protect trademarks acquired through use but takes them into account only in regard to the relationship between them and trade marks acquired by registration;

Whereas Member States also remain free to fix the provisions of procedure concerning the registration, the revocation and the invalidity of trade marks acquired by registration; whereas they can, for example, determine the form of trade mark registration and invalidity procedures, decide whether earlier rights should be invoked either in the registration procedure or in the invalidity procedure or in both and, if they allow earlier rights to be invoked in the registration procedure, have an opposition procedure or an *ex officio* examination procedure or both; whereas Member States remain free to determine the effects of revocation or invalidity of trade marks;

Whereas this Directive does not exclude the application to trade marks of provisions of law of the Member States other than trade mark law, such as the provisions relating to unfair competition, civil liability or consumer protection;

Whereas attainment of the objectives at which this approximation of laws is aiming requires that the conditions for obtaining and continuing to hold a registered trade mark are, in general, identical in all Member States; whereas, to this end, it is necessary to list examples of signs which may constitute a trade mark, provided that such signs are capable of distinguishing the goods or services of one undertaking from those of other undertakings; whereas the grounds for refusal or invalidity concerning the trade mark itself, for example, the absence of any distinctive character, or concerning conflicts between the trade mark and earlier rights, are to be listed in an exhaustive manner, even if some of these grounds are listed as an option for the Member States which will therefore be able to maintain or introduce those grounds in their legislation; whereas Member States will be able to maintain or introduce into their legislation grounds of refusal or invalidity linked to conditions for obtaining and continuing to hold a trade mark for which there is no provision of approximation, concerning, for example, the eligibility for the grant of a trade mark, the renewal of the trade mark or rules on fees, or related to the non-compliance with procedural rules;

Whereas in order to reduce the total number of trade marks registered and protected in the Community and, consequently, the number of conflicts which arise between them, it is essential to require that registered trade marks must actually be used or, if not used, be subject to revocation; whereas it is necessary to provide that a trade mark cannot be invalidated on the basis of the existence of a non-used earlier trade mark, while the Member States remain free to apply the same principle in respect of the registration of a trade mark or to provide that a trade mark may not be successfully invoked in infringement proceedings if it is established as a result of a plea that the trade mark could be revoked; whereas in all these cases it is up to the Member States to establish the applicable rules of procedure;

Whereas it is fundamental, in order to facilitate the free circulation of goods and services, to ensure that henceforth registered trade marks enjoy the same protection under the legal systems of all the Member States; whereas this should however not prevent the Member States from granting at their option extensive protection to those trade marks which have a reputation;

Whereas the protection afforded by the registered trade mark, the function of which is in particular to guarantee the trade mark as an indication of origin, is absolute in the case of identity between the mark and the sign and goods or services; whereas the protection applies also in case of similarity between the mark and the sign and the goods or services; whereas it is indispensable to give an interpretation of the concept of similarity in relation to the likelihood of confusion; whereas the likelihood of confusion, the appreciation of which depends on numerous elements and, in particular, on the recognition of the trade mark on the market, of the association which can be made with the used or registered sign, of the degree of similarity between the trade mark and the sign and between the goods or services identified, constitutes the specific condition for such protection; whereas the ways in which likelihood of confusion may be established, and in particular the onus of proof, are a matter for national Procedural rules which are not prejudiced by the Directive;

Whereas it is important, for reasons of legal certainty and without inequitably prejudicing the interests of a proprietor of an earlier trade mark, to Provide that the latter may no longer request a declaration of invalidity nor may he oppose the use of a trade mark subsequent to his own of which he has knowingly tolerated the use for a substantial length of time, unless the application for the subsequent trade mark was made in bad faith;

Whereas all Member States of the Community are bound by the Paris Convention for the Protection of Industrial Property; whereas it is necessary that the provisions of this Directive are entirely consistent with those of the Paris Convention; whereas the obligations of the Member States resulting from this Convention are not affected by this Directive; whereas, where appropriate, the second subparagraph of Article 234 of the Treaty is applicable,

HAS ADOPTED THIS DIRECTIVE:

Article 1
Scope

This Directive shall apply to every trade mark in respect of goods or services which is the subject of registration or of an application in a Member State for registration as an individual trade mark, a collective mark or a guarantee or certification mark, or which is the subject of a registration or an application for registration in the Benelux Trade Mark Office or of an international registration having effect in a Member State.

Article 2
Signs of which a trade mark may consist

A trade mark may consist of any sign capable of being represented graphically, particularly words, including personal names, designs, letters, numerals, the shape of goods or of their packaging, provided that such signs are capable of distinguishing the goods or services of one undertaking from those of other undertakings.

Article 3
Grounds for refusal or invalidity

1. The following shall not be registered or if registered shall be liable to be declared invalid:

(a) signs which cannot constitute a trade mark;

(b) trade marks which are devoid of any distinctive character;

(c) trade marks which consist exclusively of signs or indications which may serve, in trade, to designate the kind, quality, quantity, intended purpose, value, geographical origin, or the time of production of the goods or of rendering of the service, or other characteristics of the goods;

(d) trade marks which consist exclusively of signs or indications which have become customary in the current language or in the *bona fide* and established practices of the trade;

(e) signs which consist exclusively of:

- the shape which results from the nature of the goods themselves, or
- the shape of goods which is necessary to obtain a technical result, or
- the shape which gives substantial value to the goods;

(f) trade marks which are contrary to public policy or to accepted principles of morality;

(g) trade marks which are of such a nature as to deceive the public, for instance as to the nature, quality or geographical origin of the goods or service;

(h) trade marks which have not been authorized by the competent authorities and are to be refused or invalidated pursuant to Article 6*ter* of the Paris Convention for the Protection of Industrial Property, hereinafter referred to as the 'Paris Convention'.

2. Any Member State may provide that a trade mark shall not be registered or, if registered, shall be liable to be declared invalid where and to the extent that:

(a) the use of that trade mark may be prohibited pursuant to provisions of law other than trade mark law of the Member State concerned or of the Community;

(b) the trade mark covers a sign of high symbolic value, in particular a religious symbol;

(c) the trade mark includes badges, emblems and escutcheons other than those covered by Article 6*ter* of the Paris Convention and which are of Public interest, unless the consent of the appropriate authorities to its registration has been given in conformity with the legislation of the Member State;

(d) the application for registration of the trade mark was made in bad faith by the applicant.

3. A trade mark shall not be refused registration or be declared invalid in accordance with paragraph 1 (b), (c) or (d) if, before the date of application for registration and following the use which has been made of it, it has acquired a distinctive character. Any Member State may in addition provide that this provision shall also apply where the distinctive character was acquired after the date of application for registration or after the date of registration.

4. Any Member State may provide that, by derogation from the preceding paragraphs, the grounds of refusal of registration or invalidity in force in that State prior to the date on which the provisions necessary to comply with this Directive enter into force, shall apply to trade marks for which application has been made prior to that date.

Article 4
Further grounds for refusal or invalidity concerning conflicts with earlier rights

1. A trade mark shall not be registered or, if registered, shall be liable to be declared invalid:

(a) if it is identical with an earlier trade mark, and the goods or services for which the trade mark is applied for or is registered are identical with the goods or services for which the earlier trade mark is protected;

(b) if because of its identity with, or similarity to, the earlier trade mark and the identity or similarity of the goods or services covered by the trade marks, there exists a likelihood of confusion on the part of the public, which includes the likelihood of association with the earlier trade mark.

2. 'Earlier trade marks' within the meaning of paragraph 1 means:

(a) trade marks of the following kinds with a date of application for registration which is earlier than the date of application for registration of the trade mark, taking account, where appropriate, of the priorities claimed in respect of those trade marks;

(i) Community trade marks;

(ii) trade marks registered in the Member State or, in the case of Belgium, Luxembourg or the Netherlands, at the Benelux Trade Mark Office;

(iii) trade marks registered under international arrangements which have effect in the Member State;

(b) Community trade marks which validly claim seniority, in accordance with the Regulation on the Community trade mark, from a trade mark referred to in (a) (ii) and (iii), even when the latter trade mark has been surrendered or allowed to lapse;

(c) applications for the trade marks referred to in (a) and (b), subject to their registration;

(d) trade marks which, on the date of application for registration of the trade mark, or, where appropriate, of the priority claimed in respect of the application for registration of the trade mark, are well known in a Member State, in the sense in which the words 'well known' are used in Article 6bis of the Paris Convention.

3. A trade mark shall furthermore not be registered or, if registered, shall be liable to be declared invalid if it is identical with, or similar to, an earlier Community trade mark within the meaning of paragraph 2 and is to be, or has been, registered for goods or services which are not similar to those for which the earlier Community trade mark is registered, where the earlier Community trade mark has a reputation in the Community and where the use of the later trade mark without due cause would take unfair advantage of, or be detrimental to, the distinctive character or the repute of the earlier Community trade mark.

4. Any Member State may furthermore provide that a trade mark shall not be registered or, if registered, shall be liable to be declared invalid where, and to the extent that:

(a) the trade mark is identical with, or similar to, an earlier national trade mark within the meaning of paragraph 2 and is to he, or has been, registered for goods or services which are not similar to those for which the earlier trade mark is registered, where the earlier trade mark has a reputation in the Member State concerned and where the use of the later trade mark without due cause would take unfair advantage of, or be detrimental to, the distinctive character or the repute of the earlier trade mark;

(b) rights to a non-registered trade mark or to another sign used in the course of trade were acquired prior to the date of application for registration of the subsequent trade mark, or the date of the priority claimed for the application for registration of the subsequent trade mark and that non-registered trade mark or other sign confers on its proprietor the right to prohibit the use of a subsequent trade mark;

(c) the use of the trade mark may be prohibited by virtue of an earlier right other than the rights referred to in paragraphs 2 and 4 (b) and in particular:

(i)   a right to a name;

(ii)   a right of personal portrayal;

(iii) a copyright;

(iv) an industrial property right;

(d) the trade mark is identical with, or similar to, an earlier collective trade mark conferring a right which expired within a period of a maximum of three years preceding application;

(e) the trade mark is identical with, or similar to, an earlier guarantee or certification mark conferring a right which expired within a period preceding application the length of which is fixed by the Member State;

(f) the trade mark is identical with, or similar to, an earlier trade mark which was registered for identical or similar goods or services and conferred on them a right which has expired for failure to renew within a period of a maximum of two years preceding application, unless the proprietor of the earlier trade mark gave his agreement for the registration of the later mark or did not use his trade mark;

(g) the trade mark is liable to be confused with a mark which was in use abroad on the filing date of the application and which is still in use there, provided that at the date of the application the applicant was acting in bad faith.

5. The Member States may permit that in appropriate circumstances registration need not be refused or the trade mark need not be declared invalid where the proprietor of the earlier trade mark or other earlier right consents to the registration of the later trade mark.

6. Any Member State may provide that, by derogation from paragraphs 1 to 5, the grounds for refusal of registration or invalidity in force in that State prior to the date on which the provisions necessary to comply with this Directive enter into force, shall apply to trade marks for which application has been made prior to that date.

Article 5
Rights conferred by a trade mark

1. The registered trade mark shall confer on the proprietor exclusive rights therein. The proprietor shall be entitled to prevent all third parties not having his consent from using in the course of trade:

(a) any sign which is identical with the trade mark in relation to goods or services which are identical with those for which the trade mark is registered;

(b) any sign where, because of its identity with, or similarity to, the trade mark and the identity or similarity of the goods or services covered by the trade mark and the sign, there exists a likelihood of confusion on the part of the public, which includes the likelihood of association between the sign and the trade mark.

2. Any Member State may also provide that the proprietor shall be entitled to prevent all third parties not having his consent from using in the course of trade any sign which is identical with, or similar to, the trade mark in relation to goods or services which are not similar to those for which the trade mark is registered, where the latter has a reputation in the Member State and where use of that sign without due cause takes unfair advantage of, or is detrimental to, the distinctive character or the repute of the trade mark.

3. The following, *inter alia*, may be prohibited under paragraphs 1 and 2:

(a) affixing the sign to the goods or to the packaging thereof;

(b) offering the goods, or putting them on the market or stocking them for these purposes under that sign, or offering or supplying services thereunder;

(c) importing or exporting the goods under the sign;

(d) using the sign on business papers and in advertising.

4. Where, under the law of the Member State, the use of a sign under the conditions referred to in 1(b) or 2 could not be prohibited before the date on which the provisions necessary to comply with this Directive entered into force in the Member State concerned, the rights conferred by the trade mark may not be relied on to prevent the continued use of the sign.

5. Paragraphs 1 to 4 shall not affect provisions in any Member State relating to the protection against the use of a sign other than for the purposes of distinguishing goods or services, where use of that sign without due cause takes unfair advantage of, or is detrimental to, the distinctive character or the repute of the trade mark.

Article 6
Limitation of the effects of a trade mark

1. The trade mark shall not entitle the proprietor to prohibit a third party from using, in the course of trade,

(a) his own name or address;

(b) indications concerning the kind, quality, quantity, intended purpose, value, geographical origin, the time of production of goods or of rendering of the service, or other characteristics of goods or services;

(c) the trade mark where it is necessary to indicate the intended purpose of a product or service, in particular as accessories or spare parts;

provided he uses them in accordance with honest practices in industrial or commercial matters.

2. The trade mark shall not entitle the proprietor to prohibit a third party from using, in the course of trade, an earlier right which only applies in a particular locality if that right is recognized by the laws of the Member State in question and within the limits of the territory in which it is recognized.

Article 7
Exhaustion of the rights conferred by a trade mark

1. The trade mark shall not entitle the proprietor to prohibit its use in relation to goods which have been put on the market in the Community under that trade mark by the proprietor or with his consent.

2. Paragraph 1 shall not apply where there exist legitimate reasons for the proprietor to oppose further commercialization of the goods, especially where the condition of the goods is changed or impaired after they have been put on the market.

Article 8
Licensing

1. A trade mark may be licensed for some or all of the goods or services for which it is registered and for the whole or part of the Member State concerned. A license may be exclusive or non-exclusive.

2. The proprietor of a trade mark may invoke the rights conferred by that trade mark against a licensee who contravenes any provision in his licensing contract with regard to its duration, the form covered by the registration in which the trade mark may be used, the scope of the goods or services for which the licence is granted, the territory in which the trade mark may be affixed, or the quality of the goods manufactured or of the services provided by the licensee.

Article 9
Limitation in consequence of acquiescence

1. Where, in a Member State, the proprietor of an earlier trade mark as referred to in Article 4(2) has acquiesced, for a period of five successive years, in the use of a later trade mark registered in that Member State while being aware of such use, he shall no longer be entitled on the basis of the earlier trade mark either to apply for a declaration that the later trade mark is invalid or to oppose the use of the later trade mark in respect of the goods or services for which the later trade mark has been used, unless registration of the later trade mark was applied for in bad faith.

2. Any Member State may provide that paragraph 1 shall apply *mutatis mutandis* to the proprietor of an earlier trade mark referred to in Article 4(4)(a) or an other earlier right referred to in Article 4(4) (b) or (c).

3. In the cases referred to in paragraphs 1 and 2, the proprietor of a later registered trade mark shall not be entitled to oppose the use of the earlier right, even though that right may no longer be invoked against the later trade mark.

Article 10
Use of trade marks

1. If, within a period of five years following the date of the completion of the registration procedure, the proprietor has not put the trade mark to genuine use in the Member State in connection with the goods or services in respect of which it is registered, or if such use has been suspended during an uninterrupted period of five years, the trade mark shall be subject to the sanctions provided for in this Directive, unless there are proper reasons for non-use.

2. The following shall also constitute use within the meaning of paragraph 1:

(a) use of the trade mark in a form differing in elements which do not alter the distinctive character of the mark in the form in which it was registered;

(b) affixing of the trade mark to goods or to the packaging thereof in the Member State concerned solely for export purposes.

3. Use of the trade mark with the consent of the proprietor or by any person who has authority to use a collective mark or a guarantee or certification mark shall be deemed to constitute use by the proprietor.

4. In relation to trade marks registered before the date on which the provisions necessary to comply with this Directive enter into force in the Member State concerned:

(a) where a provision in force prior to that date attaches sanctions to non-use of a trade mark during an uninterrupted period, the relevant period of five years mentioned in paragraph 1 shall be deemed to have begun to run at the same time as any period of non-use which is already running at that date;

(b) where there is no use provision in force prior to that date, the periods of five years mentioned in paragraph 1 shall be deemed to run from that date at the earliest.

Article 11
Sanctions for non use of a trade mark in legal or administrative proceedings

1. A trade mark may not be declared invalid on the ground that there is an earlier conflicting trade mark if the latter does not fulfil the requirements of use set out in Article 10 (1), (2) and (3) or in Article 10(4), as the case may be.

2. Any Member State may provide that registration of a trade mark may not be refused on the ground that there is an earlier conflicting trade mark if the latter does not fulfil the requirements of use set out in Article 10 (1), (2) and (3) or in Article 10(4), as the case may be.

3. Without prejudice to the application of Article 12, where a counter-claim for revocation is made, any Member State may provide that a trade mark may not be successfully invoked in infringement proceedings if it is established as a result of a plea that the trade mark could be revoked pursuant to Article 12(1).

4. If the earlier trade mark has been used in relation to part only of the goods or services for which it is registered, it shall, for purposes of applying paragraphs 1, 2 and 3, be deemed to be registered in respect only of that part of the goods or services.

Article 12
Grounds for revocation

1. A trade mark shall be liable to revocation if, within a continuous period of five years, it has not been put to genuine use in the Member State in connection with the goods or services in respect of which it is registered, and there are no proper reasons for non-use; however, no person may claim that the proprietor's rights in a trade mark should be revoked where, during the interval between expiry of the five-year period and filing of the application for revocation, genuine use of the trade mark has been started or resumed; the commencement or resumption of use within a period of three months preceding the filing of the application for revocation which began at the earliest on expiry of the continuous period of five years of non-use, shall, however, be disregarded where preparations for the commencement or resumption occur only after the proprietor becomes aware that the application for revocation may be filed.

2. A trade mark shall also be liable to revocation if, after the date on which it was registered,

(a) in consequence of acts or inactivity of the proprietor, it has become the common name in the trade for a product or service in respect of which it is registered;

(b) in consequence of the use made of it by the proprietor of the trade mark or with his consent in respect of the goods or services for which it is registered, it is liable to mislead the public, particularly as to the nature, quality or geographical origin of those goods or services.

Article 13
Grounds for refusal or revocation or invalidity
relating to only some of the goods or services

Where grounds for refusal of registration or for revocation or invalidity of a trade mark exist in respect of only some of the goods or services for which that trade mark has been applied for or registered, refusal of registration or revocation or invalidity shall cover those goods or services only.

Article 14
Establishment a posteriori of invalidity or revocation of a trade mark

Where the seniority of an earlier trade mark which has been surrendered or allowed to lapse, is claimed for a Community trade mark, the invalidity or revocation of the earlier trade mark may be established *a posteriori*.

Article 15
Special provisions in respect of collective marks, guarantee marks and certification marks

1. Without prejudice to Article 4, Member States whose laws authorize the registration of collective marks or of guarantee or certification marks may provide that such marks shall not be registered, or shall be revoked or declared invalid, on grounds additional to those specified in Articles 3 and 12 where the function of those marks so requires.

2. By way of derogation from Article 3(1)(c), Member States may provide that signs or indications which may serve, in trade, to designate the geographical origin of the goods or services may constitute collective, guarantee or certification marks. Such a mark does not entitle the proprietor to prohibit a third party from using in the course of trade such signs or indications, provided he uses them in accordance with honest practices in industrial or commercial matters; in particular, such a mark may not be invoked against a third party who is entitled to use a geographical name.

Article 16
National provisions to be adopted pursuant to this Directive

1. The Member States shall bring into force the laws, regulations and administrative provisions necessary to comply with this Directive not later than 28 December 1991. They shall immediately inform the Commission thereof.

2. Acting on a proposal from the Commission, the Council, acting by qualified majority, may defer the date referred to in paragraph 1 until 31 December 1992 at the latest.

3. Member States shall communicate to the Commission the text of the main provisions of national law which they adopt in the field governed by this Directive.

Article 17
Addressees

This Directive is addressed to the Member States.

Done at Brussels, 21 December 1988.

EC COUNTERFEITING REGULATION

Council Regulation (EC) No 3295/94 of 22 December 1994 laying down measures to prohibit the release for free circulation, export, re-export or entry for a suspensive procedure of counterfeit and pirated goods

THE COUNCIL OF THE EUROPEAN UNION,

Having regard to the Treaty establishing the European Community, and in particular Article 113 thereof,

Having regard to the proposal from the Commission,

Having regard to the opinion of the European Parliament,

Having regard to the opinion of the Economic and Social Committee,

Whereas Council Regulation (EEC) No 3842/86 of 1 December 1986 laying down measures to prohibit the release for free circulation of counterfeit goods has been in force since 1 January 1988; whereas conclusions should be drawn from the experience gained during the early years of its implementation with a view to improving the operation of the system it set up;

Whereas the marketing of counterfeit goods and pirated goods causes considerable injury to law-abiding manufacturers and traders and to holders of the copyright or neighbouring rights and misleads consumers; whereas such goods should as far as possible be prevented from being placed on the market and measures should be adopted to that end to deal effectively with this unlawful activity without impeding to freedom of legitimate trade; whereas this objective is also being pursued through efforts being made along the same lines at international level;

Whereas, in so far as counterfeit or pirated goods and similar products are imported from third countries, it is important to prohibit their release for free circulation in the Community or their entry for a suspensive procedure and to set up an appropriate procedure enabling the customs authorities to act to ensure that such a prohibition can be properly enforced;

Whereas action by the customs authorities to prohibit the release for free circulation of counterfeit or pirated goods or their entry for a suspensive procedure should also apply to the export or re-export of such goods from the Community;

Whereas, as regards suspensive procedures and re-export subject to notification, action by the customs authorities will take place only where suspected counterfeit or pirated goods are discovered during a check;

Whereas the Community takes into account the terms of the GATT agreement on trade-related intellectual property issues, including a trade in counterfeit goods, in particular the measures to be taken at the frontier;

Whereas provision should be made that the customs authorities are empowered to take decisions on applications for action to be taken that are submitted to them;

Whereas action by the customs authorities should consist either in suspending the release for free circulation, export or re-export of goods suspected of being counterfeit or pirated or in detaining such goods when they are entered for a suspensive procedure or re-exported subject to notification for as long as is necessary to enable it to be determined whether the goods are actually counterfeit or pirated; Whereas it is appropriate to authorize the Member States to detain the goods in question for a certain period even before an application by the right holder has been lodged or approved in order to allow him to lodge an application for action by the customs authorities;

Whereas the competent authority should decide cases submitted to it by reference to the criteria which are used to determine whether goods produced in the Member State concerned infringe intellectual property rights; whereas Member States' provisions on the competence of the judicial authorities and procedures are not affected by this Regulation;

Whereas it is necessary to determine the measures to be applied to the goods in question where it is established that they are counterfeit or pirated; whereas those measures should not only deprive those responsible for trading in such goods of the economic benefits of the transaction and penalize them but also constitute an effective deterrent to further transactions of the same kind;

Whereas in order to avoid serious disruption to the clearing of goods contained in travellers' personal luggage, it is necessary to exclude from the scope of this Regulation goods which may be counterfeit or pirated which are imported from third countries within the limits laid down by Community rules in respect of relief from customs duty;

Whereas uniform application of the common rules laid down by this Regulation must be ensured and to that end a Community procedure must be established enabling measures implementing these rules to be adopted within appropriate periods and mutual assistance between the Member States, of the one part, and between the Member States and the Commission, of the other part, to be strengthened so as to ensure greater effectiveness;

Whereas it will be appropriate to consider the possibility of increasing the number of intellectual property rights covered by this Regulation in the light, inter alia, of the experience gained in its implementation;

Whereas Regulation (EEC) No 3842/86 should therefore be repealed,

HAS ADOPTED THIS REGULATION:

CHAPTER I
General

Article 1

1. This Regulation shall lay down:

(a) the conditions under which the customs authorities shall take action where goods suspected of being counterfeit or pirated are:

    — entered for free circulation, export or re-export,

    — found when checks are made on goods placed under a suspensive procedure within the meaning of Article 84(1)(a) of Council Regulation (EEC) No 2913/92 of 12 October 1992 establishing the Community Customs Code, or re-exported subject to notification; and

(b) the measures which shall be taken by the competent authorities with regard to those goods where it has been established that they are indeed counterfeit or pirated.

2. For the purposes of this Regulation:

  (a) 'counterfeit goods' means:

    — goods, including the packaging thereof, being without authorization a trade mark which is identical to the trade mark validly registered in respect of the same type of goods, or which cannot be distinguished in its essential aspects from such trade mark, and which thereby infringes the rights of the holder of the trade mark in question under Community law or the law of the Member State in which the application for action by the customs authorities is made,

    — any trade mark symbol (logo, label, sticker, brochure, instructions for use or guarantee document) whether presented separately or not, in the same circumstances as the goods referred to in the first indent,

    — packaging materials bearing the trade marks of counterfeit goods, presented separately in the same circumstances as the goods referred to in the first indent;

  (b) 'pirated goods' means goods which are or embody copies made without the consent of the holder of the copyright or neighbouring rights, or of the holder of a design right, whether registered under national law or not, or of a person duly authorized by the holder in the country of production, where the making of those copies infringes the right in question under Community law or the law of the Member State in which the application for action by the customs authorities is made;

  (c) 'holder of a right' means the holder of a trade mark, as referred to in (a), and/or one of the rights referred to in (b), or any other person authorized to use the trade mark and/or rights, or their representative;

  (d) 'declaration for release for free circulation, for export or for re-export' means declarations made in accordance with Article 61 of Regulation (EEC) No 2913/92.

3. Any mould or matrix which is specifically designed or adapted for the manufacture of a counterfeit trade mark or of goods bearing such a trade mark or of pirated goods shall be treated as 'counterfeit or pirated goods', as appropriate, provided that the use of such moulds or matrices infringes the rights of the holder of a right under Community law or the law of the Member State in which the application for action by the customs authorities is made.

4. This Regulation shall not apply to goods which bear a trade mark with

the consent of the holder of that trade mark or which are protected by a copyright or neighbouring right or a design right and which have been manufactured with the consent of the holder of the right but are placed in one of the situations referred to in paragraph 1 (a) without the latter's consent.

Nor shall it apply to goods referred to in the first subparagraph which have been manufactured or bear a trade mark under conditions other than those agreed with the holders of the rights in question.

CHAPTER II
Prohibition of the release for free circulation, export, re-export or of the placing under a suspensive procedure of counterfeit goods and pirated goods

Article 2

The release for free circulation, export, re-export or placing under a suspensive procedure of goods founds to be counterfeit or pirated on completion of the procedure provided for in Article 6 shall be prohibited.

CHAPTER III
Application for action by the customs authorities

Article 3

1. In each Member State, the holder of a right may lodge an application in writing with the competent service of the customs authority for action by the customs authorities where the goods are placed in one of the situations referred to in Article 1(1)(a).

2. The application referred to in paragraph 1 shall include:

   – a sufficiently detailed description of the goods to enable the customs authorities to recognize them,

   – proof that the applicant is the holder of the right for the goods in question.

The holder of the right must also provide all other pertinent information available to him to enable the competent customs service to take a decision in full knowledge of the facts without, however, that information being a condition of admissibility of the application.

By way of indication, in the case of pirated goods, that information shall, wherever possible, include:

   – the place where the goods are situated or the intended destination,

   – particulars identifying the consignment or packages,

   – the scheduled date of arrival or departure of the goods,

   – the means of transport used,

– the identity of the importer, exporter or holder.

3. The application must specify the length of the period during which the customs authorities are requested to take action.

4. The applicant may be charged a fee to cover the administrative costs incurred in dealing with the application. The fee shall not be disproportionate to the service provided.

5. The competent customs service with which an application drawn up pursuant to paragraph 2 has been lodged shall deal with the application and shall forthwith notify the applicant in writing of its decision.

Where that service grants the application, the service shall specify the period during which the customs authorities shall take action. That period may, upon application by the holder of the right, be extended by the service which took the initial decision.

Any refusal to grant an application shall give the reasons for refusal and may form the subject of an appeal.

6. Member States may require the holder of a right, where his application has been granted, or where action as referred to in Article 1(1)(a) has been taken pursuant to Article 6(1), to provide a security:

– to cover any liability on his part vis-à-vis the persons involved in one of the operations referred to in Article 1(1)(a) where the procedure initiated pursuant to Article 6(1) is discontinued owing to an act or omission by the holder of the right or where the goods in question are subsequently found not be counterfeit or pirated,

– to ensure payment of the costs incurred in accordance with this Regulation, in keeping the goods under customs control pursuant to Article 6.

7. The holder of the right shall be obliged to inform the service referred to in paragraph 1 should the right cease to be validly registered or should it expire.

8. Each Member State shall designate the service within the customs authority competent to receive and deal with the applications referred to in this Article.

Article 4

Where, in the course of checks made under one of the customs procedures referred to in Article 1(1)(a) and before an application by the holder of the right has been lodged or approved, it appears evident to the customs office that goods are counterfeit or pirated, the customs authority may, in accordance with the rules in force in the Member States concerned, notify the holder of the right, where known, of a possible infringement thereof. The customs authority shall be authorized to suspend release of the goods or detain them for a period of three working days to enable the holder of the right to lodge an application for action in accordance with Article 3.

Article 5

The decision granting the application by the holder of the right shall be forwarded immediately to the customs offices of the Member State which are liable to be concerned with the goods alleged in the application to be counterfeit or pirated.

CHAPTER IV
Conditions governing action by the customs authorities and by the authority competent to take a substantive decision

Article 6

1. Where a customs office to which the decision granting an application by the holder of a right has been forwarded pursuant to Article 5 is satisfied, after consulting the applicant where necessary, that goods placed in one of the situations referred to in Article 1(1)(a) correspond to the description of the counterfeit or pirated goods contained in that decision, it shall suspend release of the goods or detain them.

The customs office shall immediately inform the service which dealt with the application in accordance with Article 3. That service or the customs office, shall forthwith inform the declarant and the person who applied for action to be taken. In accordance with national provisions on the protection of personal data, commercial and industrial secrecy and professional and administrative confidentiality, the customs office or the service which dealt with the application shall notify the holder of the right, at his request, of the name and address of the declarant and, if known, of those of the consignee so as to enable the holder of the right to ask the competent authorities to take a substantive decision. The customs office shall afford the applicant and the persons involved in any of the operations referred to in Article 1(1)(a) the opportunity to inspect the goods whose release has been suspended or which have been detained.

When examining the goods the customs office may take samples in order to expedite the procedure.

2. The law in force in the Member State within the territory of which the goods are placed in one of the situations referred to in Article 1(1)(a) shall apply as regards:

(a) referral to the authority competent to take a substantive decision and immediate notification of the customs service or office referred to in paragraph 1 of that referral, unless referral is effected by that service or office;

(b) reaching the decision to be taken by that authority. In the absence of Community rules in this regard, the criteria to be used in reaching that decision shall be the same as those used to determine whether goods produced in the Member State concerned infringe the rights of the holder. Reasons shall be given for decisions adopted by the competent authority.

Article 7

1.   If, within 10 working days of notification of suspension of release or of detention, the customs office referred to in Article 6(1) has not been informed that the matter has been referred to the authority competent to take a substantive decision on the case in accordance with Article 6(2) or that the duly empowered authority has adopted interim measures, the goods shall be released, provided that all the customs formalities have been complied with and the detention order has been revoked. This period may be extended by a maximum of 10 working days in appropriate cases.

2.   In the case of goods suspected of infringing design rights, the owner, the importer or the consignee of the goods shall be able to have the goods in question released or their detention revoked against provision of a security, provided that:

–   the customs service or office referred to in Article 6(1) has been informed, within the time limit referred to in paragraph 1, that the matter has been referred to the authority competent to take a substantive decision referred to in said paragraph 1,

–   on expiry of the time limit, the authority empowered for this purpose has not imposed interim measures, and

–   all the customs formalities have been completed.

The security must be sufficient to protect the interests of the holder of the right. Payment of the security shall be without prejudice to the other remedies open to the holder of the right. Where the matter has been referred to the authority competent to take a substantive decision other than on the initiative of the holder of the right, the security shall be released if that person does not exercise his right to institute legal proceedings within 20 working days of the date on which he is notified of the suspension of release or detention. Where the second subparagraph of paragraph 1 applies, this period may be extended to a maximum of 30 working days.

3.   The conditions governing storage of the goods during the period of suspension of release or detention shall be determined by each Member State.

CHAPTER V
Provisions applicable to goods found to be counterfeit or pirated goods

Article 8

1.   Without prejudice to the other rights of action open to the holder of a trade mark which is found to have been counterfeited or the holder of a copyright or neighbouring right or of a design right which is found to have been pirated, Member States shall adopt the measures necessary to allow the competent authorities:

(a) as a general rule, and in accordance with the relevant provisions of national law, to destroy goods found to be counterfeit or pirated, or dispose of them outside commercial channels in such a way as to preclude injury to the holder of the right, without compensation of any sort and at no cost to the exchequer;

(b) to take, in respect of such goods, any other measures which effectively deprive the persons concerned of the economic benefits of the transaction.

The following in particular shall not be regarded as having such effect:

- re-exporting the counterfeit or pirated goods in the unaltered state,
- other than in exceptional cases, simply removing the trade marks which have been affixed to the counterfeit goods without authorization,
- placing the goods under a different customs procedure.

2. The counterfeit or pirated goods may be handed over to the exchequer. In that event, paragraph 1(a) shall apply.

3. In addition to the information given pursuant to the second subparagraph of Article 6(1) and under the conditions laid down therein, the customs office or the competent service shall inform the holder of the right, upon request, of the names and addresses of the consignor, of the importer or exporter and of the manufacturer of the goods found to be counterfeit or pirated and of the quantity of the goods in question.

CHAPTER VI
Final provisions

Article 9

1. Save as provided by the law of the Member State in which the application is made, the acceptance of an application drawn up in accordance with Article 3(2) shall not entitle the holder of a right to compensation where counterfeit or pirated goods are not detected by a customs office and are released or no action is taken to detain them in accordance with Article 6(1).

2. Save as provided by the law of the Member State in which the application is made, exercise by a customs office or by another duly empowered authority of the powers conferred on them in regard to combating counterfeit or pirated goods shall not render them liable to the persons involved in the operations referred to in Article 1(1)(a) or Article 4, in the event of their suffering loss or damage as a result of their action.

3. The civil liability of the holder of a right shall be governed by the law of the Member State in which the goods in question were placed in one of the situations referred to in Article 1(1)(a).

Article 10

This Regulation shall not apply to goods of a non-commercial nature contained in travellers' personal luggage within the limits laid down in respect of relief from customs duty.

Article 11

Moreover, each Member State shall introduce penalties to apply in the event of infringements of Article 2. Such penalties must be sufficiently severe to encourage compliance with the relevant provisions.

Article 12

The provisions necessary for the application of this Regulation shall be adopted in accordance with the procedure laid down in Article 13 (3) and (4).

Article 13

1. The Commission shall be assisted by the Committee set up under Article 247 of Regulation (EEC) No 2913/92.

2. The Committee shall examine any matter concerning implementation of this Regulation which its chairman may raise, either on his own initiative or at the request of the representative of a Member State.

3. The representative of the Commission shall submit to the Committee a draft of the measures to be taken. The Committee shall deliver its opinion on the draft within a time limit which the chairman may lay down according to the urgency of the measures to be taken. The opinion shall be delivered by the majority laid down in Article 148(2) of the Treaty in the case of decisions which the Council is required to adopt on a proposal from the Commission. The votes of the representatives of the Member States within the Committee shall be weighted in the manner set out in that Article. The chairman shall not vote.

4. The Commission shall adopt measures which shall apply immediately. However, if the measures are not in accordance with the opinion of the Committee, they shall be communicated by the Commission to the Council forthwith. In the event:

- the Commission shall defer application of the measures which it has decided for not more than three months from the date of their communication,
- the Council, acting by a qualified majority, may take a different decision within the time limit provided for in the first indent.

Article 14

Member States shall communicate all relevant information on the application of this Regulation to the Commission.

The Commission shall communicate that information to the other Member States.

For the purpose of the application of this Regulation, the provisions of Regulation (EEC) No 1468/81 of 19 May 1981 on mutual assistance between the administrative authorities of the Member States and cooperation between the latter and the Commission to ensure the correct application of the law on customs or agricultural matters shall apply *mutatis mutandis*.

The details of the information procedure shall be drawn up in the framework of the implementing provisions in accordance with Article 13 (2), (3) and (4).

Article 15

Within two years of the entry into force of this Regulation, the Commission shall, on the basis of the information referred to in Article 14, report to the European Parliament and the Council on the operation of the system particularly with regard to the economic and social consequences of counterfeiting and shall propose any amendments or additions required, within a period of two years from the implementation of this Regulation.

Article 16

Regulation (EEC) No 3842/86 shall be repealed as from the date of implementation of this Regulation.

Article 17

This Regulation shall enter into force on the third day following its publication in the Official Journal of the European Communities. It shall apply from 1 July 1995. This Regulation shall be binding in its entirety and directly applicable in all Member States.

Done at Brussels, 22 December 1994.

D. GEOGRAPHICAL INDICATIONS

LISBON AGREEMENT FOR THE PROTECTION OF APPELLATIONS OF ORIGIN AND THEIR INTERNATIONAL REGISTRATION
of October 31, 1958, as revised at Stockholm on July 14, 1967

Article 1
[Establishment of a Special Union; Protection of Appellations of Origin Registered at the International Bureau]*

(1) The countries to which this Agreement applies constitute a Special Union within the framework of the Union for the Protection of Industrial Property.

(2) They undertake to protect on their territories, in accordance with the terms of this Agreement, the appellations of origin of products of the other countries of the Special Union, recognized and protected as such in the country of origin and registered at the International Bureau of Intellectual Property (hereinafter designated as "the International Bureau" or "the Bureau") referred to in the Convention establishing the World Intellectual Property Organization (hereinafter designated as "the Organization").

Article 2
[Definition of Notions of Appellation of Origin and Country of Origin]

(1) In this Agreement, "appellation of origin" means the geographical name of a country, region or locality which serves to designate a product originating therein the quality and characteristics of which are due exclusively or essentially to the geographical environment, including natural and human factors.

(2) The country of origin is the country whose name, or the country in which is situated the region or locality whose name, constitutes the appellation of origin which has given the product its reputation.

Article 3
[Content of Protection]

Protection shall be ensured against any usurpation or imitation, even if the true origin of the product is indicated or if the appellation is used in translated form or accompanied by terms such as "kind," "type," "make," "imitation," or the like.

---

* Articles have been given titles by WIPO to facilitate their identification. There are no titles in the signed (French) text.

Article 4
[Protection by Virtue of Other Texts]

The Provisions of this Agreement shall in no way exclude the protection already granted to appellations of origin in each of the countries of the Special Union by virtue of other international instruments, such as the Paris Convention of March 20, 1883, for the Protection of Industrial Property and its subsequent revisions, and the Madrid Agreement of April 14, 1891, for the Repression of False or Deceptive Indications of Source on Goods and its subsequent revisions, or by virtue of national legislation or court decisions.

Article 5
[International Registration; Refusal and Opposition to Refusal; Notifications; Use Tolerated for a Fixed Period]

(1) The registration of appellations of origin shall be effected at the International Bureau, at the request of the Offices of the countries of the Special Union, in the name of any natural persons or legal entities, public or private, having, according to their national legislation, the right to use such appellations.

(2) The International Bureau shall, without delay, notify the Offices of the various countries of the Special Union of such registrations, and shall publish them in a periodical.

(3) The Office of any country may declare that it cannot ensure the protection of an appellation of origin whose registration has been notified to it, but only in so far as its declaration is notified to the International Bureau, together with an indication of the grounds therefor, within a period of one year from the receipt of the notification of registration, and provided that such declaration is not detrimental, in the country concerned, to the other forms of protection of the appellation which the owner thereof may be entitled to claim under Article 4, above.

(4) Such declaration may not be made by the Offices of the countries of the Union after the expiration of the period of one year provided for in the foregoing paragraph.

(5) The International Bureau shall, as soon as possible notify the Office of the country of origin of any declaration made under the terms of paragraph (3) by the Office of another country. The interested party, when informed by his national Office of the declaration made by another country, may resort, in that other country, to all the judicial and administrative remedies open to the nationals of that country.

(6) If an appellation which has been granted protection in a given country pursuant to notification of its international registration has already been used by third parties in that country from a date prior to such notification, the competent Office of the said country shall have the right to grant to such third parties a period not exceeding two years to terminate such use, on condition that it advise the International Bureau accordingly within three months following the expiration of the period of one year provided for in

paragraph (3), above.

Article 6
[Generic Appellations]

An appellation which has been granted protection in one of the countries of the Special Union according to the procedure under Article 5 cannot, in that country, be deemed to have become generic as long as it is protected as an appellation of origin in the country of origin.

Article 7
[Period of Validity of Registration; Fee]

(1) Registration effected at the International Bureau in conformity with Article 5 shall ensure, without renewal, protection for the whole of the period referred to in the foregoing Article.

(2) A single fee shall be paid for the registration of each appellation of origin.

Article 8
[Legal Proceedings]

Legal action required for ensuring the protection of appellations of origin may be taken in each of the countries of the Special Union under the provisions of the national legislation:

(1) at the instance of the competent Office or at the request of the public prosecutor;

(2) by any interested party, whether a natural person or a legal entity, whether public or private.

Article 9
[Assembly of the Special Union]

(1)

(a) The Special Union shall have an Assembly consisting of those countries which have ratified or acceded to this Act.

(b) The Government of each country shall be represented by one delegate, who may be assisted by alternate delegates, advisors, and experts.

(c) The expenses of each delegation shall be borne by the Government which has appointed it.

(2)

(a) The Assembly shall:

    (i)   deal with all matters concerning the maintenance and development of the Special Union and the implementation of this Agreement;

    (ii)   give directions to the International Bureau concerning the preparation for conferences of revision, due account being taken of any comments made by those countries of the Special Union which have not ratified or acceded to this Act;

(iii) modify the Regulations, including the fixation of the amount of the fee referred to in Article 7(2) and other fees relating to international registration;

(iv) review and approve the reports and activities of the Director-General of the Organization (hereinafter designated as "the Director-General") concerning the Special Union, and give him all necessary instructions concerning matters within the competence of the Special Union;

(v) determine the program and adopt the triennial budget of the Special Union, and approve its final accounts;

(vi) adopt the financial regulations of the Special Union;

(vii) establish such committees of experts and working groups as it deems appropriate to achieve the objectives of the Special Union;

(viii) determine which countries not members of the Special Union and which intergovernmental and international non-governmental organizations shall be admitted to its meetings as observers;

(ix) adopt amendments to Articles 9 to 12;

(x) take any other appropriate action designed to further the objectives of the Special Union;

(xi) perform such other functions as are appropriate under this Agreement.

(b) With respect to matters which are of interest also to other Unions administered by the Organization, the Assembly shall make its decisions after having heard the advice of the Coordination Committee of the Organization.

(3)

(a) Each country member of the Assembly shall have one vote.

(b) One-half of the countries members of the Assembly shall constitute a quorum.

(c) Notwithstanding the provisions of subparagraph (b), if, in any session, the number of countries represented is less than one-half but equal to or more than one-third of the countries members of the Assembly, the Assembly may make decisions but with the exception of decisions concerning its own procedure, all such decisions shall take effect only if the conditions set forth hereinafter are fulfilled. The International Bureau shall communicate the said decisions to the countries members of the Assembly which were not represented and shall invite them to express in writing their vote or abstention within a period of three months from the date of the communication. If, at the expiration of this period, the number of countries having thus expressed their vote or abstention attains the number of countries which was lacking for attaining the quorum in the session itself, such decisions shall take effect provided that at the same time the required majority still obtains.

(d) Subject to the provisions of the Article 12(2), the decisions of the Assembly shall require two-thirds of the votes cast.

(e) Abstentions shall not be considered as votes.

(f) A delegate may represent, and vote in the name of, one country only.

(g) Countries of the Special Union not members of the Assembly shall be admitted to the meetings of the latter as observers.

(4)

(a) The Assembly shall meet once every third calendar year in ordinary session upon convocation by the Director-General and, in the absence of exceptional circumstances, during the same period and at the same place as the General Assembly of the Organization.

(b) The Assembly shall meet in extraordinary session upon convocation by the Director-General, at the request of one-fourth of the countries members of the Assembly.

(c) The agenda of each session shall be prepared by the Director-General.

(5) The Assembly shall adopt it own rules of procedure.

Article 10
[International Bureau]

(1)

(a) International registration and related duties, as well as all other administrative tasks concerning the Special Union, shall be performed by the International Bureau.

(b) In particular, the International Bureau shall prepare the meetings and provide the secretariat of the Assembly and of such committees of experts and working groups as may have been established by the Assembly.

(c) The Director-General shall be the chief executive of the Special Union and shall represent the Special Union.

(2) The Director-General and any staff member designated by him shall participate, without the right to vote, in all meetings of the Assembly and of such committees of experts or working groups as may have been established by the Assembly. The Director-General, or a staff member designated by him, shall be ex officio secretary of those bodies.

(3)

(a) The International Bureau shall, in accordance with the directions of the Assembly, make the preparations for the conferences of revision of the provisions of the Agreement other than Articles 9 to 12.

(b) The International Bureau may consult with intergovernmental and international non-governmental organizations concerning preparations for conferences of revision.

(c) The Director-General and persons designated by him shall take part, without the right to vote, in the discussions at those conferences.

(4) The International Bureau shall carry out any other tasks assigned to it.

Article 11
[Finances]

(1)

(a) The Special Union shall have a budget.

(b) The budget of the Special Union shall include the income and expenses proper to the Special Union, its contribution to the budget of expenses common to the Unions, and, where applicable, the sum made available to the budget of the Conference of the Organization.

(c) Expenses not attributable exclusively to the Special Union but also to one or more other Unions administered by the Organization shall be considered as expenses common to the Unions. The share of the Special Union in such common expenses shall be in proportion to the interest the Special Union has in them.

(2) The budget of the Special Union shall be established with due regard to the requirements of coordination with the budgets of the other Unions administered by the Organization.

(3) The budget of the Special Union shall be financed from the following sources:

  (i)   international registration fees collected under Article 7(2) and other fees and charges due for other services rendered by the International Bureau in relation to the Special Union;

  (ii) sale of, or royalties on, the publications of the International Bureau concerning the Special Union;

  (iii) gifts, bequests, and subventions;

  (iv) rents, interests, and other miscellaneous income;

  (v)   contributions of the countries of the Special Union, if and to the extent to which receipts from the sources indicated in items (i) to (iv) do not suffice to cover the expenses of the Special Union.

(4)

(a) The amount of the fee referred to in Article 7(2) shall be fixed by the Assembly on the proposal of the Director-General.

(b) The amount of the said fee shall be so fixed that the revenue of the Special Union should, under normal circumstances, be sufficient to cover the expenses of the International Bureau for maintaining the international registration service, without requiring payment of the contributions referred to in paragraph (3)(v), above.

(5)

(a) For the purpose of establishing its contribution referred to in paragraph (3)(v), each country of the Special Union shall belong to the same class as it belongs to in the Paris Union for the Protection of Industrial Property, and shall pay its annual contributions on the basis of the same number of units as is fixed for that class in that Union.

(b) The annual contribution of each country of the Special Union shall be an amount in the same proportion to the total sum to be contributed to the budget of the Special Union by all countries as the number of its units is to the total of the units of all contributing countries.

(c) The date on which contributions are to be paid shall be fixed by the Assembly.

(d) A country which is in arrears in the payment of its contributions may not exercise its right to vote in any of the organs of the Special Union if the amount of its arrears equals or exceeds the amount of the contributions due from it for the preceding two full years. However, any organ of the Union may allow such a country to continue to exercise its right to vote in that organ if, and as long as, it is satisfied that the delay in payment is due to exceptional and unavoidable circumstances.

(e) If the budget is not adopted before the beginning of a new financial period, it shall be at the same level as the budget of the previous year, as provided in the financial regulations.

(6) Subject to the provisions of paragraph (4)(a), the amount of fees and charges due for other services rendered by the International Bureau in relation to the Special Union shall be established, and shall be reported to the Assembly, by the Director-General.

(7)

(a) The Special Union shall have a working capital fund which shall be constituted by a single payment made by each country of the Special Union. If the fund becomes insufficient, the Assembly shall decide to increase it.

(b) The amount of the initial payment of each country to the said fund or of its participation in the increase thereof shall be a proportion of the contribution of that country as a member of the Paris Union for the Protection of Industrial Property to the budget of the said Union for the year in which the fund is established or the decision to increase it is made.

(c) The proportion and the terms of payment shall be fixed by the Assembly on the proposal of the Director-General and after it has heard the advice of the Coordination Committee of the Organization.

(8)

(a) In the headquarters agreement concluded with the country on the territory of which the Organization has its headquarters, it shall be provided that, whenever the working capital fund is insufficient, such country shall grant advances. The amount of those advances and the conditions on which they are granted shall be the subject of separate agreements, in each case, between such country and the Organization.

(b) The country referred to in subparagraph (a) and the Organization shall each have the right to denounce the obligation to grant advances, by written notification. Denunciation shall take effect three years after the end of the year in which it has been notified.

(9) The auditing of the accounts shall be effected by one or more of the countries of the Special Union or by external auditors, as provided in the financial regulations. They shall be designated, with their agreement, by the Assembly.

Article 12
[Amendment of Articles 9 to 12]

(1) Proposals for the amendment of Article 9, 10, 11, and the present Article, may be initiated by any country member of the Assembly, or by the Director-General. Such proposals shall be communicated by the Director-General to the member countries of the Assembly at least six months in advance of their consideration by the Assembly.

(2) Amendment to the Articles referred to in paragraph (1) shall be adopted by the Assembly. Adoption shall require three-fourths of the votes cast, provided that any amendment to Article 9, and to the present paragraph, shall require four-fifths of the votes cast.

(3) Any amendment to the Articles referred to in paragraph (1) shall enter into force one month after written notifications of acceptance, effected in accordance with their respective constitutional processes, have been received by the Director-General from three-fourths of the countries members of the Assembly at the time it adopted the amendment. Any amendment to the said Articles thus accepted shall bind all the countries which are members of the Assembly at the time the amendment enters into force, or which become members thereof at a subsequent date, provided that any amendment increasing the financial obligations of countries of the Special Union shall bind only those countries which have notified their acceptance of such amendment.

Article 13
[Regulations; Revision]

(1) The details for carrying out this Agreement are fixed in the Regulations.

(2) This Agreement may be revised by conferences held among the delegates of the countries of the Special Union.

Article 14
[Ratification and Accession; Entry Into Force; Reference to Article 24 of Paris Convention (Territories); Accession to the Original Act of 1958]

(1) Any country of the Special Union which has signed this Act may ratify it, and, if it has not signed it, may accede to it.

(2)

(a) Any country outside the Special Union which is party to the Paris Convention for the Protection of Industrial Property may accede to this Act and thereby become a member of the Special Union.

(b) Notification of accession shall, of itself, ensure, in the territory of the acceding country, the benefits of the foregoing provisions to appellations of origin which, at the time of accession, are the subject of international registration.

(c) However, any country acceding to this Agreement may, within a period of one year, declare in regard to which appellations of origin, already registered at the International Bureau, it wishes to exercise the right provided for in Article 5(3).

(3) Instruments of ratification and accession shall be deposited with the Director-General.

(4) The provisions of Article 24 of the Paris Convention for the Protection of Industrial Property shall apply to this Agreement.

(5)

(a) With respect to the first five countries which have deposited their instruments of ratification or accession, this Act shall enter into force three months after the deposit of the fifth such instrument.

(b) With respect to any other country, this Act shall enter into force three months after the date on which its ratification or accession has been notified by the Director-General, unless a subsequent date has been indicated in the instrument of ratification or accession. In the latter case, this Act shall enter into force with respect to that country on the date thus indicated.

(6) Ratification or accession shall automatically entail acceptance of all the clauses and admission to all the advantages of this Act.

(7) After the entry into force of this Act, a country may accede to the original Act of October 31, 1958, of this Agreement only in conjunction with ratification of, or accession to, this Act.

Article 15
[Duration of the Agreement; Denunciation]

(1) This Agreement shall remain in force as long as five countries at least are party to it.

(2) Any country may denounce this Act by notification addressed to the Director-General. Such denunciation shall constitute also denunciation of the original Act of October 31, 1958, of this Agreement and shall affect only the country making it, the Agreement remaining in full force and effect as regards the other countries of the Special union.

(3) Denunciation shall take effect one year after the day on which the Director-General has received the notification.

(4) The right of denunciation provided for by this Article shall not be exercised by any country before the expiration of five years from the date upon which it becomes a member of the Special Union.

Article 16
[Application of the Original Act of 1958]

(1)

(a) This Act shall, as regards the relations between the countries of the Special Union by which it has been ratified or acceded to, replace the original Act of October 31, 1958.

(b) However, any country of the Special Union which has ratified or acceded to this Act shall be bound by the original Act of October 31, 1958, as regards its relations with countries of the Special Union which have not ratified or acceded to this Act.

(2) Countries outside the Special Union which become party to this Act shall apply it to international registrations of appellations of origin effected at the International Bureau at the request of the Office of any country of the Special Union not party to this Act, provided that such registrations satisfy, with respect to the said countries, the requirements of this Act. With regard to international registrations effected at the International Bureau at the request of the Offices of the said countries outside the Special Union which become party to this Act, such countries recognize that the aforesaid country of the Special Union may demand compliance with the requirements of the original Act of October 31, 1958.

Article 17
[Signature, Languages, Depositary Functions]

(1)

(a) This Act shall be signed in a single copy in the French language and shall be deposited with the Government of Sweden.

(b) Official texts shall be established by the Director-General, after consultation with the interested Governments, in such other languages as the Assembly may designate.

(2) This Act shall remain open for signature at Stockholm until January 13, 1968.

(3) The Director-General shall transmit two copies, certified by the Government of Sweden, of the signed text of this Act to the Governments of all countries of the Special Union and, on request, to the Government of any other country.

(4) The Director-General shall register this Act with the Secretariat of the United Nations.

(5) The Director-General shall notify the Governments of all countries of the Special Union of signatures, deposits of instruments of ratification or accession, entry into force of any provisions of this Act, denunciations, and declarations pursuant to Article 14(2)(c) and (4).

Article 18
[Transitional Provisions]

(1) Until the first Director-General assumes office, references in this Act to the International Bureau of the Organization or to the Director-General shall be construed as references to the Bureau of the Union established by the Paris Convention for the Protection of Industrial Property or its Director, respectively.

(2) Countries of the Special Union not having ratified or acceded to this Act may, until five years after the entry into force of the Convention establishing the Organization, exercise, if they so desire, the rights provided for under Articles 9 to 12 of this Act as if they were bound by those Articles. Any country desiring to exercise such rights shall give written notification to that effect to the Director-General; such notification shall be effective from the date of its receipt. Such countries shall be deemed to be members of the Assembly until the expiration of the said period.

EC REGULATION ON GEOGRAPHICAL INDICATIONS (FOODSTUFFS)

Council Regulation (EEC) No 2081/92 of 14 July 1992 on the protection of geographical indications and designations of origin for agricultural products and foodstuffs

THE COUNCIL OF THE EUROPEAN COMMUNITIES,

Having regard to the Treaty establishing the European Economic Community, and in particular Article 43,

Having regard to the proposal from the Commission,

Having regard to the opinion of the European Parliament,

Having regard to the opinion of the Economic and Social Committee,

Whereas the production, manufacture and distribution of agricultural products and foodstuffs play an important role in the Community economy;

Whereas, as part of the adjustment of the common agricultural policy the diversification of agricultural production should be encouraged so as to achieve a better balance between supply and demand on the markets; whereas the promotion of products having certain characteristics could be of considerable benefit to the rural economy, in particular to less-favoured or remote areas, by improving the incomes of farmers and by retaining the rural population in these areas;

Whereas, moreover, it has been observed in recent years that consumers are tending to attach greater importance to the quality of foodstuffs rather than to quantity; whereas this quest for specific products generates a growing demand for agricultural products or foodstuffs with an identifiable geographical origin;

Whereas in view of the wide variety of products marketed and of the abundance of information concerning them provided, consumers must, in order to be able to make the best choice, be given clear and succinct information regarding the origin of the product;

Whereas the labelling of agricultural products and foodstuffs is subject to the general rules laid down in Council Directive 79/112/EEC of 18 December 1978 on the approximation of the laws of the Member States relating to the labelling, presentation and advertising of foodstuffs; whereas, in view of their specific nature, additional special provisions should be adopted for agricultural products and foodstuffs from a specified geographical area;

Whereas the desire to protect agricultural products or foodstuffs which have an identifiable geographical origin has led certain Member States to introduce 'registered designations of origin'; whereas these have proved successful with producers, who have secured higher incomes in return for a genuine effort to improve quality, and with consumers, who can purchase high quality products with guarantees as to the method of production and origin;

Whereas, however, there is diversity in the national practices for implementing registered designations or origin and geographical indications; whereas a Community approach should be envisaged; whereas a framework of Community rules on protection will permit the development of geographical indications and designations of origin since, by providing a more uniform approach, such a framework will ensure fair competition between the producers of products bearing such indications and enhance the credibility of the products in the consumers' eyes;

Whereas the planned rules should take account of existing Community legislation on wines and spirit drinks, which provide for a higher level of protection;

Whereas the scope of this Regulation is limited to certain agricultural products and foodstuffs for which a link between product or foodstuff characteristics and geographical origin exists; whereas, however, this scope could be enlarged to encompass other products or foodstuffs;

Whereas existing practices make it appropriate to define two different types of geographical description, namely protected geographical indications and protected designations of origin;

Whereas an agricultural product or foodstuff bearing such an indication must meet certain conditions set out in a specification;

Whereas to enjoy protection in every Member State geographical indications and designations of origin must be registered at Community level; whereas entry in a register should also provide information to those involved in trade and to consumers;

Whereas the registration procedure should enable any person individually and directly concerned in a Member State to exercise his rights by notifying the Commission of his opposition;

Whereas there should be procedures to permit amendment of the specification, after registration, in the light of technological progress or withdrawal from the register of the geographical indication or designation of origin of an agricultural product or foodstuff if that product or foodstuff ceases to conform to the specification on the basis of which the geographical indication or designation of origin was granted;

Whereas provision should be made for trade with third countries offering equivalent guarantees for the issue and inspection of geographical indications or designations of origin granted on their territory;

Whereas provision should be made for a procedure establishing close cooperation between the Member States and the Commission through a Regulatory Committee set up for that purpose,

HAS ADOPTED THIS REGULATION:

Article 1

1. This Regulation lays down rules on the protection of designations of origin and geographical indications of agricultural products intended for human consumption referred to in Annex II to the Treaty and of the

foodstuffs referred to in Annex I to this Regulation and agricultural products listed in Annex II to this Regulation.

However, this Regulation shall not apply to wine products or to spirit drinks.

Annex I may be amended in accordance with the procedure set out in Article 15.

2. This Regulation shall apply without prejudice to other specific Community provisions.

3. Council Directive 83/189/EEC of 28 March 1983 laying down a procedure for the provision of information in the field of technical standards and regulations shall not apply to the designations of origin and geographical indications covered by this Regulation.

Article 2

1. Community protection of designations of origin and of geographical indications of agricultural products and foodstuffs shall be obtained in accordance with this Regulation.

2. For the purposes of this Regulation:

  (a) designation of origin: means the name of a region, a specific place or, in exceptional cases, a country, used to describe an agricultural product or a foodstuff:

    — originating in that region, specific place or country, and

    — the quality or characteristics of which are essentially or exclusively due to a particular geographical environment with its inherent natural and human factors, and the production, processing and preparation of which take place in the defined geographical area;

  (b) geographical indication: means the name of a region, a specific place or, in exceptional cases, a country, used to describe an agricultural product or a foodstuff:

    — originating in that region, specific place or country, and

    — which possesses a specific quality, reputation or other characteristics attributable to that geographical origin and the production and/or processing and/or preparation of which take place in the defined geographical area.

3. Certain traditional geographical or non-geographical names designating an agricultural product or a foodstuff originating in a region or a specific place, which fulfil the conditions referred to in the second indent of paragraph 2(a) shall also be considered as designations of origin.

4. By way of derogation from Article 2(a), certain geographical designations shall be treated as designations of origin where the raw materials of the products concerned come from a geographical area larger than or different from the processing area, provided that:

    — the production area of the raw materials is limited,

— special conditions for the production of the raw materials exist, and

— there are inspection arrangements to ensure that those conditions are adhered to.

5. For the purposes of paragraph 4, only live animals, meat and milk may be considered as raw materials. Use of other raw materials may be authorized in accordance with the procedure laid down in Article 15.

6. In order to be eligible for the derogation provided for in paragraph 4, the designations in question may be or have already been recognized as designations of origin with national protection by the Member State concerned, or, if no such scheme exists, have a proven, traditional character and an exceptional reputation and renown.

7. In order to be eligible for the derogation provided for in paragraph 4, applications for registration must be lodged within two years of the entry into force of this Regulation.

Article 3

1. Names that have become generic may not be registered.

For the purposes of this Regulation, a 'name that has become generic' means the name of an agricultural product or a foodstuff which, although it relates to the place or the region where this product or foodstuff was originally produced or marketed, has become the common name of an agricultural product or a foodstuff.

To establish whether or not a name has become generic, account shall be taken of all factors, in particular:

— the existing situation in the Member State in which the name originates and in areas of consumption,

— the existing situation in other Member States,

— the relevant national or Community laws.

Where, following the procedure laid down in Articles 6 and 7, an application of registration is rejected because a name has become generic, the Commission shall publish that decision in the Official Journal of the European Communities.

2. A name may not be registered as a designation of origin or a geographical indication where it conflicts with the name of a plant variety or an animal breed and as a result is likely to mislead the public as to the true origin of the product.

3. Before the entry into force of this Regulation, the Council, acting by a qualified majority on a proposal from the Commission, shall draw up and publish in the Official Journal of the European Communities a non-exhaustive, indicative list of the names of agricultural products or foodstuffs which are within the scope of this Regulation and are regarded under the terms of paragraph 1 as being generic and thus not able to be registered under this Regulation.

Article 4

1. To be eligible to use a protected designation of origin (PDO) or a protected geographical indication (PGI) an agricultural product or foodstuff must comply with a specification.

2. The product specification shall include at least:

(a) the name of the agricultural product or foodstuffs, including the designation of origin or the geographical indication;

(b) a description of the agricultural product or foodstuff including the raw materials, if appropriate, and principal physical, chemical, microbiological and/or organoleptic characteristics of the product or the foodstuff;

(c) the definition of the geographical area and, if appropriate, details indicating compliance with the requirements in Article 2(4);

(d) evidence that the agricultural product or the foodstuff originates in the geographical area, within the meaning of Article 2(2) (a) or (b), whichever is applicable;

(e) a description of the method of obtaining the agricultural product or foodstuff and, if appropriate, the authentic and unvarying local methods;

(f) the details bearing out the link with the geographical environment or the geographical origin within the meaning of Article 2 (2) (a) or (b), whichever is applicable;

(g) details of the inspection structures provided for in Article 10;

(h) the specific labelling details relating to the indication PDO or PGI, whichever is applicable, or the equivalent traditional national indications;

(i) any requirements laid down by Community and/or national provisions.

Article 5

1. Only a group or, subject to certain conditions to be laid down in accordance with the procedure provided for in Article 15, a natural or legal person, shall be entitled to apply for registration.

For the purposes of this Article, 'Group' means any association, irrespective of its legal form or composition, of producers and/or processors working with the same agricultural product or foodstuff. Other interested parties may participate in the group.

2. A group or a natural or legal person may apply for registration only in respect of agricultural products or foodstuffs which it produces or obtains within the meaning of Article 2(2) (a) or (b).

3. The application for registration shall include the product specification referred to in Article 4.

4. The application shall be sent to the Member State in which the geographical area is located.

5. The Member State shall check that the application is justified and shall forward the application, including the product specification referred to in Article 4 and other documents on which it has based its decision, to the

Commission, if it considers that it satisfies the requirements of this Regulation.

If the application concerns a name indicating a geographical area situated in another Member State also, that Member State shall be consulted before any decision is taken.

6. Member States shall introduce the laws, regulations and administrative provisions necessary to comply with this Article.

Article 6

1. Within a period of six months the Commission shall verify, by means of a formal investigation, whether the registration application includes all the particulars provided for in Article 4.

The Commission shall inform the Member State concerned of its findings.

2. If, after taking account of paragraph 1, the Commission concludes that the name qualifies for protection, it shall publish in the Official Journal of the European Communities the name and address of the applicant, the name of the product, the main points of the application, the references to national provisions governing the preparation, production or manufacture of the product and, if necessary, the grounds for its conclusions.

3. If no statement of objections is notified to the Commission in accordance with Article 7, the name shall be entered in a register kept by the Commission entitled 'Register of protected designations of origin and protected geographical indications`, which shall contain the names of the groups and the inspection bodies concerned.

4. The Commission shall publish in the Official Journal of the European Communities:

  − the names entered in the Register,
  − amendments to the Register made in accordance with Article 9 and 11.

5. If, in the light of the investigation provided for in paragraph 1, the Commission concludes that the name does not qualify for protection, it shall decide, in accordance with the procedure provided for in Article 15, not to proceed with the publication provided for in paragraph 2 of this Article.

Before publication as provided for in paragraphs 2 and 4 and registration as provided for in paragraph 3, the Commission may request the opinion of the Committee provided for in Article 15.

Article 7

1. Within six months of the date of publication in the Official Journal of the European Communities referred to in Article 6(2), any Member State may object to the registration.

2. The competent authorities of the Member States shall ensure that all persons who can demonstrate a legitimate economic interest are authorized

to consult the application. In addition and in accordance with the existing situation in the Member States, the Member States may provide access to other parties with a legitimate interest.

3. Any legitimately concerned natural or legal person may object to the proposed registration by sending a duly substantiated statement to the competent authority of the Member State in which he resides or is established. The competent authority shall take the necessary measures to consider these comments or objection within the deadlines laid down.

4. A statement of objection shall be admissible only if it:

- either shows non-compliance with the conditions referred to in Article 2,

- or shows that the proposed registration of a name would jeopardize the existence of an entirely or partly identical name or trade mark or the existence of products which are legally on the market at the time of publication of this regulation in the Official Journal of the European Communities,

- or indicates the features which demonstrate that the name whose registration is applied for is generic in nature.

5. Where an objection is admissible within the meaning of paragraph 4, the Commission shall ask the Member States concerned to seek agreement among themselves in accordance with their internal procedures within three months. If:

(a) agreement is reached, the Member States in question shall communicate to the Commission all the factors which made agreement possible together with the applicant's opinion and that of the objector. Where there has been no change to the information received under Article 5, the Commission shall proceed in accordance with Article 6(4). If there has been a change, it shall again initiate the procedure laid down in Article 7;

(b) no agreement is reached, the Commission shall take a decision in accordance with the procedure laid down in Article 15, having regard to traditional fair practice and of the actual likelihood of confusion. Should it decide to proceed with registration, the Commission shall carry out publication in accordance with Article 6(4).

Article 8

The indications PDO, PGI or equivalent traditional national indications may appear only on agricultural products and foodstuffs that comply with this Regulation.

Article 9

The Member State concerned may request the amendment of a specification, in particular to take account of developments in scientific and technical knowledge or to redefine the geographical area.

The Article 6 procedure shall apply *mutatis mutandis*.

The Commission may, however, decide, under the procedure laid down in Article 15, not to apply the Article 6 procedure in the case of a minor amendment.

Article 10

1. Member States shall ensure that not later than six months after the entry into force of this Regulation inspection structures are in place, the function of which shall be to ensure that agricultural products and foodstuffs bearing a protected name meet the requirements laid down in the specifications.

2. An inspection structure may comprise one or more designated inspection authorities and/or private bodies approved for that purpose by the Member State. Member States shall send the Commission lists of the authorities and/or bodies approved and their respective powers. The Commission shall publish those particulars in the Official Journal of the European Communities.

3. Designated inspection authorities and/or approved private bodies must offer adequate guarantees of objectivity and impartiality with regard to all producers or processors subject to their control and have permanently at their disposal the qualified staff and resources necessary to carry out inspection of agricultural products and foodstuffs bearing a protected name.

If an inspection structure uses the services of another body for some inspections, that body must offer the same guarantees. In that event the designated inspection authorities and/or approved private bodies shall, however, continue to be responsible vis-à-vis the Member State for all inspections.

As from 1 January 1998, in order to be approved by the Member States for the purpose of this Regulation, private bodies must fulfil the requirements laid down in standard EN 45011 of 26 June 1989.

4. If a designated inspection authority and/or private body in a Member State establishes that an agricultural product or a foodstuff bearing a protected name of origin in that Member State does not meet the criteria of the specification, they shall take the steps necessary to ensure that this Regulation is complied with. They shall inform the Member State of the measures taken in carrying out their inspections. The parties concerned must be notified of all decisions taken.

5. A Member State must withdraw approval from an inspection body where the criteria referred to in paragraphs 2 and 3 are no longer fulfilled. It shall inform the Commission, which shall publish in the Official Journal of the European Communities a revised list of approved bodies.

6. The Member States shall adopt the measures necessary to ensure that a producer who complies with this Regulation has access to the inspection system.

7. The costs of inspections provided for under this Regulation shall be

borne by the producers using the protected name.

Article 11

1. Any Member State may submit that a condition laid down in the product specification of an agricultural product or foodstuff covered by a protected name has not been met.

2. The Member State referred to in paragraph 1 shall make its submission to the Member State concerned. The Member State concerned shall examine the complaint and inform the other Member State of its findings and of any measures taken.

3. In the event of repeated irregularities and the failure of the Member States concerned to come to an agreement, a duly substantiated application must be sent to the Commission.

4. The Commission shall examine the application by consulting the Member States concerned. Where appropriate, having consulted the committee referred to in Article 15, the Commission shall take the necessary steps. These may include cancellation of the registration.

Article 12

1. Without prejudice to international agreements, this Regulation may apply to an agricultural product or foodstuff from a third country provided that:

- the third country is able to give guarantees identical or equivalent to those referred to in Article 4,
- the third country concerned has inspection arrangements equivalent to those laid down in Article 10,
- the third country concerned is prepared to provide protection equivalent to that available in the Community to corresponding agricultural products for foodstuffs coming from the Community.

2. If a protected name of a third country is identical to a Community protected name, registration shall be granted with due regard for local and traditional usage and the practical risks of confusion.

Use of such names shall be authorized only if the country of origin of the product is clearly and visibly indicated on the label.

Article 13

1. Registered names shall be protected against:

(a) any direct or indirect commercial use of a name registered in respect of products not covered by the registration in so far as those products are comparable to the products registered under that name or insofar as using the name exploits the reputation of the protected name;

(b) any misuse, imitation or evocation, even if the true origin of the product is indicated or if the protected name is translated or accompanied by an expression such as 'style', 'type', 'method', 'as produced in', 'imitation' or similar;

(c) any other false or misleading indication as to the provenance, origin, nature or essential qualities of the product, on the inner or outer packaging, advertising material or documents relating to the product concerned, and the packing of the product in a container liable to convey a false impression as to its origin;

(d) any other practice liable to mislead the public as to the true origin of the product.

Where a registered name contains within it the name of an agricultural product or foodstuff which is considered generic, the use of that generic name on the appropriate agricultural product or foodstuff shall not be considered to be contrary to (a) or (b) in the first subparagraph.

2. However, Member States may maintain national measures authorizing the use of the expressions referred to in paragraph 1 (b) for a period of not more than five years after the date of publication of this Regulation, provided that:

— the products have been marketed legally using such expressions for at least five years before the date of publication of this Regulation,

— the labelling clearly indicates the true origin of the product.

However, this exception may not lead to the marketing of products freely on the territory of a Member State where such expressions are prohibited.

3. Protected names may not become generic.

Article 14

1. Where a designation of origin or geographical indication is registered in accordance with this Regulation, the application for registration of a trade mark corresponding to one of the situations referred to in Article 13 and relating to the same type of product shall be refused, provided that the application for registration of the trade mark was submitted after the date of the publication provided for in Article 6(2).

Trade marks registered in breach of the first subparagraph shall be declared invalid.

This paragraph shall also apply where the application for registration of a trade mark was lodged before the date of publication of the application for registration provided for in Article 6(2), provided that that publication occurred before the trade mark was registered.

2. With due regard for Community law, use of a trade mark corresponding to one of the situations referred to in Article 13 which was registered in good faith before the date on which application for registration of a designation of origin or geographical indication was lodged may continue notwithstanding the registration of a designation of origin or geographical indication, where there are no grounds for invalidity or revocation of the trade mark as provided respectively by Article 3(1) (c) and (g) and Article 12(2)(b) of First

Council Directive 89/104/EEC of 21 December 1988 to approximate the laws of the Member States relating to trade marks

3. A designation of origin or geographical indication shall not be registered where, in the light of a trade mark's reputation and renown and the length of time it has been used, registration is liable to mislead the consumer as to the true identity of the product.

Article 15

The Commission shall be assisted by a committee composed of the representatives of the Member States and chaired by the representative of the Commission.

The representative of the Commission shall submit to the committee a draft of the measures to be taken. The committee shall deliver its opinion on the draft within a time limit which the chairman may lay down according to the urgency of the matter. The opinion shall be delivered by the majority laid down in Article 148(2) of the Treaty in the case of decisions which the Council is required to adopt on a proposal from the Commission. The votes of the representatives of the Member States within the committee shall be weighted in the manner set out in that Article. The chairman shall not vote.

The Commission shall adopt the measures envisaged if they are in accordance with the opinion of the committee.

If the measures envisaged are not in accordance with the opinion of the committee, or if no opinion is delivered, the Commission shall, without delay, submit to the Council a proposal relating to the measures to be taken. The Council shall act by a qualified majority.

If, on the expiry of a period of three months from the date of referral to the Council, the Council has not acted, the proposed measures shall be adopted by the Commission.

Article 16

Detailed rules for applying this Regulation shall be adopted in accordance with the procedure laid down in Article 15.

Article 17

1. Within six months of the entry into force of the Regulation, Member States shall inform the Commission which of their legally protected names or, in those Member States where there is no protection system, which of their names established by usage they wish to register pursuant to this Regulation.

2. In accordance with the procedure laid down in Article 15, the Commission shall register the names referred to in paragraph 1 which comply with Articles 2 and 4. Article 7 shall not apply. However, generic names shall not be added.

3. Member States may maintain national protection of the names

communicated in accordance with paragraph 1 until such time as a decision on registration has been taken.

Article 18

This Regulation shall enter into force twelve months after the date of its publication in the Official Journal of the European Communities.

This Regulation shall be binding in its entirety and directly applicable in all Member States.

Done at Brussels, 14 July 1992.

ANNEX I

Foodstuffs referred to in Article 1(1):

- Beer,
- Natural mineral waters and spring waters,
- Beverages made from plant extracts,
- Bread, pastry, cakes, confectionery, biscuits and other baker's wares,
- Natural gums and resins.

ANNEX II

Agricultural products referred to in Article 1(1):

- Hay
- Essential oils

E. INDUSTRIAL DESIGNS

THE HAGUE AGREEMENT CONCERNING THE INTERNATIONAL DEPOSIT OF INDUSTRIAL DESIGNS
Done November 6, 1925, revised at London June 2, 1934,
and at The Hague, November 28, 1960

Article 1

(1) The contracting States constitute a Special Union for the international deposit of industrial designs.

(2) Only States members of the International Union for the Protection of Industrial Property may become party to this Agreement.

Article 2

For the purposes of this Agreement:

"1925 Agreement" shall mean the Hague Agreement concerning the International Deposit of Industrial Designs of November 6, 1925;

"1934 Agreement" shall mean the Hague Agreement concerning the International Deposit of Industrial Designs of November 6, 1925, as revised at London on June 2, 1934;

"this Agreement" or "the present Agreement" shall mean the Hague Agreement concerning the International Deposit of Industrial Designs as established by the present Act;

"Regulations" shall mean the Regulations for carrying out this Agreement;

"International Bureau" shall mean the Bureau of the International Union for the Protection of Industrial Property;

"international deposit" shall mean a deposit made at the International Bureau;

"national deposit" shall mean a deposit made at the national Office of a contracting State;

"multiple deposit" shall mean a deposit including several designs;

"State of origin of an international deposit" shall mean the contracting State in which the applicant has a real and effective industrial or commercial establishment or, if the applicant has such establishments in several contracting States, the contracting State which he has indicated in his application; if the applicant has no such establishment in any contracting State, the contracting State in which he has his domicile; if he has no domicile in a contracting State, the contracting State of which he is a national;

"State having a novelty examination" shall mean a contracting State the domestic law of which provides for a system which involves a preliminary ex officio search and examination by its national Office as to the novelty of each deposited design.

Article 3

Nationals of contracting States and persons who, without being nationals of any contracting State, are domiciled or have a real and effective industrial or commercial establishment in the territory of a contracting State may deposit designs at the International Bureau.

Article 4

(1) International deposit may be made at the International Bureau:

   1. direct, or

   2. through the intermediary of the national Office of a contracting State if the law of that State so permits.

(2) The domestic law of any contracting State may require that international deposits of which it is deemed to be the State of origin shall be made through its national Office. Non-compliance with this requirement shall not prejudice the effects of the international deposit in the other contracting States.

Article 5

(1) The international deposit shall consist of an application and one or more photographs or other graphic representations of the design, and shall involve payment of the fees prescribed by the Regulations.

(2) The application shall contain:

   1. a list of the contracting States in which the applicant requests that the international deposit shall have effect;

   2. the designation of the article or articles in which it is intended to incorporate the design;

   3. if the applicant wishes to claim the priority provided for in Article 9, an indication of the date, the State, and the number of the deposit giving rise to the right of priority;

   4. such other particulars as the Regulations may prescribe.

(3)

   (a) In addition, the application may contain:

   1. a short description of characteristic features of the design;

   2. a declaration as to who is the true creator of the design;

   3. a request for deferment of publication as provided in Article 6(4).

   (b) The application may be accompanied also by samples or models of the article or articles incorporating the design.

(4) A multiple deposit may include several designs intended to be incorporated in articles included in the same class of the International Design Classification referred to in Article 21(2)4.

Article 6

(1) The International Bureau shall maintain the International Design Register and shall register international deposits therein.

(2) The international deposit shall be deemed to have been made on the date on which the International Bureau received the application in due form, the fees payable with the application, and the photograph or photographs or other graphic representations of the design, or, if the International Bureau received them on different dates, on the last of these dates. The registration shall bear the same date.

(3)

(a) For each international deposit, the International Bureau shall publish in a periodical bulletin:

1. reproductions in black and white or, at the request of the applicant, in color of the deposited photographs or other graphic representations;

2. the date of the international deposit;

3. the particulars prescribed by the Regulations.

(b) The International Bureau shall send the periodical bulletin to the national Offices as soon as possible.

(4)

(a) The publication referred to in paragraph (3)(a) shall, at the request of the applicant, be deferred for such period as he may request. The said period may not exceed twelve months from the date of the international deposit. However, if priority is claimed, the starting date of such period shall be the priority date.

(b) At any time during the period referred to in subparagraph (a), the applicant may request immediate publication or may withdraw his deposit. Withdrawal of the deposit may be limited to one or a few only of the contracting States and, in the case of a multiple deposit, to some only of the designs included therein.

(c) If the applicant fails to pay within the proper time the fees payable before the expiration of the period referred to in subparagraph (a), the International Bureau shall cancel the deposit and shall not effect the publication referred to in paragraph (3)(a).

(d) Until the expiration of the period referred to in subparagraph (a), the International Bureau shall keep in confidence the registration of deposits made subject to deferred publication, and the public shall have no access to any documents or articles concerning such deposits. These provisions shall apply without limitation as to time if the applicant has withdrawn his deposit before the expiration of the said period.

(5) Except as provided in paragraph (4), the Register and all documents and articles filed with the International Bureau shall be open to inspection

by the public.

Article 7

(1)

(a) A deposit registered at the International Bureau shall have the same effect in each of the contracting States designated by the applicant in his application as if all the formalities required by the domestic law for the grant of protection had been complied with by the applicant and as if all administrative acts required to that end had been accomplished by the Office of such State.

(b) Subject to the provisions of Article 11, the protection of designs the deposit of which has been registered at the International Bureau is governed in each contracting State by those provisions of the domestic law which are applicable in that State to designs for which protection has been claimed on the basis of a national deposit and in respect of which all formalities and administrative acts have been complied with and accomplished.

(2) An international deposit shall have no effect in the State of origin if the laws of that State so provide.

Article 8

(1) Notwithstanding the provisions of Article 7, the national Office of a contracting State whose domestic law provides that the national Office may, on the basis of an administrative ex officio examination or pursuant to an opposition by a third party, refuse protection shall, in case of refusal, notify the International Bureau within six months that the design does not meet the requirements of its domestic law other than the formalities and administrative acts referred to in Article 7(1). If no such refusal is notified within a period of six months the international deposit shall become effective in that State as from the date of that deposit. However, in a contracting State having a novelty examination, the international deposit, while retaining its priority, shall, if no refusal is notified within a period of six months, become effective from the expiration of the said period unless the domestic law provides for an earlier date for deposits made with its national Office.

(2) The period of six months referred to in paragraph (1) shall be computed from the date on which the national Office receives the issue of the periodical bulletin in which the registration of the international deposit has been published. The national Office shall communicate that date to any person so requesting.

(3) The applicant shall have the same remedies against the refusal of the national Office referred to in paragraph (1) as if he had deposited his design in that Office; in any case, the refusal shall be subject to a request for re-examination or appeal. Notification of such refusal shall indicate:

1. the reasons for which it has been found that the design does not meet the requirements of the domestic law;

2. the date referred to in paragraph (2);

3. the time allowed for a request for re-examination or appeal;

4. the authority to which such request or appeal may be addressed.

(4)

(a) The national Office of a contracting State whose domestic law contains provisions of the kind referred to in paragraph (1) requiring a declaration as to who is the true creator of the design or a description of the design may provide that, upon request and within a period of not less than sixty days from the dispatch of such a request by the said Office, the applicant shall file in the language of the application filed with the International Bureau:

1. a declaration as to who is the true creator of the design;

2. a short description emphasizing the essential characteristic features of the design as shown by the photographs or other graphic representations.

(b) No fees shall be charged by a national Office in connection with the filing of such declarations or descriptions, or for their possible publication by that national Office.

(5)

(a) Any contracting State whose domestic law contains provisions of the kind referred to in paragraph (1) shall notify the International Bureau accordingly.

(b) If, under its legislation, a contracting State has several systems for the protection of designs one of which provides for novelty examination, the provisions of this Agreement concerning States having a novelty examination shall apply only to the said system.

Article 9

If the international deposit of a design is made within six months of the first deposit of the same design in a State member of the International Union for the Protection of Industrial Property, and if priority is claimed for the international deposit, the priority date shall be that of the first deposit.

Article 10

(1) An international deposit may be renewed every five years by payment only, during the last year of each period of five years, of the renewal fees prescribed by the Regulations.

(2) Subject to the payment of a surcharge fixed by the Regulations, a period of grace of six months shall be granted for renewal of the international deposit.

(3) At the time of paying the renewal fees, the international deposit

number must be indicated and also, if renewal is not to be effected for all the contracting States for which the deposit is about to expire, those of the contracting States for which the renewal is to be effected.

(4) Renewal may be limited to some only of the designs included in a multiple deposit.

(5) The International Bureau shall record and publish renewals.

Article 11

(1)

(a) The term of protection granted by a contracting State to designs which have been the subject of an international deposit shall not be less than:

1. ten years from the date of the international deposit if the deposit has been renewed;

2. five years from the date of the international deposit in the absence of renewal.

(b) However, if, under the provisions of the domestic law of a contracting State having a novelty examination, protection commences at a date later than that of the international deposit, the minimum terms provided for in subparagraph (a) shall be computed from the date at which protection commences in that State. The fact that the international deposit is not renewed or is renewed only once shall in no way affect the minimum terms of protection thus defined.

(2) If the domestic law of a contracting State provides, in respect of designs which have been the subject of a national deposit, for protection whose duration, with or without renewal, is longer than ten years, protection of the same duration shall, on the basis of the international deposit and its renewals, be granted in that State to designs which have been the subject of an international deposit.

(3) A contracting State may, under its domestic law, limit the term of protection of designs which have been the subject of an international deposit to the terms provided for in paragraph (1).

(4) Subject to the provisions of paragraph (1)(b), protection in a contracting State shall terminate at the date of expiration of the international deposit, unless the domestic law of that State provides that protection shall continue after the date of expiration of the international deposit.

Article 12

(1) The International Bureau shall record and publish changes affecting ownership of a design which is the subject of an international deposit in force. It is understood that transfer of ownership may be limited to the rights arising from the international deposit in one or a few only of the contracting States and, in the case of a multiple deposit, to some only of the designs included therein.

(2) The recording referred to in paragraph (1) shall have the same effect as if it had been made in the national Offices of the contracting States.

Article 13

(1) The owner of an international deposit may, by means of a declaration addressed to the International Bureau, renounce his rights in respect of all or some only of the contracting States and, in the case of a multiple deposit, in respect of some only of the designs included therein.

(2) The International Bureau shall record and publish such declaration.

Article 14

(1) No contracting State may, as a condition of recognition of the right to protection, require that the article incorporating the design bear a sign or notice concerning the deposit of the design.

(2) If the domestic law of a contracting State provides for a notice on the article for any other purpose, such State shall regard such requirement as satisfied if all the articles offered to the public with the authorization of the owner of the rights in the design, or the tags attached to such articles, bear the international design notice.

(3) The international design notice shall consist of the symbol (D) (a capital D in a circle) accompanied by:

   1. the year of the international deposit and the name, or the usual abbreviation of the name, of the depositor, or

   2. the number of the international deposit.

(4) The mere appearance of the international design notice on the article or the tags shall in no case be interpreted as implying a waiver of protection by virtue of copyright or on any other grounds, whenever, in the absence of such notice, such protection may be claimed.

Article 15

(1) The fees prescribed by the Regulations shall consist of:

   1. fees for the International Bureau;

   2. fees for the contracting States designated by the applicant, namely:

   (a) a fee for each contracting State;

   (b) a fee for each contracting State having a novelty examination and requiring the payment of a fee for such examination.

(2) Any fees paid in respect of one and the same deposit for a contracting State under paragraph (1)2(a), shall be deducted from the amount of the fee referred to in paragraph (1)2(b), if the latter fee becomes payable for the same State.

Article 16

(1) The fees for contracting States referred to in Article 15(1)2, shall be collected by the International Bureau and paid over annually to the contracting States designated by the applicant.

(2)

  (a) Any contracting State may notify the International Bureau that it waives its right to the supplementary fees referred to in Article 15(1)2(a), in respect of international deposits of which any other contracting State making a similar waiver is deemed to be the State of origin.

  (b) Such State may make a similar waiver in respect of international deposits of which it is itself deemed to be the State of origin.

Article 17

The Regulations shall govern the details concerning the implementation of this Agreement and in particular:

1. the languages and the number of copies in which the application for deposit must be filed, and the data to be supplied in the application;

2. the amounts and the dates and method of payment of the fees for the International Bureau and for the States, including the limits imposed on the fee for contracting States having a novelty examination;

3. the number, size, and other characteristics, of the photographs or other graphic representations of each design deposited;

4. the length of the description of characteristic features of the design;

5. the limits within which and conditions under which samples or models of the articles incorporating the design may accompany the application;

6. the number of designs that may be included in a multiple deposit and other conditions governing multiple deposits;

7. all matters relating to the publication and distribution of the periodical bulletin referred to in Article 6(3)(a), including the number of copies of the bulletin which shall be given free of charge to the national Offices and the number of copies which may be sold at a reduced price to such Offices;

8. the procedure for notification by contracting States of any refusal provided for under Article 8(1), and the procedure for communication and publication of such refusals by the International Bureau;

9. the conditions for recording and publication by the International Bureau of the changes affecting the ownership of a design referred to in Article 12(1), and for the renunciations referred to in Article 13;

10. the disposal of documents and articles concerning deposits for which the possibility of renewal has ceased to exist.

Article 18

The provisions of this Agreement shall not preclude the making of a claim to the benefit of any greater protection which may be granted by domestic legislation in a contracting State, nor shall they affect in any way the protection accorded to works of art and works of applied art by international copyright treaties and conventions.

Article 19

The fees of the International Bureau for services provided for by this Agreement shall be fixed in such a manner:

(a) that the proceeds therefrom cover all the expenses of the International Design Service and all those necessitated by the preparation and holding of meetings of the International Design Committee or conferences for the revision of this Agreement;

(b) that they allow for the maintenance of the reserve fund referred to in Article 20.

Article 20

(1) There shall be a reserve fund of 250,000 Swiss francs. The amount of the reserve fund may be modified by the International Design Committee referred to in Article 21.

(2) The reserve fund shall be replenished by the surplus receipts of the International Design Service.

(3)

(a) However, at the time of the entry into force of this Agreement, the reserve fund shall be constituted by a single contribution paid by each contracting State and computed in proportion to the number of units corresponding to the class to which it belongs by virtue of Article 13(8) of the Paris Convention for the Protection of Industrial Property.

(b) States which become party to this Agreement after it enters into force shall also pay a single contribution. The contribution shall be computed according to the principles formulated in the preceding subparagraph, so that all States, whatever the date of their becoming party to the Agreement, shall pay the same contribution per unit.

(4) When the amount of the reserve fund exceeds the fixed ceiling, the surplus shall be periodically distributed among the contracting States, in proportion to the single contribution paid by each, up to the maximum amount of that contribution.

(5) When the single contributions have been fully reimbursed, the International Design Committee may decide that States subsequently becoming party to the Agreement shall not be required to pay the single contribution.

Article 21

(1) There shall be an International Design Committee consisting of representatives of all the contracting States.

(2) The Committee shall have the following duties and powers:

1. to draw up its own rules of procedure;

2. to amend the Regulations;

3. to modify the ceiling of the reserve fund referred to in Article 20;

4. to establish the International Design Classification;

5. to study matters concerning the application and possible revision of this Agreement;

6. to study all other matters concerning the international protection of designs;

7. to approve the yearly management reports of the International Bureau and to give general instructions to the International Bureau concerning the discharge of the duties assigned to it under this Agreement;

8. to draw up a report on the foreseeable expenditure of the International Bureau for each triennial period to come.

(3) The decisions of the Committee shall require four-fifths of the votes of its members present or represented and voting in the case of items (2)1, (2)2, (2)3, and (2)4, and a simple majority in all other cases. Abstentions shall not be considered as votes.

(4) The Committee shall be convened by the Director of the International Bureau:

1. at least once every three years;

2. at any time at the request of one-third of the contracting States, or, if deemed necessary, upon the initiative of the Director of the International Bureau or the Government of the Swiss Confederation.

(5) The travel expenses and subsistence allowances of members of the Committee shall be borne by their respective Governments.

Article 22

(1) The Regulations may be amended either by the Committee as prescribed in Article 21(2)2, or in accordance with the written procedure provided for in paragraph (2), below.

(2) In the case of written procedure, amendments shall be proposed by the Director of the International Bureau in a circular letter addressed to the Government of each contracting State. The amendments shall be regarded as adopted if, within one year from their communication, no contracting State has raised an objection.

Article 23

(1) This Agreement shall remain open for signature until December 31, 1961.

(2) It shall be ratified and the instruments of ratification shall be deposited with the Government of the Netherlands.

Article 24

(1) States members of the International Union for the Protection of Industrial Property which have not signed this Agreement may accede thereto.

(2) Such accessions shall be notified through diplomatic channels to the Government of the Swiss Confederation, and by the latter to the Governments of all contracting States.

Article 25

(1) Each contracting State undertakes to provide for the protection of industrial designs and to adopt, in accordance with its constitution, the measures necessary to ensure the application of this Agreement.

(2) At the time a contracting State deposits its instrument of ratification or accession, it must be in a position under its domestic law to give effect to the provisions of this Agreement.

Article 26

(1) This Agreement shall enter into force one month after the date on which the Government of the Swiss Confederation has dispatched a notification to the contracting States of the deposit of ten instruments of ratification or accession, at least four of which are those of States which, at the date of the present Agreement, are not party either to the 1925 Agreement or to the 1934 Agreement.

(2) Thereafter, the deposit of instruments of ratification and accession shall be notified to the contracting States by the Government of the Swiss Confederation. Such ratifications and accessions shall become effective one month after the date of the dispatch of such notification unless, in the case of accession, a later date is indicated in the instrument of accession.

Article 27

Any contracting State may at any time notify the Government of the Swiss Confederation that this Agreement shall also apply to all or part of those territories for the external relations of which it is responsible. Thereupon, the Government of the Swiss Confederation shall communicate such notification to the contracting States and the Agreement shall apply also to the said territories one month after the dispatch of the communication by the Government of the Swiss Confederation to the contracting States unless a later date is indicated in the notification.

Article 28

(1) Any contracting State may, by notification addressed to the Government of the Swiss Confederation, denounce this Agreement in its own name and on behalf of all or part of the territories designated in the notification under Article 27. Such notification shall take effect one year after its receipt by the Government of the Swiss Confederation.

(2) Denunciation shall not relieve any contracting State of its obligations under this Agreement in respect of designs deposited at the International Bureau prior to the date on which the denunciation takes effect.

Article 29

(1) This Agreement shall be submitted to periodical revision with a view to the introduction of amendments designed to improve the protection resulting from the international deposit of designs.

(2) Revision conferences shall be called at the request of the International Design Committee or of not less than one-half of the contracting States.

Article 30

(1) Two or more contracting States may at any time notify the Government of the Swiss Confederation that, subject to the conditions indicated in the notification:

    1. a common Office shall be substituted for the national Office of each of them;

    2. they shall be deemed to be a single State for the purposes of the application of Articles 2 to 17 of this Agreement.

(2) Such notification shall not take effect until six months after the date of dispatch of the communication thereof by the Government of the Swiss Confederation to the other contracting States.

Article 31

(1) This Agreement alone shall be applicable as regards the mutual relations of States party to both the present Agreement and the 1925 Agreement or the 1934 Agreement. However, such States shall, in their mutual relations, apply the 1925 Agreement or the 1934 Agreement, as the case may be, to designs deposited at the International Bureau prior to the date on which the present Agreement becomes applicable as regards their mutual relations.

(2)

(a) Any State party to both the present Agreement and the 1925 Agreement shall continue to apply the 1925 Agreement in its relations with States party only to the 1925 Agreement, unless the said State has denounced the 1925 Agreement.

(b) Any State party to both the present Agreement and the 1934 Agreement shall continue to apply the 1934 Agreement in its relations with States party only to the 1934 Agreement, unless the said State has denounced the 1934 Agreement.

(3) States party to the present Agreement only shall not be bound to States which, without being party to the present Agreement, are party to the 1925 Agreement or the 1934 Agreement.

Article 32

(1) Signature and ratification of, or accession to, the present Agreement by a State party, at the date of this Agreement, to the 1925 Agreement or the 1934 Agreement shall be deemed to include signature and ratification of, or accession to, the Protocol annexed to the present Agreement, unless such State makes an express declaration to the contrary at the time of signing or depositing its instrument of accession.

(2) Any contracting State having made the declaration referred to in paragraph (1), or any other contracting State not party to the 1925 Agreement or the 1934 Agreement, may sign or accede to the Protocol annexed to this Agreement. At the time of signing or depositing its instrument of accession, it may declare that it does not consider itself bound by the provisions of paragraphs 1(2)(a) or 1(2)(b) of the Protocol; in such case, the other States party to the Protocol shall be under no obligation to apply, in their relations with that State, the provisions mentioned in such declaration. The provisions of Articles 23 to 28 inclusive shall apply by analogy.

Article 33

This Act shall be signed in a single copy which shall be deposited in the archives of the Government of the Netherlands. A certified copy shall be transmitted by the latter to the Government of each State which has signed or acceded to this Agreement.

PROTOCOL

This protocol is not yet in force.

States party to this Protocol have agreed as follows:

(1) The provisions of this Protocol shall apply to designs which have been the subject of an international deposit and of which one of the States party to this Protocol is deemed to be the State of origin.

(2) In respect of designs referred to in paragraph (1), above:

    (a) the term of protection granted by States party to this Protocol to the designs referred to in paragraph (1) shall not be less than fifteen years from the date provided for in paragraphs 11(1)(a) or 11(1)(b), as the case may be;

    (b) the appearance of a notice on the articles incorporating the designs or on the tags attached thereto shall in no case be required by the States party to this Protocol, either for the exercise in their territories of rights arising from the international deposit, or for any other purpose.

THE HAGUE AGREEMENT CONCERNING THE INTERNATIONAL REGISTRATION OF INDUSTRIAL DESIGNS
Adopted at Geneva, July 2, 1999

INTRODUCTORY PROVISIONS

Article 1
Abbreviated Expressions

For the purposes of this Act:

(i) "the Hague Agreement" means the Hague Agreement Concerning the International Deposit of Industrial Designs, henceforth renamed the Hague Agreement Concerning the International Registration of Industrial Designs;

(ii) "this Act" means the Hague Agreement as established by the present Act;

(iii) "Regulations" means the Regulations under this Act;

(iv) "prescribed" means prescribed in the Regulations;

(v) "Paris Convention" means the Paris Convention for the Protection of Industrial Property, signed at Paris on March 20, 1883, as revised and amended;

(vi) "international registration" means the international registration of an industrial design effected according to this Act;

(vii) "international application" means an application for international registration;

(viii) "International Register" means the official collection of data concerning international registrations maintained by the International Bureau, which data this Act or the Regulations require or permit to be recorded, regardless of the medium in which such data are stored;

(ix) "person" means a natural person or a legal entity;

(x) "applicant" means the person in whose name an international application is filed;

(xi) "holder" means the person in whose name an international registration is recorded in the International Register;

(xii) "intergovernmental organization" means an intergovernmental organization eligible to become party to this Act in accordance with Article 27(1)(ii);

(xiii) "Contracting Party" means any State or intergovernmental organization party to this Act;

(xiv) "applicant's Contracting Party" means the Contracting Party or one of the Contracting Parties from which the applicant derives its entitlement to file an international application by virtue of satisfying, in relation to that Contracting Party, at least one of the conditions specified in

Article 3; where there are two or more Contracting Parties from which the applicant may, under Article 3, derive its entitlement to file an international application, "applicant's Contracting Party" means the one which, among those Contracting Parties, is indicated as such in the international application;

(xv) "territory of a Contracting Party" means, where the Contracting Party is a State, the territory of that State and, where the Contracting Party is an intergovernmental organization, the territory in which the constituent treaty of that intergovernmental organization applies;

(xvi) "Office" means the agency entrusted by a Contracting Party with the grant of protection for industrial designs with effect in the territory of that Contracting Party;

(xvii) "Examining Office" means an Office which *ex officio* examines applications filed with it for the protection of industrial designs at least to determine whether the industrial designs satisfy the condition of novelty;

(xviii) "designation" means a request that an international registration have effect in a Contracting Party; it also means the recording, in the International Register, of that request;

(xix) "designated Contracting Party" and "designated Office" means the Contracting Party and the Office of the Contracting Party, respectively, to which a designation applies;

(xx) "1934 Act" means the Act signed at London on June 2, 1934, of the Hague Agreement;

(xxi) "1960 Act" means the Act signed at The Hague on November 28, 1960, of the Hague Agreement;

(xxii) "1961 Additional Act" means the Act signed at Monaco on November 18, 1961, additional to the 1934 Act;

(xxiii) "Complementary Act of 1967" means the Complementary Act signed at Stockholm on July 14, 1967, as amended, of the Hague Agreement;

(xxiv) "Union" means the Hague Union established by the Hague Agreement of November 6, 1925, and maintained by the 1934 and 1960 Acts, the 1961 Additional Act, the Complementary Act of 1967 and this Act;

(xxv) "Assembly" means the Assembly referred to in Article 21(1)(a) or any body replacing that Assembly;

(xxvi) "Organization" means the World Intellectual Property Organization;

(xxvii) "Director General" means the Director General of the Organization;

(xxviii) "International Bureau" means the International Bureau of the Organization;

(xxix) "instrument of ratification" shall be construed as including instruments of acceptance or approval.

Article 2
Applicability of Other Protection Accorded by Laws of Contracting Parties and by Certain International Treaties

(1) [*Laws of Contracting Parties and Certain International Treaties*] The provisions of this Act shall not affect the application of any greater protection which may be accorded by the law of a Contracting Party, nor shall they affect in any way the protection accorded to works of art and works of applied art by international copyright treaties and conventions, or the protection accorded to industrial designs under the Agreement on Trade-Related Aspects of Intellectual Property Rights annexed to the Agreement Establishing the World Trade Organization.

(2) [*Obligation to Comply with the Paris Convention*] Each Contracting Party shall comply with the provisions of the Paris Convention which concern industrial designs.

CHAPTER I
INTERNATIONAL APPLICATION AND INTERNATIONAL REGISTRATION

Article 3
Entitlement to File an International Application

Any person that is a national of a State that is a Contracting Party or of a State member of an intergovernmental organization that is a Contracting Party, or that has a domicile, a habitual residence or a real and effective industrial or commercial establishment in the territory of a Contracting Party, shall be entitled to file an international application.

Article 4

(1) [*Direct or Indirect Filing*] (a) The international application may be filed, at the option of the applicant, either directly with the International Bureau or through the Office of the applicant's Contracting Party.

(b) Notwithstanding subparagraph (a), any Contracting Party may, in a declaration, notify the Director General that international applications may not be filed through its Office.

(2) [*Transmittal Fee in Case of Indirect Filing*] The Office of any Contracting Party may require that the applicant pay a transmittal fee to it, for its own benefit, in respect of any international application filed through it.

Article 5
Contents of the International Application

(1) [*Mandatory Contents of the International Application*] The international application shall be in the prescribed language or one of the prescribed languages and shall contain or be accompanied by

(i) a request for international registration under this Act;

(ii)   the prescribed data concerning the applicant;

(iii) the prescribed number of copies of a reproduction or, at the choice of the applicant, of several different reproductions of the industrial design that is the subject of the international application, presented in the prescribed manner; however, where the industrial design is two-dimensional and a request for deferment of publication is made in accordance with paragraph (5), the international application may, instead of containing reproductions, be accompanied by the prescribed number of specimens of the industrial design;

(iv) an indication of the product or products which constitute the industrial design or in relation to which the industrial design is to be used, as prescribed;

(v) an indication of the designated Contracting Parties;

(vi) the prescribed fees;

(vii) any other prescribed particulars.

(2) [*Additional Mandatory Contents of the International Application*] (a) Any Contracting Party whose Office is an Examining Office and whose law, at the time it becomes party to this Act, requires that an application for the grant of protection to an industrial design contain any of the elements specified in subparagraph (b) in order for that application to be accorded a filing date under that law may, in a declaration, notify the Director General of those elements.

(b) The elements that may be notified pursuant to subparagraph (a) are the following:

(i) indications concerning the identity of the creator of the industrial design that is the subject of that application;

(ii) a brief description of the reproduction or of the characteristic features of the industrial design that is the subject of that application;

(iii) a claim.

(c) Where the international application contains the designation of a Contracting Party that has made a notification under subparagraph (a), it shall also contain, in the prescribed manner, any element that was the subject of that notification.

(3) [*Other Possible Contents of the International Application*] The international application may contain or be accompanied by such other elements as are specified in the Regulations.

(4) [*Several Industrial Designs in the Same International Application*] Subject to such conditions as may be prescribed, an international application may include two or more industrial designs.

(5) [*Request for Deferred Publication*] The international application may contain a request for deferment of publication.

Article 6
Priority

(1) [*Claiming of Priority*] (a) The international application may contain a declaration claiming, under Article 4 of the Paris Convention, the priority of one or more earlier applications filed in or for any country party to that Convention or any Member of the World Trade Organization.

(b) The Regulations may provide that the declaration referred to in subparagraph (a) may be made after the filing of the international application. In such case, the Regulations shall prescribe the latest time by which such declaration may be made.

(2) [*International Application Serving as a Basis for Claiming Priority*] The international application shall, as from its filing date and whatever may be its subsequent fate, be equivalent to a regular filing within the meaning of Article 4 of the Paris Convention.

Article 7
Designation Fees

(1) [*Prescribed Designation Fee*] The prescribed fees shall include, subject to paragraph (2), a designation fee for each designated Contracting Party.

(2) [*Individual Designation Fee*] Any Contracting Party whose Office is an Examining Office and any Contracting Party that is an intergovernmental organization may, in a declaration, notify the Director General that, in connection with any international application in which it is designated, and in connection with the renewal of any international registration resulting from such an international application, the prescribed designation fee referred to in paragraph (1) shall be replaced by an individual designation fee, whose amount shall be indicated in the declaration and can be changed in further declarations. The said amount may be fixed by the said Contracting Party for the initial term of protection and for each term of renewal or for the maximum period of protection allowed by the Contracting Party concerned. However, it may not be higher than the equivalent of the amount which the Office of that Contracting Party would be entitled to receive from an applicant for a grant of protection for an equivalent period to the same number of industrial designs, that amount being diminished by the savings resulting from the international procedure.

(3) [*Transfer of Designation Fees*] The designation fees referred to in paragraphs (1) and (2) shall be transferred by the International Bureau to the Contracting Parties in respect of which those fees were paid.

Article 8
Correction of Irregularities

(1) [*Examination of the International Application*] If the International Bureau finds that the international application does not, at the time of its receipt by the International Bureau, fulfill the requirements of this Act and the Regulations, it shall invite the applicant to make the required corrections

within the prescribed time limit.

(2) [*Irregularities Not Corrected*] (a) If the applicant does not comply with the invitation within the prescribed time limit, the international application shall, subject to subparagraph (b), be considered abandoned.

(b) In the case of an irregularity which relates to Article 5(2) or to a special requirement notified to the Director General by a Contracting Party in accordance with the Regulations, if the applicant does not comply with the invitation within the prescribed time limit, the international application shall be deemed not to contain the designation of that Contracting Party.

Article 9
Filing Date of the International Application

(1) [*International Application Filed Directly*] Where the international application is filed directly with the International Bureau, the filing date shall, subject to paragraph (3), be the date on which the International Bureau receives the international application.

(2) [*International Application Filed Indirectly*] Where the international application is filed through the Office of the applicant's Contracting Party, the filing date shall be determined as prescribed.

(3) [*International Application with Certain Irregularities*] Where the international application has, on the date on which it is received by the International Bureau, an irregularity which is prescribed as an irregularity entailing a postponement of the filing date of the international application, the filing date shall be the date on which the correction of such irregularity is received by the International Bureau.

Article 10
International Registration, Date of the International Registration, Publication and Confidential Copies of the International Registration

(1) [*International Registration*] The International Bureau shall register each industrial design that is the subject of an international application immediately upon receipt by it of the international application or, where corrections are invited under Article 8, immediately upon receipt of the required corrections. The registration shall be effected whether or not publication is deferred under Article 11.

(2) [*Date of the International Registration*] (a) Subject to subparagraph (b), the date of the international registration shall be the filing date of the international application.

(b) Where the international application has, on the date on which it is received by the International Bureau, an irregularity which relates to Article 5(2), the date of the international registration shall be the date on which the correction of such irregularity is received by the International Bureau or the filing date of the international application, whichever is the later.

(3) [*Publication*] (a) The international registration shall be published by

the International Bureau. Such publication shall be deemed in all Contracting Parties to be sufficient publicity, and no other publicity may be required of the holder.

(b) The International Bureau shall send a copy of the publication of the international registration to each designated Office.

(4) [*Maintenance of Confidentiality Before Publication*] Subject to paragraph (5) and Article 11(4)(b), the International Bureau shall keep in confidence each international application and each international registration until publication.

(5) [*Confidential Copies*] (a) The International Bureau shall, immediately after registration has been effected, send a copy of the international registration, along with any relevant statement, document or specimen accompanying the international application, to each Office that has notified the International Bureau that it wishes to receive such a copy and has been designated in the international application.

(b) The Office shall, until publication of the international registration by the International Bureau, keep in confidence each international registration of which a copy has been sent to it by the International Bureau and may use the said copy only for the purpose of the examination of the international registration and of applications for the protection of industrial designs filed in or for the Contracting Party for which the Office is competent. In particular, it may not divulge the contents of any such international registration to any person outside the Office other than the holder of that international registration, except for the purposes of an administrative or legal proceeding involving a conflict over entitlement to file the international application on which the international registration is based. In the case of such an administrative or legal proceeding, the contents of the international registration may only be disclosed in confidence to the parties involved in the proceeding who shall be bound to respect the confidentiality of the disclosure.

Article 11
Deferment of Publication

(1) [*Provisions of Laws of Contracting Parties Concerning Deferment of Publication*] (a) Where the law of a Contracting Party provides for the deferment of the publication of an industrial design for a period which is less than the prescribed period, that Contracting Party shall, in a declaration, notify the Director General of the allowable period of deferment.

(b) Where the law of a Contracting Party does not provide for the deferment of the publication of an industrial design, the Contracting Party shall, in a declaration, notify the Director General of that fact.

(2) [*Deferment of Publication*] Where the international application contains a request for deferment of publication, the publication shall take place,

(i) where none of the Contracting Parties designated in the

international application has made a declaration under paragraph (1), at the expiry of the prescribed period or,

(ii) where any of the Contracting Parties designated in the international application has made a declaration under paragraph (1)(a), at the expiry of the period notified in such declaration or, where there is more than one such designated Contracting Party, at the expiry of the shortest period notified in their declarations.

(3) [*Treatment of Requests for Deferment Where Deferment Is Not Possible Under Applicable Law*] Where deferment of publication has been requested and any of the Contracting Parties designated in the international application has made a declaration under paragraph (1)(b) that deferment of publication is not possible under its law,

(i) subject to item (ii), the International Bureau shall notify the applicant accordingly; if, within the prescribed period, the applicant does not, by notice in writing to the International Bureau, withdraw the designation of the said Contracting Party, the International Bureau shall disregard the request for deferment of publication;

(ii) where, instead of containing reproductions of the industrial design, the international application was accompanied by specimens of the industrial design, the International Bureau shall disregard the designation of the said Contracting Party and shall notify the applicant accordingly.

(4) [*Request for Earlier Publication or for Special Access to the International Registration*] (a) At any time during the period of deferment applicable under paragraph (2), the holder may request publication of any or all of the industrial designs that are the subject of the international registration, in which case the period of deferment in respect of such industrial design or designs shall be considered to have expired on the date of receipt of such request by the International Bureau.

(b) The holder may also, at any time during the period of deferment applicable under paragraph (2), request the International Bureau to provide a third party specified by the holder with an extract from, or to allow such a party access to, any or all of the industrial designs that are the subject of the international registration.

(5) [*Renunciation and Limitation*] (a) If, at any time during the period of deferment applicable under paragraph (2), the holder renounces the international registration in respect of all the designated Contracting Parties, the industrial design or designs that are the subject of the international registration shall not be published.

(b) If, at any time during the period of deferment applicable under paragraph (2), the holder limits the international registration, in respect of all of the designated Contracting Parties, to one or some of the industrial designs that are the subject of the international registration, the other industrial design or designs that are the subject of the international registration shall not be published.

(6) [*Publication and Furnishing of Reproductions*] (a) At the expiration

of any period of deferment applicable under the provisions of this Article, the International Bureau shall, subject to the payment of the prescribed fees, publish the international registration. If such fees are not paid as prescribed, the international registration shall be canceled and publication shall not take place.

(b) Where the international application was accompanied by one or more specimens of the industrial design in accordance with Article 5(1)(iii), the holder shall submit the prescribed number of copies of a reproduction of each industrial design that is the subject of that application to the International Bureau within the prescribed time limit. To the extent that the holder does not do so, the international registration shall be canceled and publication shall not take place.

Article 12
Refusal

(1) [*Right to Refuse*] The Office of any designated Contracting Party may, where the conditions for the grant of protection under the law of that Contracting Party are not met in respect of any or all of the industrial designs that are the subject of an international registration, refuse the effects, in part or in whole, of the international registration in the territory of the said Contracting Party, provided that no Office may refuse the effects, in part or in whole, of any international registration on the ground that requirements relating to the form or contents of the international application that are provided for in this Act or the Regulations or are additional to, or different from, those requirements have not been satisfied under the law of the Contracting Party concerned.

(2) [*Notification of Refusal*] (a) The refusal of the effects of an international registration shall be communicated by the Office to the International Bureau in a notification of refusal within the prescribed period.

(b) Any notification of refusal shall state all the grounds on which the refusal is based.

(3) [*Transmission of Notification of Refusal; Remedies*] (a) The International Bureau shall, without delay, transmit a copy of the notification of refusal to the holder.

(b) The holder shall enjoy the same remedies as if any industrial design that is the subject of the international registration had been the subject of an application for the grant of protection under the law applicable to the Office that communicated the refusal. Such remedies shall at least consist of the possibility of a re-examination or a review of the refusal or an appeal against the refusal.

(4) [*Withdrawal of Refusal*] Any refusal may be withdrawn, in part or in whole, at any time by the Office that communicated it.

Article 13
Special Requirements Concerning Unity of Design

(1) [*Notification of Special Requirements*] Any Contracting Party whose law, at the time it becomes party to this Act, requires that designs that are the subject of the same application conform to a requirement of unity of design, unity of production or unity of use, or belong to the same set or composition of items, or that only one independent and distinct design may be claimed in a single application, may, in a declaration, notify the Director General accordingly. However, no such declaration shall affect the right of an applicant to include two or more industrial designs in an international application in accordance with Article 5(4), even if the application designates the Contracting Party that has made the declaration.

(2) [*Effect of Declaration*] Any such declaration shall enable the Office of the Contracting Party that has made it to refuse the effects of the international registration pursuant to Article 12(1) pending compliance with the requirement notified by that Contracting Party.

(3) [*Further Fees Payable on Division of Registration*] Where, following a notification of refusal in accordance with paragraph (2), an international registration is divided before the Office concerned in order to overcome a ground of refusal stated in the notification, that Office shall be entitled to charge a fee in respect of each additional international application that would have been necessary in order to avoid that ground of refusal.

Article 14
Effects of the International Registration

(1) [*Effect as Application Under Applicable Law*] The international registration shall, from the date of the international registration, have at least the same effect in each designated Contracting Party as a regularly-filed application for the grant of protection of the industrial design under the law of that Contracting Party.

(2) [*Effect as Grant of Protection Under Applicable Law*] (a) In each designated Contracting Party the Office of which has not communicated a refusal in accordance with Article 12, the international registration shall have the same effect as a grant of protection for the industrial design under the law of that Contracting Party at the latest from the date of expiration of the period allowed for it to communicate a refusal or, where a Contracting Party has made a corresponding declaration under the Regulations, at the latest at the time specified in that declaration.

(b) Where the Office of a designated Contracting Party has communicated a refusal and has subsequently withdrawn, in part or in whole, that refusal, the international registration shall, to the extent that the refusal is withdrawn, have the same effect in that Contracting Party as a grant of protection for the industrial design under the law of the said Contracting Party at the latest from the date on which the refusal was withdrawn.

(c) The effect given to the international registration under this paragraph shall apply to the industrial design or designs that are the subject of that registration as received from the International Bureau by the designated Office or, where applicable, as amended in the procedure before that Office.

(3) [*Declaration Concerning Effect of Designation of Applicant's Contracting Party*] (a) Any Contracting Party whose Office is an Examining Office may, in a declaration, notify the Director General that, where it is the applicant's Contracting Party, the designation of that Contracting Party in an international registration shall have no effect.

(b) Where a Contracting Party having made the declaration referred to in subparagraph (a) is indicated in an international application both as the applicant's Contracting Party and as a designated Contracting Party, the International Bureau shall disregard the designation of that Contracting Party.

Article 15
Invalidation

(1) [*Requirement of Opportunity of Defense*] Invalidation, by the competent authorities of a designated Contracting Party, of the effects, in part or in whole, in the territory of that Contracting Party, of the international registration may not be pronounced without the holder having, in good time, been afforded the opportunity of defending his rights.

(2) [*Notification of Invalidation*] The Office of the Contracting Party in whose territory the effects of the international registration have been invalidated shall, where it is aware of the invalidation, notify it to the International Bureau.

Article 16
Recording of Changes and Other Matters Concerning International Registrations

(1) [*Recording of Changes and Other Matters*] The International Bureau shall, as prescribed, record in the International Register

(i) any change in ownership of the international registration, in respect of any or all of the designated Contracting Parties and in respect of any or all of the industrial designs that are the subject of the international registration, provided that the new owner is entitled to file an international application under Article 3,

(ii) any change in the name or address of the holder,

(iii) the appointment of a representative of the applicant or holder and any other relevant fact concerning such representative,

(iv) any renunciation, by the holder, of the international registration, in respect of any or all of the designated Contracting Parties,

(v) any limitation, by the holder, of the international registration, in respect of any or all of the designated Contracting Parties, to one or some of the industrial designs that are the subject of the international registration,

(vi) any invalidation, by the competent authorities of a designated Contracting Party, of the effects, in the territory of that Contracting Party, of the international registration in respect of any or all of the industrial designs that are the subject of the international registration,

(vii) any other relevant fact, identified in the Regulations, concerning the rights in any or all of the industrial designs that are the subject of the international registration.

(2) [*Effect of Recording in International Register*] Any recording referred to in items (i), (ii), (iv), (v), (vi) and (vii) of paragraph (1) shall have the same effect as if it had been made in the Register of the Office of each of the Contracting Parties concerned, except that a Contracting Party may, in a declaration, notify the Director General that a recording referred to in item (i) of paragraph (1) shall not have that effect in that Contracting Party until the Office of that Contracting Party has received the statements or documents specified in that declaration.

(3) [*Fees*] Any recording made under paragraph (1) may be subject to the payment of a fee.

(4) [*Publication*] The International Bureau shall publish a notice concerning any recording made under paragraph (1). It shall send a copy of the publication of the notice to the Office of each of the Contracting Parties concerned.

Article 17
Initial Term and Renewal of the International Registration and Duration of Protection

(1) [*Initial Term of the International Registration*] The international registration shall be effected for an initial term of five years counted from the date of the international registration.

(2) [*Renewal of the International Registration*] The international registration may be renewed for additional terms of five years, in accordance with the prescribed procedure and subject to the payment of the prescribed fees.

(3) [*Duration of Protection in Designated Contracting Parties*] (a) Provided that the international registration is renewed, and subject to subparagraph (b), the duration of protection shall, in each of the designated Contracting Parties, be 15 years counted from the date of the international registration.

(b) Where the law of a designated Contracting Party provides for a duration of protection of more than 15 years for an industrial design for which protection has been granted under that law, the duration of protection shall, provided that the international registration is renewed, be the same as that provided for by the law of that Contracting Party.

(c) Each Contracting Party shall, in a declaration, notify the Director General of the maximum duration of protection provided for by its law.

(4) [*Possibility of Limited Renewal*] The renewal of the international registration may be effected for any or all of the designated Contracting

Parties and for any or all of the industrial designs that are the subject of the international registration.

(5) [*Recording and Publication of Renewal*] The International Bureau shall record renewals in the International Register and publish a notice to that effect. It shall send a copy of the publication of the notice to the Office of each of the Contracting Parties concerned.

Article 18
Information Concerning Published International Registrations

(1) [*Access to Information*] The International Bureau shall supply to any person applying therefor, upon the payment of the prescribed fee, extracts from the International Register, or information concerning the contents of the International Register, in respect of any published international registration.

(2) [*Exemption from Legalization*] Extracts from the International Register supplied by the International Bureau shall be exempt from any requirement of legalization in each Contracting Party.

CHAPTER II
ADMINISTRATIVE PROVISIONS

Article 19
Common Office of Several States

(1) [*Notification of Common Office*] If several States intending to become party to this Act have effected, or if several States party to this Act agree to effect, the unification of their domestic legislation on industrial designs, they may notify the Director General

(i) that a common Office shall be substituted for the national Office of each of them, and

(ii) that the whole of their respective territories to which the unified legislation applies shall be deemed to be a single Contracting Party for the purposes of the application of Articles 1, 3 to 18 and 31 of this Act.

(2) [*Time at Which Notification Is to Be Made*] The notification referred to in paragraph (1) shall be made,

(i) in the case of States intending to become party to this Act, at the time of the deposit of the instruments referred to in Article 27(2);

(ii) in the case of States party to this Act, at any time after the unification of their domestic legislation has been effected.

(3) [*Date of Entry into Effect of the Notification*] The notification referred to in paragraphs (1) and (2) shall take effect,

(i) in the case of States intending to become party to this Act, at the time such States become bound by this Act;

(ii) in the case of States party to this Act, three months after the date of the communication thereof by the Director General to the other Contracting Parties or at any later date indicated in the notification.

Article 20
Membership of the Hague Union

The Contracting Parties shall be members of the same Union as the States party to the 1934 Act or the 1960 Act.

Article 21
Assembly

(1) [*Composition*] (a) The Contracting Parties shall be members of the same Assembly as the States bound by Article 2 of the Complementary Act of 1967.

(b) Each member of the Assembly shall be represented in the Assembly by one delegate, who may be assisted by alternate delegates, advisors and experts, and each delegate may represent only one Contracting Party.

(c) Members of the Union that are not members of the Assembly shall be admitted to the meetings of the Assembly as observers.

(2) [*Tasks*] (a) The Assembly shall

(i) deal with all matters concerning the maintenance and development of the Union and the implementation of this Act;

(ii) exercise such rights and perform such tasks as are specifically conferred upon it or assigned to it under this Act or the Complementary Act of 1967;

(iii) give directions to the Director General concerning the preparations for conferences of revision and decide the convocation of any such conference;

(iv) amend the Regulations;

(v) review and approve the reports and activities of the Director General concerning the Union, and give the Director General all necessary instructions concerning matters within the competence of the Union;

(vi) determine the program and adopt the biennial budget of the Union, and approve its final accounts;

(vii) adopt the financial regulations of the Union;

(viii) establish such committees and working groups as it deems appropriate to achieve the objectives of the Union;

(ix) subject to paragraph (1)(c), determine which States, intergovernmental organizations and non-governmental organizations shall be admitted to its meetings as observers;

(x) take any other appropriate action to further the objectives of the Union and perform any other functions as are appropriate under this Act.

(b) With respect to matters which are also of interest to other Unions administered by the Organization, the Assembly shall make its decisions after having heard the advice of the Coordination Committee of the Organization.

(3) [*Quorum*] (a) One-half of the members of the Assembly which are States and have the right to vote on a given matter shall constitute a quorum for the purposes of the vote on that matter.

(b) Notwithstanding the provisions of subparagraph (a), if, in any session, the number of the members of the Assembly which are States, have the right to vote on a given matter and are represented is less than one-half but equal to or more than one-third of the members of the Assembly which are States and have the right to vote on that matter, the Assembly may make decisions but, with the exception of decisions concerning its own procedure, all such decisions shall take effect only if the conditions set forth hereinafter are fulfilled. The International Bureau shall communicate the said decisions to the members of the Assembly which are States, have the right to vote on the said matter and were not represented and shall invite them to express in writing their vote or abstention within a period of three months from the date of the communication. If, at the expiration of this period, the number of such members having thus expressed their vote or abstention attains the number of the members which was lacking for attaining the quorum in the session itself, such decisions shall take effect provided that at the same time the required majority still obtains.

(4) [*Taking Decisions in the Assembly*] (a) The Assembly shall endeavor to take its decisions by consensus.

(b) Where a decision cannot be arrived at by consensus, the matter at issue shall be decided by voting. In such a case,

(i) each Contracting Party that is a State shall have one vote and shall vote only in its own name, and

(ii) any Contracting Party that is an intergovernmental organization may vote, in place of its Member States, with a number of votes equal to the number of its Member States which are party to this Act, and no such intergovernmental organization shall participate in the vote if any one of its Member States exercises its right to vote, and *vice versa*.

(c) On matters concerning only States that are bound by Article 2 of the Complementary Act of 1967, Contracting Parties that are not bound by the said Article shall not have the right to vote, whereas, on matters concerning only Contracting Parties, only the latter shall have the right to vote.

(5) [*Majorities*] (a) Subject to Articles 24(2) and 26(2), the decisions of the Assembly shall require two-thirds of the votes cast.

(b) Abstentions shall not be considered as votes.

(6) [*Sessions*] (a) The Assembly shall meet once in every second calendar year in ordinary session upon convocation by the Director General and, in the absence of exceptional circumstances, during the same period and at the same place as the General Assembly of the Organization.

(b) The Assembly shall meet in extraordinary session upon convocation by the Director General, either at the request of one-fourth of the members of the Assembly or on the Director General's own initiative.

(c) The agenda of each session shall be prepared by the Director General.

(7) [*Rules of Procedure*] The Assembly shall adopt its own rules of procedure.

Article 22
International Bureau

(1) [*Administrative Tasks*] (a) International registration and related duties, as well as all other administrative tasks concerning the Union, shall be performed by the International Bureau.

(b) In particular, the International Bureau shall prepare the meetings and provide the secretariat of the Assembly and of such committees of experts and working groups as may be established by the Assembly.

(2) [*Director General*] The Director General shall be the chief executive of the Union and shall represent the Union.

(3) [*Meetings Other than Sessions of the Assembly*] The Director General shall convene any committee and working group established by the Assembly and all other meetings dealing with matters of concern to the Union.

(4) [*Role of the International Bureau in the Assembly and Other Meetings*] (a) The Director General and persons designated by the Director General shall participate, without the right to vote, in all meetings of the Assembly, the committees and working groups established by the Assembly, and any other meetings convened by the Director General under the aegis of the Union.

(b) The Director General or a staff member designated by the Director General shall be *ex officio* secretary of the Assembly, and of the committees, working groups and other meetings referred to in subparagraph (a).

(5) [*Conferences*] (a) The International Bureau shall, in accordance with the directions of the Assembly, make the preparations for any revision conferences.

(b) The International Bureau may consult with intergovernmental organizations and international and national non-governmental organizations concerning the said preparations.

(c) The Director General and persons designated by the Director General shall take part, without the right to vote, in the discussions at revision conferences.

(6) [*Other Tasks*] The International Bureau shall carry out any other tasks assigned to it in relation to this Act.

Article 23
Finances

(1) [*Budget*] (a) The Union shall have a budget.

(b) The budget of the Union shall include the income and expenses proper to the Union and its contribution to the budget of expenses common to the Unions administered by the Organization.

(c) Expenses not attributable exclusively to the Union but also to one or more other Unions administered by the Organization shall be considered to be expenses common to the Unions. The share of the Union in such common expenses shall be in proportion to the interest the Union has in them.

(2) [*Coordination with Budgets of Other Unions*] The budget of the Union shall be established with due regard to the requirements of coordination with the budgets of the other Unions administered by the Organization.

(3) [*Sources of Financing of the Budget*] The budget of the Union shall be financed from the following sources:

(i)   fees relating to international registrations;

(ii)   charges due for other services rendered by the International Bureau in relation to the Union;

(iii) sale of, or royalties on, the publications of the International Bureau concerning the Union;

(iv) gifts, bequests and subventions;

(v)   rents, interests and other miscellaneous income.

(4) [*Fixing of Fees and Charges; Level of the Budget*] (a) The amounts of the fees referred to in paragraph (3)(i) shall be fixed by the Assembly on the proposal of the Director General. Charges referred to in paragraph 3(ii) shall be established by the Director General and shall be provisionally applied subject to approval by the Assembly at its next session.

(b) The amounts of the fees referred to in paragraph (3)(i) shall be so fixed that the revenues of the Union from fees and other sources shall be at least sufficient to cover all the expenses of the International Bureau concerning the Union.

(c) If the budget is not adopted before the beginning of a new financial period, it shall be at the same level as the budget of the previous year, as provided in the financial regulations.

(5) [*Working Capital Fund*] The Union shall have a working capital fund which shall be constituted by the excess receipts and, if such excess does not suffice, by a single payment made by each member of the Union. If the fund becomes insufficient, the Assembly shall decide to increase it. The proportion and the terms of payment shall be fixed by the Assembly on the proposal of the Director General.

(6) [*Advances by Host State*] (a) In the headquarters agreement concluded with the State on the territory of which the Organization has its headquarters, it shall be provided that, whenever the working capital fund is insufficient, such State shall grant advances. The amount of those advances and the conditions on which they are granted shall be the subject of separate agreements, in each case, between such State and the Organization.

(b) The State referred to in subparagraph (a) and the Organization shall each have the right to denounce the obligation to grant advances, by written notification. Denunciation shall take effect three years after the end of the year in which it has been notified.

(7) [*Auditing of Accounts*] The auditing of the accounts shall be effected by one or more of the States members of the Union or by external auditors, as provided in the financial regulations. They shall be designated, with their agreement, by the Assembly.

Article 24
Regulations

(1) [*Subject Matter*] The Regulations shall govern the details of the implementation of this Act. They shall, in particular, include provisions concerning

(i)   matters which this Act expressly provides are to be prescribed;

(ii)   further details concerning, or any details useful in the implementation of, the provisions of this Act;

(iii) any administrative requirements, matters or procedures.

(2) [*Amendment of Certain Provisions of the Regulations*] (a) The Regulations may specify that certain provisions of the Regulations may be amended only by unanimity or only by a four-fifths majority.

(b) In order for the requirement of unanimity or a four-fifths majority no longer to apply in the future to the amendment of a provision of the Regulations, unanimity shall be required.

(c) In order for the requirement of unanimity or a four-fifths majority to apply in the future to the amendment of a provision of the Regulations, a four-fifths majority shall be required.

(3) [*Conflict Between This Act and the Regulations*] In the case of conflict between the provisions of this Act and those of the Regulations, the former shall prevail.

CHAPTER III
REVISION AND AMENDMENT

Article 25
Revision of This Act

(1) [*Revision Conferences*] This Act may be revised by a conference of the Contracting Parties.

(2) [*Revision or Amendment of Certain Articles*] Articles 21, 22, 23 and 26 may be amended either by a revision conference or by the Assembly according to the provisions of Article 26.

Article 26

Amendment of Certain Articles by the Assembly

(1) [*Proposals for Amendment*] (a) Proposals for the amendment by the Assembly of Articles 21, 22, 23 and this Article may be initiated by any Contracting Party or by the Director General.

(b) Such proposals shall be communicated by the Director General to the Contracting Parties at least six months in advance of their consideration by the Assembly.

(2) [*Majorities*] Adoption of any amendment to the Articles referred to in paragraph (1) shall require a three-fourths majority, except that adoption of any amendment to Article 21 or to the present paragraph shall require a four-fifths majority.

(3) [*Entry into Force*] (a) Except where subparagraph (b) applies, any amendment to the Articles referred to in paragraph (1) shall enter into force one month after written notifications of acceptance, effected in accordance with their respective constitutional processes, have been received by the Director General from three-fourths of those Contracting Parties which, at the time the amendment was adopted, were members of the Assembly and had the right to vote on that amendment.

(b) Any amendment to Article 21(3) or (4) or to this subparagraph shall not enter into force if, within six months of its adoption by the Assembly, any Contracting Party notifies the Director General that it does not accept such amendment.

(c) Any amendment which enters into force in accordance with the provisions of this paragraph shall bind all the States and intergovernmental organizations which are Contracting Parties at the time the amendment enters into force, or which become Contracting Parties at a subsequent date.

CHAPTER IV
FINAL PROVISIONS

Article 27
Becoming Party to This Act

(1) [*Eligibility*] Subject to paragraphs (2) and (3) and Article 28,

(i) any State member of the Organization may sign and become party to this Act;

(ii) any intergovernmental organization which maintains an Office in which protection of industrial designs may be obtained with effect in the territory in which the constituting treaty of the intergovernmental organization applies may sign and become party to this Act, provided that at least one of the member States of the intergovernmental organization is a member of the Organization and provided that such Office is not the subject of a notification under Article 19.

(2) [*Ratification or Accession*] Any State or intergovernmental organization referred to in paragraph (1) may deposit

(i) an instrument of ratification if it has signed this Act, or

(ii) an instrument of accession if it has not signed this Act.

(3) [*Effective Date of Deposit*] (a) Subject to subparagraphs (b) to (d), the effective date of the deposit of an instrument of ratification or accession shall be the date on which that instrument is deposited.

(b) The effective date of the deposit of the instrument of ratification or accession of any State in respect of which protection of industrial designs may be obtained only through the Office maintained by an intergovernmental organization of which that State is a member shall be the date on which the instrument of that intergovernmental organization is deposited if that date is later than the date on which the instrument of the said State has been deposited.

(c) The effective date of the deposit of any instrument of ratification or accession containing or accompanied by the notification referred to in Article 19 shall be the date on which the last of the instruments of the States members of the group of States having made the said notification is deposited.

(d) Any instrument of ratification or accession of a State may contain or be accompanied by a declaration making it a condition to its being considered as deposited that the instrument of one other State or one intergovernmental organization, or the instruments of two other States, or the instruments of one other State and one intergovernmental organization, specified by name and eligible to become party to this Act, is or are also deposited. The instrument containing or accompanied by such a declaration shall be considered to have been deposited on the day on which the condition indicated in the declaration is fulfilled. However, when an instrument specified in the declaration itself contains, or is itself accompanied by, a declaration of the said kind, that instrument shall be considered as deposited on the day on which the condition specified in the latter declaration is fulfilled.

(e) Any declaration made under paragraph (d) may be withdrawn, in its entirety or in part, at any time. Any such withdrawal shall become effective on the date on which the notification of withdrawal is received by the Director General.

Article 28

(1) [*Instruments to Be Taken into Consideration*] For the purposes of this Article, only instruments of ratification or accession that are deposited by States or intergovernmental organizations referred to in Article 27(1) and that have an effective date according to Article 27(3) shall be taken into consideration.

(2) [*Entry into Force of This Act*] This Act shall enter into force three months after six States have deposited their instruments of ratification or accession, provided that, according to the most recent annual statistics collected by the International Bureau, at least three of those States fulfill at least one of the following conditions:

(i) at least 3,000 applications for the protection of industrial designs have been filed in or for the State concerned, or

(ii) at least 1,000 applications for the protection of industrial designs have been filed in or for the State concerned by residents of States other than that State.

(3) [*Entry into Force of Ratifications and Accessions*] (a) Any State or intergovernmental organization that has deposited its instrument of ratification or accession three months or more before the date of entry into force of this Act shall become bound by this Act on the date of entry into force of this Act.

(b) Any other State or intergovernmental organization shall become bound by this Act three months after the date on which it has deposited its instrument of ratification or accession or at any later date indicated in that instrument.

Article 29
Prohibition of Reservations

No reservations to this Act are permitted.

Article 30
Declarations Made by Contracting Parties

(1) [*Time at Which Declarations May Be Made*] Any declaration under Articles 4(1)(b), 5(2)(a), 7(2), 11(1), 13(1), 14(3), 16(2) or 17(3)(c) may be made

(i) at the time of the deposit of an instrument referred to in Article 27(2), in which case it shall become effective on the date on which the State or intergovernmental organization having made the declaration becomes bound by this Act, or

(ii) after the deposit of an instrument referred to in Article 27(2), in which case it shall become effective three months after the date of its receipt by the Director General or at any later date indicated in the declaration but shall apply only in respect of any international registration whose date of international registration is the same as, or is later than, the effective date of the declaration.

(2) [*Declarations by States Having a Common Office*] Notwithstanding paragraph (1), any declaration referred to in that paragraph that has been made by a State which has, with another State or other States, notified the Director General under Article 19(1) of the substitution of a common Office for their national Offices shall become effective only if that other State or those other States makes or make a corresponding declaration or corresponding declarations.

(3) [*Withdrawal of Declarations*] Any declaration referred to in paragraph (1) may be withdrawn at any time by notification addressed to the Director General. Such withdrawal shall take effect three months after the date on which the Director General has received the notification or at any later date indicated in the notification. In the case of a declaration made under Article

7(2), the withdrawal shall not affect international applications filed prior to the coming into effect of the said withdrawal.

Article 31
Applicability of the 1934 and 1960 Acts

(1) [*Relations Between States Party to Both This Act and the 1934 or 1960 Acts*] This Act alone shall be applicable as regards the mutual relations of States party to both this Act and the 1934 Act or the 1960 Act. However, such States shall, in their mutual relations, apply the 1934 Act or the 1960 Act, as the case may be, to industrial designs deposited at the International Bureau prior to the date on which this Act becomes applicable as regards their mutual relations.

(2) [*Relations Between States Party to Both This Act and the 1934 or 1960 Acts and States Party to the 1934 or 1960 Acts Without Being Party to This Act*] (a) Any State that is party to both this Act and the 1934 Act shall continue to apply the 1934 Act in its relations with States that are party to the 1934 Act without being party to the 1960 Act or this Act.

(b) Any State that is party to both this Act and the 1960 Act shall continue to apply the 1960 Act in its relations with States that are party to the 1960 Act without being party to this Act.

Article 32
Denunciation of This Act

(1) [*Notification*] Any Contracting Party may denounce this Act by notification addressed to the Director General.

(2) [*Effective Date*] Denunciation shall take effect one year after the date on which the Director General has received the notification or at any later date indicated in the notification. It shall not affect the application of this Act to any international application pending and any international registration in force in respect of the denouncing Contracting Party at the time of the coming into effect of the denunciation.

Article 33
Languages of This Act; Signature

(1) [*Original Texts; Official Texts*] (a) This Act shall be signed in a single original in the English, Arabic, Chinese, French, Russian and Spanish languages, all texts being equally authentic.

(b) Official texts shall be established by the Director General, after consultation with the interested Governments, in such other languages as the Assembly may designate.

(2) [*Time Limit for Signature*] This Act shall remain open for signature at the headquarters of the Organization for one year after its adoption.

Article 34

Depositary

The Director General shall be the depositary of this Act.

EC DESIGN DIRECTIVE

Directive 98/71/EC of The European Parliament And of The Council of 13 October 1998 on the legal protection of designs

THE EUROPEAN PARLIAMENT AND THE COUNCIL OF THE EUROPEAN UNION,

Having regard to the Treaty establishing the European Community and in particular Article 100a thereof,

Having regard to the proposal by the Commission,

Having regard to the opinion of the Economic and Social Committee,

Acting in accordance with the procedure laid down in Article 189b of the Treaty, in the light of the joint text approved by the Conciliation Committee on 29 July 1998,

(1) Whereas the objectives of the Community, as laid down in the Treaty, include laying the foundations of an ever closer union among the peoples of Europe, fostering closer relations between Member States of the Community, and ensuring the economic and social progress of the Community countries by common action to eliminate the barriers which divide Europe; whereas to that end the Treaty provides for the establishment of an internal market characterised by the abolition of obstacles to the free movement of goods and also for the institution of a system ensuring that competition in the internal market is not distorted; whereas an approximation of the laws of the Member States on the legal protection of designs would further those objectives;

(2) Whereas the differences in the legal protection of designs offered by the legislation of the Member States directly affect the establishment and functioning of the internal market as regards goods embodying designs; whereas such differences can distort competition within the internal market;

(3) Whereas it is therefore necessary for the smooth functioning of the internal market to approximate the design protection laws of the Member States;

(4) Whereas, in doing so, it is important to take into consideration the solutions and the advantages with which the Community design system will provide undertakings wishing to acquire design rights;

(5) Whereas it is unnecessary to undertake a full-scale approximation of the design laws of the Member States, and it will be sufficient if approximation is limited to those national provisions of law which most directly affect the functioning of the internal market; whereas provisions on sanctions, remedies and enforcement should be left to national law; whereas the objectives of this limited approximation cannot be sufficiently achieved by the Member States acting alone;

(6) Whereas Member States should accordingly remain free to fix the procedural provisions concerning registration, renewal and

invalidation of design rights and provisions concerning the effects of such invalidity;

(7)   Whereas this Directive does not exclude the application to designs of national or Community legislation providing for protection other than that conferred by registration or publication as design, such as legislation relating to unregistered design rights, trade marks, patents and utility models, unfair competition or civil liability;

(8)   Whereas, in the absence of harmonisation of copyright law, it is important to establish the principle of cumulation of protection under specific registered design protection law and under copyright law, whilst leaving Member States free to establish the extent of copyright protection and the conditions under which such protection is conferred;

(9)   Whereas the attainment of the objectives of the internal market requires that the conditions for obtaining a registered design right be identical in all the Member States; whereas to that end it is necessary to give a unitary definition of the notion of design and of the requirements as to novelty and individual character with which registered design rights must comply;

(10) Whereas it is essential, in order to facilitate the free movement of goods, to ensure in principle that registered design rights confer upon the right holder equivalent protection in all Member States;

(11) Whereas protection is conferred by way of registration upon the right holder for those design features of a product, in whole or in part, which are shown visibly in an application and made available to the public by way of publication or consultation of the relevant file;

(12) Whereas protection should not be extended to those component parts which are not visible during normal use of a product, or to those features of such part which are not visible when the part is mounted, or which would not, in themselves, fulfil the requirements as to novelty and individual character; whereas features of design which are excluded from protection for these reasons should not be taken into consideration for the purpose of assessing whether other features of the design fulfil the requirements for protection;

(13) Whereas the assessment as to whether a design has individual character should be based on whether the overall impression produced on an informed user viewing the design clearly differs from that produced on him by the existing design corpus, taking into consideration the nature of the product to which the design is applied or in which it is incorporated, and in particular the industrial sector to which it belongs and the degree of freedom of the designer in developing the design;

(14) Whereas technological innovation should not be hampered by granting design protection to features dictated solely by a technical function; whereas it is understood that this does not entail that a design must have an aesthetic quality; whereas, likewise, the

interoperability of products of different makes should not be hindered by extending protection to the design of mechanical fittings; whereas features of a design which are excluded from protection for these reasons should not be taken into consideration for the purpose of assessing whether other features of the design fulfil the requirements for protection;

(15) Whereas the mechanical fittings of modular products may nevertheless constitute an important element of the innovative characteristics of modular products and present a major marketing asset and therefore should be eligible for protection;

(16) Whereas a design right shall not subsist in a design which is contrary to public policy or to accepted principles of morality; whereas this Directive does not constitute a harmonisation of national concepts of public policy or accepted principles of morality;

(17) Whereas it is fundamental for the smooth functioning of the internal market to unify the term of protection afforded by registered design rights;

(18) Whereas the provisions of this Directive are without prejudice to the application of the competition rules under Articles 85 and 86 of the Treaty;

(19) Whereas the rapid adoption of this Directive has become a matter of urgency for a number of industrial sectors; whereas full-scale approximation of the laws of the Member States on the use of protected designs for the purpose of permitting the repair of a complex product so as to restore its original appearance, where the product incorporating the design or to which the design is applied constitutes a component part of a complex product upon whose appearance the protected design is dependent, cannot be introduced at the present stage; whereas the lack of full-scale approximation of the laws of the Member States on the use of protected designs for such repair of a complex product should not constitute an obstacle to the approximation of those other national provisions of design law which most directly affect the functioning of the internal market; whereas for this reason Member States should in the meantime maintain in force any provisions in conformity with the Treaty relating to the use of the design of a component part used for the purpose of the repair of a complex product so as to restore its original appearance, or, if they introduce any new provisions relating to such use, the purpose of these provisions should be only to liberalise the market in such parts; whereas those Member States which, on the date of entry into force of this Directive, do not provide for protection for designs of component parts are not required to introduce registration of designs for such parts; whereas three years after the implementation date the Commission should submit an analysis of the consequences of the provisions of this Directive for Community industry, for consumers, for competition and for the functioning of the internal market;

whereas, in respect of component parts of complex products, the analysis should, in particular, consider harmonisation on the basis of possible options, including a remuneration system and a limited term of exclusivity; whereas, at the latest one year after the submission of its analysis, the Commission should, after consultation with the parties most affected, propose to the European Parliament and the Council any changes to this Directive needed to complete the internal market in respect of component parts of complex products, and any other changes which it considers necessary;

(20) Whereas the transitional provision in Article 14 concerning the design of a component part used for the purpose of the repair of a complex product so as to restore its original appearance is in no case to be construed as constituting an obstacle to the free movement of a product which constitutes such a component part;

(21) Whereas the substantive grounds for refusal of registration in those Member States which provide for substantive examination of applications prior to registration, and the substantive grounds for the invalidation of registered design rights in all the Member States, must be exhaustively enumerated,

HAVE ADOPTED THIS DIRECTIVE:

Article 1
Definitions

For the purpose of this Directive:

(a) 'design' means the appearance of the whole or a part of a product resulting from the features of, in particular, the lines, contours, colours, shape, texture and/or materials of the product itself and/or its ornamentation;

(b) 'product' means any industrial or handicraft item, including *inter alia* parts intended to be assembled into a complex product, packaging, get-up, graphic symbols and typographic typefaces, but excluding computer programs;

(c) 'complex product' means a product which is composed of multiple components which can be replaced permitting disassembly and reassembly of the product.

Article 2
Scope of application

1. This Directive shall apply to:

(a) design rights registered with the central industrial property offices of the Member States;

(b) design rights registered at the Benelux Design Office;

(c) design rights registered under international arrangements which have effect in a Member State;

(d) applications for design rights referred to under (a), (b) and (c).

2. For the purpose of this Directive, design registration shall also comprise the publication following filing of the design with the industrial property office of a Member State in which such publication has the effect of bringing a design right into existence.

Article 3
Protection requirements

1. Member States shall protect designs by registration, and shall confer exclusive rights upon their holders in accordance with the provisions of this Directive.

2. A design shall be protected by a design right to the extent that it is new and has individual character.

3. A design applied to or incorporated in a product which constitutes a component part of a complex product shall only be considered to be new and to have individual character:

(a) if the component part, once it has been incorporated into the complex product, remains visible during normal use of the latter, and

(b) to the extent that those visible features of the component part fulfil in themselves the requirements as to novelty and individual character.

4. 'Normal use' within the meaning of paragraph (3)(a) shall mean use by the end user, excluding maintenance, servicing or repair work.

Article 4
Novelty

A design shall be considered new if no identical design has been made available to the public before the date of filing of the application for registration or, if priority is claimed, the date of priority. Designs shall be deemed to be identical if their features differ only in immaterial details.

Article 5
Individual character

1. A design shall be considered to have individual character if the overall impression it produces on the informed user differs from the overall impression produced on such a user by any design which has been made available to the public before the date of filing of the application for registration or, if priority is claimed, the date of priority.

2. In assessing individual character, the degree of freedom of the designer in developing the design shall be taken into consideration.

Article 6
Disclosure

1. For the purpose of applying Articles 4 and 5, a design shall be deemed to have been made available to the public if it has been published following

registration or otherwise, or exhibited, used in trade or otherwise disclosed, except where these events could not reasonably have become known in the normal course of business to the circles specialised in the sector concerned, operating within the Community, before the date of filing of the application for registration or, if priority is claimed, the date of priority. The design shall not, however, be deemed to have been made available to the public for the sole reason that it has been disclosed to a third person under explicit or implicit conditions of confidentiality.

2. A disclosure shall not be taken into consideration for the purpose of applying Articles 4 and 5 if a design for which protection is claimed under a registered design right of a Member State has been made available to the public:

(a) by the designer, his successor in title, or a third person as a result of information provided or action taken by the designer, or his successor in title; and

(b) during the 12-month period preceding the date of filing of the application or, if priority is claimed, the date of priority.

3. Paragraph 2 shall also apply if the design has been made available to the public as a consequence of an abuse in relation to the designer or his successor in title.

Article 7
Designs dictated by their technical function and designs of interconnections

1. A design right shall not subsist in features of appearance of a product which are solely dictated by its technical function.

2. A design right shall not subsist in features of appearance of a product which must necessarily be reproduced in their exact form and dimensions in order to permit the product in which the design is incorporated or to which it is applied to be mechanically connected to or placed in, around or against another product so that either product may perform its function.

3. Notwithstanding paragraph 2, a design right shall, under the conditions set out in Articles 4 and 5, subsist in a design serving the purpose of allowing multiple assembly or connection of mutually interchangeable products within a modular system.

Article 8
Designs contrary to public policy or morality

A design right shall not subsist in a design which is contrary to public policy or to accepted principles of morality.

Article 9
Scope of protection

1. The scope of the protection conferred by a design right shall include any design which does not produce on the informed user a different overall

impression.

2. In assessing the scope of protection, the degree of freedom of the designer in developing his design shall be taken into consideration.

Article 10
Term of protection

Upon registration, a design which meets the requirements of Article 3(2) shall be protected by a design right for one or more periods of five years from the date of filing of the application. The right holder may have the term of protection renewed for one or more periods of five years each, up to a total term of 25 years from the date of filing.

Article 11
Invalidity or refusal of registration

1. A design shall be refused registration, or, if the design has been registered, the design right shall be declared invalid:

(a) if the design is not a design within the meaning of Article 1(a); or

(b) if it does not fulfil the requirements of Articles 3 to 8; or

(c) if the applicant for or the holder of the design right is not entitled to it under the law of the Member State concerned; or

(d) if the design is in conflict with a prior design which has been made available to the public after the date of filing of the application or, if priority is claimed, the date of priority, and which is protected from a date prior to the said date by a registered Community design or an application for a registered Community design or by a design right of the Member State concerned, or by an application for such a right.

2. Any Member State may provide that a design shall be refused registration, or, if the design has been registered, that the design right shall be declared invalid:

(a) if a distinctive sign is used in a subsequent design, and Community law or the law of the Member State concerned governing that sign confers on the right holder of the sign the right to prohibit such use; or

(b) if the design constitutes an unauthorised use of a work protected under the copyright law of the Member State concerned; or

(c) if the design constitutes an improper use of any of the items listed in Article 6b of the Paris Convention for the Protection of Industrial Property, or of badges, emblems and escutcheons other than those covered by Article 6b of the said Convention which are of particular public interest in the Member State concerned.

3. The ground provided for in paragraph 1(c) may be invoked solely by the person who is entitled to the design right under the law of the Member State concerned.

4. The grounds provided for in paragraph 1(d) and in paragraph 2(a) and (b) may be invoked solely by the applicant for or the holder of the conflicting

right.

5. The ground provided for in paragraph 2(c) may be invoked solely by the person or entity concerned by the use.

6. Paragraphs 4 and 5 shall be without prejudice to the freedom of Member States to provide that the grounds provided for in paragraphs 1(d) and 2(c) may also be invoked by the appropriate authority of the Member State in question on its own initiative.

7. When a design has been refused registration or a design right has been declared invalid pursuant to paragraph 1(b) or to paragraph 2, the design may be registered or the design right maintained in an amended form, if in that form it complies with the requirements for protection and the identity of the design is retained. Registration or maintenance in an amended form may include registration accompanied by a partial disclaimer by the holder of the design right or entry in the design Register of a court decision declaring the partial invalidity of the design right.

8. Any Member State may provide that, by way of derogation from paragraphs 1 to 7, the grounds for refusal of registration or for invalidation in force in that State prior to the date on which the provisions necessary to comply with this Directive enter into force shall apply to design applications which have been made prior to that date and to resulting registrations.

9. A design right may be declared invalid even after it has lapsed or has been surrendered.

Article 12
Rights conferred by the design right

1. The registration of a design shall confer on its holder the exclusive right to use it and to prevent any third party not having his consent from using it. The aforementioned use shall cover, in particular, the making, offering, putting on the market, importing, exporting or using of a product in which the design is incorporated or to which it is applied, or stocking such a product for those purposes.

2. Where, under the law of a Member State, acts referred to in paragraph 1 could not be prevented before the date on which the provisions necessary to comply with this Directive entered into force, the rights conferred by the design right may not be invoked to prevent continuation of such acts by any person who had begun such acts prior to that date.

Article 13
Limitation of the rights conferred by the design right

1. The rights conferred by a design right upon registration shall not be exercised in respect of:

(a) acts done privately and for non-commercial purposes;

(b) acts done for experimental purposes;

(c) acts of reproduction for the purposes of making citations or of teaching, provided that such acts are compatible with fair trade practice and do not unduly prejudice the normal exploitation of the design, and that mention is made of the source.

2. In addition, the rights conferred by a design right upon registration shall not be exercised in respect of:

(a) the equipment on ships and aircraft registered in another country when these temporarily enter the territory of the Member State concerned;

(b) the importation in the Member State concerned of spare parts and accessories for the purpose of repairing such craft;

(c) the execution of repairs on such craft.

Article 14
Transitional provision

Until such time as amendments to this Directive are adopted on a proposal from the Commission in accordance with the provisions of Article 18, Member States shall maintain in force their existing legal provisions relating to the use of the design of a component part used for the purpose of the repair of a complex product so as to restore its original appearance and shall introduce changes to those provisions only if the purpose is to liberalise the market for such parts.

Article 15
Exhaustion of rights

The rights conferred by a design right upon registration shall not extend to acts relating to a product in which a design included within the scope of protection of the design right is incorporated or to which it is applied, when the product has been put on the market in the Community by the holder of the design right or with his consent.

Article 16
Relationship to other forms of protection

The provisions of this Directive shall be without prejudice to any provisions of Community law or of the law of the Member State concerned relating to unregistered design rights, trade marks or other distinctive signs, patents and utility models, typefaces, civil liability or unfair competition.

Article 17
Relationship to copyright

A design protected by a design right registered in or in respect of a Member State in accordance with this Directive shall also be eligible for protection under the law of copyright of that State as from the date on which the design was created or fixed in any form. The extent to which, and the conditions under which, such a protection is conferred, including the level of originality required, shall be determined by each Member State.

Article 18
Revision

Three years after the implementation date specified in Article 19, the Commission shall submit an analysis of the consequences of the provisions of this Directive for Community industry, in particular the industrial sectors which are most affected, particularly manufacturers of complex products and component parts, for consumers, for competition and for the functioning of the internal market. At the latest one year later the Commission shall propose to the European Parliament and the Council any changes to this Directive needed to complete the internal market in respect of component parts of complex products and any other changes which it considers necessary in light of its consultations with the parties most affected.

Article 19
Implementation

1. Member States shall bring into force the laws, regulations or administrative provisions necessary to comply with this Directive not later than 28 October 2001. When Member States adopt these provisions, they shall contain a reference to this Directive or shall be accompanied by such reference on the occasion of their official publication. The methods of making such reference shall be laid down by Member States.

Member States shall communicate to the Commission the provisions of national law which they adopt in the field governed by this Directive.

Article 20
Entry into force

This Directive shall enter into force on the 20th day following its publication in the *Official Journal of the European Communities*.

Article 21
Addressees

This Directive is addressed to the Member States.

Done at Luxembourg, 13 October 1998.

EC SEMI-CONDUCTOR DIRECTIVE

Council Directive 87/54/EEC of 16 December 1986 on the legal protection of topographies of semiconductor products

THE COUNCIL OF THE EUROPEAN COMMUNITIES,

Having regard to the Treaty establishing the European Economic Community and in particular Article 100 thereof,

Having regard to the proposal from the Commission,

Having regard to the opinion of the European Parliament,

Having regard to the opinion of the Economic and Social Committee,

Whereas semiconductor products are playing an increasingly important role in a broad range of industries and semiconductor technology can accordingly be considered as being of fundamental importance for the Community's industrial development;

Whereas the functions of semiconductor products depend in large part on the topographies of such products and whereas the development of such topographies requires the investment of considerable resources, human, technical and financial, while topographies of such products can be copied at a fraction of the cost needed to develop them independently;

Whereas topographies of semiconductor products are at present not clearly protected in all Member States by existing legislation and such protection, where it exists, has different attributes;

Whereas certain existing differences in the legal protection of semiconductor products offered by the laws of the Member States have direct and negative effects on the functioning of the common market as regards semiconductor products and such differences could well become greater as Member States introduce new legislation on this subject;

Whereas existing differences having such effects need to be removed and new ones having a negative effect on the common market prevented from arising;

Whereas, in relation to extension of protection to persons outside the Community, Member States should be free to act on their own behalf in so far as Community decisions have not been taken within a limited period of time;

Whereas the Community's legal framework on the protection of topographies of semiconductor products can, in the first instance, be limited to certain basic principles by provisions specifying whom and what should be protected, the exclusive rights on which protected persons should be able to rely to authorize or prohibit certain acts, exceptions to these rights and for how long the protection should last;

Whereas other matters can for the time being be decided in accordance with national law, in particular, whether registration or deposit is required as a condition for protection and, subject to an exclusion of licences granted for the sole reason that a certain period of time has elapsed, whether and on what conditions non-voluntary licences may be granted in respect of protected topographies;

Whereas protection of topographies of semiconductor products in accordance with this Directive should be without prejudice to the application of some other forms of protection;

Whereas further measures concerning the legal protection of topographies of semiconductor products in the Community can be considered at a later stage, if necessary, while the application of common basic principles by all Member States in accordance with the provisions of this Directive is an urgent necessity,

HAS ADOPTED THIS DIRECTIVE:

CHAPTER 1
Definitions

Article 1

1. For the purposes of this Directive:

(a) a 'semiconductor product' shall mean the final or an intermediate form of any product:

  (i) consisting of a body of material which includes a layer of semiconducting material; and

  (ii) having one or more other layers composed of conducting, insulating or semiconducting material, the layers being arranged in accordance with a predetermined three-dimensional pattern; and

  (iii) intended to perform, exclusively or together with other functions, an electronic function;

(b) the 'topography' of a semiconductor product shall mean a series of related images, however fixed or encoded;

  (i) representing the three-dimensional pattern of the layers of which a semiconductor product is composed; and

  (ii) in which series, each image has the pattern or part of the pattern of a surface of the semiconductor product at any stage of its manufacture;

(c) 'commercial exploitation' means the sale, rental, leasing or any other method of commercial distribution, or an offer for these purposes. However, for the purposes of Articles 3(4), 4(1), 7 (1), (3) and (4) 'commercial exploitation' shall not include exploitation under conditions of confidentiality to the extent that no further distribution to third parties occurs, except where exploitation of a topography takes place under conditions of confidentiality required by a measure taken in conformity with Article 223(1)(b) of the Treaty.

2. The Council acting by qualified majority on a proposal from the

Commission, may amend paragraph 1(a) (i) and (ii) in order to adapt these provisions in the light of technical progress.

CHAPTER 2
Protection of topographies of semiconductor products

Article 2

1. Member States shall protect the topographies of semiconductor products by adopting legislative provisions conferring exclusive rights in accordance with the provisions of the Directive.

2. The topography of a semiconductor product shall be protected in so far as it satisfies the conditions that it is the result of its creator's own intellectual effort and is not commonplace in the semiconductor industry. Where the topography of a semiconductor product consists of elements that are commonplace in the semiconductor industry, it shall be protected only to the extent that the combination of such elements, taken as a whole, fulfils the abovementioned conditions.

Article 3

1. Subject to paragraphs 2 to 5, the right to protection shall apply in favour of persons who are the creators of the topographies of semiconductor products.

2. Member States may provide that,

(a) where a topography is created in the course of the creator's employment, the right to protection shall apply in favour of the creator's employer unless the terms of employment provide to the contrary;

(b) where a topography is created under a contract other than a contract of employment, the right to protection shall apply in favour of a party to the contract by whom the topography has been commissioned, unless the contract provides to the contrary.

3. (a) As regards the persons referred to in paragraph 1, the right to protection shall apply in favour of natural persons who are nationals of a Member State or who have their habitual residence on the territory of a Member State.

(b) Where Member States make provision in accordance with paragraph 2, the right to protection shall apply in favour of:

(i) natural persons who are nationals of a Member State or who have their habitual residence on the territory of a Member State;

(ii) companies or other legal persons which have a real and effective industrial or commercial establishment on the territory of a Member State.

4. Where no right to protection exists in accordance with other provisions of this Article, the right to protection shall also apply in favour of the persons

referred to in paragraph 3(b) (i) and (ii) who:

(a) first commercially exploit within a Member State a topography which has not yet been exploited commercially anywhere in the world; and

(b) have been exclusively authorized to exploit commercially the topography throughout the Community by the person entitled to dispose of it.

5. The right to protection shall also apply in favour of the successors in title of the persons mentioned in paragraphs 1 to 4.

6. Subject to paragraph 7, Member States may negotiate and conclude agreements or understandings with third States and multilateral Conventions concerning the legal protection of topographies of semiconductor products whilst respecting Community law and in particular the rules laid down in this Directive.

7. Member States may enter into negotiations which third States with a view to extending the right to protection to persons who do not benefit from the right to protection according to the provisions of this Directive. Member States who enter into such negotiations shall inform the Commission thereof.

When a Member State wishes to extend protection to persons who otherwise do not benefit from the right to protection according to the provisions of this Directive or to conclude an agreement or understanding on the extension of protection with a non-Member State it shall notify the Commission. The Commission shall inform the other Member States thereof.

The Member State shall hold the extension of protection or the conclusion of the agreement or understanding in abeyance for one month from the date on which it notifies the Commission. However, if within that period the Commission notifies the Member State concerned of its intention to submit a proposal to the Council for all Member States to extend protection in respect of the persons or non-Member State concerned, the Member State shall hold the extension of protection or the conclusion of the agreement or understanding in abeyance for a period of two months from the date of the notification by the Member State.

Where, before the end of this two-month period, the Commission submits such a proposal to the Council, the Member State shall hold the extension of protection or the conclusion of the agreement or understanding in abeyance for a further period of four months from the date on which the proposal was submitted.

In the absence of a Commission notification or proposal or a Council decision within the time limits prescribed above, the Member State may extend protection or conclude the agreement or understanding.

A proposal by the Commission to extend protection, whether or not it is made following a notification by a Member State in accordance with the preceding paragraphs shall be adopted by the Council acting by qualified majority.

A Decision of the Council on the basis of a Commission proposal shall not prevent a Member State from extending protection to persons, in addition to those to benefit from protection in all Member States, who were included in the envisaged extension, agreement or understanding as notified, unless the Council acting by qualified majority has decided otherwise.

8. Commission proposals and Council decisions pursuant to paragraph 7 shall be published for information in the *Official Journal of the European Communities.*

Article 4

1. Member States may provide that the exclusive rights conferred in conformity with Article 2 shall not come into existence or shall no longer apply to the topography of a semiconductor product unless an application for registration in due form has been filed with a public authority within two years of its first commercial exploitation. Member States may require in addition to such registration that material identifying or exemplifying the topography or any combination thereof has been deposited with a public authority, as well as a statement as to the date of first commercial exploitation of the topography where it precedes the date of the application for registration.

2. Member States shall ensure that material deposited in conformity with paragraph 1 is not made available to the public where it is a trade secret. This provision shall be without prejudice to the disclosure of such material pursuant to an order of a court or other competent authority to persons involved in litigation concerning the validity or infringement of the exclusive rights referred to in Article 2.

3. Member States may require that transfers of rights in protected topographies be registered.

4. Member States may subject registration and deposit in accordance with paragraphs 1 and 3 to the payment of fees not exceeding their administrative costs.

5. Conditions prescribing the fulfilment of additional formalities for obtaining or maintaining protection shall not be admitted.

6. Member States which require registration shall provide for legal remedies in favour of a person having the right to protection in accordance with the provisions of this Directive who can prove that another person has applied for or obtained the registration of a topography without his authorization.

Article 5

1. The exclusive rights referred to in Article 2 shall include the rights to authorize or prohibit any of the following acts:

(a) reproduction of a topography in so far as it is protected under Article 2 (2);

(b) commercial exploitation or the importation for that purpose of a topography or of a semiconductor product manufactured by using the topography.

2. Notwithstanding paragraph 1, a Member State pay permit the reproduction of a topography privately for non commercial aims.

3. The exclusive rights referred to in paragraph 1(a) shall not apply to reproduction for the purpose of analyzing, evaluating or teaching the concepts, processes, systems or techniques embodied in the topography or the topography itself.

4. The exclusive rights referred to in paragraph 1 shall not extend to any such act in relation to a topography meeting the requirements of Article 2(2) and created on the basis of an analysis and evaluation of another topography, carried out in conformity with paragraph 3.

5. The exclusive rights to authorize or prohibit the acts specified in paragraph 1(b) shall not apply to any such act committed after the topography or the semiconductor product has been put on the market in a Member State by the person entitled to authorize its marketing or with his consent.

6. A person who, when he acquires a semiconductor product, does not know, or has no reasonable grounds to believe, that the product is protected by an exclusive right conferred by a Member State in conformity with this Directive shall not be prevented from commercially exploiting that product.

However, for acts committed after that person knows, or has reasonable grounds to believe, that the semiconductor product is so protected, Member States shall ensure that on the demand of the rightholder a tribunal may require, in accordance with the provisions of the national law applicable, the payment of adequate remuneration.

7. The provisions of paragraph 6 shall apply to the successors in title of the person referred to in the first sentence of that paragraph.

Article 6

Member States shall not subject the exclusive rights referred to in Article 2 to licences granted, for the sole reason that a certain period of time has elapsed, automatically, and by operation of law.

Article 7

1. Member States shall provide that the exclusive rights referred to in Article 2 shall come into existence:

(a) where registration is the condition for the coming into existence of the exclusive rights in accordance with Article 4, on the earlier of the following dates:

(i) the date when the topography is first commercially exploited anywhere in the world;

(ii) the date when an application or registration has been filed in due form; or

(b) when the topography is first commercially exploited anywhere in the world; or

(c) when the topography is first fixed or encoded.

2. Where the exclusive rights come into existence in accordance with paragraph 1 (a) or (b), the Member States shall provide, for the period prior to those rights coming into existence, legal remedies in favour of a person having the right to protection in accordance with the provisions of this Directive who can prove that another person has fraudulently reproduced or commercially exploited or imported for that purpose a topography. This paragraph shall be without prejudice to legal remedies made available to enforce the exclusive rights conferred in conformity with Article 2.

3. The exclusive rights shall come to an end 10 years from the end of the calendar year in which the topography is first commercially exploited anywhere in the world or, where registration is a condition for the coming into existence or continuing application of the exclusive rights, 10 years from the earlier of the following dates:

(a) the end of the calendar year in which the topography is first commercially exploited anywhere in the world;

(b) the end of the calendar year in which the application for registration has been filed in due form.

4. Where a topography has not been commercially exploited anywhere in the world within a period of 15 years from its first fixation or encoding, any exclusive rights in existence pursuant to paragraph 1 shall come to an end and no new exclusive rights shall come into existence unless an application for registration in due form has been filed within that period in those Member States where registration is a condition for the coming into existence or continuing application of the exclusive rights.

Article 8

The protection granted to the topographies of semiconductor products in accordance with Article 2 shall not extend to any concept, process, system, technique or encoded information embodied in the topography other than the topography itself.

Article 9

Where the legislation of Member States provides that semiconductor products manufactured using protected topographies may carry an indication, the indication to be used shall be a capital T as follows: T, 'T', [T], T*, or [T]

CHAPTER 3
Continued application of other legal provisions

Article 10

1. The provisions of this Directive shall be without prejudice to legal provisions concerning patent and utility model rights.

2. The provisions of this Directive shall be without prejudice:

(a) to rights conferred by the Member States in fulfilment of their obligations under international agreements, including provisions extending such rights to nationals of, or residents in, the territory of the Member State concerned;

(b) to the law of copyright in Member States, restricting the reproduction of drawing or other artistic representations of topographies by copying them in two dimensions.

3. Protection granted by national law to topographies of semiconductor products fixed or encoded before the entry into force of the national provisions enacting the Directive, but no later than the date set out in Article 11(1), shall not be affected by the provisions of this Directive.

CHAPTER 4
Final provisions

Article 11

1. Member States shall bring into force the laws, regulations or administrative provisions necessary to comply with this Directive by 7 November 1987.

2. Member States shall ensure that they communicate to the Commission the texts of the main provisions of national law which they adopt in the field covered by this Directive.

Article 12

This Directive is addressed to the Member States.

Done at Brussels, 16 December 1986.

F. PATENT LAW

PATENT COOPERATION TREATY
Done at Washington on June 19, 1970, amended on September 28, 1979,
and modified on February 3, 1984

The Contracting States,

Desiring to make a contribution to the progress of science and technology,

Desiring to perfect the legal protection of inventions,

Desiring to simplify and render more economical the obtaining of protection for inventions where protection is sought in several countries,

Desiring to facilitate and accelerate access by the public to the technical information contained in documents describing new inventions,

Desiring to foster and accelerate the economic development of developing countries through the adoption of measures designed to increase the efficiency of their legal systems, whether national or regional, instituted for the protection of inventions by providing easily accessible information on the availability of technological solutions applicable to their special needs and by facilitating access to the ever expanding volume of modern technology,

Convinced that cooperation among nations will greatly facilitate the attainment of these aims,

Have concluded the present Treaty.

INTRODUCTORY PROVISIONS

Article 1
Establishment of a Union

(1) The States party to this Treaty (hereinafter called "the Contracting States") constitute a Union for cooperation in the filing, searching, and examination, of applications for the protection of inventions, and for rendering special technical services. The Union shall be known as the International Patent Cooperation Union.

(2) No provision of this Treaty shall be interpreted as diminishing the rights under the Paris Convention for the Protection of Industrial Property of any national or resident of any country party to that Convention.

Article 2
Definitions

For the purposes of this Treaty and the Regulations and unless expressly stated otherwise:

(i) "application" means an application for the protection of an invention; references to an "application" shall be construed as references to applications for patents for inventions, inventors' certificates, utility certificates, utility models, patents or certificates of addition, inventors' certificates of addition, and utility certificates of addition;

(ii) references to a "patent" shall be construed as references to patents for inventions, inventors' certificates, utility certificates, utility models, patents or certificates of addition, inventors' certificates of addition, and utility certificates of addition;

(iii) "national patent" means a patent granted by a national authority;

(iv) "regional patent" means a patent granted by a national or an intergovernmental authority having the power to grant patents effective in more than one State;

(v) "regional application" means an application for a regional patent;

(vi) references to a "national application" shall be construed as references to applications for national patents and regional patents, other than applications filed under this Treaty;

(vii) "international application" means an application filed under this Treaty;

(viii) references to an "application" shall be construed as references to international applications and national applications;

(ix) references to a "patent" shall be construed as references to national patents and regional patents;

(x) references to "national law" shall be construed as references to the national law of a Contracting State or, where a regional application or a regional patent is involved, to the treaty providing for the filing of regional applications or the granting of regional patents;

(xi) "priority date," for the purposes of computing time limits, means:

(a) where the international application contains a priority claim under Article 8, the filing date of the application whose priority is so claimed;

(b) where the international application contains several priority claims under Article 8, the filing date of the earliest application whose priority is so claimed;

(c) where the international application does not contain any priority claim under Article 8, the international filing date of such application;

(xii) "national Office" means the government authority of a Contracting State entrusted with the granting of patents; references to a "national Office" shall be construed as referring also to any intergovernmental authority which several States have entrusted with the task of granting regional patents, provided that at least one of those States is a Contracting State, and provided that the said States have authorized that authority to assume the obligations and exercise the powers which this Treaty and the Regulations provide for in respect of national Offices;

(xiii) "designated Office" means the national Office of or acting for the State designated by the applicant under Chapter I of this Treaty;

(xiv) "elected Office" means the national Office of or acting for the State elected by the applicant under Chapter II of this Treaty;

(xv) "receiving Office" means the national Office or the intergovernmental organization with which the international application has been filed;

(xvi) "Union" means the International Patent Cooperation Union;

(xvii) "Assembly" means the Assembly of the Union;

(xviii) "Organization" means the World Intellectual Property Organization;

(xix) "International Bureau" means the International Bureau of the Organization and, as long as it subsists, the United International Bureaux for the Protection of Intellectual Property (BIRPI);

(xx) "Director General" means the Director General of the Organization and, as long as BIRPI subsists, the Director of BIRPI.

CHAPTER I
INTERNATIONAL APPLICATION AND INTERNATIONAL SEARCH

Article 3
The International Application

(1) Applications for the protection of inventions in any of the Contracting States may be filed as international applications under this Treaty.

(2) An international application shall contain, as specified in this Treaty and the Regulations, a request, a description, one or more claims, one or more drawings (where required), and an abstract.

(3) The abstract merely serves the purpose of technical information and cannot be taken into account for any other purpose, particularly not for the purpose of interpreting the scope of the protection sought.

(4) The international application shall:

(i) be in a prescribed language;

(ii) comply with the prescribed physical requirements;

(iii) comply with the prescribed requirement of unity of invention;

(iv) be subject to the payment of the prescribed fees.

Article 4
The Request

(1) The request shall contain:

(i) a petition to the effect that the international application be processed according to this Treaty;

(ii) the designation of the Contracting State or States in which protection for the invention is desired on the basis of the international application ("designated States"); if for any designated State a regional patent is available and the applicant wishes to obtain a regional patent rather than a national patent, the request shall so indicate; if, under a treaty concerning a regional patent, the applicant cannot limit his application to certain of the States party to that treaty, designation of one of those States and the indication of the wish to obtain the regional patent shall be treated as designation of all the States party to that treaty; if, under the national law of the designated State, the designation of that State has the effect of an application for a regional patent, the designation of the said State shall be treated as an indication of the wish to obtain the regional patent;

(iii) the name of and other prescribed data concerning the applicant and the agent (if any);

(iv) the title of the invention;

(v) the name of and other prescribed data concerning the inventor where the national law of at least one of the designated States requires that these indications be furnished at the time of filing a national application. Otherwise, the said indications may be furnished either in the request or in separate notices addressed to each designated Office whose national law requires the furnishing of the said indications but allows that they be furnished at a time later than that of the filing of a national application.

(2) Every designation shall be subject to the payment of the prescribed fee within the prescribed time limit.

(3) Unless the applicant asks for any of the other kinds of protection referred to in Article 43, designation shall mean that the desired protection consists of the grant of a patent by or for the designated State. For the purposes of this paragraph, Article 2(ii) shall not apply.

(4) Failure to indicate in the request the name and other prescribed data concerning the inventor shall have no consequence in any designated State whose national law requires the furnishing of the said indications but allows that they be furnished at a time later than that of the filing of a national application. Failure to furnish the said indications in a separate notice shall have no consequence in any designated State whose national law does not require the furnishing of the said indications.

Article 5
The Description

The description shall disclose the invention in a manner sufficiently clear and complete for the invention to be carried out by a person skilled in the art.

Article 6
The Claims

The claim or claims shall define the matter for which protection is sought. Claims shall be clear and concise. They shall be fully supported by the description.

Article 7
The Drawings

(1) Subject to the provisions of paragraph (2)(ii), drawings shall be required

when they are necessary for the understanding of the invention.

(2) Where, without being necessary for the understanding of the invention, the nature of the invention admits of illustration by drawings:

(i) the applicant may include such drawings in the international application when filed,

(ii) any designated Office may require that the applicant file such drawings with it within the prescribed time limit.

Article 8
Claiming Priority

(1) The international application may contain a declaration, as prescribed in the Regulations, claiming the priority of one or more earlier applications filed in or for any country party to the Paris Convention for the Protection of Industrial Property.

(2) (a) Subject to the provisions of subparagraph (b), the conditions for, and the effect of, any priority claim declared under paragraph (1) shall be as provided in Article 4 of the Stockholm Act of the Paris Convention for the Protection of Industrial Property.

(b) The international application for which the priority of one or more earlier applications filed in or for a Contracting State is claimed may contain the designation of that State. Where, in the international application, the priority of one or more national applications filed in or for a designated State is claimed, or where the priority of an international application having designated only one State is claimed, the conditions for, and the effect of, the priority claim in that State shall be governed by the national law of that State.

Article 9
The Applicant

(1) Any resident or national of a Contracting State may file an international application.

(2) The Assembly may decide to allow the residents and the nationals of any country party to the Paris Convention for the Protection of Industrial Property which is not party to this Treaty to file international applications.

(3) The concepts of residence and nationality, and the application of those concepts in cases where there are several applicants or where the applicants are not the same for all the designated States, are defined in the Regulations.

Article 10
The Receiving Office

The international application shall be filed with the prescribed receiving Office, which will check and process it as provided in this Treaty and the Regulations.

Article 11
Filing Date and Effects of the International Application

(1) The receiving Office shall accord as the international filing date the date of receipt of the international application, provided that that Office has found that, at the time of receipt:

(i) the applicant does not obviously lack, for reasons of residence or nationality, the right to file an international application with the receiving Office,

(ii) the international application is in the prescribed language,

(iii) the international application contains at least the following elements:

(a) an indication that it is intended as an international application,

(b) the designation of at least one Contracting State,

(c) the name of the applicant, as prescribed,

(d) a part which on the face of it appears to be a description,

(e) a part which on the face of it appears to be a claim or claims.

(2) (a) If the receiving Office finds that the international application did not, at the time of receipt, fulfill the requirements listed in paragraph (1), it shall, as provided in the Regulations, invite the applicant to file the required correction.

(b) If the applicant complies with the invitation, as provided in the Regulations, the receiving Office shall accord as the international filing date the date of receipt of the required correction.

(3) Subject to Article 64(4), any international application fulfilling the requirements listed in items (i) to (iii) of paragraph (1) and accorded an international filing date shall have the effect of a regular national application in each designated State as of the international filing date, which date shall be considered to be the actual filing date in each designated State.

(4) Any international application fulfilling the requirements listed in items (i) to (iii) of paragraph (1) shall be equivalent to a regular national filing within the meaning of the Paris Convention for the Protection of Industrial Property.

Article 12
Transmittal of the International Application to the International Bureau and the International Searching Authority

(1) One copy of the international application shall be kept by the receiving Office ("home copy"), one copy ("record copy") shall be transmitted to the International Bureau, and another copy ("search copy") shall be transmitted to the competent International Searching Authority referred to in Article 16, as provided in the Regulations.

(2) The record copy shall be considered the true copy of the international application.

(3) The international application shall be considered withdrawn if the

record copy has not been received by the International Bureau within the prescribed time limit.

Article 13
Availability of Copy of the International Application to Designated Offices

(1) Any designated Office may ask the International Bureau to transmit to it a copy of the international application prior to the communication provided for in Article 20, and the International Bureau shall transmit such copy to the designated Office as soon as possible after the expiration of one year from the priority date.

(2) (a) The applicant may, at any time, transmit a copy of his international application to any designated Office.

(b) The applicant may, at any time, ask the International Bureau to transmit a copy of his international application to any designated Office, and the International Bureau shall transmit such copy to the designated Office as soon as possible.

(c) Any national Office may notify the International Bureau that it does not wish to receive copies as provided for in subparagraph (b), in which case that subparagraph shall not be applicable in respect of that Office.

Article 14
Certain Defects in the International Application

(1)(a) The receiving Office shall check whether the international application contains any of the following defects, that is to say:

(i) it is not signed as provided in the Regulations;

(ii) it does not contain the prescribed indications concerning the applicant;

(iii) it does not contain a title;

(iv) it does not contain an abstract;

(v) it does not comply to the extent provided in the Regulations with the prescribed physical requirements.

(b) If the receiving Office finds any of the said defects, it shall invite the applicant to correct the international application within the prescribed time limit, failing which that application shall be considered withdrawn and the receiving Office shall so declare.

(2) If the international application refers to drawings which, in fact, are not included in that application, the receiving Office shall notify the applicant accordingly and he may furnish them within the prescribed time limit and, if he does, the international filing date shall be the date on which the drawings are received by the receiving Office. Otherwise, any reference to the said drawings shall be considered non-existent.

(3) (a) If the receiving Office finds that, within the prescribed time limits, the fees prescribed under Article 3(4)(iv) have not been paid, or no fee

prescribed under Article 4(2) has been paid in respect of any of the designated States, the international application shall be considered withdrawn and the receiving Office shall so declare.

(b) If the receiving Office finds that the fee prescribed under Article 4(2) has been paid in respect of one or more (but less than all) designated States within the prescribed time limit, the designation of those States in respect of which it has not been paid within the prescribed time limit shall be considered withdrawn and the receiving Office shall so declare.

(4) If, after having accorded an international filing date to the international application, the receiving Office finds, within the prescribed time limit, that any of the requirements listed in items (i) to (iii) of Article 11(1) was not complied with at that date, the said application shall be considered withdrawn and the receiving Office shall so declare.

Article 15
The International Search

(1) Each international application shall be the subject of international search.

(2) The objective of the international search is to discover relevant prior art.

(3) International search shall be made on the basis of the claims, with due regard to the description and the drawings (if any).

(4) The International Searching Authority referred to in Article 16 shall endeavor to discover as much of the relevant prior art as its facilities permit, and shall, in any case, consult the documentation specified in the Regulations.

(5) (a) If the national law of the Contracting State so permits, the applicant who files a national application with the national Office of or acting for such State may, subject to the conditions provided for in such law, request that a search similar to an international search ("international-type search") be carried out on such application.

(b) If the national law of the Contracting State so permits, the national Office of or acting for such State may subject any national application filed with it to an international-type search.

(c) The international-type search shall be carried out by the International Searching Authority referred to in Article 16 which would be competent for an international search if the national application were an international application and were filed with the Office referred to in subparagraphs (a) and (b). If the national application is in a language which the International Searching Authority considers it is not equipped to handle, the international-type search shall be carried out on a translation prepared by the applicant in a language prescribed for international applications and which the International Searching Authority has undertaken to accept for international applications. The national application and the translation, when required, shall be presented in the form prescribed for international applications.

Article 16
The International Searching Authority

(1) International search shall be carried out by an International Searching Authority, which may be either a national Office or an intergovernmental organization, such as the International Patent Institute, whose tasks include the establishing of documentary search reports on prior art with respect to inventions which are the subject of applications.

(2) If, pending the establishment of a single International Searching Authority, there are several International Searching Authorities, each receiving Office shall, in accordance with the provisions of the applicable agreement referred to in paragraph (3)(b), specify the International Searching Authority or Authorities competent for the searching of international applications filed with such Office.

(3) (a) International Searching Authorities shall be appointed by the Assembly. Any national Office and any intergovernmental organization satisfying the requirements referred to in subparagraph (c) may be appointed as International Searching Authority.

(b) Appointment shall be conditional on the consent of the national Office or intergovernmental organization to be appointed and the conclusion of an agreement, subject to approval by the Assembly, between such Office or organization and the International Bureau. The agreement shall specify the rights and obligations of the parties, in particular, the formal undertaking by the said Office or organization to apply and observe all the common rules of international search.

(c) The Regulations prescribe the minimum requirements, particularly as to manpower and documentation, which any Office or organization must satisfy before it can be appointed and must continue to satisfy while it remains appointed.

(d) Appointment shall be for a fixed period of time and may be extended for further periods.

(e) Before the Assembly makes a decision on the appointment of any national Office or intergovernmental organization, or on the extension of its appointment, or before it allows any such appointment to lapse, the Assembly shall hear the interested Office or organization and seek the advice of the Committee for Technical Cooperation referred to in Article 56 once that Committee has been established.

Article 17
Procedure Before the International Searching Authority

(1) Procedure before the International Searching Authority shall be governed by the provisions of this Treaty, the Regulations, and the agreement which the International Bureau shall conclude, subject to this Treaty and the Regulations, with the said Authority.

(2) (a) If the International Searching Authority considers

(i) that the international application relates to a subject matter which the International Searching Authority is not required, under the Regulations, to search, and in the particular case decides not to search, or

(ii) that the description, the claims, or the drawings, fail to comply with the prescribed requirements to such an extent that a meaningful search could not be carried out, the said Authority shall so declare and shall notify the applicant and the International Bureau that no international search report will be established.

(b) If any of the situations referred to in subparagraph (a) is found to exist in connection with certain claims only, the international search report shall so indicate in respect of such claims, whereas, for the other claims, the said report shall be established as provided in Article 18.

(3) (a) If the International Searching Authority considers that the international application does not comply with the requirement of unity of invention as set forth in the Regulations, it shall invite the applicant to pay additional fees. The International Searching Authority shall establish the international search report on those parts of the international application which relate to the invention first mentioned in the claims ("main invention") and, provided the required additional fees have been paid within the prescribed time limit, on those parts of the international application which relate to inventions in respect of which the said fees were paid.

(b) The national law of any designated State may provide that, where the national Office of that State finds the invitation, referred to in subparagraph (a), of the International Searching Authority justified and where the applicant has not paid all additional fees, those parts of the international application which consequently have not been searched shall, as far as effects in that State are concerned, be considered withdrawn unless a special fee is paid by the applicant to the national Office of that State.

Article 18
The International Search Report

(1) The international search report shall be established within the prescribed time limit and in the prescribed form.

(2) The international search report shall, as soon as it has been established, be transmitted by the International Searching Authority to the applicant and the International Bureau.

(3) The international search report or the declaration referred to in Article 17(2)(a) shall be translated as provided in the Regulations. The translations shall be prepared by or under the responsibility of the International Bureau.

Article 19
Amendment of the Claims Before the International Bureau

(1) The applicant shall, after having received the international search report, be entitled to one opportunity to amend the claims of the international application by filing amendments with the International Bureau within the prescribed time limit. He may, at the same time, file a

brief statement, as provided in the Regulations, explaining the amendments and indicating any impact that such amendments might have on the description and the drawings.

(2) The amendments shall not go beyond the disclosure in the international application as filed.

(3) If the national law of any designated State permits amendments to go beyond the said disclosure, failure to comply with paragraph (2) shall have no consequence in that State.

Article 20
Communication to Designated Offices

(1) (a) The international application, together with the international search report (including any indication referred to in Article 17(2)(b)) or the declaration referred to in Article 17(2)(a), shall be communicated to each designated Office, as provided in the Regulations, unless the designated Office waives such requirement in its entirety or in part.

(b) The communication shall include the translation (as prescribed) of the said report or declaration.

(2) If the claims have been amended by virtue of Article 19(1), the communication shall either contain the full text of the claims both as filed and as amended or shall contain the full text of the claims as filed and specify the amendments, and shall include the statement, if any, referred to in Article 19(1).

(3) At the request of the designated Office or the applicant, the International Searching Authority shall send to the said Office or the applicant, respectively, copies of the documents cited in the international search report, as provided in the Regulations.

Article 21
International Publication

(1) The International Bureau shall publish international applications.

(2) (a) Subject to the exceptions provided for in subparagraph (b) and in Article 64(3), the international publication of the international application shall be effected promptly after the expiration of 18 months from the priority date of that application.

(b) The applicant may ask the International Bureau to publish his international application any time before the expiration of the time limit referred to in subparagraph (a). The International Bureau shall proceed accordingly, as provided in the Regulations.

(3) The international search report or the declaration referred to in Article 17(2)(a) shall be published as prescribed in the Regulations.

(4) The language and form of the international publication and other details are governed by the Regulations.

(5) There shall be no international publication if the international

application is withdrawn or is considered withdrawn before the technical preparations for publication have been completed.

(6) If the international application contains expressions or drawings which, in the opinion of the International Bureau, are contrary to morality or public order, or if, in its opinion, the international application contains disparaging statements as defined in the Regulations, it may omit such expressions, drawings, and statements, from its publications, indicating the place and number of words or drawings omitted, and furnishing, upon request, individual copies of the passages omitted.

Article 22
Copy, Translation, and Fee, to Designated Offices

(1) The applicant shall furnish a copy of the international application (unless the communication provided for in Article 20 has already taken place) and a translation thereof (as prescribed), and pay the national fee (if any), to each designated Office not later than at the expiration of 20 months from the priority date. Where the national law of the designated State requires the indication of the name of and other prescribed data concerning the inventor but allows that these indications be furnished at a time later than that of the filing of a national application, the applicant shall, unless they were contained in the request, furnish the said indications to the national Office of or acting for the State not later than at the expiration of 20 months from the priority date.

(2) Where the International Searching Authority makes a declaration, under Article 17(2)(a), that no international search report will be established, the time limit for performing the acts referred to in paragraph (1) of this Article shall be the same as that provided for in paragraph (1).

(3) Any national law may, for performing the acts referred to in paragraphs (1) or (2), fix time limits which expire later than the time limit provided for in those paragraphs.

Article 23
Delaying of National Procedure

(1) No designated Office shall process or examine the international application prior to the expiration of the applicable time limit under Article 22.

(2) Notwithstanding the provisions of paragraph (1), any designated Office may, on the express request of the applicant, process or examine the international application at any time.

Article 24
Possible Loss of Effect in Designated States

(1) Subject, in case (ii) below, to the provisions of Article 25, the effect of the international application provided for in Article 11(3) shall cease in any designated State with the same consequences as the withdrawal of any

national application in that State:

(i) if the applicant withdraws his international application or the designation of that State;

(ii) if the international application is considered withdrawn by virtue of Articles 12(3), 14(1)(b), 14(3)(a), or 14(4), or if the designation of that State is considered withdrawn by virtue of Article 14(3)(b);

(iii) if the applicant fails to perform the acts referred to in Article 22 within the applicable time limit.

(2) Notwithstanding the provisions of paragraph (1), any designated Office may maintain the effect provided for in Article 11(3) even where such effect is not required to be maintained by virtue of Article 25(2).

Article 25
Review by Designated Offices

(1) (a) Where the receiving Office has refused to accord an international filing date or has declared that the international application is considered withdrawn, or where the International Bureau has made a finding under Article 12(3), the International Bureau shall promptly send, at the request of the applicant, copies of any document in the file to any of the designated Offices named by the applicant.

(b) Where the receiving Office has declared that the designation of any given State is considered withdrawn, the International Bureau shall promptly send, at the request of the applicant, copies of any document in the file to the national Office of such State.

(c) The request under subparagraphs (a) or (b) shall be presented within the prescribed time limit.

(2) (a) Subject to the provisions of subparagraph (b), each designated Office shall, provided that the national fee (if any) has been paid and the appropriate translation (as prescribed) has been furnished within the prescribed time limit, decide whether the refusal, declaration, or finding, referred to in paragraph (1) was justified under the provisions of this Treaty and the Regulations, and, if it finds that the refusal or declaration was the result of an error or omission on the part of the receiving Office or that the finding was the result of an error or omission on the part of the International Bureau, it shall, as far as effects in the State of the designated Office are concerned, treat the international application as if such error or omission had not occurred.

(b) Where the record copy has reached the International Bureau after the expiration of the time limit prescribed under Article 12(3) on account of any error or omission on the part of the applicant, the provisions of subparagraph (a) shall apply only under the circumstances referred to in Article 48(2).

Article 26
Opportunity to Correct Before Designated Offices

No designated Office shall reject an international application on the grounds of non-compliance with the requirements of this Treaty and the Regulations without first giving the applicant the opportunity to correct the said application to the extent and according to the procedure provided by the national law for the same or comparable situations in respect of national applications.

Article 27
National Requirements

(1) No national law shall require compliance with requirements relating to the form or contents of the international application different from or additional to those which are provided for in this Treaty and the Regulations.

(2) The provisions of paragraph (1) neither affect the application of the provisions of Article 7(2) nor preclude any national law from requiring, once the processing of the international application has started in the designated Office, the furnishing:

(i) when the applicant is a legal entity, of the name of an officer entitled to represent such legal entity,

(ii) of documents not part of the international application but which constitute proof of allegations or statements made in that application, including the confirmation of the international application by the signature of the applicant when that application, as filed, was signed by his representative or agent.

(3) Where the applicant, for the purposes of any designated State, is not qualified according to the national law of that State to file a national application because he is not the inventor, the international application may be rejected by the designated Office.

(4) Where the national law provides, in respect of the form or contents of national applications, for requirements which, from the viewpoint of applicants, are more favorable than the requirements provided for by this Treaty and the Regulations in respect of international applications, the national Office, the courts and any other competent organs of or acting for the designated State may apply the former requirements, instead of the latter requirements, to international applications, except where the applicant insists that the requirements provided for by this Treaty and the Regulations be applied to his international application.

(5) Nothing in this Treaty and the Regulations is intended to be construed as prescribing anything that would limit the freedom of each Contracting State to prescribe such substantive conditions of patentability as it desires. In particular, any provision in this Treaty and the Regulations concerning the definition of prior art is exclusively for the purposes of the international procedure and, consequently, any Contracting State is free to apply, when determining the patentability of an invention claimed in an international application, the criteria of its national law in respect of prior art and other conditions of patentability not constituting requirements as to the form and contents of applications.

(6) The national law may require that the applicant furnish evidence in respect of any substantive condition of patentability prescribed by such law.

(7) Any receiving Office or, once the processing of the international application has started in the designated Office, that Office may apply the national law as far as it relates to any requirement that the applicant be represented by an agent having the right to represent applicants before the said Office and/or that the applicant have an address in the designated State for the purpose of receiving notifications.

(8) Nothing in this Treaty and the Regulations is intended to be construed as limiting the freedom of any Contracting State to apply measures deemed necessary for the preservation of its national security or to limit, for the protection of the general economic interests of that State, the right of its own residents or nationals to file international applications.

Article 28
Amendment of the Claims, the Description, and the Drawings, Before Designated Offices

(1) The applicant shall be given the opportunity to amend the claims, the description, and the drawings, before each designated Office within the prescribed time limit. No designated Office shall grant a patent, or refuse the grant of a patent, before such time limit has expired except with the express consent of the applicant.

(2) The amendments shall not go beyond the disclosure in the international application as filed unless the national law of the designated State permits them to go beyond the said disclosure.

(3) The amendments shall be in accordance with the national law of the designated State in all respects not provided for in this Treaty and the Regulations.

(4) Where the designated Office requires a translation of the international application, the amendments shall be in the language of the translation.

Article 29
Effects of the International Publication

(1) As far as the protection of any rights of the applicant in a designated State is concerned, the effects, in that State, of the international publication of an international application shall, subject to the provisions of paragraphs (2) to (4), be the same as those which the national law of the designated State provides for the compulsory national publication of unexamined national applications as such.

(2) If the language in which the international publication has been effected is different from the language in which publications under the national law are effected in the designated State, the said national law may provide that the effects provided for in paragraph (1) shall be applicable only from such time as:

(i) a translation into the latter language has been published as provided by the national law, or

(ii) a translation into the latter language has been made available to the public, by laying open for public inspection as provided by the national law, or

(iii) a translation into the latter language has been transmitted by the applicant to the actual or prospective unauthorized user of the invention claimed in the international application, or

(iv) both the acts described in (i) and (iii), or both the acts described in (ii) and (iii), have taken place.

(3) The national law of any designated State may provide that, where the international publication has been effected, on the request of the applicant, before the expiration of 18 months from the priority date, the effects provided for in paragraph (1) shall be applicable only from the expiration of 18 months from the priority date.

(4) The national law of any designated State may provide that the effects provided for in paragraph (1) shall be applicable only from the date on which a copy of the international application as published under Article 21 has been received in the national Office of or acting for such State. The said Office shall publish the date of receipt in its gazette as soon as possible.

Article 30
Confidential Nature of the International Application

(1) (a) Subject to the provisions of subparagraph (b), the International Bureau and the International Searching Authorities shall not allow access by any person or authority to the international application before the international publication of that application, unless requested or authorized by the applicant.

(b) The provisions of subparagraph (a) shall not apply to any transmittal to the competent International Searching Authority, to transmittals provided for under Article 13, and to communications provided for under Article 20.

(2) (a) No national Office shall allow access to the international application by third parties, unless requested or authorized by the applicant, before the earliest of the following dates:

(i) date of the international publication of the international application,

(ii) date of the receipt of the communication of the international application under Article 20,

(iii) date of the receipt of a copy of the international application under Article 22.

(b) The provisions of subparagraph (a) shall not prevent any national Office from informing third parties that it has been designated, or from publishing that fact. Such information or publication may, however, contain only the following data: identification of the receiving Office, name of the applicant, international filing date, international application number, and title of the invention.

(c) The provisions of subparagraph (a) shall not prevent any designated Office from allowing access to the international application for the purposes of the judicial authorities.

(3) The provisions of paragraph (2)(a) shall apply to any receiving Office except as far as transmittals provided for under Article 12(1) are concerned.

(4) For the purposes of this Article, the term "access" covers any means by which third parties may acquire cognizance, including individual communication and general publication, provided, however, that no national Office shall generally publish an international application or its translation before the international publication or, if international publication has not taken place by the expiration of 20 months from the priority date, before the expiration of 20 months from the said priority date.

CHAPTER II
INTERNATIONAL PRELIMINARY EXAMINATION

Article 31
Demand for International Preliminary Examination

(1) On the demand of the applicant, his international application shall be the subject of an international preliminary examination as provided in the following provisions and the Regulations.

(2) (a) Any applicant who is a resident or national, as defined in the Regulations, of a Contracting State bound by Chapter II, and whose international application has been filed with the receiving Office of or acting for such State, may make a demand for international preliminary examination.

(b) The Assembly may decide to allow persons entitled to file international applications to make a demand for international preliminary examination even if they are residents or nationals of a State not party to this Treaty or not bound by Chapter II.

(3) The demand for international preliminary examination shall be made separately from the international application. The demand shall contain the prescribed particulars and shall be in the prescribed language and form.

(4) (a) The demand shall indicate the Contracting State or States in which the applicant intends to use the results of the international preliminary examination ("elected States"). Additional Contracting States may be elected later. Election may relate only to Contracting States already designated under Article 4.

(b) Applicants referred to in paragraph (2)(a) may elect any Contracting State bound by Chapter II. Applicants referred to in paragraph (2)(b) may elect only such Contracting States bound by Chapter II as have declared that they are prepared to be elected by such applicants.

(5) The demand shall be subject to the payment of the prescribed fees within the prescribed time limit.

(6) (a) The demand shall be submitted to the competent International Preliminary Examining Authority referred to in Article 32.

(b) Any later election shall be submitted to the International Bureau.

(7) Each elected Office shall be notified of its election.

Article 32
The International Preliminary Examining Authority

(1) International preliminary examination shall be carried out by the International Preliminary Examining Authority.

(2) In the case of demands referred to in Article 31(2)(a), the receiving Office, and, in the case of demands referred to in Article 31(2)(b), the Assembly, shall, in accordance with the applicable agreement between the interested International Preliminary Examining Authority or Authorities and the International Bureau, specify the International Preliminary Examining Authority or Authorities competent for the preliminary examination.

(3) The provisions of Article 16(3) shall apply, *mutatis mutandis*, in respect of International Preliminary Examining Authorities.

Article 33
The International Preliminary Examination

(1) The objective of the international preliminary examination is to formulate a preliminary and non-binding opinion on the questions whether the claimed invention appears to be novel, to involve an inventive step (to be non-obvious), and to be industrially applicable.

(2) For the purposes of the international preliminary examination, a claimed invention shall be considered novel if it is not anticipated by the prior art as defined in the Regulations.

(3) For the purposes of the international preliminary examination, a claimed invention shall be considered to involve an inventive step if, having regard to the prior art as defined in the Regulations, it is not, at the prescribed relevant date, obvious to a person skilled in the art.

(4) For the purposes of the international preliminary examination, a claimed invention shall be considered industrially applicable if, according to its nature, it can be made or used (in the technological sense) in any kind of industry. "Industry" shall be understood in its broadest sense, as in the Paris Convention for the Protection of Industrial Property.

(5) The criteria described above merely serve the purposes of international preliminary examination. Any Contracting State may apply additional or different criteria for the purpose of deciding whether, in that State, the claimed invention is patentable or not.

(6) The international preliminary examination shall take into consideration

all the documents cited in the international search report. It may take into consideration any additional documents considered to be relevant in the particular case.

Article 34
Procedure Before the International Preliminary Examining Authority

(1) Procedure before the International Preliminary Examining Authority shall be governed by the provisions of this Treaty, the Regulations, and the agreement which the International Bureau shall conclude, subject to this Treaty and the Regulations, with the said Authority.

(2) (a) The applicant shall have a right to communicate orally and in writing with the International Preliminary Examining Authority.

(b) The applicant shall have a right to amend the claims, the description, and the drawings, in the prescribed manner and within the prescribed time limit, before the international preliminary examination report is established. The amendment shall not go beyond the disclosure in the international application as filed.

(c) The applicant shall receive at least one written opinion from the International Preliminary Examining Authority unless such Authority considers that all of the following conditions are fulfilled:

(i) the invention satisfies the criteria set forth in Article 33(1),

(ii) the international application complies with the requirements of this Treaty and the Regulations in so far as checked by that Authority,

(iii) no observations are intended to be made under Article 35(2), last sentence.

(d) The applicant may respond to the written opinion.

(3) (a) If the International Preliminary Examining Authority considers that the international application does not comply with the requirement of unity of invention as set forth in the Regulations, it may invite the applicant, at his option, to restrict the claims so as to comply with the requirement or to pay additional fees.

(b) The national law of any elected State may provide that, where the applicant chooses to restrict the claims under subparagraph (a), those parts of the international application which, as a consequence of the restriction, are not to be the subject of international preliminary examination shall, as far as effects in that State are concerned, be considered withdrawn unless a special fee is paid by the applicant to the national Office of that State.

(c) If the applicant does not comply with the invitation referred to in subparagraph (a) within the prescribed time limit, the International Preliminary Examining Authority shall establish an international preliminary examination report on those parts of the international application which relate to what appears to be the main invention and shall indicate the relevant facts in the said report. The national law of any elected State may provide that, where its national Office finds the invitation of the

International Preliminary Examining Authority justified, those parts of the international application which do not relate to the main invention shall, as far as effects in that State are concerned, be considered withdrawn unless a special fee is paid by the applicant to that Office.

(4) (a) If the International Preliminary Examining Authority considers

(i) that the international application relates to a subject matter on which the International Preliminary Examining Authority is not required, under the Regulations, to carry out an international preliminary examination, and in the particular case decides not to carry out such examination, or

(ii) that the description, the claims, or the drawings, are so unclear, or the claims are so inadequately supported by the description, that no meaningful opinion can be formed on the novelty, inventive step (non-obviousness), or industrial applicability, of the claimed invention, the said Authority shall not go into the questions referred to in Article 33(1) and shall inform the applicant of this opinion and the reasons therefor.

(b) If any of the situations referred to in subparagraph (a) is found to exist in, or in connection with, certain claims only, the provisions of that subparagraph shall apply only to the said claims.

Article 35
The International Preliminary Examination Report

(1) The international preliminary examination report shall be established within the prescribed time limit and in the prescribed form.

(2) The international preliminary examination report shall not contain any statement on the question whether the claimed invention is or seems to be patentable or unpatentable according to any national law. It shall state, subject to the provisions of paragraph (3), in relation to each claim, whether the claim appears to satisfy the criteria of novelty, inventive step (non-obviousness), and industrial applicability, as defined for the purposes of the international preliminary examination in Article 33(1) to (4). The statement shall be accompanied by the citation of the documents believed to support the stated conclusion with such explanations as the circumstances of the case may require. The statement shall also be accompanied by such other observations as the Regulations provide for.

(3)(a) If, at the time of establishing the international preliminary examination report, the International Preliminary Examining Authority considers that any of the situations referred to in Article 34(4)(a) exists, that report shall state this opinion and the reasons therefor. It shall not contain any statement as provided in paragraph (2).

(b) If a situation under Article 34(4)(b) is found to exist, the international preliminary examination report shall, in relation to the claims in question, contain the statement as provided in subparagraph (a), whereas, in relation to the other claims, it shall contain the statement as provided in paragraph (2).

Article 36
Transmittal, Translation, and Communication, of the International Preliminary Examination Report

(1) The international preliminary examination report, together with the prescribed annexes, shall be transmitted to the applicant and to the International Bureau.

(2) (a) The international preliminary examination report and its annexes shall be translated into the prescribed languages.

(b) Any translation of the said report shall be prepared by or under the responsibility of the International Bureau, whereas any translation of the said annexes shall be prepared by the applicant.

(3) (a) The international preliminary examination report, together with its translation (as prescribed) and its annexes (in the original language), shall be communicated by the International Bureau to each elected Office.

(b) The prescribed translation of the annexes shall be transmitted within the prescribed time limit by the applicant to the elected Offices.

(4) The provisions of Article 20(3) shall apply, *mutatis mutandis*, to copies of any document which is cited in the international preliminary examination report and which was not cited in the international search report.

Article 37
Withdrawal of Demand or Election

(1) The applicant may withdraw any or all elections.

(2) If the election of all elected States is withdrawn, the demand shall be considered withdrawn.

(3) (a) Any withdrawal shall be notified to the International Bureau.

(b) The elected Offices concerned and the International Preliminary Examining Authority concerned shall be notified accordingly by the International Bureau.

(4) (a) Subject to the provisions of subparagraph (b), withdrawal of the demand or of the election of a Contracting State shall, unless the national law of that State provides otherwise, be considered to be withdrawal of the international application as far as that State is concerned.

(b) Withdrawal of the demand or of the election shall not be considered to be withdrawal of the international application if such withdrawal is effected prior to the expiration of the applicable time limit under Article 22; however, any Contracting State may provide in its national law that the aforesaid shall apply only if its national Office has received, within the said time limit, a copy of the international application, together with a translation (as prescribed), and the national fee.

Article 38
Confidential Nature of the International

Preliminary Examination

(1) Neither the International Bureau nor the International Preliminary Examining Authority shall, unless requested or authorized by the applicant, allow access within the meaning, and with the proviso, of Article 30(4) to the file of the international preliminary examination by any person or authority at any time, except by the elected Offices once the international preliminary examination report has been established.

(2) Subject to the provisions of paragraph (1) and Articles 36(1) and (3) and 37(3)(b), neither the International Bureau nor the International Preliminary Examining Authority shall, unless requested or authorized by the applicant, give information on the issuance or nonissuance of an international preliminary examination report and on the withdrawal or nonwithdrawal of the demand or of any election.

Article 39
Copy, Translation, and Fee, to Elected Offices

(1) (a) If the election of any Contracting State has been effected prior to the expiration of the 19th month from the priority date, the provisions of Article 22 shall not apply to such State and the applicant shall furnish a copy of the international application (unless the communication under Article 20 has already taken place) and a translation thereof (as prescribed), and pay the national fee (if any), to each elected Office not later than at the expiration of 30 months from the priority date.

(b) Any national law may, for performing the acts referred to in subparagraph (a), fix time limits which expire later than the time limit provided for in that subparagraph.

(2) The effect provided for in Article 11(3) shall cease in the elected State with the same consequences as the withdrawal of any national application in that State if the applicant fails to perform the acts referred to in paragraph (1)(a) within the time limit applicable under paragraph (1)(a) or (b).

(3) Any elected Office may maintain the effect provided for in Article 11(3) even where the applicant does not comply with the requirements provided for in paragraph (1)(a) or (b).

Article 40
Delaying of National Examination and Other Processing

(1) If the election of any Contracting State has been effected prior to the expiration of the 19th month from the priority date, the provisions of Article 23 shall not apply to such State and the national Office of or acting for that State shall not proceed, subject to the provisions of paragraph (2), to the examination and other processing of the international application prior to the expiration of the applicable time limit under Article 39.

(2) Notwithstanding the provisions of paragraph (1), any elected Office may, on the express request of the applicant, proceed to the examination and

other processing of the international application at any time.

Article 41
Amendment of the Claims, the Description, and the Drawings, Before Elected Offices

(1) The applicant shall be given the opportunity to amend the claims, the description, and the drawings, before each elected Office within the prescribed time limit. No elected Office shall grant a patent, or refuse the grant of a patent, before such time limit has expired, except with the express consent of the applicant.

(2) The amendments shall not go beyond the disclosure in the international application as filed, unless the national law of the elected State permits them to go beyond the said disclosure.

(3) The amendments shall be in accordance with the national law of the elected State in all respects not provided for in this Treaty and the Regulations.

(4) Where an elected Office requires a translation of the international application, the amendments shall be in the language of the translation.

Article 42
Results of National Examination in Elected Offices

No elected Office receiving the international preliminary examination report may require that the applicant furnish copies, or information on the contents, of any papers connected with the examination relating to the same international application in any other elected Office.

CHAPTER III
COMMON PROVISIONS

Article 43
Seeking Certain Kinds of Protection

In respect of any designated or elected State whose law provides for the grant of inventors' certificates, utility certificates, utility models, patents or certificates of addition, inventors' certificates of addition, or utility certificates of addition, the applicant may indicate, as prescribed in the Regulations, that his international application is for the grant, as far as that State is concerned, of an inventor's certificate, a utility certificate, or a utility model, rather than a patent, or that it is for the grant of a patent or certificate of addition, an inventor's certificate of addition, or a utility certificate of addition, and the ensuing effect shall be governed by the applicant's choice. For the purposes of this Article and any Rule thereunder, Article 2(ii) shall not apply.

Article 44
Seeking Two Kinds of Protection

In respect of any designated or elected State whose law permits an application, while being for the grant of a patent or one of the other kinds of protection referred to in Article 43, to be also for the grant of another of the said kinds of protection, the applicant may indicate, as prescribed in the Regulations, the two kinds of protection he is seeking, and the ensuing effect shall be governed by the applicant's indications. For the purposes of this Article, Article 2(ii) shall not apply.

Article 45
Regional Patent Treaties

(1) Any treaty providing for the grant of regional patents ("regional patent treaty"), and giving to all persons who, according to Article 9, are entitled to file international applications the right to file applications for such patents, may provide that international applications designating or electing a State party to both the regional patent treaty and the present Treaty may be filed as applications for such patents.

(2) The national law of the said designated or elected State may provide that any designation or election of such State in the international application shall have the effect of an indication of the wish to obtain a regional patent under the regional patent treaty.

Article 46
Incorrect Translation of the International Application

If, because of an incorrect translation of the international application, the scope of any patent granted on that application exceeds the scope of the international application in its original language, the competent authorities of the Contracting State concerned may accordingly and retroactively limit the scope of the patent, and declare it null and void to the extent that its scope has exceeded the scope of the international application in its original language.

Article 47
Time Limits

(1) The details for computing time limits referred to in this Treaty are governed by the Regulations.

(2) (a) All time limits fixed in Chapters I and II of this Treaty may, outside any revision under Article 60, be modified by a decision of the Contracting States.

(b) Such decisions shall be made in the Assembly or through voting by correspondence and must be unanimous.

(c) The details of the procedure are governed by the Regulations.

Article 48
Delay in Meeting Certain Time Limits

(1) Where any time limit fixed in this Treaty or the Regulations is not met

because of interruption in the mail service or unavoidable loss or delay in the mail, the time limit shall be deemed to be met in the cases and subject to the proof and other conditions prescribed in the Regulations.

(2) (a) Any Contracting State shall, as far as that State is concerned, excuse, for reasons admitted under its national law, any delay in meeting any time limit.

(b) Any Contracting State may, as far as that State is concerned, excuse, for reasons other than those referred to in subparagraph (a), any delay in meeting any time limit.

Article 49
Right to Practice Before International Authorities

Any attorney, patent agent, or other person, having the right to practice before the national Office with which the international application was filed, shall be entitled to practice before the International Bureau and the competent International Searching Authority and competent International Preliminary Examining Authority in respect of that application.

CHAPTER IV
TECHNICAL SERVICES

Article 50
Patent Information Services

(1) The International Bureau may furnish services by providing technical and any other pertinent information available to it on the basis of published documents, primarily patents and published applications (referred to in this Article as "the information services").

(2) The International Bureau may provide these information services either directly or through one or more International Searching Authorities or other national or international specialized institutions, with which the International Bureau may reach agreement.

(3) The information services shall be operated in a way particularly facilitating the acquisition by Contracting States which are developing countries of technical knowledge and technology, including available published know-how.

(4) The information services shall be available to Governments of Contracting States and their nationals and residents. The Assembly may decide to make these services available also to others.

(5) (a) Any service to Governments of Contracting States shall be furnished at cost, provided that, when the Government is that of a Contracting State which is a developing country, the service shall be furnished below cost if the difference can be covered from profit made on services furnished to others than Governments of Contracting States or from the sources referred to in Article 51(4).

(b) The cost referred to in subparagraph (a) is to be understood as cost over and above costs normally incident to the performance of the services of a national Office or the obligations of an International Searching Authority.

(6) The details concerning the implementation of the provisions of this Article shall be governed by decisions of the Assembly and, within the limits to be fixed by the Assembly, such working groups as the Assembly may set up for that purpose.

(7) The Assembly shall, when it considers it necessary, recommend methods of providing financing supplementary to those referred to in paragraph (5).

Article 51
Technical Assistance

(1) The Assembly shall establish a Committee for Technical Assistance (referred to in this Article as "the Committee").

(2)(a) The members of the Committee shall be elected among the Contracting States, with due regard to the representation of developing countries.

(b) The Director General shall, on his own initiative or at the request of the Committee, invite representatives of intergovernmental organizations concerned with technical assistance to developing countries to participate in the work of the Committee.

(3) (a) The task of the Committee shall be to organize and supervise technical assistance for Contracting States which are developing countries in developing their patent systems individually or on a regional basis.

(b) The technical assistance shall comprise, among other things, the training of specialists, the loaning of experts, and the supply of equipment both for demonstration and for operational purposes.

(4) The International Bureau shall seek to enter into agreements, on the one hand, with international financing organizations and intergovernmental organizations, particularly the United Nations, the agencies of the United Nations, and the Specialized Agencies connected with the United Nations concerned with technical assistance, and, on the other hand, with the Governments of the States receiving the technical assistance, for the financing of projects pursuant to this Article.

(5) The details concerning the implementation of the provisions of this Article shall be governed by decisions of the Assembly and, within the limits to be fixed by the Assembly, such working groups as the Assembly may set up for that purpose.

Article 52
Relations with Other Provisions of the Treaty

Nothing in this Chapter shall affect the financial provisions contained in any other Chapter of this Treaty. Such provisions are not applicable to the present Chapter or to its implementation.

CHAPTER V
ADMINISTRATIVE PROVISIONS

Article 53
Assembly

(1) (a) The Assembly shall, subject to Article 57(8), consist of the Contracting States.

(b) The Government of each Contracting State shall be represented by one delegate, who may be assisted by alternate delegates, advisors, and experts.

(2) (a) The Assembly shall:

(i) deal with all matters concerning the maintenance and development of the Union and the implementation of this Treaty;

(ii) perform such tasks as are specifically assigned to it under other provisions of this Treaty;

(iii) give directions to the International Bureau concerning the preparation for revision conferences;

(iv) review and approve the reports and activities of the Director General concerning the Union, and give him all necessary instructions concerning matters within the competence of the Union;

(v) review and approve the reports and activities of the Executive Committee established under paragraph (9), and give instructions to such Committee;

(vi) determine the program and adopt the triennial budget of the Union, and approve its final accounts;

(vii) adopt the financial regulations of the Union;

(viii) establish such committees and working groups as it deems appropriate to achieve the objectives of the Union;

(ix) determine which States other than Contracting States and, subject to the provisions of paragraph (8), which intergovernmental and international non-governmental organizations shall be admitted to its meetings as observers;

(x) take any other appropriate action designed to further the objectives of the Union and perform such other functions as are appropriate under this Treaty.

(b) With respect to matters which are of interest also to other Unions administered by the Organization, the Assembly shall make its decisions after having heard the advice of the Coordination Committee of the Organization.

(3) A delegate may represent, and vote in the name of, one State only.

(4) Each Contracting State shall have one vote.

(5) (a) One-half of the Contracting States shall constitute a quorum.

(b) In the absence of the quorum, the Assembly may make decisions but, with the exception of decisions concerning its own procedure, all such decisions shall take effect only if the quorum and the required majority are attained through voting by correspondence as provided in the Regulations.

(6) (a) Subject to the provisions of Articles 47(2)(b), 58(2)(b), 58(3) and 61(2)(b), the decisions of the Assembly shall require two-thirds of the votes cast.

(b) Abstentions shall not be considered as votes.

(7) In connection with matters of exclusive interest to States bound by Chapter II, any reference to Contracting States in paragraphs (4), (5), and (6), shall be considered as applying only to States bound by Chapter II.

(8) Any intergovernmental organization appointed as International Searching or Preliminary Examining Authority shall be admitted as observer to the Assembly.

(9) When the number of Contracting States exceeds forty, the Assembly shall establish an Executive Committee. Any reference to the Executive Committee in this Treaty and the Regulations shall be construed as references to such Committee once it has been established.

(10) Until the Executive Committee has been established, the Assembly shall approve, within the limits of the program and triennial budget, the annual programs and budgets prepared by the Director General.

(11) (a) The Assembly shall meet in every second calendar year in ordinary session upon convocation by the Director General and, in the absence of exceptional circumstances, during the same period and at the same place as the General Assembly of the Organization.

(b) The Assembly shall meet in extraordinary session upon convocation by the Director General, at the request of the Executive Committee, or at the request of one-fourth of the Contracting States.

(12) The Assembly shall adopt its own rules of procedure.

Article 54
Executive Committee

(1) When the Assembly has established an Executive Committee, that Committee shall be subject to the provisions set forth hereinafter.

(2) (a) The Executive Committee shall, subject to Article 57(8), consist of States elected by the Assembly from among States members of the Assembly.

(b) The Government of each State member of the Executive Committee shall be represented by one delegate, who may be assisted by alternate delegates, advisors, and experts.

(3) The number of States members of the Executive Committee shall correspond to one-fourth of the number of States members of the Assembly. In establishing the number of seats to be filled, remainders after division by four shall be disregarded.

(4) In electing the members of the Executive Committee, the Assembly shall have due regard to an equitable geographical distribution.

(5) (a) Each member of the Executive Committee shall serve from the close of the session of the Assembly which elected it to the close of the next ordinary session of the Assembly.

(b) Members of the Executive Committee may be re-elected but only up to a maximum of two-thirds of such members.

(c) The Assembly shall establish the details of the rules governing the election and possible re-election of the members of the Executive Committee.

(6) (a) The Executive Committee shall:

(i) prepare the draft agenda of the Assembly;

(ii) submit proposals to the Assembly in respect of the draft program and biennial budget of the Union prepared by the Director General;

(iii) *[deleted]*

(iv) submit, with appropriate comments, to the Assembly the periodical reports of the Director General and the yearly audit reports on the accounts;

(v) take all necessary measures to ensure the execution of the program of the Union by the Director General, in accordance with the decisions of the Assembly and having regard to circumstances arising between two ordinary sessions of the Assembly;

(vi) perform such other functions as are allocated to it under this Treaty.

(b) With respect to matters which are of interest also to other Unions administered by the Organization, the Executive Committee shall make its decisions after having heard the advice of the Coordination Committee of the Organization.

(7) (a) The Executive Committee shall meet once a year in ordinary session upon convocation by the Director General, preferably during the same period and at the same place as the Coordination Committee of the Organization.

(b) The Executive Committee shall meet in extraordinary session upon convocation by the Director General, either on his own initiative or at the request of its Chairman or one-fourth of its members.

(8) (a) Each State member of the Executive Committee shall have one vote.

(b) One-half of the members of the Executive Committee shall constitute a quorum.

(c) Decisions shall be made by a simple majority of the votes cast.

(d) Abstentions shall not be considered as votes.

(e) A delegate may represent, and vote in the name of, one State only.

(9) Contracting States not members of the Executive Committee shall be admitted to its meetings as observers, as well as any intergovernmental organization appointed as International Searching or Preliminary Examining Authority.

(10) The Executive Committee shall adopt its own rules of procedure.

Article 55
International Bureau

(1) Administrative tasks concerning the Union shall be performed by the International Bureau.

(2) The International Bureau shall provide the secretariat of the various organs of the Union.

(3) The Director General shall be the chief executive of the Union and shall represent the Union.

(4) The International Bureau shall publish a Gazette and other publications provided for by the Regulations or required by the Assembly.

(5) The Regulations shall specify the services that national Offices shall perform in order to assist the International Bureau and the International Searching and Preliminary Examining Authorities in carrying out their tasks under this Treaty.

(6) The Director General and any staff member designated by him shall participate, without the right to vote, in all meetings of the Assembly, the Executive Committee and any other committee or working group established under this Treaty or the Regulations. The Director General, or a staff member designated by him, shall be *ex officio* secretary of these bodies.

(7) (a) The International Bureau shall, in accordance with the directions of the Assembly and in cooperation with the Executive Committee, make the preparations for the revision conferences.

(b) The International Bureau may consult with intergovernmental and international non-governmental organizations concerning preparations for revision conferences.

(c) The Director General and persons designated by him shall take part, without the right to vote, in the discussions at revision conferences.

(8) The International Bureau shall carry out any other tasks assigned to it.

Article 56
Committee for Technical Cooperation

(1) The Assembly shall establish a Committee for Technical Cooperation (referred to in this Article as "the Committee").

(2) (a) The Assembly shall determine the composition of the Committee and appoint its members, with due regard to an equitable representation of developing countries.

(b) The International Searching and Preliminary Examining Authorities shall be *ex officio* members of the Committee. In the case where such an Authority is the national Office of a Contracting State, that State shall not be additionally represented on the Committee.

(c) If the number of Contracting States so allows, the total number of members of the Committee shall be more than double the number of *ex officio* members.

(d) The Director General shall, on his own initiative or at the request of the Committee, invite representatives of interested organizations to participate in discussions of interest to them.

(3) The aim of the Committee shall be to contribute, by advice and recommendations:

(i) to the constant improvement of the services provided for under this Treaty,

(ii) to the securing, so long as there are several International Searching Authorities and several International Preliminary Examining Authorities, of the maximum degree of uniformity in their documentation and working methods and the maximum degree of uniformly high quality in their reports, and

(iii) on the initiative of the Assembly or the Executive Committee, to the solution of the technical problems specifically involved in the establishment of a single International Searching Authority.

(4) Any Contracting State and any interested international organization may approach the Committee in writing on questions which fall within the competence of the Committee.

(5) The Committee may address its advice and recommendations to the Director General or, through him, to the Assembly, the Executive Committee, all or some of the International Searching and Preliminary Examining Authorities, and all or some of the receiving Offices.

(6) (a) In any case, the Director General shall transmit to the Executive Committee the texts of all the advice and recommendations of the Committee. He may comment on such texts.

(b) The Executive Committee may express its views on any advice, recommendation, or other activity of the Committee, and may invite the Committee to study and report on questions falling within its competence. The Executive Committee may submit to the Assembly, with appropriate comments, the advice, recommendations and report of the Committee.

(7) Until the Executive Committee has been established, references in paragraph (6) to the Executive Committee shall be construed as references to the Assembly.

(8) The details of the procedure of the Committee shall be governed by the decisions of the Assembly.

Article 57
Finances

(1) (a) The Union shall have a budget.

(b) The budget of the Union shall include the income and expenses proper to the Union and its contribution to the budget of expenses common to the Unions administered by the Organization.

(c) Expenses not attributable exclusively to the Union but also to one or more other Unions administered by the Organization shall be considered as expenses common to the Unions. The share of the Union in such common expenses shall be in proportion to the interest the Union has in them.

(2) The budget of the Union shall be established with due regard to the requirements of coordination with the budgets of the other Unions administered by the Organization.

(3) Subject to the provisions of paragraph (5), the budget of the Union shall be financed from the following sources:

(i) fees and charges due for services rendered by the International Bureau in relation to the Union;

(ii) sale of, or royalties on, the publications of the International Bureau concerning the Union;

(iii) gifts, bequests, and subventions;

(iv) rents, interests, and other miscellaneous income.

(4) The amounts of fees and charges due to the International Bureau and the prices of its publications shall be so fixed that they should, under normal circumstances, be sufficient to cover all the expenses of the International Bureau connected with the administration of this Treaty.

(5) (a) Should any financial year close with a deficit, the Contracting States shall, subject to the provisions of subparagraphs (b) and (c), pay contributions to cover such deficit.

(b) The amount of the contribution of each Contracting State shall be decided by the Assembly with due regard to the number of international applications which has emanated from each of them in the relevant year.

(c) If other means of provisionally covering any deficit or any part thereof are secured, the Assembly may decide that such deficit be carried forward and that the Contracting States should not be asked to pay contributions.

(d) If the financial situation of the Union so permits, the Assembly may decide that any contributions paid under subparagraph (a) be reimbursed to the Contracting States which have paid them.

(e) A Contracting State which has not paid, within two years of the due date as established by the Assembly, its contribution under subparagraph (b) may not exercise its right to vote in any of the organs of the Union. However, any organ of the Union may allow such a State to continue to exercise its right to vote in that organ so long as it is satisfied that the delay in payment is due to exceptional and unavoidable circumstances.

(6) If the budget is not adopted before the beginning of a new financial period, it shall be at the same level as the budget of the previous year, as provided in the financial regulations.

(7) (a) The Union shall have a working capital fund which shall be constituted by a single payment made by each Contracting State. If the fund becomes insufficient, the Assembly shall arrange to increase it. If part of the fund is no longer needed, it shall be reimbursed.

(b) The amount of the initial payment of each Contracting State to the said fund or of its participation in the increase thereof shall be decided by the

Assembly on the basis of principles similar to those provided for under paragraph (5)(b).

(c) The terms of payment shall be fixed by the Assembly on the proposal of the Director General and after it has heard the advice of the Coordination Committee of the Organization.

(d) Any reimbursement shall be proportionate to the amounts paid by each Contracting State, taking into account the dates at which they were paid.

(8) (a) In the headquarters agreement concluded with the State on the territory of which the Organization has its headquarters, it shall be provided that, whenever the working capital fund is insufficient, such State shall grant advances. The amount of these advances and the conditions on which they are granted shall be the subject of separate agreements, in each case, between such State and the Organization. As long as it remains under the obligation to grant advances, such State shall have an *ex officio* seat in the Assembly and on the Executive Committee.

(b) The State referred to in subparagraph (a) and the Organization shall each have the right to denounce the obligation to grant advances, by written notification. Denunciation shall take effect three years after the end of the year in which it has been notified.

(9) The auditing of the accounts shall be effected by one or more of the Contracting States or by external auditors, as provided in the financial regulations. They shall be designated, with their agreement, by the Assembly.

Article 58
Regulations

(1) The Regulations annexed to this Treaty provide Rules:

(i)   concerning matters in respect of which this Treaty expressly refers to the Regulations or expressly provides that they are or shall be prescribed,

(ii) concerning any administrative requirements, matters, or procedures,

(iii) concerning any details useful in the implementation of the provisions of this Treaty.

(2) (a) The Assembly may amend the Regulations.

(b) Subject to the provisions of paragraph (3), amendments shall require three-fourths of the votes cast.

(3) (a) The Regulations specify the Rules which may be amended

(i) only by unanimous consent, or

(ii) only if none of the Contracting States whose national Office acts as an International Searching or Preliminary Examining Authority dissents, and, where such Authority is an intergovernmental organization, if the Contracting State member of that organization authorized for that purpose by the other member States within the competent body of such organization does not dissent.

(b) Exclusion, for the future, of any such Rules from the applicable requirement shall require the fulfillment of the conditions referred to in subparagraph (a)(i) or (a)(ii), respectively.

(c) Inclusion, for the future, of any Rule in one or the other of the requirements referred to in subparagraph (a) shall require unanimous consent.

(4) The Regulations provide for the establishment, under the control of the Assembly, of Administrative Instructions by the Director General.

(5) In the case of conflict between the provisions of the Treaty and those of the Regulations, the provisions of the Treaty shall prevail.

CHAPTER VI
DISPUTES

Article 59
Disputes

Subject to Article 64(5), any dispute between two or more Contracting States concerning the interpretation or application of this Treaty or the Regulations, not settled by negotiation, may, by any one of the States concerned, be brought before the International Court of Justice by application in conformity with the Statute of the Court, unless the States concerned agree on some other method of settlement. The Contracting State bringing the dispute before the Court shall inform the International Bureau; the International Bureau shall bring the matter to the attention of the other Contracting States.

CHAPTER VII
REVISION AND AMENDMENT

Article 60
Revision of the Treaty

(1) This Treaty may be revised from time to time by a special conference of the Contracting States.

(2) The convocation of any revision conference shall be decided by the Assembly.

(3) Any intergovernmental organization appointed as International Searching or Preliminary Examining Authority shall be admitted as observer to any revision conference.

(4) Articles 53(5), (9) and (11), 54, 55(4) to (8), 56, and 57, may be amended either by a revision conference or according to the provisions of Article 61.

Article 61

Amendment of Certain Provisions of the Treaty

(1) (a) Proposals for the amendment of Articles 53(5), (9) and (11), 54, 55(4) to (8), 56, and 57, may be initiated by any State member of the Assembly, by the Executive Committee, or by the Director General.

(b) Such proposals shall be communicated by the Director General to the Contracting States at least six months in advance of their consideration by the Assembly.

(2) (a) Amendments to the Articles referred to in paragraph (1) shall be adopted by the Assembly.

(b) Adoption shall require three-fourths of the votes cast.

(3)(a) Any amendment to the Articles referred to in paragraph (1) shall enter into force one month after written notifications of acceptance, effected in accordance with their respective constitutional processes, have been received by the Director General from three-fourths of the States members of the Assembly at the time it adopted the amendment.

(b) Any amendment to the said Articles thus accepted shall bind all the States which are members of the Assembly at the time the amendment enters into force, provided that any amendment increasing the financial obligations of the Contracting States shall bind only those States which have notified their acceptance of such amendment.

(c) Any amendment accepted in accordance with the provisions of subparagraph (a) shall bind all States which become members of the Assembly after the date on which the amendment entered into force in accordance with the provisions of subparagraph (a).

CHAPTER VIII
FINAL PROVISIONS

Article 62
Becoming Party to the Treaty

(1) Any State member of the International Union for the Protection of Industrial Property may become party to this Treaty by:

(i) signature followed by the deposit of an instrument of ratification, or

(ii) deposit of an instrument of accession.

(2) Instruments of ratification or accession shall be deposited with the Director General.

(3) The provisions of Article 24 of the Stockholm Act of the Paris Convention for the Protection of Industrial Property shall apply to this Treaty.

(4) Paragraph (3) shall in no way be understood as implying the recognition or tacit acceptance by a Contracting State of the factual situation concerning a territory to which this Treaty is made applicable by another Contracting State by virtue of the said paragraph.

Article 63
Entry into Force of the Treaty

(1) (a) Subject to the provisions of paragraph (3), this Treaty shall enter into force three months after eight States have deposited their instruments of ratification or accession, provided that at least four of those States each fulfill any of the following conditions:

(i) the number of applications filed in the State has exceeded 40,000 according to the most recent annual statistics published by the International Bureau,

(ii) the nationals or residents of the State have filed at least 1,000 applications in one foreign country according to the most recent annual statistics published by the International Bureau,

(iii) the national Office of the State has received at least 10,000 applications from nationals or residents of foreign countries according to the most recent annual statistics published by the International Bureau.

(b) For the purposes of this paragraph, the term "applications" does not include applications for utility models.

(2) Subject to the provisions of paragraph (3), any State which does not become party to this Treaty upon entry into force under paragraph (1) shall become bound by this Treaty three months after the date on which such State has deposited its instrument of ratification or accession.

(3) The provisions of Chapter II and the corresponding provisions of the Regulations annexed to this Treaty shall become applicable, however, only on the date on which three States each of which fulfill at least one of the three requirements specified in paragraph (1) have become party to this Treaty without declaring, as provided in Article 64(1), that they do not intend to be bound by the provisions of Chapter II. That date shall not, however, be prior to that of the initial entry into force under paragraph (1).

Article 64
Reservations

(1) (a) Any State may declare that it shall not be bound by the provisions of Chapter II.

(b) States making a declaration under subparagraph (a) shall not be bound by the provisions of Chapter II and the corresponding provisions of the Regulations.

(2) (a) Any State not having made a declaration under paragraph (1)(a) may declare that:

(i) it shall not be bound by the provisions of Article 39(1) with respect to the furnishing of a copy of the international application and a translation thereof (as prescribed),

(ii) the obligation to delay national processing, as provided for under Article 40, shall not prevent publication, by or through its national Office, of the international application or a translation thereof, it being understood, however, that it is not exempted from the limitations provided for in Articles 30 and 38.

(b) States making such a declaration shall be bound accordingly.

(3) (a) Any State may declare that, as far as it is concerned, international publication of international applications is not required.

(b) Where, at the expiration of 18 months from the priority date, the international application contains the designation only of such States as have made declarations under subparagraph (a), the international application shall not be published by virtue of Article 21(2).

(c) Where the provisions of subparagraph (b) apply, the international application shall nevertheless be published by the International Bureau:

(i) at the request of the applicant, as provided in the Regulations,

(ii) when a national application or a patent based on the international application is published by or on behalf of the national Office of any designated State having made a declaration under subparagraph (a), promptly after such publication but not before the expiration of 18 months from the priority date.

(4) (a) Any State whose national law provides for prior art effect of its patents as from a date before publication, but does not equate for prior art purposes the priority date claimed under the Paris Convention for the Protection of Industrial Property to the actual filing date in that State, may declare that the filing outside that State of an international application designating that State is not equated to an actual filing in that State for prior art purposes.

(b) Any State making a declaration under subparagraph (a) shall to that extent not be bound by the provisions of Article 11(3).

(c) Any State making a declaration under subparagraph (a) shall, at the same time, state in writing the date from which, and the conditions under which, the prior art effect of any international application designating that State becomes effective in that State. This statement may be modified at any time by notification addressed to the Director General.

(5) Each State may declare that it does not consider itself bound by Article 59. With regard to any dispute between any Contracting State having made such a declaration and any other Contracting State, the provisions of Article 59 shall not apply.

(6) (a) Any declaration made under this Article shall be made in writing. It may be made at the time of signing this Treaty, at the time of depositing the instrument of ratification or accession, or, except in the case referred to in paragraph (5), at any later time by notification addressed to the Director General. In the case of the said notification, the declaration shall take effect six months after the day on which the Director General has received the notification, and shall not affect international applications filed prior to the expiration of the said six-month period.

(b) Any declaration made under this Article may be withdrawn at any time by notification addressed to the Director General. Such withdrawal shall take effect three months after the day on which the Director General has received the notification and, in the case of the withdrawal of a declaration made under paragraph (3), shall not affect international applications filed prior to the expiration of the said three-month period.

(7) No reservations to this Treaty other than the reservations under paragraphs (1) to (5) are permitted.

Article 65
Gradual Application

(1) If the agreement with any International Searching or Preliminary Examining Authority provides, transitionally, for limits on the number or kind of international applications that such Authority undertakes to process, the Assembly shall adopt the measures necessary for the gradual application of this Treaty and the Regulations in respect of given categories of international applications. This provision shall also apply to requests for an international-type search under Article 15(5).

(2) The Assembly shall fix the dates from which, subject to the provision of paragraph (1), international applications may be filed and demands for international preliminary examination may be submitted. Such dates shall not be later than six months after this Treaty has entered into force according to the provisions of Article 63(1), or after Chapter II has become applicable under Article 63(3), respectively.

Article 66
Denunciation

(1) Any Contracting State may denounce this Treaty by notification addressed to the Director General.

(2) Denunciation shall take effect six months after receipt of the said notification by the Director General. It shall not affect the effects of the international application in the denouncing State if the international application was filed, and, where the denouncing State has been elected, the election was made, prior to the expiration of the said six-month period.

Article 67
Signature and Languages

(1) (a) This Treaty shall be signed in a single original in the English and French languages, both texts being equally authentic.

(b) Official texts shall be established by the Director General, after consultation with the interested Governments, in the German, Japanese, Portuguese, Russian and Spanish languages, and such other languages as the Assembly may designate.

(2) This Treaty shall remain open for signature at Washington until December 31, 1970.

Article 68
Depositary Functions

(1) The original of this Treaty, when no longer open for signature, shall be deposited with the Director General.

(2) The Director General shall transmit two copies, certified by him, of this Treaty and the Regulations annexed hereto to the Governments of all States party to the Paris Convention for the Protection of Industrial Property and, on request, to the Government of any other State.

(3) The Director General shall register this Treaty with the Secretariat of the United Nations.

(4) The Director General shall transmit two copies, certified by him, of any amendment to this Treaty and the Regulations to the Governments of all Contracting States and, on request, to the Government of any other State.

Article 69
Notifications

The Director General shall notify the Governments of all States party to the Paris Convention for the Protection of Industrial Property of:

(i) signatures under Article 62,

(ii) deposits of instruments of ratification or accession under Article 62,

(iii) the date of entry into force of this Treaty and the date from which Chapter II is applicable in accordance with Article 63(3),

(iv) any declarations made under Article 64(1) to (5),

(v) withdrawals of any declarations made under Article 64(6)(b),

(vi) denunciations received under Article 66, and

(vii) any declarations made under Article 31(4).

PATENT LAW TREATY
Done at Geneva, June 2, 2000

Article 1
Abbreviated Expressions

For the purposes of this Treaty, unless expressly stated otherwise:

(i) "Office" means the authority of a Contracting Party entrusted with the granting of patents or with other matters covered by this Treaty;

(ii) "application" means an application for the grant of a patent, as referred to in Article 3;

(iii) "patent" means a patent as referred to in Article 3;

(iv) references to a "person" shall be construed as including, in particular, a natural person and a legal entity;

(v) "communication" means any application, or any request, declaration, document, correspondence or other information relating to an application or patent, whether relating to a procedure under this Treaty or not, which is filed with the Office;

(vi) "records of the Office" means the collection of information maintained by the Office, relating to and including the applications filed with, and the patents granted by, that Office or another authority with effect for the Contracting Party concerned, irrespective of the medium in which such information is maintained;

(vii) "recordation" means any act of including information in the records of the Office;

(viii) "applicant" means the person whom the records of the Office show, pursuant to the applicable law, as the person who is applying for the patent, or as another person who is filing or prosecuting the application;

(ix) "owner" means the person whom the records of the Office show as the owner of the patent;

(x) "representative" means a representative under the applicable law;

(xi) "signature" means any means of self-identification;

(xii) "a language accepted by the Office" means any one language accepted by the Office for the relevant procedure before the Office;

(xiii) "translation" means a translation into a language or, where appropriate, a transliteration into an alphabet or character set, accepted by the Office;

(xiv) "procedure before the Office" means any procedure in proceedings before the Office with respect to an application or patent;

(xv) except where the context indicates otherwise, words in the singular include the plural, and *vice versa*, and masculine personal pronouns include the feminine;

(xvi) "Paris Convention" means the Paris Convention for the Protection of Industrial Property, signed on March 20, 1883, as revised and amended;

(xvii) "Patent Cooperation Treaty" means the Patent Cooperation Treaty, signed on June 19, 1970, together with the Regulations and the Administrative Instructions under that Treaty, as revised, amended and modified;

(xviii) "Contracting Party" means any State or intergovernmental organization that is party to this Treaty;

(xix) "applicable law" means, where the Contracting Party is a State, the law of that State and, where the Contracting Party is an intergovernmental organization, the legal enactments under which that intergovernmental organization operates;

(xx) "instrument of ratification" shall be construed as including instruments of acceptance or approval;

(xxi) "Organization" means the World Intellectual Property Organization;

(xxii) "International Bureau" means the International Bureau of the Organization;

(xxiii) "Director General" means the Director General of the Organization.

Article 2
General Principles

(1) [*More Favorable Requirements*] A Contracting Party shall be free to provide for requirements which, from the viewpoint of applicants and owners, are more favorable than the requirements referred to in this Treaty and the Regulations, other than Article 5.

(2) [*No Regulation of Substantive Patent Law*] Nothing in this Treaty or the Regulations is intended to be construed as prescribing anything that would limit the freedom of a Contracting Party to prescribe such requirements of the applicable substantive law relating to patents as it desires.

Article 3
Applications and Patents to Which the Treaty Applies

(1) [*Applications*] (a) The provisions of this Treaty and the Regulations shall apply to national and regional applications for patents for invention and for patents of addition, which are filed with or for the Office of a Contracting Party, and which are:

(i) types of applications permitted to be filed as international applications under the Patent Cooperation Treaty;

(ii) divisional applications of the types of applications referred to in item (i), for patents for invention or for patents of addition, as referred to in Article 4G(1) or (2) of the Paris Convention.

(b) Subject to the provisions of the Patent Cooperation Treaty, the provisions of this Treaty and the Regulations shall apply to international applications, for patents for invention and for patents of addition, under the Patent Cooperation Treaty:

(i) in respect of the time limits applicable under Articles 22 and 39(1) of the Patent Cooperation Treaty in the Office of a Contracting Party;

(ii) in respect of any procedure commenced on or after the date on which processing or examination of the international application may start under Article 23 or 40 of that Treaty.

(2)[*Patents*] The provisions of this Treaty and the Regulations shall apply to national and regional patents for invention, and to national and regional patents of addition, which have been granted with effect for a Contracting Party.

Article 4
Security Exception

Nothing in this Treaty and the Regulations shall limit the freedom of a Contracting Party to take any action it deems necessary for the preservation of essential security interests.

Article 5
Filing Date

(1)[*Elements of Application*] (a) Except as otherwise prescribed in the Regulations, and subject to paragraphs (2) to (8), a Contracting Party shall provide that the filing date of an application shall be the date on which its Office has received all of the following elements, filed, at the option of the applicant, on paper or as otherwise permitted by the Office for the purposes of the filing date:

(i) an express or implicit indication to the effect that the elements are intended to be an application;

(ii) indications allowing the identity of the applicant to be established or allowing the applicant to be contacted by the Office;

(iii) a part which on the face of it appears to be a description.

(b) A Contracting Party may, for the purposes of the filing date, accept a drawing as the element referred to in subparagraph (a)(iii).

(c) For the purposes of the filing date, a Contracting Party may require both information allowing the identity of the applicant to be established and information allowing the applicant to be contacted by the Office, or it may accept evidence allowing the identity of the applicant to be established or allowing the applicant to be contacted by the Office, as the element referred to in subparagraph (a)(ii).

(2)[*Language*] (a) A Contracting Party may require that the indications referred to in paragraph (1)(a)(i) and (ii) be in a language accepted by the Office.

(b) The part referred to in paragraph (1)(a)(iii) may, for the purposes of the filing date, be filed in any language.

(3)[*Notification*] Where the application does not comply with one or more of the requirements applied by the Contracting Party under paragraphs (1) and (2), the Office shall, as soon as practicable, notify the applicant, giving the opportunity to comply with any such requirement, and to make observations, within the time limit prescribed in the Regulations.

(4)[*Subsequent Compliance with Requirements*] (a) Where one or more of the requirements applied by the Contracting Party under paragraphs (1) and (2) are not complied with in the application as initially filed, the filing date shall, subject to subparagraph (b) and paragraph (6), be the date on which all of the requirements applied by the Contracting Party under paragraphs (1) and (2) are subsequently complied with.

(b) A Contracting Party may provide that, where one or more of the requirements referred to in subparagraph (a) are not complied with within the time limit prescribed in the Regulations, the application shall be deemed not to have been filed. Where the application is deemed not to have been filed, the Office shall notify the applicant accordingly, indicating the reasons therefor.

(5)[*Notification Concerning Missing Part of Description or Drawing*] Where, in establishing the filing date, the Office finds that a part of the description appears to be missing from the application, or that the application refers to a drawing which appears to be missing from the application, the Office shall promptly notify the applicant accordingly.

(6)[*Filing Date Where Missing Part of Description or Drawing Is Filed*] (a) Where a missing part of the description or a missing drawing is filed with the Office within the time limit prescribed in the Regulations, that part of the description or drawing shall be included in the application, and, subject to subparagraphs (b) and (c), the filing date shall be the date on which the Office has received that part of the description or that drawing, or the date on which all of the requirements applied by the Contracting Party under paragraphs (1) and (2) are complied with, whichever is later.

(b) Where the missing part of the description or the missing drawing is filed under subparagraph (a) to rectify its omission from an application which, at the date on which one or more elements referred to in paragraph (1)(a) were first received by the Office, claims the priority of an earlier application, the filing date shall, upon the request of the applicant filed within a time limit prescribed in the Regulations, and subject to the requirements prescribed in the Regulations, be the date on which all the requirements applied by the Contracting Party under paragraphs (1) and (2) are complied with.

(c) Where the missing part of the description or the missing drawing filed under subparagraph (a) is withdrawn within a time limit fixed by the Contracting Party, the filing date shall be the date on which the requirements applied by the Contracting Party under paragraphs (1) and (2) are complied with.

(7)[*Replacing Description and Drawings by Reference to a Previously Filed Application*] (a) Subject to the requirements prescribed in the Regulations, a reference, made upon the filing of the application, in a language accepted by the Office, to a previously filed application shall, for the purposes of the filing date of the application, replace the description and any drawings.

(b) Where the requirements referred to in subparagraph (a) are not complied with, the application may be deemed not to have been filed. Where the application is deemed not to have been filed, the Office shall notify the applicant accordingly, indicating the reasons therefor.

(8)[*Exceptions*] Nothing in this Article shall limit:

(i) the right of an applicant under Article 4G(1) or (2) of the Paris Convention to preserve, as the date of a divisional application referred to in that Article, the date of the initial application referred to in that Article and the benefit of the right of priority, if any;

(ii) the freedom of a Contracting Party to apply any requirements necessary to accord the benefit of the filing date of an earlier application to an application of any type prescribed in the Regulations.

<h1 style="text-align:center">Article 6
Application</h1>

(1)[*Form or Contents of Application*] Except where otherwise provided for by this Treaty, no Contracting Party shall require compliance with any requirement relating to the form or contents of an application different from or additional to:

(i) the requirements relating to form or contents which are provided for in respect of international applications under the Patent Cooperation Treaty;

(ii) the requirements relating to form or contents compliance with which, under the Patent Cooperation Treaty, may be required by the Office of, or acting for, any State party to that Treaty once the processing or examination of an international application, as referred to in Article 23 or 40 of the said Treaty, has started;

(iii) any further requirements prescribed in the Regulations.

(2)[*Request Form*] (a) A Contracting Party may require that the contents of an application which correspond to the contents of the request of an international application under the Patent Cooperation Treaty be presented on a request Form prescribed by that Contracting Party. A Contracting Party may also require that any further contents allowed under paragraph (1)(ii) or prescribed in the Regulations pursuant to paragraph (1)(iii) be contained in that request Form.

(b) Notwithstanding subparagraph (a), and subject to Article 8(1), a Contracting Party shall accept the presentation of the contents referred to in subparagraph (a) on a request Form provided for in the Regulations.

(3)[*Translation*] A Contracting Party may require a translation of any part of the application that is not in a language accepted by its Office. A Contracting Party may also require a translation of the parts of the application, as prescribed in the Regulations, that are in a language accepted by the Office, into any other languages accepted by that Office.

(4)[*Fees*] A Contracting Party may require that fees be paid in respect of the application. A Contracting Party may apply the provisions of the Patent Cooperation Treaty relating to payment of application fees.

(5)[*Priority Document*] Where the priority of an earlier application is claimed, a Contracting Party may require that a copy of the earlier application, and a translation where the earlier application is not in a language accepted by the Office, be filed in accordance with the requirements prescribed in the Regulations.

(6)[*Evidence*] A Contracting Party may require that evidence in respect of any matter referred to in paragraph (1) or (2) or in a declaration of priority, or any translation referred to in paragraph (3) or (5), be filed with its Office in the course of the processing of the application only where that Office may reasonably doubt the veracity of that matter or the accuracy of that translation.

(7)[*Notification*] Where one or more of the requirements applied by the Contracting Party under paragraphs (1) to (6) are not complied with, the Office shall notify the applicant, giving the opportunity to comply with any such requirement, and to make observations, within the time limit prescribed in the Regulations.

(8)[*Non-Compliance with Requirements*] (a) Where one or more of the requirements applied by the Contracting Party under paragraphs (1) to (6) are not complied with within the time limit prescribed in the Regulations, the Contracting Party may, subject to subparagraph (b) and Articles 5 and 10, apply such sanction as is provided for in its law.

(b) Where any requirement applied by the Contracting Party under paragraph (1), (5) or (6) in respect of a priority claim is not complied with within the time limit prescribed in the Regulations, the priority claim may, subject to Article 13, be deemed non-existent. Subject to Article 5(7)(b), no other sanctions may be applied.

Article 7
Representation

(1)[*Representatives*]   (a)   A Contracting Party may require that a representative appointed for the purposes of any procedure before the Office:

(i) have the right, under the applicable law, to practice before the Office in respect of applications and patents;

(ii) provide, as his address, an address on a territory prescribed by the Contracting Party.

(b) Subject to subparagraph (c), an act, with respect to any procedure before the Office, by or in relation to a representative who complies with the requirements applied by the Contracting Party under subparagraph (a), shall have the effect of an act by or in relation to the applicant, owner or other interested person who appointed that representative.

(c) A Contracting Party may provide that, in the case of an oath or declaration or the revocation of a power of attorney, the signature of a representative shall not have the effect of the signature of the applicant, owner or other interested person who appointed that representative.

(2)[*Mandatory Representation*] (a) A Contracting Party may require that an applicant, owner or other interested person appoint a representative for the purposes of any procedure before the Office, except that an assignee of an application, an applicant, owner or other interested person may act himself before the Office for the following procedures:

(i) the filing of an application for the purposes of the filing date;

(ii) the mere payment of a fee;

(iii) any other procedure as prescribed in the Regulations;

(iv) the issue of a receipt or notification by the Office in respect of any procedure referred to in items (i) to (iii).

(b) A maintenance fee may be paid by any person.

(3)[*Appointment of Representative*] A Contracting Party shall accept that the appointment of the representative be filed with the Office in a manner prescribed in the Regulations.

(4)[*Prohibition of Other Requirements*] No Contracting Party may require that formal requirements other than those referred to in paragraphs (1) to (3) be complied with in respect of the matters dealt with in those paragraphs, except where otherwise provided for by this Treaty or prescribed in the Regulations.

(5)[*Notification*] Where one or more of the requirements applied by the Contracting Party under paragraphs (1) to (3) are not complied with, the Office shall notify the assignee of the application, applicant, owner or other interested person, giving the opportunity to comply with any such requirement, and to make observations, within the time limit prescribed in the Regulations.

(6)[*Non-Compliance with Requirements*] Where one or more of the requirements applied by the Contracting Party under paragraphs (1) to (3) are not complied with within the time limit prescribed in the Regulations, the Contracting Party may apply such sanction as is provided for in its law.

Article 8
Communications; Addresses

(1)[*Form and Means of Transmittal of Communications*] (a) Except for the establishment of a filing date under Article 5(1), and subject to Article 6(1), the Regulations shall, subject to subparagraphs (b) to (d), set out the requirements which a Contracting Party shall be permitted to apply as regards the form and means of transmittal of communications.

(b) No Contracting Party shall be obliged to accept the filing of communications other than on paper.

(c) No Contracting Party shall be obliged to exclude the filing of communications on paper.

(d) A Contracting Party shall accept the filing of communications on paper for the purpose of complying with a time limit.

(2)[*Language of Communications*] A Contracting Party may, except where otherwise provided for by this Treaty or the Regulations, require that a communication be in a language accepted by the Office.

(3)[*Model International Forms*] Notwithstanding paragraph (1)(a), and subject to paragraph (1)(b) and Article 6(2)(b), a Contracting Party shall accept the presentation of the contents of a communication on a Form which corresponds to a Model International Form in respect of such a communication provided for in the Regulations, if any.

(4)[*Signature of Communications*] (a) Where a Contracting Party requires a signature for the purposes of any communication, that Contracting Party shall accept any signature that complies with the requirements prescribed in the Regulations.

(b) No Contracting Party may require the attestation, notarization, authentication, legalization or other certification of any signature which is communicated to its Office, except in respect of any quasi-judicial proceedings or as prescribed in the Regulations.

(c) Subject to subparagraph (b), a Contracting Party may require that evidence be filed with the Office only where the Office may reasonably doubt the authenticity of any signature.

(5)[*Indications in Communications*] A Contracting Party may require that any communication contain one or more indications prescribed in the Regulations.

(6)[*Address for Correspondence, Address for Legal Service and Other Address*] A Contracting Party may, subject to any provisions prescribed in the Regulations, require that an applicant, owner or other interested person indicate in any communication:

(i) an address for correspondence;

(ii) an address for legal service;

(iii) any other address provided for in the Regulations.

(7)[*Notification*] Where one or more of the requirements applied by the Contracting Party under paragraphs (1) to (6) are not complied with in respect of communications, the Office shall notify the applicant, owner or other interested person, giving the opportunity to comply with any such requirement, and to make observations, within the time limit prescribed in the Regulations.

(8)[*Non-Compliance with Requirements*] Where one or more of the requirements applied by the Contracting Party under paragraphs (1) to (6) are not complied with within the time limit prescribed in the Regulations, the Contracting Party may, subject to Articles 5 and 10 and to any exceptions prescribed in the Regulations, apply such sanction as is provided for in its law.

Article 9
Notifications

(1)[*Sufficient Notification*] Any notification under this Treaty or the Regulations which is sent by the Office to an address for correspondence or address for legal service indicated under Article 8(6), or any other address provided for in the Regulations for the purpose of this provision, and which complies with the provisions with respect to that notification, shall constitute a sufficient notification for the purposes of this Treaty and the Regulations.

(2)[*If Indications Allowing Contact Were Not Filed*] Nothing in this Treaty and in the Regulations shall oblige a Contracting Party to send a notification to an applicant, owner or other interested person, if indications allowing that applicant, owner or other interested person to be contacted have not been filed with the Office.

(3)[*Failure to Notify*] Subject to Article 10(1), where an Office does not notify an applicant, owner or other interested person of a failure to comply with any requirement under this Treaty or the Regulations, that absence of notification does not relieve that applicant, owner or other interested person of the obligation to comply with that requirement.

Article 10
Validity of Patent; Revocation

(1)[*Validity of Patent Not Affected by Non-Compliance with Certain Formal Requirements*] Non-compliance with one or more of the formal requirements referred to in Articles 6(1), (2), (4) and (5) and 8(1) to (4) with respect to an application may not be a ground for revocation or invalidation of a patent, either totally or in part, except where the non-compliance with the formal requirement occurred as a result of a fraudulent intention.

(2)[*Opportunity to Make Observations, Amendments or Corrections in Case of Intended Revocation or Invalidation*] A patent may not be revoked or invalidated, either totally or in part, without the owner being given the opportunity to make observations on the intended revocation or invalidation, and to make amendments and corrections where permitted under the applicable law, within a reasonable time limit.

(3)[*No Obligation for Special Procedures*] Paragraphs (1) and (2) do not create any obligation to put in place judicial procedures for the enforcement of patent rights distinct from those for the enforcement of law in general.

Article 11
Relief in Respect of Time Limits

(1)[*Extension of Time Limits*] A Contracting Party may provide for the extension, for the period prescribed in the Regulations, of a time limit fixed by the Office for an action in a procedure before the Office in respect of an application or a patent, if a request to that effect is made to the Office in accordance with the requirements prescribed in the Regulations, and the request is filed, at the option of the Contracting Party:

(i) prior to the expiration of the time limit; or

(ii) after the expiration of the time limit, and within the time limit prescribed in the Regulations.

(2)[*Continued Processing*] Where an applicant or owner has failed to comply with a time limit fixed by the Office of a Contracting Party for an action in a procedure before the Office in respect of an application or a patent, and that Contracting Party does not provide for extension of a time limit under paragraph (1)(ii), the Contracting Party shall provide for continued processing with respect to the application or patent and, if necessary, reinstatement of the rights of the applicant or owner with respect to that application or patent, if:

(i) a request to that effect is made to the Office in accordance with the requirements prescribed in the Regulations;

(ii) the request is filed, and all of the requirements in respect of which the time limit for the action concerned applied are complied with, within the time limit prescribed in the Regulations.

(3)[*Exceptions*] No Contracting Party shall be required to provide for the relief referred to in paragraph (1) or (2) with respect to the exceptions prescribed in the Regulations.

(4)[*Fees*] A Contracting Party may require that a fee be paid in respect of a request under paragraph (1) or (2).

(5)[*Prohibition of Other Requirements*] No Contracting Party may require that requirements other than those referred to in paragraphs (1) to (4) be complied with in respect of the relief provided for under paragraph (1) or (2), except where otherwise provided for by this Treaty or prescribed in the Regulations.

(6)[*Opportunity to Make Observations in Case of Intended Refusal*] A request under paragraph (1) or (2) may not be refused without the applicant or owner being given the opportunity to make observations on the intended refusal within a reasonable time limit.

Article 12
Reinstatement of Rights After a Finding of Due Care or Unintentionality by the Office

(1)[*Request*] A Contracting Party shall provide that, where an applicant or owner has failed to comply with a time limit for an action in a procedure before the Office, and that failure has the direct consequence of causing a loss of rights with respect to an application or patent, the Office shall reinstate the rights of the applicant or owner with respect to the application or patent concerned, if:

(i) a request to that effect is made to the Office in accordance with the requirements prescribed in the Regulations;

(ii) the request is filed, and all of the requirements in respect of which the time limit for the said action applied are complied with, within the time limit prescribed in the Regulations;

(iii) the request states the reasons for the failure to comply with the time limit; and

(iv) the Office finds that the failure to comply with the time limit occurred in spite of due care required by the circumstances having been taken or, at the option of the Contracting Party, that any delay was unintentional.

(2)[*Exceptions*] No Contracting Party shall be required to provide for the reinstatement of rights under paragraph (1) with respect to the exceptions prescribed in the Regulations.

(3)[*Fees*] A Contracting Party may require that a fee be paid in respect of a request under paragraph (1).

(4)[*Evidence*] A Contracting Party may require that a declaration or other evidence in support of the reasons referred to in paragraph (1)(iii) be filed with the Office within a time limit fixed by the Office.

(5)[*Opportunity to Make Observations in Case of Intended Refusal*] A request under paragraph (1) may not be refused, totally or in part, without the requesting party being given the opportunity to make observations on the intended refusal within a reasonable time limit.

Article 13
Correction or Addition of Priority Claim;
Restoration of Priority Right

(1)[*Correction or Addition of Priority Claim*] Except where otherwise prescribed in the Regulations, a Contracting Party shall provide for the correction or addition of a priority claim with respect to an application ("the subsequent application"), if:

(i) a request to that effect is made to the Office in accordance with the requirements prescribed in the Regulations;

(ii) the request is filed within the time limit prescribed in the Regulations; and

(iii) the filing date of the subsequent application is not later than the date of the expiration of the priority period calculated from the filing date of the earliest application whose priority is claimed.

(2)[*Delayed Filing of the Subsequent Application*] Taking into consideration Article 15, a Contracting Party shall provide that, where an application ("the subsequent application") which claims or could have claimed the priority of an earlier application has a filing date which is later than the date on which the priority period expired, but within the time limit prescribed in the Regulations, the Office shall restore the right of priority, if:

(i)   a request to that effect is made to the Office in accordance with the requirements prescribed in the Regulations;

(ii)   the request is filed within the time limit prescribed in the Regulations;

(iii) the request states the reasons for the failure to comply with the priority period; and

(iv) the Office finds that the failure to file the subsequent application within the priority period occurred in spite of due care required by the circumstances having been taken or, at the option of the Contracting Party, was unintentional.

(3) [*Failure to File a Copy of Earlier Application*] A Contracting Party shall provide that, where a copy of an earlier application required under Article 6(5) is not filed with the Office within the time limit prescribed in the Regulations pursuant to Article 6, the Office shall restore the right of priority, if:

(i) a request to that effect is made to the Office in accordance with the requirements prescribed in the Regulations;

(ii) the request is filed within the time limit for filing the copy of the earlier application prescribed in the Regulations pursuant to Article 6(5);

(iii) the Office finds that the request for the copy to be provided had been filed with the Office with which the earlier application was filed, within the time limit prescribed in the Regulations; and

(iv) a copy of the earlier application is filed within the time limit prescribed in the Regulations.

(4) [*Fees*] A Contracting Party may require that a fee be paid in respect of a request under paragraphs (1) to (3).

(5)[*Evidence*] A Contracting Party may require that a declaration or other evidence in support of the reasons referred to in paragraph (2)(iii) be filed with the Office within a time limit fixed by the Office.

(6)[*Opportunity to Make Observations in Case of Intended Refusal*] A request under paragraphs (1) to (3) may not be refused, totally or in part, without the requesting party being given the opportunity to make observations on the intended refusal within a reasonable time limit.

Article 14
Regulations

(1)[*Content*] (a) The Regulations annexed to this Treaty provide rules concerning:

(i) matters which this Treaty expressly provides are to be "prescribed in the Regulations";

(ii) details useful in the implementation of the provisions of this Treaty;

(iii) administrative requirements, matters or procedures.

(b) The Regulations also provide rules concerning the formal requirements which a Contracting Party shall be permitted to apply in respect of requests for:

(i) recordation of change in name or address;

(ii) recordation of change in applicant or owner;

(iii) recordation of a license or a security interest;

(iv) correction of a mistake.

(c) The Regulations also provide for the establishment of Model International Forms, and for the establishment of a request Form for the purposes of Article 6(2)(b), by the Assembly, with the assistance of the International Bureau.

(2)[*Amending the Regulations*] Subject to paragraph (3), any amendment of the Regulations shall require three-fourths of the votes cast.

(3)[*Requirement of Unanimity*] (a) The Regulations may specify provisions of the Regulations which may be amended only by unanimity.

(b) Any amendment of the Regulations resulting in the addition of provisions to, or the deletion of provisions from, the provisions specified in the Regulations pursuant to subparagraph (a) shall require unanimity.

(c) In determining whether unanimity is attained, only votes actually cast shall be taken into consideration. Abstentions shall not be considered as votes.

(4)[*Conflict Between the Treaty and the Regulations*] In the case of conflict between the provisions of this Treaty and those of the Regulations, the former shall prevail.

Article 15
Relation to the Paris Convention

(1)[*Obligation to Comply with the Paris Convention*] Each Contracting Party shall comply with the provisions of the Paris Convention which concern patents.

(2)[*Obligations and Rights Under the Paris Convention*] (a) Nothing in this Treaty shall derogate from obligations that Contracting Parties have to each other under the Paris Convention.

(b) Nothing in this Treaty shall derogate from rights that applicants and owners enjoy under the Paris Convention.

Article 16
Effect of Revisions, Amendments and Modifications
of the Patent Cooperation Treaty

(1)[*Applicability of Revisions, Amendments and Modifications of the Patent Cooperation Treaty*] Subject to paragraph (2), any revision, amendment or modification of the Patent Cooperation Treaty made after June 2, 2000, which is consistent with the Articles of this Treaty, shall apply for the purposes of this Treaty and the Regulations if the Assembly so decides, in the particular case, by three-fourths of the votes cast.

(2)[*Non-Applicability of Transitional Provisions of the Patent Cooperation Treaty*] Any provision of the Patent Cooperation Treaty, by virtue of which a revised, amended or modified provision of that Treaty does not apply to a State party to it, or to the Office of or acting for such a State, for as long as the latter provision is incompatible with the law applied by that State or Office, shall not apply for the purposes of this Treaty and the Regulations.

Article 17
Assembly

(1)[*Composition*] (a) The Contracting Parties shall have an Assembly.

(b) Each Contracting Party shall be represented in the Assembly by one delegate, who may be assisted by alternate delegates, advisors and experts. Each delegate may represent only one Contracting Party.

(2)[*Tasks*] The Assembly shall:

(i) deal with matters concerning the maintenance and development of this Treaty and the application and operation of this Treaty;

(ii) establish Model International Forms, and the request Form, referred to in Article 14(1)(c), with the assistance of the International Bureau;

(iii) amend the Regulations;

(iv) determine the conditions for the date of application of each Model International Form, and the request Form, referred to in item (ii), and each amendment referred to in item (iii);

(v) decide, pursuant to Article 16(1), whether any revision, amendment or modification of the Patent Cooperation Treaty shall apply for the purposes of this Treaty and the Regulations;

(vi) perform such other functions as are appropriate under this Treaty.

(3)[*Quorum*] (a) One-half of the members of the Assembly which are States shall constitute a quorum.

(b) Notwithstanding subparagraph (a), if, in any session, the number of the members of the Assembly which are States and are represented is less than one-half but equal to or more than one-third of the members of the Assembly which are States, the Assembly may make decisions but, with the exception of decisions concerning its own procedure, all such decisions shall take effect only if the conditions set forth hereinafter are fulfilled. The International Bureau shall communicate the said decisions to the members of the Assembly which are States and were not represented and shall invite them to express in writing their vote or abstention within a period of three months from the date of the communication. If, at the expiration of this period, the number of such members having thus expressed their vote or abstention attains the number of the members which was lacking for attaining the quorum in the session itself, such decisions shall take effect, provided that at the same time the required majority still obtains.

(4)[*Taking Decisions in the Assembly*] (a) The Assembly shall endeavor to take its decisions by consensus.

(b)Where a decision cannot be arrived at by consensus, the matter at issue shall be decided by voting. In such a case:

(i) each Contracting Party that is a State shall have one vote and shall vote only in its own name; and

(ii) any Contracting Party that is an intergovernmental organization may participate in the vote, in place of its Member States, with a number of votes equal to the number of its Member States which are party to this Treaty. No such intergovernmental organization shall participate in the vote if any one of its Member States exercises its right to vote and *vice versa*. In addition, no such intergovernmental organization shall participate in the vote if any one of its Member States party to this Treaty is a Member State of another such intergovernmental organization and that other intergovernmental organization participates in that vote.

(5)[*Majorities*] (a) Subject to Articles 14(2) and (3), 16(1) and 19(3), the decisions of the Assembly shall require two-thirds of the votes cast.

(b) In determining whether the required majority is attained, only votes actually cast shall be taken into consideration. Abstentions shall not be considered as votes.

(6)[*Sessions*] The Assembly shall meet in ordinary session once every two years upon convocation by the Director General.

(7)[*Rules of Procedure*] The Assembly shall establish its own rules of procedure, including rules for the convocation of extraordinary sessions.

Article 18
International Bureau

(1)[*Administrative Tasks*] (a) The International Bureau shall perform the administrative tasks concerning this Treaty.

(b) In particular, the International Bureau shall prepare the meetings and provide the secretariat of the Assembly and of such committees of experts and working groups as may be established by the Assembly.

(2)[*Meetings Other than Sessions of the Assembly*] The Director General shall convene any committee and working group established by the Assembly.

(3)[*Role of the International Bureau in the Assembly and Other Meetings*]
(a) The Director General and persons designated by the Director General shall participate, without the right to vote, in all meetings of the Assembly, the committees and working groups established by the Assembly.

(b) The Director General or a staff member designated by the Director General shall be *ex officio* secretary of the Assembly, and of the committees and working groups referred to in subparagraph (a).

(4)[*Conferences*] (a) The International Bureau shall, in accordance with the directions of the Assembly, make the preparations for any revision conferences.

(b) The International Bureau may consult with member States of the Organization, intergovernmental organizations and international and national non-governmental organizations concerning the said preparations.

(c) The Director General and persons designated by the Director

General shall take part, without the right to vote, in the discussions at revision conferences.

(5)[*Other Tasks*] The International Bureau shall carry out any other tasks assigned to it in relation to this Treaty.

Article 19
Revisions

(1)[*Revision of the Treaty*] Subject to paragraph (2), this Treaty may be revised by a conference of the Contracting Parties. The convocation of any revision conference shall be decided by the Assembly.

(2)[*Revision or Amendment of Certain Provisions of the Treaty*] Article 17(2) and (6) may be amended either by a revision conference, or by the Assembly according to the provisions of paragraph (3).

(3)[*Amendment by the Assembly of Certain Provisions of the Treaty*] (a) Proposals for the amendment by the Assembly of Article 17(2) and (6) may be initiated by any Contracting Party or by the Director General. Such proposals shall be communicated by the Director General to the Contracting Parties at least six months in advance of their consideration by the Assembly.

(b) Adoption of any amendment to the provisions referred to in subparagraph (a) shall require three-fourths of the votes cast.

(c) Any amendment to the provisions referred to in subparagraph (a) shall enter into force one month after written notifications of acceptance, effected in accordance with their respective constitutional processes, have been received by the Director General from three-fourths of the Contracting Parties which were members of the Assembly at the time the Assembly adopted the amendment. Any amendment to the said provisions thus accepted shall bind all the Contracting Parties at the time the amendment enters into force, and States and intergovernmental organizations which become Contracting Parties at a subsequent date.

Article 20
Becoming Party to the Treaty

(1)[*States*] Any State which is party to the Paris Convention or which is a member of the Organization, and in respect of which patents may be granted, either through the State's own Office or through the Office of another State or intergovernmental organization, may become party to this Treaty.

(2)[*Intergovernmental Organizations*] Any intergovernmental organization may become party to this Treaty if at least one member State of that intergovernmental organization is party to the Paris Convention or a member of the Organization, and the intergovernmental organization declares that it has been duly authorized, in accordance with its internal procedures, to become party to this Treaty, and declares that:

(i) it is competent to grant patents with effect for its member States; or

(ii) it is competent in respect of, and has its own legislation binding on all its member States concerning, matters covered by this Treaty, and it has, or has charged, a regional Office for the purpose of granting patents with effect in its territory in accordance with that legislation.

Subject to paragraph (3), any such declaration shall be made at the time of the deposit of the instrument of ratification or accession.

(3)[*Regional Patent Organizations*] The European Patent Organisation, the Eurasian Patent Organization and the African Regional Industrial Property Organization, having made the declaration referred to in paragraph (2)(i) or (ii) in the Diplomatic Conference that has adopted this Treaty, may become party to this Treaty as an intergovernmental organization, if it declares, at the time of the deposit of the instrument of ratification or accession that it has been duly authorized, in accordance with its internal procedures, to become party to this Treaty.

(4)[*Ratification or Accession*] Any State or intergovernmental organization satisfying the requirements in paragraph (1), (2) or (3) may deposit:

(i) an instrument of ratification if it has signed this Treaty; or

(ii) an instrument of accession if it has not signed this Treaty.

Article 21
Entry into Force; Effective Dates of Ratifications and Accessions

(1)[*Entry into Force of this Treaty*] This Treaty shall enter into force three months after ten instruments of ratification or accession by States have been deposited with the Director General.

(2)[*Effective Dates of Ratifications and Accessions*] This Treaty shall bind:

(i) the ten States referred to in paragraph (1), from the date on which this Treaty has entered into force;

(ii) each other State, from the expiration of three months after the date on which the State has deposited its instrument of ratification or accession with the Director General, or from any later date indicated in that instrument, but no later than six months after the date of such deposit;

(iii) each of the European Patent Organisation, the Eurasian Patent Organization and the African Regional Industrial Property Organization, from the expiration of three months after the deposit of its instrument of ratification or accession, or from any later date indicated in that instrument, but no later than six months after the date of such deposit, if such instrument has been deposited after the entry into force of this Treaty according to paragraph (1), or three months after the entry into force of this Treaty if such instrument has been deposited before the entry into force of this Treaty;

(iv) any other intergovernmental organization that is eligible to become party to this Treaty, from the expiration of three months after the deposit of its instrument of ratification or accession, or from any later date indicated in that instrument, but no later than six months after the date of such deposit.

Article 22
Application of the Treaty to Existing Applications and Patents

(1)[*Principle*] Subject to paragraph (2), a Contracting Party shall apply the provisions of this Treaty and the Regulations, other than Articles 5 and 6(1) and (2) and related Regulations, to applications which are pending, and to patents which are in force, on the date on which this Treaty binds that Contracting Party under Article 21.

(2)[*Procedures*]   No Contracting Party shall be obliged to apply the provisions of this Treaty and the Regulations to any procedure in proceedings with respect to applications and patents referred to in paragraph (1), if such procedure commenced before the date on which this Treaty binds that Contracting Party under Article 21.

Article 23
Reservations

(1)[*Reservation*] Any State or intergovernmental organization may declare through a reservation that the provisions of Article 6(1) shall not apply to any requirement relating to unity of invention applicable under the Patent Cooperation Treaty to an international application.

(2)[*Modalities*] Any reservation under paragraph (1) shall be made in a declaration accompanying the instrument of ratification of, or accession to, this Treaty of the State or intergovernmental organization making the reservation.

(3)[*Withdrawal*] Any reservation under paragraph (1) may be withdrawn at any time.

(4)[*Prohibition of Other Reservations*] No reservation to this Treaty other than the reservation allowed under paragraph (1) shall be permitted.

Article 24
Denunciation of the Treaty

(1)[*Notification*] Any Contracting Party may denounce this Treaty by notification addressed to the Director General.

(2)[*Effective Date*] Any denunciation shall take effect one year from the date on which the Director General has received the notification or at any later date indicated in the notification. It shall not affect the application of this Treaty to any application pending or any patent in force in respect of the denouncing Contracting Party at the time of the coming into effect of the denunciation.

Article 25
Languages of the Treaty

(1)[*Authentic Texts*] This Treaty is signed in a single original in the English, Arabic, Chinese, French, Russian and Spanish languages, all texts being equally and exclusively authentic.

(2)[*Official Texts*] An official text in any language other than those referred to in paragraph (1) shall be established by the Director General, after consultation with the interested parties. For the purposes of this paragraph, interested party means any State which is party to the Treaty, or is eligible to become party to the Treaty under Article 20(1), whose official language, or one of whose official languages, is involved, and the European Patent Organisation, the Eurasian Patent Organization and the African Regional Industrial Property Organization and any other intergovernmental organization that is party to the Treaty, or may become party to the Treaty, if one of its official languages is involved.

(3)[*Authentic Texts to Prevail*]   In case of differences of opinion on interpretation between authentic and official texts, the authentic texts shall prevail.

Article 26
Signature of the Treaty

The Treaty shall remain open for signature by any State that is eligible for becoming party to the Treaty under Article 20(1) and by the European Patent Organisation, the Eurasian Patent Organization and the African Regional Industrial Property Organization at the headquarters of the Organization for one year after its adoption.

Article 27
Depositary; Registration

(1)[*Depositary*]   The Director General is the depositary of this Treaty.

(2)[*Registration*]   The Director General shall register this Treaty with the Secretariat of the United Nations.

AGREED STATEMENTS

1.   When adopting Article 1(xiv), the Diplomatic Conference understood that the words "procedure before the Office" would not cover judicial procedures under the applicable law.

2.   When adopting Articles 1(xvii), 16 and 17(2)(v), the Diplomatic Conference understood that:

(1) The PLT Assembly would, when appropriate, be convened in conjunction with meetings of the PCT Assembly.

(2) Contracting Parties of the PLT would be consulted, when appropriate, in addition to States party to the PCT, in relation to proposed modifications of the PCT Administrative Instructions.

(3) The Director General shall propose, for the determination of the PCT Assembly, that Contracting Parties of the PLT which are not party to the PCT be invited as observers to PCT Assembly meetings and to

meetings of other PCT bodies, when appropriate.

(4) When the PLT Assembly decides, under Article 16, that a revision, amendment or modification of the PCT shall apply for the purposes of the PLT, the Assembly may provide for transitional provisions under the PLT in the particular case.

3. When adopting Articles 6(5) and 13(3), and Rules 4 and 14, the Diplomatic Conference urged the World Intellectual Property Organization to expedite the creation of a digital library system for priority documents. Such a system would be of benefit to patent owners and others wanting access to priority documents.

4. With a view to facilitating the implementation of Rule 8(1)(a) of this Treaty, the Diplomatic Conference requests the General Assembly of the World Intellectual Property Organization (WIPO) and the Contracting Parties to provide the developing and least developed countries and countries in transition with additional technical assistance to meet their obligations under this Treaty, even before the entry into force of the Treaty.

The Diplomatic Conference further urges industrialized market economy countries to provide, on request and on mutually agreed terms and conditions, technical and financial cooperation in favour of developing and least developed countries and countries in transition.

The Diplomatic Conference requests the WIPO General Assembly, once the Treaty has entered into force, to monitor and evaluate the progress of that cooperation every ordinary session.

5. When adopting Rules 12(5)(vi) and 13(3)(iv), the Diplomatic Conference understood that, while it was appropriate to exclude actions in relation to *inter partes* proceedings from the relief provided by Articles 11 and 12, it was desirable that the applicable law of Contracting Parties provide appropriate relief in those circumstances which takes into account the competing interests of third parties, as well as those interests of others who are not parties to the proceedings.

6. It was agreed that any dispute arising between two or more Contracting Parties concerning the interpretation or the application of this Treaty and its Regulations may be settled amicably through consultation or mediation under the auspices of the Director General.

THE STRASBOURG AGREEMENT
CONCERNING THE INTERNATIONAL PATENT
CLASSIFICATION
of March 24, 1971, as amended on September 28, 1979

The Contracting Parties,

Considering that the universal adoption of a uniform system of classification of patents, inventors' certificates, utility models and utility certificates is in the general interest and is likely to establish closer international cooperation in the industrial property field, and to contribute to the harmonization of national legislation in that field,

Recognizing the importance of the European Convention on the International Classification of Patents for Invention, of December 19, 1954, under which the Council of Europe created the International Classification of Patents for Invention,

Having regard to the universal value of this Classification, and to its importance to all countries party to the Paris Convention for the Protection of Industrial Property,

Having regard to the importance to developing countries of this Classification, which gives them easier access to the ever-expanding volume of modern technology,

Having regard to Article 19 of the Paris Convention for the Protection of Industrial Property of March 20, 1883, as revised at Brussels on December 14, 1900, at Washington on June 2, 1911, at The Hague on November 6, 1925, at London on June 2, 1934, at Lisbon on October 31, 1958, and at Stockholm on July 14, 1967,

Agree as follows:

Article 1
Establishment of a Special Union;
Adoption of an International Classification

The countries to which this Agreement applies constitute a Special Union and adopt a common classification for patents for invention, inventors' certificates, utility models and utility certificates, to be known as the "International Patent Classification" (hereinafter designated as the "Classification").

Article 2
Definition of the Classification

(1)

   (a) The Classification comprises:

      (i)   the text which was established pursuant to the provisions of the European Convention on the International Classification of Patents for Invention of December 19, 1954 (hereinafter designated as the "European Convention"), and which came into force and was published by the Secretary General of the Council of Europe on September 1, 1968;

(ii) the amendments which have entered into force pursuant to Article 2(2) of the European Convention prior to the entry into force of this Agreement;

(iii) the amendments made thereafter in accordance with Article 5 which enter into force pursuant to the provisions of Article 6.

(b) The Guide and the notes included in the text of the Classification are an integral part thereof.

(2)

(a) The text referred to in paragraph (1)(a)(i) is contained in two authentic copies, each in the English and French languages, deposited, at the time that this Agreement is opened for signature, one with the Secretary General of the Council of Europe and the other with the Director General of the World Intellectual Property Organization (hereinafter respectively designated "Director General" and "Organization") established by the Convention of July 14, 1967.

(b) The amendments referred to in paragraph (1)(a)(ii) shall be deposited in two authentic copies, each in the English and French languages, one with the Secretary General of the Council of Europe and the other with the Director General.

(c) The amendments referred to in paragraph (1)(a)(iii) shall be deposited in one authentic copy only, in the English and French languages, with the Director General.

Article 3
Languages of the Classification

(1) The Classification shall be established in the English and French languages, both texts being equally authentic.

(2) Official texts of the Classification, in German, Japanese, Portuguese, Russian, Spanish and in such other languages as the Assembly referred to in Article 7 may designate, shall be established by the International Bureau of the Organization (hereinafter designated as the "International Bureau"), in consultation with the interested Governments and either on the basis of a translation submitted by those Governments or by any other means which do not entail financial implications for the budget of the Special Union or for the Organization.

Article 4
Use of the Classification

(1) The Classification shall be solely of an administrative character.

(2) Each country of the Special Union shall have the right to use the Classification either as a principal or as a subsidiary system.

(3) The competent authorities of the countries of the Special Union shall include in

(i) patents, inventors' certificates, utility models and utility certificates issued by them, and in applications relating thereto, whether published or only laid open for public inspection by them, and

(ii) notices, appearing in official periodicals, of the publication or laying open of the documents referred to in subparagraph (i)

the complete symbols of the Classification applied to the invention to which the document referred to in subparagraph (i) relates.

(4) When signing this Agreement or when depositing its instrument of ratification or accession:

(i) any country may declare that it does not undertake to include the symbols relating to groups or subgroups of the Classification in applications as referred to in paragraph (3) which are only laid open for public inspection and in notices relating thereto, and

(ii) any country which does not proceed to an examination as to novelty, whether immediate or deferred, and in which the procedure for the grant of patents or other kinds of protection does not provide for a search into the state of the art, may declare that it does not undertake to include the symbols relating to the groups and subgroups of the Classification in the documents and notices referred to in paragraph (3). If these conditions exist only in relation to certain kinds of protection or certain fields of technology, the country in question may only make this reservation to the extent that the conditions apply.

(5) The symbols of the Classification, preceded by the words "International Patent Classification" or an abbreviation thereof to be determined by the Committee of Experts referred to in Article 5, shall be printed in heavy type, or in such a manner that they are clearly visible, in the heading of each document referred to in paragraph (3)(i) in which they are to be included.

(6) If any country of the Special Union entrusts the grant of patents to an intergovernmental authority, it shall take all possible measures to ensure that this authority uses the Classification in accordance with this Article.

Article 5
Committee of Experts

(1) A Committee of Experts shall be set up in which each country of the Special Union shall be represented.

(2)

(a) The Director General shall invite intergovernmental organizations specialized in the patent field, and of which at least one of the member countries is party to this Agreement, to be represented by observers at meetings of the Committee of Experts.

(b) The Director General may, and, if requested by the Committee of Experts, shall, invite representatives of other intergovernmental and international non-governmental organizations to participate in discussions of interest to them.

(3) The Committee of Experts shall:

(i) amend the Classification;

(ii) address recommendations to the countries of the Special Union for the purpose of facilitating the use of the Classification and promoting its uniform application;

(iii) assist in the promotion of international cooperation in the reclassification of documentation used for the examination of inventions, taking in particular the needs of developing countries into account;

(iv) take all other measures which, without entailing financial implications for the budget of the Special Union or for the Organization, contribute towards facilitating the application of the Classification by developing countries;

(v) have the right to establish subcommittees and working groups.

(4) The Committee of Experts shall adopt its own Rules of Procedure. These shall allow for the possibility of participation of intergovernmental organizations, referred to in paragraph (2)(a), which can perform substantial work in the development of the Classification, in meetings of its subcommittees and working groups.

(5) Proposals for amendments to the Classification may be made by the competent authority of any country of the Special Union, the International Bureau, any intergovernmental organization represented in the Committee of Experts pursuant to paragraph (2)(a) and any other organization specially invited by the Committee of Experts to submit such proposals. The proposals shall be communicated to the International Bureau which shall submit them to the members of the Committee of Experts and to the observers not later than two months before the session of the Committee of Experts at which the said proposals are to be considered.

(6)

(a) Each country member of the Committee of Experts shall have one vote.

(b) The decisions of the Committee of Experts shall require a simple majority of the countries represented and voting.

(c) Any decision which is regarded by one-fifth of the countries represented and voting as giving rise to a modification in the basic structure of the Classification or as entailing a substantial work of reclassification shall require a majority of three-fourths of the countries represented and voting.

(d) Abstentions shall not be considered as votes.

Article 6
Notification, Entry into Force and Publication of Amendments and Other Decisions

(1) Every decision of the Committee of Experts concerning the adoption of amendments to the Classification and recommendations of the Committee of Experts shall be notified by the International Bureau to the competent authorities of the countries of the Special Union. The amendments shall enter into force six months from the date of dispatch of the notification.

(2) The International Bureau shall incorporate in the Classification the amendments which have entered into force. Announcements of the amendments shall be published in such periodicals as are designated by the Assembly referred to in Article 7.

Article 7
Assembly of the Special Union

(1)

(a) The Special Union shall have an Assembly consisting of the countries of the Special Union.

(b) The Government of each country of the Special Union shall be represented by one delegate, who may be assisted by alternate delegates, advisors and experts.

(c) Any intergovernmental organization referred to in Article 5(2)(a) may be represented by an observer in the meetings of the Assembly, and, if the Assembly so decides, in those of such committees or working groups as may have been established by the Assembly.

(d) The expenses of each delegation shall be borne by the Government which has appointed it.

(2)

(a) Subject to the provisions of Article 5, the Assembly shall:

(i) deal with all matters concerning the maintenance and development of the Special Union and the implementation of this Agreement;

(ii) give directions to the International Bureau concerning the preparation for conferences of revision;

(iii) review and approve the reports and activities of the Director General concerning the Special Union, and give him all necessary instructions concerning matters within the competence of the Special Union;

(iv) determine the program and adopt the biennial budget of the Special Union, and approve its final accounts;

(v) adopt the financial regulations of the Special Union;

(vi) decide on the establishment of official texts of the Classification in languages other than English, French and those listed in Article 3(2);

(vii) establish such committees and working groups as it deems appropriate to achieve the objectives of the Special Union;

(viii) determine, subject to paragraph (1)(c), which countries not members of the Special Union and which intergovernmental and international non-governmental organizations shall be admitted as observers to its meetings, and to those of any committee or working group established by it;

(ix) take any other appropriate action designed to further the objectives of the Special Union;

(x) perform such other functions as are appropriate under this Agreement.

(b) With respect to matters which are of interest also to other Unions administered by the Organization, the Assembly shall make its decisions after having heard the advice of the Coordination Committee of the Organization.

(3)

(a) Each country member of the Assembly shall have one vote.

(b) One-half of the countries members of the Assembly shall constitute a quorum.

(c) In the absence of the quorum, the Assembly may make decisions but, with the exception of decisions concerning its own procedure, all such decisions shall take effect only if the conditions set forth hereinafter are fulfilled. The International Bureau shall communicate the said decisions to the countries members of the Assembly which were not represented and shall invite them to express in writing their vote or abstention within a period of three months from the date of the communication. If, at the expiration of this period, the number of countries having thus expressed their vote or abstention attains the number of countries which was lacking for attaining the quorum in the session itself, such decisions shall take effect provided that at the same time the required majority still obtains.

(d) Subject to the provisions of Article 11(2), the decisions of the Assembly shall require two-thirds of the votes cast.

(e) Abstentions shall not be considered as votes.

(f) A delegate may represent, and vote in the name of, one country only.

(4)

(a) The Assembly shall meet once in every second calendar year in ordinary session upon convocation by the Director General and, in the absence of exceptional circumstances, during the same period and at the same place as the General Assembly of the Organization.

(b) The Assembly shall meet in extraordinary session upon convocation by the Director General, at the request of one-fourth of the countries members of the Assembly.

(c) The agenda of each session shall be prepared by the Director General.

(5) The Assembly shall adopt its own Rules of Procedure.

Article 8
International Bureau

(1)

(a) Administrative tasks concerning the Special Union shall be performed by the International Bureau.

(b) In particular, the International Bureau shall prepare the meetings and provide the secretariat of the Assembly, the Committee of Experts and such other committees or working groups as may have been established by the Assembly or the Committee of Experts.

(c) The Director General shall be the chief executive of the Special Union and shall represent the Special Union.

(2) The Director General and any staff member designated by him shall participate, without the right to vote, in all meetings of the Assembly, the Committee of Experts and such other committees or working groups as may have been established by the Assembly or the Committee of Experts. The Director General, or a staff member designated by him, shall be ex officio secretary of those bodies.

(3)

(a) The International Bureau shall, in accordance with the directions of the Assembly, make the preparations for revision conferences.

(b) The International Bureau may consult with intergovernmental and international non-governmental organizations concerning preparations for revision conferences.

(c) The Director General and persons designated by him shall take part, without the right to vote, in the discussions at revision conferences.

(4) The International Bureau shall carry out any other tasks assigned to it.

Article 9
Finances

(1)

(a) The Special Union shall have a budget.

(b) The budget of the Special Union shall include the income and expenses proper to the Special Union, its contribution to the budget of expenses common to the Unions and, where applicable, the sum made available to the budget of the Conference of the Organization.

(c) Expenses not attributable exclusively to the Special Union but also to one or more other Unions administered by the Organization shall be considered as expenses common to the Unions. The share of the Special Union in such common expenses shall be in proportion to the interest the Special Union has in them.

(2) The budget of the Special Union shall be established with due regard to the requirements of coordination with the budgets of the other Unions

administered by the Organization.

(3) The budget of the Special Union shall be financed from the following sources:

    (i)   contributions of the countries of the Special Union;

    (ii)   fees and charges due for services rendered by the International Bureau in relation to the Special Union;

    (iii)   sale of, or royalties on, the publications of the International Bureau concerning the Special Union;

    (iv)   gifts, bequests and subventions;

    (v)   rents, interests and other miscellaneous income.

(4)

(a) For the purpose of establishing its contribution referred to in paragraph (3)(i), each country of the Special Union shall belong to the same class as it belongs to in the Paris Union for the Protection of Industrial Property, and shall pay its annual contribution on the basis of the same number of units as is fixed for that class in that Union.

(b) The annual contribution of each country of the Special Union shall be an amount in the same proportion to the total sum to be contributed to the budget of the Special Union by all countries as the number of its units is to the total of the units of all contributing countries.

(c) Contributions shall become due on the first of January of each year.

(d) A country which is in arrears in the payment of its contributions may not exercise its right to vote in any organ of the Special Union if the amount of its arrears equals or exceeds the amount of the contributions due from it for the preceding two full years. However, any organ of the Special Union may allow such a country to continue to exercise its right to vote in that organ if, and as long as, it is satisfied that the delay in payment is due to exceptional and unavoidable circumstances.

(e) If the budget is not adopted before the beginning of a new financial period, it shall be at the same level as the budget of the previous year, as provided in the financial regulations.

(5) The amount of the fees and charges due for services rendered by the International Bureau in relation to the Special Union shall be established, and shall be reported to the Assembly, by the Director General.

(6)

(a) The Special Union shall have a working capital fund which shall be constituted by a single payment made by each country of the Special Union. If the fund becomes insufficient, the Assembly shall decide to increase it.

(b) The amount of the initial payment of each country to the said fund or of its participation in the increase thereof shall be a proportion of the contribution of that country for the year in which the fund is established or the decision to increase it is made.

(c) The proportion and the terms of payment shall be fixed by the

Assembly on the proposal of the Director General and after it has heard the advice of the Coordination Committee of the Organization.

(7)

(a) In the headquarters agreement concluded with the country on the territory of which the Organization has its headquarters, it shall be provided that, whenever the working capital fund is insufficient, such country shall grant advances. The amount of those advances and the conditions on which they are granted shall be the subject of separate agreements, in each case, between such country and the Organization.

(b) The country referred to in subparagraph (a) and the Organization shall each have the right to denounce the obligation to grant advances, by written notification. Denunciation shall take effect three years after the end of the year in which it was notified.

(8) The auditing of the accounts shall be effected by one or more of the countries of the Special Union or by external auditors, as provided in the financial regulations. They shall be designated, with their agreement, by the Assembly.

Article 10
Revision of the Agreement

(1) This Agreement may be revised from time to time by a special conference of the countries of the Special Union.

(2) The convocation of any revision conference shall be decided by the Assembly.

(3) Articles 7, 8, 9 and 11 may be amended either by a revision conference or according to the provisions of Article 11.

Article 11
Amendment of Certain Provisions of the Agreement

(1) Proposals for the amendment of Articles 7, 8, 9 and of the present Article may be initiated by any country of the Special Union or by the Director General. Such proposals shall be communicated by the Director General to the countries of the Special Union at least six months in advance of their consideration by the Assembly.

(2) Amendments to the Articles referred to in paragraph (1) shall be adopted by the Assembly. Adoption shall require three-fourths of the votes cast, provided that any amendment to Article 7 and to the present paragraph shall require four-fifths of the votes cast.

(3)

(a) Any amendment to the Articles referred to in paragraph (1) shall enter into force one month after written notifications of acceptance, effected in accordance with their respective constitutional processes, have been received by the Director General from three-fourths of the countries members of the Special Union at the time the amendment was adopted.

(b) Any amendment to the said Articles thus accepted shall bind all the countries which are members of the Special Union at the time the amendment enters into force, provided that any amendment increasing the financial obligations of countries of the Special Union shall bind only those countries which have notified their acceptance of such amendment.

(c) Any amendment accepted in accordance with the provisions of subparagraph (a) shall bind all countries which become members of the Special Union after the date on which the amendment entered into force in accordance with the provisions of subparagraph (a).

Article 12
Becoming Party to the Agreement

(1) Any country party to the Paris Convention for the Protection of Industrial Property may become party to this Agreement by:

(i)   signature followed by the deposit of an instrument of ratification, or

(ii)   deposit of an instrument of accession.

(2) Instruments of ratification or accession shall be deposited with the Director General.

(3) The provisions of Article 24 of the Stockholm Act of the Paris Convention for the Protection of Industrial Property shall apply to this Agreement.

(4) Paragraph (3) shall in no way be understood as implying the recognition or tacit acceptance, by a country of the Special Union, of the factual situation concerning a territory to which this Agreement is made applicable by another country by virtue of the said paragraph.

Article 13
Entry into Force of the Agreement

(1)

(a) This Agreement shall enter into force one year after instruments of ratification or accession have been deposited by:

(i)   two-thirds of the countries party to the European Convention on the date on which this Agreement is opened for signature, and

(ii)   three countries party to the Paris Convention for the Protection of Industrial Property, which were not previously party to the European Convention and of which at least one is a country where, according to the most recent annual statistics published by the International Bureau on the date of deposit of its instrument of ratification or accession, more than 40,000 applications for patents or inventors' certificates have been filed.

(b) With respect to any country other than those for which this Agreement has entered into force pursuant to subparagraph (a), it shall enter into force one year after the date on which the ratification or accession of that country was notified by the Director General, unless a subsequent date has been indicated in the instrument of ratification or accession. In the latter case, this Agreement shall enter into force with respect to that country on the date thus indicated.

(c) Countries party to the European Convention which ratify this Agreement or accede to it shall be obliged to denounce the said Convention, at the latest, with effect from the day on which this Agreement enters into force with respect to those countries.

(2) Ratification or accession shall automatically entail acceptance of all the clauses and admission to all the advantages of this Agreement.

Article 14
Duration of the Agreement

This Agreement shall have the same duration as the Paris Convention for the Protection of Industrial Property.

Article 15
Denunciation

(1) Any country of the Special Union may denounce this Agreement by notification addressed to the Director General.

(2) Denunciation shall take effect one year after the day on which the Director General has received the notification.

(3) The right of denunciation provided by this Article shall not be exercised by any country before the expiration of five years from the date upon which it becomes a member of the Special Union.

Article 16
Signature, Languages, Notification, Depositary Functions

(1)

(a) This Agreement shall be signed in a single original in the English and French languages, both texts being equally authentic.

(b) This Agreement shall remain open for signature at Strasbourg until September 30, 1971.

(c) The original of this Agreement, when no longer open for signature, shall be deposited with the Director General.

(2) Official texts shall be established by the Director General, after consultation with the interested Governments, in German, Japanese, Portuguese, Russian, Spanish and such other languages as the Assembly may designate.

(3)

(a) The Director General shall transmit two copies, certified by him, of the signed text of this Agreement to the Governments of the countries that have signed it and, on request, to the Government of any other country. He shall also transmit a copy, certified by him, to the Secretary General of the Council of Europe.

(b) The Director General shall transmit two copies, certified by him, of any amendment to this Agreement to the Governments of all countries of the Special Union and, on request, to the Government of any other country. He shall also transmit a copy, certified by him, to the Secretary General of the Council of Europe.

(c) The Director General shall, on request, furnish the Government of any country that has signed this Agreement, or that accedes to it, with a copy of the Classification, certified by him, in the English or French language.

(4) The Director General shall register this Agreement with the Secretariat of the United Nations.

(5) The Director General shall notify the Governments of all countries party to the Paris Convention for the Protection of Industrial Property and the Secretariat General of the Council of Europe of:

(i)   signatures;

(ii)   deposits of instruments of ratification or accession;

(iii)   the date of entry into force of this Agreement;

(iv)   reservations on the use of the Classification;

(v)   acceptances of amendments to this Agreement;

(vi)   the dates on which such amendments enter into force;

(vii)   denunciations received.

Article 17
Transitional Provisions

(1) During the two years following the entry into force of this Agreement, the countries party to the European Convention which are not yet members of the Special Union may enjoy, if they so wish, the same rights in the Committee of Experts as if they were members of the Special Union.

(2) During the three years following the expiration of the period referred to in paragraph (1), the countries referred to in the said paragraph may be represented by observers in the meetings of the Committee of Experts and, if the said Committee so decides, in any subcommittee or working group established by it. During the same period they may submit proposals for amendments to the Classification, in accordance with Article 5(5), and shall be notified of the decisions and recommendations of the Committee of Experts, in accordance with Article 6(1).

(3) During the five years following the entry into force of this Agreement, the countries party to the European Convention which are not yet members of the Special Union may be represented by observers in the meetings of the Assembly and, if the Assembly so decides, in any committee or working group established by it.

INTERNATIONAL CONVENTION FOR THE PROTECTION OF NEW VARIETIES OF PLANTS (UPOV 1978)

Done December 2, 1961, as revised at Geneva on November 10, 1972, and on October 23, 1978

THE CONTRACTING PARTIES,

Considering that the International Convention for the Protection of New Varieties of Plants of December 2, 1961, amended by the Additional Act of November 10, 1972, has proved a valuable instrument for international cooperation in the field of the protection of the rights of the breeders,

Reaffirming the principles contained in the Preamble to the Convention to the effect that:

(a) they are convinced of the importance attaching to the protection of new varieties of plants not only for the development of agriculture in their territory but also for safeguarding the interests of breeders,

(b) they are conscious of the special problems arising from the recognition and protection of the rights of breeders and particularly of the limitations that the requirements of the public interest may impose on the free exercise of such a right,

(c) they deem it highly desirable that these problems, to which very many States rightly attach importance, should be resolved by each of them in accordance with uniform and clearly defined principles,

Considering that the idea of protecting the rights of breeders has gained general acceptance in many States which have not yet acceded to the Convention,

Considering that certain amendments in the Convention are necessary in order to facilitate the joining of the Union by these States,

Considering that some provisions concerning the administration of the Union created by the Convention require amendment in the light of experience,

Considering that these objectives may be best achieved by a new revision of the Convention,

Have agreed as follows:

Article 1
Purpose of the Convention; Constitution of a Union;
Seat of the Union

(1) The purpose of this Convention is to recognise and to ensure to the breeder of a new plant variety or to his successor in title (both hereinafter referred to as "the breeder") a right under the conditions hereinafter defined.

(2) The States parties to this Convention (hereinafter referred to as "the member States of the Union") constitute a Union for the Protection of New Varieties of Plants.

(3) The seat of the Union and its permanent organs shall be at Geneva.

Article 2
Forms of Protection

(1) Each member State of the Union may recognise the right of the breeder provided for in this Convention by the grant either of a special title of protection or of a patent. Nevertheless, a member State of the Union whose national law admits of protection under both these forms may provide only one of them for one and the same botanical genus or species.

(2) Each member State of the Union may limit the application of this Convention within a genus or species to varieties with a particular manner of reproduction or multiplication, or a certain end-use.

Article 3
National Treatment; Reciprocity

(1) Without prejudice to the rights specially provided for in this Convention, natural and legal persons resident or having their registered office in one of the member States of the Union shall, in so far as the recognition and protection of the right of the breeder are concerned, enjoy in the other member States of the Union the same treatment as is accorded or may hereafter be accorded by the respective laws of such States to their own nationals, provided that such persons comply with the conditions and formalities imposed on such nationals.

(2) Nationals of member States of the Union not resident or having their registered office in one of those States shall likewise enjoy the same rights provided that they fulfil such obligations as may be imposed on them for the purpose of enabling the varieties which they have bred to be examined and the multiplication of such varieties to be checked.

(3) Notwithstanding the provisions of paragraph (1) and paragraph (2), any member State of the Union applying this Convention to a given genus or species shall be entitled to limit the benefit of the protection to the nationals of those member States of the Union which apply this Convention to that genus or species and to natural and legal persons resident or having their registered office in any of those States.

Article 4
Botanical Genera and Species Which Must
or May be Protected

(1) This Convention may be applied to all botanical genera and species.

(2) The member States of the Union undertake to adopt all measures necessary for the progressive application of the provisions of this Convention to the largest possible number of botanical genera and species.

(3) (a) Each member State of the Union shall, on the entry into force of this Convention in its territory, apply the provisions of this Convention to at least five genera or species.

(b) Subsequently, each member State of the Union shall apply the said provisions to additional genera or species within the following periods from the date of the entry into force of this Convention in its territory:

(i) within three years, to at least ten genera or species in all;

(ii) within six years, to at least eighteen genera or species in all;

(iii) within eight years, to at least twenty-four genera or species in all.

(c) If a member State of the Union has limited the application of this Convention within a genus or species in accordance with the provisions of Article 2(2), that genus or species shall nevertheless, for the purposes of subparagraph (a) and subparagraph (b), be considered as one genus or species.

(4) At the request of any State intending to ratify, accept, approve or accede to this Convention, the Council may, in order to take account of special economic or ecological conditions prevailing in that State, decide, for the purpose of that State, to reduce the minimum numbers referred to in paragraph (3), or to extend the periods referred to in that paragraph, or to do both.

(5) At the request of any member State of the Union, the Council may, in order to take account of special difficulties encountered by that State in the fulfilment of the obligations under paragraph (3)(b), decide, for the purposes of that State, to extend the periods referred to in paragraph (3)(b).

Article 5
Rights Protected; Scope of Protection

(1) The effect of the right granted to the breeder is that his prior authorisation shall be required for

- the production for purposes of commercial marketing
- the offering for sale
- the marketing

of the reproductive or vegetative propagating material, as such, of the variety.

Vegetative propagating material shall be deemed to include whole plants. The right of the breeder shall extend to ornamental plants or parts thereof normally marketed for purposes other than propagation when they are used commercially as propagating material in the production of ornamental plants or cut flowers.

(2) The authorisation given by the breeder may be made subject to such conditions as he may specify.

(3) Authorisation by the breeder shall not be required either for the utilisation of the variety as an initial source of variation for the purpose of creating other varieties or for the marketing of such varieties. Such authorisation shall be required, however, when the repeated use of the variety is necessary for the commercial production of another variety.

(4) Any member State of the Union may, either under its own law or by means of special agreements under Article 29, grant to breeders, in respect of certain botanical genera or species, a more extensive right than that set out in paragraph (1), extending in particular to the marketed product. A member State of the Union which grants such a right may limit the benefit of it to the nationals of member States of the Union which grant an identical right and to natural and legal persons resident or having their registered office in any of those States.

Article 6
Conditions Required for Protection

(1) The breeder shall benefit from the protection provided for in this Convention when the following conditions are satisfied:

(a) Whatever may be the origin, artificial or natural, of the initial variation from which it has resulted, the variety must be clearly distinguishable by one or more important characteristics from any other variety whose existence is a matter of common knowledge at the time when protection is applied for. Common knowledge may be established by reference to various factors such as: cultivation or marketing already in progress, entry in an official register of varieties already made or in the course of being made, inclusion in a reference collection, or precise description in a publication. The characteristics which permit a variety to be defined and distinguished must be capable of precise recognition and description.

(b) At the date on which the application for protection in a member State of the Union is filed, the variety

(i) must not or, where the law of that State so provides, must not for longer than one year have been offered for sale or marketed, with the agreement of the breeder, in the territory of that State, and

(ii) must not have been offered for sale or marketed, with the agreement of the breeder, in the territory of any other State for longer than six years in the case of vines, forest trees, fruit trees and ornamental trees, including, in each case, their rootstocks, or for longer than four years in the case of all other plants.

Trials of the variety not involving offering for sale or marketing shall not affect the right to protection. The fact that the variety has become a matter of common knowledge in ways other than through offering for sale or marketing shall also not affect the right of the breeder to protection.

(c) The variety must be sufficiently homogeneous, having regard to the particular features of its sexual reproduction or vegetative propagation.

(d) The variety must be stable in its essential characteristics, that is to say, it must remain true to its description after repeated reproduction or propagation or, where the breeder has defined a particular cycle of reproduction or multiplication, at the end of each cycle.

(e) The variety shall be given a denomination as provided in Article 13.

(2) Provided that the breeder shall have complied with the formalities provided for by the national law of the member State of the Union in which the application for protection was filed, including the payment of fees, the grant of protection may not be made subject to conditions other than those set forth above.

Article 7
Official Examination of Varieties; Provisional Protection

(1) Protection shall be granted after examination of the variety in the light of the criteria defined in Article 6. Such examination shall be appropriate to each botanical genus or species.

(2) For the purposes of such examination, the competent authorities of each member State of the Union may require the breeder to furnish all the necessary information, documents, propagating material or seeds.

(3) Any member State of the Union may provide measures to protect the breeder against abusive acts of third parties committed during the period between the filing of the application for protection and the decision thereon.

Article 8
Period of Protection

The right conferred on the breeder shall be granted for a limited period. This period may not be less than fifteen years, computed from the date of issue of the title of protection. For vines, forest trees, fruit trees and ornamental trees, including, in each case, their rootstocks, the period of protection may not be less than eighteen years, computed from the said date.

Article 9
Restrictions in the Exercise of Rights Protected

(1) The free exercise of the exclusive right accorded to the breeder may not be restricted otherwise than for reasons of public interest.

(2) When any such restriction is made in order to ensure the widespread distribution of the variety, the member State of the Union concerned shall take all measures necessary to ensure that the breeder receives equitable remuneration.

Article 10
Nullity and Forfeiture of the Rights Protected

(1) The right of the breeder shall be declared null and void, in accordance with the provisions of the national law of each member State of the Union, if it is established that the conditions laid down in Article 6(1)(a) and Article 6(1)(b) were not effectively complied with at the time when the title of protection was issued.

(2) The right of the breeder shall become forfeit when he is no longer in a position to provide the competent authority with reproductive or propagating material capable of producing the variety with its characteristics

as defined when the protection was granted.

(3) The right of the breeder may become forfeit if:

(a) after being requested to do so and within a prescribed period, he does not provide the competent authority with the reproductive or propagating material, the documents and the information deemed necessary for checking the variety, or he does not allow inspection of the measures which have been taken for the maintenance of the variety; or

(b) he has failed to pay within the prescribed period such fees as may be payable to keep his rights in force.

(4) The right of the breeder may not be annulled or become forfeit except on the grounds set out in this Article.

Article 11
Free Choice of the Member State in Which the First Application is Filed; Application in Other Member States; Independence of Protection in Different Member States

(1) The breeder may choose the member State of the Union in which he wishes to file his first application for protection.

(2) The breeder may apply to other member States of the Union for protection of his right without waiting for the issue to him of a title of protection by the member State of the Union in which he filed his first application.

(3) The protection applied for in different member States of the Union by natural or legal persons entitled to benefit under this Convention shall be independent of the protection obtained for the same variety in other States whether or not such States are members of the Union.

Article 12
Right of Priority

(1) Any breeder who has duly filed an application for protection in one of the member States of the Union shall, for the purpose of filing in the other member States of the Union, enjoy a right of priority for a period of twelve months. This period shall be computed from the date of filing of the first application. The day of filing shall not be included in such period.

(2) To benefit from the provisions of paragraph (1), the further filing must include an application for protection, a claim in respect of the priority of the first application and, within a period of three months, a copy of the documents which constitute that application, certified to be a true copy by the authority which received it.

(3) The breeder shall be allowed a period of four years after the expiration of the period of priority in which to furnish, to the member State of the Union with which he has filed an application for protection in accordance with the terms of paragraph (2), the additional documents and material required by the laws and regulations of that State. Nevertheless, that State may require the additional documents and material to be furnished within an adequate

period in the case where the application whose priority is claimed is rejected or withdrawn.

(4) Such matters as the filing of another application of the publication or use of the subject of the application, occurring within the period provided for in paragraph (1), shall not constitute grounds for objection to an application filed in accordance with the foregoing conditions. Such matters may not give rise to any right in favour of a third party or to any right of personal possession.

Article 13
Variety Denomination

(1) The variety shall be designated by a denomination destined to be its generic designation. Each member State of the Union shall ensure that subject to paragraph (4) no rights in the designation registered as the denomination of the variety shall hamper the free use of the denomination in connection with the variety, even after the expiration of the protection.

(2) The denomination must enable the variety to be identified. It may not consist solely of figures except where this is an established practice for designating varieties. It must not be liable to mislead or to cause confusion concerning the characteristics, value or identity of the variety or the identity of the breeder. In particular, it must be different from every denomination which designates, in any member State of the Union, an existing variety of the same botanical species or of a closely related species.

(3) The denomination of the variety shall be submitted by the breeder to the authority referred to in Article 30(1)(b). If it is found that such denomination does not satisfy the requirements of paragraph (2), that authority shall refuse to register it and shall require the breeder to propose another denomination within a prescribed period. The denomination shall be registered at the same time as the title of protection is issued in accordance with the provisions of Article 7.

(4) Prior rights of third parties shall not be affected. If, by reason of a prior right, the use of the denomination of a variety is forbidden to a person who, in accordance with the provisions of paragraph (7), is obliged to use it, the authority referred to in Article 30(1)(b) shall require the breeder to submit another denomination for the variety.

(5) A variety must be submitted in member States of the Union under the same denomination. The authority referred to in Article 30(1)(b) shall register the denomination so submitted, unless it considers that denomination unsuitable in its State. In the latter case, it may require the breeder to submit another denomination.

(6) The authority referred to in Article 30(1)(b) shall ensure that all the other such authorities are informed of matters concerning variety denominations, in particular the submission, registration and cancellation of denominations. Any authority referred to in Article 30(1)(b) may address its observations, if any, on the registration of a denomination to the authority which communicated that denomination.

(7) Any person who, in a member State of the Union, offers for sale or markets reproductive or vegetative propagating material of a variety protected in that State shall be obliged to use the denomination of that variety, even after the expiration of the protection of that variety, in so far as, in accordance with the provisions of paragraph (4), prior rights do not prevent such use.

(8) When the variety is offered for sale or marketed, it shall be permitted to associate a trade mark, trade name or other similar identification with a registered variety denomination. If such an indication is so associated, the denomination must nevertheless be easily recognizable.

Article 14
Protection Independent of Measures Regulating Production, Certification and Marketing

(1) The right accorded to the breeder in pursuance of the provisions of this Convention shall be independent of the measures taken by each member State of the Union to regulate the production, certification and marketing of seeds and propagating material.

(2) However, such measures shall, as far as possible, avoid hindering the application of the provisions of this Convention.

Article 15
Organs of the Union

The permanent organs of the Union shall be:

(a) the Council;

(b) the Secretariat General, entitled the Office of the International Union for the Protection of New Varieties of Plants.

Article 16
Composition of the Council; Votes

(1) The Council shall consist of the representatives of the member States of the Union. Each member State of the Union shall appoint one representative to the Council and one alternate.

(2) Representatives or alternates may be accompanied by assistants or advisers.

(3) Each member State of the Union shall have one vote in the Council.

Article 17
Observers in Meetings of the Council

(1) States not members of the Union which have signed this Act shall be invited as observers to meetings of the Council.

(2) Other observers or experts may also be invited to such meetings.

Article 18
President and Vice-Presidents of the Council

(1) The Council shall elect a President and a first Vice-President from among its members. It may elect other Vice-Presidents. The first Vice-President shall take the place of the President if the latter is unable to officiate.

(2) The President shall hold office for three years.

Article 19
Sessions of the Council

(1) The Council shall meet upon convocation by its President.

(2) An ordinary session of the Council shall be held annually. In addition, the President may convene the Council at his discretion; he shall convene it, within a period of three months, if one-third of the member States of the Union so request.

Article 20
Rules of Procedure of the Council; Administrative and Financial Regulations of the Union

The Council shall establish its rules of procedure and the administrative and financial regulations of the Union.

Article 21
Tasks of the Council

The tasks of the Council shall be to:

(a) study appropriate measures to safeguard the interests and to encourage the development of the Union;

(b) appoint the Secretary-General and, if it finds it necessary, a Vice Secretary-General and determine the terms of appointment of each;

(c) examine the annual report on the activities of the Union and lay down the programme for its future work;

(d) give to the Secretary-General, whose functions are set out in Article 23, all necessary directions for the accomplishment of the tasks of the Union;

(e) examine and approve the budget of the Union and fix the contribution of each member State of the Union in accordance with the provisions of Article 26;

(f) examine and approve the accounts presented by the Secretary-General;

(g) fix, in accordance with the provisions of Article 27, the date and place of the conferences referred to in that Article and take the measures necessary for their preparation; and

(h) in general, take all necessary decisions to ensure the efficient functioning of the Union.

Article 22
Majorities Required for Decisions of the Council

Any decision of the Council shall require a simple majority of the votes of the members present and voting, provided that any decision of the Council under Article 4(4), Article 20, Article 21(e), Article 26(5)(b), Article 27(1), Article 28(3) or Article 32(3) shall require three-fourths of the votes of the members present and voting. Abstentions shall not be considered as votes.

Article 23
Tasks of the Office of the Union; Responsibilities of the Secretary-General; Appointment of Staff

(1) The Office of the Union shall carry out all the duties and tasks entrusted to it by the Council. It shall be under the direction of the Secretary-General.

(2) The Secretary-General shall be responsible to the Council; he shall be responsible for carrying out the decisions of the Council. He shall submit the budget for the approval of the Council and shall be responsible for its implementation. He shall make an annual report to the Council on his administration and a report on the activities and financial position of the Union.

(3) Subject to the provisions of Article 21(b), the conditions of appointment and employment of the staff necessary for the efficient performance of the tasks of the Office of the Union shall be fixed in the administrative and financial regulations referred to in Article 20.

Article 24
Legal Status

(1) The Union shall have legal personality.

(2) The Union shall enjoy on the territory of each member State of the Union, in conformity with the laws of that State, such legal capacity as may be necessary for the fulfilment of the objectives of the Union and for the exercise of its functions.

(3) The Union shall conclude a headquarters agreement with the Swiss Confederation.

Article 25
Auditing of the Accounts

The auditing of the accounts of the Union shall be effected by a member State of the Union as provided in the administrative and financial regulations referred to in Article 20. Such State shall be designated, with its agreement, by the Council.

Article 26
Finances

(1) The expenses of the Union shall be met from:

— the annual contributions of the member States of the Union;

— payments received for services rendered;

— miscellaneous receipts.

(2) (a) The share of each member State of the Union in the total amount of the annual contributions shall be determined by reference to the total expenditure to be met from the contributions of the member States of the Union and to the number of contribution units applicable to it under paragraph (3). The said share shall be computed according to paragraph (4).

(b) The number of contribution units shall be expressed in whole numbers or fractions thereof, provided that such number shall not be less than one-fifth.

(3) (a) As far as any State is concerned which is a member State of the Union on the date on which this Act enters into force with respect to that State, the number of contribution units applicable to it shall be the same as was applicable to it, immediately before the said date, according to the Convention of 1961 as amended by the Additional Act of 1972.

(b) As far as any other State is concerned, that State shall, on joining the Union, indicate, in a declaration addressed to the Secretary-General, the number of contribution units applicable to it.

(c) Any member State of the Union may, at any time, indicate, in a declaration addressed to the Secretary-General, a number of contribution units different from the number applicable to it under subparagraph (a) or subparagraph (b). Such declaration, if made during the first six months of a calendar year, shall take effect from the beginning of the subsequent calendar year; otherwise it shall take effect from the beginning of the second calendar year which follows the year in which the declaration was made.

(4) (a) For each budgetary period, the amount corresponding to one contribution unit shall be obtained by dividing the total amount of the expenditure to be met in that period from the contributions of the member States of the Union by the total number of units applicable to those States.

(b) The amount of the contribution of each member State of the Union shall be obtained by multiplying the amount corresponding to one contribution unit by the number of contribution units applicable to that State.

(5) (a) A member State of the Union which is in arrears in the payment of its contributions may not, subject to paragraph (b), exercise its right to vote in the Council if the amount of its arrears equals or exceeds the amount of the contributions due from it for the preceding two full years. The suspension of the right to vote does not relieve such State of its obligations under this Convention and does not deprive it of any other rights thereunder.

(b) The Council may allow the said State to continue to exercise its right to vote if, and as long as, the Council is satisfied that the delay in payment is due to exceptional and unavoidable circumstances.

Article 27
Revision of the Convention

(1) This Convention may be revised by a conference of the member States of the Union. The convocation of such conference shall be decided by the Council.

(2) The proceedings of a conference shall be effective only if at least half of the member States of the Union are represented at it. A majority of five-sixths of the member States of the Union represented at the conference shall be required for the adoption of a revised text of the Convention.

Article 28
Languages Used by the Office and in Meetings of the Council

(1) The English, French and German languages shall be used by the Office of the Union in carrying out its duties.

(2) Meetings of the Council and of revision conferences shall be held in the three languages.

(3) If the need arises, the Council may decide that further languages shall be used.

Article 29
Special Agreements for the Protection of New Varieties of Plants

Member States of the Union reserve the right to conclude among themselves special agreements for the protection of new varieties of plants, in so far as such agreements do not contravene the provisions of this Convention.

Article 30
Implementation of the Convention on the Domestic Level; Contracts on the Joint Utilisation of Examination Services

(1) Each member State of the Union shall adopt all measures necessary for the application of this Convention; in particular, it shall:

(a) provide for appropriate legal remedies for the effective defence of the rights provided for in this Convention;

(b) set up a special authority for the protection of new varieties of plants or entrust such protection to an existing authority;

(c) ensure that the public is informed of matters concerning such protection, including as a minimum the periodical publication of the list of titles of protection issued.

(2) Contracts may be concluded between the competent authorities of the member States of the Union, with a view to the joint utilisation of the

services of the authorities entrusted with the examination of varieties in accordance with the provisions of Article 7 and with assembling the necessary reference collections and documents.

(3) It shall be understood that, on depositing its instrument of ratification, acceptance, approval or accession, each State must be in a position, under its own domestic law, to give effect to the provisions of this Convention.

Article 31
Signature

This Act shall be open for signature by any member State of the Union and any other State which was represented in the Diplomatic Conference adopting this Act. It shall remain open for signature until October 31, 1979.

Article 32
Ratification, Acceptance or Approval; Accession

(1) Any State shall express its consent to be bound by this Act by the deposit of:

(a) its instrument of ratification, acceptance or approval, if it has signed this Act; or

(b) its instrument of accession, if it has not signed this Act.

(2) Instruments of ratification, acceptance, approval or accession shall be deposited with the Secretary-General.

(3) Any State which is not a member of the Union and which has not signed this Act shall, before depositing its instrument of accession, ask the Council to advise it in respect of the conformity of its laws with the provisions of this Act. If the decision embodying the advice is positive, the instrument of accession may be deposited.

Article 33
Entry into Force; Closing of Earlier Texts

(1) This Act shall enter into force one month after the following two conditions are fulfilled:

(a) the number of instruments of ratification, acceptance, approval or accession deposited is not less than five; and

(b) at least three of the said instruments are instruments deposited by States parties to the Convention of 1961.

(2) With respect to any State which deposits its instrument of ratification, acceptance, approval or accession after the conditions referred to in paragraph (1)(a) and paragraph (1)(b) have been fulfilled, this Act shall enter into force one month after the deposit of the instrument of the said State.

(3) Once this Act enters into force according to paragraph (1), no State may accede to the Convention of 1961 as amended by the Additional Act of 1972.

Article 34
Relations Between States Bound by Different Texts

(1) Any member State of the Union which, on the day on which this Act enters into force with respect to that State, is bound by the Convention of 1961 as amended by the Additional Act of 1972 shall, in its relations with any other member State of the Union which is not bound by this Act, continue to apply, until the present Act enters into force also with respect to that other State, the said Convention as amended by the said Additional Act.

(2) Any member State of the Union not bound by this Act ("the former State") may declare, in a notification addressed to the Secretary-General, that it will apply the Convention of 1961 as amended by the Additional Act of 1972 in its relations with any State bound by this Act which becomes a member of the Union through ratification, acceptance or approval of or accession to this Act ("the latter State"). As from the beginning of one month after the date of any such notification and until the entry into force of this Act with respect to the former State, the former State shall apply the Convention of 1961 as amended by the Additional Act of 1972 in its relations with any such latter State, whereas any such latter State shall apply this Act in its relations with the former State.

Article 35
Communications Concerning the Genera and Species Protected; Information to be Published

(1) When depositing its instrument of ratification, acceptance or approval of or accession to this Act, each State which is not a member of the Union shall notify the Secretary-General of the list of genera and species to which, on the entry into force of this Act with respect to that State, it will apply the provisions of this Convention.

(2) The Secretary-General shall, on the basis of communications received from each member State of the Union concerned, publish information on:

(a) the extension of the application of the provisions of this Convention to additional genera and species after the entry into force of this Act with respect to that State;

(b) any use of the faculty provided for in Article 3(3);

(c) the use of any faculty granted by the Council pursuant to Article 4(4) or Article 4(5);

(d) any use of the faculty provided for in Article 5(4), first sentence, with an indication of the nature of the more extensive rights and with a specification of the genera and species to which such rights apply;

(e) any use of the faculty provided for in Article 5(4), second sentence;

(f) the fact that the law of the said State contains a provision as permitted under Article 6(1)(b)(i), and the length of the period permitted;

(g) the length of the period referred to in Article 8 if such period is longer than the fifteen years and the eighteen years, respectively, referred to in that Article.

Article 36
Territories

(1) Any State may declare in its instrument of ratification, acceptance, approval or accession, or may inform the Secretary-General by written notification any time thereafter, that this Act shall be applicable to all or part of the territories designated in the declaration or notification.

(2) Any State which has made such a declaration or given such a notification may, at any time, notify the Secretary-General that this Act shall cease to be applicable to all or part of such territories.

(3) (a) Any declaration made under paragraph (1) shall take effect on the same date as the ratification, acceptance, approval or accession in the instrument of which it was included, and any notification given under that paragraph shall take effect three months after its notification by the Secretary-General.

(b) Any notification given under paragraph (2) shall take effect twelve months after its receipt by the Secretary-General.

Article 37
Exceptional Rules for Protection Under Two Forms

(1) Notwithstanding the provisions of Article 2(1), any State which, prior to the end of the period during which this Act is open for signature, provides for protection under the different forms referred to in Article 2(1) for one and the same genus or species, may continue to do so if, at the time of signing this Act or of depositing its instrument of ratification, acceptance or approval of or accession to this Act, it notifies the Secretary-General of that fact.

(2) Where, in a member State of the Union to which paragraph (1) applies, protection is sought under patent legislation, the said State may apply the patentability criteria and the period of protection of the patent legislation to the varieties protected thereunder, notwithstanding the provisions of Article 6(1)(a), Article 6(1)(b) and Article 8.

(3) The said State may, at any time, notify the Secretary-General of the withdrawal of the notification it has given under paragraph (1). Such withdrawal shall take effect on the date which the State shall indicate in its notification of withdrawal.

Article 38
Transitional Limitation of the Requirement of Novelty

Notwithstanding the provisions of Article 6, any member State of the Union may, without thereby creating an obligation for other member States of the Union, limit the requirement of novelty laid down in that Article, with regard to varieties of recent creation existing at the date on which such State applies the provisions of this Convention for the first time to the genus or species to which such varieties belong.

Article 39
Preservation of Existing Rights

This Convention shall not affect existing rights under the national laws of member States of the Union or under agreements concluded between such States.

Article 40
Reservations

No reservations to this Convention are permitted.

Article 41
Duration and Denunciation of the Convention

(1) This Convention is of unlimited duration.

(2) Any member State of the Union may denounce this Convention by notification addressed to the Secretary-General. The Secretary-General shall promptly notify all member States of the Union of the receipt of that notification.

(3) The denunciation shall take effect at the end of the calendar year following the year in which the notification was received by the Secretary-General.

(4) The denunciation shall not affect any rights acquired in a variety by reason of this Convention prior to the date on which the denunciation becomes effective.

Article 42
Languages; Depositary Functions

(1) This Act shall be signed in a single original in the French, English and German languages, the French text prevailing in case of any discrepancy among the various texts. The original shall be deposited with the Secretary-General.

(2) The Secretary-General shall transmit two certified copies of this Act to the Governments of all States which were represented in the Diplomatic Conference that adopted it and, on request, to the Government of any other State.

(3) The Secretary-General shall, after consultation with the Governments of the interested States which were represented in the said Conference, establish official texts in the Arabic, Dutch, Italian, Japanese and Spanish languages and such other languages as the Council may designate.

(4) The Secretary-General shall register this Act with the Secretariat of the United Nations.

(5) The Secretary-General shall notify the Governments of the member States of the Union and of the States which, without being members of the Union, were represented in the Diplomatic Conference that adopted it of the

signatures of this Act, the deposit of instruments of ratification, acceptance, approval and accession, any notification received under Article 34(2), Article 36(1), Article 37(1) and Article 37(3) or Article 41(2) and any declaration made under Article 36(1).

INTERNATIONAL CONVENTION FOR THE PROTECTION OF NEW VARIETIES OF PLANTS (UPOV 1991)

of December 2, 1961, as Revised at Geneva on November 10, 1972, on October 23, 1978, and on March 19, 1991

CHAPTER I
DEFINITIONS

Article 1
Definitions

For the purposes of this Act:

(i)   "this Convention" means the present (1991) Act of the International Convention for the Protection of New Varieties of Plants;

(ii)   "Act of 1961/1972" means the International Convention for the Protection of New Varieties of Plants of December 2, 1961, as amended by the Additional Act of November 10, 1972;

(iii) "Act of 1978" means the Act of October 23, 1978, of the International Convention for the Protection of New Varieties of Plants;

(iv) "breeder" means

- the person who bred, or discovered and developed, a variety,

- the person who is the employer of the aforementioned person or who has commissioned the latter's work, where the laws of the relevant Contracting Party so provide, or

- the successor in title of the first or second aforementioned person, as the case may be;

(v) "breeder's right" means the right of the breeder provided for in this Convention;

(vi) "variety" means a plant grouping within a single botanical taxon of the lowest known rank, which grouping, irrespective of whether the conditions for the grant of a breeder's right are fully met, can be

- defined by the expression of the characteristics resulting from a given genotype or combination of genotypes,

- distinguished from any other plant grouping by the expression of at least one of the said characteristics and

- considered as a unit with regard to its suitability for being propagated unchanged;

(vii) "Contracting Party" means a State or an intergovernmental organization party to this Convention;

(viii) "territory," in relation to a Contracting Party, means, where the Contracting Party is a State, the territory of that State and, where the Contracting Party is an intergovernmental organization, the territory in which the constituting treaty of that intergovernmental organization applies;

(ix) "authority" means the authority referred to in Article 30(1)(ii);

(x) "Union" means the Union for the Protection of New Varieties of Plants founded by the Act of 1961 and further mentioned in the Act of 1972, the Act of 1978 and in this Convention;

(xi) "member of the Union" means a State party to the Act of 1961/1972 or the Act of 1978, or a Contracting Party.

CHAPTER II
GENERAL OBLIGATIONS OF THE CONTRACTING PARTIES

Article 2
Basic Obligation of the Contracting Parties

Each Contracting Party shall grant and protect breeders' rights.

Article 3
Genera and Species to be Protected

(1) [*States already members of the Union*] Each Contracting Party which is bound by the Act of 1961/1972 or the Act of 1978 shall apply the provisions of this Convention,

(i) at the date on which it becomes bound by this Convention, to all plant genera and species to which it applies, on the said date, the provisions of the Act of 1961/1972 or the Act of 1978 and,

(ii) at the latest by the expiration of a period of five years after the said date, to all plant genera and species.

(2) [*New members of the Union*] Each Contracting Party which is not bound by the Act of 1961/1972 or the Act of 1978 shall apply the provisions of this Convention,

(i) at the date on which it becomes bound by this Convention, to at least 15 plant genera or species and,

(ii) at the latest by the expiration of a period of 10 years from the said date, to all plant genera and species.

Article 4
National Treatment

(1) [*Treatment*] Without prejudice to the rights specified in this Convention, nationals of a Contracting Party as well as natural persons resident and legal entities having their registered offices within the territory of a Contracting Party shall, insofar as the grant and protection of breeders' rights are concerned, enjoy within the territory of each other Contracting Party the same treatment as is accorded or may hereafter be accorded by the laws of each such other Contracting Party to its own nationals, provided that the said nationals, natural persons or legal entities comply with the conditions and formalities imposed on the nationals of the said other Contracting Party.

(2) [*"Nationals"*] For the purposes of the preceding paragraph, "nationals"

means, where the Contracting Party is a State, the nationals of that State and, where the Contracting Party is an intergovernmental organization, the nationals of the States which are members of that organization.

CHAPTER III
CONDITIONS FOR THE GRANT OF THE BREEDER'S RIGHT

Article 5
Conditions of Protection

(1) [*Criteria to be satisfied*] The breeder's right shall be granted where the variety is

(i) new,

(ii) distinct,

(iii) uniform and

(iv) stable.

(2) [*Other conditions*] The grant of the breeder's right shall not be subject to any further or different conditions, provided that the variety is designated by a denomination in accordance with the provisions of Article 20, that the applicant complies with the formalities provided for by the law of the Contracting Party with whose authority the application has been filed and that he pays the required fees.

Article 6
Novelty

(1) [*Criteria*] The variety shall be deemed to be new if, at the date of filing of the application for a breeder's right, propagating or harvested material of the variety has not been sold or otherwise disposed of to others, by or with the consent of the breeder, for purposes of exploitation of the variety

(i) in the territory of the Contracting Party in which the application has been filed earlier than one year before that date and

(ii) in a territory other than that of the Contracting Party in which the application has been filed earlier than four years or, in the case of trees or of vines, earlier than six years before the said date.

(2) [*Varieties of recent creation*] Where a Contracting Party applies this Convention to a plant genus or species to which it did not previously apply this Convention or an earlier Act, it may consider a variety of recent creation existing at the date of such extension of protection to satisfy the condition of novelty defined in paragraph (1) even where the sale or disposal to others described in that paragraph took place earlier than the time limits defined in that paragraph.

(3) [*"Territory" in certain cases*] For the purposes of paragraph (1), all the Contracting Parties which are member States of one and the same intergovernmental organization may act jointly, where the regulations of that organization so require, to assimilate acts done on the territories of the

States members of that organization to acts done on their own territories and, should they do so, shall notify the Secretary-General accordingly.

Article 7
Distinctness

The variety shall be deemed to be distinct if it is clearly distinguishable from any other variety whose existence is a matter of common knowledge at the time of the filing of the application. In particular, the filing of an application for the granting of a breeder's right or for the entering of another variety in an official register of varieties, in any country, shall be deemed to render that other variety a matter of common knowledge from the date of the application, provided that the application leads to the granting of a breeder's right or to the entering of the said other variety in the official register of varieties, as the case may be.

Article 8
Uniformity

The variety shall be deemed to be uniform if, subject to the variation that may be expected from the particular features of its propagation, it is sufficiently uniform in its relevant characteristics.

Article 9
Stability

The variety shall be deemed to be stable if its relevant characteristics remain unchanged after repeated propagation or, in the case of a particular cycle of propagation, at the end of each such cycle.

CHAPTER IV
APPLICATION FOR THE GRANT OF THE BREEDER'S RIGHT

Article 10
Filing of Applications

(1) [*Place of first application*] The breeder may choose the Contracting Party with whose authority he wishes to file his first application for a breeder's right.

(2) [*Time of subsequent applications*] The breeder may apply to the authorities of other Contracting Parties for the grant of breeders' rights without waiting for the grant to him of a breeder's right by the authority of the Contracting Party with which the first application was filed.

(3) [*Independence of protection*] No Contracting Party shall refuse to grant a breeder's right or limit its duration on the ground that protection for the same variety has not been applied for, has been refused or has expired in any other State or intergovernmental organization.

Article 11
Right of Priority

(1) [*The right; its period*] Any breeder who has duly filed an application for the protection of a variety in one of the Contracting Parties (the "first application") shall, for the purpose of filing an application for the grant of a breeder's right for the same variety with the authority of any other Contracting Party (the "subsequent application"), enjoy a right of priority for a period of twelve months. This period shall be computed from the date of filing of the first application. The day of filing shall not be included in the latter period.

(2) [*Claiming the right*] In order to benefit from the right of priority, the breeder shall, in the subsequent application, claim the priority of the first application. The authority with which the subsequent application has been filed may require the breeder to furnish, within a period of not less than three months from the filing date of the subsequent application, a copy of the documents which constitute the first application, certified to be a true copy by the authority with which that application was filed, and samples or other evidence that the variety which is the subject matter of both applications is the same.

(3) [*Documents and material*] The breeder shall be allowed a period of two years after the expiration of the period of priority or, where the first application is rejected or withdrawn, an appropriate time after such rejection or withdrawal, in which to furnish, to the authority of the Contracting Party with which he has filed the subsequent application, any necessary information, document or material required for the purpose of the examination under Article 12, as required by the laws of that Contracting Party.

(4) [*Events occurring during the period*] Events occurring within the period provided for in paragraph (1), such as the filing of another application or the publication or use of the variety that is the subject of the first application, shall not constitute a ground for rejecting the subsequent application. Such events shall also not give rise to any third-party right.

Article 12
Examination of the Application

Any decision to grant a breeder's right shall require an examination for compliance with the conditions under Article 5 to Article 9. In the course of the examination, the authority may grow the variety or carry out other necessary tests, cause the growing of the variety or the carrying out of other necessary tests, or take into account the results of growing tests or other trials which have already been carried out. For the purposes of examination, the authority may require the breeder to furnish all the necessary information, documents or material.

Article 13
Provisional Protection

Each Contracting Party shall provide measures designed to safeguard the interests of the breeder during the period between the filing or the publication of the application for the grant of a breeder's right and the grant of that right. Such measures shall have the effect that the holder of a breeder's right shall at least be entitled to equitable remuneration from any person who, during the said period, has carried out acts which, once the right is granted, require the breeder's authorization as provided in Article 14. A Contracting Party may provide that the said measures shall only take effect in relation to persons whom the breeder has notified of the filing of the application.

CHAPTER V
THE RIGHTS OF THE BREEDER

Article 14
Scope of the Breeder's Right

(1) [*Acts in respect of the propagating material*] (a) Subject to Article 15 and Article 16, the following acts in respect of the propagating material of the protected variety shall require the authorization of the breeder:

(i) production or reproduction (multiplication),

(ii) conditioning for the purpose of propagation,

(iii) offering for sale,

(iv) selling or other marketing,

(v) exporting,

(vi) importing,

(vii) stocking for any of the purposes mentioned in (i) to (vi), above.

(b) The breeder may make his authorization subject to conditions and limitations.

(2) [*Acts in respect of the harvested material*] Subject to Article 15 and Article 16, the acts referred to in items paragraph (1)(a)(i) to paragraph (1)(a)(vii) in respect of harvested material, including entire plants and parts of plants, obtained through the unauthorized use of propagating material of the protected variety shall require the authorization of the breeder, unless the breeder has had reasonable opportunity to exercise his right in relation to the said propagating material.

(3) [*Acts in respect of certain products*] Each Contracting Party may provide that, subject to Article 15 and Article 16, the acts referred to in items paragraph (1)(a)(i) to paragraph (1)(a)(vii) in respect of products made directly from harvested material of the protected variety falling within the provisions of paragraph (2) through the unauthorized use of the said harvested material shall require the authorization of the breeder, unless the breeder has had reasonable opportunity to exercise his right in relation to

the said harvested material.

(4) [*Possible additional acts*] Each Contracting Party may provide that, subject to Article 15 and Article 16, acts other than those referred to in items paragraph (1)(a)(i) to paragraph (1)(a)(vii) shall also require the authorization of the breeder.

(5) [*Essentially derived and certain other varieties*] (a) The provisions of paragraph (1) to paragraph (4) shall also apply in relation to

(i) varieties which are essentially derived from the protected variety, where the protected variety is not itself an essentially derived variety,

(ii) varieties which are not clearly distinguishable in accordance with Article 7 from the protected variety and

(iii) varieties whose production requires the repeated use of the protected variety.

(b) For the purposes of subparagraph (a)(i), a variety shall be deemed to be essentially derived from another variety ("the initial variety") when

(i) it is predominantly derived from the initial variety, or from a variety that is itself predominantly derived from the initial variety, while retaining the expression of the essential characteristics that result from the genotype or combination of genotypes of the initial variety,

(ii) it is clearly distinguishable from the initial variety and

(iii) except for the differences which result from the act of derivation, it conforms to the initial variety in the expression of the essential characteristics that result from the genotype or combination of genotypes of the initial variety.

(c) Essentially derived varieties may be obtained for example by the selection of a natural or induced mutant, or of a somaclonal variant, the selection of a variant individual from plants of the initial variety, backcrossing, or transformation by genetic engineering.

Article 15
Exceptions to the Breeder's Right

(1) [*Compulsory exceptions*] The breeder's right shall not extend to

(i) acts done privately and for non-commercial purposes,

(ii) acts done for experimental purposes and

(iii) acts done for the purpose of breeding other varieties, and, except where the provisions of Article 14(5) apply, acts referred to in Article 14(1) to Article 14(4) in respect of such other varieties.

(2) [*Optional exception*] Notwithstanding Article 14, each Contracting Party may, within reasonable limits and subject to the safeguarding of the legitimate interests of the breeder, restrict the breeder's right in relation to any variety in order to permit farmers to use for propagating purposes, on their own holdings, the product of the harvest which they have obtained by planting, on their own holdings, the protected variety or a variety covered by Article 14(5)(a)(i) or Article 14(5)(a)(ii).

Article 16
Exhaustion of the Breeder's Right

(1) [*Exhaustion of right*] The breeder's right shall not extend to acts concerning any material of the protected variety, or of a variety covered by the provisions of Article 14(5), which has been sold or otherwise marketed by the breeder or with his consent in the territory of the Contracting Party concerned, or any material derived from the said material, unless such acts

(i) involve further propagation of the variety in question or

(ii) involve an export of material of the variety, which enables the propagation of the variety, into a country which does not protect varieties of the plant genus or species to which the variety belongs, except where the exported material is for final consumption purposes.

(2) [*Meaning of "material"*] For the purposes of paragraph (1), "material" means, in relation to a variety,

(i) propagating material of any kind,

(ii) harvested material, including entire plants and parts of plants, and

(iii) any product made directly from the harvested material.

(3)[*"Territory" in certain cases*] For the purposes of paragraph (1), all the Contracting Parties which are member States of one and the same intergovernmental organization may act jointly, where the regulations of that organization so require, to assimilate acts done on the territories of the States members of that organization to acts done on their own territories and, should they do so, shall notify the Secretary-General accordingly.

Article 17
Restrictions on the Exercise of the Breeder's Right

(1) [*Public interest*] Except where expressly provided in this Convention, no Contracting Party may restrict the free exercise of a breeder's right for reasons other than of public interest.

(2) [*Equitable remuneration*] When any such restriction has the effect of authorizing a third party to perform any act for which the breeder's authorization is required, the Contracting Party concerned shall take all measures necessary to ensure that the breeder receives equitable remuneration.

Article 18
Measures Regulating Commerce

The breeder's right shall be independent of any measure taken by a Contracting Party to regulate within its territory the production, certification and marketing of material of varieties or the importing or exporting of such material. In any case, such measures shall not affect the application of the provisions of this Convention.

Article 19
Duration of the Breeder's Right

(1) [*Period of protection*] The breeder's right shall be granted for a fixed period.

(2) [*Minimum period*] The said period shall not be shorter than 20 years from the date of the grant of the breeder's right. For trees and vines, the said period shall not be shorter than 25 years from the said date.

CHAPTER VI
VARIETY DENOMINATION

Article 20
Variety Denomination

(1) [*Designation of varieties by denominations; use of the denomination*] (a)

The variety shall be designated by a denomination which will be its generic designation.

(b) Each Contracting Party shall ensure that, subject to paragraph (4), no rights in the designation registered as the denomination of the variety shall hamper the free use of the denomination in connection with the variety, even after the expiration of the breeder's right.

(2) [*Characteristics of the denomination*] The denomination must enable the variety to be identified. It may not consist solely of figures except where this is an established practice for designating varieties. It must not be liable to mislead or to cause confusion concerning the characteristics, value or identity of the variety or the identity of the breeder. In particular, it must be different from every denomination which designates, in the territory of any Contracting Party, an existing variety of the same plant species or of a closely related species.

(3) [*Registration of the denomination*] The denomination of the variety shall be submitted by the breeder to the authority. If it is found that the denomination does not satisfy the requirements of paragraph (2), the authority shall refuse to register it and shall require the breeder to propose another denomination within a prescribed period. The denomination shall be registered by the authority at the same time as the breeder's right is granted.

(4) [*Prior rights of third persons*] Prior rights of third persons shall not be affected. If, by reason of a prior right, the use of the denomination of a variety is forbidden to a person who, in accordance with the provisions of paragraph (7), is obliged to use it, the authority shall require the breeder to submit another denomination for the variety.

(5) [*Same denomination in all Contracting Parties*] A variety must be submitted to all Contracting Parties under the same denomination. The authority of each Contracting Party shall register the denomination so submitted, unless it considers the denomination unsuitable within its territory. In the latter case, it shall require the breeder to submit another

denomination.

(6) [*Information among the authorities of Contracting Parties*] The authority of a Contracting Party shall ensure that the authorities of all the other Contracting Parties are informed of matters concerning variety denominations, in particular the submission, registration and cancellation of denominations. Any authority may address its observations, if any, on the registration of a denomination to the authority which communicated that denomination.

(7) [*Obligation to use the denomination*] Any person who, within the territory of one of the Contracting Parties, offers for sale or markets propagating material of a variety protected within the said territory shall be obliged to use the denomination of that variety, even after the expiration of the breeder's right in that variety, except where, in accordance with the provisions of paragraph (4), prior rights prevent such use.

(8) [*Indications used in association with denominations*] When a variety is offered for sale or marketed, it shall be permitted to associate a trademark, trade name or other similar indication with a registered variety denomination. If such an indication is so associated, the denomination must nevertheless be easily recognizable.

CHAPTER VII
NULLITY AND CANCELLATION OF THE BREEDER'S RIGHT

Article 21
Nullity of the Breeder's Right

(1) [*Reasons of nullity*] Each Contracting Party shall declare a breeder's right granted by it null and void when it is established

(i) that the conditions laid down in Article 6 or Article 7 were not complied with at the time of the grant of the breeder's right,

(ii) that, where the grant of the breeder's right has been essentially based upon information and documents furnished by the breeder, the conditions laid down in Article 8 or Article 9 were not complied with at the time of the grant of the breeder's right, or

(iii) that the breeder's right has been granted to a person who is not entitled to it, unless it is transferred to the person who is so entitled.

(2) [*Exclusion of other reasons*] No breeder's right shall be declared null and void for reasons other than those referred to in paragraph (1).

Article 22
Cancellation of the Breeder's Right

(1) [*Reasons for cancellation*] (a) Each Contracting Party may cancel a breeder's right granted by it if it is established that the conditions laid down in Article 8 or Article 9 are no longer fulfilled.

(b) Furthermore, each Contracting Party may cancel a breeder's right granted by it if, after being requested to do so and within a prescribed period,

(i) the breeder does not provide the authority with the information, documents or material deemed necessary for verifying the maintenance of the variety,

(ii) the breeder fails to pay such fees as may be payable to keep his right in force, or

(iii) the breeder does not propose, where the denomination of the variety is cancelled after the grant of the right, another suitable denomination.

(2) [*Exclusion of other reasons*] No breeder's right shall be cancelled for reasons other than those referred to in paragraph (1).

CHAPTER VIII
THE UNION

Article 23
Members

The Contracting Parties shall be members of the Union.

Article 24
Legal Status and Seat

(1) [*Legal personality*] The Union has legal personality.

(2) [*Legal capacity*] The Union enjoys on the territory of each Contracting Party, in conformity with the laws applicable in the said territory, such legal capacity as may be necessary for the fulfillment of the objectives of the Union and for the exercise of its functions.

(3) [*Seat*] The seat of the Union and its permanent organs are at Geneva.

(4) [*Headquarters agreement*] The Union has a headquarters agreement with the Swiss Confederation.

Article 25
Organs

The permanent organs of the Union are the Council and the Office of the Union.

Article 26
The Council

(1) [*Composition*] The Council shall consist of the representatives of the members of the Union. Each member of the Union shall appoint one representative to the Council and one alternate. Representatives or alternates may be accompanied by assistants or advisers.

(2) [*Officers*] The Council shall elect a President and a first Vice-President from among its members. It may elect other Vice-Presidents. The first Vice-

President shall take the place of the President if the latter is unable to officiate. The President shall hold office for three years.

(3) [*Sessions*] The Council shall meet upon convocation by its President. An ordinary session of the Council shall be held annually. In addition, the President may convene the Council at his discretion; he shall convene it, within a period of three months, if one-third of the members of the Union so request.

(4) [*Observers*] States not members of the Union may be invited as observers to meetings of the Council. Other observers, as well as experts, may also be invited to such meetings.

(5) [*Tasks*] The tasks of the Council shall be to:

(i) study appropriate measures to safeguard the interests and to encourage the development of the Union;

(ii) establish its rules of procedure;

(iii) appoint the Secretary-General and, if it finds it necessary, a Vice Secretary-General and determine the terms of appointment of each;

(iv) examine an annual report on the activities of the Union and lay down the programme for its future work;

(v) give to the Secretary-General all necessary directions for the accomplishment of the tasks of the Union;

(vi) establish the administrative and financial regulations of the Union;

(vii) examine and approve the budget of the Union and fix the contribution of each member of the Union;

(viii) examine and approve the accounts presented by the Secretary-General;

(ix) fix the date and place of the conferences referred to in Article 38 and take the measures necessary for their preparation; and

(x) in general, take all necessary decisions to ensure the efficient functioning of the Union.

(6) [*Votes*] (a) Each member of the Union that is a State shall have one vote in the Council.

(b) Any Contracting Party that is an intergovernmental organization may, in matters within its competence, exercise the rights to vote of its member States that are members of the Union. Such an intergovernmental organization shall not exercise the rights to vote of its member States if its member States exercise their right to vote, and vice versa.

(7) [*Majorities*] Any decision of the Council shall require a simple majority of the votes cast, provided that any decision of the Council under paragraph (5)(ii), paragraph (5)(vi) and paragraph (5)(vii) and under Article 28(3), Article 29(5)(b) and Article 38(1) shall require three-fourths of the votes cast. Abstentions shall not be considered as votes.

Article 27
The Office of the Union

(1) [*Tasks and direction of the Office*] The Office of the Union shall carry out all the duties and tasks entrusted to it by the Council. It shall be under the direction of the Secretary-General.

(2) [*Duties of the Secretary-General*] The Secretary-General shall be responsible to the Council; he shall be responsible for carrying out the decisions of the Council. He shall submit the budget of the Union for the approval of the Council and shall be responsible for its implementation. He shall make reports to the Council on his administration and the activities and financial position of the Union.

(3) [*Staff*] Subject to the provisions of Article 26(5)(iii), the conditions of appointment and employment of the staff necessary for the efficient performance of the tasks of the Office of the Union shall be fixed in the administrative and financial regulations.

Article 28
Languages

(1) [*Languages of the Office*] The English, French, German and Spanish languages shall be used by the Office of the Union in carrying out its duties.

(2) [*Languages in certain meetings*] Meetings of the Council and of revision conferences shall be held in the four languages.

(3) [*Further languages*] The Council may decide that further languages shall be used.

Article 29
Finances

(1) [*Income*] The expenses of the Union shall be met from

(i) the annual contributions of the States members of the Union,

(ii) payments received for services rendered,

(iii) miscellaneous receipts.

(2) [*Contributions: units*] (a) The share of each State member of the Union in the total amount of the annual contributions shall be determined by reference to the total expenditure to be met from the contributions of the States members of the Union and to the number of contribution units applicable to it under paragraph (3). The said share shall be computed according to paragraph (4).

(b) The number of contribution units shall be expressed in whole numbers or fractions thereof, provided that no fraction shall be smaller than one-fifth.

(3) [*Contributions: share of each member*] (a) The number of contribution units applicable to any member of the Union which is party to the Act of 1961/1972 or the Act of 1978 on the date on which it becomes bound by this Convention shall be the same as the number applicable to it immediately before the said date.

(b) Any other State member of the Union shall, on joining the Union, indicate, in a declaration addressed to the Secretary-General, the number of contribution units applicable to it.

(c) Any State member of the Union may, at any time, indicate, in a declaration addressed to the Secretary-General, a number of contribution units different from the number applicable to it under subparagraph (a) or subparagraph (b). Such declaration, if made during the first six months of a calendar year, shall take effect from the beginning of the subsequent calendar year; otherwise, it shall take effect from the beginning of the second calendar year which follows the year in which the declaration was made.

(4) [*Contributions: computation of shares*] (a) For each budgetary period, the amount corresponding to one contribution unit shall be obtained by dividing the total amount of the expenditure to be met in that period from the contributions of the States members of the Union by the total number of units applicable to those States members of the Union.

(b) The amount of the contribution of each State member of the Union shall be obtained by multiplying the amount corresponding to one contribution unit by the number of contribution units applicable to that State member of the Union.

(5) [*Arrears in contributions*] (a) A State member of the Union which is in arrears in the payment of its contributions may not, subject to subparagraph (b), exercise its right to vote in the Council if the amount of its arrears equals or exceeds the amount of the contribution due from it for the preceding full year. The suspension of the right to vote shall not relieve such State member of the Union of its obligations under this Convention and shall not deprive it of any other rights thereunder.

(b) The Council may allow the said State member of the Union to continue to exercise its right to vote if, and as long as, the Council is satisfied that the delay in payment is due to exceptional and unavoidable circumstances.

(6) [*Auditing of the accounts*] The auditing of the accounts of the Union shall be effected by a State member of the Union as provided in the administrative and financial regulations. Such State member of the Union shall be designated, with its agreement, by the Council.

(7) [*Contributions of intergovernmental* organizations] Any Contracting Party which is an intergovernmental organization shall not be obliged to pay contributions. If, nevertheless, it chooses to pay contributions, the provisions of paragraph (1) to paragraph (4) shall be applied accordingly.

CHAPTER IX
IMPLEMENTATION OF THE CONVENTION; OTHER AGREEMENTS

Article 30
Implementation of the Convention

(1) [*Measures of implementation*] Each Contracting Party shall adopt all

measures necessary for the implementation of this Convention; in particular, it shall:

(i) provide for appropriate legal remedies for the effective enforcement of breeders' rights;

(ii) maintain an authority entrusted with the task of granting breeders' rights or entrust the said task to an authority maintained by another Contracting Party;

(iii) ensure that the public is informed through the regular publication of information concerning

— applications for and grants of breeders' rights, and

— proposed and approved denominations.

(2) [*Conformity of laws*] It shall be understood that, on depositing its instrument of ratification, acceptance, approval or accession, as the case may be, each State or intergovernmental organization must be in a position, under its laws, to give effect to the provisions of this Convention.

Article 31
Relations Between Contracting Parties and States Bound by Earlier Acts

(1) [*Relations between States bound by this Convention*] Between States members of the Union which are bound both by this Convention and any earlier Act of the Convention, only this Convention shall apply.

(2) [*Possible relations with States not bound by this Convention*] Any State member of the Union not bound by this Convention may declare, in a notification addressed to the Secretary-General, that, in its relations with each member of the Union bound only by this Convention, it will apply the latest Act by which it is bound. As from the expiration of one month after the date of such notification and until the State member of the Union making the declaration becomes bound by this Convention, the said member of the Union shall apply the latest Act by which it is bound in its relations with each of the members of the Union bound only by this Convention, whereas the latter shall apply this Convention in respect of the former.

Article 32
Special Agreements

Members of the Union reserve the right to conclude among themselves special agreements for the protection of varieties, insofar as such agreements do not contravene the provisions of this Convention.

CHAPTER X
FINAL PROVISIONS

Article 33
Signature

This Convention shall be open for signature by any State which is a member of the Union at the date of its adoption. It shall remain open for signature until March 31, 1992.

Article 34
Ratification, Acceptance or Approval; Accession

(1) [*States and certain intergovernmental organizations*] (a) Any State may, as provided in this Article, become party to this Convention.

(b) Any intergovernmental organization may, as provided in this Article, become party to this Convention if it

(i) has competence in respect of matters governed by this Convention,

(ii) has its own legislation providing for the grant and protection of breeders' rights binding on all its member States and

(iii) has been duly authorized, in accordance with its internal procedures, to accede to this Convention.

(2) [*Instrument of adherence*] Any State which has signed this Convention shall become party to this Convention by depositing an instrument of ratification, acceptance or approval of this Convention. Any State which has not signed this Convention and any intergovernmental organization shall become party to this Convention by depositing an instrument of accession to this Convention. Instruments of ratification, acceptance, approval or accession shall be deposited with the Secretary-General.

(3) [*Advice of the Council*] Any State which is not a member of the Union and any intergovernmental organization shall, before depositing its instrument of accession, ask the Council to advise it in respect of the conformity of its laws with the provisions of this Convention. If the decision embodying the advice is positive, the instrument of accession may be deposited.

Article 35
Reservations

(1) [*Principle*] Subject to paragraph (2), no reservations to this Convention are permitted.

(2) [*Possible exception*] (a) Notwithstanding the provisions of Article 3(1), any State which, at the time of becoming party to this Convention, is a party to the Act of 1978 and which, as far as varieties reproduced asexually are concerned, provides for protection by an industrial property title other than a breeder's right shall have the right to continue to do so without applying this Convention to those varieties.

(b) Any State making use of the said right shall, at the time of depositing its instrument of ratification, acceptance, approval or accession, as the case may be, notify the Secretary-General accordingly. The same State may, at any time, withdraw the said notification.

Article 36
Communications Concerning Legislation and the Genera and Species Protected; Information to be Published

(1) [*Initial notification*] When depositing its instrument of ratification, acceptance or approval of or accession to this Convention, as the case may be, any State or intergovernmental organization shall notify the Secretary-General of

(i) its legislation governing breeder's rights and

(ii) the list of plant genera and species to which, on the date on which it will become bound by this Convention, it will apply the provisions of this Convention.

(2) [Notification of changes] Each Contracting Party shall promptly notify the Secretary-General of

(i) any changes in its legislation governing breeders' rights and

(ii) any extension of the application of this Convention to additional plant genera and species.

(3) [*Publication of the information*] The Secretary-General shall, on the basis of communications received from each Contracting Party concerned, publish information on

(i) the legislation governing breeders' rights and any changes in that legislation, and

(ii) the list of plant genera and species referred to in paragraph (1)(ii) and any extension referred to in paragraph (2)(ii).

Article 37
Entry into Force; Closing of Earlier Acts

(1) [*Initial entry into force*] This Convention shall enter into force one month after five States have deposited their instruments of ratification, acceptance, approval or accession, as the case may be, provided that at least three of the said instruments have been deposited by States party to the Act of 1961/1972 or the Act of 1978.

(2) [*Subsequent entry into force*] Any State not covered by paragraph (1) or any intergovernmental organization shall become bound by this Convention one month after the date on which it has deposited its instrument of ratification, acceptance, approval or accession, as the case may be.

(3) [*Closing of the 1978 Act*] No instrument of accession to the Act of 1978 may be deposited after the entry into force of this Convention according to paragraph (1), except that any State that, in conformity with the established

practice of the General Assembly of the United Nations, is regarded as a developing country may deposit such an instrument until December 31, 1995, and that any other State may deposit such an instrument until December 31, 1993, even if this Convention enters into force before that date.

Article 38
Revision of the Convention

(1) *[Conference]* This Convention may be revised by a conference of the members of the Union. The convocation of such conference shall be decided by the Council.

(2) *[Quorum and majority]* The proceedings of a conference shall be effective only if at least half of the States members of the Union are represented at it. A majority of three-quarters of the States members of the Union present and voting at the conference shall be required for the adoption of any revision.

Article 39
Denunciation

(1) *[Notifications]* Any Contracting Party may denounce this Convention by notification addressed to the Secretary-General. The Secretary-General shall promptly notify all members of the Union of the receipt of that notification.

(2) *[Earlier Acts]* Notification of the denunciation of this Convention shall be deemed also to constitute notification of the denunciation of any earlier Act by which the Contracting Party denouncing this Convention is bound.

(3) *[Effective date]* The denunciation shall take effect at the end of the calendar year following the year in which the notification was received by the Secretary-General.

(4) *[Acquired rights]* The denunciation shall not affect any rights acquired in a variety by reason of this Convention or any earlier Act prior to the date on which the denunciation becomes effective.

Article 40
Preservation of Existing Rights

This Convention shall not limit existing breeders' rights under the laws of Contracting Parties or by reason of any earlier Act or any agreement other than this Convention concluded between members of the Union.

Article 41
Original and Official Texts of the Convention

(1) *[Original]* This Convention shall be signed in a single original in the English, French and German languages, the French text prevailing in case of any discrepancy among the various texts. The original shall be deposited with the Secretary-General.

(2) [*Official texts*] The Secretary-General shall, after consultation with the interested Governments, establish official texts of this Convention in the Arabic, Dutch, Italian, Japanese and Spanish languages and such other languages as the Council may designate.

Article 42
Depositary Functions

(1) [*Transmittal of copies*] The Secretary-General shall transmit certified copies of this Convention to all States and intergovernmental organizations which were represented in the Diplomatic Conference that adopted this Convention and, on request, to any other State or intergovernmental organization.

(2) [*Registration*] The Secretary-General shall register this Convention with the Secretariat of the United Nations.

Resolution on Article 14(5)

The Diplomatic Conference for the Revision of the International Convention for the Protection of New Varieties of Plants held from March 4 to 19, 1991, requests the Secretary-General of UPOV to start work immediately after the Conference on the establishment of draft standard guidelines, for adoption by the Council of UPOV, on essentially derived varieties.

Recommendation Relating to Article 15(2)

The Diplomatic Conference recommends that the provisions laid down in Article 15(2) of the International Convention for the Protection of New Varieties of Plants of December 2, 1961, as Revised at Geneva on November 10, 1972, on October 23, 1978, and on March 19, 1991, should not be read so as to be intended to open the possibility of extending the practice commonly called "farmer's privilege" to sectors of agricultural or horticultural production in which such a privilege is not a common practice on the territory of the Contracting Party concerned.

Common Statement Relating to Article 34

The Diplomatic Conference noted and accepted a declaration by the Delegation of Denmark and a declaration by the Delegation of the Netherlands according to which the Convention adopted by the Diplomatic Conference will not, upon its ratification, acceptance, approval or accession by Denmark or the Netherlands, be automatically applicable, in the case of Denmark, in Greenland and the Faroe Islands and, in the case of the Netherlands, in Aruba and the Netherlands Antilles. The said Convention will only apply in the said territories if and when Denmark or the Netherlands, as the case may be, expressly so notifies the Secretary-General.

PART I

GENERAL AND INSTITUTIONAL PROVISIONS

Chapter I
General provisions

Article 1
European law for the grant of patents

Article 2
European patents

CONVENTION ON THE GRANT OF EUROPEAN PATENTS (EUROPEAN PATENT CONVENTION)

Done at Munich, October 5, 1973, as amended December 21, 1978[*]

PREAMBLE

The Contracting States,

DESIRING to strengthen co-operation between the States of Europe in respect of the protection of inventions,

DESIRING that such protection may be obtained in those States by a single procedure for the grant of patents and by the establishment of certain standard rules governing patents so granted,

DESIRING, for this purpose, to conclude a Convention which establishes a European Patent Organisation and which constitutes a special agreement within the meaning of Article 19 of the Convention for the Protection of Industrial Property, signed in Paris on 20 March 1883 and last revised on 14 July 1967, and a regional patent treaty within the meaning of Article 45, paragraph 1, of the Patent Cooperation Treaty of 19 June 1970,

HAVE AGREED on the following provisions:

PART I
GENERAL AND INSTITUTIONAL PROVISIONS

Chapter I
General provisions

Article 1
European law for the grant of patents

A system of law, common to the Contracting States, for the grant of patents for invention is hereby established.

Article 2
European patent

(1) Patents granted by virtue of this Convention shall be called European patents.

(2) The European patent shall, in each of the Contracting States for which it is granted, have the effect of and be subject to the same conditions as a

---

* The EPC was revised in November 2000, which caused the renumbering of certain articles. The 2000 revisions are unlikely to be implemented for some time, however, and thus we have used the existing numbering throughout the casebook. The one exception to this occurs when we have included an except from the EPC, namely at page 499-500 (and the Question thereon at page 504) The renumbering is noted in a footnote accompanying the excerpt.

national patent granted by that State, unless otherwise provided in this Convention.

Article 3
Territorial effect

The grant of a European patent may be requested for one or more of the Contracting States.

Article 4
European Patent Organisation

(1) A European Patent Organisation, hereinafter referred to as the Organisation, is established by this Convention. It shall have administrative and financial autonomy.

(2) The organs of the Organisation shall be:

(a) a European Patent Office;

(b) an Administrative Council.

(3) The task of the Organisation shall be to grant European patents. This shall be carried out by the European Patent Office supervised by the Administrative Council.

Chapter II
The European Patent Organisation

Article 5
Legal status

(1) The Organisation shall have legal personality.

(2) In each of the Contracting States, the Organisation shall enjoy the most extensive legal capacity accorded to legal persons under the national law of that State; it may in particular acquire or dispose of movable and immovable property and may be a party to legal proceedings.

(3) The President of the European Patent Office shall represent the Organisation.

Article 6
Seat

(1) The Organisation shall have its seat at Munich.

(2) The European Patent Office shall be set up at Munich. It shall have a branch at The Hague.

Article 7
Sub-offices of the European Patent Office

By decision of the Administrative Council, suboffices of the European Patent Office may be created if need be, for the purpose of information and liaison, in the Contracting States and with inter-governmental organisations in the field of industrial property, subject to the approval of the Contracting State or organisation concerned.

Article 8
Privileges and immunities

The Protocol on Privileges and Immunities annexed to this Convention shall define the conditions under which the Organisation, the members of the Administrative Council, the employees of the European Patent Office and such other persons specified in that Protocol as take part in the work of the Organisation, shall enjoy, in the territory of each Contracting State, the privileges and immunities necessary for the performance of their duties.

Article 9
Liability

(1) The contractual liability of the Organisation shall be governed by the law applicable to the relevant contract.

(2) The non-contractual liability of the Organisation in respect of any damage caused by it or by the employees of the European Patent Office in the performance of their duties shall be governed by the provisions of the law of the Federal Republic of Germany. Where the damage is caused by the branch at The Hague or a sub-office or employees attached thereto, the provisions of the law of the Contracting State in which such branch or sub-office is located shall apply.

(3) The personal liability of the employees of the European Patent Office towards the Organisation shall be laid down in their Service Regulations or conditions of employment.

(4) The courts with jurisdiction to settle disputes under paragraphs 1 and 2 shall be:

(a) for disputes under paragraph 1, the courts of competent jurisdiction in the Federal Republic of Germany, unless the contract concluded between the parties designates the courts of another State;

(b) for disputes under paragraph 2, either the courts of competent jurisdiction in the Federal Republic of Germany, or the courts of competent jurisdiction in the State in which the branch or sub-office is located.

Chapter III
The European Patent Office

Article 10
Direction

(1) The European Patent Office shall be directed by the President who shall be responsible for its activities to the Administrative Council.

(2) To this end, the President shall have in particular the following

functions and powers:

(a) he shall take all necessary steps, including the adoption of internal administrative instructions and the publication of guidance for the public, to ensure the functioning of the European Patent Office;

(b) in so far as this Convention contains no provisions in this respect, he shall prescribe which transactions are to be carried out at the European Patent Office at Munich and its branch at The Hague respectively;

(c) he may place before the Administrative Council any proposal for amending this Convention and any proposal for general regulations or decisions which come within the competence of the Administrative Council;

(d) he shall prepare and implement the budget and any amending or supplementary budget;

(e) he shall submit a management report to the Administrative Council each year;

(f) he shall exercise supervisory authority over the personnel;

(g) subject to the provisions of Article 11, he shall appoint and promote the employees;

(h) he shall exercise disciplinary authority over the employees other than those referred to in Article 11, and may propose disciplinary action to the Administrative Council with regard to employees referred to in Article 11, paragraphs 2 and 3;

(i) he may delegate his functions and powers.

(3) The President shall be assisted by a number of Vice-Presidents. If the President is absent or indisposed, one of the Vice-Presidents shall take his place in accordance with the procedure laid down by the Administrative Council.

Article 11
Appointment of senior employees

(1) The President of the European Patent Office shall be appointed by decision of the Administrative Council.

(2) The Vice-Presidents shall be appointed by decision of the Administrative Council after the President has been consulted.

(3) The members, including the Chairmen, of the Boards of Appeal and of the Enlarged Board of Appeal shall be appointed by decision of the Administrative Council, taken on a proposal from the President of the European Patent Office. They may be re-appointed by decision of the Administrative Council after the President of the European Patent Office has been consulted.

(4) The Administrative Council shall exercise disciplinary authority over the employees referred to in paragraphs 1 to 3.

Article 12
Duties of office

The employees of the European Patent Office shall be bound, even after the termination of their employment, neither to disclose nor to make use of information which by its nature is a professional secret.

Article 13
Disputes between the Organisation and the employees
of the European Patent Office

(1) Employees and former employees of the European Patent Office or their successors in title may apply to the Administrative Tribunal of the International Labour Organisation in the case of disputes with the European Patent Organisation in accordance with the Statute of the Tribunal and within the limits and subject to the conditions laid down in the Service Regulations for permanent employees or the Pension Scheme Regulations or arising from the conditions of employment of other employees.

(2) An appeal shall only be admissible if the person concerned has exhausted such other means of appeal as are available to him under the Service Regulations, the Pension Scheme Regulations or the conditions of employment, as the case may be.

Article 14
Languages of the European Patent Office

(1) The official languages of the European Patent Office shall be English, French and German. European patent applications must be filed in one of these languages.

(2) However, natural or legal persons having their residence or principal place of business within the territory of a Contracting State having a language other than English, French or German as an official language, and nationals of that State who are resident abroad, may file European patent applications in an official language of that State. Nevertheless, a translation in one of the official languages of the European Patent Office must be filed within the time limit prescribed in the Implementing Regulations; throughout the proceedings before the European Patent Office, such translation may be brought into conformity with the original text of the application.

(3) The official language of the European Patent Office in which the European patent application is filed or, in the case referred to in paragraph 2, that of the translation, shall be used as the language of the proceedings in all proceedings before the European Patent Office concerning the application or the resulting patent, unless otherwise provided in the Implementing Regulations.

(4) The persons referred to in paragraph 2 may also file documents which have to be filed within a time limit in an official language of the Contracting State concerned. They must however file a translation in the language of the

proceedings within the time limit prescribed in the Implementing Regulations; in the cases provided for in the Implementing Regulations, they may file a translation in a different official language of the European Patent Office.

(5) If any document, other than those making up the European patent application, is not filed in the language prescribed by this Convention, or if any translation required by virtue of this Convention is not filed in due time, the document shall be deemed not to have been received.

(6) European patent applications shall be published in the language of the proceedings.

(7) The specifications of European patents shall be published in the language of the proceedings; they shall include a translation of the claims in the two other official languages of the European Patent Office.

(8) There shall be published in the three official languages of the European Patent Office:

(a) the European Patent Bulletin;

(b) the Official Journal of the European Patent Office.

(9) Entries in the Register of European Patents shall be made in the three official languages of the European Patent Office. In cases of doubt, the entry in the language of the proceedings shall be authentic.

Article 15
The departments charged with the procedure

For implementing the procedures laid down in this Convention, there shall be set up within the European Patent Office:

(a) a Receiving Section;

(b) Search Divisions;

(c) Examining Divisions;

(d) Opposition Divisions;

(e) a Legal Division;

(f) Boards of Appeal;

(g) an Enlarged Board of Appeal.

Article 16
Receiving Section

The Receiving Section shall be in the branch at The Hague. It shall be responsible for the examination on filing and the examination as to formal requirements of each European patent application up to the time when a request for examination has been made or the applicant has indicated under Article 96, paragraph 1, that he desires to proceed further with his application. It shall also be responsible for the publication of the European patent application and of the European search report.

Article 17
Search Divisions

The Search Divisions shall be in the branch at The Hague. They shall be responsible for drawing up European search reports.

Article 18
Examining Divisions

(1) An Examining Division shall be responsible for the examination of each European patent application from the time when the Receiving Section ceases to be responsible.

(2) An Examining Division shall consist of three technical examiners. Nevertheless, the examination prior to a final decision shall, as a general rule, be entrusted to one member of the Division. Oral proceedings shall be before the Examining Division itself. If the Examining Division considers that the nature of the decision so requires, it shall be enlarged by the addition of a legally qualified examiner. In the event of parity of votes, the vote of the Chairman of the Division shall be decisive.

Article 19
Opposition Divisions

(1) An Opposition Division shall be responsible for the examination of oppositions against any European patent.

(2) An Opposition Division shall consist of three technical examiners, at least two of whom shall not have taken part in the proceedings for grant of the patent to which the opposition relates. An examiner who has taken part in the proceedings for the grant of the European patent shall not be the Chairman. Prior to the taking of a final decision on the opposition, the Opposition Division may entrust the examination of the opposition to one of its members. Oral proceedings shall be before the Opposition Division itself. If the Opposition Division considers that the nature of the decision so requires, it shall be enlarged by the addition of a legally qualified examiner who shall not have taken part in the proceedings for grant of the patent. In the event of parity of votes, the vote of the Chairman of the Division shall be decisive.

Article 20
Legal Division

(1) The Legal Division shall be responsible for decisions in respect of entries in the Register of European Patents and in respect of registration on, and deletion from, the list of professional representatives.

(2) Decisions of the Legal Division shall be taken by one legally qualified member.

Article 21
Boards of Appeal

(1) The Boards of Appeal shall be responsible for the examination of appeals from the decisions of the Receiving Section, Examining Divisions, Opposition Divisions and of the Legal Division.

(2) For appeals from a decision of the Receiving Section or the Legal Division, a Board of Appeal shall consist of three legally qualified members.

(3) For appeals from a decision of an Examining Division, a Board of Appeal shall consist of:

(a) two technically qualified members and one legally qualified member, when the decision concerns the refusal of a European patent application or the grant of a European patent and was taken by an Examining Division consisting of less than four members;

(b) three technically qualified members and two legally qualified members, when the decision was taken by an Examining Division consisting of four members or when the Board of Appeal considers that the nature of the appeal so requires;

(c) three legally qualified members in all other cases.

(4) For appeals from a decision of an Opposition Division, a Board of Appeal shall consist of:

(a) two technically qualified members and one legally qualified member, when the decision was taken by an Opposition Division consisting of three members;

(b) three technically qualified members and two legally qualified members, when the decision was taken by an Opposition Division consisting of four members or when the Board of Appeal considers that the nature of the appeal so requires.

Article 22
Enlarged Board of Appeal

(1) The Enlarged Board of Appeal shall be responsible for:

(a) deciding points of law referred to it by Boards of Appeal;

(b) giving opinions on points of law referred to it by the President of the European Patent Office under the conditions laid down in Article 112.

(2) For giving decisions or opinions, the Enlarged Board of Appeal shall consist of five legally qualified members and two technically qualified members. One of the legally qualified members shall be the Chairman.

Article 23
Independence of the members of the Boards

(1) The members of the Enlarged Board of Appeal and of the Boards of Appeal shall be appointed for a term of five years and may not be removed from office during this term, except if there are serious grounds for such removal and if the Administrative Council, on a proposal from the Enlarged

Board of Appeal, takes a decision to this effect.

(2) The members of the Boards may not be members of the Receiving Section, Examining Divisions, Opposition Divisions or of the Legal Division.

(3) In their decisions the members of the Boards shall not be bound by any instructions and shall comply only with the provisions of this Convention.

(4) The Rules of Procedure of the Boards of Appeal and the Enlarged Board of Appeal shall be adopted in accordance with the provisions of the Implementing Regulations. They shall be subject to the approval of the Administrative Council.

Article 24
Exclusion and objection

(1) Members of the Boards of Appeal or of the Enlarged Board of Appeal may not take part in any appeal if they have any personal interest therein, if they have previously been involved as representatives of one of the parties, or if they participated in the decision under appeal.

(2) If, for one of the reasons mentioned in paragraph 1, or for any other reason, a member of a Board of Appeal or of the Enlarged Board of Appeal considers that he should not take part in any appeal, he shall inform the Board accordingly.

(3) Members of a Board of Appeal or of the Enlarged Board of Appeal may be objected to by any party for one of the reasons mentioned in paragraph 1, or if suspected of partiality. An objection shall not be admissible if, while being aware of a reason for objection, the party has taken a procedural step. No objection may be based upon the nationality of members.

(4) The Boards of Appeal and the Enlarged Board of Appeal shall decide as to the action to be taken in the cases specified in paragraphs 2 and 3 without the participation of the member concerned. For the purposes of taking this decision the member objected to shall be replaced by his alternate.

Article 25
Technical opinion

At the request of the competent national court trying an infringement or revocation action, the European Patent Office shall be obliged, against payment of an appropriate fee, to give a technical opinion concerning the European patent which is the subject of the action. The Examining Division shall be responsible for the issue of such opinions.

Chapter IV
The Administrative Council

Article 26
Membership

(1) The Administrative Council shall be composed of the Representatives

and the alternate Representatives of the Contracting States. Each Contracting State shall be entitled to appoint one Representative and one alternate Representative to the Administrative Council.

(2) The members of the Administrative Council may, subject to the provisions of its Rules of Procedure, be assisted by advisers or experts.

Article 27
Chairmanship

(1) The Administrative Council shall elect a Chairman and a Deputy Chairman from among the Representatives and alternate Representatives of the Contracting States. The Deputy Chairman shall ex officio replace the Chairman in the event of his being prevented from attending to his duties.

(2) The duration of the terms of office of the Chairman and the Deputy Chairman shall be three years. The terms of office shall be renewable.

Article 28
Board

(1) When there are at least eight Contracting States, the Administrative Council may set up a Board composed of five of its members.

(2) The Chairman and the Deputy Chairman of the Administrative Council shall be members of the Board ex officio; the other three members shall be elected by the Administrative Council.

(3) The term of office of the members elected by the Administrative Council shall be three years. This term of office shall not be renewable.

(4) The Board shall perform the duties given to it by the Administrative Council in accordance with the Rules of Procedure.

Article 29
Meetings

(1) Meetings of the Administrative Council shall be convened by its Chairman.

(2) The President of the European Patent Office shall take part in the deliberations of the Administrative Council.

(3) The Administrative Council shall hold an ordinary meeting once each year. In addition, it shall meet on the initiative of its Chairman or at the request of one-third of the Contracting States.

(4) The deliberations of the Administrative Council shall be based on an agenda, and shall be held in accordance with its Rules of Procedure.

(5) The provisional agenda shall contain any question whose inclusion is requested by any Contracting State in accordance with the Rules of Procedure.

Article 30
Attendance of observers

(1) The World Intellectual Property Organization shall be represented at the meetings of the Administrative Council, in accordance with the provisions of an agreement to be concluded between the European Patent Organisation and the World Intellectual Property Organization.

(2) Any other inter-governmental organisation charged with the implementation of international procedures in the field of patents with which the Organisation has concluded an agreement shall be represented at the meetings of the Administrative Council, in accordance with any provisions contained in such agreement.

(3) Any other inter-governmental and international non-governmental organisations exercising an activity of interest to the Organisation may be invited by the Administrative Council to arrange to be represented at its meetings during any discussion of matters of mutual interest.

Article 31
Languages of the Administrative Council

(1) The languages in use in the deliberations of the Administrative Council shall be English, French and German.

(2) Documents submitted to the Administrative Council, and the minutes of its deliberations, shall be drawn up in the three languages mentioned in paragraph 1.

Article 32
Staff, premises and equipment

The European Patent Office shall place at the disposal of the Administrative Council and any body established by it such staff, premises and equipment as may be necessary for the performance of their duties.

Article 33
Competence of the Administrative Council in certain cases

(1) The Administrative Council shall be competent to amend the following provisions of this Convention:

(a) the time limits laid down in this Convention; this shall apply to the time limit laid down in Article 94 only in the conditions laid down in Article 95;

(b) the Implementing Regulations.

(2) The Administrative Council shall be competent, in conformity with this Convention, to adopt or amend the following provisions:

(a) the Financial Regulations;

(b) the Service Regulations for permanent employees and the conditions of employment of other employees of the European Patent Office, the salary scales of the said permanent and other employees, and also the nature, and rules for the grant, of any supplementary benefits;

(c) the Pension Scheme Regulations and any appropriate increases in existing pensions to correspond to increases in salaries;

(d) the Rules relating to Fees;

(e) its Rules of Procedure.

(3) Notwithstanding Article 18, paragraph 2, the Administrative Council shall be competent to decide, in the light of experience, that in certain categories of cases Examining Divisions shall consist of one technical examiner. Such decision may be rescinded.

(4) The Administrative Council shall be competent to authorise the President of the European Patent Office to negotiate and, with its approval, to conclude agreements on behalf of the European Patent Organisation with States, with intergovernmental organisations and with documentation centres set up by virtue of agreements with such organisations.

Article 34
Voting rights

(1) The right to vote in the Administrative Council shall be restricted to the Contracting States.

(2) Each Contracting State shall have one vote, subject to the application of the provisions of Article 36.

Article 35
Voting rules

(1) The Administrative Council shall take its decisions other than those referred to in paragraph 2 by a simple majority of the Contracting States represented and voting.

(2) A majority of three-quarters of the votes of the Contracting States represented and voting shall be required for the decisions which the Administrative Council is empowered to take under Article 7, Article 11, paragraph 1, Article 33, Article 39, paragraph 1, Article 40, paragraphs 2 and 4, Article 46, Article 87, Article 95, Article 134, Article 151, paragraph 3, Article 154, paragraph 2, Article 155, paragraph 2, Article 156, Article 157, paragraphs 2 to 4, Article 160, paragraph 1, second sentence, Article 162, Article 163, Article 166, Article 167 and Article 172.

(3) Abstentions shall not be considered as votes.

Article 36
Weighting of votes

(1) In respect of the adoption or amendment of the Rules relating to Fees and, if the financial contribution to be made by the Contracting States would thereby be increased, the adoption of the budget of the Organisation and of any amending or supplementary budget, any Contracting State may require, following a first ballot in which each Contracting State shall have one vote,

and whatever the result of this ballot, that a second ballot be taken immediately, in which votes shall be given to the States in accordance with paragraph 2. The decision shall be determined by the result of this second ballot.

(2) The number of votes that each Contracting State shall have in the second ballot shall be calculated as follows:

(a) the percentage obtained for each Contracting State in respect of the scale for the special financial contributions, pursuant to Article 40, paragraphs 3 and 4, shall be multiplied by the number of Contracting States and divided by five;

(b) the number of votes thus given shall be rounded upwards to the next higher whole number;

(c) five additional votes shall be added to this number;

(d) nevertheless no Contracting State shall have more than 30 votes.

Chapter V
Financial provisions

Article 37
Cover for expenditure

The expenditure of the Organisation shall be covered:

(a) by the Organisation's own resources;

(b) by payments made by the Contracting States in respect of renewal fees for European patents levied in these States;

(c) where necessary, by special financial contributions made by the Contracting States;

(d) where appropriate, by the revenue provided for in Article 146.

Article 38
The Organisation's own resources

The Organisation's own resources shall be the yield from the fees laid down in this Convention, and also all receipts, whatever their nature.

Article 39
Payments by the Contracting States in respect of renewal fees for European patents

(1) Each Contracting State shall pay to the Organisation in respect of each renewal fee received for a European patent in that State an amount equal to a proportion of that fee, to be fixed by the Administrative Council; the proportion shall not exceed 75 per cent and shall be the same for all Contracting States. However, if the said proportion corresponds to an amount which is less than a uniform minimum amount fixed by the Administrative Council, the Contracting State shall pay that minimum to the Organisation.

(2) Each Contracting State shall communicate to the Organisation such information as the Administrative Council considers to be necessary to determine the amount of its payments.

(3) The due dates for these payments shall be determined by the Administrative Council.

(4) If a payment is not remitted fully by the due date, the Contracting State shall pay interest from the due date on the amount remaining unpaid.

Article 40
Level of fees and payments—Special financial contributions

(1) The amounts of the fees referred to under Article 38 and the proportion referred to under Article 39 shall be fixed at such a level as to ensure that the revenue in respect thereof is sufficient for the budget of the Organisation to be balanced.

(2) However, if the Organisation is unable to balance its budget under the conditions laid down in paragraph 1, the Contracting States shall remit to the Organisation special financial contributions, the amount of which shall be determined by the Administrative Council for the accounting period in question.

(3) These special financial contributions shall be determined in respect of any Contracting State on the basis of the number of patent applications filed in the last year but one prior to that of entry into force of this Convention, and calculated in the following manner:

(a) one half in proportion to the number of patent applications filed in that Contracting State;

(b) one half in proportion to the second highest number of patent applications filed in the other Contracting States by natural or legal persons having their residence or principal place of business in that Contracting State.

However, the amounts to be contributed by States in which the number of patent applications filed exceeds 25 000 shall then be taken as a whole and a new scale drawn up determined in proportion to the total number of patent applications filed in these States.

(4) Where, in respect of any Contracting State, its scale position cannot be established in accordance with paragraph 3, the Administrative Council shall, with the consent of that State, decide its scale position.

(5) Article 39, paragraphs 3 and 4, shall apply *mutatis mutandis* to the special financial contributions.

(6) The special financial contributions shall be repaid together with interest at a rate which shall be the same for all Contracting States. Repayments shall be made in so far as it is possible to provide for this purpose in the budget; the amount thus provided shall be distributed among the Contracting States in accordance with the scale mentioned in paragraphs 3 and 4 above.

(7) The special financial contributions remitted in any accounting period shall be wholly repaid before any such contributions or parts thereof remitted in any subsequent accounting period are repaid.

Article 41
Advances

(1) At the request of the President of the European Patent Office, the Contracting States shall make advances to the Organisation, on account of their payments and contributions, within the limit of the amount fixed by the Administrative Council. Such advances shall be apportioned in proportion to the amounts due by the Contracting States for the accounting period in question.

(2) Article 39, paragraphs 3 and 4, shall apply *mutatis mutandis* to the advances.

Article 42
Budget

(1) Income and expenditure of the Organisation shall form the subject of estimates in respect of each accounting period and shall be shown in the budget. If necessary, there may be amending or supplementary budgets.

(2) The budget shall be balanced as between income and expenditure.

(3) The budget shall be drawn up in the unit of account fixed in the Financial Regulations.

Article 43
Authorisation for expenditure

(1) The expenditure entered in the budget shall be authorised for the duration of one accounting period, unless any provisions to the contrary are contained in the Financial Regulations.

(2) Subject to the conditions to be laid down in the Financial Regulations, any appropriations, other than those relating to staff costs, which are unexpended at the end of the accounting period may be carried forward, but not beyond the end of the following accounting period.

(3) Appropriations shall be set out under different headings according to type and purpose of the expenditure and subdivided, as far as necessary, in accordance with the Financial Regulations.

Article 44
Appropriations for unforeseeable expenditure

(1) The budget of the Organisation may contain appropriations for unforeseeable expenditure.

(2) The employment of these appropriations by the Organisation shall be subject to the prior approval of the Administrative Council.

Article 45
Accounting period

The accounting period shall commence on 1 January and end on 31 December.

Article 46
Preparation and adoption of the budget

(1) The President of the European Patent Office shall lay the draft budget before the Administrative Council not later than the date prescribed in the Financial Regulations.

(2) The budget and any amending or supplementary budget shall be adopted by the Administrative Council.

Article 47
Provisional budget

(1) If, at the beginning of the accounting period, the budget has not been adopted by the Administrative Council, expenditures may be effected on a monthly basis per heading or other division of the budget, according to the provisions of the Financial Regulations, up to one-twelfth of the budget appropriations for the preceding accounting period, provided that the appropriations thus made available to the President of the European Patent Office shall not exceed one-twelfth of those provided for in the draft budget.

(2) The Administrative Council may, subject to the observance of the other provisions laid down in paragraph 1, authorise expenditure in excess of one-twelfth of the appropriations.

(3) The payments referred to in Article 37, sub-paragraph (b), shall continue to be made, on a provisional basis, under the conditions determined under Article 39 for the year preceding that to which the draft budget relates.

(4) The Contracting States shall pay each month, on a provisional basis and in accordance with the scale referred to in Article 40, paragraphs 3 and 4, any special financial contributions necessary to ensure implementation of paragraphs 1 and 2 above. Article 39, paragraph 4, shall apply *mutatis mutandis* to these contributions.

Article 48
Budget implementation

(1) The President of the European Patent Office shall implement the budget and any amending or supplementary budget on his own responsibility and within the limits of the allocated appropriations.

(2) Within the budget, the President of the European Patent Office may, subject to the limits and conditions laid down in the Financial Regulations, transfer funds as between the various headings or sub-headings.

Article 49
Auditing of accounts

(1) The income and expenditure account and a balance sheet of the Organisation shall be examined by auditors whose independence is beyond doubt, appointed by the Administrative Council for a period of five years, which shall be renewable or extensible.

(2) The audit, which shall be based on vouchers and shall take place, if necessary, in situ, shall ascertain that all income has been received and all expenditure effected in a lawful and proper manner and that the financial management is sound. The auditors shall draw up a report after the end of each accounting period.

(3) The President of the European Patent Office shall annually submit to the Administrative Council the accounts of the preceding accounting period in respect of the budget and the balance sheet showing the assets and liabilities of the Organisation together with the report of the auditors.

(4) The Administrative Council shall approve the annual accounts together with the report of the auditors and shall give the President of the European Patent Office a discharge in respect of the implementation of the budget.

Article 50
Financial Regulations

The Financial Regulations shall in particular establish:

(a) the procedure relating to the establishment and implementation of the budget and for the rendering and auditing of accounts;

(b) the method and procedure whereby the payments and contributions provided for in Article 37 and the advances provided for in Article 41 are to be made available to the Organisation by the Contracting States;

(c) the rules concerning the responsibilities of accounting and paying officers and the arrangements for their supervision;

(d) the rates of interest provided for in Articles 39, 40 and 47;

(e) the method of calculating the contributions payable by virtue of Article 146;

(f) the composition of and duties to be assigned to a Budget and Finance Committee which should be set up by the Administrative Council.

Article 51
Rules relating to Fees

The Rules relating to Fees shall determine in particular the amounts of the fees and the ways in which they are to be paid.

PART II
SUBSTANTIVE PATENT LAW

Chapter I
Patentability

Article 52
Patentable inventions

(1) European patents shall be granted for any inventions which are susceptible of industrial application, which are new and which involve an inventive step.

(2) The following in particular shall not be regarded as inventions within the meaning of paragraph 1:

(a) discoveries, scientific theories and mathematical methods;

(b) aesthetic creations;

(c) schemes, rules and methods for performing mental acts, playing games or doing business, and programs for computers;

(d) presentations of information.

(3) The provisions of paragraph 2 shall exclude patentability of the subject-matter or activities referred to in that provision only to the extent to which a European patent application or European patent relates to such subject-matter or activities as such.

(4) Methods for treatment of the human or animal body by surgery or therapy and diagnostic methods practised on the human or animal body shall not be regarded as inventions which are susceptible of industrial application within the meaning of paragraph 1. This provision shall not apply to products, in particular substances or compositions, for use in any of these methods.

Article 53
Exceptions to patentability

European patents shall not be granted in respect of:

(a) inventions the publication or exploitation of which would be contrary to ``ordre public" or morality, provided that the exploitation shall not be deemed to be so contrary merely because it is prohibited by law or regulation in some or all of the Contracting States;

(b) plant or animal varieties or essentially biological processes for the production of plants or animals; this provision does not apply to microbiological processes or the products thereof.

Article 54
Novelty

(1) An invention shall be considered to be new if it does not form part of the state of the art.

(2) The state of the art shall be held to comprise everything made available to the public by means of a written or oral description, by use, or in any other way, before the date of filing of the European patent application.

(3) Additionally, the content of European patent applications as filed, of which the dates of filing are prior to the date referred to in paragraph 2 and which were published under Article 93 on or after that date, shall be considered as comprised in the state of the art.

(4) Paragraph 3 shall be applied only in so far as a Contracting State designated in respect of the later application, was also designated in respect of the earlier application as published.

(5) The provisions of paragraphs 1 to 4 shall not exclude the patentability of any substance or composition, comprised in the state of the art, for use in a method referred to in Article 52, paragraph 4, provided that its use for any method referred to in that paragraph is not comprised in the state of the art.

Article 55
Non-prejudicial disclosures

(1) For the application of Article 54 a disclosure of the invention shall not be taken into consideration if it occurred no earlier than six months preceding the filing of the European patent application and if it was due to, or in consequence of:

(a) an evident abuse in relation to the applicant or his legal predecessor, or

(b) the fact that the applicant or his legal predecessor has displayed the invention at an official, or officially recognised, international exhibition falling within the terms of the Convention on international exhibitions signed at Paris on 22 November 1928 and last revised on 30 November 1972.

(2) In the case of paragraph 1(b), paragraph 1 shall apply only if the applicant states, when filing the European patent application, that the invention has been so displayed and files a supporting certificate within the period and under the conditions laid down in the Implementing Regulations.

Article 56
Inventive step

An invention shall be considered as involving an inventive step if, having regard to the state of the art, it is not obvious to a person skilled in the art. If the state of the art also includes documents within the meaning of Article 54, paragraph 3, these documents are not to be considered in deciding whether there has been an inventive step.

Article 57
Industrial application

An invention shall be considered as susceptible of industrial application if it can be made or used in any kind of industry, including agriculture.

Chapter II
Persons entitled to apply for and obtain European patents—Mention of the inventor

Article 58
Entitlement to file a European patent application

A European patent application may be filed by any natural or legal person, or any body equivalent to a legal person by virtue of the law governing it.

Article 59
Multiple applicants

A European patent application may also be filed either by joint applicants or by two or more applicants designating different Contracting States.

Article 60
Right to a European patent

(1) The right to a European patent shall belong to the inventor or his successor in title. If the inventor is an employee the right to the European patent shall be determined in accordance with the law of the State in which the employee is mainly employed; if the State in which the employee is mainly employed cannot be determined, the law to be applied shall be that of the State in which the employer has his place of business to which the employee is attached.

(2) If two or more persons have made an invention independently of each other, the right to the European patent shall belong to the person whose European patent application has the earliest date of filing; however, this provision shall apply only if this first application has been published under Article 93 and shall only have effect in respect of the Contracting States designated in that application as published.

(3) For the purposes of proceedings before the European Patent Office, the applicant shall be deemed to be entitled to exercise the right to the European patent.

Article 61
European patent applications by persons not having the right to a European patent

(1) If by a final decision it is adjudged that a person referred to in Article 60, paragraph 1, other than the applicant, is entitled to the grant of a European patent, that person may, within a period of three months after the decision has become final, provided that the European patent has not yet been granted, in respect of those Contracting States designated in the European patent application in which the decision has been taken or recognised, or has to be recognised on the basis of the Protocol on Recognition annexed to this Convention:

(a) prosecute the application as his own application in place of the applicant,

(b) file a new European patent application in respect of the same invention, or

(c) request that the application be refused.

(2) The provisions of Article 76, paragraph 1, shall apply *mutatis mutandis* to a new application filed under paragraph 1.

(3) The procedure to be followed in carrying out the provisions of paragraph 1, the special conditions applying to a new application filed under paragraph 1 and the time limit for paying the filing, search and designation fees on it are laid down in the Implementing Regulations.

Article 62
Right of the inventor to be mentioned

The inventor shall have the right, vis-à-vis the applicant for or proprietor of a European patent, to be mentioned as such before the European Patent Office.

Chapter III
Effects of the European patent and the European patent application

Article 63
Term of the European patent

(1) The term of the European patent shall be 20 years as from the date of filing of the application.

(2) Nothing in the preceding paragraph shall limit the right of a Contracting State to extend the term of a European patent, or to grant corresponding protection which follows immediately on expiry of the term of the patent, under the same conditions as those applying to national patents:

(a) in order to take account of a state of war or similar emergency conditions affecting that State;

(b) if the subject-matter of the European patent is a product or a process of manufacturing a product or a use of a product which has to undergo an administrative authorisation procedure required by law before it can be put on the market in that State.

(3) Paragraph 2 shall apply *mutatis mutandis* to European patents granted jointly for a group of Contracting States in accordance with Article 142.

(4) A Contracting State which makes provision for extension of the term or corresponding protection under paragraph 2(b) may, in accordance with an agreement concluded with the Organisation, entrust to the European Patent Office tasks associated with implementation of the relevant provisions.

Article 64
Rights conferred by a European patent

(1) A European patent shall, subject to the provisions of paragraph 2, confer on its proprietor from the date of publication of the mention of its grant, in each Contracting State in respect of which it is granted, the same rights as would be conferred by a national patent granted in that State.

(2) If the subject-matter of the European patent is a process, the protection conferred by the patent shall extend to the products directly obtained by such process.

(3) Any infringement of a European patent shall be dealt with by national law.

Article 65
Translation of the specification of the European patent

(1) Any Contracting State may prescribe that if the text, in which the European Patent Office intends to grant a European patent or maintain a European patent as amended for that State, is not drawn up in one of its official languages, the applicant for or proprietor of the patent shall supply to its central industrial property office a translation of this text in one of its official languages at his option or, where that State has prescribed the use of one specific official language, in that language. The period for supplying the translation shall end three months after the date on which the mention of the grant of the European patent or of the maintenance of the European patent as amended is published in the European Patent Bulletin, unless the State concerned prescribes a longer period.

(2) Any Contracting State which has adopted provisions pursuant to paragraph 1 may prescribe that the applicant for or proprietor of the patent must pay all or part of the costs of publication of such translation within a period laid down by that State.

(3) Any Contracting State may prescribe that in the event of failure to observe the provisions adopted in accordance with paragraphs 1 and 2, the European patent shall be deemed to be void ab initio in that State.

Article 66
Equivalence of European filing with national filing

A European patent application which has been accorded a date of filing shall, in the designated Contracting States, be equivalent to a regular national filing, where appropriate with the priority claimed for the European patent application.

Article 67
Rights conferred by a European patent application after publication

(1) A European patent application shall, from the date of its publication under Article 93, provisionally confer upon the applicant such protection as

is conferred by Article 64, in the Contracting States designated in the application as published.

(2) Any Contracting State may prescribe that a European patent application shall not confer such protection as is conferred by Article 64. However, the protection attached to the publication of the European patent application may not be less than that which the laws of the State concerned attach to the compulsory publication of unexamined national patent applications. In any event, every State shall ensure at least that, from the date of publication of a European patent application, the applicant can claim compensation reasonable in the circumstances from any person who has used the invention in the said State in circumstances where that person would be liable under national law for infringement of a national patent.

(3) Any Contracting State which does not have as an official language the language of the proceedings, may prescribe that provisional protection in accordance with paragraphs 1 and 2 above shall not be effective until such time as a translation of the claims in one of its official languages at the option of the applicant or, where that State has prescribed the use of one specific official language, in that language:

(a) has been made available to the public in the manner prescribed by national law, or

(b) has been communicated to the person using the invention in the said State.

(4) The European patent application shall be deemed never to have had the effects set out in paragraphs 1 and 2 above when it has been withdrawn, deemed to be withdrawn or finally refused. The same shall apply in respect of the effects of the European patent application in a Contracting State the designation of which is withdrawn or deemed to be withdrawn.

Article 68
Effect of revocation of the European patent

The European patent application and the resulting patent shall be deemed not to have had, as from the outset, the effects specified in Articles 64 and 67, to the extent that the patent has been revoked in opposition proceedings.

Article 69
Extent of protection

(1) The extent of the protection conferred by a European patent or a European patent application shall be determined by the terms of the claims. Nevertheless, the description and drawings shall be used to interpret the claims.

(2) For the period up to grant of the European patent, the extent of the protection conferred by the European patent application shall be determined by the latest filed claims contained in the publication under Article 93. However, the European patent as granted or as amended in opposition proceedings shall determine retroactively the protection conferred by the

European patent application, in so far as such protection is not thereby extended.

Article 70
Authentic text of a European patent application or European patent

(1) The text of a European patent application or a European patent in the language of the proceedings shall be the authentic text in any proceedings before the European Patent Office and in any Contracting State.

(2) However, in the case referred to in Article 14, paragraph 2, the original text shall, in proceedings before the European Patent Office, constitute the basis for determining whether the subject-matter of the application or patent extends beyond the content of the application as filed.

(3) Any Contracting State may provide that a translation, as provided for in this Convention, in an official language of that State, shall in that State be regarded as authentic, except for revocation proceedings, in the event of the application or patent in the language of the translation conferring protection which is narrower than that conferred by it in the language of the proceedings.

(4) Any Contracting State which adopts a provision under paragraph 3:

(a) must allow the applicant for or proprietor of the patent to file a corrected translation of the European patent application or European patent. Such corrected translation shall not have any legal effect until any conditions established by the Contracting State under Article 65, paragraph 2, and Article 67, paragraph 3, have been complied with *mutatis mutandis*;

(b) may prescribe that any person who, in that State, in good faith is using or has made effective and serious preparations for using an invention the use of which would not constitute infringement of the application or patent in the original translation may, after the corrected translation takes effect, continue such use in the course of his business or for the needs thereof without payment.

Chapter IV
The European patent application as an object of property

Article 71
Transfer and constitution of rights

A European patent application may be transferred or give rise to rights for one or more of the designated Contracting States.

Article 72
Assignment

An assignment of a European patent application shall be made in writing and shall require the signature of the parties to the contract.

Article 73
Contractual licensing

A European patent application may be licensed in whole or in part for the whole or part of the territories of the designated Contracting States.

Article 74
Law applicable

Unless otherwise specified in this Convention, the European patent application as an object of property shall, in each designated Contracting State and with effect for such State, be subject to the law applicable in that State to national patent applications

PART III
APPLICATION FOR EUROPEAN PATENTS

Chapter I
Filing and requirements of the European patent application

Article 75
Filing of the European patent application

(1) A European patent application may be filed:

(a) at the European Patent Office at Munich or its branch at The Hague, or

(b) if the law of a Contracting State so permits, at the central industrial property office or other competent authority of that State. An application filed in this way shall have the same effect as if it had been filed on the same date at the European Patent Office.

(2) The provisions of paragraph 1 shall not preclude the application of legislative or regulatory provisions which, in any Contracting State:

(a) govern inventions which, owing to the nature of their subject-matter, may not be communicated abroad without the prior authorisation of the competent authorities of that State, or

(b) prescribe that each application is to be filed initially with a national authority or make direct filing with another authority subject to prior authorisation.

(3) No Contracting State may provide for or allow the filing of European divisional applications with an authority referred to in paragraph 1(b).

Article 76
European divisional applications

(1) A European divisional application must be filed directly with the European Patent Office at Munich or its branch at The Hague. It may be filed only in respect of subject-matter which does not extend beyond the

content of the earlier application as filed; in so far as this provision is complied with, the divisional application shall be deemed to have been filed on the date of filing of the earlier application and shall have the benefit of any right to priority.

(2) The European divisional application shall not designate Contracting States which were not designated in the earlier application.

(3) The procedure to be followed in carrying out the provisions of paragraph 1, the special conditions to be complied with by a divisional application and the time limit for paying the filing, search and designation fees are laid down in the Implementing Regulations.

Article 77
Forwarding of European patent applications

(1) The central industrial property office of a Contracting State shall be obliged to forward to the European Patent Office, in the shortest time compatible with the application of national law concerning the secrecy of inventions in the interests of the State, any European patent applications which have been filed with that office or with other competent authorities in that State.

(2) The Contracting States shall take all appropriate steps to ensure that European patent applications, the subject of which is obviously not liable to secrecy by virtue of the law referred to in paragraph 1, shall be forwarded to the European Patent Office within six weeks after filing.

(3) European patent applications which require further examination as to their liability to secrecy shall be forwarded in such manner as to reach the European Patent Office within four months after filing, or, where priority has been claimed, fourteen months after the date of priority.

(4) A European patent application, the subject of which has been made secret, shall not be forwarded to the European Patent Office.

(5) European patent applications which do not reach the European Patent Office before the end of the fourteenth month after filing or, if priority has been claimed, after the date of priority, shall be deemed to be withdrawn. The filing, search and designation fees shall be refunded.

Article 78
Requirements of the European patent application

(1) A European patent application shall contain:

(a) a request for the grant of a European patent;

(b) a description of the invention;

(c) one or more claims;

(d) any drawings referred to in the description or the claims;

(e) an abstract.

(2) A European patent application shall be subject to the payment of the filing fee and the search fee within one month after the filing of the

application.

(3) A European patent application must satisfy the conditions laid down in the Implementing Regulations.

Article 79
Designation of Contracting States

(1) The request for the grant of a European patent shall contain the designation of the Contracting State or States in which protection for the invention is desired.

(2) The designation of a contracting state shall be subject to the payment of the designation fee. The designation fees shall be paid within six months of the date on which the European Patent Bulletin mentions the publication of the European search report.

(3) The designation of a Contracting State may be withdrawn at any time up to the grant of the European patent. Withdrawal of the designation of all the Contracting States shall be deemed to be a withdrawal of the European patent application. Designation fees shall not be refunded.

Article 80
Date of filing

The date of filing of a European patent application shall be the date on which documents filed by the applicant contain:

(a) an indication that a European patent is sought;

(b) the designation of at least one Contracting State;

(c) information identifying the applicant;

(d) a description and one or more claims in one of the languages referred to in Article 14, paragraphs 1 and 2, even though the description and the claims do not comply with the other requirements of this Convention.

Article 81
Designation of the inventor

The European patent application shall designate the inventor. If the applicant is not the inventor or is not the sole inventor, the designation shall contain a statement indicating the origin of the right to the European patent.

Article 82
Unity of invention

The European patent application shall relate to one invention only or to a group of inventions so linked as to form a single general inventive concept.

Article 83
Disclosure of the invention

The European patent application must disclose the invention in a manner sufficiently clear and complete for it to be carried out by a person skilled in the art.

Article 84
The claims

The claims shall define the matter for which protection is sought. They shall be clear and concise and be supported by the description.

Article 85
The abstract

The abstract shall merely serve for use as technical information; it may not be taken into account for any other purpose, in particular not for the purpose of interpreting the scope of the protection sought nor for the purpose of applying Article 54, paragraph 3.

Article 86
Renewal fees for European patent applications

(1) Renewal fees shall be paid to the European Patent Office in accordance with the Implementing Regulations in respect of European patent applications. These fees shall be due in respect of the third year and each subsequent year, calculated from the date of filing of the application.

(2) When a renewal fee has not been paid on or before the due date, the fee may be validly paid within six months of the said date, provided that the additional fee is paid at the same time.

(3) If the renewal fee and any additional fee have not been paid in due time the European patent application shall be deemed to be withdrawn. The European Patent Office alone shall be competent to decide this.

(4) The obligation to pay renewal fees shall terminate with the payment of the renewal fee due in respect of the year in which the mention of the grant of the European patent is published.

Chapter II
Priority

Article 87
Priority right

(1) A person who has duly filed in or for any State party to the Paris Convention for the Protection of Industrial Property, an application for a patent or for the registration of a utility model or for a utility certificate or for an inventor's certificate, or his successors in title, shall enjoy, for the purpose of filing a European patent application in respect of the same invention, a right of priority during a period of twelve months from the date of filing of the first application.

(2) Every filing that is equivalent to a regular national filing under the

national law of the State where it was made or under bilateral or multilateral agreements, including this Convention, shall be recognised as giving rise to a right of priority.

(3) By a regular national filing is meant any filing that is sufficient to establish the date on which the application was filed, whatever may be the outcome of the application.

(4) A subsequent application for the same subject-matter as a previous first application and filed in or in respect of the same State shall be considered as the first application for the purposes of determining priority, provided that, at the date of filing the subsequent application, the previous application has been withdrawn, abandoned or refused, without being open to public inspection and without leaving any rights outstanding, and has not served as a basis for claiming a right of priority. The previous application may not thereafter serve as a basis for claiming a right of priority.

(5) If the first filing has been made in a State which is not a party to the Paris Convention for the Protection of Industrial Property, paragraphs 1 to 4 shall apply only in so far as that State, according to a notification published by the Administrative Council, and by virtue of bilateral or multilateral agreements, grants on the basis of a first filing made at the European Patent Office as well as on the basis of a first filing made in or for any Contracting State and subject to conditions equivalent to those laid down in the Paris Convention, a right of priority having equivalent effect.

Article 88
Claiming priority

(1) An applicant for a European patent desiring to take advantage of the priority of a previous application shall file a declaration of priority, a copy of the previous application and, if the language of the latter is not one of the official languages of the European Patent Office, a translation of it in one of such official languages. The procedure to be followed in carrying out these provisions is laid down in the Implementing Regulations.

(2) Multiple priorities may be claimed in respect of a European patent application, notwithstanding the fact that they originated in different countries. Where appropriate, multiple priorities may be claimed for any one claim. Where multiple priorities are claimed, time limits which run from the date of priority shall run from the earliest date of priority.

(3) If one or more priorities are claimed in respect of a European patent application, the right of priority shall cover only those elements of the European patent application which are included in the application or applications whose priority is claimed.

(4) If certain elements of the invention for which priority is claimed do not appear among the claims formulated in the previous application, priority may nonetheless be granted, provided that the documents of the previous application as a whole specifically disclose such elements.

Article 89
Effect of priority right

The right of priority shall have the effect that the date of priority shall count as the date of filing of the European patent application for the purposes of Article 54, paragraphs 2 and 3, and Article 60, paragraph 2.

PART IV
PROCEDURE UP TO GRANT

Article 90
Examination on filing

(1) The Receiving Section shall examine whether:

(a) the European patent application satisfies the requirements for the accordance of a date of filing;

(b) the filing fee and the search fee have been paid in due time;

(c) in the case provided for in Article 14, paragraph 2, the translation of the European patent application in the language of the proceedings has been filed in due time.

(2) If a date of filing cannot be accorded, the Receiving Section shall give the applicant an opportunity to correct the deficiencies in accordance with the Implementing Regulations. If the deficiencies are not remedied in due time, the application shall not be dealt with as a European patent application.

(3) If the filing fee and the search fee have not been paid in due time or, in the case provided for in Article 14, paragraph 2, the translation of the application in the language of the proceedings has not been filed in due time, the application shall be deemed to be withdrawn

Article 91
Examination as to formal requirements

(1) If a European patent application has been accorded a date of filing, and is not deemed to be withdrawn by virtue of Article 90, paragraph 3, the Receiving Section shall examine whether:

(a) the requirements of Article 133, paragraph 2, have been satisfied;

(b) the application meets the physical requirements laid down in the Implementing Regulations for the implementation of this provision;

(c) the abstract has been filed;

(d) the request for the grant of a European patent satisfies the mandatory provisions of the Implementing Regulations concerning its content and, where appropriate, whether the requirements of this Convention concerning the claim to priority have been satisfied;

(e) the designation fees have been paid;

(f) the designation of the inventor has been made in accordance with

Article 81;

(g) the drawings referred to in Article 78, paragraph 1(d), were filed on the date of filing of the application.

(2) Where the Receiving Section notes that there are deficiencies which may be corrected, it shall give the applicant an opportunity to correct them in accordance with the Implementing Regulations.

(3) If any deficiencies noted in the examination under paragraph 1(a) to (d) are not corrected in accordance with the Implementing Regulations, the application shall be refused; where the provisions referred to in paragraph 1(d) concern the right of priority, this right shall be lost for the application.

(4) Where, in the case referred to in paragraph 1(e), the designation fee has not been paid in due time in respect of any designated State, the designation of that State shall be deemed to be withdrawn.

(5) Where, in the case referred to in paragraph 1(f), the omission of the designation of the inventor is not, in accordance with the Implementing Regulations and subject to the exceptions laid down therein, corrected within 16 months after the date of filing of the European patent application or, if priority is claimed, after the date of priority, the application shall be deemed to be withdrawn.

(6) Where, in the case referred to in paragraph 1(g), the drawings were not filed on the date of filing of the application and no steps have been taken to correct the deficiency in accordance with the Implementing Regulations, either the application shall be re-dated to the date of filing of the drawings or any reference to the drawings in the application shall be deemed to be deleted, according to the choice exercised by the applicant in accordance with the Implementing Regulations.

Article 92
The drawing up of the European search report

(1) If a European patent application has been accorded a date of filing and is not deemed to be withdrawn by virtue of Article 90, paragraph 3, the Search Division shall draw up the European search report on the basis of the claims, with due regard to the description and any drawings, in the form prescribed in the Implementing Regulations.

(2) Immediately after it has been drawn up, the European search report shall be transmitted to the applicant together with copies of any cited documents.

Article 93
Publication of a European patent application

(1) A European patent application shall be published as soon as possible after the expiry of a period of eighteen months from the date of filing or, if priority has been claimed, as from the date of priority. Nevertheless, at the request of the applicant the application may be published before the expiry of the period referred to above. It shall be published simultaneously with the

publication of the specification of the European patent when the grant of the patent has become effective before the expiry of the period referred to above.

(2) The publication shall contain the description, the claims and any drawings as filed and, in an annex, the European search report and the abstract, in so far as the latter are available before the termination of the technical preparations for publication. If the European search report and the abstract have not been published at the same time as the application, they shall be published separately.

Article 94
Request for examination

(1) The European Patent Office shall examine, on written request, whether a European patent application and the invention to which it relates meet the requirements of this Convention.

(2) A request for examination may be filed by the applicant up to the end of six months after the date on which the European Patent Bulletin mentions the publication of the European search report. The request shall not be deemed to be filed until after the examination fee has been paid. The request may not be withdrawn.

(3) If no request for examination has been filed by the end of the period referred to in paragraph 2, the application shall be deemed to be withdrawn.

Article 95
Extension of the period within which requests for examination may be filed

(1) The Administrative Council may extend the period within which requests for examination may be filed if it is established that European patent applications cannot be examined in due time.

(2) If the Administrative Council extends the period, it may decide that third parties will be entitled to make requests for examination. In such cases, it shall determine the appropriate rules in the Implementing Regulations.

(3) Any decision of the Administrative Council to extend the period shall apply only in respect of applications filed after the publication of such decision in the Official Journal of the European Patent Office.

(4) If the Administrative Council extends the period, it must lay down measures with a view to restoring the original period as soon as possible.

Article 96
Examination of the European patent application

(1) If the applicant for a European patent has filed the request for examination before the European search report has been transmitted to him, the European Patent Office shall invite him after the transmission of the report to indicate, within a period to be determined, whether he desires to proceed further with the European patent application.

(2) If the examination of a European patent application reveals that the application or the invention to which it relates does not meet the requirements of this Convention, the Examining Division shall invite the applicant, in accordance with the Implementing Regulations and as often as necessary, to file his observations within a period to be fixed by the Examining Division.

(3) If the applicant fails to reply in due time to any invitation under paragraph 1 or paragraph 2, the application shall be deemed to be withdrawn.

Article 97
Refusal or grant

(1) The Examining Division shall refuse a European patent application if it is of the opinion that such application or the invention to which it relates does not meet the requirements of this Convention, except where a different sanction is provided for by this Convention.

(2) If the Examining Division is of the opinion that the application and the invention to which it relates meet the requirements of this Convention, it shall decide to grant the European patent for the designated Contracting States provided that:

(a) it is established, in accordance with the provisions of the Implementing Regulations, that the applicant approves the text in which the Examining Division intends to grant the patent;

(b) the fees for grant and printing are paid within the time limit prescribed in the Implementing Regulations;

(c) the renewal fees and any additional fees already due have been paid.

(3) If the fees for grant and printing are not paid in due time, the application shall be deemed to be withdrawn.

(4) The decision to grant a European patent shall not take effect until the date on which the European Patent Bulletin mentions the grant. This mention shall be published at least 3 months after the start of the time limit referred to in paragraph 2(b).

(5) Provision may be made in the Implementing Regulations for the applicant to file a translation, in the two official languages of the European Patent Office other than the language of the proceedings, of the claims appearing in the text in which the Examining Division intends to grant the patent. In such case, the period laid down in paragraph 4 shall be at least five months. If the translation has not been filed in due time, the application shall be deemed to be withdrawn.

(6) At the request of the applicant, mention of grant of the European patent shall be published before expiry of the time limit under paragraph 4 or 5. Such request may only be made if the requirements pursuant to paragraphs 2 and 5 are met.

Article 98
Publication of a specification of the European patent

At the same time as it publishes the mention of the grant of the European patent, the European Patent Office shall publish a specification of the European patent containing the description, the claims and any drawings.

PART V
OPPOSITION PROCEDURE

Article 99
Opposition

(1) Within nine months from the publication of the mention of the grant of the European patent, any person may give notice to the European Patent Office of opposition to the European patent granted. Notice of opposition shall be filed in a written reasoned statement. It shall not be deemed to have been filed until the opposition fee has been paid.

(2) The opposition shall apply to the European patent in all the Contracting States in which that patent has effect.

(3) An opposition may be filed even if the European patent has been surrendered or has lapsed for all the designated States.

(4) Opponents shall be parties to the opposition proceedings as well as the proprietor of the patent.

(5) Where a person provides evidence that in a Contracting State, following a final decision, he has been entered in the patent register of such State instead of the previous proprietor, such person shall, at his request, replace the previous proprietor in respect of such State. By derogation from Article 118, the previous proprietor and the person making the request shall not be deemed to be joint proprietors unless both so request.

Article 100
Grounds for opposition

Opposition may only be filed on the grounds that:

(a) the subject-matter of the European patent is not patentable within the terms of Articles 52 to 57;

(b) the European patent does not disclose the invention in a manner sufficiently clear and complete for it to be carried out by a person skilled in the art;

(c) the subject-matter of the European patent extends beyond the content of the application as filed, or, if the patent was granted on a divisional application or on a new application filed in accordance with Article 61, beyond the content of the earlier application as filed

Article 101
Examination of the opposition

(1) If the opposition is admissible, the Opposition Division shall examine whether the grounds for opposition laid down in Article 100 prejudice the maintenance of the European patent.

(2) In the examination of the opposition, which shall be conducted in accordance with the provisions of the Implementing Regulations, the Opposition Division shall invite the parties, as often as necessary, to file observations, within a period to be fixed by the Opposition Division, on communications from another party or issued by itself.

Article 102
Revocation or maintenance of the European patent

(1) If the Opposition Division is of the opinion that the grounds for opposition mentioned in Article 100 prejudice the maintenance of the European patent, it shall revoke the patent.

(2) If the Opposition Division is of the opinion that the grounds for opposition mentioned in Article 100 do not prejudice the maintenance of the patent unamended, it shall reject the opposition.

(3) If the Opposition Division is of the opinion that, taking into consideration the amendments made by the proprietor of the patent during the opposition proceedings, the patent and the invention to which it relates meet the requirements of this Convention, it shall decide to maintain the patent as amended, provided that:

(a) it is established, in accordance with the provisions of the Implementing Regulations, that the proprietor of the patent approves the text in which the Opposition Division intends to maintain the patent;

(b) the fee for the printing of a new specification of the European patent is paid within the time limit prescribed in the Implementing Regulations.

(4) If the fee for the printing of a new specification is not paid in due time, the patent shall be revoked.

(5) Provision may be made in the Implementing Regulations for the proprietor of the patent to file a translation of any amended claims in the two official languages of the European Patent Office other than the language of the proceedings. If the translation has not been filed in due time the patent shall be revoked.

Article 103
Publication of a new specification of the European patent

If a European patent is amended under Article 102, paragraph 3, the European Patent Office shall, at the same time as it publishes the mention of the opposition decision, publish a new specification of the European patent containing the description, the claims and any drawings, in the amended form.

Article 104
Costs

(1) Each party to the proceedings shall meet the costs he has incurred unless a decision of an Opposition Division or Board of Appeal, for reasons of equity, orders, in accordance with the Implementing Regulations, a different apportionment of costs incurred during taking of evidence or in oral proceedings.

(2) On request, the registry of the Opposition Division shall fix the amount of the costs to be paid under a decision apportioning them. The fixing of the costs by the registry may be reviewed by a decision of the Opposition Division on a request filed within the period laid down in the Implementing Regulations.

(3) Any final decision of the European Patent Office fixing the amount of costs shall be dealt with, for the purpose of enforcement in the Contracting States, in the same way as a final decision given by a civil court of the State in the territory of which enforcement is to be carried out. Verification of such decision shall be limited to its authenticity.

Article 105
Intervention of the assumed infringer

(1) In the event of an opposition to a European patent being filed, any third party who proves that proceedings for infringement of the same patent have been instituted against him may, after the opposition period has expired, intervene in the opposition proceedings, if he gives notice of intervention within three months of the date on which the infringement proceedings were instituted. The same shall apply in respect of any third party who proves both that the proprietor of the patent has requested that he cease alleged infringement of the patent and that he has instituted proceedings for a court ruling that he is not infringing the patent.

(2) Notice of intervention shall be filed in a written reasoned statement. It shall not be deemed to have been filed until the opposition fee has been paid. Thereafter the intervention shall, subject to any exceptions laid down in the Implementing Regulations, be treated as an opposition.

PART VI
APPEALS PROCEDURE

Article 106
Decisions subject to appeal

(1) An appeal shall lie from decisions of the Receiving Section, Examining Divisions, Opposition Divisions and the Legal Division. It shall have suspensive effect.

(2) An appeal may be filed against the decision of the Opposition Division even if the European patent has been surrendered or has lapsed for all the

designated States.

(3) A decision which does not terminate proceedings as regards one of the parties can only be appealed together with the final decision, unless the decision allows separate appeal.

(4) The apportionment of costs of opposition proceedings cannot be the sole subject of an appeal.

(5) A decision fixing the amount of costs of opposition proceedings cannot be appealed unless the amount is in excess of that laid down in the Rules relating to Fees.

Article 107
Persons entitled to appeal and to be parties to appeal proceedings

Any party to proceedings adversely affected by a decision may appeal. Any other parties to the proceedings shall be parties to the appeal proceedings as of right.

Article 108
Time limit and form of appeal

Notice of appeal must be filed in writing at the European Patent Office within two months after the date of notification of the decision appealed from. The notice shall not be deemed to have been filed until after the fee for appeal has been paid. Within four months after the date of notification of the decision, a written statement setting out the grounds of appeal must be filed.

Article 109
Interlocutory revision

(1) If the department whose decision is contested considers the appeal to be admissible and well founded, it shall rectify its decision. This shall not apply where the appellant is opposed by another party to the proceedings.

(2) If the appeal is not allowed within three months after receipt of the statement of grounds, it shall be remitted to the Board of Appeal without delay, and without comment as to its merit

Article 110
Examination of appeals

(1) If the appeal is admissible, the Board of Appeal shall examine whether the appeal is allowable.

(2) In the examination of the appeal, which shall be conducted in accordance with the provisions of the Implementing Regulations, the Board of Appeal shall invite the parties, as often as necessary, to file observations, within a period to be fixed by the Board of Appeal, on communications from another party or issued by itself.

(3) If the applicant fails to reply in due time to an invitation under

paragraph 2, the European patent application shall be deemed to be withdrawn, unless the decision under appeal was taken by the Legal Division.

Article 111
Decision in respect of appeals

(1) Following the examination as to the allowability of the appeal, the Board of Appeal shall decide on the appeal. The Board of Appeal may either exercise any power within the competence of the department which was responsible for the decision appealed or remit the case to that department for further prosecution.

(2) If the Board of Appeal remits the case for further prosecution to the department whose decision was appealed, that department shall be bound by the ratio decidendi of the Board of Appeal, in so far as the facts are the same. If the decision which was appealed emanated from the Receiving Section, the Examining Division shall similarly be bound by the ratio decidendi of the Board of Appeal.

Article 112
Decision or opinion of the Enlarged Board of Appeal

(1) In order to ensure uniform application of the law, or if an important point of law arises:

(a) the Board of Appeal shall, during proceedings on a case and either of its own motion or following a request from a party to the appeal, refer any question to the Enlarged Board of Appeal if it considers that a decision is required for the above purposes. If the Board of Appeal rejects the request, it shall give the reasons in its final decision;

(b) the President of the European Patent Office may refer a point of law to the Enlarged Board of Appeal where two Boards of Appeal have given different decisions on that question.

(2) In the cases covered by paragraph 1(a) the parties to the appeal proceedings shall be parties to the proceedings before the Enlarged Board of Appeal.

(3) The decision of the Enlarged Board of Appeal referred to in paragraph 1(a) shall be binding on the Board of Appeal in respect of the appeal in question.

PART VII
COMMON PROVISIONS

Chapter I
Common provisions governing procedure

Article 113
Basis of decisions

(1) The decisions of the European Patent Office may only be based on grounds or evidence on which the parties concerned have had an opportunity to present their comments.

(2) The European Patent Office shall consider and decide upon the European patent application or the European patent only in the text submitted to it, or agreed, by the applicant for or proprietor of the patent.

Article 114
Examination by the European Patent Office of its own motion

(1) In proceedings before it, the European Patent Office shall examine the facts of its own motion; it shall not be restricted in this examination to the facts, evidence and arguments provided by the parties and the relief sought.

(2) The European Patent Office may disregard facts or evidence which are not submitted in due time by the parties concerned.

Article 115
Observations by third parties

(1) Following the publication of the European patent application, any person may present observations concerning the patentability of the invention in respect of which the application has been filed. Such observations must be filed in writing and must include a statement of the grounds on which they are based. That person shall not be a party to the proceedings before the European Patent Office.

(2) The observations referred to in paragraph 1 shall be communicated to the applicant for or proprietor of the patent who may comment on them.

Article 116
Oral proceedings

(1) Oral proceedings shall take place either at the instance of the European Patent Office if it considers this to be expedient or at the request of any party to the proceedings. However, the European Patent Office may reject a request for further oral proceedings before the same department where the parties and the subject of the proceedings are the same.

(2) Nevertheless, oral proceedings shall take place before the Receiving Section at the request of the applicant only where the Receiving Section considers this to be expedient or where it envisages refusing the European

patent application.

(3) Oral proceedings before the Receiving Section, the Examining Divisions and the Legal Division shall not be public.

(4) Oral proceedings, including delivery of the decision, shall be public, as regards the Boards of Appeal and the Enlarged Board of Appeal, after publication of the European patent application, and also before the Opposition Divisions, in so far as the department before which the proceedings are taking place does not decide otherwise in cases where admission of the public could have serious and unjustified disadvantages, in particular for a party to the proceedings.

Article 117
Taking of evidence

(1) In any proceedings before an Examining Division, an Opposition Division, the Legal Division or a Board of Appeal the means of giving or obtaining evidence shall include the following:

(a) hearing the parties;

(b) requests for information;

(c) the production of documents;

(d) hearing the witnesses;

(e) opinions by experts;

(f) inspection;

(g) sworn statements in writing.

(2) The Examining Division, Opposition Division or Board of Appeal may commission one of its members to examine the evidence adduced.

(3) If the European Patent Office considers it necessary for a party, witness or expert to give evidence orally, it shall either:

(a) issue a summons to the person concerned to appear before it, or

(b) request, in accordance with the provisions of Article 131, paragraph 2, the competent court in the country of residence of the person concerned to take such evidence.

(4) A party, witness or expert who is summoned before the European Patent Office may request the latter to allow his evidence to be heard by a competent court in his country of residence. On receipt of such a request, or if there has been no reply to the summons by the expiry of a period fixed by the European Patent Office in the summons, the European Patent Office may, in accordance with the provisions of Article 131, paragraph 2, request the competent court to hear the person concerned.

(5) If a party, witness or expert gives evidence before the European Patent Office, the latter may, if it considers it advisable for the evidence to be given on oath or in an equally binding form, request the competent court in the country of residence of the person concerned to re-examine his evidence under such conditions.

(6) When the European Patent Office requests a competent court to take evidence, it may request the court to take the evidence on oath or in an equally binding form and to permit a member of the department concerned to attend the hearing and question the party, witness or expert either through the intermediary of the court or directly.

Article 118
Unity of the European patent application or European patent

Where the applicants for or proprietors of a European patent are not the same in respect of different designated Contracting States, they shall be regarded as joint applicants or proprietors for the purposes of proceedings before the European Patent Office. The unity of the application or patent in these proceedings shall not be affected; in particular the text of the application or patent shall be uniform for all designated Contracting States unless otherwise provided for in this Convention.

Article 119
Notification

The European Patent Office shall, as a matter of course, notify those concerned of decisions and summonses, and of any notice or other communication from which a time limit is reckoned, or of which those concerned must be notified under other provisions of this Convention, or of which notification has been ordered by the President of the European Patent Office. Notifications may, where exceptional circumstances so require, be given through the intermediary of the central industrial property offices of the Contracting States.

Article 120
Time limits

The Implementing Regulations shall specify:

(a) the manner of computation of time limits and the conditions under which such time limits may be extended, either because the European Patent Office or the authorities referred to in Article 75, paragraph 1(b), are not open to receive documents or because mail is not delivered in the localities in which the European Patent Office or such authorities are situated or because postal services are generally interrupted or subsequently dislocated;

(b) the minima and maxima for time limits to be determined by the European Patent Office.

Article 121
Further processing of the European patent application

(1) If the European patent application is to be refused or is refused or deemed to be withdrawn following failure to reply within a time limit set by the European Patent Office, the legal consequence provided for shall not ensue or, if it has already ensued, shall be retracted if the applicant requests

further processing of the application.

(2) The request shall be filed in writing within two months of the date on which either the decision to refuse the application or the communication that the application is deemed to be withdrawn was notified. The omitted act must be completed within this time limit. The request shall not be deemed to have been filed until the fee for further processing has been paid.

(3) The department competent to decide on the omitted act shall decide on the request

Article 122
Restitutio in integrum

(1) The applicant for or proprietor of a European patent who, in spite of all due care required by the circumstances having been taken, was unable to observe a time limit vis-à-vis the European Patent Office shall, upon application, have his rights re-established if the non-observance in question has the direct consequence, by virtue of this Convention, of causing the refusal of the European patent application, or of a request, or the deeming of the European patent application to have been withdrawn, or the revocation of the European patent, or the loss of any other right or means of redress.

(2) The application must be filed in writing within two months from the removal of the cause of non-compliance with the time limit. The omitted act must be completed within this period. The application shall only be admissible within the year immediately following the expiry of the unobserved time limit. In the case of non-payment of a renewal fee, the period specified in Article 86, paragraph 2, shall be deducted from the period of one year.

(3) The application must state the grounds on which it is based, and must set out the facts on which it relies. It shall not be deemed to be filed until after the fee for re-establishment of rights has been paid.

(4) The department competent to decide on the omitted act shall decide upon the application.

(5) The provisions of this Article shall not be applicable to the time limits referred to in paragraph 2 of this Article, Article 61, paragraph 3, Article 76, paragraph 3, Article 78, paragraph 2, Article 79, paragraph 2, Article 87, paragraph 1, and Article 94, paragraph 2.

(6) Any person who, in a designated Contracting State, in good faith has used or made effective and serious preparations for using an invention which is the subject of a published European patent application or a European patent in the course of the period between the loss of rights referred to in paragraph 1 and publication of the mention of re-establishment of those rights, may without payment continue such use in the course of his business or for the needs thereof.

(7) Nothing in this Article shall limit the right of a Contracting State to grant restitutio in integrum in respect of time limits provided for in this

Convention and to be observed vis-à-vis the authorities of such State.

Article 123
Amendments

(1) The conditions under which a European patent application or a European patent may be amended in proceedings before the European Patent Office are laid down in the Implementing Regulations. In any case, an applicant shall be allowed at least one opportunity of amending the description, claims and drawings of his own volition.

(2) A European patent application or a European patent may not be amended in such a way that it contains subject-matter which extends beyond the content of the application as filed.

(3) The claims of the European patent may not be amended during opposition proceedings in such a way as to extend the protection conferred.

Article 124
Information concerning national patent applications

(1) The Examining Division or the Board of Appeal may invite the applicant to indicate, within a period to be determined by it, the States in which he has made applications for national patents for the whole or part of the invention to which the European patent application relates, and to give the reference numbers of the said applications.

(2) If the applicant fails to reply in due time to an invitation under paragraph 1, the European patent application shall be deemed to be withdrawn.

Article 125
Reference to general principles

In the absence of procedural provisions in this Convention, the European Patent Office shall take into account the principles of procedural law generally recognised in the Contracting States.

Article 126
Termination of financial obligations

(1) Rights of the Organisation to the payment of a fee to the European Patent Office shall be extinguished after four years from the end of the calendar year in which the fee fell due.

(2) Rights against the Organisation for the refunding by the European Patent Office of fees or sums of money paid in excess of a fee shall be extinguished after four years from the end of the calendar year in which the right arose.

(3) The period laid down in paragraphs 1 and 2 shall be interrupted in the case covered by paragraph 1 by a request for payment of the fee and in the case covered by paragraph 2 by a reasoned claim in writing. On interruption

it shall begin again immediately and shall end at the latest six years after the end of the year in which it originally began, unless, in the meantime, judicial proceedings to enforce the right have begun; in this case the period shall end at the earliest one year after the judgment enters into force.

Chapter II
Information to the public or official authorities

Article 127
Register of European Patents

The European Patent Office shall keep a register, to be known as the Register of European Patents, which shall contain those particulars the registration of which is provided for by this Convention. No entry shall be made in the Register prior to the publication of the European patent application. The Register shall be open to public inspection.

Article 128
Inspection of files

(1) The files relating to European patent applications, which have not yet been published, shall not be made available for inspection without the consent of the applicant.

(2) Any person who can prove that the applicant for a European patent has invoked the rights under the application against him may obtain inspection of the files prior to the publication of that application and without the consent of the applicant.

(3) Where a European divisional application or a new European patent application filed under Article 61, paragraph 1, is published, any person may obtain inspection of the files of the earlier application prior to the publication of that application and without the consent of the relevant applicant.

(4) Subsequent to the publication of the European patent application, the files relating to such application and the resulting European patent may be inspected on request, subject to the restrictions laid down in the Implementing Regulations.

(5) Even prior to the publication of the European patent application, the European Patent Office may communicate the following bibliographic data to third parties or publish them:

(a) the number of the European patent application;

(b) the date of filing of the European patent application and, where the priority of a previous application is claimed, the date, State and file number of the previous application;

(c) the name of the applicant;

(d) the title of the invention;

(e) the Contracting States designated.

Article 129
Periodical publications

The European Patent Office shall periodically publish:

(a) a European Patent Bulletin containing entries made in the Register of European Patents, as well as other particulars the publication of which is prescribed by this Convention;

(b) an Official Journal of the European Patent Office, containing notices and information of a general character issued by the President of the European Patent Office, as well as any other information relevant to this Convention or its implementation.

Article 130
Exchanges of information

(1) The European Patent Office and, subject to the application of the legislative or regulatory provisions referred to in Article 75, paragraph 2, the central industrial property office of any Contracting State shall, on request, communicate to each other any useful information regarding the filing of European or national patent applications and regarding any proceedings concerning such applications and the resulting patents.

(2) The provisions of paragraph 1 shall apply to the communication of information by virtue of working agreements between the European Patent Office and:

(a) the central industrial property office of any State which is not a party to this Convention;

(b) any inter-governmental organisation entrusted with the task of granting patents;

(c) any other organisation.

(3) The communications under paragraphs 1 and 2(a) and (b) shall not be subject to the restrictions laid down in Article 128. The Administrative Council may decide that communications under paragraph 2(c) shall not be subject to such restrictions, provided that the organisation concerned shall treat the information communicated as confidential until the European patent application has been published.

Article 131
Administrative and legal co-operation

(1) Unless otherwise provided in this Convention or in national laws, the European Patent Office and the courts or authorities of Contracting States shall on request give assistance to each other by communicating information or opening files for inspection. Where the European Patent Office lays files open to inspection by courts, Public Prosecutors' Offices or central industrial property offices, the inspection shall not be subject to the restrictions laid down in Article 128.

(2) Upon receipt of letters rogatory from the European Patent Office, the

courts or other competent authorities of Contracting States shall undertake, on behalf of that Office and within the limits of their jurisdiction, any necessary enquiries or other legal measures.

Article 132
Exchange of publications

(1) The European Patent Office and the central industrial property offices of the Contracting States shall despatch to each other on request and for their own use one or more copies of their respective publications free of charge.

(2) The European Patent Office may conclude agreements relating to the exchange or supply of publications.

Chapter III
Representation

Article 133
General principles of representation

(1) Subject to the provisions of paragraph 2, no person shall be compelled to be represented by a professional representative in proceedings established by this Convention.

(2) Natural or legal persons not having either a residence or their principal place of business within the territory of one of the Contracting States must be represented by a professional representative and act through him in all proceedings established by this Convention, other than in filing the European patent application; the Implementing Regulations may permit other exceptions.

(3) Natural or legal persons having their residence or principal place of business within the territory of one of the Contracting States may be represented in proceedings established by this Convention by an employee, who need not be a professional representative but who must be authorised in accordance with the Implementing Regulations. The Implementing Regulations may provide whether and under what conditions an employee of such a legal person may also represent other legal persons which have their principal place of business within the territory of one of the Contracting States and which have economic connections with the first legal person.

(4) The Implementing Regulations may prescribe special provisions concerning the common representation of parties acting in common.

Article 134
Professional representatives

(1) Professional representation of natural or legal persons in proceedings established by this Convention may only be undertaken by professional representatives whose names appear on a list maintained for this purpose by the European Patent Office.

(2) Any natural person who fulfils the following conditions may be entered on the list of professional representatives:

(a) he must be a national of one of the Contracting States;

(b) he must have his place of business or employment within the territory of one of the Contracting States;

(c) he must have passed the European qualifying examination.

(3) Entry shall be effected upon request, accompanied by certificates which must indicate that the conditions laid down in paragraph 2 are fulfilled.

(4) Persons whose names appear on the list of professional representatives shall be entitled to act in all proceedings established by this Convention.

(5) For the purpose of acting as a professional representative, any person whose name appears on the list referred to in paragraph 1 shall be entitled to establish a place of business in any Contracting State in which proceedings established by this Convention may be conducted, having regard to the Protocol on Centralisation annexed to this Convention. The authorities of such State may remove that entitlement in individual cases only in application of legal provisions adopted for the purpose of protecting public security and law and order. Before such action is taken, the President of the European Patent Office shall be consulted.

(6) The President of the European Patent Office may, in special circumstances, grant exemption from the requirement of paragraph 2(a).

(7) Professional representation in proceedings established by this Convention may also be undertaken, in the same way as by a professional representative, by any legal practitioner qualified in one of the Contracting States and having his place of business within such State, to the extent that he is entitled, within the said State, to act as a professional representative in patent matters. Paragraph 5 shall apply *mutatis mutandis*.

(8) The Administrative Council may adopt provisions governing:

(a) the qualifications and training required of a person for admission to the European qualifying examination and the conduct of such examination;

(b) the establishment or recognition of an institute constituted by the persons entitled to act as professional representatives by virtue of either the European qualifying examination or the provisions of Article 163, paragraph 7;

(c) any disciplinary power to be exercised by that institute or the European Patent Office on such persons.

PART VIII
IMPACT ON NATIONAL LAW

Chapter I
Conversion into a national patent application

Article 135
Request for the application of national procedure

(1) The central industrial property office of a designated Contracting State shall apply the procedure for the grant of a national patent only at the request of the applicant for or proprietor of a European patent, and in the following circumstances:

(a) when the European patent application is deemed to be withdrawn pursuant to Article 77, paragraph 5, or Article 162, paragraph 4;

(b) in such other cases as are provided for by the national law in which the European patent application is refused or withdrawn or deemed to be withdrawn, or the European patent is revoked under this Convention.

(2) The request for conversion shall be filed within three months after the European patent application has been withdrawn or after notification has been made that the application is deemed to be withdrawn, or after a decision has been notified refusing the application or revoking the European patent. The effect referred to in Article 66 shall lapse if the request is not filed in due time.

Article 136
Submission and transmission of the request

(1) A request for conversion shall be filed with the European Patent Office and shall specify the Contracting States in which application of the procedure for the grant of a national patent is desired. The request shall not be deemed to be filed until the conversion fee has been paid. The European Patent Office shall transmit the request to the central industrial property offices of the Contracting States specified therein, accompanied by a copy of the files relating to the European patent application or the European patent.

(2) However, if the applicant is notified that the European patent application has been deemed to be withdrawn pursuant to Article 77, paragraph 5, the request shall be filed with the central industrial property office with which the application has been filed. That office shall, subject to the provisions of national security, transmit the request, together with a copy of the European patent application, directly to the central industrial property offices of the Contracting States specified by the applicant in the request. The effect referred to in Article 66 shall lapse if such transmission is not made within twenty months after the date of filing or, if a priority has been claimed, after the date of priority.

Article 137
Formal requirements for conversion

(1) A European patent application transmitted in accordance with Article 136 shall not be subjected to formal requirements of national law which are different from or additional to those provided for in this Convention.

(2) Any central industrial property office to which the application is transmitted may require that the applicant shall, within not less than two months:

(a) pay the national application fee;

(b) file a translation in one of the official languages of the State in question of the original text of the European patent application and, where appropriate, of the text, as amended during proceedings before the European Patent Office, which the applicant wishes to submit to the national procedure.

Chapter II
Revocation and prior rights

Article 138
Grounds for revocation

(1) Subject to the provisions of Article 139, a European patent may only be revoked under the law of a Contracting State, with effect for its territory, on the following grounds:

(a) if the subject-matter of the European patent is not patentable within the terms of Articles 52 to 57;

(b) if the European patent does not disclose the invention in a manner sufficiently clear and complete for it to be carried out by a person skilled in the art;

(c) if the subject-matter of the European patent extends beyond the content of the application as filed or, if the patent was granted on a divisional application or on a new application filed in accordance with Article 61, beyond the content of the earlier application as filed;

(d) if the protection conferred by the European patent has been extended;

(e) if the proprietor of the European patent is not entitled under Article 60, paragraph 1.

(2) If the grounds for revocation only affect the European patent in part, revocation shall be pronounced in the form of a corresponding limitation of the said patent. If the national law so allows, the limitation may be effected in the form of an amendment to the claims, the description or the drawings.

Article 139
Rights of earlier date or the same date

(1) In any designated Contracting State a European patent application and

a European patent shall have with regard to a national patent application and a national patent the same prior right effect as a national patent application and a national patent.

(2) A national patent application and a national patent in a Contracting State shall have with regard to a European patent in which that Contracting State is designated the same prior right effect as they have with regard to a national patent.

(3) Any Contracting State may prescribe whether and on what terms an invention disclosed in both a European patent application or patent and a national application or patent having the same date of filing or, where priority is claimed, the same date of priority, may be protected simultaneously by both applications or patents.

Chapter III
Miscellaneous effects

Article 140
National utility models and utility certificates

Article 66, Article 124, Articles 135 to 137 and Article 139 shall apply to utility models and utility certificates and to applications for utility models and utility certificates registered or deposited in the Contracting States whose laws make provision for such models or certificates.

Article 141
Renewal fees for European patents

(1) Renewal fees in respect of a European patent may only be imposed for the years which follow that referred to in Article 86, paragraph 4.

(2) Any renewal fees falling due within two months after the publication of the mention of the grant of the European patent shall be deemed to have been validly paid if they are paid within that period. Any additional fee provided for under national law shall not be charged.

PART IX
SPECIAL AGREEMENTS
Article 142
Unitary patents

(1) Any group of Contracting States, which has provided by a special agreement that a European patent granted for those States has a unitary character throughout their territories, may provide that a European patent may only be granted jointly in respect of all those States.

(2) Where any group of Contracting States has availed itself of the authorisation given in paragraph 1, the provisions of this Part shall apply.

Article 143
Special departments of the European Patent Office

(1) The group of Contracting States may give additional tasks to the European Patent Office.

(2) Special departments common to the Contracting States in the group may be set up within the European Patent Office in order to carry out the additional tasks. The President of the European Patent Office shall direct such special departments; Article 10, paragraphs 2 and 3, shall apply *mutatis mutandis*.

Article 144
Representation before special departments

The group of Contracting States may lay down special provisions to govern representation of parties before the departments referred to in Article 143, paragraph 2.

Article 145
Select committee of the Administrative Council

(1) The group of Contracting States may set up a select committee of the Administrative Council for the purpose of supervising the activities of the special departments set up under Article 143, paragraph 2; the European Patent Office shall place at its disposal such staff, premises and equipment as may be necessary for the performance of its duties. The President of the European Patent Office shall be responsible for the activities of the special departments to the select committee of the Administrative Council.

(2) The composition, powers and functions of the select committee shall be determined by the group of Contracting States.

Article 146
Cover for expenditure for carrying out special tasks

Where additional tasks have been given to the European Patent Office under Article 143, the group of Contracting States shall bear the expenses incurred by the Organisation in carrying out these tasks. Where special departments have been set up in the European Patent Office to carry out these additional tasks, the group shall bear the expenditure on staff, premises and equipment chargeable in respect of these departments. Article 39, paragraphs 3 and 4, Article 41 and Article 47 shall apply *mutatis mutandis*.

Article 147
Payments in respect of renewal fees for unitary patents

If the group of Contracting States has fixed a common scale of renewal fees in respect of European patents the proportion referred to in Article 39, paragraph 1, shall be calculated on the basis of the common scale; the minimum amount referred to in Article 39, paragraph 1, shall apply to the unitary patent. Article 39, paragraphs 3 and 4, shall apply *mutatis mutandis*.

Article 148
The European patent application as an object of property

(1) Article 74 shall apply unless the group of Contracting States has specified otherwise.

(2) The group of Contracting States may provide that a European patent application for which these Contracting States are designated may only be transferred, mortgaged or subjected to any legal means of execution in respect of all the Contracting States of the group and in accordance with the provisions of the special agreement.

Article 149
Joint designation

(1) The group of Contracting States may provide that these States may only be designated jointly, and that the designation of one or some only of such States shall be deemed to constitute the designation of all the States of the group.

(2) Where the European Patent Office acts as a designated Office under Article 153, paragraph 1, paragraph 1 shall apply if the applicant has indicated in the international application that he wishes to obtain a European patent for one or more of the designated States of the group. The same shall apply if the applicant designates in the international application one of the Contracting States in the group, whose national law provides that the designation of that State shall have the effect of the application being for a European patent.

PART X
INTERNATIONAL APPLICATION PURSUANT TO THE PATENT COOPERATION TREATY

Article 150
Application of the Patent Cooperation Treaty

(1) The Patent Cooperation Treaty of 19 June 1970, hereinafter referred to as the Cooperation Treaty, shall be applied in accordance with the provisions of this Part.

(2) International applications filed under the Cooperation Treaty may be the subject of proceedings before the European Patent Office. In such proceedings, the provisions of that Treaty shall be applied, supplemented by the provisions of this Convention. In case of conflict, the provisions of the Cooperation Treaty shall prevail. In particular, for an international application the time limit within which a request for examination must be filed under Article 94, paragraph 2, of this Convention shall not expire before the time prescribed by Article 22 or Article 39 of the Cooperation Treaty as the case maybe.

(3) An international application, for which the European Patent Office acts as designated Office or elected Office, shall be deemed to be a European patent application.

(4) Where reference is made in this Convention to the Cooperation Treaty, such reference shall include the Regulations under that Treaty.

Article 151
The European Patent Office as a receiving Office

(1) The European Patent Office may act as a receiving Office within the meaning of Article 2(xv) of the Cooperation Treaty if the applicant is a resident or national of a Contracting State to this Convention in respect of which the Cooperation Treaty has entered into force.

(2) The European Patent Office may also act as a receiving Office if the applicant is a resident or national of a State which is not a Contracting State to this Convention, but which is a Contracting State to the Cooperation Treaty and which has concluded an agreement with the Organisation whereby the European Patent Office acts as a receiving Office, in accordance with the provisions of the Cooperation Treaty, in place of the national office of that State.

(3) Subject to the prior approval of the Administrative Council, the European Patent Office may also act as a receiving Office for any other applicant, in accordance with an agreement concluded between the Organisation and the International Bureau of the World Intellectual Property Organization.

Article 152
Filing and transmittal of the international application

(1) If the applicant chooses the European Patent Office as a receiving Office for his international application, he shall file it directly with the European Patent Office. Article 75, paragraph 2, shall nevertheless apply *mutatis mutandis*.

(2) In the event of an international application being filed with the European Patent Office through the intermediary of the competent central industrial property office, the Contracting State concerned shall take all necessary measures to ensure that the application is transmitted to the European Patent Office in time for the latter to be able to comply in due time with the conditions for transmittal under the Cooperation Treaty.

(3) Each international application shall be subject to the payment of the transmittal fee, which shall be payable within one month after receipt of the application.

Article 153
The European Patent Office as a designated Office

(1) The European Patent Office shall act as a designated Office within the meaning of Article 2(xiii) of the Cooperation Treaty for those Contracting

States to this Convention in respect of which the Cooperation Treaty has entered into force and which are designated in the international application if the applicant informs the receiving Office in the international application that he wishes to obtain a European patent for these States. The same shall apply if, in the international application, the applicant designates a Contracting State of which the national law provides that designation of that State shall have the effect of the application being for a European patent.

(2) When the European Patent Office acts as a designated Office, the Examining Division shall be competent to take decisions which are required under Article 25, paragraph 2(a), of the Cooperation Treaty.

Article 154
The European Patent Office as an International Searching Authority

(1) The European Patent Office shall act as an International Searching Authority within the meaning of Chapter I of the Cooperation Treaty for applicants who are residents or nationals of a Contracting State in respect of which the Cooperation Treaty has entered into force, subject to the conclusion of an agreement between the Organisation and the International Bureau of the World Intellectual Property Organization.

(2) Subject to the prior approval of the Administrative Council, the European Patent Office shall also act as an International Searching Authority for any other applicant, in accordance with an agreement concluded between the Organisation and the International Bureau of the World Intellectual Property Organization.

(3) The Boards of Appeal shall be responsible for deciding on a protest made by an applicant against an additional fee charged by the European Patent Office under the provisions of Article 17, paragraph 3(a), of the Cooperation Treaty.

Article 155
The European Patent Office as an International Preliminary Examining Authority

(1) The European Patent Office shall act as an International Preliminary Examining Authority within the meaning of Chapter II of the Cooperation Treaty for applicants who are residents or nationals of a Contracting State bound by that Chapter, subject to the conclusion of an agreement between the Organisation and the International Bureau of the World Intellectual Property Organization.

(2) Subject to the prior approval of the Administrative Council, the European Patent Office shall also act as an International Preliminary Examining Authority for any other applicant, in accordance with an agreement concluded between the Organisation and the International Bureau of the World Intellectual Property Organization.

(3) The Boards of Appeal shall be responsible for deciding on a protest

made by an applicant against an additional fee charged by the European Patent Office under the provisions of Article 34, paragraph 3(a), of the Cooperation Treaty.

Article 156
The European Patent Office as an elected Office

The European Patent Office shall act as an elected Office within the meaning of Article 2(xiv) of the Cooperation Treaty if the applicant has elected any of the designated States referred to in Article 153, paragraph 1, or Article 149, paragraph 2, for which Chapter II of that Treaty has become binding. Subject to the prior approval of the Administrative Council, the same shall apply where the applicant is a resident or national of a State which is not a party to that Treaty or which is not bound by Chapter II of that Treaty, provided that he is one of the persons whom the Assembly of the International Patent Cooperation Union has decided to allow, pursuant to Article 31, paragraph 2(b), of the Cooperation Treaty, to make a demand for international preliminary examination.

Article 157
International search report

(1) Without prejudice to the provisions of paragraphs 2 to 4, the international search report under Article 18 of the Cooperation Treaty or any declaration under Article 17, paragraph 2(a), of that Treaty and their publication under Article 21 of that Treaty shall take the place of the European search report and the mention of its publication in the European Patent Bulletin.

(2) Subject to the decisions of the Administrative Council referred to in paragraph 3:

(a) a supplementary European search report shall be drawn up in respect of all international applications;

(b) the applicant shall pay the search fee, which shall be paid at the same time as the national fee provided for in Article 22, paragraph 1, or Article 39, paragraph 1, of the Cooperation Treaty. If the search fee is not paid in due time the application shall be deemed to be withdrawn.

(3) The Administrative Council may decide under what conditions and to what extent:

(a) the supplementary European search report is to be dispensed with;

(b) the search fee is to be reduced.

(4) The Administrative Council may at any time rescind the decisions taken pursuant to paragraph 3.

Article 158
Publication of the international application
and its supply to the European Patent Office

(1) Publication under Article 21 of the Cooperation Treaty of an international application for which the European Patent Office is a designated Office shall, subject to paragraph 3, take the place of the publication of a European patent application and shall be mentioned in the European Patent Bulletin. Such an application shall not however be considered as comprised in the state of the art in accordance with Article 54, paragraph 3, if the conditions laid down in paragraph 2 are not fulfilled.

(2) The international application shall be supplied to the European Patent Office in one of its official languages. The applicant shall pay to the European Patent Office the national fee provided for in Article 22, paragraph 1, or Article 39, paragraph 1, of the Cooperation Treaty.

(3) If the international application is published in a language other than one of the official languages of the European Patent Office, that Office shall publish the international application, supplied as specified in paragraph 2. Subject to the provisions of Article 67, paragraph 3, the provisional protection in accordance with Article 67, paragraphs 1 and 2, shall be effective from the date of that publication.

PART XI
TRANSITIONAL PROVISIONS

Article 159
Administrative Council during a transitional period

(1) The States referred to in Article 169, paragraph 1, shall appoint their representatives to the Administrative Council; on the invitation of the Government of the Federal Republic of Germany, the Administrative Council shall meet no later than two months after the entry into force of this Convention, particularly for the purpose of appointing the President of the European Patent Office.

(2) The duration of the term of office of the first Chairman of the Administrative Council appointed after the entry into force of this Convention shall be four years.

(3) The term of office of two of the elected members of the first Board of the Administrative Council set up after the entry into force of this Convention shall be five and four years respectively.

Article 160
Appointment of employees during a transitional period

(1) Until such time as the Service Regulations for permanent employees and the conditions of employment of other employees of the European Patent Office have been adopted, the Administrative Council and the President of the European Patent Office, each within their respective powers, shall

recruit the necessary employees and shall conclude short-term contracts to that effect. The Administrative Council may lay down general principles in respect of recruitment.

(2) During a transitional period, the expiry of which shall be determined by the Administrative Council, the Administrative Council, after consulting the President of the European Patent Office, may appoint as members of the Enlarged Board of Appeal or of the Boards of Appeal technically or legally qualified members of national courts and authorities of Contracting States who may continue their activities in their national courts or authorities. They may be appointed for a term of less than five years, though this shall not be less than one year, and may be reappointed.

Article 161
First accounting period

(1) The first accounting period of the Organisation shall extend from the date of entry into force of this Convention to 31 December of the same year. If that date falls within the second half of the year, the accounting period shall extend until 31 December of the following year.

(2) The budget for the first accounting period shall be drawn up as soon as possible after the entry into force of this Convention. Until contributions provided for in Article 40 due in accordance with the first budget are received by the Organisation, the Contracting States shall, upon the request of and within the limit of the amount fixed by the Administrative Council, make advances which shall be deducted from their contributions in respect of that budget. The advances shall be determined in accordance with the scale referred to in Article 40. Article 39, paragraphs 3 and 4, shall apply *mutatis mutandis* to the advances.

Article 162
Progressive expansion of the field of activity of the European Patent Office

(1) European patent applications may be filed with the European Patent Office from the date fixed by the Administrative Council on the recommendation of the President of the European Patent Office.

(2) The Administrative Council may, on the recommendation of the President of the European Patent Office, decide that, as from the date referred to in paragraph 1, the processing of European patent applications may be restricted. Such restriction may be in respect of certain areas of technology. However, examination shall in any event be made as to whether European patent applications can be accorded a date of filing.

(3) If a decision has been taken under paragraph 2, the Administrative Council may not subsequently further restrict the processing of European patent applications.

(4) Where, as a result of the procedure being restricted under paragraph 2, a European patent application cannot be further processed, the European

Patent Office shall communicate this to the applicant and shall point out that he may make a request for conversion. The European patent application shall be deemed to be withdrawn on receipt of such communication.

Article 163
Professional representatives during a transitional period

(1) During a transitional period, the expiry of which shall be determined by the Administrative Council [October 7, 1981], notwithstanding the provisions of Article 134, paragraph 2, any natural person who fulfils the following conditions may be entered on the list of professional representatives:

(a) he must be a national of a Contracting State;

(b) he must have his place of business or employment within the territory of one of the Contracting States;

(c) he must be entitled to represent natural or legal persons in patent matters before the central industrial property office of the Contracting State in which he has his place of business or employment.

(2) Entry shall be effected upon request, accompanied by a certificate, furnished by the central industrial property office, which must indicate that the conditions laid down in paragraph 1 are fulfilled.

(3) When, in any Contracting State, the entitlement referred to in paragraph 1(c) is not conditional upon the requirement of special professional qualifications, persons applying to be entered on the list who act in patent matters before the central industrial property office of the said State must have habitually so acted for at least five years. However, persons whose professional qualification to represent natural or legal persons in patent matters before the central industrial property office of one of the Contracting States is officially recognised in accordance with the regulations laid down by such State shall not be subject to the condition of having exercised the profession. The certificate furnished by the central industrial property office must indicate that the applicant satisfies one of the conditions referred to in the present paragraph.

(4) The President of the European Patent Office may grant exemption from:

(a) the requirement of paragraph 3, first sentence, if the applicant furnishes proof that he has acquired the requisite qualification in another way;

(b) the requirement of paragraph 1(a) in special circumstances.

(5) The President of the European Patent Office shall grant exemption from the requirement of paragraph 1(a) if on 5 October 1973 the applicant fulfilled the requirements of paragraph 1(b) and (c).

(6) Persons having their places of business or employment in a State which acceded to this Convention less than one year before the expiry of the transitional period referred to in paragraph 1 or after the expiry of the transitional period may, under the conditions laid down in paragraphs 1 to 5, during a period of one year calculated from the date of entry into force of the accession of that State, be entered on the list of professional

representatives.

(7) After the expiry of the transitional period, any person whose name was entered on the list of professional representatives during that period shall, without prejudice to any disciplinary measures taken under Article 134, paragraph 8(c), remain thereon or, on request, be restored thereto, provided that he then fulfils the requirement of paragraph 1(b).

PART XII
FINAL PROVISIONS

Article 164
Implementing Regulations and Protocols

(1) The Implementing Regulations, the Protocol on Recognition, the Protocol on Privileges and Immunities, the Protocol on Centralisation and the Protocol on the Interpretation of Article 69 shall be integral parts of this Convention.

(2) In the case of conflict between the provisions of this Convention and those of the Implementing Regulations, the provisions of this Convention shall prevail.

Article 165
Signature—Ratification

(1) This Convention shall be open for signature until 5 April 1974 by the States which took part in the Inter-Governmental Conference for the setting up of a European System for the Grant of Patents or were informed of the holding of that conference and offered the option of taking part therein.

(2) This Convention shall be subject to ratification; instruments of ratification shall be deposited with the Government of the Federal Republic of Germany.

Article 166
Accession

(1) This Convention shall be open to accession by:

(a) the States referred to in Article 165, paragraph 1;

(b) any other European State at the invitation of the Administrative Council.

(2) Any State which has been a party to the Convention and has ceased so to be as a result of the application of Article 172, paragraph 4, may again become a party to the Convention by acceding to it.

(3) Instruments of accession shall be deposited with the Government of the Federal Republic of Germany.

Article 167
Reservations

(1) Each Contracting State may, at the time of signature or when depositing its instrument of ratification or accession, make only the reservations specified in paragraph 2.

(2) Each Contracting State may reserve the right to provide that:

(a) European patents, in so far as they confer protection on chemical, pharmaceutical or food products, as such, shall, in accordance with the provisions applicable to national patents, be ineffective or revocable; this reservation shall not affect protection conferred by the patent in so far as it involves a process of manufacture or use of a chemical product or a process of manufacture of a pharmaceutical or food product;

(b) European patents, in so far as they confer protection on agricultural or horticultural processes other than those to which Article 53, sub-paragraph (b), applies, shall, in accordance with the provisions applicable to national patents, be ineffective or revocable;

(c) European patents shall have a term shorter than twenty years, in accordance with the provisions applicable to national patents;

(d) it shall not be bound by the Protocol on Recognition.

(3) Any reservation made by a Contracting State shall have effect for a period of not more than ten years from the entry into force of this Convention. However, where a Contracting State has made any of the reservations referred to in paragraph 2(a) and (b), the Administrative Council may, in respect of such State, extend the period by not more than five years for all or part of any reservation made, if that State submits, at the latest one year before the end of the ten-year period, a reasoned request which satisfies the Administrative Council that the State is not in a position to dispense with that reservation by the expiry of the ten-year period.

(4) Any Contracting State that has made a reservation shall withdraw this reservation as soon as circumstances permit. Such withdrawal shall be made by notification addressed to the Government of the Federal Republic of Germany and shall take effect one month from the date of receipt of such notification.

(5) Any reservation made in accordance with paragraph 2(a), (b) or (c) shall apply to European patents granted on European patent applications filed during the period in which the reservation has effect. The effect of the reservation shall continue for the term of the patent.

(6) Without prejudice to paragraphs 4 and 5, any reservation shall cease to have effect on expiry of the period referred to in paragraph 3, first sentence, or, if the period is extended, on expiry of the extended period.

Article 168
Territorial field of application

(1) Any Contracting State may declare in its instrument of ratification or accession, or may inform the Government of the Federal Republic of

Germany by written notification any time thereafter, that this Convention shall be applicable to one or more of the territories for the external relations of which it is responsible. European patents granted for that Contracting State shall also have effect in the territories for which such a declaration has taken effect.

(2) If the declaration referred to in paragraph 1 is contained in the instrument of ratification or accession, it shall take effect on the same date as the ratification or accession; if the declaration is made in a notification after the deposit of the instrument of ratification or accession, such notification shall take effect six months after the date of its receipt by the Government of the Federal Republic of Germany.

(3) Any Contracting State may at any time declare that the Convention shall cease to apply to some or to all of the territories in respect of which it has given a notification pursuant to paragraph 1. Such declaration shall take effect one year after the date on which the Government of the Federal Republic of Germany received notification thereof.

Article 169
Entry into force

(1) This Convention shall enter into force three months after the deposit of the last instrument of ratification or accession by six States on whose territory the total number of patent applications filed in 1970 amounted to at least 180 000 for all the said States.

(2) Any ratification or accession after the entry into force of this Convention shall take effect on the first day of the third month after the deposit of the instrument of ratification or accession.

Article 170
Initial contribution

(1) Any State which ratifies or accedes to this Convention after its entry into force shall pay to the Organisation an initial contribution, which shall not be refunded.

(2) The initial contribution shall be 5% of an amount calculated by applying the percentage obtained for the State in question, on the date on which ratification or accession takes effect, in accordance with the scale provided for in Article 40, paragraphs 3 and 4, to the sum of the special financial contributions due from the other Contracting States in respect of the accounting periods preceding the date referred to above.

(3) In the event that special financial contributions were not required in respect of the accounting period immediately preceding the date referred to in paragraph 2, the scale of contributions referred to in that paragraph shall be the scale that would have been applicable to the State concerned in respect of the last year for which financial contributions were required.

Article 171
Duration of the Convention

The present Convention shall be of unlimited duration.

Article 172
Revision

(1) This Convention may be revised by a Conference of the Contracting States.

(2) The Conference shall be prepared and convened by the Administrative Council. The Conference shall not be deemed to be validly constituted unless at least three-quarters of the Contracting States are represented at it. In order to adopt the revised text there must be a majority of three-quarters of the Contracting States represented and voting at the Conference. Abstentions shall not be considered as votes.

(3) The revised text shall enter into force when it has been ratified or acceded to by the number of Contracting States specified by the Conference, and at the time specified by that Conference.

(4) Such States as have not ratified or acceded to the revised text of the Convention at the time of its entry into force shall cease to be parties to this Convention as from that time.

Article 173
Disputes between Contracting States

(1) Any dispute between Contracting States concerning the interpretation or application of the present Convention which is not settled by negotiation shall be submitted, at the request of one of the States concerned, to the Administrative Council, which shall endeavour to bring about agreement between the States concerned.

(2) If such agreement is not reached within six months from the date when the Administrative Council was seized of the dispute, any one of the States concerned may submit the dispute to the International Court of Justice for a binding decision.

Article 174
Denunciation

Any Contracting State may at any time denounce this Convention. Notification of denunciation shall be given to the Government of the Federal Republic of Germany. Denunciation shall take effect one year after the date of receipt of such notification.

Article 175
Preservation of acquired rights

(1) In the event of a State ceasing to be party to this Convention in accordance with Article 172, paragraph 4, or Article 174, rights already

acquired pursuant to this Convention shall not be impaired.

(2) A European patent application which is pending when a designated State ceases to be party to the Convention shall be processed by the European Patent Office, in so far as that State is concerned, as if the Convention in force thereafter were applicable to that State.

(3) The provisions of paragraph 2 shall apply to European patents in respect of which, on the date mentioned in that paragraph, an opposition is pending or the opposition period has not expired.

(4) Nothing in this Article shall affect the right of any State that has ceased to be a party to this Convention to treat any European patent in accordance with the text to which it was a party.

Article 176
Financial rights and obligations of a former Contracting State

(1) Any State which has ceased to be a party to this Convention in accordance with Article 172, paragraph 4, or Article 174, shall have the special financial contributions which it has paid pursuant to Article 40, paragraph 2, refunded to it by the Organisation only at the time and under the conditions whereby the Organisation refunds special financial contributions paid by other States during the same accounting period.

(2) The State referred to in paragraph 1 shall, even after ceasing to be a party to this Convention, continue to pay the proportion pursuant to Article 39 of renewal fees in respect of European patents remaining in force in that State, at the rate current on the date on which it ceased to be a party.

Article 177
Languages of the Convention

(1) This Convention, drawn up in a single original, in the English, French and German languages, shall be deposited in the archives of the Government of the Federal Republic of Germany, the three texts being equally authentic.

(2) The texts of this Convention drawn up in official languages of Contracting States other than those referred to in paragraph 1 shall, if they have been approved by the Administrative Council, be considered as official texts. In the event of conflict on the interpretation of the various texts, the texts referred to in paragraph 1 shall be authentic.

Article 178
Transmission and notifications

(1) The Government of the Federal Republic of Germany shall draw up certified true copies of this Convention and shall transmit them to the Governments of all signatory or acceding States.

(2) The Government of the Federal Republic of Germany shall notify to the Governments of the States referred to in paragraph 1:

(a) any signature;

(b) the deposit of any instrument of ratification or accession;

(c) any reservation or withdrawal of reservation pursuant to the provisions of Article 167;

(d) any declaration or notification received pursuant to the provisions of Article 168;

(e) the date of entry into force of this Convention;

(f) any denunciation received pursuant to the provisions of Article 174 and the date on which such denunciation comes into force.

(3) The Government of the Federal Republic of Germany shall register this Convention with the Secretariat of the United Nations.

IN WITNESS WHEREOF, the Plenipotentiaries authorised thereto, having presented their Full Powers, found to be in good and due form, have signed this Convention.

Done at Munich this fifth day of October one thousand nine hundred and seventy-three.

EUROPEAN PATENT CONVENTION
Protocol on the Interpretation of Article 69 of the Convention
adopted at the Munich Diplomatic Conference for the setting up of a European System for the Grant of Patents on 5 October 1973

Article 69 should not be interpreted in the sense that the extent of the protection conferred by a European patent is to be understood as that defined by the strict, literal meaning of the wording used in the claims, the description and drawings being employed only for the purpose of resolving an ambiguity found in the claims. Neither should it be interpreted in the sense that the claims serve only as a guideline and that the actual protection conferred may extend to what, from a consideration of the description and drawings by a person skilled in the art, the patentee has contemplated. On the contrary, it is to be interpreted as defining a position between these extremes which combines a fair protection for the patentee with a reasonable degree of certainty for third parties.

(The Protocol shall be an integral part of the Convention pursuant to Article 164, paragraph 1.)

CONVENTION FOR THE UNIFICATION OF CERTAIN POINTS OF SUBSTANTIVE LAW ON PATENTS FOR INVENTION

Done at Strasbourg, November 27, 1963[*]

The member States of the Council of Europe, signatory hereto,

Considering that the aim of the Council of Europe is to achieve a greater unity between its members for the purpose, among others, of facilitating their economic and social progress by agreements and common action in economic, social, cultural, scientific, legal and administrative matters;

Considering that the unification of certain points of substantive law on patents for invention is likely to assist industry and inventors, to promote technical progress and contribute to the creation of an international patent;

Having regard to Article 15 of the Convention for the Protection of Industrial Property signed at Paris on 20th March 1883, revised at Brussels on 14th December 1900, at Washington on 2nd June 1911, at The Hague on 6th November 1925, at London on 2nd June 1934 and at Lisbon on 31st October 1958,

Have agreed as follows:

Article 1

In the Contracting States, patents shall be granted for any inventions which are susceptible of industrial application, which are new and which involve an inventive step. An invention which does not comply with these conditions shall not be the subject of a valid patent. A patent declared invalid because the invention does not comply with these conditions shall be considered invalid *ab initio*.

Article 2

The Contracting States shall not be bound to provide for the grant of patents in respect of:

(*a*) inventions the publication or exploitation of which would be contrary to "*ordre public*" or morality, provided that the exploitation shall not be deemed to be so contrary merely because it is prohibited by a law or regulation;

(*b*) plant or animal varieties or essentially biological processes for the production of plants or animals; this provision does not apply to micro-biological processes and the products thereof.

Article 3

An invention shall be considered as susceptible of industrial application if

---

* This Convention entered into force on August 1, 1980. Denmark, the Federal Republic of Germany, France, Ireland, Italy, Liechtenstein, Luxembourg, Netherlands, Sweden, Switzerland and the United Kingdom are bound by the terms of this Convention.

it can be made or used in any kind of industry including agriculture.

Article 4

1. An invention shall be considered to be new if it does not form part of the state of the art.

2. Subject to the provisions of paragraph 4 of this Article, the state of the art shall be held to comprise everything made available to the public by means of a written or oral description, by use, or in any other way, before the date of the patent application or of a foreign application, the priority of which is validly claimed.

3. Any Contracting State may consider the contents of applications for patents made, or of patents granted, in that State, which have been officially published on or after the date referred to in paragraph 2 of this Article, as comprised in the state of the art, to the extent to which such contents have an earlier priority date.

4. A patent shall not be refused or held invalid by virtue only of the fact that the invention was made public, within six months preceding the filing of the application, if the disclosure was due to, or in consequence of:

   (a) an evident abuse in relation to the applicant or his legal predecessor, or

   (b) the fact that the applicant or his legal predecessor has displayed the invention at official, or officially recognized, international exhibitions falling within the terms of the Convention on international exhibitions signed at Paris on November 22, 1928, and amended on May 10, 1948.

Article 5

An invention shall be considered as involving an inventive step if it is not obvious having regard to the state of the art. However, for the purposes of considering whether or not an invention involves an inventive step, the law of any Contracting State may, either generally or in relation to particular classes of patents or patent applications, for example patents of addition, provide that the state of the art shall not include all or any of the patents or patent applications mentioned in paragraph 3 of Article 4.

Article 6

Any Contracting State which does not apply the provisions of paragraph 3 of Article 4 shall nevertheless provide that no invention shall be validly protected in so far as it includes matter which is or has been validly protected by a patent in that State which, though not comprised in the state of the art, has, in respect of that matter, an earlier priority date.

Article 7

Any group of Contracting States who provide for a common patent application may be regarded as a single State for the purposes of paragraph 3 of Article 4, or of Article 6.

Article 8

1. The patent application shall contain a description of the invention with the necessary drawings referred to therein and one or more claims defining the protection applied for.

2. The description must disclose the invention in a manner sufficiently clear and complete for it to be carried out by a person skilled in the art.

3. The extent of the protection conferred by the patent shall be determined by the terms of the claims. Nevertheless, the description and drawings shall be used to interpret the claims.

Article 9

1. This Convention shall be open for signature by the member States of the Council of Europe. It shall be subject to ratification or acceptance. Instruments of ratification or acceptance shall be deposited with the Secretary-General of the Council of Europe.

2. This Convention shall enter into force three months after the date of deposit of the eighth instrument of ratification or acceptance.

3. In respect of a signatory State ratifying or accepting subsequently, the Convention shall come into force three months after the date of deposit of its instrument of ratification or acceptance.

Article 10

1. After the entry into force of this Convention, the Committee of Ministers of the Council of Europe may invite any Member of the International Union for the Protection of Industrial Property which is not a Member of the Council of Europe to accede thereto.

2. Such accession shall be effected by depositing with the Secretary General of the Council of Europe an instrument of accession which ; shall take effect three months after the date of its deposit.

Article 11

1. Any Contracting Party may at the time of signature or when depositing its instrument of ratification, acceptance or accession, specify the territory or territories to which this Convention shall apply.

2. Any Contracting Party may, when depositing its instrument of ratification, acceptance or accession or at any later date, by notification addressed to the Secretary-General of the Council of Europe, extend this Convention to any other territory or territories specified in the

declaration and for whose international relations it is responsible or on whose behalf it is authorized to give undertakings.

3. Any declaration made in pursuance of the preceding paragraph may, in respect of any territory mentioned in such declaration, be withdrawn according to the procedure laid down in Article 13 of this Convention.

Article 12

1. Notwithstanding anything in this Convention, each Contracting Party may, at the time of signature or when depositing its instrument of ratification, acceptance or accession, temporarily reserve, for the limited period stated below, the right:

(a) not to provide for the grant of patents in respect of food and pharmaceutical products, as such, and agricultural or horticultural processes other than those to which paragraph (b) of Article 2 applies:

(b) to grant valid patents for inventions disclosed within the six months preceding the ruling of the application, either, apart from the case referred to in paragraph 4(b) of Article 4, by the inventor himself, or, apart from the case referred to in paragraph 4(a) of Article 4, by a third party as a result of information derived from the inventor.

2. The limited period referred to in paragraph 1 of this Article shall be ten years in the case of sub-paragraph (a) and five years in the case of sub-paragraph (b). It shall start from the entry into force of this Convention for the Contracting Party considered.

3. Any contracting Party which makes a reservation under this Article shall withdraw the said reservation as soon as circumstances permit. Such withdrawal shall be made by notification addressed to the Secretary-General of the Council of Europe and shall take effect one month from the date of receipt of such notification..

Article 13

1. This Convention shall remain in force indefinitely.

2. Any Contracting Party may, in so far as it is concerned, denounce this Convention by means of a notification addressed to the Secretary-General of the Council of Europe.

3. Such denunciation shall take effect six months after the date of receipt by the Secretary-General of such notification.

Article 14

The Secretary-General of the Council of Europe shall notify the member States of the Council, any State which has acceded to this Convention and the Director of the International Bureau for the Protection of Industrial Property of:

(a) any signature;

(b) any deposit of an instrument of ratification, acceptance or accession;

(c) any date of entry into force of this Convention;

(d) any declaration and notification received in pursuance of the provisions of paragraphs 2 and 3 of Article 11;

(e) any reservation made in pursuance of the provisions of paragraph 1 of Article 12;

(f) the withdrawal of any reservation carried out in pursuance of the provisions of paragraph 3 of Article 12;

(g) any notification received in pursuance of the provisions of paragraph 2 of Article 13 and the date on which denunciation takes effect.

In witness whereof the undersigned, being duly authorised thereto, have signed this Convention.

Done at Strasbourg, this 27th day of November 1963, in English and in French, both texts being equally authoritative, in a single copy which shall remain deposited in the archives of the Council of Europe. The Secretary General shall transmit certified copies to each of the signatory and acceding States and to the Director of the International Bureau for the Protection of Industrial Property.

CONVENTION
FOR THE EUROPEAN PATENT FOR THE COMMON MARKET
(Community Patent Convention)

Done at Luxembourg, 1973

PART I
GENERAL AND INSTITUTIONAL PROVISIONS

CHAPTER I
GENERAL PROVISIONS

Article 1
Common system of law for patents

1. A system of law, common to the Contracting States, concerning patents for invention is hereby established.

2. The common system of law shall govern the European patents granted for the Contracting States in accordance with the Convention on the Grant of European Patents, hereinafter referred to as 'the European Patent Convention', and the European patent applications in which such States are designated.

Article 2
Community patent

1. European patents granted for the Contracting States shall be called Community patents.

2. Community patents shall have a unitary character. They shall have equal effect throughout the

territories to which this Convention applies and may only be granted, transferred, revoked or allowed to lapse in respect of the whole of such territories. The same shall apply *mutatis mutandis* to applications for European patents in which the Contracting States are designated.

3. Community patents shall have an autonomous character. They shall be subject only to the provisions of this Convention and those provisions of the European Patent Convention which are binding upon every European patent and which shall consequently be deemed to be provisions of this Convention.

Article 3
Joint designation

Designation of the States parties to this Convention in accordance with Article 79 of the European Patent Convention shall be effected jointly. Designation of one or some only of these States shall be deemed to be designation of all of these States.

Article 4
Setting up of special departments

The following bodies common to the Contracting States shall implement the procedures laid down in this Convention:

(a) special departments which are set up within the European Patent Office and whose work shall be supervised by a Select Committee of the Administrative Council of the European Patent Organization;

(b) the Common Appeal Court established by the Protocol on the Settlement of Litigation concerning the Infringement and Validity of Community Patents, hereinafter referred to as 'the Protocol on Litigation'.

Article 5
National patents

This Convention shall be without prejudice to the right of the Contracting States to grant national patents.

CHAPTER II
SPECIAL DEPARTMENTS OF THE EUROPEAN PATENT OFFICE

Article 6
The special departments

The special departments shall be as follows:

(a) a Patent Administration Division;

(b) one or more Revocation Divisions.

Article 7
Patent Administration Division

1. The Patent Administration Division shall be responsible for all acts of the European Patent Office relating to Community patents, in so far as these acts are not the responsibility of other departments of the Office. It shall in particular be responsible for decisions in respects of entries in the Register of Community Patents.

2. Decisions of the Patent Administration Division shall be taken by one legally qualified member.

3. The members of the Patent Administration Division may not be members of the Boards of Appeal or the Enlarged Board of Appeal set up under the European Patent Convention.

Article 8
Revocation Divisions

1. The Revocation Divisions shall be responsible for the examination of

requests for the limitation of and applications for the revocation of Community patents, and for determining compensation under Article 43(5).

2. A Revocation Division shall consist of one legally qualified member who shall be the Chairman, and two technically qualified members. Prior to the taking of a final decision on the request or application, the Revocation Division may entrust the examination of the request or application to one of its members. Oral proceedings shall be before the Revocation Division itself.

Article 9
Exclusion and objection

1. Members of the Revocation Divisions may not take part in any proceedings if they have any personal interest therein, if they have previously been involved as representatives of one of the parties, or if they have participated in the final decision on the case in the proceedings for grant or opposition proceedings.

2. If, for one of the reasons mentioned in paragraph 1 or for any other reason, a member of a Revocation Division considers that he should not take part in any proceedings, he shall inform the division accordingly.

3. Members of a Revocation Division may be objected to by any party for one of the reasons mentioned in paragraph 1, or if suspected of partiality. An objection shall not be admissible if, while being aware of a reason for objection, the party has taken a procedural step. No objection may be based upon the nationality of members.

4. The Revocation Divisions shall decide as to the action to be taken in the cases specified in paragraphs 2 and 3 without the participation of the member concerned. For the purpose of taking this decision the member objected to shall be replaced by his alternate.

Article 10
Languages for proceedings and publications

1. The official languages of the European Patent Office shall also be the official languages of the special departments.

2. Throughout the proceedings before the special departments, a translation filed in accordance with Article 14(2), second sentence, of the European Patent Convention may be brought into conformity with the original text of the European patent application.

3. The official language of the European Patent Office in which the Community patent is granted shall be used as the language of the proceedings in all proceedings before the special departments concerning the Community patent, unless otherwise provided in the Implementing Regulations.

4. However, natural or legal persons having their residence or principal place of business within the territory of a Contracting State having a language other than one of the official languages of the European Patent

Office as an official language, and nationals of that State who are resident abroad, may file documents which have to be filed within a time limit in an official language of the Contracting State concerned. They must, however, file a translation in the language of the proceedings within the time limit prescribed in the Implementing Regulations; in the cases provided for in the Implementing Regulations, they may file a translation in a different official language of the European Patent Office.

5. If any document is not filed in the language prescribed by this Convention, or if any translation required by virtue of this Convention is not filed in due time, the document shall be deemed not to have been received.

6. New specifications of Community patents published following limitation or revocation proceedings shall be published in the language of the proceedings; they shall include a translation of the amended claims in one of the official languages of each of the Contracting States which do not have as an official language the language of the proceedings.

7. The Community Patent Bulletin shall be published in the three official languages of the European Patent Office.

8. Entries in the Register of Community Patents shall be made in the three official languages of the European Patent Office. In cases of doubt, the entry in the language of the proceedings shall be authentic.

9. No State party to this Convention may avail itself of the authorizations given in Articles 65, 67 (3) and 70 (3) of the European Patent Convention.

CHAPTER III
THE SELECT COMMITTEE OF THE ADMINISTRATIVE COUNCIL

Article 11
Membership

1. The Select Committee of the Administrative Council shall be composed of the Representatives of the Contracting States, the Representative of the Commission of the European Communities and their alternate Representatives. Each Contracting State and the Commission shall be entitled to appoint one Representative and one alternate Representative to the Select Committee. The same members shall represent the Contracting States on the Administrative Council and on the Select Committee.

2. The members of the Select Committee may, subject to the provisions of its Rules of Procedure, be assisted by advisers or experts.

Article 12
Chairmanship

1. The Select Committee of the Administrative Council shall elect a Chairman and a Deputy Chairman from among the Representatives and alternate Representatives of the Contracting States. The Deputy Chairman

shall ex officio replace the Chairman in the event of his being prevented from attending to his duties.

2. The duration of the terms of office of the Chairman and the Deputy Chairman shall be three years. The terms of office shall be renewable.

Article 13
Board

1. The Select Committee of the Administrative Council may set up a Board composed of five of its members.

2. The chairman and the deputy chairman of the Select Committee shall be members of the board ex officio; the other three members shall be elected by the Select Committee.

3. The term of office of the members elected by the Select Committee shall be three years. This term of office shall be three years. This term of office shall not be renewable.

4. The board shall perform the duties given to it by the Select Committee in accordance with the Rules of Procedure.

Article 14
Meetings

1. Meetings of the Select Committee of the Administrative Council shall be convened by its chairman.

2. The President of the European Patent Office shall take part in the deliberations of the Select Committee.

3. The Select Committee shall hold an ordinary meeting once each year. In addition, it shall meet on the initiative of its chairman or at the request of one-third of the Contracting States.

4. The deliberations of the Select Committee shall be based on an agenda, and shall be held in accordance with its Rules of Procedure.

5. The provisional agenda shall contain any question whose inclusion is requested by any Contracting State in accordance with the Rules of Procedure.

Article 15
Languages of the Select Committee

1. The languages in use in the deliberations of the Select Committee of the Administrative Council shall be English, French and German.

2. Documents submitted to the Select Committee, and the minutes of its deliberations, shall be drawn up in the three languages mentioned in paragraph 1.

Article 16
Competence of the Select Committee in certain cases

1. The Select Committee of the Administrative Council shall be competent to amend the following provisions of this Convention:

(a) the time limits laid down in the Convention which are to be observed vis-à-vis the European Patent Office;

(b) the Implementing Regulations.

2. The Select Committee shall be competent, in conformity with this Convention, to adopt or amend the following provisions:

(a) the Financial Regulations;

(b) the Rules relating to Fees;

(c) its Rules of Procedure.

Article 17
Voting rights

1. The right to vote in the Select Committee of the Administrative Council shall be restricted to the Contracting States.

2. Each Contracting State shall have one vote, subject to the application of the provisions of Article 19.

Article 18
Voting rules

1. The Select Committee of the Administrative Council shall take its decisions other than those referred to in paragraph 2 by a simple majority of the Contracting States represented and voting.

2. A majority of three-quarters of the votes of the Contracting States represented and voting shall be required for the decisions which the Select Committee is empowered to take under Article 16 and Article 21 (a).

3. Abstentions shall not be considered as votes.

Article 19
Weighting of votes

In respect of the adoption or amendment of the rules relating to fees and, if the financial contribution to be made by the Contracting States would thereby be increased, the approval referred to in Article 21(a), voting shall be conducted according to Article 36 of the European Patent Convention. The term 'Contracting States' in that Article shall be understood as meaning the States parties to this Convention.

CHAPTER IV
FINANCIAL PROVISIONS

Article 20
Financial obligations and benefits

1. The amount payable by the States parties to this Convention pursuant to Article 146 of the European Patent Convention shall be covered by financial contributions determined in respect of each State in accordance with the scale laid down in paragraph 3.

2. Both the revenue derived from fees paid in accordance with the rules relating to fees, less the payments to the European Patent Organization pursuant to Articles 39 and 147 of the European Patent Convention, and all other receipts of the European Patent Organization obtained in implementation of this convention shall be distributed among the States parties to this convention in accordance with the scale laid down in paragraph 3.

3. The scale referred to in paragraphs 1 and 2 shall be as follows:

- Belgium   5,25 %
- Denmark   5,20 %
- Germany   20,40 %
- Greece   4,40 %
- Spain   6,30 %
- France   12,80 %
- Ireland   3,45 %
- Italy   7,00 %
- Luxembourg   3,00 %
- Netherlands   11,80 %
- Portugal   3,50 %
- United Kingdom   16,90 %

4. The scale laid down in paragraph 3 may be amended by decision of the Council of the European Communities, acting on a proposal from the Commission of the European Communities, or on a request from at least three Contracting States, following a review to be conducted by the Select Committee of the Administrative Council of the European Patent Organization five years after the entry into force of the Agreement relating to Community Patents.

5. The decision referred to in paragraph 4 shall require:

(a) unanimity from the sixth to the 10th year inclusive from the date of entry into force of the Agreement relating to Community Patents;

(b) after the expiry of that period, a qualified majority; this majority shall be that specified in the first indent of the second subparagraph of Article 148 (2) of the Treaty establishing the European Economic

Community.

6. Five years after the entry into force of the Agreement relating to Community Patents the necessary work shall be commenced in order to examine under what conditions and at what date the system of financing provided for in paragraphs 1 to 5 may be replaced by another system based, having regard to developments in the European Communities, on Community financing. This system may include the amounts payable by the States parties to this Convention pursuant to the European Patent Convention and the amounts accruing to these States pursuant to that Convention. When this work has been concluded, this Article and, if appropriate, Article 19 may be amended by a decision of the Council of the European Communities acting unanimously on a proposal from the Commission.

Article 21
Powers of the Select Committee of the Administrative Council in budgetary matters

The Select Committee of the Administrative Council shall:

(a) approve annually the forecasts of expenditure and revenue relating to the implementation of this Convention and any amendments or additions made to these forecasts, submitted to it by the President of the European Patent Office, and supervise the implementation thereof;

(b) grant the authorization provided for in Article 47(2) of the European Patent Convention, in so far as the expenditure involved relates to the implementation of this Convention;

(c) approve the annual accounts of the European Patent Organization which relate to the implementation of this Convention and that part of the report of the auditors appointed under Article 49(1) of the European Patent Convention which relates to these accounts, and give the President of the European Patent Office a discharge.

Article 22
Rules relating to Fees

The Rules relating to Fees shall determine in particular the amounts of the fees and the ways in which they are to be paid.

PART II
SUBSTANTIVE PATENT LAW

CHAPTER I
RIGHT TO THE COMMUNITY PATENT

Article 23
Claiming the right to the Community patent

1. If a Community patent has been granted to a person who is not entitled to it under Article 60(1) of the European Patent Convention, the person entitled to it under that provision may, without prejudice to any other remedy which may be open to him, claim to have the patent transferred to him.

2. Where a person is entitled to only part of the Community patent, that person may, in accordance with paragraph 1, claim to be made a joint proprietor.

3. Legal proceedings in respect of the rights specified in paragraphs 1 and 2 may be instituted only within a period of not more than two years after the date on which the European Patent Bulletin mentions the grant of the European patent. This provision shall not apply if the proprietor of the patent knew, at the time when the patent was granted or transferred to him, that he was not entitled to the patent.

4. The fact that legal proceedings have been instituted shall be entered in the Register of Community Patents. Entry shall also be made of the final decision in, or of any other termination of, the proceedings.

Article 24
Effect of change of proprietorship

1. Where there is a complete change of proprietorship of a Community patent as a result of legal proceedings under Article 23, licences and other rights shall lapse upon the registration of the person entitled to the patent in the Register of Community Patents.

2. If, before the institution of legal proceedings has been registered,

(a) the proprietor of the patent has used the invention within the territory of any of the Contracting States or made effective and serious preparations to do so, or

(b) a licensee of the patent has obtained his licence and has used the invention within the territory of any of the Contracting States or made effective and serious preparations to do so,

he may continue such use provided that he requests a non-exclusive licence of the patent from the new proprietor whose name is entered in the Register of Community Patents.

Such request must be made within the period prescribed in the Implementing Regulations. The licence shall be granted for a reasonable period and upon reasonable terms.

3. Paragraph 2 shall not apply if the proprietor of the patent or the licensee, as the case may be, was acting in bad faith at the time when he began to use the invention or to make preparations to do so.

CHAPTER II
EFFECTS OF THE COMMUNITY PATENT AND THE EUROPEAN PATENT APPLICATION

Article 25
Prohibition of direct use of the invention

A Community patent shall confer on its proprietor the right to prevent all third parties not having his consent:

(a) from making, offering, putting on the market or using a product which is the subject-matter of the patent, or importing or stocking the product for these purposes;

(b) from using a process which is the subject-matter of the patent or, when the third party knows, or it is obvious in the circumstances, that the use of the process is prohibited without the consent of the proprietor of the patent, from offering the process for use within the territories of the Contracting States;

(c) from offering, putting on the market, using, or importing or stocking for these purposes the product obtained directly by a process which is the subject-matter of the patent.

Article 26
Prohibition of indirect use of the invention

1. A Community patent shall also confer on its proprietor the right to prevent all third parties not having his consent from supplying or offering to supply within the territories of the Contracting States a person, other than a party entitled to exploit the patented invention, with means, relating to an essential element of that invention, for putting it into effect therein, when the third party knows, or it is obvious in the circumstances, that these means are suitable and intended for putting that invention into effect.

2. Paragraph 1 shall not apply when the means are staple commercial products, except when the third party induces the person supplied to commit acts prohibited by Article 25.

3. Persons performing the acts referred to in Article 27 (a) to (c) shall not be considered to be parties entitled to exploit the invention within the meaning of paragraph 1.

Article 27
Limitation of the effects of the Community patent

The rights conferred by a Community patent shall not extend to:

(a) acts done privately and for non-commercial purposes;

(b) acts done for experimental purposes relating to the subject-matter of the patented invention;

(c) the extemporaneous preparation for individual cases in a pharmacy of a medicine in accordance with a medical prescription nor acts concerning the medicine so prepared;

(d) the use on board vessels of the countries of the Union of Paris for the Protection of Industrial Property, other than the Contracting States, of the patented invention, in the body of the vessel, in the machinery, tackle, gear and other accessories, when such vessels temporarily or accidentally enter the waters of Contracting States, provided that the invention is used there exclusively for the needs of the vessel;

(e) the use of the patented invention in the construction or operation of aircraft or land vehicles of countries of the Union of Paris for the Protection of Industrial Property, other than the Contracting States, or of accessories to such aircraft or land vehicles, when these temporarily or accidentally enter the territory of Contracting States;

(f) the acts specified in Article 27 of the Convention on International Civil Aviation of 7 December 1944, where these acts concern the aircraft of a State, other than the Contracting States, benefiting from the provisions of that Article.

Article 28
Exhaustion of the rights conferred by the Community patent

The rights conferred by a Community patent shall not extend to acts concerning a product covered by that patent which are done within the territories of the Contracting States after that product has been put on the market in one of these States by the proprietor of the patent or with his express consent, unless there are grounds which, under Community law, would justify the extension to such acts of the rights conferred by the patent.

Article 29
Translation of the claims in examination or opposition proceedings

1. The applicant shall file with the European Patent Office within the time limit prescribed in the Implementing Regulations a translation of the claims on which the grant of the European patent is to be based in one of the official languages of each of the Contracting States which does not have English, French or German as an official language.

2. Paragraph 1 shall apply *mutatis mutandis* in respect of claims which are amended during opposition proceedings.

3. The translations of the claims shall be published by the European Patent Office.

4. The applicant for or proprietor of the patent shall pay the fee for the publication of the translations of the claims within the time limits prescribed in the Implementing Regulations.

5. If the translations prescribed in paragraph 1 are not filed in due time or if the fee for the publication of the translations of the claims is not paid in due time the European patent application shall be deemed to be withdrawn in respects of the designated Contracting States. If the translations prescribed in paragraph 2 are not filed in due time or if the fee for the publication of the translations of the claims is not paid in due time the Community patent shall be revoked.

6. Where a translation of the claims prescribed in paragraph 1 or 2, or a translation of the claims in the two official languages of the European Patent Office which are not the language of the proceedings, is defective, the applicant for or the proprietor of the patent may file a corrected translation with the European Patent Office. The corrected translation shall not have any legal effect until the conditions prescribed in the Implementing Regulations have been complied with.

7. Where the translation of the claims in one of the official languages of a Contracting State is defective, any person who, in that State, is using or has made effective and serious preparations for using an invention the use of which would not constitute infringement of the patent in the defective translation of the claims, may, after the corrected translation takes effect, continue such use without payment. This shall not apply if it is established that the person concerned did not act in good faith.

Article 30
Translation of the specification of the Community patent

1. In addition to the translations prescribed in Article 29(1) the applicant shall file with the European Patent Office, before the end of the period prescribed in the Implementing Regulations, a translation of the text of the application which forms the basis for the grant of the Community patent in one of the official languages of each of the Contracting States in which the language of the proceedings is not an official language.

2. Paragraph 1 shall apply *mutatis mutandis* to the text of the Community patent which forms the basis for its maintenance in amended form during opposition proceedings.

3. The European Patent Office shall, within the time limit laid down in the Implementing Regulations, forward to each of the central industrial property offices of the Contracting States which have so requested a copy of the translations referred to in paragraphs 1 and 2 in the relevant language or languages. The applicant must for that purpose file a sufficient number of copies of the translations.

4. The translations prescribed in paragraphs 1 and 2 shall be made

available to the public by the European Patent Office and shall be forwarded in due time and free of charge to the central industrial property offices of the Contracting States concerned in a suitable form for adequate and inexpensive dissemination.

5. If the translations prescribed in paragraph 1 are filed in due time, the proprietor of the patent may avail himself from the date of publication of the mention of the grant of the patent of the rights conferred by the patent.

6. If the translations prescribed in paragraphs 1 or 2 are not filed in due time, the Community patent shall be deemed to be void ab initio. However, the proprietor may, instead of the Community patent, obtain a European patent for the Contracting States for which he has filed translations in due time. He must for that purpose notify his intention in writing to the European Patent Office within a period of two months from the expiry of the applicable time limit and pay within the same period the fees referred to in Article 81(1).

7. Article 29 (6) and (7) shall apply *mutatis mutandis* to the translations prescribed in paragraphs 1 and 2.

Article 31
Status of translations

The translations provided for in Articles 29 and 30 which have been carried out by persons authorized under the law of a Contracting State shall be deemed in that State to be in conformity with the original, until proved to the contrary.

Article 32
Rights conferred by a European patent application after publication

1. Compensation reasonable in the circumstances may be claimed from a third party who, in the period between the date of publication of a European patent application in which the Contracting States are designated and the date of publication of the mention of the grant of the European patent, has made any use of the invention which, after that period, would be prohibited by virtue of the Community patent.

2. Any Contracting State which does not have as an official language the language of the proceedings of a European patent application in which the Contracting States are designated may prescribe that such application shall not confer, in respect of use of the invention within its territory, the right referred to in paragraph 1 until such time as the applicant, at his option, has:

(a) supplied a translation of the claims in one of its official languages to the competent authority of that State and the translation has been published in accordance with the law of that State; or

(b) communicated such a translation to the person using the invention within that State.

3. Any Contracting State referred to in paragraph 2 may prescribe that, where the applicant avails himself of the option provided for in subparagraph 2(b), the right conferred by the application in respect of use of the invention within the territory of the State concerned may be invoked only if the applicant supplies a copy of the translation to the competent authority of that State within 15 days after it has been communicated to the person using the invention within that State. The Contracting State may prescribe that the authority shall publish the translation, in accordance with the law of that State.

4. Any Contracting State which adopts a provision under paragraph 2 may prescribe that, where the translation of the claims is defective, any person who, in that State, has used or made effective and serious preparations for using the invention the use of which would not constitute infringement of the application in the original translation of the claims shall be liable for reasonable compensation in accordance with paragraph 1 only from the moment when the corrected translation of the claims has been published or has been received by him, unless it is established that he did not act in good faith, in which case he shall be liable for reasonable compensation in accordance with paragraph 1 from the moment when the requirements of paragraph 2 were fulfilled.

Article 33
Effect of revocation of the Community patent

1. A European patent application in which the Contracting States are designated and the resulting Community patent shall be deemed not to have had, as from the outset, the effects specified in this Chapter, to the extent that the patent has been revoked.

2. Subject to the national provisions relating either to claims for compensation for damage caused by negligence or lack of good faith on the part of the proprietor of the patent, or to unjust enrichment, the retroactive effect of the revocation of the patent as a result of opposition or revocation proceedings shall not effect:

(a) any decision on infringement which has acquired the authority of a final decision and been enforced prior to the revocation decision;

(b) any contract concluded prior to the revocation decision, in so far as it has been performed before that decision; however, repayment, to an extent justified by the circumstances, of sums paid under the relevant contract, may be claimed on grounds of equity.

Article 34
Complementary application of national law regarding infringement

1. The effects of a Community patent shall be governed solely by the provisions of this Convention. In other respects, infringement of a Community patent shall be governed by the national law relating to

infringement of a national patent, in accordance with and subject to the provisions of the Protocol on Litigation.

2. Paragraph 1 shall apply *mutatis mutandis* to a European patent application which may result in the grant of a Community patent.

Article 35
Burden of proof

1. If the subject-matter of a Community patent is a process for obtaining a new product, the same product when produced by any other party shall, in the absence of proof to the contrary, be deemed to have been obtained by the patented process.

2. In the adduction of proof to the contrary, the legitimate interests of the defendant in protecting his manufacturing and business secrets shall be taken into account.

CHAPTER III
NATIONAL RIGHTS

Article 36
National prior right

1. With regard to a Community patent having a date of filing or, where priority has been claimed, a date of priority later than that of a national patent application or national patent made public in a Contracting State on or after that date, the national patent application or patent shall, for that Contracting State, have the same prior right effect as a published European patent application designating that Contracting State.

2. If, in a Contracting State, a national patent application or patent, which is unpublished by reason of the national law of that State concerning the secrecy of inventions, has a prior right effect with regard to a national patent in that State having a later date of filing, or where priority has been claimed a later date of priority, the same shall apply in that State with regard to a Community patent.

Article 37
Right based on prior use and right of personal possession

1. Any person who, if a national patent had been granted in respect of an invention, would have had, in one of the Contracting States, a right based on prior use of that invention or a right of personal possession of that invention, shall enjoy, in that State, the same rights in respect of a Community patent for the same invention.

2. The rights conferred by a Community patent shall not extend to acts concerning a product covered by that patent which are done within the territory of the State concerned after that product has been put on the market in that State by the person referred to in paragraph 1, in so far as the

national law of that State makes provision to the same effect in respect of national patents.

CHAPTER IV
THE COMMUNITY PATENT AS AN OBJECT OF PROPERTY

Article 38
Dealing with the Community patent as a national patent

1. Unless otherwise specified in this Convention, a Community patent as an object of property shall be dealt with in its entirety, and for the whole of the territories in which it is effective, as a national patent of the Contracting State in which, according to the Register of European Patents provided for in the European Patent Convention:

(a) the applicant for the patent had his residence or principal place of business on the date of filing of the European patent application;

(b) where subparagraph (a) does not apply, the applicant had a place of business on that date; or

(c) where neither subparagraph (a) nor subparagraph (b) applies, the applicant's representative whose name is entered first in the Register of European Patents had his place of business on the date of that entry.

2. Where subparagraphs (a), (b) and (c) of paragraph 1 do not apply, the Contracting State referred to in that paragraph shall be the Federal Republic of Germany.

3. If two or more persons are mentioned in the Register of European Patents as joint applicants, paragraph 1 shall apply to the joint applicant first mentioned; if this is not possible, it shall apply to the joint applicant next mentioned in respect of whom it is applicable. Where paragraph 1 does not apply to any of the joint applicants, paragraph 2 shall apply.

4. If in a Contracting State as determined by the preceding paragraphs a right in respect of a national patent is effective only after entry in the national patent register, such a right in respect of a Community patent shall be effective only after entry in the Register of Community Patents.

Article 39
Transfer

1. An assignment of a Community patent shall be made in writing and shall require the signature of the parties to the contract, except when it is a result of a judgment.

2. Subject to Article 24(1) a transfer shall not affect rights acquired by third parties before the date of transfer.

3. A transfer shall, to the extent to which it is verified by the papers referred to in the Implementing Regulations, only have effect vis-à-vis third parties after entry in the Register of Community Patents. Nevertheless, a

transfer, before it is so entered, shall have effect vis-à-vis third parties who have acquired rights after the date of the transfer but who knew of the transfer at the date on which the rights were acquired.

Article 40
Enforcement proceedings

The courts and other authorities of the Contracting State determined in accordance with Article 38 shall have exclusive jurisdiction in respect of proceedings relating to judgments or other official acts in so far as they are being enforced against Community patents.

Article 41
Bankruptcy or like proceedings

1. Until such time as common rules for the Contracting States in this field enter into force, the only Contracting State in which a Community patent may be involved in bankruptcy or like proceedings shall be that in which such proceedings are opened first.

2. Paragraph 1 shall apply *mutatis mutandis* in the case of joint proprietorship of a Community patent to the share of the joint proprietor.

Article 42
Contractual licensing

1. A Community patent may be licensed in whole or in part for the whole or part of the territories in which it is effective. A licence may be exclusive or non-exclusive.

2. The rights conferred by the Community patent may be invoked against a licensee who contravenes any restriction in his licence which is covered by paragraph 1.

3. Article 39 (2) and (3) shall apply *mutatis mutandis* to the grant or transfer of a licence in respect of a Community patent.

Article 43
Licences of right

1. Where the proprietor of a Community patent files a written statement with the European Patent Office that he is prepared to allow any person to use the invention as a licensee in return for appropriate compensation, the renewal fees for the Community patent which fall due after receipt of the statement shall be reduced; the amount of the reduction shall be fixed in the rules relating to fees. Where there is a complete change of proprietorship of the patent as a result of legal proceedings under Article 23, the statement shall be deemed withdrawn upon the entry of the name of the person entitled to the patent in the Register of Community Patents.

2. The statement may be withdrawn at any time upon written notification to this effect to the European Patent Office, provided that no-one has

informed the proprietor of the patent of his intention to use the invention. Such withdrawal shall take effect from the date of its notification. The amount by which the renewal fees were reduced shall be paid within one month after withdrawal; Article 48(2) shall apply, but the six-month period shall start upon expiry of the above period.

3. The statement may not be filed while an exclusive licence is recorded in the Register of Community Patents or a request for the recording of such a licence is before the European Patent Office.

4. On the basis of the statement, any person shall be entitled to use the invention as a licensee under the conditions laid down in the Implementing Regulations. A licence so obtained shall, for the purposes of this Convention, be treated as a contractual licence.

5. On written request by one of the parties, a Revocation Division shall determine the appropriate compensation or review it if circumstances have arisen or become known which render the compensation determined obviously inappropriate. The provisions governing revocation proceedings shall apply *mutatis mutandis*, unless they are inapplicable as a result of the particular nature of revocation proceedings. The request shall not be deemed to have been made until such time as an administrative fee has been paid.

6. No request for recording an exclusive licence in the Register of Community Patents shall be admissible after the statement has been filed, unless it is withdrawn or deemed withdrawn.

Article 44
The European patent application as an object of property

1. Articles 38 to 42 shall apply *mutatis mutandis* to a European patent application in which the Contracting States are designated, the reference to the Register of Community Patents being understood as referring to the Register of European Patents provided for in the European Patent Convention.

2. The rights acquired by third parties in respect of a European patent application referred to in paragraph 1 shall continue to be effective with regard to the Community patent granted upon that application.

CHAPTER V
COMPULSORY LICENCES IN RESPECT OF
A COMMUNITY PATENT

Article 45
Compulsory licences

1. Any provision in the law of a Contracting State for the grant of compulsory licences in respect of national patents shall be applicable to Community patents. The extent and effect of compulsory licences granted in respect of Community patents shall be restricted to the territory of the State

concerned. Article 28 shall not apply.

2. Each Contracting State shall, at least in respect of compensation under a compulsory licence, provide for a final appeal to a court of law.

3. As far as practicable national authorities shall notify the European Patent Office of the grant of any compulsory licence in respect of a Community patent.

4. For the purposes of this Convention, the term 'compulsory licences' shall be construed as including official licences and any right to use patented inventions in the public interest.

Article 46
Compulsory licences for lack or insufficiency of exploitation

A compulsory licence may not be granted in respect of a Community patent on the ground of lack or insufficiency of exploitation if the product covered by the patent, which is manufactured in a Contracting State, is put on the market in the territory of any other Contracting State, for which such a licence has been requested, in sufficient quantity to satisfy needs in the territory of that other Contracting State. This provision shall not apply to compulsory licences granted in the public interest.

Article 47
Compulsory licences in respect of dependent patents

Any provisions in the law of a Contracting State for the grant of compulsory licences in respect of earlier patents in favour of subsequent dependent patents shall be applicable to the relationship between Community patents and national patents and to the relationship between Community patents themselves.

PART III
RENEWAL, LAPSE, LIMITATION AND REVOCATION
OF THE COMMUNITY PATENT

CHAPTER I
RENEWAL AND LAPSE

Article 48
Renewal fees

1. Renewal fees in respect of Community patents shall be paid to the European Patent Office in accordance with the Implementing Regulations. These fees shall be due in respect of the years following the year referred to in Article 86(4) of the European Patent Convention, provided that no renewal fees shall be due in respect of the first two years, calculated from the date of filing of the application.

2. When a renewal fee has not been paid on or before the due date, the fee may be validly paid within six months of that date, provided that the additional fee is paid at the same time.

3. Any renewal fee in respect of a Community patent falling due within two months after the publication of the mention of the grant of the European patent shall be deemed to have been validly paid if it is paid within that period. No additional fee shall be charged.

Article 49
Surrender

1. A Community patent may be surrendered only in its entirety.

2. Surrender must be declared in writing to the European Patent Office by the proprietor of the patent. It shall not have effect until it is entered in the Register of Community Patents.

3. Surrender will be entered in the Register of Community Patents only with the agreement of any third party who has a right in rem recorded in the Register or in respect of whom there is an entry in the Register pursuant to Article 23(4), first sentence. If a licence is recorded in the Register, surrender will be entered only if the proprietor of the patent proves that he has previously informed the licensee of his intention to surrender; this entry will be made on expiry of the period laid down in the Implementing Regulations.

Article 50
Lapse

1. A Community patent shall lapse:

   (a) at the end of the term laid down in Article 63 of the European Patent Convention;

   (b) if the proprietor of the patent surrenders it in accordance with Article 49;

   (c) if a renewal fee and any additional fee have not been paid in due time.

2. The Community patent shall lapse on the date mentioned in Article 53(4) to the extent that it is not maintained.

3. The lapse of a patent for failure to pay a renewal fee and any additional fee within the due period shall be deemed to have occurred on the date on which the renewal fee was due.

4. The lapse of a Community patent shall, if necessary, be decided by the Patent Administration Division or, if proceedings in respect of that patent are pending before it, a Revocation Division.

CHAPTER II
LIMITATION PROCEDURE

Article 51
Request for limitation

1. At the request of the proprietor, a Community patent may be limited in the form of an amendment to the claims, the description or the drawings. Limitation in respect of one or some of the Contracting States may be requested only where Article 36(1) applies.

2. The request may not be filed during the period within which an opposition may be filed or while opposition proceedings or revocation proceedings are pending.

3. The request shall be filed in writing with the European Patent Office. It shall not be deemed to have been filed until the fee for limitation has been paid.

4. Article 49(3) shall apply *mutatis mutandis* to the filing of the request.

5. Where an application for revocation of the Community patent is filed during limitation proceedings, the Revocation Division shall stay the limitation proceedings until a final decision is given in respect of the application for revocation.

Article 52
Examination of the request

1. The Revocation Division shall examine whether the grounds for revocation mentioned in Article 56(1) (a) to (d) would prejudice the maintenance of the Community patent as amended.

2. In the examination of the request, which shall be conducted in accordance with the Implementing Regulations, the Revocation Division shall invite the proprietor of the patent, as often as necessary, to file observations, within a period to be fixed by the Revocation Division, on communications issued by itself.

3. If the proprietor of the patent fails to reply in due time to any invitation under paragraph 2, the request shall be deemed to be withdrawn.

Article 53
Rejection of the request or limitation of the Community patent

1. If, following the examination provided for in Article 52, the Revocation Division is of the opinion that the amendments are not acceptable, it shall reject the request.

2. If the Revocation Division is of the opinion that, taking into consideration the amendments made by the proprietor of the patent during the limitation proceedings, the grounds for revocation mentioned in Article 56 do not prejudice the maintenance of the Community patent, it shall decide to limit the patent accordingly, provided that:

(a) it is established, in accordance with the Implementing Regulations, that the proprietor of the patent approves the text in which the Revocation Division intends to limit the patent;

(b) a translation of all amendments to the patent specification in one of the official languages of each of the Contracting States which does not have as an official language the language of the proceedings is filed within the time limit prescribed in the Implementing Regulations;

(c) the fee for the printing of a new specification is paid within the time limit prescribed in the Implementing Regulations.

3. If a translation is not filed in due time or if the fee for the printing of a new specification is not paid in due time, the request shall be deemed to be withdrawn, unless these acts are done and the additional fee is paid within a further period as prescribed in the Implementing Regulations.

4. The decision to limit a Community patent shall not take effect until the date on which the Community Patent Bulletin mentions the limitation.

Article 54
Publication of a new specification following limitation proceedings

If a Community patent is limited under Article 53(2) the European Patent Office shall, at the same time as it publishes the mention of the decision to limit, publish a new specification of the Community patent containing the description, the claims and any drawings, in the amended form. Article 30 (3) and (4) shall apply *mutatis mutandis*.

CHAPTER III
REVOCATION PROCEDURE

Article 55
Application for revocation

1. Any person may file with the European Patent Office an application for revocation of a Community patent; however, in the case specified in Article 56(1)(e) the application may be filed only by a person entitled to be entered in the Register of Community Patents as the sole proprietor of the patent or by all the persons entitled to be entered as joint proprietors of it in accordance with Article 23 acting jointly.

2. The application may not be filed in the cases specified in Article 56(1) (a) to (d) during the period within which an opposition may be filed or while opposition proceedings are pending.

3. An application may be filed even if the Community patent has lapsed.

4. The application shall be filed in a written reasoned statement. It shall not be deemed to have been filed until the revocation fee has been paid.

5. Applicants shall be parties to the revocation proceedings as well as the proprietor of the patent.

6. If the applicant has neither his residence nor his principal place of business within the territory of one of the Contracting States, he shall, at the request of the proprietor of the patent, furnish security for the costs of the proceedings. The Revocation Division shall fix at a reasonable figure the amount of the security and the period within which it must be deposited. If the security is not deposited within the period specified, the application shall be deemed to be withdrawn.

Article 56
Grounds for revocation

1. An application for revocation of a Community patent may be filed only on the grounds that:

(a) the subject-matter of the patent is not patentable within the terms of Articles 52 to 57 of the European Patent Convention;

(b) the patent does not disclose the invention in a manner sufficiently clear and complete for it to be carried out by a person skilled in the art;

(c) the subject-matter of the patent extends beyond the content of the European patent application as filed, or, if the patent was granted on a European divisional application or on a new European application filed in accordance with Article 61 of the European Patent Convention, beyond the content of the earlier application as filed;

(d) the protection conferred by the patent has been extended;

(e) the proprietor of the patent is not, having regard to a decision which has to be recognized in all the Contracting States, entitled under Article 60(1) of the European Patent Convention;

(f) the subject-matter of the patent is not patentable within the terms of Article 36(1).

2. If the grounds for revocation affect the patent only partially, revocation shall be pronounced in the form of a corresponding limitation of the patent. The limitation may be effected in the form of an amendment to the claims, the description or the drawings.

3. In the case specified in paragraph 1(f), revocation shall be pronounced only in respect of the Contracting State in which the national patent application or national patent has been made public.

Article 57
Examination of the application

1. If the application for revocation of the Community patent is admissible, the Revocation Division shall examine whether the grounds for revocation mentioned in Article 56 prejudice the maintenance of the patent.

2. In the examination of the application, which shall be conducted in accordance with the Implementing Regulations, the Revocation Division shall invite the parties, as often as necessary, to file observations, within a

period to be fixed by the Revocation Division, on communications from another party or issued by itself.

Article 58
Revocation or maintenance of the Community patent

1. If the Revocation Division is of the opinion that the grounds for revocation mentioned in Article 56 prejudice the maintenance of the Community patent, it shall revoke the patent.

2. If the Revocation Division is of the opinion that the grounds for revocation mentioned in Article 56 do not prejudice the maintenance of the patent unamended, it shall reject the application.

3. If the Revocation Division is of the opinion that, taking into consideration the amendments made by the proprietor of the patent during the revocation proceedings, the grounds for revocation mentioned in Article 56 do not prejudice the maintenance of the patent, it shall decide to maintain the patent as amended, provided that:

(a) it is established, in accordance with the Implementing Regulations, that the proprietor of the patent approves the text in which the Revocation Division intends to maintain the patent;

(b) a translation of all amendments to the patent specification in one of the official languages of each of the Contracting States which does not have as an official language the language of the proceedings is filed within the time limit prescribed in the Implementing Regulations;

(c) the fee for the printing of a new specification is paid within the time limit prescribed in the Implementing Regulations.

4. If a translation is not filed in due time or if the fee for the printing of a new specification is not paid in due time, the patent shall be revoked, unless these acts are done and the additional fee is paid within a further period as prescribed in the Implementing Regulations.

Article 59
Publication of a new specification following revocation proceedings

If a Community patent is amended under Article 58(3) the European Patent Office shall, at the same time as it publishes the mention of the decision on the application for revocation, publish a new specification of the Community patent containing the description, the claims and any drawings, in the amended form. Article 30 (3) and (4) shall apply *mutatis mutandis*.

Article 60
Costs

1. Each party to revocation proceedings shall meet the costs he has incurred unless a decision of a Revocation Division in accordance with the Implementing Regulations or of the Common Appeal Court in accordance

with its Rules of Procedure, for reasons of equity, orders a different apportionment of costs incurred during taking of evidence or in oral proceedings. A decision on the apportionment of the costs may also be taken on request when the application for revocation is withdrawn or when the Community patent lapses.

2. On request, the registry of the Revocation Division shall fix the amount of the costs to be paid under a decision apportioning them. The fixing of the costs by the registry may be reviewed by a decision of the Revocation Division on a request filed within the period laid down in the Implementing Regulations.

3. Article 104(3) of the European Patent Convention shall apply *mutatis mutandis*.

PART IV
APPEALS PROCEDURE

Article 61
Appeal

1. An appeal shall lie from decisions of the Revocation Division and the Patent Administration Division.

2. Articles 106 to 109 of the European Patent Convention shall apply *mutatis mutandis* to this appeals procedure in so far as the Rules of Procedure of the Common Appeal Court or the Rules relating to Fees do not provide otherwise.

PART V
COMMON PROVISIONS

Article 62
Common provisions governing procedure and representation

1. The provisions of Part VII, Chapters I and III, of the European Patent Convention, other than Article 124, shall apply *mutatis mutandis* to this Convention, subject to the following:

   (a) Article 114(1) shall apply only to the Revocation Divisions;

   (b) Article 116 (2) and (3) shall apply only to the Patent Administration Division, and paragraph 4 shall apply only to the Revocation Divisions;

   (c) Article 122 shall also apply to all other parties to proceedings before the special departments;

   (d) Article 123(3) shall apply to limitation and revocation proceedings before the Revocation Divisions;

   (e) the term 'Contracting States' shall be understood as meaning the States parties to this Convention.

2. Notwithstanding paragraph 1(e), a person whose name appears on the list of professional representatives maintained by the European Patent Office who is not a national of one of the States parties to this Convention or does not have his place of business or employment within the territory of one of these States, shall be entitled to act as a professional representative for a party to proceedings relating to a Community patent before the special departments, provided that:

(a) he was, according to the Register of European Patents, the person last authorized to act as the professional representative for the same party or his predecessor in title in proceedings pursuant to the European Patent Convention which relate to this Community patent or to the European patent application on which it is based; and

(b) the State of which he is a national or within the territory of which he has his place of business or employment applies rules, as regards representation before the central industrial property office of the State concerned, which comply, in respect of reciprocity, with such conditions as the Select Committee of the Administrative Council may prescribe.

Article 63
Register of Community Patents

The European Patent Office shall keep a register, to be known as the Register of Community Patents, which shall contain those particulars the registration of which is provided for by this Convention. The Register shall be open to public inspection.

Article 64
Community Patent Bulletin

The European Patent Office shall periodically publish a Community Patent Bulletin containing entries made in the Register of Community Patents, as well as other particulars, the publication of which is prescribed by this Convention.

Article 65
Information to the public or official authorities

Articles 128 (4) and 130 to 132 of the European Patent Convention shall apply *mutatis mutandis*, the term 'Contracting States' being understood as meaning the States parties to this Convention.

PART VI
JURISDICTION AND PROCEDURE IN ACTIONS RELATING TO COMMUNITY PATENTS OTHER THAN THOSE GOVERNED BY THE PROTOCOL ON LITIGATION

CHAPTER I
JURISDICTION AND ENFORCEMENT

Article 66
General provisions

Unless otherwise specified in this Convention, the Convention on Jurisdiction and Enforcement of Judgments in Civil and Commercial Matters, signed at Brussels on 27 September 1968, as amended by the Conventions on the Accession to that Convention of the States acceding to the European Communities, the whole of which Convention and of which Conventions of Accession are hereinafter referred to as the 'Convention on Jurisdiction and Enforcement', shall apply to actions relating to Community patents, other than those to which the Protocol on Litigation applies, and to decisions given in respect of such actions.

Article 67
Jurisdiction of national courts concerning actions relating to Community patents

The following courts shall have exclusive jurisdiction:

(a) in actions relating to compulsory licences in respect of a Community patent, the courts of the Contracting State the national law of which is applicable to the licence;

(b) in actions relating to the right to a patent in which an employer and an employee are in dispute, the courts of the Contracting State under whose law the right to a European patent is determined in accordance with Article 60(1), second sentence, of the European Patent Convention. Any agreement conferring jurisdiction shall be valid only in so far as the national law governing the contract of employment allows the agreement in question.

Article 68
Supplementary provisions on jurisdiction

1. Within the Contracting State whose courts have jurisdiction under Articles 66 and 67, those courts shall have jurisdiction which would have jurisdiction *ratione loci* and *ratione materiae* in the case of actions relating to a national patent granted in that State.

2. Articles 66 and 67 shall apply to actions relating to a European patent application in which the Contracting States are designated, except in so far as the right to the grant of a European patent is claimed.

3. Actions relating to a Community patent for which no court has jurisdiction under Articles 66 and 67 and paragraphs 1 and 2 may be heard before the courts of the Federal Republic of Germany.

Article 69
Supplementary provisions on recognition and enforcement

1. Article 27 (3) and (4) of the Convention on Jurisdiction and Enforcement shall not apply to decisions relating to the right to the Community patent.

2. In the case of irreconcilable decisions relating to the right to a Community patent given in proceedings between the same parties, only the decision of the court first seised of the matter shall be recognized. Neither party may invoke any other decision even in the Contracting State in which it was given.

Article 70
National authorities

For actions relating to the right to a Community patent or to compulsory licences in respect of a Community patent the term 'courts' in this Convention and the Convention on Jurisdiction and Enforcement shall include authorities which, under the national law of a Contracting State, have jurisdiction to decide such actions relating to a national patent granted in that State. The Contracting State concerned shall notify the European Patent Office of any authority on which such jurisdiction is conferred and the European Patent Office shall inform the other Contracting States accordingly.

CHAPTER II
PROCEDURE

Article 71
Rules of procedure

Unless otherwise specified in this Convention, the actions referred to in Articles 66 to 68 shall be subject to the national rules of procedure governing the same type of action relating to a national patent.

Article 72
Obligation of the national court

A national court which is dealing with an action relating to a Community patent, other than the actions governed by the Protocol on Litigation, shall treat the patent as valid.

Article 73
Stay of proceedings

1. If the decision in an action before a national court relating to a European patent application which may result in the grant of a Community patent, other than an action governed by the Protocol on Litigation, depends upon the patentability of the invention, that decision may be given only after the European Patent Office has granted a Community patent or refused the European patent application. Paragraph 2 shall apply after the grant of the Community patent.

2. Where an opposition has been filed or a request for the limitation or an application for the revocation of a Community patent has been made, the national court may, at the request of one of the parties and after hearing the other parties, stay proceedings relating to the Community patent, in so far as its decision depends upon validity. At the request of one of the parties the court shall instruct that the documentary evidence of the opposition, limitation or revocation proceedings be communicated to it, in order to give a ruling on the request for a stay of proceedings.

Article 74
Penal sanctions for infringement

The national penal provisions in the matter of infringement shall be applicable in the case of infringement of a Community patent, to the extent that like acts of infringement would be punishable if they similarly affected a national patent.

PART VII
IMPACT ON NATIONAL LAW

Article 75
Prohibition of simultaneous protection

1. Where a national patent granted in a Contracting State relates to an invention for which a Community patent has been granted to the same inventor or to his successor in title with the same date of filing, or, if priority has been claimed, with the same date of priority, that national patent shall be ineffective to the extent that it covers the same invention as the Community patent, from the date on which:

(a) the period for filing an opposition to the Community patent has expired without any opposition being filed;

(b) the opposition proceedings are concluded with a decision to maintain the Community patent; or

(c) the national patent is granted, where this date is subsequent to the date referred to in subparagraph (a) or (b), as the case may be.

2. The subsequent lapse or revocation of the Community patent shall not affect the provisions of paragraph 1.

3. Each Contracting State may prescribe the procedure whereby the loss of effect of the national patent is determined and, where appropriate, the extent of that loss. It may also prescribe that the loss of effect shall apply as from the outset.

4. Prior to the date applicable under paragraph 1, simultaneous protection by a Community patent or a European patent application and a national patent or a national patent application shall exist unless any Contracting State provides otherwise.

Article 76
Exhaustion of the rights conferred by a national patent

1. The rights conferred by a national patent in a Contracting State shall not extend to acts concerning a product covered by that patent which are done within the territory of that Contracting State after that product has been put on the market in any Contracting State by the proprietor of the patent or with his express consent, unless there are grounds which, under Community law, would justify the extension to such acts of the rights conferred by the patent.

2. Paragraph 1 shall also apply with regard to a product put on the market by the proprietor of a national patent, granted for the same invention in another Contracting State, who has economic connections with the proprietor of the patent referred to in paragraph 1. For the purpose of this paragraph, two persons shall be deemed to have economic connections where one of them is in a position to exert a decisive influence on the other, directly or indirectly, with regard to the exploitation of a patent, or where a third party is in a position to exercise such an influence on both persons.

3. The preceding paragraph shall not apply in the case of a product put on the market under a compulsory licence.

Article 77
Compulsory licences in respect of national patents

Article 46 shall apply *mutatis mutandis* to the grant of compulsory licences for lack or insufficiency of exploitation of a national patent.

Article 78
Effect of unpublished national applications or patents

1. Where Article 36(2) applies, the Community patent shall be ineffective in the Contracting State concerned to the extent that it covers the same invention as the national patent application or patent.

2. The procedure confirming that, pursuant to paragraph 1, the Community patent is ineffective in the Contracting State shall, in that State, be that according to which, if the Community patent had been a national patent, it could have been revoked or made ineffective.

Article 79
National utility models and utility certificates

1. Articles 36, 75 and 76 shall apply to utility models and utility certificates and to applications for utility models and utility certificates in the Contracting States whose laws make provision for such models or certificates.

2. If a Contracting State provides in its law that a person may not exercise the rights conferred by a patent so long as there exists a utility model having an earlier date of filing or, where priority has been claimed an earlier date of priority, the same shall, notwithstanding paragraph 1, apply also to the Community patent in that State.

PART VIII
TRANSITIONAL PROVISIONS
Article 80
Application of the Convention on Jurisdiction and Enforcement

The provisions of the Convention on Jurisdiction and Enforcement rendered applicable by the preceding Articles shall not have effect in respect of any Contracting State for which that Convention has not yet entered into force until such entry into force.

Article 81
Option between a Community patent and a European patent

1. This Convention shall, subject to paragraph 3, not apply to a European patent application filed during a transitional period nor to any resulting European patent provided that, within the time limit prescribed in the Implementing Regulations, the applicant files with the European Patent Office a statement indicating that he does not wish to obtain a Community patent and identifying the Contracting States the designation of which is to be maintained. The statement shall not be deemed to be filed until after the prescribed fees have been paid. The statement may not be withdrawn.

2. Article 54 (3) and (4) of the European Patent Convention shall apply where a European patent application in which the Contracting States are designated or a Community patent has a date of filing or, where priority has been claimed, a date of priority later than that of a European patent application in which one or some of the Contracting States are designated. In the event of limitation or revocation of the Community patent on this ground, limitation or revocation shall be pronounced only in respect of the Contracting States designated in the earlier European patent application as published.

3. Articles 75 to 77 and 79 shall apply to a European patent as referred to in paragraph 1, the references in Articles 75 and 79 to a Community patent and the references in Articles 76 and 77 to a national patent being understood as references to such a European patent.

4. The transitional period referred to in paragraph 1 may be terminated by

decision of the Council of the European Communities, acting on a proposal from the Commission of the European Communities or from a Contracting State.

5. The decision referred to in paragraph 4 shall require unanimity.

Article 82
Subsequent choice of a Community patent

This Convention shall apply to a European patent granted in respect of a European patent application in which all the Contracting States are designated and which is filed prior to the entry into force of this Convention, provided that prior to the expiry of the time limit mentioned in Article 97(2)(b) of the European Patent Convention the applicant files with the European Patent Office a written statement that he wishes to obtain a Community patent.

Article 83
Reservation in respect of compulsory licences

1. Any signatory State may, at the time of signature or when depositing its instrument of ratification, declare that it reserves the right to provide that Articles 46 and 77 shall not apply within its territory to Community patents or to European patents granted for, or to national patents granted by, that State.

2. Any reservation made by a signatory State under paragraph 1 shall have effect until the end of the 10th year at the latest after the entry into force of the Agreement relating to Community Patents. However, the Council of the European Communities may, acting by a qualified majority on a proposal from a signatory State, extend the period in respect of a signatory State making such a reservation by not more than five years. This majority shall be that specified in the second indent of the second subparagraph of Article 148(2) of the Treaty establishing the European Economic Community.

3. Any reservation made under paragraph 1 shall cease to apply when common rules on the granting of compulsory licences in respect of Community patents have become operative.

4. Any signatory State that has made a reservation under paragraph 1 may withdraw it at any time. Such withdrawal shall be made by notification addressed to the Secretary-General of the Council of the European Communities and shall take effect one month from the date of receipt of such notification.

5. Termination of the effect of the reservation shall not affect compulsory licences granted before the date on which the reservation ceased to have effect.

Article 84
Other transitional provisions

1. Articles 159, 161 and 163 of the European Patent Convention shall apply *mutatis mutandis*, subject to the following:

   (a) the first meeting of the Select Committee of the Administrative Council shall be on the invitation of the Secretary-General of the Council of the European Communities;

   (b) the term 'Contracting State' shall be understood as meaning the States parties to this Convention.

2. Notwithstanding paragraph 1(b), Article 62(2) shall apply.

PART IX
FINAL PROVISIONS

Article 85
Implementing Regulations

1. The Implementing Regulations shall be an integral part of this Convention.

2. In the case of conflict between the provisions of this Convention and those of the Implementing Regulations, the provisions of this Convention shall prevail.

EC BIOTECHNOLOGY DIRECTIVE

Directive 98/44/EC of the European Parliament and of the Council of 6 July 1998 on the legal protection of biotechnological inventions

THE EUROPEAN PARLIAMENT AND THE COUNCIL OF THE EUROPEAN UNION,

Having regard to the Treaty establishing the European Community, and in particular Article 100a thereof,

Having regard to the proposal from the Commission,

Having regard to the opinion of the Economic and Social Committee,

Acting in accordance with the procedure laid down in Article 189b of the Treaty,

(1) Whereas biotechnology and genetic engineering are playing an increasingly important role in a broad range of industries and the protection of biotechnological inventions will certainly be of fundamental importance for the Community's industrial development

(2) Whereas, in particular in the field of genetic engineering, research and development require a considerable amount of high-risk investment and therefore only adequate legal protection can make them profitable

(3) Whereas effective and harmonised protection throughout the Member States is essential in order to maintain and encourage investment in the field of biotechnology

(4) Whereas following the European Parliament's rejection of the joint text, approved by the Conciliation Committee, for a European Parliament and Council Directive on the legal protection of biotechnological inventions, the European Parliament and the Council have determined that the legal protection of biotechnological inventions requires clarification

(5) Whereas differences exist in the legal protection of biotechnological inventions offered by the laws and practices of the different Member States whereas such differences could create barriers to trade and hence impede the proper functioning of the internal market

(6) Whereas such differences could well become greater as Member States adopt new and different legislation and administrative practices, or whereas national case-law interpreting such legislation develops differently

(7) Whereas uncoordinated development of national laws on the legal protection of biotechnological inventions in the Community could lead to further disincentives to trade, to the detriment of the industrial development of such inventions and of the smooth operation of the internal market

(8) Whereas legal protection of biotechnological inventions does not necessitate the creation of a separate body of law in place of the rules of national patent law whereas the rules of national patent law remain the essential basis for the legal protection of biotechnological inventions given that they must be adapted or added to in certain specific respects in order to

take adequate account of technological developments involving biological material which also fulfil the requirements for patentability

(9) Whereas in certain cases, such as the exclusion from patentability of plant and animal varieties and of essentially biological processes for the production of plants and animals, certain concepts in national laws based upon international patent and plant variety conventions have created uncertainty regarding the protection of biotechnological and certain microbiological inventions whereas harmonisation is necessary to clarify the said uncertainty

(10) Whereas regard should be had to the potential of the development of biotechnology for the environment and in particular the utility of this technology for the development of methods of cultivation which are less polluting and more economical in their use of ground whereas the patent system should be used to encourage research into, and the application of, such processes

(11) Whereas the development of biotechnology is important to developing countries, both in the field of health and combating major epidemics and endemic diseases and in that of combating hunger in the world whereas the patent system should likewise be used to encourage research in these fields whereas international procedures for the dissemination of such technology in the Third World and to the benefit of the population groups concerned should be promoted

(12) Whereas the Agreement on Trade-Related Aspects of Intellectual Property Rights (TRIPs) signed by the European Community and the Member States, has entered into force and provides that patent protection must be guaranteed for products and processes in all areas of technology

(13) Whereas the Community's legal framework for the protection of biotechnological inventions can be limited to laying down certain principles as they apply to the patentability of biological material as such, such principles being intended in particular to determine the difference between inventions and discoveries with regard to the patentability of certain elements of human origin, to the scope of protection conferred by a patent on a biotechnological invention, to the right to use a deposit mechanism in addition to written descriptions and lastly to the option of obtaining non-exclusive compulsory licences in respect of interdependence between plant varieties and inventions, and conversely

(14) Whereas a patent for invention does not authorise the holder to implement that invention, but merely entitles him to prohibit third parties from exploiting it for industrial and commercial purposes whereas, consequently, substantive patent law cannot serve to replace or render superfluous national, European or international law which may impose restrictions or prohibitions or which concerns the monitoring of research and of the use or commercialisation of its results, notably from the point of view of the requirements of public health, safety, environmental protection, animal welfare, the preservation of genetic diversity and compliance with certain ethical standards

(15) Whereas no prohibition or exclusion exists in national or European patent law (Munich Convention) which precludes a priori the patentability of biological matter

(16) Whereas patent law must be applied so as to respect the fundamental principles safeguarding the dignity and integrity of the person whereas it is important to assert the principle that the human body, at any stage in its formation or development, including germ cells, and the simple discovery of one of its elements or one of its products, including the sequence or partial sequence of a human gene, cannot be patented whereas these principles are in line with the criteria of patentability proper to patent law, whereby a mere discovery cannot be patented

(17) Whereas significant progress in the treatment of diseases has already been made thanks to the existence of medicinal products derived from elements isolated from the human body and/or otherwise produced, such medicinal products resulting from technical processes aimed at obtaining elements similar in structure to those existing naturally in the human body and whereas, consequently, research aimed at obtaining and isolating such elements valuable to medicinal production should be encouraged by means of the patent system

(18) Whereas, since the patent system provides insufficient incentive for encouraging research into and production of biotechnological medicines which are needed to combat rare or 'orphan. diseases, the Community and the Member States have a duty to respond adequately to this problem

(19) Whereas account has been taken of Opinion No. 8 of the Group of Advisers on the Ethical Implications of Biotechnology to the European Commission

(20) Whereas, therefore, it should be made clear that an invention based on an element isolated from the human body or otherwise produced by means of a technical process, which is susceptible of industrial application, is not excluded from patentability, even where the structure of that element is identical to that of a natural element, given that the rights conferred by the patent do not extend to the human body and its elements in their natural environment

(21) Whereas such an element isolated from the human body or otherwise produced is not excluded from patentability since it is, for example, the result of technical processes used to identify, purify and classify it and to reproduce it outside the human body, techniques which human beings alone are capable of putting into practice and which nature is incapable of accomplishing by itself

(22) Whereas the discussion on the patentability of sequences or partial sequences of genes is controversial whereas, according to this Directive, the granting of a patent for inventions which concern such sequences or partial sequences should be subject to the same criteria of patentability as in all other areas of technology: novelty, inventive step and industrial application whereas the industrial application of a sequence or partial sequence must be disclosed in the patent application as filed

(23) Whereas a mere DNA sequence without indication of a function does not contain any technical information and is therefore not a patentable invention

(24) Whereas, in order to comply with the industrial application criterion it is necessary in cases where a sequence or partial sequence of a gene is used to produce a protein or part of a protein, to specify which protein or part of a protein is produced or what function it performs

(25) Whereas, for the purposes of interpreting rights conferred by a patent, when sequences overlap only in parts which are not essential to the invention, each sequence will be considered as an independent sequence in patent law terms

(26) Whereas if an invention is based on biological material of human origin or if it uses such material, where a patent application is filed, the person from whose body the material is taken must have had an opportunity of expressing free and informed consent thereto, in accordance with national law

(27) Whereas if an invention is based on biological material of plant or animal origin or if it uses such material, the patent application should, where appropriate, include information on the geographical origin of such material, if known whereas this is without prejudice to the processing of patent applications or the validity of rights arising from granted patents

(28) Whereas this Directive does not in any way affect the basis of current patent law, according to which a patent may be granted for any new application of a patented product

(29) Whereas this Directive is without prejudice to the exclusion of plant and animal varieties from patentability whereas on the other hand inventions which concern plants or animals are patentable provided that the application of the invention is not technically confined to a single plant or animal variety

(30) Whereas the concept 'plant variety. is defined by the legislation protecting new varieties, pursuant to which a variety is defined by its whole genome and therefore possesses individuality and is clearly distinguishable from other varieties

(31) Whereas a plant grouping which is characterised by a particular gene (and not its whole genome) is not covered by the protection of new varieties and is therefore not excluded from patentability even if it comprises new varieties of plants

(32) Whereas, however, if an invention consists only in genetically modifying a particular plant variety, and if a new plant variety is bred, it will still be excluded from patentability even if the genetic modification is the result not of an essentially biological process but of a biotechnological process

(33) Whereas it is necessary to define for the purposes of this Directive when a process for the breeding of plants and animals is essentially biological

(34) Whereas this Directive shall be without prejudice to concepts of invention and discovery, as developed by national, European or international

patent law

(35) Whereas this Directive shall be without prejudice to the provisions of national patent law whereby processes for treatment of the human or animal body by surgery or therapy and diagnostic methods practised on the human or animal body are excluded from patentability

(36) Whereas the TRIPs Agreement provides for the possibility that members of the World Trade Organisation may exclude from patentability inventions, the prevention within their territory of the commercial exploitation of which is necessary to protect ordre public or morality, including to protect human, animal or plant life or health or to avoid serious prejudice to the environment, provided that such exclusion is not made merely because the exploitation is prohibited by their law

(37) Whereas the principle whereby inventions must be excluded from patentability where their commercial exploitation offends against ordre public or morality must also be stressed in this Directive

(38) Whereas the operative part of this Directive should also include an illustrative list of inventions excluded from patentability so as to provide national courts and patent offices with a general guide to interpreting the reference to ordre public and morality whereas this list obviously cannot presume to be exhaustive whereas processes, the use of which offend against human dignity, such as processes to produce chimeras from germ cells or totipotent cells of humans and animals, are obviously also excluded from patentability

(39) Whereas ordre public and morality correspond in particular to ethical or moral principles recognised in a Member State, respect for which is particularly important in the field of biotechnology in view of the potential scope of inventions in this field and their inherent relationship to living matter whereas such ethical or moral principles supplement the standard legal examinations under patent law regardless of the technical field of the invention

(40) Whereas there is a consensus within the Community that interventions in the human germ line and the cloning of human beings offends against ordre public and morality whereas it is therefore important to exclude unequivocally from patentability processes for modifying the germ line genetic identity of human beings and processes for cloning human beings

(41) Whereas a process for cloning human beings may be defined as any process, including techniques of embryo splitting, designed to create a human being with the same nuclear genetic information as another living or deceased human being

(42) Whereas, moreover, uses of human embryos for industrial or commercial purposes must also be excluded from patentability whereas in any case such exclusion does not affect inventions for therapeutic or diagnostic purposes which are applied to the human embryo and are useful to it

(43) Whereas pursuant to Article F(2) of the Treaty on European Union, the

Union is to respect fundamental rights, as guaranteed by the European Convention for the Protection of Human Rights and Fundamental Freedoms signed in Rome on 4 November 1950 and as they result from the constitutional traditions common to the Member States, as general principles of Community law

(44) Whereas the Commission's European Group on Ethics in Science and New Technologies evaluates all ethical aspects of biotechnology whereas it should be pointed out in this connection that that Group may be consulted only where biotechnology is to be evaluated at the level of basic ethical principles, including where it is consulted on patent law

(45) Whereas processes for modifying the genetic identity of animals which are likely to cause them suffering without any substantial medical benefit in terms of research, prevention, diagnosis or therapy to man or animal, and also animals resulting from such processes, must be excluded from patentability

(46) Whereas, in view of the fact that the function of a patent is to reward the inventor for his creative efforts by granting an exclusive but time-bound right, and thereby encourage inventive activities, the holder of the patent should be entitled to prohibit the use of patented self-reproducing material in situations analogous to those where it would be permitted to prohibit the use of patented, non-self-reproducing products, that is to say the production of the patented product itself

(47) Whereas it is necessary to provide for a first derogation from the rights of the holder of the patent when the propagating material incorporating the protected invention is sold to a farmer for farming purposes by the holder of the patent or with his consent whereas that initial derogation must authorise the farmer to use the product of his harvest for further multiplication or propagation on his own farm whereas the extent and the conditions of that derogation must be limited in accordance with the extent and conditions set out in Council Regulation (EC) No 2100/94 of 27 July 1994 on Community plant variety rights;

(48) Whereas only the fee envisaged under Community law relating to plant variety rights as a condition for applying the derogation from Community plant variety rights can be required of the farmer

(49) Whereas, however, the holder of the patent may defend his rights against a farmer abusing the derogation or against a breeder who has developed a plant variety incorporating the protected invention if the latter fails to adhere to his commitments

(50) Whereas a second derogation from the rights of the holder of the patent must authorise the farmer to use protected livestock for agricultural purposes

(51) Whereas the extent and the conditions of that second derogation must be determined by national laws, regulations and practices, since there is no Community legislation on animal variety rights

(52) Whereas, in the field of exploitation of new plant characteristics

resulting from genetic engineering, guaranteed access must, on payment of a fee, be granted in the form of a compulsory licence where, in relation to the genus or species concerned, the plant variety represents significant technical progress of considerable economic interest compared to the invention claimed in the patent

(53) Whereas, in the field of the use of new plant characteristics resulting from new plant varieties in genetic engineering, guaranteed access must, on payment of a fee, be granted in the form of a compulsory licence where the invention represents significant technical progress of considerable economic interest

(54) Whereas Article 34 of the TRIPs Agreement contains detailed provisions on the burden of proof which is binding on all Member States whereas, therefore, a provision in this Directive is not necessary

(55) Whereas following Decision 93/626/EEC the Community is party to the Convention on Biological Diversity of 5 June 1992 whereas, in this regard, Member States must give particular weight to Article 3 and Article 8(j), the second sentence of Article 16(2) and Article 16(5) of the Convention when bringing into force the laws, regulations and administrative provisions necessary to comply with this Directive

(56) Whereas the Third Conference of the Parties to the Biodiversity Convention, which took place in November 1996, noted in Decision III/17 that 'further work is required to help develop a common appreciation of the relationship between intellectual property rights and the relevant provisions of the TRIPs Agreement and the Convention on Biological Diversity, in particular on issues relating to technology transfer and conservation and sustainable use of biological diversity and the fair and equitable sharing of benefits arising out of the use of genetic resources, including the protection of knowledge, innovations and practices of indigenous and local communities embodying traditional lifestyles relevant for the conservation and sustainable use of biological diversity.,

HAVE ADOPTED THIS DIRECTIVE:

CHAPTER I
Patentability

Article 1

1. Member States shall protect biotechnological inventions under national patent law. They shall, if necessary, adjust their national patent law to take account of the provisions of this Directive.

2. This Directive shall be without prejudice to the obligations of the Member States pursuant to international agreements, and in particular the TRIPs Agreement and the Convention on Biological Diversity.

Article 2

1. For the purposes of this Directive,

(a) 'biological material. means any material containing genetic information and capable of reproducing itself or being reproduced in a biological system

(b) 'microbiological process. means any process involving or performed upon or resulting in microbiological material.

2. A process for the production of plants or animals is essentially biological if it consists entirely of natural phenomena such as crossing or selection.

3. The concept of 'plant variety. is defined by Article 5 of Regulation (EC) No 2100/94.

Article 3

1. For the purposes of this Directive, inventions which are new, which involve an inventive step and which are susceptible of industrial application shall be patentable even if they concern a product consisting of or containing biological material or a process by means of which biological material is produced, processed or used.

2. Biological material which is isolated from its natural environment or produced by means of a technical process may be the subject of an invention even if it previously occurred in nature.

Article 4

1. The following shall not be patentable:

(a) plant and animal varieties

(b) essentially biological processes for the production of plants or animals.

2. Inventions which concern plants or animals shall be patentable if the technical feasibility of the invention is not confined to a particular plant or animal variety.

3. Paragraph 1(b) shall be without prejudice to the patentability of inventions which concern a microbiological or other technical process or a product obtained by means of such a process.

Article 5

1. The human body, at the various stages of its formation and development, and the simple discovery of one of its elements, including the sequence or partial sequence of a gene, cannot constitute patentable inventions.

2. An element isolated from the human body or otherwise produced by means of a technical process, including the sequence or partial sequence of a gene, may constitute a patentable invention, even if the structure of that element is identical to that of a natural element.

3. The industrial application of a sequence or a partial sequence of a gene must be disclosed in the patent application.

Article 6

1. Inventions shall be considered unpatentable where their commercial exploitation would be contrary to ordre public or morality however, exploitation shall not be deemed to be so contrary merely because it is prohibited by law or regulation.

2. On the basis of paragraph 1, the following, in particular, shall be considered unpatentable:

(a) processes for cloning human beings

(b) processes for modifying the germ line genetic identity of human beings

(c) uses of human embryos for industrial or commercial purposes

(d) processes for modifying the genetic identity of animals which are likely to cause them suffering without any substantial medical benefit to man or animal, and also animals resulting from such processes.

Article 7

The Commission's European Group on Ethics in Science and New Technologies evaluates all ethical aspects of biotechnology.

CHAPTER II
Scope of protection

Article 8

1. The protection conferred by a patent on a biological material possessing specific characteristics as a result of the invention shall extend to any biological material derived from that biological material through propagation or multiplication in an identical or divergent form and possessing those same characteristics.

2. The protection conferred by a patent on a process that enables a biological material to be produced possessing specific characteristics as a result of the invention shall extend to biological material directly obtained through that process and to any other biological material derived from the directly obtained biological material through propagation or multiplication in an identical or divergent form and possessing those same characteristics.

Article 9

The protection conferred by a patent on a product containing or consisting of genetic information shall extend to all material, save as provided in Article 5(1), in which the product in incorporated and in which the genetic information is contained and performs its function.

Article 10

The protection referred to in Articles 8 and 9 shall not extend to biological material obtained from the propagation or multiplication of biological material placed on the market in the territory of a Member State by the holder of the patent or with his consent, where the multiplication or propagation necessarily results from the application for which the biological material was marketed, provided that the material obtained is not subsequently used for other propagation or multiplication.

Article 11

1. By way of derogation from Articles 8 and 9, the sale or other form of commercialisation of plant propagating material to a farmer by the holder of the patent or with his consent for agricultural use implies authorisation for the farmer to use the product of his harvest for propagation or multiplication by him on his own farm, the extent and conditions of this derogation corresponding to those under Article 14 of Regulation (EC) No 2100/94.

2. By way of derogation from Articles 8 and 9, the sale or any other form of commercialisation of breeding stock or other animal reproductive material to a farmer by the holder of the patent or with his consent implies authorisation for the farmer to use the protected livestock for an agricultural purpose. This includes making the animal or other animal reproductive material available for the purposes of pursuing his agricultural activity but not sale within the framework or for the purpose of a commercial reproduction activity.

3. The extent and the conditions of the derogation provided for in paragraph 2 shall be determined by national laws, regulations and practices.

CHAPTER III
Compulsory cross-licensing
Article 12

1. Where a breeder cannot acquire or exploit a plant variety right without infringing a prior patent, he may apply for a compulsory licence for non-exclusive use of the invention protected by the patent inasmuch as the licence is necessary for the exploitation of the plant variety to be protected, subject to payment of an appropriate royalty. Member States shall provide that, where such a licence is granted, the holder of the patent will be entitled to a cross-licence on reasonable terms to use the protected variety.

2. Where the holder of a patent concerning a biotechnological invention cannot exploit it without infringing a prior plant variety right, he may apply for a compulsory licence for non-exclusive use of the plant variety protected by that right, subject to payment of an appropriate royalty. Member States shall provide that, where such a licence is granted, the holder of the variety right will be entitled to a cross-licence on reasonable terms to use the protected invention.

3. Applicants for the licences referred to in paragraphs 1 and 2 must demonstrate that:

(a) they have applied unsuccessfully to the holder of the patent or of the plant variety right to obtain a contractual licence

(b) the plant variety or the invention constitutes significant technical progress of considerable economic interest compared with the invention claimed in the patent or the protected plant variety.

4.   Each Member State shall designate the authority or authorities responsible for granting the licence. Where a licence for a plant variety can be granted only by the Community Plant Variety Office, Article 29 of Regulation (EC) No 2100/94 shall apply.

CHAPTER IV
Deposit, access and re-deposit of a biological material

Article 13

1. Where an invention involves the use of or concerns biological material which is not available to the public and which cannot be described in a patent application in such a manner as to enable the invention to be reproduced by a person skilled in the art, the description shall be considered inadequate for the purposes of patent law unless:

(a) the biological material has been deposited no later than the date on which the patent application was filed with a recognised depositary institution. At least the international depositary authorities which acquired this status by virtue of Article 7 of the Budapest Treaty of 28 April 1977 on the international recognition of the deposit of micro-organisms for the purposes of patent procedure, hereinafter referred to as the 'Budapest Treaty, shall be recognised

(b) the application as filed contains such relevant information as is available to the applicant on the characteristics of the biological material deposited

(c) the patent application states the name of the depository institution and the accession number.

2. Access to the deposited biological material shall be provided through the supply of a sample:

(a) up to the first publication of the patent application, only to those persons who are authorised under national patent law

(b) between the first publication of the application and the granting of the patent, to anyone requesting it or, if the applicant so requests, only to an independent expert

(c) after the patent has been granted, and notwithstanding revocation or cancellation of the patent, to anyone requesting it.

3. The sample shall be supplied only if the person requesting it undertakes, for the term during which the patent is in force:

(a) not to make it or any material derived from it available to third parties and

(b) not to use it or any material derived from it except for experimental purposes, unless the applicant for or proprietor of the patent, as applicable, expressly waives such an undertaking.

4. At the applicant's request, where an application is refused or withdrawn, access to the deposited material shall be limited to an independent expert for 20 years from the date on which the patent application was filed. In that case, paragraph 3 shall apply.

5. The applicant's requests referred to in point (b) of paragraph 2 and in paragraph 4 may only be made up to the date on which the technical preparations for publishing the patent application are deemed to have been completed.

Article 14

1. If the biological material deposited in accordance with Article 13 ceases to be available from the recognised depositary institution, a new deposit of the material shall be permitted on the same terms as those laid down in the Budapest Treaty.

2. Any new deposit shall be accompanied by a statement signed by the depositor certifying that the newly deposited biological material is the same as that originally deposited.

CHAPTER V
Final provisions
Article 15

1. Member States shall bring into force the laws, regulations and administrative provisions necessary to comply with this Directive not later than 30 July 2000. They shall forthwith inform the Commission thereof.

When Member States adopt these measures, they shall contain a reference to this Directive or shall be accompanied by such reference on the occasion of their official publication. The methods of making such reference shall be laid down by Member States.

2. Member States shall communicate to the Commission the text of the provisions of national law which they adopt in the field covered by this Directive.

Article 16

The Commission shall send the European Parliament and the Council:

(a) every five years as from the date specified in Article 15(1) a report on any problems encountered with regard to the relationship between this Directive and international agreements on the protection of human rights to which the Member States have acceded.

(b) within two years of entry into force of this Directive, a report assessing the implications for basic genetic engineering research of failure to publish, or late publication of, papers on subjects which could be patentable

(c) annually as from the date specified in Article 15(1), a report on the development and implications of patent law in the field of biotechnology and genetic engineering.

Article 17

This Directive shall enter into force on the day of its publication in the Official Journal of the European Communities.

Article 18

This Directive is addressed to the Member States.

Done at Brussels, 6 July 1998.

EC BLOCK EXEMPTION ON TECHNOLOGY TRANSFER
Commission Regulation (EC) 240/96 of 31 January 1996
On the application of Article 85(3) of the Treaty to certain categories of technology transfer agreements

THE COMMISSION OF THE EUROPEAN COMMUNITIES,

Having regard to the Treaty establishing the European Community,

Having regard to Council Regulation No. 19/65/EEC of 2 March 1965 on the application of Article 85(3) of the Treaty to certain categories of agreements and concerted practices, as last amended by the Act of Accession of Austria, Finland and Sweden, and in particular Article 1 thereof,

Having published a draft of this Regulation,

After consulting the Advisory Committee on Restrictive Practices and Dominant Positions,

Whereas:

(1)   Regulation No 19/65/EEC empowers the Commission to apply Article 85(3) of the Treaty by regulation to certain categories of agreements and concerted practices falling within the scope of Article 85(1) which include restrictions imposed in relation to the acquisition or use of industrial property rights—in particular of patents, utility models, designs or trademarks—or to the rights arising out of contracts for assignment of, or the right to use, a method of manufacture of knowledge relating to use or to the application of industrial processes.

(2)   The Commission has made use of this power by adopting Regulation (EEC) No 2349/84 of 23 July 1984 on the application of Article 85(3) of the Treaty to certain categories of patent licensing agreements, as last amended by Regulation (EC) No 2131/95, and Regulation (EEC) No 556/89 of 30 November 1988 on the application of Article 85(3) of the Treaty to certain categories of know-how licensing agreements, as last amended by the Act of Accession of Austria, Finland and Sweden.

(3)   These two block exemptions ought to be combined into a single regulation covering technology transfer agreements, and the rules governing patent licensing agreements and agreements for the licensing of know-how ought to be harmonized and simplified as far as possible, in order to encourage the dissemination of technical knowledge in the Community and to promote the manufacture of technically more sophisticated products. In those circumstances Regulation (EEC) No 556/89 should be repealed.

(4)   This Regulation should apply to the licensing of Member States' own patents, Community patents and European patents ('pure' patent licensing agreements). It should also apply to agreements for the licensing of non-patented technical information such as descriptions of manufacturing processes, recipes, formulae, designs or drawings, commonly termed 'know-how' ('pure' know-how licensing agreements), and to combined patent and know-how licensing agreements ('mixed'

agreements), which are playing an increasing important role in the transfer of technology. For the purposes of this Regulation, a number of terms are defined in Article 10.

(5)   Patent or know-how licensing agreements are agreements whereby one undertaking which holds a patent or know-how ('the licensor') permits another undertaking ('the licensee') to exploit the patent thereby licensed, or communicates the know-how to it, in particular for purposes of manufacture, use or putting on the market. In the light of experience acquired so far, it is possible to define a category of licensing agreements covering all or part of the common market which are capable of falling within the scope of Article 85(1) but which can normally be regarded as satisfying the conditions laid down in Article 85(3), where patents are necessary for the achievement of the objects of the licensed technology by a mixed agreement or where know how—whether it is ancillary to patents or independent of them—is secret, substantial and identified in any appropriate form. These criteria are intended only to ensure that the licensing of the know-how or the grant of the patent licence justifies a block exemption of obligations restricting competition. This is without prejudice to the right of the parties to include in the contract provisions regarding other obligations, such as the obligation to pay royalties, even if the block exemption no longer applies.

(6)   It is appropriate to extend the scope of this Regulation to pure or mixed agreements containing the licensing of intellectual property rights other than patents (in particular, trademarks, design rights and copyright, especially software protection), when such additional licensing contributes to the achievement of the objects of the licensed technology and contains only ancillary provisions.

(7)   Where such pure or mixed licensing agreements contain not only obligations relating to territories within the common market but also obligations relating to non-member countries, the presence of the latter does not prevent this Regulation from applying to the obligations relating to territories within the common market. Where licensing agreements for non member countries or for territories which extend beyond the frontiers of the Community have effects within the common market which may fall within the scope of Article 85(1), such agreements should be covered by this Regulation to the same extent as would agreements for territories within the common market.

(8)   The objective being to facilitate the dissemination of technology and the improvement of manufacturing processes, this Regulation should apply only where the licensee himself manufactures the licensed products or has them manufactured for his account, or where the licensed product is a service, provides the service himself or has the service provided for his account, irrespective of whether or not the licensee is also entitled to use confidential information provided by the licensor for the promotion and sale of the licensed product. The

scope of this Regulation should therefore exclude agreements solely for the purpose of sale. Also to be excluded from the scope of this Regulation are agreements relating to marketing know-how communicated in the context of franchising arrangements and certain licensing agreements entered into in connection with arrangements such as joint ventures or patent pools and other arrangements in which a licence is granted in exchange for other licences not related to improvements to or new applications of the licensed technology. Such agreements pose different problems which cannot at present be dealt with in a single regulation (Article 5).

(9) Given the similarity between sale and exclusive licensing, and the danger that the requirements of this Regulation might be evaded by presenting as assignments what are in fact exclusive licenses restrictive of competition, this Regulation should apply to agreements concerning the assignment and acquisition of patents or know-how where the risk associated with exploitation remains with the assignor. It should also apply to licensing agreements in which the licensor is not the holder of the patent or know-how but is authorized by the holder to grant the licence (as in the case of sub-licences) and to licensing agreements in which the parties' rights or obligations are assumed by connected undertakings (Article 6).

(10) Exclusive licensing agreements, i.e. agreements in which the licensor undertakes not to exploit the licensed technology in the licensed territory himself or to grant further licences there, may not be in themselves incompatible with Article 85(1) where they are concerned with the introduction and protection of a new technology in the licensed territory, by reason of the scale of the research which has been undertaken, of the increase in the level of competition, in particular inter-brand competition, and of the competitiveness of the undertakings concerned resulting from the dissemination of innovation within the Community. In so far as agreements of this kind fall, in other circumstances, within the scope of Article 85(1), it is appropriate to include them in Article 1 in order that they may also benefit from the exemption.

(11) The exemption of export bans on the licensor and on the licensees does not prejudice any developments in the case law of the Court of Justice in relation to such agreements, notably with respect to Articles 30 to 36 and Article 85(1). This is also the case, in particular, regarding the prohibition on the licensee from selling the licensed product in territories granted to other licensees (passive competition).

(12) The obligations listed in Article 1 generally contribute to improving the production of goods and to promoting technical progress. They make the holders of patents or know-how more willing to grant licences and licensees more inclined to undertake the investment required to manufacture, use and put on the market a new product or to use a new process. Such obligations may be permitted under this Regulation in respect of territories where the licensed product is

protected by patents as long as these remain in force.

(13) Since the point at which the know-how ceases to be secret can be difficult to determine, it is appropriate, in respect of territories where the licensed technology comprises know-how only, to limit such obligations to a fixed number of years. Moreover, in order to provide sufficient periods of protection, it is appropriate to take as the starting-point for such periods the date on which the product is first put on the market in the Community by a licensee.

(14) Exemption under Article 85(3) of longer periods of territorial protection for know-how agreements, in particular in order to protect expensive and risky investment or where the parties were not competitors at the date of the grant of the licence, can be granted only by individual decision. On the other hand, parties are free to extend the term of their agreements in order to exploit any subsequent improvement and to provide for the payment of additional royalties. However, in such cases, further periods of territorial protection may be allowed only starting from the date of licensing of the secret improvements in the Community, and by individual decision. Where the research for improvements results in innovations which are distinct from the licensed technology the parties may conclude a new agreement benefitting from an exemption under this Regulation.

(15) Provision should also be made for exemption of an obligation on the licensee not to put the product on the market in the territories of other licensees, the permitted period for such an obligation (this obligation would ban not just active competition but passive competition too) should, however, be limited to a few years from the date on which the licensed product is first put on the market in the Community by a licensee, irrespective of whether the licensed technology comprises know-how, patents or both in the territories concerned.

(16) The exemption of territorial protection should apply for the whole duration of the periods thus permitted, as long as the patents remain in force or the know-how remains secret and substantial. The parties to a mixed patent and know-how licensing agreement must be able to take advantage in a particular territory of the period of protection conferred by a patent or by the know-how, whichever is the longer.

(17) The obligations listed in Article 1 also generally fulfil the other conditions for the application of Article 85(3). Consumers will, as a rule, be allowed a fair share of the benefit resulting from the improvement in the supply of goods on the market. To safeguard this effect, however, it is right to exclude from the application of Article 1 cases where the parties agree to refuse to meet demand from users or resellers within their respective territories who would resell for export, or to take other steps to impede parallel imports. The obligations referred to above thus only impose restrictions which are indispensable to the attainment of their objectives.

(18) It is desirable to list in this Regulation a number of obligations that are commonly found in licensing agreements but are normally not restrictive of competition, and to provide that in the event that because of the particular economic or legal circumstances they should fall within Article 85(1), they too will be covered by the exemption. This list, in Article 2, is not exhaustive.

(19) This Regulation must also specify what restrictions or provisions may not be included in licensing agreements if these are to benefit from the block exemption. The restrictions listed in Article 3 may fall under the prohibition of Article 85(1), but in their case there can be no general presumption that, although they relate to the transfer of technology, they will lead to the positive effects required by Article 85(3), as would be necessary for the granting of a block exemption. Such restrictions can be declared exempt only by an individual decision, taking account of the market position of the undertakings concerned and the degree of concentration on the relevant market.

(20) The obligations on the licensee to cease using the licensed technology after the termination of the agreement (Article 2(1)(3)) and to make improvements available to the licensor (Article 2(1)(4)) do not generally restrict competition. The post-term use ban may be regarded as a normal feature of licensing, as otherwise the licensor would be forced to transfer his know-how or patents in perpetuity. Undertakings by the licensee to grant back to the licensor a licence for improvements to the licensed know-how and/or patents are generally not restrictive of competition if the licensee is entitled by the contract to share in future experience and inventions made by the licensor. On the other hand, a restrictive effect on competition arises where the agreement obliges the licensee to assign to the licensor rights to improvements of the originally licensed technology that he himself has brought about (Article 3(6)).

(21) The list of clauses which do not prevent exemption also includes an obligation on the licensee to keep paying royalties until the end of the agreement independently of whether or not the licensed know-how has entered into the public domain through the action of third parties or of the licensee himself (Article 2(1)(7)). Moreover, the parties must be free, in order to facilitate payment, to spread the royalty payments for the use of the licensed technology over a period extending beyond the duration of the licensed patents, in particular by setting lower royalty rates. As a rule, parties do not need to be protected against the foreseeable financial consequences of an agreement freely entered into, and they should therefore be free to choose the appropriate means of financing the technology transfer and sharing between them the risks of such use. However, the setting of rates of royalty so as to achieve one of the restrictions listed in Article 3 renders the agreement ineligible for the block exemption.

(22) An obligation on the licensee to restrict his exploitation of the licensed technology to one or more technical fields of application ('fields of use')

or to one or more product markets is not caught by Article 85(1) either, since the licensor is entitled to transfer the technology only for a limited purpose (Article 2(1)(8)).

(23) Clauses whereby the parties allocate customers within the same technological field of use or the same product market, either by an actual prohibition on supplying certain classes of customer or through an obligation with an equivalent effect, would also render the agreement ineligible for the block exemption where the parties are competitors for the contract products (Article 3(4)). Such restrictions between undertakings which are not competitors remain subject to the opposition procedure. Article 3 does not apply to cases where the patent or know-how licence is granted in order to provide a single customer with a second source of supply. In such a case, a prohibition on the second licensee from supplying persons other than the customer concerned is an essential condition for the grant of a second licence, since the purpose of the transaction is not to create an independent supplier in the market. The same applies to limitations on the quantities the licensee may supply to the customer concerned (Article 2(1)(13)).

(24) Besides the clauses already mentioned, the list of restrictions which render the block exemption inapplicable also includes restrictions regarding the selling prices of the licensed product or the quantities to be manufactured or sold, since they seriously limit the extent to which the licensee can exploit the licensed technology and since quantity restrictions particularly may have the same effect as export bans (Article 3(1) and (5)). This does not apply where a licence is granted for use of the technology in specific production facilities and where both a specific technology is communicated for the setting-up, operation and maintenance of these facilities and the licensee is allowed to increase the capacity of the facilities or to set up further facilities for its own use on normal commercial terms. On the other hand, the licensee may lawfully be prevented from using the transferred technology to set up facilities for third parties, since the purpose of the agreement is not to permit the licensee to give other producers access to the licensor's technology while it remains secret or protected by patent (Article 2(1)(12)).

(25) Agreements which are not automatically covered by the exemption because they contain provisions that are not expressly exempted by this Regulation and not expressly excluded from exemption, including those listed in Article 4(2), may, in certain circumstances, nonetheless be presumed to be eligible for application of the block exemption. It will be possible for the Commission rapidly to establish whether this is the case on the basis of the information undertakings are obliged to provide under Commission Regulation (EC) No 3385/94. The Commission may waive the requirement to supply specific information required in form A/B but which it does not deem necessary. The Commission will generally be content with

communication of the text of the agreement and with an estimate, based on directly available data, of the market structure and of the licensee's market share. Such agreements should therefore be deemed to be covered by the exemption provided for in this Regulation where they are notified to the Commission and the Commission does not oppose the application of the exemption within a specified period of time.

(26) Where agreements exempted under this Regulation nevertheless have effects incompatible with Article 85(3), the Commission may withdraw the block exemption, in particular where the licensed products are not faced with real competition in the licensed territory (Article 7). This could also be the case where the licensee has a strong position on the market. In assessing the competition the Commission will pay special attention to cases where the licensee has more than 40% of the whole market for the licensed products and of all the products or services which customers consider interchangeable or substitutable on account of their characteristics, prices and intended use.

(27) Agreements which come within the terms of Articles 1 and 2 and which have neither the object nor the effect of restricting competition in any other way need no longer be notified. Nevertheless, undertakings will still have the right to apply in individual cases for negative clearance or for exemption under Article 85(3) in accordance with Council Regulation No 17 as last amended by the Act of Accession of Austria, Finland and Sweden. They can in particular notify agreements obliging the licensor not to grant other licences in the territory, where the licensee's market share exceeds or is likely to exceed 40%,

HAS ADOPTED THIS REGULATION:

Article 1

1. Pursuant to Article 85(3) of the Treaty and subject to the conditions set out below, it is hereby declared that Article 85(1) of the Treaty shall not apply to pure patent licensing or know-how licensing agreements and to mixed patent and know-how licensing agreements, including those agreements containing ancillary provisions relating to intellectual property rights other than patents, to which only two undertakings are party and which include one or more of the following obligations:

(1) an obligation on the licensor not to license other undertakings to exploit the licensed technology in the licensed territory;

(2) an obligation on the licensor not to exploit the licensed technology in the licensed territory himself;

(3) an obligation on the licensee not to exploit the licensed technology in the territory of the licensor within the common market;

(4) an obligation on the licensee not to manufacture or use the licensed

product, or use the licensed process, in territories within the common market which are licensed to other licensees;

(5) an obligation on the licensee not to pursue an active policy of putting the licensed product on the market in the territories within the common market which are licensed to other licensees, and in particular not to engage in advertising specifically aimed at those territories or to establish any branch or maintain an distribution depot there;

(6) an obligation on the licensee not to put the licensed product on the market in the territories licensed to other licensees within the common market in response to unsolicited orders;

(7) an obligation on the licensee to use only the licensor's trademark or get up to distinguish the licensed product during the term of the agreement, provided that the licensee is not prevented from identifying himself as the manufacturer of the licensed products;

(8) an obligation on the licensee to limit his production of the licensed product to the quantities he requires in manufacturing his own products and to sell the licensed product only as an integral part of or a replacement part for his own products or otherwise in connection with the sale of his own products, provided that such quantities are freely determined by the licensee.

2. Where the agreement is a pure patent licensing agreement, the exemption of the obligations referred to in paragraph 1 is granted only to the extent that and for as long as the licensed product is protected by parallel patents, in the territories respectively of the licensee (points (1), (2), (7) and (8)), the licensor (point (3)) and other licensees (points (4) and (5)). The exemption of the obligation referred to in point (6) of paragraph 1 is granted for a period not exceeding five years from the date when the licensed product is first put on the market within the common market by one of the licensees, to the extent that and for as long as, in these territories, this product is protected by parallel patents.

3. Where the agreement is a pure know-how licensing agreement, the period for which the exemption of the obligations referred to in points (1) to (5) of paragraph 1 is granted may not exceed ten years from the date when the licensed product is first put on the market within the common market by one of the licensees.

The exemption of the obligation referred to in point (6) of paragraph 1 is granted for a period not exceeding five years from the date when the licensed product is first put on the market within the common market by one of the licensees.

The obligations referred to in points (7) and (8) of paragraph 1 are exempted during the lifetime of the agreement for as long as the know-how remains secret and substantial.

However, the exemption in paragraph 1 shall apply only where the parties have identified in any appropriate form the initial know-how and any subsequent improvements to it which become available to one party and are communicated to the other party pursuant to the terms of the agreement and to the purpose thereof, and only for as long as the know-how remains secret and substantial.

4. Where the agreement is a mixed patent and know-how licensing agreement, the exemption of the obligations referred to in points (1) to (5) of paragraph 1 shall apply in Member States in which the licensed technology is protected by necessary patents for as long as the licensed product is protected in those Member States by such patents if the duration of such protection exceeds the periods specified in paragraph 3.

The duration of the exemption provided in point (6) of paragraph 1 may not exceed the five-year period provided for in paragraphs 2 and 3.

However, such agreements qualify for the exemption referred to in paragraph 1 only for as long as the patents remain in force or to the extent that the know-how is identified and for as long as it remains secret and substantial whichever period is the longer.

5. The exemption provided for in paragraph 1 shall also apply where in a particular agreement the parties undertake obligations of the types referred to in that paragraph but with a more limited scope than is permitted by that paragraph.

Article 2

1. Article 1 shall apply notwithstanding the presence in particular of any of the following clauses, which are generally not restrictive of competition:

(1) an obligation on the licensee not to divulge the know-how communicated by the licensor; the licensee may be held to this obligation after the agreement has expired;

(2) an obligation on the licensee not to grant sublicences or assign the licence;

(3) an obligation on the licensee not to exploit the licensed know-how or patents after termination of the agreement in so far and as long as the know-how is still secret or the patents are still in force;

(4) an obligation on the licensee to grant to the licensor a licence in respect of his own improvements to or his new applications of the licensed technology, provided:

— that, in the case of severable improvements, such a licence is not exclusive, so that the licensee is free to use his own improvements or to license them to third parties, in so far as that does not involve disclosure of the know-how communicated by the licensor that is still secret,

— and that the licensor undertakes to grant an exclusive or non-exclusive licence of his own improvements to the licensee;

(5) an obligation on the licensee to observe minimum quality specifications, including technical specifications, for the licensed

product or to procure goods or services from the licensor or from an undertaking designated by the licensor, in so far as these quality specifications, products or services are necessary for:

(a) a technically proper exploitation of the licensed technology; or

(b) ensuring that the product of the licensee conforms to the minimum quality specifications that are applicable to the licensor and other licensees;

and to allow the licensor to carry out related checks;

(6) obligations:

(a) to inform the licensor of misappropriation of the know-how or of infringements of the licensed patents; or

(b) to take or to assist the licensor in taking legal action against such misappropriation or infringements;

(7) an obligation on the licensee to continue paying the royalties;

(a) until the end of the agreement in the amounts, for the periods and according to the methods freely determined by the parties, in the event of the know-how becoming publicly known other than by action of the licensor, without prejudice to the payment of any additional damages in the event of the know-how becoming publicly known by the action of the licensee in breach of the agreement;

(b) over a period going beyond the duration of the licensed patents, in order to facilitate payment;

(8) an obligation on the licensee to restrict his exploitation of the licensed technology to one or more technical fields of application covered by the licensed technology or to one or more product markets;

(9) an obligation on the licensee to pay a minimum royalty or to produce a minimum quantity of the licensed product or to carry out a minimum number of operations exploiting the licensed technology;

(10) an obligation on the licensor to grant the licensee any more favourable terms that the licensor may grant to another undertaking after the agreement is entered into;

(11) an obligation on the licensee to mark the licensed product with an indication of the licensor's name or of the licensed patent;

(12) an obligation on the licensee not to use the licensor's technology to construct facilities for third parties; this is without prejudice to the right of the licensee to increase the capacity of his facilities or to set up additional facilities for his own use on normal commercial terms, including the payment of additional royalties;

(13) an obligation on the licensee to supply only a limited quantity of the licensed product to a particular customer, where the licence was granted so that the customer might have a second source of supply inside the licensed territory; this provision shall also apply where the customer is the licensee, and the licence which was granted in order to provide a second source of supply provides that the

customer is himself to manufacture the licensed products or to have them manufactured by a subcontractor;

(14) a reservation by the licensor of the right to exercise the rights conferred by a patent to oppose the exploitation of the technology by the licensee outside the licensed territory;

(15) a reservation by the licensor of the right to terminate the agreement if the licensee contests the secret or substantial nature of the licensed know-how or challenges the validity of licensed patents within the common market belonging to the licensor or undertakings connected with it;

(16) a reservation by the licensor of the right to terminate the licence agreement of a patent if the licensee raises the claim that such a patent is not necessary;

(17) an obligation on the licensee to use his best endeavours to manufacture and market the licensed product;

(18) a reservation by the licensor of the right to terminate the exclusivity granted to the licensee and to stop licensing improvements to him when the licensee enters into competition within the common market with the licensor, with undertakings connected with the licensor or with other undertakings in respect of research and development, production, use or distribution of competing products, and to require the licensee to prove that the licensed know-how is not being used for the production of products and the provision of services other than those licensed.

2. In the event that, because of particular circumstances, the clauses referred to in paragraph 1 fall within the scope of Article 85(1), they shall also be exempted even if they are not accompanied by any of the obligations exempted by Article 1.

3. The exemption in paragraph 2 shall also apply where an agreement contains clauses of the types referred to in paragraph 1 but with a more limited scope than is permitted by that paragraph.

Article 3

Article 1 and Article 2(2) shall not apply where:

(1) one party is restricted in the determination of prices, components of prices or discounts for the licensed products;

(2) one party is restricted from competing within the common market with the other party, with undertakings connected with the other party or with other undertakings in respect of research and development, production, use or distribution of competing products without prejudice to the provisions of Article 2(1)(17) and (18);

(3) one or both of the parties are required without any objectively justified reason:

  (a) to refuse to meet orders from users or resellers in their respective territories who would market products in other territories within the common market;

(b) to make it difficult for users or resellers to obtain the products from other resellers within the common market, and n particular to exercise intellectual property rights or take measures so as to prevent users or resellers from obtaining outside, or from putting on the market in the licensed territory products which have been lawfully put on the market within the common market by the licensor or with his consent; or do so as a result of a concerted practice between them;

(4) the parties were already competing manufacturers before the grant of the licence and one of them is restricted, within the same technical field of use or within the same product market, as to the customers he may serve, in particular by being prohibited from supplying certain classes of user, employing certain forms of distribution or, with the aim of sharing customers, using certain types of packaging for the products, save as provided in Article 1(1)(7) and Article 2(1)(13);

(5) the quantity of the licensed products one party may manufacture or sell or the number of operations exploiting the licensed technology he may carry out are subject to limitations, save as provided in Article (1)(8) and Article 2(1)(13);

(6) the licensee is obliged to assign in whole or in part to the licensor rights to improvements to or new applications of the licensed technology;

(7) the licensor is required, albeit in separate agreements or through automatic prolongation of the initial duration of the agreement by the inclusion of any new improvements, for a period exceeding that referred to in Article 1(2) and (3) not to license other undertakings to exploit the licensed technology in the licensed territory, or a party is required for a period exceeding that referred to in Article 1(2) and (3) or Article 1(4) not to exploit the licensed technology in the territory of the other party or of other licensees.

Article 4

1. The exemption provided for in Articles 1 and 2 shall also apply to agreements containing obligations restrictive of competition which are not covered by those Articles and do not fall within the scope of Article 3, on condition that the agreements in question are notified to the Commission in accordance with the provisions of Articles 1, 2 and 3 of Regulation (EC) No 3385/94 and that the Commission does not oppose such exemption within a period of four months.

2. Paragraph 1 shall apply, in particular, where:

a. the licensee is obliged at the time the agreement is entered into to accept quality specifications or further licences or to procure goods or services which are not necessary for a technically satisfactory exploitation of the licensed technology or for ensuring that the production of the licensee conforms to the quality standards that are respected by the licensor and other licensees;

    b. the licensee is prohibited from contesting the secrecy or the substantiality of the licensed know-how or from challenging the validity of patents licensed within the common market belonging to the licensor or undertakings connected with him.

3. The period of four months referred to in paragraph 1 shall run from the date on which the notification takes effect in accordance with Article 4 of Regulation (EC) No 3385/94.

4. The benefit of paragraphs 1 and 2 may be claimed for agreements notified before the entry into force of this Regulation by submitting a communication to the Commission referring expressly to this Article and to the notification. Paragraph 3 shall apply *mutatis mutandis*.

5. The Commission may oppose the exemption within a period of four months. It shall oppose exemption if it receives a request to do so from a Member State within two months of the transmission to the Member State of the notification referred to in paragraph 1 or of the communication referred to in paragraph 4. This request must be justified on the basis of considerations relating to the competition rules of the Treaty.

6. The Commission may withdraw the opposition to the exemption at any time. However, where the opposition was raised at the request of a Member State and this request is maintained, it may be withdrawn only after consultation of the Advisory Committee on Restrictive Practices and Dominant Positions.

7. If the opposition is withdrawn because the undertakings concerned have shown that the conditions of Article 85(3) are satisfied, the exemption shall apply from the date of notification.

8. If the opposition is withdrawn because the undertakings concerned have amended the agreement so that the conditions of Article 85(3) are satisfied, the exemption shall apply from the date on which the amendments take effect.

9. If the Commission opposes exemption and the opposition is not withdrawn, the effects of the notification shall be governed by the provisions of Regulation No 17.

Article 5

1. This Regulation shall not apply to:

    (1) agreements between members of a patent or know-how pool which relate to the pooled technologies;

    (2) licensing agreements between competing undertakings which hold interests in a joint venture, or between one of them and the joint venture, if the licensing agreements relate to the activities of the joint venture;

(3) agreements under which one party grants the other a patent and/or know-how licence and in exchange the other party, albeit in separate agreements or through connected undertakings, grants the first party a patent, trademark or know-how licence or exclusive sales rights, where the parties are competitors in relation to the products covered by those agreements;

(4) licensing agreements containing provisions relating to intellectual property rights other than patents which are not ancillary;

(5) agreements entered into solely for the purpose of sale.

2. This Regulation shall nevertheless apply:

(1) to agreements to which paragraph 1(2) applies, under which a parent undertaking grants the joint venture a patent or know-how licence, provided that the licensed products and the other goods and services of the participating undertakings which are considered by users to be interchangeable or substitutable in view of their characteristics, price and intended use represent:

— in case of a licence limited to production, not more than 20%, and

— in case of a licence covering production and distribution, not more than 10%;

of the market for the licensed products and all interchangeable or substitutable goods and services;

(2) to agreements to which paragraph 1(1) applies and to reciprocal licences within the meaning of paragraph 1(3), provided the parties are not subject to any territorial restriction within the common market with regard to the manufacture, use or putting on the market of the licensed products or to the use of the licensed or pooled technologies.

3. This Regulation shall continue to apply where, for two consecutive financial years, the market shares in paragraph 2(1) are not exceeded by more than one-tenth; where that limit is exceeded, this Regulation shall continue to apply for a period of six months from the end of the year in which the limit was exceeded.

Article 6

This Regulation shall also apply to:

(1) agreements where the licensor is not the holder of the know-how or the patentee, but is authorized by the holder or the patentee to grant a licence;

(2) assignments of know-how, patents or both where the risk associated with exploitation remains with the assignor, in particular where the sum payable in consideration of the assignment is dependent on the turnover obtained by the assignee in respect of products made using the know-how or the patents, the quantity of such products manufactured or the number of operations carried out employing the

know-how or the patents;

(3) licensing agreements in which the rights or obligations of the licensor or the licensee are assumed by undertakings connected with them.

Article 7

The Commission may withdraw the benefit of this Regulation, pursuant to Article 7 of Regulation No 19/65/EEC, where it finds in a particular case that an agreement exempted by this Regulation nevertheless has certain effects which are incompatible with the conditions laid down in Article 85(3) of the Treaty, and in particular where:

(1) the effect of the agreement is to prevent the licensed products from being exposed to effective competition in the licensed territory from identical goods or services or from goods or services considered by users as interchangeable or substitutable in view of their characteristics, price and intended use, which may in particular occur where the licensee's market share exceeds 40%;

(2) without prejudice to Article 1(1)(6), the licensee refuses, without any objectively justified reason, to meet unsolicited orders from users or resellers in the territory of other licensees;

(3) the parties:

  (a) without any objectively justified reason, refuse to meet orders from users or resellers in their respective territories who would market the products in other territories within the common market; or

  (b) make it difficult for users or resellers to obtain the products from other resellers within the common market, and in particular where they exercise intellectual property rights or take measures so as to prevent resellers or users from obtaining outside, or from putting on the market in the licensed territory products which have been lawfully put on the market within the common market by the licensee or with his consent;

(4) the parties were competing manufacturers at the date of the grant of the licence and obligations on the licensee to produce a minimum quantity or to use his best endeavours as referred to in Article 2(1), (9) and (17) respectively have the effect of preventing the licensee from using competing technologies.

Article 8

1. For purposes of this Regulation:

  (a) patent applications;

  (b) utility models;

  (c) applications for registration of utility models;

  (d) topographies of semiconductor products;

  (e) certificats d'utilite and certificats d'addition under French law;

   (f) applications for certificats d'utilite and certificats d'addition under French law;

   (g) supplementary protection certificates for medicinal products or other products for which such supplementary protection certificates may be obtained;

   (h) plant breeder's certificates, shall be deemed to be patents.

2. This Regulation shall also apply to agreements relating to the exploitation of an invention if an application within the meaning of paragraph 1 is made in respect of the invention for a licensed territory after the date when the agreements were entered into but within the time-limits set by the national law or the international convention to be applied.

3. This Regulation shall furthermore apply to pure patent or know-how licensing agreements or to mixed agreements whose initial duration is automatically prolonged by the inclusion of any new improvements, whether patented or not, communicated by the licensor, provided that the licensee has the right to refuse such improvements or each party has the right to terminate the agreement at the expiry of the initial term of an agreement and at least every three years thereafter.

Article 9

1. Information acquired pursuant to Article 4 shall be used only for the purposes of this Regulation.

2. The Commission and the authorities of the Member States, their officials and other servants shall not disclose information acquired by them pursuant to this Regulation of the kind covered by the obligation of professional secrecy.

3. The provisions of paragraphs 1 and 2 shall not prevent publication of general information or surveys which do not contain information relating to particular undertakings or associations of undertakings.

Article 10

For purposes of this Regulation:

   (1) 'know-how' means a body of technical information that is secret, substantial and identified in any appropriate form;

   (2) 'secret' means that the know-how package as a body or in the precise configuration and assembly of its components is not generally known or easily accessible, so that part of its value consists in the lead which the licensee gains when it is communicated to him; it is not limited to the narrow sense that each individual component of the know-how should be totally unknown or unobtainable outside the licensor's business;

   (3) 'substantial' means that the know-how includes information which must be useful, i.e. can reasonably be expected at the date of conclusion of the agreement to be capable of improving the

competitive position of the licensee, for example by helping him to enter a new market or giving him an advantage in competition with other manufacturers or providers of services who do not have access to the licensed secret know-how or other comparable secret know-how;

(4) 'identified' means that the know-how is described or recorded in such a manner as to make it possible to verify that it satisfies the criteria of secrecy and substantiality and to ensure that the licensee is not unduly restricted in his exploitation of how own technology, to be identified the know-how can either be set out in the licence agreement or in a separate document or recorded in any other appropriate form at the latest when the know-how is transferred or shortly thereafter, provided that the separate document or other record can be made available if the need arises;

(5) 'necessary patents' are patents where a licence under the patent is necessary for the putting into effect of the licensed technology in so far as, in the absence of such a licence, the realization of the licensed technology would not be possible or would be possible only to a lesser extent or in more difficult or costly conditions. Such patents must therefore be of technical, legal or economic interest to the licensee;

(6) 'licensing agreement' means pure patent licensing agreements and pure know-how licensing agreements as well as mixed patent and know-how licensing agreements;

(7) 'licensed technology' means the initial manufacturing know-how or the necessary product and process patents, or both, existing at the time the first licensing agreement is concluded, and improvements subsequently made to the know-how or patents, irrespective of whether and to what extent they are exploited by the parties or by other licensees;

(8) 'the licensed products' are goods or services the production or provision of which requires the use of the licensed technology;

(9) 'the licensee's market share' means the proportion which the licensed products and other goods or services provided by the licensee, which are considered by users to be interchangeable or substitutable for the licensed products in view of their characteristics, price and intended use, represent the entire market for the licensed products and all other interchangeable or substitutable goods and services in the common market or a substantial part of it;

(10) 'exploitation' refers to any use of the licensed technology in particular in the production, active or passive sales in a territory even if not coupled with manufacture in that territory, or leasing of the licensed products;

(11) 'the licensed territory' is the territory covering all or at least part of the common market where the licensee is entitled to exploit the licensed technology;

(12) 'territory of the licensor' means territories in which the licensor has

not granted any licences for patents and/or know-how covered by the licensing agreement;

(13) 'parallel patents' means patents which, in spite of the divergences which remain in the absence of any unification of national rules concerning industrial property, protect the same invention in various Member States;

(14) 'connected undertakings' means:

  (a) undertakings in which a party to the agreement, directly or indirectly:

   — owns more than half the capital or business assets, or

   — has the power to exercise more than half the voting rights, or

   — has the power to appoint more than half the members of the supervisory board, board of directors or bodies legally representing the undertaking, or

   — has the right to manage the affairs of the undertaking;

  (b) undertakings which, directly or indirectly, have in or over a party to the agreement the rights or powers listed in (a);

  (c) undertakings in which an undertaking referred to in (b), directly or indirectly, has the rights of powers listed in (a);

  (d) undertakings in which the parties to the agreement or undertakings connected with them jointly have the rights or powers listed in (a): such jointly controlled undertakings are considered to be connected with each of the parties to the agreement;

(15) 'ancillary provisions' are provisions relating to the exploitation of intellectual property rights other than patents, which contain no obligations restrictive of competition other than those also attached to the licensed know-how or patents and exempted under this Regulation;

(16) 'obligation' means both contractual obligation and a concerted practice;

(17) 'competing manufacturers' or manufacturers of 'competing products' means manufacturers who sell products which, in view of their characteristics, price and intended use, are considered by users to be interchangeable or substitutable for the licensed products.

Article 11

1. Regulation (EEC) No 556/89 is hereby repealed with effect from 1 April 1996.

2. Regulation (EEC) No 2349/84 shall continue to apply until 31 March 1996.

3. The prohibition in Article 85(1) of the Treaty shall not apply to agreements in force on 31 March 1996 which fulfil the exemption requirements laid down by Regulation (EEC) No 2349/84 and (EEC) No

556/89.

Article 12

1. The Commission shall undertake regular assessments of the application of this Regulation, and in particular of the opposition procedure provided for in Article 4.

2. The Commission shall draw up a report on the operation of this Regulation before the end of the fourth year following its entry into force and shall, on that basis, assess whether any adaptation of the Regulation is desirable.

Article 13

This Regulation shall enter into force on 1 April 1996. It shall apply until 31 March 2006.

Article 11(2) of this Regulation shall, however, enter into force on 1 January 1996.

This Regulation shall be binding in its entirety and directly applicable in all Member States.

Done at Brussels, 31 January 1996.

EURASIAN PATENT CONVENTION
done at Moscow, Sept. 9, 1994

The states party to this Convention History (hereinafter referred to as "the Contracting States") represented by Governments,

Desiring to strengthen cooperation in the field of the protection of inventions,

Striving to establish an interstate system for obtaining such protection on the basis of a common patent having legal effect on the territory of all the Contracting States,

Desiring to conclude, for this purpose, a Convention which constitutes a special agreement within the meaning of Article 19 of the Paris Convention for the Protection of Industrial Property of March 20, 1883, and a regional patent agreement within the meaning of Article 45(1) of the Patent Cooperation Treaty of June 19, 1970,

Have agreed as follows:

Part I
The Eurasian Patent System

Article 1
Establishment of the Eurasian Patent System

(1) The Contracting States, maintaining their complete sovereignty to develop their national systems for protection of inventions, hereby establish a Eurasian Patent System.

(2) No provision of this Convention shall be interpreted as diminishing the rights under the Paris Convention for the Protection of Industrial Property of any national or resident of any country party to the Paris Convention.

Part II
The Eurasian Patent Organization

Article 2
Establishment of the Eurasian Patent Organization

(1) The Eurasian Patent Organization (hereinafter referred to as "the Organization") is established in order to administer the functioning of the Eurasian Patent System and the grant of Eurasian patents.

(2) All Contracting States shall be members of the Organization.

(3) The organs of the Organization are the Administrative Council and the Eurasian Patent Office(hereinafter referred to as "the Eurasian Office").

(4) The Eurasian Office is headed by the President who is the chief executive of the Organization and represents the Organization.

(5) The Organization is an intergovernmental organization having the status of legal entity. The Organization shall, in each Contracting State, enjoy the legal capacity attributed to legal entities in conformity with the national law of that State. The Organization may acquire or dispose of movable property or real estate and may defend its rights in court. The headquarters of the Organization shall be at Moscow, Russian Federation.

(6) The official language of the Organization shall be Russian.

(7) The Organization, the plenipotentiary representatives of the Contracting States and their deputies, the staff of the Eurasian Office and other persons engaged in carrying out the tasks of the Organization shall enjoy on the territory of every Contracting States the rights, the privileges and immunities granted by such Contracting States to any other international organization and its staff, and on the territory of the Russian Federation also regulated by the special headquarters agreement of the Organization concluded between the Organization and the Government of the Russian Federation.

Article 3
Administrative Council

(1) Each Contracting State shall be represented in the Administrative Council. Each Contracting State shall have one vote in the Administrative Council. Two-thirds of the Contracting States shall constitute a quorum. Decisions shall be made by consensus or, failing that, by a simple majority of the voting plenipotentiary representatives of the Contracting States, with the exception of those cases where this Convention requires unanimity or a majority of two-thirds of the votes cast.

(2) The Administrative Council shall meet in ordinary sessions in each calendar year and in extraordinary session on the initiative of at least three Contracting States, the Chairman of the Administrative Council or the President of the Eurasian Office. The sessions shall be convened by the President of the Eurasian Office.

(3) The Administrative Council shall

(i) adopt its own Rules of Procedure;

(ii) elect the Chairman of the Administrative Council for a renewable term of two years;

(iii) appoint the President of the Eurasian Office for a renewable term of six years; the conditions of appointment shall be fixed in a contract between the Organization and the future President;

(iv) give advice to the President of the Eurasian Office in respect of the appointment, by the President, of Vice Presidents of the Eurasian Office;

(v) approve the headquarters agreement of the Organization concluded by the Organization with the Government of the Russian Federation;

(vi) approve agreements concluded by the Organization with States and international organizations;

(vii) adopt by a majority of two thirds the Patent Regulations, the Financial Regulations, and the Administrative Regulations;

(viii) establish by a majority of two-thirds the yearly budget, examine the yearly report and approve the yearly accounts of the Organization;

(ix) take any other action aimed at performing the tasks of the Organization.

(4) The World Intellectual Property Organization (hereinafter referred to as "WIPO") shall be represented at the meetings of the Administrative Council in an advisory capacity in conformity with the provisions of an agreement concluded between the Organization and WIPO.

Article 4
Eurasian Office

(1) The Eurasian Office shall carry out all administrative tasks of the Organization. It shall be the secretariat of the Organization.

(2) The President of the Eurasian Office shall determine its structure and shall appoint the staff. He may participate in all meetings of the Administrative Council.

(3) Each Contracting State shall have its quota in respect of the staff of the Eurasian Office, which shall be determined in the Administrative Regulations.

(4) The Eurasian Office shall be located at Moscow, Russian Federation.

Article 5
Finances

(1) The Organization shall be self-supporting in that its expenses shall be covered from fees and other income earned by it. No Contracting State shall be obliged to pay contributions to the Organization.

(2) The budget of the Organization shall be financed from the following sources:

(i) the proceeds from fees and charges for services rendered by the Eurasian Office;

(ii) the proceeds from the publishing activities of the Eurasian Office;

(iii) gifts, bequests and subventions given to the Organization;

(iv) rents, interests and other miscellaneous income of the Organization.

(3) Any excess of income of the Organization over its expenditure shall be used for the development of the Eurasian Office.

(4) In the headquarters agreement of the Organization referred to in Article 3(3)(v), it shall be provided that, whenever the financial means of the Organization are insufficient for its activities, the Russian Federation shall grant advances to the Organization. The amount of those advances and the conditions on which they are granted shall be the subject of separate agreements, in each case, between the Organization and the Government of

the Russian Federation.

Part III
Substantive Patent Law

Article 6
Patentable Inventions

The Eurasian Office shall grant a Eurasian patent for any invention that is new, involves an inventive step and is industrially applicable.

Article 7
Persons Entitled to a Eurasian Patent

(1) The right to a Eurasian patent shall belong to the inventor or his successor in title. Where the inventor is an employee, the right to a Eurasian patent shall be determined in accordance with the law of the State in which the employee is mainly employed; if the State in which the employee is mainly employed cannot be determined, the law to be applied shall be that of the State in which the employer has a place of business to which the employee is attached.

(2) For the purposes of proceedings before the Eurasian Office, the applicant shall be deemed to be entitled to the Eurasian patent.

Article 8
Right of Priority

The right of priority shall be recognized in conformity with the Paris Convention for the Protection of Industrial Property.

Article 9
Patent Rights

(1) The owner of a Eurasian patent shall have the exclusive right to use, and also to authorize the use or prohibit others from using, the patented invention.

(2) The owner of a Eurasian patent may assign or license his rights.

(3) After an application for the grant of a Eurasian patent (hereinafter referred to as "the Eurasian application") has been published, the applicant shall enjoy provisional protection in conformity with the national legislation of the Contracting States.

Article 10
Extent of Legal Protection

The extent of the legal protection conferred by a Eurasian patent shall be determined by the claims. The description and drawings shall serve only to interpret the claims.

Article 11
Term of Eurasian Patent

The term of a Eurasian patent shall be 20 years from the filing date of the Eurasian application.

Article 12
Compulsory Licenses

(1) Compulsory licenses for the use of a Eurasian patent by third parties may be granted in conformity with the Paris Convention for the Protection of Industrial Property by the competent authority of a Contracting State with effect in the territory of that State.

(2) A decision to grant a compulsory license may be contested in the courts or other competent authorities of the contracting State in the territory of which the compulsory license has been granted.

Article 13
Validity of Eurasian Patent and Enforcement of Rights

(1) Any dispute arising from the validity, in a given Contracting State, or the infringement, in a given Contracting State, of a Eurasian patent shall be resolved by the national courts or other competent authorities of that State on the basis of this Convention and the Patent Regulations. The decision shall have effect only in the territory of the Contracting State.

(2) Each Contracting State shall, in the case of infringement of a Eurasian patent, provide for the same civil or other liability as in the case of a national patent.

(3) Any national court or other competent authority of a Contracting State may require that the plaintiff furnish to it a translation of the Eurasian patent in the state language of the Contracting State.

Article 14
Patent Regulations. Substantive Provisions

The Patent regulations shall provide for the details concerning substantive patent law, and in particular the following:

(i) the definition of the criteria of patentability of an invention, including the definition of novelty, inventive step and industrial applicability, and the requirement of the disclosure of the invention,

(ii) disclosures that do not affect the patentability of the invention,

(iii) the requirement of unity of invention,

(iv) the definition and effects of the right of priority,

(v) the definition of the exclusive right in the patented invention,

(vi) the right of the prior user,

(vii) the interpretation of the claims,

(viii) the right of the inventor to be mentioned in the Eurasian application and Eurasian patent,

(ix) the assignment and other transfer of the right to a Eurasian application or patent,

(x) the confidentiality in processing Eurasian applications.

Part IV
Procedural Patent Law

Article 15
Eurasian Application and Grant of the Eurasian Patent

(1) The Eurasian application may be filed:

(i) with the Eurasian Office subject to subparagraph(ii) of this Article;

(ii) in the case of an applicant from a Contracting State, the Eurasian application shall be filed through the national Patent Office of that State(hereinafter referred to as ("the National Office") where provided in the legislation of the Contracting State. The Eurasian application filed through a national Office shall have the same effect as if it had been filed with the Eurasian Office on the same date, provided that it is transmitted to the Eurasian Office within the time limit prescribed in the Patent Regulations. The national Office shall verify the compliance of the application with the requirements prescribed by this Convention and the Patent Regulations with regard to the examination as to form of the Eurasian application and, where the examination finding is that the application complies with the said requirements, it shall transmit the application to the Eurasian Office for further processing.

(2) Where the Eurasian application is filed with the Eurasian Office, a unitary procedural fee for filing, search, publication and other processing shall be payable to that Office at the time of filing. Where the Eurasian application is filed through a national Office, a fee shall be payable to the national Office at the time of the filing for examination as to form and transmittal of the application, whereas the unitary procedural fee shall be payable to the Eurasian Office at the time of the transmittal of the Eurasian application to that Office.

(3) The Eurasian Office shall verify the compliance of the Eurasian application with the requirements prescribed by this Convention and the Patent Regulations with regard to the examination as to form and shall carry out a search in relation to the said application. The search shall result in a search report which shall be forwarded to the applicant.

(4) The Eurasian Office shall publish the Eurasian application together with the search report promptly after the expiry of 18 months from the filing date or, where priority is claimed, from the priority date. At the request of the applicant, the Eurasian Office shall publish the Eurasian application earlier. In that case, the search report will be published separately as soon as it is available.

(5) At the request of the applicant, to be filed with the Eurasian Office

before the expiry of six months from the date of publication of the search report, the Eurasian Office shall carry out the substantive examination of the Eurasian application.

(6) The filing of the request referred to in paragraph(5) of this Article shall be subject to the payment of an examination fee to the Eurasian Office.

(7) The decision to grant a Eurasian patent or reject the Eurasian application shall be made, on behalf of the Eurasian Office, by collegia composed of three examiners each, who shall be staff members of the Eurasian Office and, unless otherwise decided by the unanimous decision of the Administrative Council, nationals of different Contracting States.

(8) Where the applicant disagrees with the decision of the Eurasian Office to refuse the grant of a Eurasian patent, he may, within three months following the date of receipt of the notice of refusal, lodge an appeal with the Office which shall be examined by a collegium of the Eurasian Office to be composed in conformity with paragraph(7) of this Article. The collegium shall include at least two examiners who did not participate in the taking of the decision on the subject matter of the said appeal.

(9) The lodging of the appeal referred to in paragraph(8) of this Article shall be subject to the payment of a fee to the Eurasian Office.

(10) The grant of a Eurasian patent shall be subject to the payment of a fee to the Eurasian Office within three months after the date on which the applicant receives notice from the Eurasian Office that it is ready to grant the Eurasian patent.

(11) Subject to the provisions of Article 17, a Eurasian patent shall have effect on the territory of all Contracting States from the date of its publication.

(12) Any person who has the right to be a representative before the national Office of a Contracting State and who is registered with the Eurasian Office as a patent agent may act as representative before the Eurasian Office. Where the applicant does not have his residence or principal place of business in the territory of any Contracting State, he shall be required to be represented by such a patent agent. Persons having their residence or principal place of business in the territory of any Contracting State may file Eurasian applications and act in all proceedings before the Eurasian Office, either personally or through patent agents or through representatives who are not patent agents.

Article 16
Conversion of Eurasian Applications Into National Patent Applications

(1) Before the expiry of six months from the date on which the applicant receives notice of the Eurasian Office's refusal to grant a Eurasian patent or of its refusal to allow an appeal lodged in accordance with Article 15(8), the applicant may file a request with the Eurasian Office designating those Contracting States in which he wishes to obtain national patents according

to the national procedure.

(2) The Eurasian application in respect of which such a decision has been taken and which is the subject of such request shall be treated in any Contracting State so designated as a regular national application filed with the national Office and having the filing date and the priority date, if any, of the Eurasian application, with all the consequences provided in the national legislation, and it shall be further processed by the national Office, provided that the applicant pays the prescribed national fees to the said national Office.

Article 17
Maintenance of Eurasian Patents

(1) The maintenance of the Eurasian patent shall be subject to the annual payment of fees.

(2) The maintenance fees shall be payable in each of the years following the grant of the Eurasian patent by the date corresponding to the filing date of the Eurasian application.

(3) The continuing effect of a Eurasian patent in each Contracting State shall require that the owner of the patent designate to that end, by name, each Contracting State in which the owner wishes the effect to continue. Such designation shall be addressed to the Eurasian Office and shall be made at the same time as the maintenance fee is paid. Such fee shall be payable in respect of each designated Contracting State.

Article 18
Fees

(1) Fees concerning any Eurasian application or patent, and all charges for services rendered by the Eurasian Office, shall be payable to the Eurasian Office and, subject to the provisions of paragraph(2) of this Article, shall belong to the Organization. The fee referred to in Article 15(2) for the examination as to form and transmittal of the Eurasian application is payable to and belongs to the national Office with which the Eurasian application was filed.

(2) All fees for maintenance of a Eurasian patent shall be payable to the Eurasian Office. The ratio of distribution of the maintenance fees between the Organization and the designated Contracting States shall be fixed by the Administrative Council by a majority of two-thirds of the votes cast, provided that at least one-fifth of the fee received for each designation of a Contracting State shall belong to the Organization; the remaining part of the fee shall be transferred to the national Office of the designated Contracting State.

(3) The amount of the fee for maintenance of a Eurasian patent with respect to each Contracting State shall be fixed by that State. The currency in which the fee for maintenance of a Eurasian patent is to be paid shall be determined by the Administrative Council.

Article 19
Patent Regulations. Procedural Provisions

The Patent Regulations shall provide for details concerning Eurasian patent procedure, and in particular the following:

(i) requirements as to the form and contents of the Eurasian application;

(ii) requirements as to patent agents, procedures for their certification and registration as a patent agent;

(iii) the filing date;

(iv) calculation of time limits;

(v) claiming of priority;

(vi) the currencies and the procedures for the payment of fees;

(vii) amendment or correction of the Eurasian application;

(viii) patent search and examination;

(ix) the documentation and information services rendered by the Eurasian Office;

(x) the publication of Eurasian applications and patents;

(xi) the Register of Eurasian patents;

(xii) the Gazette of the Eurasian Office;

(xiii) the conditions and procedures for the administrative revocation of Eurasian patents;

(xiv) the conversion of Eurasian applications into national patent applications;

(xv) the application of the relevant provisions where there are several inventors, applicants, patent owners or representatives;

(xvi) the contacts of the Eurasian Office with applicants, patent owners, patent agents and other third parties and the procedure for consultation of the files of the Eurasian Office by the said persons.

Part V
Application of the Patent Cooperation Treaty(PCT)

Article 20
Application of the Patent Cooperation Treaty

The Patent Cooperation Treaty and its Regulations shall be applied in the Eurasian Patent System and, in the case of conflict between them and this Convention and its Regulations, the former shall prevail. The Eurasian Office shall be a receiving Office, and also a designated and an elected Office, under the Patent Cooperation Treaty and may, with the authorization of the Administrative Council, apply for the status of International searching and Preliminary Examining Authority under the Treaty.

Part VI
Transitional Provisions

Article 21
Search. Collegia

(1) The Eurasian Office may, with the authorization of the Administrative Council, conclude with a national or regional patent office an agreement for carrying out, as long as may be deemed necessary, searches in relation to Eurasian applications by that national or regional patent office, provided that the national or regional patent office is capable of carrying out searches of the same type as those carried out under the Patent Cooperation Treaty in all or selected fields of technology.

(2) As long as may be deemed necessary, the collegia of three examiners referred to in Article 15(7) may also consist of examiners recommended by the national Offices of the Contracting States.

Part VII
Miscellaneous Provisions

Article 22
Independence of National Patent Systems

(1) This Convention shall not prejudice the right of any Contracting State to grant national patents.

(2) This Convention shall not prevent any Contracting State from participating, on its own, in any international organization or from developing various forms of international cooperation in the field of protection of industrial property.

Article 23
Revision of the Convention

(1) This Convention may be revised at any time by the Contracting States.

(2) The Administrative Council shall decide on the convocation of conferences of the Contracting States for the purpose of revising the Convention. It shall also decide on the rules of procedure and other details of revision conferences.

Article 24
Settlement of Disputes

Where any dispute arises concerning the interpretation or implementation of this Convention, the Director General of WIPO shall, at the request of any of the parties to the dispute, mediate in order to lead the parties to a settlement of the dispute.

Part VIII
Information Services

Article 25
Dissemination of Patent Information

(1) Each Contracting State shall receive, free of charge, the Gazette of the Eurasian Office and the descriptions of Eurasian applications and patents.

(2) Subject to paragraph(1) of this Article, no publication of the Eurasian Office may be disseminated free of charge without the authorization of the Administrative Council.

Part IX
Final Clauses

Article 26
Signature. Entry Into Force of the Convention

(1) This Convention shall be signed in the Russian language.

(2) Any State may become party to this Convention that is a member of the United Nations and bound by the Paris Convention for the Protection of Industrial Property and the Patent Cooperation Treaty. To become party to this Convention, a State shall either sign this Convention and deposit an instrument of ratification, or deposit an instrument of accession.

(3) No reservations to this Convention are permitted.

(4) This Convention shall enter into force, in respect of the first three States to ratify it or accede to it, three months after the third instrument of ratification or accession has been deposited with the Director General of WIPO. In respect of any other State, this Convention shall enter into force three months after such State has deposited its instrument of ratification or accession.

Article 27
Denunciation of the Convention

Any Contracting State may denounce this Convention by notification addressed to the Director General of WIPO. Denunciation shall take effect six months after the day on which the Director General received the notification.

Article 28
Depositary

The Director General of WIPO shall be the depositary of this Convention.

CONVENTION ON BIOLOGICAL DIVERSITY
Concluded at Rio de Janeiro, 6 June 1992
[selected provisions]

Preamble.

The Contracting Parties,

Conscious of the intrinsic value of biological diversity and of the ecological, genetic, social, economic, scientific, educational, cultural, recreational and aesthetic values of biological diversity and its components,

Conscious also of the importance of biological diversity for evolution and for maintaining life sustaining systems of the biosphere,

Affirming that the conservation of biological diversity is a common concern of humankind,

Reaffirming that States have sovereign rights over their own biological resources,

Reaffirming also that States are responsible for conserving their biological diversity and for using their biological resources in a sustainable manner,

Concerned that biological diversity is being significantly reduced by certain human activities,

Aware of the general lack of information and knowledge regarding biological diversity and of the urgent need to develop scientific, technical and institutional capacities to provide the basic understanding upon which to plan and implement appropriate measures,

Noting that it is vital to anticipate, prevent and attack the causes of significant reduction or loss of biological diversity at source,

Noting also that where there is a threat of significant reduction or loss of biological diversity, lack of full scientific certainty should not be used as a reason for postponing measures to avoid or minimize such a threat,

Noting further that the fundamental requirement for the conservation of biological diversity is the in-situ conservation of ecosystems and natural habitats and the maintenance and recovery of viable populations of species in their natural surroundings,

Noting further that ex-situ measures, preferably in the country of origin, also have an important role to play,

Recognizing the close and traditional dependence of many indigenous and local communities embodying traditional lifestyles on biological resources, and the desirability of sharing equitably benefits arising from the use of traditional knowledge, innovations and practices relevant to the conservation of biological diversity and the sustainable use of its components,

Recognizing also the vital role that women play in the conservation and sustainable use of biological diversity and affirming the need for the full participation of women at all levels of policy-making and implementation for biological diversity conservation,

Stressing the importance of, and the need to promote, international, regional and global cooperation among States and intergovernmental organizations and the non-governmental sector for the conservation of biological diversity and the sustainable use of its components,

Acknowledging that the provision of new and additional financial resources and appropriate access to relevant technologies can be expected to make a substantial difference in the world's ability to address the loss of biological diversity,

Acknowledging further that special provision is required to meet the needs of developing countries, including the provision of new and additional financial resources and appropriate access to relevant technologies,

Noting in this regard the special conditions of the least developed countries and small island States,

Acknowledging that substantial investments are required to conserve biological diversity and that there is the expectation of a broad range of environmental, economic and social benefits from those investments,

Recognizing that economic and social development and poverty eradication are the first and overriding priorities of developing countries,

Aware that conservation and sustainable use of biological diversity is of critical importance for meeting the food, health and other needs of the growing world population, for which purpose access to and sharing of both genetic resources and technologies are essential,

Noting that, ultimately, the conservation and sustainable use of biological diversity will strengthen friendly relations among States and contribute to peace for humankind,

Desiring to enhance and complement existing international arrangements for the conservation of biological diversity and sustainable use of its components, and

Determined to conserve and sustainably use biological diversity for the benefit of present and future generations,

Have agreed as follows:

Article 1. Objectives

The objectives of this Convention, to be pursued in accordance with its relevant provisions, are the conservation of biological diversity, the sustainable use of its components and the fair and equitable sharing of the benefits arising out of the utilization of genetic resources, including by appropriate access to genetic resources and by appropriate transfer of relevant technologies, taking into account all rights over those resources and to technologies, and by appropriate funding.

Article 2. Use of Terms

For the purposes of this Convention:

"Biological diversity" means the variability among living organisms from all sources including, inter alia, terrestrial, marine and other aquatic ecosystems and the ecological complexes of which they are part; this includes diversity within species, between species and of ecosystems.

"Biological resources" includes genetic resources, organisms or parts thereof, populations, or any other biotic component of ecosystems with actual or potential use or value for humanity.

"Biotechnology" means any technological application that uses biological systems, living organisms, or derivatives thereof, to make or modify products or processes for specific use.

"Country of origin of genetic resources" means the country which possesses those genetic resources in in-situ conditions.

"Country providing genetic resources" means the country supplying genetic resources collected from in-situ sources, including populations of both wild and domesticated species, or taken from ex-situ sources, which may or may not have originated in that country.

"Domesticated or cultivated species" means species in which the evolutionary process has been influenced by humans to meet their needs.

"Ecosystem" means a dynamic complex of plant, animal and micro-organism communities and their non-living environment interacting as a functional unit.

"Ex-situ conservation" means the conservation of components of biological diversity outside their natural habitats.

"Genetic material" means any material of plant, animal, microbial or other origin containing functional units of heredity.

"Genetic resources" means genetic material of actual or potential value.

"Habitat" means the place or type of site where an organism or population naturally occurs.

"In-situ conditions" means conditions where genetic resources exist within ecosystems and natural habitats, and, in the case of domesticated or cultivated species, in the surroundings where they have developed their distinctive properties. "In-situ conservation" means the conservation of ecosystems and natural habitats and the maintenance and recovery of viable populations of species in their natural surroundings and, in the case of domesticated or cultivated species, in the surroundings where they have developed their distinctive properties.

"Protected area" means a geographically defined area which is designated or regulated and managed to achieve specific conservation objectives.

"Regional economic integration organization" means an organization constituted by sovereign States of a given region, to which its member States have transferred competence in respect of matters governed by this Convention and which has been duly authorized, in accordance with its internal procedures, to sign, ratify, accept, approve or accede to it.

"Sustainable use" means the use of components of biological diversity in a way and at a rate that does not lead to the long-term decline of biological diversity, thereby maintaining its potential to meet the needs and aspirations of present and future generations.

"Technology" includes biotechnology.

Article 3. Principle

States have, in accordance with the Charter of the United Nations and the principles of international law, the sovereign right to exploit their own resources pursuant to their own environmental policies, and the responsibility to ensure that activities within their jurisdiction or control do not cause damage to the environment of other States or of areas beyond the limits of national jurisdiction.

Article 4. Jurisdictional Scope

Subject to the rights of other States, and except as otherwise expressly provided in this Convention, the provisions of this Convention apply, in relation to each Contracting Party:

(a) In the case of components of biological diversity, in areas within the limits of its national jurisdiction; and

(b) In the case of processes and activities, regardless of where their effects occur, carried out under its jurisdiction or control, within the area of its national jurisdiction or beyond the limits of national jurisdiction.

Article 5. Cooperation

Each Contracting Party shall, as far as possible and as appropriate, cooperate with other Contracting Parties, directly or, where appropriate, through competent international organizations, in respect of areas beyond national jurisdiction and on other matters of mutual interest, for the conservation and sustainable use of biological diversity.

. . .

Article 7. Identification and Monitoring

Each Contracting Party shall, as far as possible and as appropriate, in particular for the purposes of Articles 8 to 10:

(a) Identify components of biological diversity important for its conservation and sustainable use having regard to the indicative list of categories set down in Annex I;

(b) Monitor, through sampling and other techniques, the components of biological diversity identified pursuant to subparagraph (a) above, paying particular attention to those requiring urgent conservation measures and those which offer the greatest potential for sustainable use;

(c) Identify processes and categories of activities which have or are likely to have significant adverse impacts on the conservation and sustainable use of biological diversity, and monitor their effects through sampling and other techniques; and

(d) Maintain and organize, by any mechanism data, derived from identification and monitoring activities pursuant to subparagraphs (a), (b) and (c)) above.

Article 8. In-situ Conservation

Each Contracting Party shall, as far as possible and as appropriate:

(a) Establish a system of protected areas or areas where special measures need to be taken to conserve biological diversity;

(b) Develop, where necessary, guidelines for the selection, establishment and management of protected areas or areas where special measures need to be taken to conserve biological diversity;

(c) Regulate or manage biological resources important for the conservation of biological diversity whether within or outside protected areas, with a view to ensuring their conservation and sustainable use;

(d) Promote the protection of ecosystems, natural habitats and the maintenance of viable populations of species in natural surroundings;

(e) Promote environmentally sound and sustainable development in areas adjacent to protected areas with a view to furthering protection of these areas;

(f) Rehabilitate and restore degraded ecosystems and promote the recovery of threatened species, inter alia, through the development and implementation of plans or other management strategies;

(g) Establish or maintain means to regulate, manage or control the risks associated with the use and release of living modified organisms resulting from biotechnology which are likely to have adverse environmental impacts that could affect the conservation and sustainable use of biological diversity, taking also into account the risks to human health;

(h) Prevent the introduction of, control or eradicate those alien species which threaten ecosystems, habitats or species;

(i) Endeavour to provide the conditions needed for compatibility between present uses and the conservation of biological diversity and the sustainable use of its components;

(j) Subject to its national legislation, respect, preserve and maintain knowledge, innovations and practices of indigenous and local communities embodying traditional lifestyles relevant for the conservation and sustainable use of biological diversity and promote their wider application with the approval and involvement of the holders of such knowledge, innovations and practices and encourage the equitable sharing of the benefits arising from the utilization of such knowledge, innovations and practices;

(k) Develop or maintain necessary legislation and/or other regulatory provisions for the protection of threatened species and populations;

(l) Where a significant adverse effect on biological diversity has been determined pursuant to Article 7, regulate or manage the relevant processes and categories of activities; and

(m) Cooperate in providing financial and other support for in-situ conservation outlined in subparagraphs (a) to (l) above, particularly to developing countries.

. . . .

Article 11. Incentive Measures

Each Contracting Party shall, as far as possible and as appropriate, adopt economically and socially sound measures that act as incentives for the conservation and sustainable use of components of biological diversity.

. . . .

Article 15. Access to Genetic Resources

1. Recognizing the sovereign rights of States over their natural resources, the authority to determine access to genetic resources rests with the national governments and is subject to national legislation.

2. Each Contracting Party shall endeavour to create conditions to facilitate access to genetic resources for environmentally sound uses by other Contracting Parties and not to impose restrictions that run counter to the objectives of this Convention.

3. For the purpose of this Convention, the genetic resources being provided by a Contracting Party, as referred to in this Article and Articles 16 and 19, are only those that are provided by Contracting Parties that are countries of origin of such resources or by the Parties that have acquired the genetic resources in accordance with this Convention.

4. Access, where granted, shall be on mutually agreed terms and subject to the provisions of this Article.

5. Access to genetic resources shall be subject to prior informed consent of the Contracting Party providing such resources, unless otherwise determined by that Party.

6. Each Contracting Party shall endeavour to develop and carry out scientific research based on genetic resources provided by other Contracting Parties with the full participation of, and where possible in, such Contracting Parties.

7. Each Contracting Party shall take legislative, administrative or policy measures, as appropriate, and in accordance with Articles 16 and 19 and, where necessary, through the financial mechanism established by Articles 20 and 21 with the aim of sharing in a fair and equitable way the results of research and development and the benefits arising from the commercial and other utilization of genetic resources with the Contracting Party providing such resources. Such sharing shall be upon mutually agreed terms.

Article 16. Access to and Transfer of technology

1. Each Contracting Party, recognizing that technology includes biotechnology, and that both access to and transfer of technology among Contracting Parties are essential elements for the attainment of the objectives of this Convention, undertakes subject to the provisions of this Article to provide and/or facilitate access for and transfer to other Contracting Parties of technologies that are relevant to the conservation and sustainable use of biological diversity or make use of genetic resources and do not cause significant damage to the environment.

2. Access to and transfer of technology referred to in paragraph 1 above to developing countries shall be provided and/or facilitated under fair and most favourable terms, including on concessional and preferential terms where mutually agreed, and, where necessary, in accordance with the financial mechanism established by Articles 20 and 21. In the case of technology subject to patents and other intellectual property rights, such access and transfer shall be provided on terms which recognize and are consistent with the adequate and effective protection of intellectual property rights. The application of this paragraph shall be consistent with paragraphs 3, 4 and 5 below.

3. Each Contracting Party shall take legislative, administrative or policy measures, as appropriate, with the aim that Contracting Parties, in particular those that are developing countries, which provide genetic resources are provided access to and transfer of technology which makes use of those resources, on mutually agreed terms, including technology protected by patents and other intellectual property rights, where necessary, through the provisions of Articles 20 and 21 and in accordance with international law and consistent with paragraphs 4 and 5 below.

4. Each Contracting Party shall take legislative, administrative or policy measures, as appropriate, with the aim that the private sector facilitates access to, joint development and transfer of technology referred to in paragraph 1 above for the benefit of both governmental institutions and the private sector of developing countries and in this regard shall abide by the obligations included in paragraphs 1, 2 and 3 above.

5. The Contracting Parties, recognizing that patents and other intellectual property rights may have an influence on the implementation of this Convention, shall cooperate in this regard subject to national legislation and international law in order to ensure that such rights are supportive of and do not run counter to its objectives.

G. COPYRIGHT & RELATED RIGHTS

BERNE CONVENTION FOR THE PROTECTION OF LITERARY AND ARTISTIC WORKS

Done September 9, 1886, completed at Paris on May 4, 1896, revised at
Berlin on November 13, 1908, completed at Berne on March 20, 1914,
revised at Rome on June 2, 1928, at Brussels on June 26, 1948,
at Stockholm on July 14, 1967, and at Paris on July 24, 1971,
and amended on September 28, 1979.

The countries of the Union, being equally animated by the desire to
protect, in as effective and uniform a manner as possible, the rights of
authors in their literary and artistic works,

Recognizing the importance of the work of the Revision Conference held
at Stockholm in 1967,

Have resolved to revise the Act adopted by the Stockholm Conference,
while maintaining without change Articles 1 to 20 and 22 to 26 of that Act.

Consequently, the undersigned Plenipotentiaries, having presented their
full powers, recognized as in good and due form, have agreed as follows:

Article 1
*[Establishment of a Union]**

The countries to which this Convention applies constitute a Union for the
protection of the rights of authors in their literary and artistic works.

Article 2
[Protected Works: 1. "Literary and artistic works"; 2. Possible requirement of fixation; 3. Derivative works; 4. Official texts; 5. Collections; 6. Obligation to protect; beneficiaries of protection; 7. Works of applied art and industrial designs; 8. News]

(1) The expression "literary and artistic works" shall include every
production in the literary, scientific and artistic domain, whatever may be
the mode or form of its expression, such as books, pamphlets and other
writings; lectures, addresses, sermons and other works of the same nature;
dramatic or dramatico-musical works; choreographic works and
entertainments in dumb show; musical compositions with or without words;
cinematographic works to which are assimilated works expressed by a
process analogous to cinematography; works of drawing, painting,
architecture, sculpture, engraving and lithography; photographic works to
which are assimilated works expressed by a process analogous to

---

* Articles have been given titles by WIPO to facilitate their identification. There are no titles in the signed (English) text.

photography; works of applied art; illustrations, maps, plans, sketches and three-dimensional works relative to geography, topography, architecture or science.

(2) It shall, however, be a matter for legislation in the countries of the Union to prescribe that works in general or any specified categories of works shall not be protected unless they have been fixed in some material form.

(3) Translations, adaptations, arrangements of music and other alterations of a literary or artistic work shall be protected as original works without prejudice to the copyright in the original work.

(4) It shall be a matter for legislation in the countries of the Union to determine the protection to be granted to official texts of a legislative, administrative and legal nature, and to official translations of such texts.

(5) Collections of literary or artistic works such as encyclopaedias and anthologies which, by reason of the selection and arrangement of their contents, constitute intellectual creations shall be protected as such, without prejudice to the copyright in each of the works forming part of such collections.

(6) The works mentioned in this Article shall enjoy protection in all countries of the Union. This protection shall operate for the benefit of the author and his successors in title.

(7) Subject to the provisions of Article 7(4) of this Convention, it shall be a matter for legislation in the countries of the Union to determine the extent of the application of their laws to works of applied art and industrial designs and models, as well as the conditions under which such works, designs and models shall be protected. Works protected in the country of origin solely as designs and models shall be entitled in another country of the Union only to such special protection as is granted in that country to designs and models; however, if no such special protection is granted in that country, such works shall be protected as artistic works.

(8) The protection of this Convention shall not apply to news of the day or to miscellaneous facts having the character of mere items of press information.

Article 2bis
[Possible Limitation of Protection of Certain Works: 1. Certain speeches; 2. Certain uses of lectures and addresses; 3. Right to make collections of such works]

(1) It shall be a matter for legislation in the countries of the Union to exclude, wholly or in part, from the protection provided by the preceding Article political speeches and speeches delivered in the course of legal proceedings.

(2) It shall also be a matter for legislation in the countries of the Union to determine the conditions under which lectures, addresses and other works of the same nature which are delivered in public may be reproduced by the press, broadcast, communicated to the public by wire and made the subject

of public communication as envisaged in Article 11*bis*(1) of this Convention, when such use is justified by the informatory purpose.

(3) Nevertheless, the author shall enjoy the exclusive right of making a collection of his works mentioned in the preceding paragraphs.

Article 3
[*Criteria of Eligibility for Protection:* 1. Nationality of author; place of publication of work; 2. Residence of author; 3. "Published" works; 4. "Simultaneously published" works]

(1) The protection of this Convention shall apply to:

(a) authors who are nationals of one of the countries of the Union, for their works, whether published or not;

(b) authors who are not nationals of one of the countries of the Union, for their works first published in one of those countries, or simultaneously in a country outside the Union and in a country of the Union.

(2) Authors who are not nationals of one of the countries of the Union but who have their habitual residence in one of them shall, for the purposes of this Convention, be assimilated to nationals of that country.

(3) The expression "published works" means works published with the consent of their authors, whatever may be the means of manufacture of the copies, provided that the availability of such copies has been such as to satisfy the reasonable requirements of the public, having regard to the nature of the work. The performance of a dramatic, dramatico-musical, cinematographic or musical work, the public recitation of a literary work, the communication by wire or the broadcasting of literary or artistic works, the exhibition of a work of art and the construction of a work of architecture shall not constitute publication.

(4) A work shall be considered as having been published simultaneously in several countries if it has been published in two or more countries within thirty days of its first publication.

Article 4
[*Criteria of Eligibility for Protection of Cinematographic Works, Works of Architecture and Certain Artistic Works*]

The protection of this Convention shall apply, even if the conditions of Article 3 are not fulfilled, to:

(a) authors of cinematographic works the maker of which has his headquarters or habitual residence in one of the countries of the Union;

(b) authors of works of architecture erected in a country of the Union or of other artistic works incorporated in a building or other structure located in a country of the Union.

Article 5

[*Rights Guaranteed:* 1. and 2. Outside the country of origin; 3. In the country of origin; 4. "Country of origin"]

(1) Authors shall enjoy, in respect of works for which they are protected under this Convention, in countries of the Union other than the country of origin, the rights which their respective laws do now or may hereafter grant to their nationals, as well as the rights specially granted by this Convention.

(2) The enjoyment and the exercise of these rights shall not be subject to any formality; such enjoyment and such exercise shall be independent of the existence of protection in the country of origin of the work. Consequently, apart from the provisions of this Convention, the extent of protection, as well as the means of redress afforded to the author to protect his rights, shall be governed exclusively by the laws of the country where protection is claimed.

(3) Protection in the country of origin is governed by domestic law. However, when the author is not a national of the country of origin of the work for which he is protected under this Convention, he shall enjoy in that country the same rights as national authors.

(4) The country of origin shall be considered to be:

(a) in the case of works first published in a country of the Union, that country; in the case of works published simultaneously in several countries of the Union which grant different terms of protection, the country whose legislation grants the shortest term of protection;

(b) in the case of works published simultaneously in a country outside the Union and in a country of the Union, the latter country;

(c) in the case of unpublished works or of works first published in a country outside the Union, without simultaneous publication in a country of the Union, the country of the Union of which the author is a national, provided that:

    (i) when these are cinematographic works the maker of which has his headquarters or his habitual residence in a country of the Union, the country of origin shall be that country, and

    (ii) when these are works of architecture erected in a country of the Union or other artistic works incorporated in a building or other structure located in a country of the Union, the country of origin shall be that country.

Article 6

[*Possible Restriction of Protection in Respect of Certain Works of Nationals of Certain Countries Outside the Union:* 1. In the country of the first publication and in other countries; 2. No retroactivity; 3. Notice]

(1) Where any country outside the Union fails to protect in an adequate manner the works of authors who are nationals of one of the countries of the Union, the latter country may restrict the protection given to the works of authors who are, at the date of the first publication thereof, nationals of the

other country and are not habitually resident in one of the countries of the Union. If the country of first publication avails itself of this right, the other countries of the Union shall not be required to grant to works thus subjected to special treatment a wider protection than that granted to them in the country of first publication.

(2) No restrictions introduced by virtue of the preceding paragraph shall affect the rights which an author may have acquired in respect of a work published in a country of the Union before such restrictions were put into force.

(3) The countries of the Union which restrict the grant of copyright in accordance with this Article shall give notice thereof to the Director General of the World Intellectual Property Organization (hereinafter designated as "the Director General") by a written declaration specifying the countries in regard to which protection is restricted, and the restrictions to which rights of authors who are nationals of those countries are subjected. The Director General shall immediately communicate this declaration to all the countries of the Union.

Article 6*bis*
[Moral Rights: 1. To claim authorship; to object to certain modifications and other derogatory actions; 2. After the author's death; 3. Means of redress]

(1) Independently of the author's economic rights, and even after the transfer of the said rights, the author shall have the right to claim authorship of the work and to object to any distortion, mutilation or other modification of, or other derogatory action in relation to, the said work, which would be prejudicial to his honor or reputation.

(2) The rights granted to the author in accordance with the preceding paragraph shall, after his death, be maintained, at least until the expiry of the economic rights, and shall be exercisable by the persons or institutions authorized by the legislation of the country where protection is claimed. However, those countries whose legislation, at the moment of their ratification of or accession to this Act, does not provide for the protection after the death of the author of all the rights set out in the preceding paragraph may provide that some of these rights may, after his death, cease to be maintained.

(3) The means of redress for safeguarding the rights granted by this Article shall be governed by the legislation of the country where protection is claimed.

Article 7

[*Term of Protection:* 1. Generally; 2. For cinematographic works; 3. For anonymous and pseudonymous works; 4. For photographic works and works of applied art; 5. Starting date of computation; 6. Longer terms; 7. Shorter terms; 8. Applicable law; "comparison" of terms]

(1) The term of protection granted by this Convention shall be the life of the author and fifty years after his death.

(2) However, in the case of cinematographic works, the countries of the Union may provide that the term of protection shall expire fifty years after the work has been made available to the public with the consent of the author, or, failing such an event within fifty years from the making of such a work, fifty years after the making.

(3) In the case of anonymous or pseudonymous works, the term of protection granted by this Convention shall expire fifty years after the work has been lawfully made available to the public. However, when the pseudonym adopted by the author leaves no doubt as to his identity, the term of protection shall be that provided in paragraph (1). If the author of an anonymous or pseudonymous work discloses his identity during the above-mentioned period, the term of protection applicable shall be that provided in paragraph (1). The countries of the Union shall not be required to protect anonymous or pseudonymous works in respect of which it is reasonable to presume that their author has been dead for fifty years.

(4) It shall be a matter for legislation in the countries of the Union to determine the term of protection of photographic works and that of works of applied art in so far as they are protected as artistic works; however, this term shall last at least until the end of a period of twenty-five years from the making of such a work.

(5) The term of protection subsequent to the death of the author and the terms provided by paragraph (2), paragraph (3) and paragraph (4) shall run from the date of death or of the event referred to in those paragraphs, but such terms shall always be deemed to begin on the first of January of the year following the death or such event.

(6) The countries of the Union may grant a term of protection in excess of those provided by the preceding paragraphs.

(7) Those countries of the Union bound by the Rome Act of this Convention which grant, in their national legislation in force at the time of signature of the present Act, shorter terms of protection than those provided for in the preceding paragraphs shall have the right to maintain such terms when ratifying or acceding to the present Act.

(8) In any case, the term shall be governed by the legislation of the country where protection is claimed; however, unless the legislation of that country otherwise provides, the term shall not exceed the term fixed in the country of origin of the work.

Article 7bis
[Term of Protection for Works of Joint Authorship]

The provisions of the preceding Article shall also apply in the case of a work of joint authorship, provided that the terms measured from the death of the author shall be calculated from the death of the last surviving author.

Article 8
[Right of Translation]

Authors of literary and artistic works protected by this Convention shall enjoy the exclusive right of making and of authorizing the translation of their works throughout the term of protection of their rights in the original works.

Article 9
[Right of Reproduction: 1. Generally; 2. Possible exceptions; 3. Sound and visual recordings]

(1) Authors of literary and artistic works protected by this Convention shall have the exclusive right of authorizing the reproduction of these works, in any manner or form.

(2) It shall be a matter for legislation in the countries of the Union to permit the reproduction of such works in certain special cases, provided that such reproduction does not conflict with a normal exploitation of the work and does not unreasonably prejudice the legitimate interests of the author.

(3) Any sound or visual recording shall be considered as a reproduction for the purposes of this Convention.

Article 10
[Certain Free Uses of Works: 1. Quotations; 2. Illustrations for teaching; 3. Indication of source and author]

(1) It shall be permissible to make quotations from a work which has already been lawfully made available to the public, provided that their making is compatible with fair practice, and their extent does not exceed that justified by the purpose, including quotations from newspaper articles and periodicals in the form of press summaries.

(2) It shall be a matter for legislation in the countries of the Union, and for special agreements existing or to be concluded between them, to permit the utilization, to the extent justified by the purpose, of literary or artistic works by way of illustration in publications, broadcasts or sound or visual recordings for teaching, provided such utilization is compatible with fair practice.

(3) Where use is made of works in accordance with the preceding paragraphs of this Article, mention shall be made of the source, and of the name of the author if it appears thereon.

Article 10*bis*
[*Further Possible Free Uses of Works:* 1. Of certain articles and broadcast works; 2. Of works seen or heard in connection with current events]

(1) It shall be a matter for legislation in the countries of the Union to permit the reproduction by the press, the broadcasting or the communication to the public by wire of articles published in newspapers or periodicals on current economic, political or religious topics, and of broadcast works of the same character, in cases in which the reproduction, broadcasting or such communication thereof is not expressly reserved. Nevertheless, the source must always be clearly indicated; the legal consequences of a breach of this obligation shall be determined by the legislation of the country where protection is claimed.

(2) It shall also be a matter for legislation in the countries of the Union to determine the conditions under which, for the purpose of reporting current events by means of photography, cinematography, broadcasting or communication to the public by wire, literary or artistic works seen or heard in the course of the event may, to the extent justified by the informatory purpose, be reproduced and made available to the public.

Article 11
[*Certain Rights in Dramatic and Musical Works*: 1. Right of public performance and of communication to the public of a performance; 2. In respect of translations]

(1) Authors of dramatic, dramatico-musical and musical works shall enjoy the exclusive right of authorizing:

    (i)   the public performance of their works, including such public performance by any means or process;

    (ii)   any communication to the public of the performance of their works.

(2) Authors of dramatic or dramatico-musical works shall enjoy, during the full term of their rights in the original works, the same rights with respect to translations thereof.

Article 11*bis*
[*Broadcasting and Related Rights:* 1. Broadcasting and other wireless communications, public communication of broadcast by wire or rebroadcast, public communication of broadcast by loudspeaker or analogous instruments; 2. Compulsory licenses; 3. Recording; ephemeral recordings]

(1) Authors of literary and artistic works shall enjoy the exclusive right of authorizing:

    (i)   the broadcasting of their works or the communication thereof to the public by any other means of wireless diffusion of signs, sounds or images;

    (ii)   any communication to the public by wire or by rebroadcasting of the broadcast of the work, when this communication is made by an organization other than the original one;

    (iii)   the public communication by loudspeaker or any other analogous instrument transmitting, by signs, sounds or images, the broadcast of the work.

(2) It shall be a matter for legislation in the countries of the Union to determine the conditions under which the rights mentioned in the paragraph 1 may be exercised, but these conditions shall apply only in the countries where they have been prescribed. They shall not in any circumstances be prejudicial to the moral rights of the author, nor to his right to obtain equitable remuneration which, in the absence of agreement, shall be fixed by competent authority.

(3) In the absence of any contrary stipulation, permission granted in accordance with paragraph (1) of this Article shall not imply permission to record, by means of instruments recording sounds or images, the work broadcast. It shall, however, be a matter for legislation in the countries of the Union to determine the regulations for ephemeral recordings made by a broadcasting organization by means of its own facilities and used for its own broadcasts. The preservation of these recordings in official archives may, on the ground of their exceptional documentary character, be authorized by such legislation.

Article 11ter
[Certain Rights in Literary Works: 1. Right of public recitation and of communication to the public of a recitation; 2. In respect of translations]

(1) Authors of literary works shall enjoy the exclusive right of authorizing:

    (i)   the public recitation of their works, including such public recitation by any means or process;

    (ii)   any communication to the public of the recitation of their works.

(2) Authors of literary works shall enjoy, during the full term of their rights in the original works, the same rights with respect to translations thereof.

Article 12
[Right of Adaptation, Arrangement and Other Alteration]

Authors of literary or artistic works shall enjoy the exclusive right of authorizing adaptations, arrangements and other alterations of their works.

Article 13
[*Possible Limitation of the Right of Recording of Musical Works and Any Words Pertaining Thereto:* 1. Compulsory licenses; 2. Transitory measures; 3. Seizure on importation of copies made without the author's permission]

(1) Each country of the Union may impose for itself reservations and conditions on the exclusive right granted to the author of a musical work and to the author of any words, the recording of which together with the musical work has already been authorized by the latter, to authorize the sound recording of that musical work, together with such words, if any; but all such reservations and conditions shall apply only in the countries which have imposed them and shall not, in any circumstances, be prejudicial to the rights of these authors to obtain equitable remuneration which, in the absence of agreement, shall be fixed by competent authority.

(2) Recordings of musical works made in a country of the Union in accordance with Article 13(3) of the Conventions signed at Rome on June 2, 1928, and at Brussels on June 26, 1948, may be reproduced in that country without the permission of the author of the musical work until a date two years after that country becomes bound by this Act.

(3) Recordings made in accordance with paragraph (1) and paragraph (2) of this Article and imported without permission from the parties concerned into a country where they are treated as infringing recordings shall be liable to seizure.

Article 14
[*Cinematographic and Related Rights:* 1. Cinematographic adaptation and reproduction; distribution; public performance and public communication by wire of works thus adapted or reproduced; 2. Adaptation of cinematographic productions; 3. No compulsory licenses]

(1) Authors of literary or artistic works shall have the exclusive right of authorizing:

- (i) the cinematographic adaptation and reproduction of these works, and the distribution of the works thus adapted or reproduced;
- (ii) the public performance and communication to the public by wire of the works thus adapted or reproduced.

(2) The adaptation into any other artistic form of a cinematographic production derived from literary or artistic works shall, without prejudice to the authorization of the author of the cinematographic production, remain subject to the authorization of the authors of the original works.

(3) The provisions of Article 13(1) shall not apply.

Article 14*bis*
[*Special Provisions Concerning Cinematographic Works:* 1. Assimilation to "original" works; 2. Ownership; limitation of certain rights of certain contributors; 3. Certain other contributors]

(1) Without prejudice to the copyright in any work which may have been adapted or reproduced, a cinematographic work shall be protected as an original work. The owner of copyright in a cinematographic work shall enjoy the same rights as the author of an original work, including the rights referred to in the preceding Article.

(2)

(a) Ownership of copyright in a cinematographic work shall be a matter for legislation in the country where protection is claimed.

(b) However, in the countries of the Union which, by legislation, include among the owners of copyright in a cinematographic work authors who have brought contributions to the making of the work, such authors, if they have undertaken to bring such contributions, may not, in the absence of any contrary or special stipulation, object to the reproduction, distribution, public performance, communication to the public by wire, broadcasting or any other communication to the public, or to the subtitling or dubbing of texts, of the work.

(c) The question whether or not the form of the undertaking referred to above should, for the application of the preceding subparagraph (b), be in a written agreement or a written act of the same effect shall be a matter for the legislation of the country where the maker of the cinematographic work has his headquarters or habitual residence. However, it shall be a matter for the legislation of the country of the Union where protection is claimed to provide that the said undertaking shall be in a written agreement or a written act of the same effect. The countries whose legislation so provides shall notify the Director General by means of a written declaration, which will be immediately communicated by him to all the other countries of the Union.

(d) By "contrary or special stipulation" is meant any restrictive condition which is relevant to the aforesaid undertaking.

(3) Unless the national legislation provides to the contrary, the provisions of paragraph (2)(b) above shall not be applicable to authors of scenarios, dialogues and musical works created for the making of the cinematographic work, or to the principal director thereof. However, those countries of the Union whose legislation does not contain rules providing for the application of the said paragraph (2)(b) to such director shall notify the Director General by means of a written declaration, which will be immediately communicated by him to all the other countries of the Union.

Article 14*ter*
[*"Droit de suite" in Works of Art and Manuscripts:* 1. Right to an interest in resales; 2. Applicable law; 3. Procedure]

(1) The author, or after his death the persons or institutions authorized by national legislation, shall, with respect to original works of art and original manuscripts of writers and composers, enjoy the inalienable right to an interest in any sale of the work subsequent to the first transfer by the author of the work.

(2) The protection provided by the preceding paragraph may be claimed in a country of the Union only if legislation in the country to which the author belongs so permits, and to the extent permitted by the country where this protection is claimed.

(3) The procedure for collection and the amounts shall be matters for determination by national legislation.

Article 15
[*Right to Enforce Protected Rights:* 1. Where author's name is indicated or where pseudonym leaves no doubt as to author's identity; 2. In the case of cinematographic works; 3. In the case of anonymous and pseudonymous works; 4. In the case of certain unpublished works of unknown authorship]

(1) In order that the author of a literary or artistic work protected by this Convention shall, in the absence of proof to the contrary, be regarded as such, and consequently be entitled to institute infringement proceedings in the countries of the Union, it shall be sufficient for his name to appear on the work in the usual manner. This paragraph shall be applicable even if this name is a pseudonym, where the pseudonym adopted by the author leaves no doubt as to his identity.

(2) The person or body corporate whose name appears on a cinematographic work in the usual manner shall, in the absence of proof to the contrary, be presumed to be the maker of the said work.

(3) In the case of anonymous and pseudonymous works, other than those referred to in paragraph (1) above, the publisher whose name appears on the work shall, in the absence of proof to the contrary, be deemed to represent the author, and in this capacity he shall be entitled to protect and enforce the author's rights. The provisions of this paragraph shall cease to apply when the author reveals his identity and establishes his claim to authorship of the work.

(4)

(a) In the case of unpublished works where the identity of the author is unknown, but where there is every ground to presume that he is a national of a country of the Union, it shall be a matter for legislation in that country to designate the competent authority which shall represent the author and shall be entitled to protect and enforce his rights in the countries of the Union.

(b) Countries of the Union which make such designation under the terms of this provision shall notify the Director General by means of a written declaration giving full information concerning the authority thus designated. The Director General shall at once communicate this declaration to all other countries of the Union.

Article 16
[*Infringing Copies:* 1. Seizure; 2. Seizure on importation; 3. Applicable law]

(1) Infringing copies of a work shall be liable to seizure in any country of the Union where the work enjoys legal protection.

(2) The provisions of the preceding paragraph shall also apply to reproductions coming from a country where the work is not protected, or has ceased to be protected.

(3) The seizure shall take place in accordance with the legislation of each country.

Article 17
[*Possibility of Control of Circulation, Presentation and Exhibition of Works*]

The provisions of this Convention cannot in any way affect the right of the Government of each country of the Union to permit, to control, or to prohibit, by legislation or regulation, the circulation, presentation, or exhibition of any work or production in regard to which the competent authority may find it necessary to exercise that right.

Article 18
[*Works Existing on Convention's Entry Into Force:* 1. Protectable where protection not yet expired in country of origin; 2. Non-protectable where protection already expired in country where it is claimed; 3. Application of these principles; 4. Special cases]

(1) This Convention shall apply to all works which, at the moment of its coming into force, have not yet fallen into the public domain in the country of origin through the expiry of the term of protection.

(2) If, however, through the expiry of the term of protection which was previously granted, a work has fallen into the public domain of the country where protection is claimed, that work shall not be protected anew.

(3) The application of this principle shall be subject to any provisions contained in special conventions to that effect existing or to be concluded between countries of the Union. In the absence of such provisions, the respective countries shall determine, each in so far as it is concerned, the conditions of application of this principle.

(4) The preceding provisions shall also apply in the case of new accessions to the Union and to cases in which protection is extended by the application of Article 7 or by the abandonment of reservations.

Article 19
[Protection Greater than Resulting from Convention]

The provisions of this Convention shall not preclude the making of a claim to the benefit of any greater protection which may be granted by legislation in a country of the Union.

Article 20
[Special Agreements Among Countries of the Union]

The Governments of the countries of the Union reserve the right to enter into special agreements among themselves, in so far as such agreements grant to authors more extensive rights than those granted by the Convention, or contain other provisions not contrary to this Convention. The provisions of existing agreements which satisfy these conditions shall remain applicable.

Article 21
[Special Provisions Regarding Developing Countries: 1. Reference to Appendix; 2. Appendix part of Act]

(1) Special provisions regarding developing countries are included in the Appendix.

(2) Subject to the provisions of Article 28(1)(b), the Appendix forms an integral part of this Act.

Article 22
[Assembly: 1. Constitution and composition; 2. Tasks; 3. Quorum, voting, observers; 4. Convocation; 5. Rules of procedure]

(1)

(a) The Union shall have an Assembly consisting of those countries of the Union which are bound by Article 22 to Article 26.

(b) The Government of each country shall be represented by one delegate, who may be assisted by alternate delegates, advisors, and experts.

(c) The expenses of each delegation shall be borne by the Government which has appointed it.

(2)

(a) The Assembly shall:

    (i)   deal with all matters concerning the maintenance and development of the Union and the implementation of this Convention;

    (ii)   give directions concerning the preparation for conferences of revision to the International Bureau of Intellectual Property (hereinafter designated as "the International Bureau") referred to in the Convention Establishing the World Intellectual Property Organization (hereinafter designated as "the

Organization"), due account being taken of any comments made by those countries of the Union which are not bound by Article 22 to Article 26;

(iii) review and approve the reports and activities of the Director General of the Organization concerning the Union, and give him all necessary instructions concerning matters within the competence of the Union;

(iv) elect the members of the Executive Committee of the Assembly;

(v) review and approve the reports and activities of its Executive Committee, and give instructions to such Committee;

(vi) determine the program and adopt the biennial budget of the Union, and approve its final accounts;

(vii) adopt the financial regulations of the Union;

(viii) establish such committees of experts and working groups as may be necessary for the work of the Union;

(ix) determine which countries not members of the Union and which intergovernmental and international non-governmental organizations shall be admitted to its meetings as observers;

(x) adopt amendments to Article 22 to Article 26;

(xi) take any other appropriate action designed to further the objectives of the Union;

(xii) exercise such other functions as are appropriate under this Convention;

(xiii) subject to its acceptance, exercise such rights as are given to it in the Convention establishing the Organization.

(b) With respect to matters which are of interest also to other Unions administered by the Organization, the Assembly shall make its decisions after having heard the advice of the Coordination Committee of the Organization.

(3)

(a) Each country member of the Assembly shall have one vote.

(b) One-half of the countries members of the Assembly shall constitute a quorum.

(c) Notwithstanding the provisions of subparagraph (b), if, in any session, the number of countries represented is less than one-half but equal to or more than one-third of the countries members of the Assembly, the Assembly may make decisions but, with the exception of decisions concerning its own procedure, all such decisions shall take effect only if the following conditions are fulfilled. The International Bureau shall communicate the said decisions to the countries members of the Assembly which were not represented and shall invite them to express in writing their vote or abstention within a period of three months from the date of the communication. If, at the expiration of this period, the number of countries having thus expressed their vote or abstention attains the number of countries which was lacking for attaining the quorum in the session itself, such decisions shall take effect provided that at the same time the required majority still obtains.

(d) Subject to the provisions of Article 26(2), the decisions of the Assembly shall require two-thirds of the votes cast.

(e) Abstentions shall not be considered as votes.

(f) A delegate may represent, and vote in the name of, one country only.

(g) Countries of the Union not members of the Assembly shall be admitted to its meetings as observers.

(4)

(a) The Assembly shall meet once in every second calendar year in ordinary session upon convocation by the Director General and, in the absence of exceptional circumstances, during the same period and at the same place as the General Assembly of the Organization.

(b) The Assembly shall meet in extraordinary session upon convocation by the Director General, at the request of the Executive Committee or at the request of one-fourth of the countries members of the Assembly.

(5) The Assembly shall adopt its own rules of procedure.

Article 23
[*Executive Committee:* 1. Constitution; 2. Composition; 3. Number of members; 4. Geographical distribution; special agreements; 5. Term, limits of re-eligibility, rules of election; 6. Tasks; 7. Convocation; 8. Quorum, voting; 9. Observers; 10. Rules of procedure]

(1) The Assembly shall have an Executive Committee.

(2)

(a) The Executive Committee shall consist of countries elected by the Assembly from among countries members of the Assembly. Furthermore, the country on whose territory the Organization has its headquarters shall, subject to the provisions of Article 25(7)(b), have an ex officio seat on the Committee.

(b) The Government of each country member of the Executive Committee shall be represented by one delegate, who may be assisted by alternate delegates, advisors, and experts.

(c) The expenses of each delegation shall be borne by the Government which has appointed it.

(3) The number of countries members of the Executive Committee shall correspond to one-fourth of the number of countries members of the Assembly. In establishing the number of seats to be filled, remainders after division by four shall be disregarded.

(4) In electing the members of the Executive Committee, the Assembly shall have due regard to an equitable geographical distribution and to the need for countries party to the Special Agreements which might be

established in relation with the Union to be among the countries constituting the Executive Committee.

(5)

(a) Each member of the Executive Committee shall serve from the close of the session of the Assembly which elected it to the close of the next ordinary session of the Assembly.

(b) Members of the Executive Committee may be re-elected, but not more than two-thirds of them.

(c) The Assembly shall establish the details of the rules governing the election and possible re-election of the members of the Executive Committee.

(6)

(a) The Executive Committee shall:

(i)   prepare the draft agenda of the Assembly;

(ii)   submit proposals to the Assembly respecting the draft program and biennial budget of the Union prepared by the Director General;

(iii)   [deleted]

(iv)   submit, with appropriate comments, to the Assembly the periodical reports of the Director General and the yearly audit reports on the accounts;

(v)   in accordance with the decisions of the Assembly and having regard to circumstances arising between two ordinary sessions of the Assembly, take all necessary measures to ensure the execution of the program of the Union by the Director General;

(vi)   perform such other functions as are allocated to it under this Convention.

(b) With respect to matters which are of interest also to other Unions administered by the Organization, the Executive Committee shall make its decisions after having heard the advice of the Coordination Committee of the Organization.

(7)

(a) The Executive Committee shall meet once a year in ordinary session upon convocation by the Director General, preferably during the same period and at the same place as the Coordination Committee of the Organization.

(b) The Executive Committee shall meet in extraordinary session upon convocation by the Director General, either on his own initiative, or at the request of its Chairman or one-fourth of its members.

(8)

(a) Each country member of the Executive Committee shall have one vote.

(b) One-half of the members of the Executive Committee shall constitute a quorum.

(c) Decisions shall be made by a simple majority of the votes cast.

(d) Abstentions shall not be considered as votes.

(e) A delegate may represent, and vote in the name of, one country only.

(9) Countries of the Union not members of the Executive Committee shall be admitted to its meetings as observers.

(10) The Executive Committee shall adopt its own rules of procedure.

Article 24
[*International Bureau:* 1. Tasks in general, Director General; 2. General information; 3. Periodical; 4. Information to countries; 5. Studies and services; 6. Participation in meetings; 7. Conferences of revision; 8. Other tasks]

(1)

(a) The administrative tasks with respect to the Union shall be performed by the International Bureau, which is a continuation of the Bureau of the Union united with the Bureau of the Union established by the International Convention for the Protection of Industrial Property.

(b) In particular, the International Bureau shall provide the secretariat of the various organs of the Union.

(c) The Director General of the Organization shall be the chief executive of the Union and shall represent the Union.

(2) The International Bureau shall assemble and publish information concerning the protection of copyright. Each country of the Union shall promptly communicate to the International Bureau all new laws and official texts concerning the protection of copyright.

(3) The International Bureau shall publish a monthly periodical.

(4) The International Bureau shall, on request, furnish information to any country of the Union on matters concerning the protection of copyright.

(5) The International Bureau shall conduct studies, and shall provide services, designed to facilitate the protection of copyright.

(6) The Director General and any staff member designated by him shall participate, without the right to vote, in all meetings of the Assembly, the Executive Committee and any other committee of experts or working group. The Director General, or a staff member designated by him, shall be ex officio secretary of these bodies.

(7)

(a) The International Bureau shall, in accordance with the directions of the Assembly and in cooperation with the Executive Committee, make the preparations for the conferences of revision of the provisions of the Convention other than Article 22 to Article 26.

(b) The International Bureau may consult with intergovernmental and international non-governmental organizations concerning preparations for conferences of revision.

(c) The Director General and persons designated by him shall take part, without the right to vote, in the discussions at these conferences.

(8) The International Bureau shall carry out any other tasks assigned to it.

Article 25
[*Finances:* 1. Budget; 2. Coordination with other Unions; 3. Resources; 4. Contributions; possible extension of previous budget; 5. Fees and charges; 6. Working capital fund; 7. Advances by host Government; 8. Auditing of accounts]

(1)

(a) The Union shall have a budget.

(b) The budget of the Union shall include the income and expenses proper to the Union, its contribution to the budget of expenses common to the Unions, and, where applicable, the sum made available to the budget of the Conference of the Organization.

(c) Expenses not attributable exclusively to the Union but also to one or more other Unions administered by the Organization shall be considered as expenses common to the Unions. The share of the Union in such common expenses shall be in proportion to the interest the Union has in them.

(2) The budget of the Union shall be established with due regard to the requirements of coordination with the budgets of the other Unions administered by the Organization.

(3) The budget of the Union shall be financed from the following sources:

(i)   contributions of the countries of the Union;

(ii)   fees and charges due for services performed by the International Bureau in relation to the Union;

(iii) sale of, or royalties on, the publications of the International Bureau concerning the Union;

(iv)   gifts, bequests, and subventions;

(v)   rents, interests, and other miscellaneous income.

(4)

(a) For the purpose of establishing its contribution towards the budget, each country of the Union shall belong to a class, and shall pay its annual contributions on the basis of a number of units fixed as follows:

Class I 25

Class II 20

Class III 15

Class IV 10

Class V 5

Class VI 3

Class VII 1

(b) Unless it has already done so, each country shall indicate, concurrently with depositing its instrument of ratification or accession, the class to which it wishes to belong. Any country may change class. If it chooses a lower class, the country must announce it to the Assembly at one of its ordinary sessions. Any such change shall take effect at the beginning of the calendar year following the session.

(c) The annual contribution of each country shall be an amount in the same proportion to the total sum to be contributed to the annual budget of the Union by all countries as the number of its units is to the total of the units of all contributing countries.

(d) Contributions shall become due on the first of January of each year.

(e) A country which is in arrears in the payment of its contributions shall have no vote in any of the organs of the Union of which it is a member if the amount of its arrears equals or exceeds the amount of the contributions due from it for the preceding two full years. However, any organ of the Union may allow such a country to continue to exercise its vote in that organ if, and as long as, it is satisfied that the delay in payment is due to exceptional and unavoidable circumstances.

(f) If the budget is not adopted before the beginning of a new financial period, it shall be at the same level as the budget of the previous year, in accordance with the financial regulations.

(5) The amount of the fees and charges due for services rendered by the International Bureau in relation to the Union shall be established, and shall be reported to the Assembly and the Executive Committee, by the Director General.

(6)

(a) The Union shall have a working capital fund which shall be constituted by a single payment made by each country of the Union. If the fund becomes insufficient, an increase shall be decided by the Assembly.

(b) The amount of the initial payment of each country to the said fund or of its participation in the increase thereof shall be a proportion of the contribution of that country for the year in which the fund is established or the increase decided.

(c) The proportion and the terms of payment shall be fixed by the Assembly on the proposal of the Director General and after it has heard the advice of the Coordination Committee of the Organization.

(7)

(a) In the headquarters agreement concluded with the country on the territory of which the Organization has its headquarters, it shall be provided that, whenever the working capital fund is insufficient, such country shall grant advances. The amount of these advances and the conditions on which they are granted shall be the subject of separate agreements, in each case, between such country and the Organization. As long as it remains under the obligation to grant advances, such country shall have an ex officio seat on the Executive Committee.

(b) The country referred to in subparagraph (a) and the Organization shall each have the right to denounce the obligation to grant advances, by written notification. Denunciation shall take effect three years after the end of the year in which it has been notified.

(8) The auditing of the accounts shall be effected by one or more of the countries of the Union or by external auditors, as provided in the financial regulations. They shall be designated, with their agreement, by the Assembly.

Article 26
[*Amendments:* 1. Provisions susceptible of amendment by the Assembly; proposals; 2. Adoption; 3. Entry into force]

(1) Proposals for the amendment of Article 22, Article 23, Article 24, Article 25, and the present Article, may be initiated by any country member of the Assembly, by the Executive Committee, or by the Director General. Such proposals shall be communicated by the Director General to the member countries of the Assembly at least six months in advance of their consideration by the Assembly.

(2) Amendments to the Articles referred to in paragraph (1) shall be adopted by the Assembly. Adoption shall require three-fourths of the votes cast, provided that any amendment of Article 22, and of the present paragraph, shall require four-fifths of the votes cast.

(3) Any amendment to the Articles referred to in paragraph (1) shall enter into force one month after written notifications of acceptance, effected in accordance with their respective constitutional processes, have been received by the Director General from three-fourths of the countries members of the Assembly at the time it adopted the amendment. Any amendment to the said Articles thus accepted shall bind all the countries which are members of the Assembly at the time the amendment enters into force, or which become members thereof at a subsequent date, provided that any amendment increasing the financial obligations of countries of the Union shall bind only those countries which have notified their acceptance of such amendment.

Article 27
[*Revision:* 1. Objective; 2. Conferences; 3. Adoption]

(1) This Convention shall be submitted to revision with a view to the introduction of amendments designed to improve the system of the Union.

(2) For this purpose, conferences shall be held successively in one of the countries of the Union among the delegates of the said countries.

(3) Subject to the provisions of Article 26 which apply to the amendment of Article 22 to Article 26, any revision of this Act, including the Appendix, shall require the unanimity of the votes cast.

Article 28
[Acceptance and Entry Into Force of Act for Countries of the Union: 1. Ratification, accession; possibility of excluding certain provisions; withdrawal of exclusion; 2. Entry into force of Articles 1 to 21 and Appendix; 3. Entry into force of Articles 22 to 38]

(1)

(a) Any country of the Union which has signed this Act may ratify it, and, if it has not signed it, may accede to it. Instruments of ratification or accession shall be deposited with the Director General.

(b) Any country of the Union may declare in its instrument of ratification or accession that its ratification or accession shall not apply to Article 1 to Article 21 and the Appendix, provided that, if such country has previously made a declaration under Article VI(1) of the Appendix, then it may declare in the said instrument only that its ratification or accession shall not apply to Article 1 to Article 20.

(c) Any country of the Union which, in accordance with subparagraph (b), has excluded provisions therein referred to from the effects of its ratification or accession may at any later time declare that it extends the effects of its ratification or accession to those provisions. Such declaration shall be deposited with the Director General.

(2)

(a) Article 1 to Article 21 and the Appendix shall enter into force three months after both of the following two conditions are fulfilled:

(i) at least five countries of the Union have ratified or acceded to this Act without making a declaration under paragraph (1)(b),

(ii) France, Spain, the United Kingdom of Great Britain and Northern Ireland, and the United States of America, have become bound by the Universal Copyright Convention as revised at Paris on July 24, 1971.

(b) The entry into force referred to in subparagraph (a) shall apply to those countries of the Union which, at least three months before the said entry into force, have deposited instruments of ratification or accession not containing a declaration under paragraph (1)(b).

(c) With respect to any country of the Union not covered by subparagraph (b) and which ratifies or accedes to this Act without making a declaration under paragraph (1)(b), Article 1 to Article 21 and the Appendix shall enter into force three months after the date on which the Director General has notified the deposit of the relevant instrument of ratification or accession, unless a subsequent date has been indicated in the instrument deposited. In the latter case, Article 1 to Article 21 and the Appendix shall enter into force with respect to that country on the date thus indicated.

(d) The provisions of subparagraph (a) to subparagraph (c) do not affect the application of Article VI of the Appendix.

(3) With respect to any country of the Union which ratifies or accedes to this Act with or without a declaration made under paragraph (1)(b), Article

22 to Article 38 shall enter into force three months after the date on which the Director General has notified the deposit of the relevant instrument of ratification or accession, unless a subsequent date has been indicated in the instrument deposited. In the latter case, Article 22 to Article 38 shall enter into force with respect to that country on the date thus indicated.

Article 29
[Acceptance and Entry Into Force for Countries Outside the Union: 1. Accession; 2. Entry into force]

(1) Any country outside the Union may accede to this Act and thereby become party to this Convention and a member of the Union. Instruments of accession shall be deposited with the Director General.

(2)

(a) Subject to subparagraph (b), this Convention shall enter into force with respect to any country outside the Union three months after the date on which the Director General has notified the deposit of its instrument of accession, unless a subsequent date has been indicated in the instrument deposited. In the latter case, this Convention shall enter into force with respect to that country on the date thus indicated.

(b) If the entry into force according to subparagraph (a) precedes the entry into force of Article 1 to Article 21 and the Appendix according to Article 28(2)(a), the said country shall, in the meantime, be bound, instead of by Article 1 to Article 21 and the Appendix, by Article 1 to Article 20 of the Brussels Act of this Convention.

Article 29bis
[Effect of Acceptance of Act for the Purposes of Article 14(2) of the WIPO Convention]

Ratification of or accession to this Act by any country not bound by Article 22 to Article 38 of the Stockholm Act of this Convention shall, for the sole purposes of Article 14(2) of the Convention establishing the Organization, amount to ratification of or accession to the said Stockholm Act with the limitation set forth in Article 28(1)(b)(i) thereof.

Article 30
[Reservations: 1. Limits of possibility of making reservations; 2. Earlier reservations; reservation as to the right of translation; withdrawal of reservation]

(1) Subject to the exceptions permitted by paragraph (2) of this Article, by Article 28(1)(b), by Article 33(2), and by the Appendix, ratification or accession shall automatically entail acceptance of all the provisions and admission to all the advantages of this Convention.

(2)

(a) Any country of the Union ratifying or acceding to this Act may, subject to Article V(2) of the Appendix, retain the benefit of the reservations it has previously formulated on condition that it makes a declaration to that effect at the time of the deposit of its instrument of ratification or accession.

(b) Any country outside the Union may declare, in acceding to this Convention and subject to Article V(2) of the Appendix, that it intends to substitute, temporarily at least, for Article 8 of this Act concerning the right of translation, the provisions of Article 5 of the Union Convention of 1886, as completed at Paris in 1896, on the clear understanding that the said provisions are applicable only to translations into a language in general use in the said country. Subject to Article I(6)(b) of the Appendix, any country has the right to apply, in relation to the right of translation of works whose country of origin is a country availing itself of such a reservation, a protection which is equivalent to the protection granted by the latter country.

(c) Any country may withdraw such reservations at any time by notification addressed to the Director General.

Article 31
[*Applicability to Certain Territories:* 1. Declaration; 2. Withdrawal of declaration; 3. Effective date; 4. Acceptance of factual situations not implied]

(1) Any country may declare in its instrument of ratification or accession, or may inform the Director General by written notification at any time thereafter, that this Convention shall be applicable to all or part of those territories, designated in the declaration or notification, for the external relations of which it is responsible.

(2) Any country which has made such a declaration or given such a notification may, at any time, notify the Director General that this Convention shall cease to be applicable to all or part of such territories.

(3)

(a) Any declaration made under paragraph (1) shall take effect on the same date as the ratification or accession in which it was included, and any notification given under that paragraph shall take effect three months after its notification by the Director General.

(b) Any notification given under paragraph (2) shall take effect twelve months after its receipt by the Director General.

(4) This Article shall in no way be understood as implying the recognition or tacit acceptance by a country of the Union of the factual situation concerning a territory to which this Convention is made applicable by another country of the Union by virtue of a declaration under paragraph (1).

Article 32
[*Applicability of this Act and of Earlier Acts:* 1. As between countries already members of the Union; 2. As between a country becoming a member of the Union and other countries members of the Union; 3. Applicability of the Appendix in certain relations]

(1) This Act shall, as regards relations between the countries of the

Union, and to the extent that it applies, replace the Berne Convention of September 9, 1886, and the subsequent Acts of revision. The Acts previously in force shall continue to be applicable, in their entirety or to the extent that this Act does not replace them by virtue of the preceding sentence, in relations with countries of the Union which do not ratify or accede to this Act.

(2) Countries outside the Union which become party to this Act shall, subject to paragraph (3), apply it with respect to any country of the Union not bound by this Act or which, although bound by this Act, has made a declaration pursuant to Article 28(1)(b). Such countries recognize that the said country of the Union, in its relations with them:

(i) may apply the provisions of the most recent Act by which it is bound, and

(ii) subject to Article I(6) of the Appendix, has the right to adapt the protection to the level provided for by this Act.

(3) Any country which has availed itself of any of the faculties provided for in the Appendix may apply the provisions of the Appendix relating to the faculty or faculties of which it has availed itself in its relations with any other country of the Union which is not bound by this Act, provided that the latter country has accepted the application of the said provisions.

Article 33
[*Disputes:* 1. Jurisdiction of the International Court of Justice; 2. Reservation as to such jurisdiction; 3. Withdrawal of reservation]

(1) Any dispute between two or more countries of the Union concerning the interpretation or application of this Convention, not settled by negotiation, may, by any one of the countries concerned, be brought before the International Court of Justice by application in conformity with the Statute of the Court, unless the countries concerned agree on some other method of settlement. The country bringing the dispute before the Court shall inform the International Bureau; the International Bureau shall bring the matter to the attention of the other countries of the Union.

(2) Each country may, at the time it signs this Act or deposits its instrument of ratification or accession, declare that it does not consider itself bound by the provisions of paragraph (1). With regard to any dispute between such country and any other country of the Union, the provisions of paragraph (1) shall not apply.

(3) Any country having made a declaration in accordance with the provisions of paragraph (2) may, at any time, withdraw its declaration by notification addressed to the Director General.

Article 34
[*Closing of Certain Earlier Provisions:* 1. Of earlier Acts; 2. Of the Protocol to the Stockholm Act]

(1) Subject to Article 29*bis*, no country may ratify or accede to earlier Acts

of this Convention once Article 1 to Article 21 and the Appendix have entered into force.

(2) Once Article 1 to Article 21 and the Appendix have entered into force, no country may make a declaration under Article 5 of the Protocol Regarding Developing Countries attached to the Stockholm Act.

Article 35
[*Duration of the Convention; Denunciation:* 1. Unlimited duration; 2. Possibility of denunciation; 3. Effective date of denunciation; 4. Moratorium on denunciation]

(1) This Convention shall remain in force without limitation as to time.

(2) Any country may denounce this Act by notification addressed to the Director General. Such denunciation shall constitute also denunciation of all earlier Acts and shall affect only the country making it, the Convention remaining in full force and effect as regards the other countries of the Union.

(3) Denunciation shall take effect one year after the day on which the Director General has received the notification.

(4) The right of denunciation provided by this Article shall not be exercised by any country before the expiration of five years from the date upon which it becomes a member of the Union.

Article 36
[*Application of the Convention:* 1. Obligation to adopt the necessary measures; 2. Time from which obligation exists]

(1) Any country party to this Convention undertakes to adopt, in accordance with its constitution, the measures necessary to ensure the application of this Convention.

(2) It is understood that, at the time a country becomes bound by this Convention, it will be in a position under its domestic law to give effect to the provisions of this Convention.

Article 37
[*Final Clauses:* 1. Languages of the Act; 2. Signature; 3. Certified copies; 4. Registration; 5. Notifications]

(1)

(a) This Act shall be signed in a single copy in the French and English languages and, subject to paragraph (2), shall be deposited with the Director General.

(b) Official texts shall be established by the Director General, after consultation with the interested Governments, in the Arabic, German, Italian, Portuguese and Spanish languages, and such other languages as the Assembly may designate.

(c) In case of differences of opinion on the interpretation of the various texts, the French text shall prevail.

(2) This Act shall remain open for signature until January 31, 1972. Until that date, the copy referred to in paragraph (1)(a) shall be deposited with the Government of the French Republic.

(3) The Director General shall certify and transmit two copies of the signed text of this Act to the Governments of all countries of the Union and, on request, to the Government of any other country.

(4) The Director General shall register this Act with the Secretariat of the United Nations.

(5) The Director General shall notify the Governments of all countries of the Union of signatures, deposits of instruments of ratification or accession and any declarations included in such instruments or made pursuant to Article 28(1)(c), Article 30(2)(a) and Article 30(2)(b), and Article 33(2), entry into force of any provisions of this Act, notifications of denunciation, and notifications pursuant to Article 30(2)(c), Article 31(1) and Article 31(2), Article 33(3), and Article 38(1), as well as the Appendix.

Article 38
[*Transitory Provisions:* 1. Exercise of the "five-year privilege"; 2. Bureau of the Union, Director of the Bureau; 3. Succession of Bureau of the Union]

(1) Countries of the Union which have not ratified or acceded to this Act and which are not bound by Article 22 to Article 26 of the Stockholm Act of this Convention may, until April 26, 1975, exercise, if they so desire, the rights provided under the said Articles as if they were bound by them. Any country desiring to exercise such rights shall give written notification to this effect to the Director General; this notification shall be effective on the date of its receipt. Such countries shall be deemed to be members of the Assembly until the said date.

(2) As long as all the countries of the Union have not become Members of the Organization, the International Bureau of the Organization shall also function as the Bureau of the Union, and the Director General as the Director of the said Bureau.

(3) Once all the countries of the Union have become Members of the Organization, the rights, obligations, and property, of the Bureau of the Union shall devolve on the International Bureau of the Organization.

APPENDIX
[SPECIAL PROVISIONS REGARDING DEVELOPING COUNTRIES]

Article I
[Faculties Open to Developing Countries: 1. Availability of certain faculties; declaration: 2. Duration of effect of declaration, 3. Cessation of developing country status; 4. Existing stocks of copies; 5. Declarations concerning certain territories; 6. Limits of reciprocity]

(1) Any country regarded as a developing country in conformity with the established practice of the General Assembly of the United Nations which ratifies or accedes to this Act, of which this Appendix forms an integral part, and which, having regard to its economic situation and its social or cultural needs, does not consider itself immediately in a position to make provision for the protection of all the rights as provided for in this Act, may, by a notification deposited with the Director General at the time of depositing its instrument of ratification or accession or, subject to Article V(1)(c), at any time thereafter, declare that it will avail itself of the faculty provided for in Article II, or of the faculty provided for in Article III, or of both of those faculties. It may, instead of availing itself of the faculty provided for in Article II, make a declaration according to Article V(1)(a).

(2)

(a) Any declaration under paragraph (1) notified before the expiration of the period of ten years from the entry into force of Article 1 to Article 21 and this Appendix according to Article 28(2) shall be effective until the expiration of the said period. Any such declaration may be renewed in whole or in part for periods of ten years each by a notification deposited with the Director General not more than fifteen months and not less than three months before the expiration of the ten-year period then running.

(b) Any declaration under paragraph (1) notified after the expiration of the period of ten years from the entry into force of Article 1 to Article 21 and this Appendix according to Article 28(2) shall be effective until the expiration of the ten-year period then running. Any such declaration may be renewed as provided for in the second sentence of subparagraph (a).

(3) Any country of the Union which has ceased to be regarded as a developing country as referred to in paragraph (1) shall no longer be entitled to renew its declaration as provided in paragraph (2), and, whether or not it formally withdraws its declaration, such country shall be precluded from availing itself of the faculties referred to in paragraph (1) from the expiration of the ten-year period then running or from the expiration of a period of three years after it has ceased to be regarded as a developing country, whichever period expires later.

(4) Where, at the time when the declaration made under paragraph (1) or paragraph (2) ceases to be effective, there are copies in stock which were made under a license granted by virtue of this Appendix, such copies may

continue to be distributed until their stock is exhausted.

(5) Any country which is bound by the provisions of this Act and which has deposited a declaration or a notification in accordance with Article 31(1) with respect to the application of this Act to a particular territory, the situation of which can be regarded as analogous to that of the countries referred to in paragraph (1), may, in respect of such territory, make the declaration referred to in paragraph (1) and the notification of renewal referred to in paragraph (2). As long as such declaration or notification remains in effect, the provisions of this Appendix shall be applicable to the territory in respect of which it was made.

(6)

(a) The fact that a country avails itself of any of the faculties referred to in paragraph (1) does not permit another country to give less protection to works of which the country of origin is the former country than it is obliged to grant under Article 1 to Article 20.

(b) The right to apply reciprocal treatment provided for in Article 30(2)(b), second sentence, shall not, until the date on which the period applicable under Article I(3) expires, be exercised in respect of works the country of origin of which is a country which has made a declaration according to Article V(1)(a).

Article II
[Limitations on the Right of Translation: 1. Licenses grantable by competent authority; 2. to 4. Conditions allowing the grant of such licenses; 5. Purposes for which licenses may be granted; 6. Termination of licenses; 7. Works composed mainly of illustrations; 8. Works withdrawn from circulation; 9. Licenses for broadcasting organizations]

(1) Any country which has declared that it will avail itself of the faculty provided for in this Article shall be entitled, so far as works published in printed or analogous forms of reproduction are concerned, to substitute for the exclusive right of translation provided for in Article 8 a system of non-exclusive and non-transferable licenses, granted by the competent authority under the following conditions and subject to Article IV.

(2)

(a) Subject to paragraph (3), if, after the expiration of a period of three years, or of any longer period determined by the national legislation of the said country, commencing on the date of the first publication of the work, a translation of such work has not been published in a language in general use in that country by the owner of the right of translation, or with his authorization, any national of such country may obtain a license to make a translation of the work in the said language and publish the translation in printed or analogous forms of reproduction.

(b) A license under the conditions provided for in this Article may also be granted if all the editions of the translation published in the language concerned are out of print.

(3)

(a) In the case of translations into a language which is not in general use in one or more developed countries which are members of the Union, a period of one year shall be substituted for the period of three years referred to in paragraph (2)(a).

(b) Any country referred to in paragraph (1) may, with the unanimous agreement of the developed countries which are members of the Union and in which the same language is in general use, substitute, in the case of translations into that language, for the period of three years referred to in paragraph (2)(a) a shorter period as determined by such agreement but not less than one year. However, the provisions of the foregoing sentence shall not apply where the language in question is English, French or Spanish. The Director General shall be notified of any such agreement by the Governments which have concluded it.

(4)

(a) No license obtainable after three years shall be granted under this Article until a further period of six months has elapsed, and no license obtainable after one year shall be granted under this Article until a further period of nine months has elapsed

    (i)   from the date on which the applicant complies with the requirements mentioned in Article IV(1), or

    (ii)   where the identity or the address of the owner of the right of translation is unknown, from the date on which the applicant sends, as provided for in Article IV(2), copies of his application submitted to the authority competent to grant the license.

(b) If, during the said period of six or nine months, a translation in the language in respect of which the application was made is published by the owner of the right of translation or with his authorization, no license under this Article shall be granted.

(5) Any license under this Article shall be granted only for the purpose of teaching, scholarship or research.

(6) If a translation of a work is published by the owner of the right of translation or with his authorization at a price reasonably related to that normally charged in the country for comparable works, any license granted under this Article shall terminate if such translation is in the same language and with substantially the same content as the translation published under the license. Any copies already made before the license terminates may continue to be distributed until their stock is exhausted.

(7) For works which are composed mainly of illustrations, a license to make and publish a translation of the text and to reproduce and publish the illustrations may be granted only if the conditions of Article III are also fulfilled.

(8) No license shall be granted under this Article when the author has withdrawn from circulation all copies of his work.

(9)

(a) A license to make a translation of a work which has been published in printed or analogous forms of reproduction may also be granted to any broadcasting organization having its headquarters in a country referred to in paragraph (1), upon an application made to the competent authority of that country by the said organization, provided that all of the following conditions are met:

(i) the translation is made from a copy made and acquired in accordance with the laws of the said country;

(ii) the translation is only for use in broadcasts intended exclusively for teaching or for the dissemination of the results of specialized technical or scientific research to experts in a particular profession;

(iii) the translation is used exclusively for the purposes referred to in condition (ii) through broadcasts made lawfully and intended for recipients on the territory of the said country, including broadcasts made through the medium of sound or visual recordings lawfully and exclusively made for the purpose of such broadcasts;

(iv) all uses made of the translation are without any commercial purpose.

(b) Sound or visual recordings of a translation which was made by a broadcasting organization under a license granted by virtue of this paragraph may, for the purposes and subject to the conditions referred to in subparagraph (a) and with the agreement of that organization, also be used by any other broadcasting organization having its headquarters in the country whose competent authority granted the license in question.

(c) Provided that all of the criteria and conditions set out in subparagraph (a) are met, a license may also be granted to a broadcasting organization to translate any text incorporated in an audio-visual fixation where such fixation was itself prepared and published for the sole purpose of being used in connection with systematic instructional activities.

(d) Subject to subparagraph (a) to subparagraph (c), the provisions of the preceding paragraphs shall apply to the grant and exercise of any license granted under this paragraph.

Article III
[Limitation on the Right of Reproduction: 1. Licenses grantable by competent authority; 2. to 5. Conditions allowing the grant of such licenses; 6. Termination of licenses; 7. Works to which this Article applies]

(1) Any country which has declared that it will avail itself of the faculty provided for in this Article shall be entitled to substitute for the exclusive right of reproduction provided for in Article 9 a system of non-exclusive and non-transferable licenses, granted by the competent authority under the

following conditions and subject to Article IV.

(2)

(a) If, in relation to a work to which this Article applies by virtue of paragraph (7), after the expiration of

(i)   the relevant period specified in paragraph (3), commencing on the date of first publication of a particular edition of the work, or

(ii)   any longer period determined by national legislation of the country referred to in paragraph (1), commencing on the same date,

copies of such edition have not been distributed in that country to the general public or in connection with systematic instructional activities, by the owner of the right of reproduction or with his authorization, at a price reasonably related to that normally charged in the country for comparable works, any national of such country may obtain a license to reproduce and publish such edition at that or a lower price for use in connection with systematic instructional activities.

(b) A license to reproduce and publish an edition which has been distributed as described in subparagraph (a) may also be granted under the conditions provided for in this Article if, after the expiration of the applicable period, no authorized copies of that edition have been on sale for a period of six months in the country concerned to the general public or in connection with systematic instructional activities at a price reasonably related to that normally charged in the country for comparable works.

(3) The period referred to in paragraph (2)(a)(i) shall be five years, except that

(i)   for works of the natural and physical sciences, including mathematics, and of technology, the period shall be three years;

(ii)   for works of fiction, poetry, drama and music, and for art books, the period shall be seven years.

(4)

(a) No license obtainable after three years shall be granted under this Article until a period of six months has elapsed

(i)   from the date on which the applicant complies with the requirements mentioned in Article IV(1), or

(ii)   where the identity or the address of the owner of the right of reproduction is unknown, from the date on which the applicant sends, as provided for in Article IV(2), copies of his application submitted to the authority competent to grant the license.

(b) Where licenses are obtainable after other periods and Article IV(2) is applicable, no license shall be granted until a period of three months has elapsed from the date of the dispatch of the copies of the application.

(c) If, during the period of six or three months referred to in subparagraph (a) and subparagraph (b), a distribution as described in paragraph (2)(a) has taken place, no license shall be granted under this

Article.

(d) No license shall be granted if the author has withdrawn from circulation all copies of the edition for the reproduction and publication of which the license has been applied for.

(5) A license to reproduce and publish a translation of a work shall not be granted under this Article in the following cases:

(i) where the translation was not published by the owner of the right of translation or with his authorization, or

(ii) where the translation is not in a language in general use in the country in which the license is applied for.

(6) If copies of an edition of a work are distributed in the country referred to in paragraph (1) to the general public or in connection with systematic instructional activities, by the owner of the right of reproduction or with his authorization, at a price reasonably related to that normally charged in the country for comparable works, any license granted under this Article shall terminate if such edition is in the same language and with substantially the same content as the edition which was published under the said license. Any copies already made before the license terminates may continue to be distributed until their stock is exhausted.

(7)

(a) Subject to subparagraph (b), the works to which this Article applies shall be limited to works published in printed or analogous forms of reproduction.

(b) This Article shall also apply to the reproduction in audio-visual form of lawfully made audio-visual fixations including any protected works incorporated therein and to the translation of any incorporated text into a language in general use in the country in which the license is applied for, always provided that the audio-visual fixations in question were prepared and published for the sole purpose of being used in connection with systematic instructional activities.

Article IV
[Provisions Common to Licenses Under Articles II and III: 1 and 2. Procedure; 3. Indication of author and title of work; 4. Exportation of copies; 5. Notice; 6. Compensation]

(1) A license under Article II or Article III may be granted only if the applicant, in accordance with the procedure of the country concerned, establishes either that he has requested, and has been denied, authorization by the owner of the right to make and publish the translation or to reproduce and publish the edition, as the case may be, or that, after due diligence on his part, he was unable to find the owner of the right. At the same time as making the request, the applicant shall inform any national or international information center referred to in paragraph (2).

(2) If the owner of the right cannot be found, the applicant for a license shall send, by registered airmail, copies of his application, submitted to the

authority competent to grant the license, to the publisher whose name appears on the work and to any national or international information center which may have been designated, in a notification to that effect deposited with the Director General, by the Government of the country in which the publisher is believed to have his principal place of business.

(3) The name of the author shall be indicated on all copies of the translation or reproduction published under a license granted under Article II or Article III. The title of the work shall appear on all such copies. In the case of a translation, the original title of the work shall appear in any case on all the said copies.

(4)

(a) No license granted under Article II or Article III shall extend to the export of copies, and any such license shall be valid only for publication of the translation or of the reproduction, as the case may be, in the territory of the country in which it has been applied for.

(b) For the purposes of subparagraph (a), the notion of export shall include the sending of copies from any territory to the country which, in respect of that territory, has made a declaration under Article I(5).

(c) Where a governmental or other public entity of a country which has granted a license to make a translation under Article II into a language other than English, French or Spanish sends copies of a translation published under such license to another country, such sending of copies shall not, for the purposes of subparagraph (a), be considered to constitute export if all of the following conditions are met:

> (i) the recipients are individuals who are nationals of the country whose competent authority has granted the license, or organizations grouping such individuals;

> (ii) the copies are to be used only for the purpose of teaching, scholarship or research;

> (iii) the sending of the copies and their subsequent distribution to recipients is without any commercial purpose; and

> (iv) the country to which the copies have been sent has agreed with the country whose competent authority has granted the license to allow the receipt, or distribution, or both, and the Director General has been notified of the agreement by the Government of the country in which the license has been granted.

(5) All copies published under a license granted by virtue of Article II or Article III shall bear a notice in the appropriate language stating that the copies are available for distribution only in the country or territory to which the said license applies.

(6)

(a) Due provision shall be made at the national level to ensure

> (i) that the license provides, in favour of the owner of the right of translation or of reproduction, as the case may be, for just

compensation that is consistent with standards of royalties normally operating on licenses freely negotiated between persons in the two countries concerned, and

(ii) payment and transmittal of the compensation: should national currency regulations intervene, the competent authority shall make all efforts, by the use of international machinery, to ensure transmittal in internationally convertible currency or its equivalent.

(b) Due provision shall be made by national legislation to ensure a correct translation of the work, or an accurate reproduction of the particular edition, as the case may be.

Article V
[Alternative Possibility for Limitation of the Right of Translation: 1. Regime provided for under the 1886 and 1896 Acts; 2. No possibility of change to regime under Article II; 3. Time limit for choosing the alternative possibility]

(1)

(a) Any country entitled to make a declaration that it will avail itself of the faculty provided for in Article II may, instead, at the time of ratifying or acceding to this Act:

(i) if it is a country to which Article 30(2)(a) applies, make a declaration under that provision as far as the right of translation is concerned;

(ii) if it is a country to which Article 30(2)(a) does not apply, and even if it is not a country outside the Union, make a declaration as provided for in Article 30(2)(b), first sentence.

(b) In the case of a country which ceases to be regarded as a developing country as referred to in Article I(1), a declaration made according to this paragraph shall be effective until the date on which the period applicable under Article I(3) expires.

(c) Any country which has made a declaration according to this paragraph may not subsequently avail itself of the faculty provided for in Article II even if it withdraws the said declaration.

(2) Subject to paragraph (3), any country which has availed itself of the faculty provided for in Article II may not subsequently make a declaration according to paragraph (1).

(3) Any country which has ceased to be regarded as a developing country as referred to in Article I(1) may, not later than two years prior to the expiration of the period applicable under Article I(3), make a declaration to the effect provided for in Article 30(2)(b), first sentence, notwithstanding the fact that it is not a country outside the Union. Such declaration shall take effect at the date on which the period applicable under Article I(3) expires.

Article VI
[Possibilities of Applying, or Admitting the Application of, Certain Provisions of the Appendix Before Becoming Bound by It: 1. Declaration; 2. Depository and effective date of declaration]

(1) Any country of the Union may declare, as from the date of this Act, and at any time before becoming bound by Article 1 to Article 21 and this Appendix:

    (i) if it is a country which, were it bound by Article 1 to Article 21 and this Appendix, would be entitled to avail itself of the faculties referred to in Article I(1), that it will apply the provisions of Article II or of Article III or of both to works whose country of origin is a country which, pursuant to (ii) below, admits the application of those Articles to such works, or which is bound by Article 1 to Article 21 and this Appendix; such declaration may, instead of referring to Article II, refer to Article V;

    (ii) that it admits the application of this Appendix to works of which it is the country of origin by countries which have made a declaration under (i) above or a notification under Article I.

(2) Any declaration made under paragraph (1) shall be in writing and shall be deposited with the Director General. The declaration shall become effective from the date of its deposit.

UNIVERSAL COPYRIGHT CONVENTION
Done at Geneva, September 6, 1952, and revised at Paris, July 24, 1971

The Contracting States,

Moved by the desire to ensure in all countries copyright protection of literary, scientific and artistic works,

Convinced that a system of copyright protection appropriate to all nations of the world and expressed in a universal convention, additional to, and without impairing international systems already in force, will ensure respect for the rights of the individual and encourage the development of literature, the sciences and the arts,

Persuaded that such a universal copyright system will facilitate a wider dissemination of works of the human mind and increase international understanding,

Have resolved to revise the Universal Copyright Convention as signed at Geneva on 6 September 1952 (hereinafter called "the 1952 Convention"), and consequently,

Have agreed as follows:

Article I

Each Contracting State undertakes to provide for the adequate and effective protection of the rights of authors and other copyright proprietors in literary, scientific and artistic works, including writings, musical, dramatic and cinematographic works, and paintings, engravings and sculpture.

Article II

1. Published works of nationals of any Contracting State and works first published in that State shall enjoy in each other Contracting State the same protection as that other State accords to works of its nationals first published in its own territory, as well as the protection specially granted by this Convention.

2. Unpublished works of nationals of each Contracting State shall enjoy in each other Contracting State the same protection as that other State accords to unpublished works of its own nationals, as well as the protection specially granted by this Convention.

3. For the purposed of this Convention any Contracting State may, by domestic legislation, assimilate to its own nationals any person domiciled in that State.

Article III

1. Any Contracting State which, under its domestic law, requires as a condition of copyright, compliance with formalities such as deposit,

registration, notice notarial certificates, payment of fees or manufacture or publication in that Contracting State, shall regard these requirements as satisfied with respect to all works protected in accordance with this Convention and first published outside its territory and the author of which is not one of its nationals, if from the time of the first publication all the copies of the work published with the authority of the author or other copyright proprietor bear the symbol of a lower case "c" inside of a circle accompanied by the name of the copyright proprietor and the year of first publication placed in such manner and location as to give reasonable notice of claim of copyright.

2. The provisions of paragraph 1 shall not preclude any Contracting State from requiring formalities or other conditions for the acquisition and enjoyment of copyright in respect of works first published in its territory or works of its nationals wherever published.

3. The provisions of paragraph 1 shall not preclude any Contracting State from providing that a person seeking judicial relief must, in bringing the action, comply with procedural requirements, such as that the complainant must appear through domestic counsel or that the complainant must deposit with the court or an administrative office, or both, a copy of the work involved in the litigation; provided that failure to comply with such requirements shall not affect the validity of the copyright, nor shall any such requirement be imposed upon a national of another Contracting State if such requirement is not imposed on nationals of the State in which protection is claimed.

4. In each Contracting State there shall be legal means of protecting without formalities the unpublished work of nationals of other Contracting States.

5. If a Contracting State grants protection for more than one term of copyright and the first term is for a period longer than one of the minimum periods prescribed in Article IV, such State shall not be required to comply with the provisions of paragraph 1 of this Article in respect of the second or any subsequent term of copyright.

Article IV

1. The duration of protection of a work shall be governed, in accordance with the provisions of Article II and this Article, by the law of the Contracting State in which protection is claimed.

2. (a) The term of protection for works protected under this Convention shall not be less that the life of the author and twenty-five years after his death. However, any Contracting State which, on the effective date of this Convention in that State, has limited this term for certain classes of works to a period computed from this first publication of the work, shall be entitled to maintain these exceptions and to extend them to other classes of works. For all these classes the term of protection shall not be less than twenty-five years from the date of first publication.

(b) Any Contracting State which, upon the effective date of this Convention in that State, does not compute the term of protection upon the basis of the life of the author, shall be entitled to compute the term of protection from the date of the first publication of the work or from its registration prior to publication, as the case may be, provided the term of protection shall not be less than twenty-five years from the date of first publication or from its registration prior to publication, as the case may be.

(c) If the legislation of a Contracting State grants two or more successive terms of protection, the duration of the first term shall not be less than one of the minimum periods specified in subparagraphs (a) and (b).

3. The provisions of paragraph 2 shall not apply to photographic works or to works of applied art; provided, however, that the term of protection in those Contracting States which protect photographic works, or works of applied art in so far as they are protected as artistic works, shall not be less than ten years for each of said classes of works.

4. (a) No Contracting State shall be obliged to grant protection to a work for a period longer than that fixed for the class of works to which the work in question belongs, in the case of unpublished works by the law of the Contracting State of which the author is a national, and in the case of published works by the law of the Contracting State in which the work has been first published.

(b) For the purposes of the application of subparagraph (a), if the law of any Contracting State grants two or more successive terms of protection, the period of protection of that State shall be considered to be the aggregate of those terms. However, if a specified work is not protected by such State during the second or any subsequent term for any reason, the other Contracting States shall not be obliged to protect it during the second or any subsequent term.

5. For the purposes of the application of paragraph 4, the work of a national of a Contracting State, first published in a non-Contracting State, shall be treated as though first published in the Contracting State of which the author is a national.

6. For the purposes of the application of paragraph 4, in case of simultaneous publication in two or more Contracting States, the work shall be treated as though first published in the State which affords the shortest term; any work published in two or more Contracting States within thirty days of its first publication shall be considered as having been published simultaneously in said Contracting States.

Article IVbis

1. The rights referred to in Article I shall include the basic rights ensuring the author's economic interests, including the exclusive right to authorize reproduction by any means, public performance and broadcasting. The provisions of this Article shall extend to works protected under this Convention either in their original form or in any form recognizably derived

from the original.

2. However, any Contracting State may, by its domestic legislation, make exceptions that do not conflict with the spirit and provisions of this Convention, to the rights mentioned in paragraph 1 of this Article. Any State whose legislation so provides, shall nevertheless accord a reasonable degree of effective protection to each of the rights to which exception has been made.

Article V

1. The rights referred to in Article I shall include the exclusive right of the author to make, publish and authorize the making and publication of translations of works protected under this Convention.

2. However, any Contracting State may, by its domestic legislation, restrict the right of translation of writings, but only subject to the following provisions:

(a) If, after the expiration of a period of seven years from the date of the first publication of a writing, a translation of such writing has not been published in a language in general use in the Contracting State, by the owner of the right of translation or with his authorization, any national of such Contracting State may obtain a non-exclusive licence from the competent authority thereof to translate the work into that language and publish the work so translated.

(b) Such national shall in accordance with the procedure of the State concerned, establish either that he has requested, and been denied, authorization by the proprietor of the right to make and publish the translation, or that, after due diligence on his part, he was unable to find the owner of the right. A licence may also be granted on the same conditions if all previous editions of a translation in a language in general use in the Contracting State are out of print.

(c) If the owner of the right of translation cannot be found, then the applicant for a licence shall send copies of his application to the publisher whose name appears on the work and, if the nationality of the owner of the right of translation is known, to the diplomatic or consular representative of the State of which such owner is a national, or to the organization which may have been designated by the government of that State. The licence shall not be granted before the expiration of a period of two months from the date of the dispatch of the copies of the application.

(d) Due provision shall be made by domestic legislation to ensure to the owner of the right of translation a compensation which is just and conforms to international standards, to ensure payment and transmittal of such compensation, and to ensure a correct translation of the work.

(e) The original title and the name of the author of the work shall be printed on all copies of the published translation. The licence shall be valid only for publication of the translation in the territory of the Contracting State where it has been applied for. Copies so published may be imported and sold in another Contracting State if a language in general use in such other State is the same language as that into which the work has been so translated, and if the domestic law in such other State makes provision for such licenses and does not prohibit such importation and sale. Where the foregoing conditions do not exist, the importation and sale of such copies in a Contracting State shall be governed by its domestic law and its agreements. The licence shall not be transferred by the licensee.

(f) The licence shall not be granted when the author has withdrawn from circulation all copies of the work.

Article V*bis*

1. Any Contracting State regarded as a developing country in conformity with the established practice of the General Assembly of the United Nations may, by a notification deposited with the Director-General of the United Nations Educational, Scientific and Cultural Organization (hereinafter called "the Director-General") at the time of its ratification, acceptance or accession or thereafter, avail itself of any or all of the exceptions provided for in Articles V*ter* and V*quater*.

2. Any such notification shall be effective for ten years from the date of coming into force of this Convention, or for such part of that ten-year period as remains at the date of deposit of the notification, and may be renewed in whole or in part for further periods of ten years each if, not more than fifteen or less than three months before the expiration of the relevant ten-year period, the contracting State deposits a further notification with the Director-General. Initial notifications may also be made during these further periods of ten years in accordance with the provisions of this Article.

3. Notwithstanding the provisions of paragraph 2, a Contracting State that has ceased to be regarded as a developing country as referred to in paragraph 1 shall no longer be entitled to renew its notification made under the provisions of paragraph 1 or 2, and whether or not it formally withdraws the notification such State shall be precluded from availing itself of the exceptions provided for in Articles V*ter* and V*quater* at the end of the current ten-year period, or at the end of three years after it has ceased to be regarded as a developing country, whichever period expires later.

4. Any copies of a work already made under the exceptions provided for in Articles V*ter* and V*quater* may continue to be distributed after the expiration of the period for which notifications under this Article were effective until their stock is exhausted.

5. Any Contracting State that has deposited a notification in accordance with Article XIII with respect to the application of this Convention to a particular country or territory, the situation of which can be regarded as analogous to that of the States referred to in paragraph 1 of this Article, may also deposit notifications and renew them in accordance with the provisions of this Article with respect to any such country or territory. During the effective period of such notifications, the provisions of Articles V*ter* and V*quater* may be applied with respect to such country or territory. The sending of copies from the country or territory to the Contracting State shall

be considered as export within the meaning of Articles V*ter* and V*quater*.

Article V*ter*

1. (a) Any Contracting State to which Article V*bis*(1) applies may substitute for the period of seven years provided for in Article V(2) a period of three years or any longer period prescribed by its legislation. However, in the case of a translation into a language not in general use in one or more developed countries that are party to this Convention or only the 1952 Convention, the period shall be one year instead of three.

(b) A Contracting State to which Article V*bis*(1) applies may, with the unanimous agreement of the developed countries party to this Convention or only the 1952 Convention and in which the same language is in general use, substitute, in the case of translation into that language, for the period of three years provided for in sub-paragraph (a) another period as determined be such agreement but not shorter than one year. However, this sub-paragraph shall not apply where the language in question is English, French or Spanish. Notification of any such agreement shall be made to the Director-General.

(c) The licence may only be granted if the applicant, in accordance with the procedure of the State concerned, establishes either that he has requested, and been denied, authorization by the owner of the right of translation, or that, after due diligence on his part, he was unable to find the owner of the right. At the same time as he makes his request he shall inform either the International Copyright Information Centre established by the United Nations Educational, Scientific and Cultural Organization or any national or regional information centre which may have been designated in a notification to that effect deposited with the Director-General by the government of the State in which the publisher is believed to have his principal place of business.

(d) If the owner of the right of translation cannot be found, the applicant for a licence shall send, by registered airmail, copies of his application to the publisher whose name appears on the work and to any national or regional information centre as mentioned in sub-paragraph (c). If no such centre is notified he shall also send a copy to the international copyright information centre established by the United Nations Educational, Scientific and Cultural Organization.

2. (a) Licenses obtainable after three years shall not be granted under this Article until a further period of six months has elapsed and licenses obtainable after one year until a further period of nine months has elapsed. The further period shall begin either from the date of the request for permission to translate mentioned in paragraph 1(c) or, if the identity or address of the owner of the right of translation is not known, from the date of dispatch of the copies of the application for a licence mentioned in paragraph 1(d).

(b) Licenses shall not be granted if a translation has been published by the owner of the right of translation or with his authorization during the said period of six or nine months.

3. Any licence under this Article shall be granted only for the purpose of teaching, scholarship or research.

4. (a) Any licence granted under this Article shall not extend to the export of copies and shall be valid only for publication in the territory of the Contracting State where it has been applied for.

(b) Any copy published in accordance with a licence granted under this Article shall bear a notice in the appropriate language stating that the copy is available for distribution only in the Contracting State Granting the licence. If the writing bears the notice specified in Article III (1) the copies shall bear the same notice.

(c) The prohibition of export provided for in sub-paragraph (a) shall not apply where a governmental or other public entity of a State which has granted a licence under this Article to translate a work into a language other than English, French or Spanish sends copies of a translation prepared under such licence to another country if:

(i)   the recipients are individuals who are nationals of the Contracting State granting the licence, or organizations grouping such individuals;

(ii)   the copies are to be used only for the purpose of teaching, scholarship or research;

(iii)   the sending of the copies and their subsequent distribution to recipients is without the object of commercial purpose; and

(iv)   the country to which the copies have been sent has agreed with the Contracting State to allow the receipt, distribution or both and the Director-General has been notified of such agreement by any one of the governments which have concluded it.

5. Due provision shall be made at the national level to ensure:

(a) that the licence provides for just compensation that is consistent with standards of royalties normally operating in the case of licenses freely negotiated between persons in the two countries concerned; and

(b) payment and transmittal of the compensation; however, should national currency regulations intervene, the competent authority shall make all efforts, by the use of international machinery, to ensure transmittal in internationally convertible currency or its equivalent.

6. Any licence granted by a Contracting State under this Article shall terminate if a translation of the work in the same language with substantially the same content as the edition in respect of which the licence was granted is published in the said State by the owner of the right of translation or with his authorization, at a price reasonably related to that normally charged in the same State for comparable works. Any copies already made before the licence is terminated may continue to be distributed until their stock is exhausted.

7. For works which are composed mainly of illustrations a licence to

translate the text and to reproduce the illustrations may be granted only if the conditions of Article V*quater* are also fulfilled.

8. (a) A licence to translate a work protected under this Convention, published in printed or analogous forms of reproduction, may also be granted to a broadcasting organization having its headquarters in a Contracting State to which Article V*bis* (1) applies, upon an application made in that State by the said organization under the following conditions:

(i) the translation is made from a copy made and acquired in accordance with the laws of the Contracting State;

(ii) the translation is for use only in broadcasts intended exclusively for teaching or for the dissemination of the results of specialized technical or scientific research to experts in a particular profession;

(iii) the translation is used exclusively for the purposes set out in condition (ii), through broadcasts lawfully made which are intended for recipients on the territory of the Contracting State, including broadcasts made through the medium of sound or visual recordings lawfully and exclusively made for the purpose of such broadcasts;

(iv) sound or visual recordings of the translation may be exchanged only between broadcasting organizations having their headquarters in the Contracting State granting the licence; and

(v) all uses made of the translation are without any commercial purpose.

(b) Provided all of the criteria and conditions set out in subparagraph (a) are met, a licence may also be granted to a broadcasting organization to translate any text incorporated in an audio-visual fixation which was itself prepared and published for the sole purpose of being used in connexion with systematic instructional activities.

(c) Subject to sub-paragraphs (a) and (b), the other provisions of this Article shall apply to the grant and exercise of the licence.

9. Subject to the provisions of this Article, any licence granted under this Article shall be governed by the provisions of Article V, and shall continue to be governed by the provisions of Article V and of this Article, even after the seven-year period provided for in Article V(2) has expired. However, after the said period has expired, the licensee shall be free to request that the said licence be replaced by a new licence governed exclusively by the provisions of Article V.

Article V*quater*

1. Any Contracting State to which Article V*bis*(1) applies may adopt the following provisions:

(a) If, after the expiration of (i) the relevant period specified in sub-paragraph (c) commencing from the date of first publication of a particular edition of a literary, scientific or artistic work referred to in paragraph 3, or (ii) any longer period determined by national legislation of the State, copies of such edition have not been distributed in that State to the general public or in connexion with systematic instructional activities at a price reasonably related to that normally charged in the State for comparable works, by the owner of the right of reproduction or with his authorization, any national of such State may obtain a non-exclusive licence from the competent authority to publish such edition at that or a lower price for use in connexion with systematic instructional activities. The licence may only be granted if such national, in accordance with the procedure of the State concerned, established either that he has requested, and been denied, authorization by the proprietor of the right to publish such work, or that, after due diligence on his part, he was unable to find the owner of the right. At the same time as he makes his request he shall inform either the international copyright information centre established by the United Nations Educational, Scientific and Cultural Organization or any national or regional information centre referred to in sub-paragraph (d).

(b) A licence may also be granted on the same conditions if, for a period of six months, no authorized copies of the edition in question have been on sale in the State concerned to the general public or in connexion with systematic instructional activities at a price reasonably related to that normally charged in the State for comparable works.

(c) The period referred to in sub-paragraph (a) shall be five years except that:

(i)   for works of the natural and physical sciences, including mathematics, and of technology, the period shall be three years;

(ii) for works of fiction, poetry, drama and music, and for art books, the period shall be seven years.

(d) If the owner of the right of reproduction cannot be found, the applicant for a licence shall send, by registered air mail, copies of his application to the publisher whose name appears on the work and to any national or regional information centre identified as such in a notification deposited with the Director-General by the State in which the publisher is believed to have his principal place of business. In the absence of any such notification, he shall also send a copy to the international copyright information centre established by the United Nations Education, Scientific and Cultural Organization. The licence shall not be granted before the expiration of a period of three months from the date of dispatch of the copies of the application.

(e) Licenses obtainable after three years shall not be granted under this Article:

(i)   until a period of six months has elapsed from the date of the request for permission referred to in sub-paragraph (a) or, if the identity or address of the owner of the right of reproduction is unknown, from the date of the dispatch of the copies of the application for a licence referred to in sub-paragraph (d);

(ii) if any such distribution of copies of the edition as is mentioned in sub-paragraph (a) has taken place during that period.

(f) The name of the author and the title of the particular edition of the work shall be printed on all copies of the published reproduction. The licence shall not extend to the export of copies and shall be valid only for publication in the territory of the Contracting State where it has been applied for. The licence shall not be transferable by the licensee.

(g) Due provision shall be made by domestic legislation to ensure an accurate reproduction of the particular edition in question.

(h) A licence to reproduce and publish a translation of a work shall not be granted under this Article in the following cases:

    (i)   where the translation was not published by the owner of the right of translation or with his authorization;

    (ii)   where the translation is not in a language in general use in the State with power to grant the licence.

2. The exceptions provided for in paragraph 1 are subject to the following additional provisions:

(a) Any copy published in accordance with a licence granted under this Article shall bear a notice in the appropriate language stating that the copy is available for distribution only in the Contracting State to which the said licence applies. If the edition bears the notice specified in Article III(1), the copies shall bear the same notice.

(b) Due provision shall be made at the national level to ensure:

    (i)   that the licence provides for just compensation that is consistent with standards of royalties normally operating in the case licenses freely negotiated between persons in the two countries concerned; and

    (ii)   payment and transmittal of the compensation; however, should national currency regulations intervene, the competent authority shall make all efforts, by the use of international machinery, to ensure transmittal in internationally convertible currency or its equivalent.

(c) Whenever copies of an edition of a work are distributed in the Contracting State to the general public or in connexion with systematic instructional activities, by the owner of the right of reproduction or with his authorization, at a price reasonably related to that normally charged in the State for comparable works, any licence granted under this Article shall terminate if such edition is in the same language and is substantially the same in content as the edition published under the licence. Any copies already made before the licence is terminated may continue to be distributed until their stock is exhausted.

(d) No licence shall be granted when the author has withdrawn from circulation all copies of the edition in question.

3. (a) Subject to sub-paragraph (b), the literary, scientific or artistic works to which this Article applies shall be limited to works published in printed

or analogous forms of reproduction.

(b) The provisions of this Article shall also apply to reproduction in audio-visual form of lawfully made audio-visual fixations including any protected works incorporated therein and to the translation of any incorporated text into a language in general use in the State with power to grant the licence; always provided that the audio-visual fixations in question were prepared and published for the sole purpose of being used in connexion with systematic instructional activities.

Article VI

"Publication", as used in this Convention, means the reproduction in tangible form and the general distribution to the public of copies of a work from which it can be read or otherwise visually perceived.

Article VII

This Convention shall not apply to works or rights in works which, at the effective date of this Convention in a Contracting State where protection is claimed, are permanently in the public domain in the said Contracting State.

Article VIII

1. This Convention, which shall bear the date of 24 July 1971, shall be deposited with the Director-General and shall remain open for signature by all States party to the 1952 Convention for a period of 120 days after the date of this Convention. It shall be subject to ratification or acceptance by the signatory States.

2. Any State which has not signed this Convention may accede thereto.

3. Ratification, acceptance or accession shall be effected by the deposit of an instrument to that effect with the Director-General.

Article IX

1. This Convention shall come into force three months after the deposit of twelve instruments of ratification, acceptance or accession.

2. Subsequently, this Convention shall come into force in respect of each State three months after that State has deposited its instrument of ratification, acceptance or accession.

3. Accession to this Convention by a State not party to the 1952 Convention shall also constitute accession to that Convention; however, if its instrument of accession is deposited before this Convention comes into force, such State may make its accession to the 1952 Convention conditional upon the coming into force of this Convention. After the coming into force of this Convention, no State may accede solely to the 1952 Convention.

4. Relations between States party to this Convention and States that are party only to the 1952 Convention, shall be governed by the 1952

Convention. However, any State party only to the 1952 Convention may, by a notification deposited with the Director-General, declare that it will admit the application of the 1971 Convention to works of its nationals or works first published in its territory by all States party to this Convention.

Article X

1. Each Contracting State undertakes to adopt, in accordance with its Constitution, such measures as are necessary to ensure the application of this Convention.

2. It is understood that at the date this Convention comes into force in respect of any State, that State must be in a position under its domestic law to give effect to the terms of this Convention.

Article XI

1. An Intergovernmental Committee is hereby established with the following duties:

(a) to study the problems concerning the application and operation of the Universal Copyright Convention;

(b) to make preparation for periodic revisions of this Convention;

(c) to study any other problems concerning the international protection of copyright, in co-operation with the various interested international organizations, such as the United Nations Educational, Scientific and Cultural Organization, the International Union for the Protection of Literary and Artistic Works and the Organization of American States;

(d) to inform States party to the Universal Copyright Convention as to its activities.

2. The Committee shall consist of the representatives of eighteen States party to this Convention or only to the 1952 Convention.

3. The Committee shall be selected with due consideration to a fair balance of national interests on the basis of geographical location, population, languages and stage of development.

4. The Director-General of the United Nations Educational, Scientific and Cultural Organization, the Director-General of the World Intellectual Property Organization and the Secretary-General of the Organization of American States, or their representatives, may attend meetings of the Committee in an advisory capacity.

Article XII

The Intergovernmental Committee shall convene a conference for revision whenever it deems necessary, or at the request of at least ten States party to this Convention.

Article XIII

1. Any Contracting State may, at the time of deposit of its instrument of ratification, acceptance or accession, or at any time thereafter, declare by notification addressed to the Director-General that this Convention shall apply to all or any of the countries or territories for the international relations of which it is responsible and this Convention shall thereupon apply to the countries or territories named in such notification after the expiration of the term of three months provided for in Article IX. In the absence of such notification, this Convention shall not apply to any such country or territory.

2. However, nothing in this Article shall be understood as implying the recognition or tacit acceptance by a Contracting State of the factual situation concerning a country or territory to which this Convention is made applicable by another Contracting State in accordance with the provisions of this Article.

Article XIV

1. Any Contracting State may denounce this Convention in its own name or on behalf of all or any of the countries or territories with respect to which a notification has been given under Article XIII. The denunciation shall be made by notification addressed to the Director-General. Such denunciation shall also constitute denunciation of the 1952 Convention.

2. Such denunciation shall operate only in respect of the State or of the country or territory on whose behalf it was made and shall not take effect until twelve months after the date of receipt of the notification.

Article XV

A dispute between two or more Contracting States concerning the interpretation or application of this Convention, not settled by negotiation, shall, unless the States concerned agree on some other method of settlement, be brought before the International Court of Justice for determination by it.

Article XVI

1. This Convention shall be established in English, French, and Spanish. The three texts shall be signed and shall be equally authoritative.

2. Official texts of this Convention shall be established by the Director-General, after consultation with the governments concerned, in Arabic, German, Italian, and Portuguese.

3. Any Contracting State or group of Contracting States shall be entitled to have established by the Director-General other texts in the language of its choice by arrangement with the Director-General.

4. All such texts shall be annexed to the signed texts of this Convention.

Article XVII

1. This Convention shall not in any way affect the provisions of the Berne

Convention for the Protection of Literary and Artistic Works or membership in the Union created by that Convention.

2. In application of the foregoing paragraph, a declaration has been annexed to the present Article. This declaration is an integral part of this Convention for the States bound by the Berne Convention on 1 January 1951, or which have or may become bound to it at a later date. The signature of this Convention by such States shall also constitute signature of the said declaration, and ratification, acceptance or accession by such States shall include the declaration, as well as this Convention.

Article XVIII

This Convention shall not abrogate multilateral or bilateral copyright conventions or arrangements that are or may be in effect exclusively between two or more American Republics. In the event of any difference either between the provisions of such existing conventions or arrangements and the provisions of this Convention, or between the provisions of this Convention and those of any new convention or arrangement which may be formulated between two or more American Republics after this Convention comes into force, the convention or arrangement most recently formulated shall prevail between the parties thereto. Rights in works acquired in any Contracting State under existing conventions or arrangements before the date this Convention comes into force in such State shall not be affected.

Article XIX

This Convention shall not abrogate multilateral or bilateral conventions or arrangements in effect between two or more Contracting States. In the event of any difference between the provisions of such existing conventions or arrangements and the provisions of this Convention, the provisions of this Convention shall prevail. Rights in works acquired in any Contracting State under existing conventions or arrangements before the date on which this Convention comes into force in such State shall not be affected. Nothing in this Article shall affect the provisions of Articles XVII and XVIII.

Article XX

Reservations to this Convention shall not be permitted.

Article XXI

1. The Director-General shall send duly certified copies of this Convention to the States interested and to the Secretary-General of the United Nations for registration by him.

2. He shall also inform all interested States of the ratifications, acceptances, accessions which have been deposited, the date on which this Convention comes into force, the notifications under this Convention and denunciations under Article XIV.

Appendix Declaration relating to Article XVII

The States which are members of the International Union for the Protection of Literary and Artistic Works (hereinafter called "the Berne Union") and which are signatories of this Convention,

Desiring to reinforce their mutual relations on the basis of the said Union and to avoid any conflict which might result from the coexistence of the Berne Convention and the Universal Copyright Convention,

Recognizing the temporary need of some States to adjust their level of copyright protection in accordance with their stage of cultural, social and economic development,

Have, by common agreement, accepted the terms of the following declaration:

(a) Except as provided by paragraph (b), works which, according to the Berne Convention, have as their country of origin a country which has withdrawn from the Berne Union after 1 January 1951, shall not be protected by the Universal Copyright Convention in the countries of the Berne Union;

(b) Where a Contracting State is regarded as a developing country in conformity with the established practice of the General Assembly of the United Nations, and has deposited with the Director-General of the United Nations Educational, Scientific and Cultural Organization, at the time of its withdrawal from the Berne Union, a notification to the effect that it regards itself as a developing country, the provisions of paragraph (a) shall not be applicable as long as such State may avail itself of the exceptions provided for by this Convention in accordance with Article V*bis*;

(c) The Universal Copyright Convention shall not be applicable to the relationships among countries of the Berne Union in so far as it relates to the protection of works having as their country of origin, within the meaning of the Berne Convention, a country of the Berne Union.

Resolution Concerning Article XI

The Conference for Revision of the Universal Copyright Convention,

Having considered the problems relating to the Intergovernmental Committee provided for in Article XI of this Convention, to which this resolution is annexed,

Resolves that:

1. At its inception, the Committee shall include representative of the twelve States members of the Intergovernmental Committee established under Article XI of the 1952 Convention and the resolution annexed to it, and, in addition, representatives of the following States: Algeria, Australia, Japan, Mexico, Senegal and Yugoslavia.

2. Any States that are not party to the 1952 Convention and have not acceded to this Convention before the first ordinary session of the Committee

following the entry into force of this Convention shall be replaced by other States to be selected by the Committee at its first ordinary session in conformity with the provisions of Article XI (2) and (3).

3. As soon as this Convention comes into force the Committee as provided for in paragraph 1 shall be deemed to be constituted in accordance with Article XI of this Convention.

4. A session of the Committee shall take place with one year after the coming into force of this Convention; thereafter the Committee shall meet in ordinary session at intervals of not more than two years.

5. The Committee shall elect its Chairman and two Vice-Chairmen. It shall establish its Rules of Procedure having regard to the following principles:

(a) The normal duration of the term of office of the members represented on the Committee shall be six years with one-third retiring every two years, it being however understood that, of the original terms of office, one-third shall expire at the end of the Committee's second ordinary session which will follow the entry into force of this Convention, a further third at the end of its third ordinary session, and the remaining third at the end of its fourth ordinary session.

(b) The rules governing the procedure whereby the Committee shall fill vacancies, the order in which terms of membership expire, eligibility for reelection, and election procedures, shall be based upon a balancing of the needs for continuity of membership and rotation of representation, as well as the considerations set out in Article XI (3).

Expresses the wish that the United Nations Educational, Scientific and Cultural Organization provide its Secretariat.

In faith whereof the undersigned, having deposited their respective full powers, have signed this Convention.

DONE at Paris, this twenty-fourth day of July 1971, in a single copy.

PROTOCOL 1

Annexed to the Universal Copyright Convention as revised at Paris on 24 July 1971 concerning the application of that Convention to works of Stateless persons and refugees

The States party hereto, being also party to the Universal Copyright Convention as revised at Paris on 24 July 1971 (hereinafter called "the 1971 Convention"),

Have accepted the following provisions:

1. Stateless persons and refugees who have their habitual residence in a State party to this Protocol shall, for the purposes of the 1971 Convention, be assimilated to the nationals of that State.

2. (a) This Protocol shall be signed and shall be subject to ratification or acceptance, or may be acceded to, as if the provisions of Article VIII of the 1971 Convention applied hereto.

(b) This Protocol shall enter into force in respect of each State, on the date of deposit of the instrument of ratification, acceptance or accession of the State concerned or on the date of entry into force of the 1971 Convention with respect to such State, whichever is the later.

(c) On the entry into force of this Protocol in respect of a State not party to Protocol 1 annexed to the 1952 Convention, the latter Protocol shall be deemed to enter into force in respect of such State.

In faith whereof the undersigned, being duly authorized thereto, have signed this Protocol.

Done at Paris this twenty-fourth day of July 1971, in the English, French and Spanish languages, the three texts being equally authoritative, in a single copy which shall be deposited with the Director-General of the United Nations Educational, Scientific and Cultural Organization. The Director-General shall send certified copies to the signatory States, and to the Secretary-General of the United Nations for registration.

PROTOCOL 2
Annexed to the Universal Copyright convention as revised at Paris on 24 July 1971 concerning the application of that Convention to the works of certain international organizations

The States party hereto, being also party to the Universal Copyright Convention as revised at Paris on 24 July 1971 (hereinafter called "the 1971 Convention"),

Have accepted the following provisions:

1. (a) The protection provided for in Article II (1) of the 1971 Convention shall apply to works published for the first time by the United Nations by the Specialized Agencies in relationship therewith, or by the Organization of American States.

(b) Similarly, Article II (2) of the 1971 Convention shall apply to the said organization or agencies.

2. (a) This Protocol shall be signed and shall be subject to ratification or acceptance, or may be acceded to, as if the provisions of Article VIII of the 1971 Convention applied hereto.

(b) This Protocol shall enter into force for each State on the date of deposit of the instrument of ratification, acceptance or accession of the State concerned or on the date of entry into force of the 1971 Convention with respect to such State, whichever is the later.

In faith whereof the undersigned, being duly authorized thereto, have signed this Protocol.

Done at Paris, this twenty-fourth day of July 1971, in the English, French and Spanish languages, the three texts being equally authoritative, in a single copy which shall be deposited with the Director-General of the United Nations Educational, Scientific and Cultural Organization. The Director-General shall send certified copies to the signatory States, and to the

Secretary-General of the United Nations for registration.

WIPO COPYRIGHT TREATY
Done at Geneva, December 20, 1996

Preamble

The Contracting Parties,

Desiring to develop and maintain the protection of the rights of authors in their literary and artistic works in a manner as effective and uniform as possible,

Recognizing the need to introduce new international rules and clarify the interpretation of certain existing rules in order to provide adequate solutions to the questions raised by new economic, social, cultural and technological developments,

Recognizing the profound impact of the development and convergence of information and communication technologies on the creation and use of literary and artistic works,

Emphasizing the outstanding significance of copyright protection as an incentive for literary and artistic creation,

Recognizing the need to maintain a balance between the rights of authors and the larger public interest, particularly education, research and access to information, as reflected in the Berne Convention,

Have agreed as follows:

Article 1
Relation to the Berne Convention

(1) This Treaty is a special agreement within the meaning of Article 20 of the Berne Convention for the Protection of Literary and Artistic Works, as regards Contracting Parties that are countries of the Union established by that Convention. This Treaty shall not have any connection with treaties other than the Berne Convention, nor shall it prejudice any rights and obligations under any other treaties.

(2) Nothing in this Treaty shall derogate from existing obligations that Contracting Parties have to each other under the Berne Convention for the Protection of Literary and Artistic Works.

(3) Hereinafter, "Berne Convention" shall refer to the Paris Act of July 24, 1971 of the Berne Convention for the Protection of Literary and Artistic Works.

(4) Contracting Parties shall comply with Articles 1 to 21 and the Appendix of the Berne Convention. [See the agreed statement concerning Article 1(4).]

Article 2
Scope of Copyright Protection

Copyright protection extends to expressions and not to ideas, procedures, methods of operation or mathematical concepts as such.

Article 3
Application of Articles 2 to 6 of the Berne Convention

Contracting Parties shall apply *mutatis mutandis* the provisions of Articles 2 to 6 of the Berne Convention in respect of the protection provided for in this Treaty. [See the agreed statement concerning Article 3.]

Article 4
Computer Programs

Computer programs are protected as literary works within the meaning of Article 2 of the Berne Convention. Such protection applies to computer programs, whatever may be the mode or form of their expression. [See the agreed statement concerning Article 4.]

Article 5
Compilations of Data (Databases)

Compilations of data or other material, in any form, which by reason of the selection or arrangement of their contents constitute intellectual creations, are protected as such. This protection does not extend to the data or the material itself and is without prejudice to any copyright subsisting in the data or material contained in the compilation. [See the agreed statement concerning Article 5.]

Article 6
Right of Distribution

(1) Authors of literary and artistic works shall enjoy the exclusive right of authorizing the making available to the public of the original and copies of their works through sale or other transfer of ownership.

(2) Nothing in this Treaty shall affect the freedom of Contracting Parties to determine the conditions, if any, under which the exhaustion of the right in paragraph (1) applies after the first sale or other transfer of ownership of the original or a copy of the work with the authorization of the author. [See the agreed statement concerning Articles 6 and 7.]

Article 7
Right of Rental

(1) Authors of

(i)   computer programs;

(ii) cinematographic works; and

(iii) works embodied in phonograms, as determined in the national law of Contracting Parties, shall enjoy the exclusive right of authorizing commercial rental to the public of the originals or copies of their works.

(2) Paragraph (1) shall not apply

(i) in the case of computer programs, where the program itself is not the essential object of the rental; and

(ii) in the case of cinematographic works, unless such commercial rental has led to widespread copying of such works materially impairing the exclusive right of reproduction.

(3) Notwithstanding the provisions of paragraph (1), a Contracting Party that, on April 15, 1994, had and continues to have in force a system of equitable remuneration of authors for the rental of copies of their works embodied in phonograms may maintain that system provided that the commercial rental of works embodied in phonograms is not giving rise to the material impairment of the exclusive right of reproduction of authors. [See the agreed statement concerning Articles 6 and 7, and the agreed statement concerning Article 7.]

Article 8
Right of Communication to the Public

Without prejudice to the provisions of Articles 11(1)(ii), 11*bis*(1)(i) and (ii), 11*ter*(1)(ii), 14(1)(ii) and 14*bis*(1) of the Berne Convention, authors of literary and artistic works shall enjoy the exclusive right of authorizing any communication to the public of their works, by wire or wireless means, including the making available to the public of their works in such a way that members of the public may access these works from a place and at a time individually chosen by them. [See the agreed statement concerning Article 8.]

Article 9
Duration of the Protection of Photographic Works

In respect of photographic works, the Contracting Parties shall not apply the provisions of Article 7(4) of the Berne Convention.

Article 10
Limitations and Exceptions

(1) Contracting Parties may, in their national legislation, provide for limitations of or exceptions to the rights granted to authors of literary and artistic works under this Treaty in certain special cases that do not conflict with a normal exploitation of the work and do not unreasonably prejudice the legitimate interests of the author.

(2) Contracting Parties shall, when applying the Berne Convention, confine any limitations of or exceptions to rights provided for therein to certain special cases that do not conflict with a normal exploitation of the work and do not unreasonably prejudice the legitimate interests of the author. [See the agreed statement concerning Article 10.]

Article 11
Obligations concerning Technological Measures

Contracting Parties shall provide adequate legal protection and effective legal remedies against the circumvention of effective technological measures that are used by authors in connection with the exercise of their rights under this Treaty or the Berne Convention and that restrict acts, in respect of their works, which are not authorized by the authors concerned or permitted by law.

Article 12
Obligations concerning Rights Management Information

(1)   Contracting Parties shall provide adequate and effective legal remedies against any person knowingly performing any of the following acts knowing, or with respect to civil remedies having reasonable grounds to know, that it will induce, enable, facilitate or conceal an infringement of any right covered by this Treaty or the Berne Convention:

(i) to remove or alter any electronic rights management information without authority;

(ii) to distribute, import for distribution, broadcast or communicate to the public, without authority, works or copies of works knowing that electronic rights management information has been removed or altered without authority.

(2) As used in this Article, "rights management information" means information which identifies the work, the author of the work, the owner of any right in the work, or information about the terms and conditions of use of the work, and any numbers or codes that represent such information, when any of these items of information is attached to a copy of a work or appears in connection with the communication of a work to the public. [See the agreed statement concerning Article 12.]

Article 13
Application in Time

Contracting Parties shall apply the provisions of Article 18 of the Berne Convention to all protection provided for in this Treaty.

Article 14
Provisions on Enforcement of Rights

(1) Contracting Parties undertake to adopt, in accordance with their legal systems, the measures necessary to ensure the application of this Treaty.

(2) Contracting Parties shall ensure that enforcement procedures are available under their law so as to permit effective action against any act of infringement of rights covered by this Treaty, including expeditious remedies to prevent infringements and remedies which constitute a deterrent to further infringements.

Article 15
Assembly

(1)

(a) The Contracting Parties shall have an Assembly.

(b) Each Contracting Party shall be represented by one delegate who may be assisted by alternate delegates, advisors and experts.

(c) The expenses of each delegation shall be borne by the Contracting Party that has appointed the delegation. The Assembly may ask the World Intellectual Property Organization (hereinafter referred to as "WIPO") to grant financial assistance to facilitate the participation of delegations of Contracting Parties that are regarded as developing countries in conformity with the established practice of the General Assembly of the United Nations or that are countries in transition to a market economy.

(2)

(a) The Assembly shall deal with matters concerning the maintenance and development of this Treaty and the application and operation of this Treaty.

(b) The Assembly shall perform the function allocated to it under Article 17(2) in respect of the admission of certain intergovernmental organizations to become party to this Treaty.

(c) The Assembly shall decide the convocation of any diplomatic conference for the revision of this Treaty and give the necessary instructions to the Director General of WIPO for the preparation of such diplomatic conference.

(3)

(a) Each Contracting Party that is a State shall have one vote and shall vote only in its own name.

(b) Any Contracting Party that is an intergovernmental organization may participate in the vote, in place of its Member States, with a number of votes equal to the number of its Member States which are party to this Treaty. No such intergovernmental organization shall participate in the vote if any one of its Member States exercises its right to vote and *vice versa*.

(4) The Assembly shall meet in ordinary session once every two years upon convocation by the Director General of WIPO.

(5) The Assembly shall establish its own rules of procedure, including the convocation of extraordinary sessions, the requirements of a quorum and, subject to the provisions of this Treaty, the required majority for various kinds of decisions.

Article 16
International Bureau

The International Bureau of WIPO shall perform the administrative tasks concerning the Treaty.

Article 17
Eligibility for Becoming Party to the Treaty

(1) Any Member State of WIPO may become party to this Treaty.

(2) The Assembly may decide to admit any intergovernmental organization to become party to this Treaty which declares that it is competent in respect of, and has its own legislation binding on all its Member States on, matters covered by this Treaty and that it has been duly authorized, in accordance with its internal procedures, to become party to this Treaty.

(3) The European Community, having made the declaration referred to in the preceding paragraph in the Diplomatic Conference that has adopted this Treaty, may become party to this Treaty.

Article 18
Rights and Obligations under the Treaty

Subject to any specific provisions to the contrary in this Treaty, each Contracting Party shall enjoy all of the rights and assume all of the obligations under this Treaty.

Article 19
Signature of the Treaty

This Treaty shall be open for signature until December 31, 1997, by any Member State of WIPO and by the European Community.

Article 20
Entry into Force of the Treaty

This Treaty shall enter into force three months after 30 instruments of ratification or accession by States have been deposited with the Director General of WIPO.

Article 21
Effective Date of Becoming Party to the Treaty

This Treaty shall bind

(i)   the 30 States referred to in Article 20, from the date on which this Treaty has entered into force;

(ii) each other State from the expiration of three months from the date on which the State has deposited its instrument with the Director General of WIPO;

(iii) the European Community, from the expiration of three months after the deposit of its instrument of ratification or accession if such instrument has been deposited after the entry into force of this Treaty according to Article 20, or, three months after the entry into force of this Treaty if such instrument has been deposited before the entry into force of this Treaty;

(iv)   any other intergovernmental organization that is admitted to become party to this Treaty, from the expiration of three months after the deposit of its instrument of accession.

Article 22
No Reservations to the Treaty

No reservation to this Treaty shall be admitted.

Article 23
Denunciation of the Treaty

This Treaty may be denounced by any Contracting Party by notification addressed to the Director General of WIPO. Any denunciation shall take effect one year from the date on which the Director General of WIPO received the notification.

Article 24
Languages of the Treaty

(1) This Treaty is signed in a single original in English, Arabic, Chinese, French, Russian and Spanish languages, the versions in all these languages being equally authentic.

(2)   An official text in any language other than those referred to in paragraph (1) shall be established by the Director General of WIPO on the request of an interested party, after consultation with all the interested parties. For the purposes of this paragraph, "interested party" means any Member State of WIPO whose official language, or one of whose official languages, is involved and the European Community, and any other intergovernmental organization that may become party to this Treaty, if one of its official languages is involved.

Article 25
Depositary

The Director General of WIPO is the depositary of this Treaty.

AGREED STATEMENTS CONCERNING THE WIPO COPYRIGHT TREATY
adopted by the Diplomatic Conference on December 20, 1996

Concerning Article 1(4)

The reproduction right, as set out in Article 9 of the Berne Convention, and the exceptions permitted thereunder, fully apply in the digital environment, in particular to the use of works in digital form. It is understood that the storage of a protected work in digital form in an electronic medium constitutes a reproduction within the meaning of Article 9 of the Berne Convention.

Concerning Article 3

It is understood that in applying Article 3 of this Treaty, the expression "country of the Union" in Articles 2 to 6 of the Berne Convention will be read as if it were a reference to a Contracting Party to this Treaty, in the application of those Berne Articles in respect of protection provided for in this Treaty. It is also understood that the expression "country outside the Union" in those Articles in the Berne Convention will, in the same circumstances, be read as if it were a reference to a country that is not a Contracting Party to this Treaty, and that "this Convention" in Articles 2(8), 2*bis*(2), 3, 4 and 5 of the Berne Convention will be read as if it were a reference to the Berne Convention and this Treaty. Finally, it is understood that a reference in Articles 3 to 6 of the Berne Convention to a "national of one of the countries of the Union" will, when these Articles are applied to this Treaty, mean, in regard to an intergovernmental organization that is a Contracting Party to this Treaty, a national of one of the countries that is member of that organization.

Concerning Article 4

The scope of protection for computer programs under Article 4 of this Treaty, read with Article 2, is consistent with Article 2 of the Berne Convention and on a par with the relevant provisions of the TRIPS Agreement.

Concerning Article 5

The scope of protection for compilations of data (databases) under Article 5 of this Treaty, read with Article 2, is consistent with Article 2 of the Berne Convention and on a par with the relevant provisions of the TRIPS Agreement.

Concerning Articles 6 and 7

As used in these Articles, the expressions "copies" and "original and copies," being subject to the right of distribution and the right of rental under the said Articles, refer exclusively to fixed copies that can be put into circulation as tangible objects.

Concerning Article 7

It is understood that the obligation under Article 7(1) does not require a Contracting Party to provide an exclusive right of commercial rental to authors who, under that Contracting Party"s law, are not granted rights in respect of phonograms. It is understood that this obligation is consistent with Article 14(4) of the TRIPS Agreement.

Concerning Article 8

It is understood that the mere provision of physical facilities for enabling or making a communication does not in itself amount to communication within the meaning of this Treaty or the Berne Convention. It is further understood that nothing in Article 8 precludes a Contracting Party from applying Article 11*bis*(2).

Concerning Article 10

It is understood that the provisions of Article 10 permit Contracting Parties to carry forward and appropriately extend into the digital environment limitations and exceptions in their national laws which have been considered acceptable under the Berne Convention. Similarly, these provisions should be understood to permit Contracting Parties to devise new exceptions and limitations that are appropriate in the digital network environment.

It is also understood that Article 10(2) neither reduces nor extends the scope of applicability of the limitations and exceptions permitted by the Berne Convention.

Concerning Article 12

It is understood that the reference to "infringement of any right covered by this Treaty or the Berne Convention" includes both exclusive rights and rights of remuneration.

It is further understood that Contracting Parties will not rely on this Article to devise or implement rights management systems that would have the effect of imposing formalities which are not permitted under the Berne Convention or this Treaty, prohibiting the free movement of goods or impeding the enjoyment of rights under this Treaty.

WIPO PERFORMANCES AND PHONOGRAMS TREATY
Done at Geneva, December 20, 1996

Preamble

The Contracting Parties,

Desiring to develop and maintain the protection of the rights of performers and producers of phonograms in a manner as effective and uniform as possible,

Recognizing the need to introduce new international rules in order to provide adequate solutions to the questions raised by economic, social, cultural and technological developments,

Recognizing the profound impact of the development and convergence of information and communication technologies on the production and use of performances and phonograms,

Recognizing the need to maintain a balance between the rights of performers and producers of phonograms and the larger public interest, particularly education, research and access to information,

Have agreed as follows:

CHAPTER I
GENERAL PROVISIONS

Article 1
Relation to Other Conventions

(1) Nothing in this Treaty shall derogate from existing obligations that Contracting Parties have to each other under the International Convention for the Protection of Performers, Producers of Phonograms and Broadcasting Organizations done in Rome, October 26, 1961 (hereinafter the "Rome Convention").

(2) Protection granted under this Treaty shall leave intact and shall in no way affect the protection of copyright in literary and artistic works. Consequently, no provision of this Treaty may be interpreted as prejudicing such protection.

(3) This Treaty shall not have any connection with, nor shall it prejudice any rights and obligations under, any other treaties.

Article 2
Definitions

For the purposes of this Treaty:

(a) "performers" are actors, singers, musicians, dancers, and other persons who act, sing, deliver, declaim, play in, interpret, or otherwise perform literary or artistic works or expressions of folklore;

(b) "phonogram" means the fixation of the sounds of a performance or of other sounds, or of a representation of sounds, other than in the form of a fixation incorporated in a cinematographic or other audiovisual work;

(c) "fixation" means the embodiment of sounds, or of the representations thereof, from which they can be perceived, reproduced or communicated through a device;

(d) "producer of a phonogram" means the person, or the legal entity, who or which takes the initiative and has the responsibility for the first fixation of the sounds of a performance or other sounds, or the representations of sounds;

(e) "publication" of a fixed performance or a phonogram means the offering of copies of the fixed performance or the phonogram to the public, with the consent of the rightholder, and provided that copies are offered to the public in reasonable quantity;

(f) "broadcasting" means the transmission by wireless means for public reception of sounds or of images and sounds or of the representations thereof; such transmission by satellite is also ""broadcasting""; transmission of encrypted signals is ""broadcasting"" where the means for decrypting are provided to the public by the broadcasting organization or with its consent;

(g) "communication to the public" of a performance or a phonogram means the transmission to the public by any medium, otherwise than by broadcasting, of sounds of a performance or the sounds or the representations of sounds fixed in a phonogram. For the purposes of Article 15, "communication to the public" includes making the sounds or representations of sounds fixed in a phonogram audible to the public.

Article 3
Beneficiaries of Protection under this Treaty

(1) Contracting Parties shall accord the protection provided under this Treaty to the performers and producers of phonograms who are nationals of other Contracting Parties.

(2) The nationals of other Contracting Parties shall be understood to be those performers or producers of phonograms who would meet the criteria for eligibility for protection provided under the Rome Convention, were all the Contracting Parties to this Treaty Contracting States of that Convention. In respect of these criteria of eligibility, Contracting Parties shall apply the relevant definitions in Article 2 of this Treaty.

(3) Any Contracting Party availing itself of the possibilities provided in Article 5(3) of the Rome Convention or, for the purposes of Article 5 of the same Convention, Article 17 thereof shall make a notification as foreseen in those provisions to the Director General of the World Intellectual Property Organization (WIPO).

Article 4
National Treatment

(1) Each Contracting Party shall accord to nationals of other Contracting

Parties, as defined in Article 3(2), the treatment it accords to its own nationals with regard to the exclusive rights specifically granted in this Treaty, and to the right to equitable remuneration provided for in Article 15 of this Treaty.

(2) The obligation provided for in paragraph (1) does not apply to the extent that another Contracting Party makes use of the reservations permitted by Article 15(3) of this Treaty.

CHAPTER II
RIGHTS OF PERFORMERS

Article 5
Moral Rights of Performers

(1) Independently of a performer's economic rights, and even after the transfer of those rights, the performer shall, as regards his live aural performances or performances fixed in phonograms, have the right to claim to be identified as the performer of his performances, except where omission is dictated by the manner of the use of the performance, and to object to any distortion, mutilation or other modification of his performances that would be prejudicial to his reputation.

(2) The rights granted to a performer in accordance with paragraph (1) shall, after his death, be maintained, at least until the expiry of the economic rights, and shall be exercisable by the persons or institutions authorized by the legislation of the Contracting Party where protection is claimed. However, those Contracting Parties whose legislation, at the moment of their ratification of or accession to this Treaty, does not provide for protection after the death of the performer of all rights set out in the preceding paragraph may provide that some of these rights will, after his death, cease to be maintained.

(3) The means of redress for safeguarding the rights granted under this Article shall be governed by the legislation of the Contracting Party where protection is claimed.

Article 6
Economic Rights of Performers in their Unfixed Performances

Performers shall enjoy the exclusive right of authorizing, as regards their performances:

(i) the broadcasting and communication to the public of their unfixed performances except where the performance is already a broadcast performance; and

(ii) the fixation of their unfixed performances.

Article 7
Right of Reproduction

Performers shall enjoy the exclusive right of authorizing the direct or indirect reproduction of their performances fixed in phonograms, in any manner or form.

Article 8
Right of Distribution

(1) Performers shall enjoy the exclusive right of authorizing the making available to the public of the original and copies of their performances fixed in phonograms through sale or other transfer of ownership.

(2) Nothing in this Treaty shall affect the freedom of Contracting Parties to determine the conditions, if any, under which the exhaustion of the right in paragraph (1) applies after the first sale or other transfer of ownership of the original or a copy of the fixed performance with the authorization of the performer.

Article 9
Right of Rental

(1) Performers shall enjoy the exclusive right of authorizing the commercial rental to the public of the original and copies of their performances fixed in phonograms as determined in the national law of Contracting Parties, even after distribution of them by, or pursuant to, authorization by the performer.

(2) Notwithstanding the provisions of paragraph (1), a Contracting Party that, on April 15, 1994, had and continues to have in force a system of equitable remuneration of performers for the rental of copies of their performances fixed in phonograms, may maintain that system provided that the commercial rental of phonograms is not giving rise to the material impairment of the exclusive right of reproduction of performers.

Article 10
Right of Making Available of Fixed Performances

Performers shall enjoy the exclusive right of authorizing the making available to the public of their performances fixed in phonograms, by wire or wireless means, in such a way that members of the public may access them from a place and at a time individually chosen by them.

CHAPTER III
RIGHTS OF PRODUCERS OF PHONOGRAMS

Article 11
Right of Reproduction

Producers of phonograms shall enjoy the exclusive right of authorizing the direct or indirect reproduction of their phonograms, in any manner or form.

Article 12
Right of Distribution

(1) Producers of phonograms shall enjoy the exclusive right of authorizing the making available to the public of the original and copies of their phonograms through sale or other transfer of ownership.

(2) Nothing in this Treaty shall affect the freedom of Contracting Parties to determine the conditions, if any, under which the exhaustion of the right in paragraph (1) applies after the first sale or other transfer of ownership of the original or a copy of the phonogram with the authorization of the producer of the phonogram.

Article 13
Right of Rental

(1) Producers of phonograms shall enjoy the exclusive right of authorizing the commercial rental to the public of the original and copies of their phonograms, even after distribution of them by or pursuant to authorization by the producer.

(2) Notwithstanding the provisions of paragraph (1), a Contracting Party that, on April 15, 1994, had and continues to have in force a system of equitable remuneration of producers of phonograms for the rental of copies of their phonograms, may maintain that system provided that the commercial rental of phonograms is not giving rise to the material impairment of the exclusive rights of reproduction of producers of phonograms.

Article 14
Right of Making Available of Phonograms

Producers of phonograms shall enjoy the exclusive right of authorizing the making available to the public of their phonograms, by wire or wireless means, in such a way that members of the public may access them from a place and at a time individually chosen by them.

CHAPTER IV
COMMON PROVISIONS

Article 15
Right to Remuneration for Broadcasting and Communication to the Public

(1) Performers and producers of phonograms shall enjoy the right to a single equitable remuneration for the direct or indirect use of phonograms published for commercial purposes for broadcasting or for any communication to the public.

(2) Contracting Parties may establish in their national legislation that the single equitable remuneration shall be claimed from the user by the performer or by the producer of a phonogram or by both. Contracting Parties

may enact national legislation that, in the absence of an agreement between the performer and the producer of a phonogram, sets the terms according to which performers and producers of phonograms shall share the single equitable remuneration.

(3) Any Contracting Party may in a notification deposited with the Director General of WIPO, declare that it will apply the provisions of paragraph (1) only in respect of certain uses, or that it will limit their application in some other way, or that it will not apply these provisions at all.

(4) For the purposes of this Article, phonograms made available to the public by wire or wireless means in such a way that members of the public may access them from a place and at a time individually chosen by them shall be considered as if they had been published for commercial purposes.

Article 16
Limitations and Exceptions

(1) Contracting Parties may, in their national legislation, provide for the same kinds of limitations or exceptions with regard to the protection of performers and producers of phonograms as they provide for, in their national legislation, in connection with the protection of copyright in literary and artistic works.

(2) Contracting Parties shall confine any limitations of or exceptions to rights provided for in this Treaty to certain special cases which do not conflict with a normal exploitation of the performance or phonogram and do not unreasonably prejudice the legitimate interests of the performer or of the producer of the phonogram.

Article 17
Term of Protection

(1) The term of protection to be granted to performers under this Treaty shall last, at least, until the end of a period of 50 years computed from the end of the year in which the performance was fixed in a phonogram.

(2) The term of protection to be granted to producers of phonograms under this Treaty shall last, at least, until the end of a period of 50 years computed from the end of the year in which the phonogram was published, or failing such publication within 50 years from fixation of the phonogram, 50 years from the end of the year in which the fixation was made.

Article 18
Obligations concerning Technological Measures

Contracting Parties shall provide adequate legal protection and effective legal remedies against the circumvention of effective technological measures that are used by performers or producers of phonograms in connection with the exercise of their rights under this Treaty and that restrict acts, in respect of their performances or phonograms, which are not authorized by the performers or the producers of phonograms concerned or permitted by law.

Article 19
Obligations concerning Rights Management Information

(1) Contracting Parties shall provide adequate and effective legal remedies against any person knowingly performing any of the following acts knowing, or with respect to civil remedies having reasonable grounds to know, that it will induce, enable, facilitate or conceal an infringement of any right covered by this Treaty:

    (i) to remove or alter any electronic rights management information without authority;

    (ii) to distribute, import for distribution, broadcast, communicate or make available to the public, without authority, performances, copies of fixed performances or phonograms knowing that electronic rights management information has been removed or altered without authority.

(2) As used in this Article, "rights management information" means information which identifies the performer, the performance of the performer, the producer of the phonogram, the phonogram, the owner of any right in the performance or phonogram, or information about the terms and conditions of use of the performance or phonogram, and any numbers or codes that represent such information, when any of these items of information is attached to a copy of a fixed performance or a phonogram or appears in connection with the communication or making available of a fixed performance or a phonogram to the public.

Article 20
Formalities

The enjoyment and exercise of the rights provided for in this Treaty shall not be subject to any formality.

Article 21
Reservations

Subject to the provisions of Article 15(3), no reservations to this Treaty shall be permitted.

Article 22
Application in Time

(1) Contracting Parties shall apply the provisions of Article 18 of the Berne Convention, *mutatis mutandis*, to the rights of performers and producers of phonograms provided for in this Treaty.

(2) Notwithstanding paragraph (1), a Contracting Party may limit the application of Article 5 of this Treaty to performances which occurred after the entry into force of this Treaty for that Party.

Article 23
Provisions on Enforcement of Rights

(1) Contracting Parties undertake to adopt, in accordance with their legal systems, the measures necessary to ensure the application of this Treaty.

(2) Contracting Parties shall ensure that enforcement procedures are available under their law so as to permit effective action against any act of infringement of rights covered by this Treaty, including expeditious remedies to prevent infringements and remedies which constitute a deterrent to further infringements.

CHAPTER V
ADMINISTRATIVE AND FINAL CLAUSES

Article 24
Assembly

(1)

(a) The Contracting Parties shall have an Assembly.

(b) Each Contracting Party shall be represented by one delegate who may be assisted by alternate delegates, advisors and experts.

(c) The expenses of each delegation shall be borne by the Contracting Party that has appointed the delegation. The Assembly may ask WIPO to grant financial assistance to facilitate the participation of delegations of Contracting Parties that are regarded as developing countries in conformity with the established practice of the General Assembly of the United Nations or that are countries in transition to a market economy.

(2)

(a) The Assembly shall deal with matters concerning the maintenance and development of this Treaty and the application and operation of this Treaty.

(b) The Assembly shall perform the function allocated to it under Article 26(2) in respect of the admission of certain intergovernmental organizations to become party to this Treaty.

(c) The Assembly shall decide the convocation of any diplomatic conference for the revision of this Treaty and give the necessary instructions to the Director General of WIPO for the preparation of such diplomatic conference.

(3)

(a) Each Contracting Party that is a State shall have one vote and shall vote only in its own name.

(b) Any Contracting Party that is an intergovernmental organization may participate in the vote, in place of its Member States, with a number of votes equal to the number of its Member States which are party to this Treaty. No such intergovernmental organization shall participate in the vote if any one of its Member States exercises its right to vote and vice versa.

(4) The Assembly shall meet in ordinary session once every two years upon convocation by the Director General of WIPO.

(5) The Assembly shall establish its own rules of procedure, including the convocation of extraordinary sessions, the requirements of a quorum and, subject to the provisions of this Treaty, the required majority for various kinds of decisions.

Article 25
International Bureau

The International Bureau of WIPO shall perform the administrative tasks concerning the Treaty.

Article 26
Eligibility for Becoming Party to the Treaty

(1) Any Member State of WIPO may become party to this Treaty.

(2) The Assembly may decide to admit any intergovernmental organization to become party to this Treaty which declares that it is competent in respect of, and has its own legislation binding on all its Member States on, matters covered by this Treaty and that it has been duly authorized, in accordance with its internal procedures, to become party to this Treaty.

(3) The European Community, having made the declaration referred to in the preceding paragraph in the Diplomatic Conference that has adopted this Treaty, may become party to this Treaty.

Article 27
Rights and Obligations under the Treaty

Subject to any specific provisions to the contrary in this Treaty, each Contracting Party shall enjoy all of the rights and assume all of the obligations under this Treaty.

Article 28
Signature of the Treaty

This Treaty shall be open for signature until December 31, 1997, by any Member State of WIPO and by the European Community.

Article 29
Entry into Force of the Treaty

This Treaty shall enter into force three months after 30 instruments of ratification or accession by States have been deposited with the Director General of WIPO.

Article 30
Effective Date of Becoming Party to the Treaty

This Treaty shall bind

(i)   the 30 States referred to in Article 29, from the date on which this Treaty has entered into force;

(ii)   each other State from the expiration of three months from the date on which the State has deposited its instrument with the Director General of WIPO;

(iii)   the European Community, from the expiration of three months after the deposit of its instrument of ratification or accession if such instrument has been deposited after the entry into force of this Treaty according to Article 29, or, three months after the entry into force of this Treaty if such instrument has been deposited before the entry into force of this Treaty;

(iv)   any other intergovernmental organization that is admitted to become party to this Treaty, from the expiration of three months after the deposit of its instrument of accession.

Article 31
Denunciation of the Treaty

This Treaty may be denounced by any Contracting Party by notification addressed to the Director General of WIPO. Any denunciation shall take effect one year from the date on which the Director General of WIPO received the notification.

Article 32
Languages of the Treaty

(1) This Treaty is signed in a single original in English, Arabic, Chinese, French, Russian and Spanish languages, the versions in all these languages being equally authentic.

(2) An official text in any language other than those referred to in paragraph (1) shall be established by the Director General of WIPO on the request of an interested party, after consultation with all the interested parties. For the purposes of this paragraph, ""interested party"" means any Member State of WIPO whose official language, or one of whose official languages, is involved and the European Community, and any other intergovernmental organization that may become party to this Treaty, if one of its official languages is involved.

Article 33
Depositary

The Director General of WIPO is the depositary of this Treaty.

AGREED STATEMENTS
Adopted at the Diplomatic Conference, December 20, 1996

Concerning Article 1

It is understood that Article 1(2) clarifies the relationship between rights in phonograms under this Treaty and copyright in works embodied in the phonograms. In cases where authorization is needed from both the author of a work embodied in the phonogram and a performer or producer owning rights in the phonogram, the need for the authorization of the author does not cease to exist because the authorization of the performer or producer is also required, and vice versa.

It is further understood that nothing in Article 1(2) precludes a Contracting Party from providing exclusive rights to a performer or producer of phonograms beyond those required to be provided under this Treaty.

Concerning Article 2(b)

It is understood that the definition of phonogram provided in Article 2(b) does not suggest that rights in the phonogram are in any way affected through their incorporation into a cinematographic or other audiovisual work.

Concerning Articles 2(e), 8, 9, 12, and 13

As used in these Articles, the expressions "copies" and "original and copies," being subject to the right of distribution and the right of rental under the said Articles, refer exclusively to fixed copies that can be put into circulation as tangible objects.

Concerning Article 3

It is understood that the reference in Articles 5(a) and 16(a)(iv) of the Rome Convention to "national of another Contracting State" will, when applied to this Treaty, mean, in regard to an intergovernmental organization that is a Contracting Party to this Treaty, a national of one of the countries that is a member of that organization.

Concerning Article 3(2)

For the application of Article 3(2), it is understood that fixation means the finalization of the master tape ("bande-mère").

Concerning Articles 7, 11 and 16

The reproduction right, as set out in Articles 7 and 11, and the exceptions permitted thereunder through Article 16, fully apply in the digital environment, in particular to the use of performances and phonograms in digital form. It is understood that the storage of a protected performance or phonogram in digital form in an electronic medium constitutes a reproduction within the meaning of these Articles.

Concerning Article 15

It is understood that Article 15 does not represent a complete resolution of the level of rights of broadcasting and communication to the public that should be enjoyed by performers and phonogram producers in the digital age. Delegations were unable to achieve consensus on differing proposals for aspects of exclusivity to be provided in certain circumstances or for rights to be provided without the possibility of reservations, and have therefore left the issue to future resolution.

Concerning Article 15

It is understood that Article 15 does not prevent the granting of the right conferred by this Article to performers of folklore and producers of phonograms recording folklore where such phonograms have not been published for commercial gain.

Concerning Article 16

The agreed statement concerning Article 10 (on Limitations and Exceptions) of the WIPO Copyright Treaty is applicable *mutatis mutandis* also to Article 16 (on Limitations and Exceptions) of the WIPO Performances and Phonograms Treaty.

Concerning Article 19

The agreed statement concerning Article 12 (on Obligations concerning Rights Management Information) of the WIPO Copyright Treaty is applicable *mutatis mutandis* also to Article 19 (on Obligations concerning Rights Management Information) of the WIPO Performances and Phonograms Treaty.

INTERNATIONAL CONVENTION FOR THE PROTECTION OF PERFORMERS, PRODUCERS OF PHONOGRAMS AND BROADCASTING ORGANISATIONS

Done at Rome on October 26, 1961

The Contracting States, moved by the desire to protect the rights of performers, producers of phonograms, and broadcasting organisations,

Have agreed as follows:

Article 1
[Safeguard of Copyright Proper]*

Protection granted under this Convention shall leave intact and shall in no way affect the protection of copyright in literary and artistic works. Consequently, no provision of this Convention may be interpreted as prejudicing such protection.

Article 2
[Protection given by the Convention. Definition of National Treatment]

1.   For the purposes of this Convention, national treatment shall mean the treatment accorded by the domestic law of the Contracting State in which protection is claimed:

(a) to performers who are its nationals, as regards performances taking place, broadcast, or first fixed, on its territory;

(b) to producers of phonograms who are its nationals, as regards phonograms first fixed or first published on its territory;

(c) to broadcasting organisations which have their headquarters on its territory, as regards broadcasts transmitted from transmitters situated on its territory.

2.   National treatment shall be subject to the protection specifically guaranteed, and the limitations specifically provided for, in this Convention.

Article 3
[Definitions: (a) Performers; (b) Phonogram; (c) Producers of Phonograms; (d) Publication; (e) Reproduction; (f) Broadcasting; (g) Rebroadcasting]

For the purposes of this Convention:

(a) "performers" means actors, singers, musicians, dancers, and other persons who act, sing, deliver, declaim, play in, or otherwise perform literary or artistic works;

---

* Articles have been given titles by WIPO to facilitate their identification. There are no titles in the signed text.

(b) "phonogram" means any exclusively aural fixation of sounds of a performance or of other sounds;

(c) "producer of phonograms" means the person who, or the legal entity which, first fixes the sounds of a performance or other sounds;

(d) "publication" means the offering of copies of a phonogram to the public in reasonable quantity;

(e) "reproduction" means the making of a copy or copies of a fixation;

(f) "broadcasting" means the transmission by wireless means for public reception of sounds or of images and sounds;

(g) "rebroadcasting" means the simultaneous broadcasting by one broadcasting organisation of the broadcast of another broadcasting organisation.

Article 4
[Performances Protected. Points of Attachment for Performers]

Each Contracting State shall grant national treatment to performers if any of the following conditions is met:

(a) the performance takes place in another Contracting State;

(b) the performance is incorporated in a phonogram which is protected under Article 5 of this Convention;

(c) the performance, not being fixed on a phonogram, is carried by a broadcast which is protected by Article 6 of this Convention.

Article 5
[Protected Phonograms: 1. Points of Attachment for Producers of Phonograms; 2. Simultaneous Publication; 3. Power to exclude certain Criteria]

1. Each Contracting State shall grant national treatment to producers of phonograms if any of the following conditions is met:

(a) the producer of the phonogram is a national of another Contracting State (criterion of nationality);

(b) the first fixation of the sound was made in another Contracting State (criterion of fixation);

(c) the phonogram was first published in another Contracting State (criterion of publication).

2. If a phonogram was first published in a non-contracting State but if it was also published, within thirty days of its first publication, in a Contracting State (simultaneous publication), it shall be considered as first published in the Contracting State.

3. By means of a notification deposited with the Secretary-General of the United Nations, any Contracting State may declare that it will not apply the criterion of publication or, alternatively, the criterion of fixation. Such notification may be deposited at the time of ratification, acceptance or

accession, or at any time thereafter; in the last case, it shall become effective six months after it has been deposited.

Article 6
[Protected Broadcasts: 1. Points of Attachment for Broadcasting Organizations; 2. Power to Reserve]

1. Each Contracting State shall grant national treatment to broadcasting organisations if either of the following conditions is met:

(a) the headquarters of the broadcasting organisation is situated in another Contracting State;

(b) the broadcast was transmitted from a transmitter situated in another Contracting State.

2. By means of a notification deposited with the Secretary-General of the United Nations, any Contracting State may declare that it will protect broadcasts only if the headquarters of the broadcasting organisation is situated in another Contracting State and the broadcast was transmitted from a transmitter situated in the same Contracting State. Such notification may be deposited at the time of ratification, acceptance or accession, or at any time thereafter; in the last case, it shall become effective six months after it has been deposited.

Article 7
[Minimum Protection for Performers: 1. Particular Rights; 2. Relations between Performers and Broadcasting Organizations]

1.   The protection provided for performers by this Convention shall include the possibility of preventing:

(a)   the broadcasting and the communication to the public, without their consent, of their performance, except where the performance used in the broadcasting or the public communication is itself already a broadcast performance or is made from a fixation;

(b)   the fixation, without their consent, of their unfixed performance;

(c)   the reproduction, without their consent, of a fixation of their performance:

(i)   if the original fixation itself was made without their consent;

(ii)   if the reproduction is made for purposes different from those for which the performers gave their consent;

(iii) if the original fixation was made in accordance with the provisions of Article 15, and the reproduction is made for purposes different from those referred to in those provisions.

2.

(1) If broadcasting was consented to by the performers, it shall be a matter for the domestic law of the Contracting State where protection is claimed to regulate the protection against rebroadcasting, fixation for broadcasting purposes and the reproduction of such fixation for broadcasting

purposes.

(2) The terms and conditions governing the use by broadcasting organisations of fixations made for broadcasting purposes shall be determined in accordance with the domestic law of the Contracting State where protection is claimed.

(3) However, the domestic law referred to in sub-paragraphs (1) and (2) of this paragraph shall not operate to deprive performers of the ability to control, by contract, their relations with broadcasting organisations.

Article 8
[Performers acting jointly]

Any Contracting State may, by its domestic laws and regulations, specify the manner in which performers will be represented in connexion with the exercise of their rights if several of them participate in the same performance.

Article 9
[Variety and Circus Artists]

Any Contracting State may, by its domestic laws and regulations, extend the protection provided for in this Convention to artists who do not perform literary or artistic works.

Article 10
[Right of Reproduction for Phonogram Producers]

Producers of phonograms shall enjoy the right to authorise or prohibit the direct or indirect reproduction of their phonograms.

Article 11
[Formalities for Phonograms]

If, as a condition of protecting the rights of producers of phonograms, or of performers, or both, in relation to phonograms, a Contracting State, under its domestic law, requires compliance with formalities, these shall be considered as fulfilled if all the copies in commerce of the published phonogram or their containers bear a notice consisting of the symbol (P), accompanied by the year date of the first publication, placed in such a manner as to give reasonable notice of claim of protection; and if the copies or their containers do not identify the producer or the licensee of the producer (by carrying his name, trade mark or other appropriate designation), the notice shall also include the name of the owner of the rights of the producer; and, furthermore, if the copies or their containers do not identify the principal performers, the notice shall also include the name of the person who, in the country in which the fixation was effected, owns the rights of such performers.

Article 12
[Secondary Uses of Phonograms]

If a phonogram published for commercial purposes, or a reproduction of such phonogram, is used directly for broadcasting or for any communication to the public, a single equitable remuneration shall be paid by the user to the performers, or to the producers of the phonograms, or to both. Domestic law may, in the absence of agreement between these parties, lay down the conditions as to the sharing of this remuneration.

Article 13
[Minimum Rights for Broadcasting Organizations]

Broadcasting organisations shall enjoy the right to authorise or prohibit:

(a) the rebroadcasting of their broadcasts;

(b) the fixation of their broadcasts;

(c) the reproduction:

  (i)   of fixations, made without their consent, of their broadcasts;

  (ii)   of fixations, made in accordance with the provisions of Article 15, of their broadcasts, if the reproduction is made for purposes different from those referred to in those provisions;

(d) the communication to the public of their television broadcasts if such communication is made in places accessible to the public against payment of an entrance fee; it shall be a matter for the domestic law of the State where protection of this right is claimed to determine the conditions under which it may be exercised.

Article 14
[Minimum Duration of Protection]

The term of protection to be granted under this Convention shall last at least until the end of a period of twenty years computed from the end of the year in which:

(a) the fixation was made-for phonograms and for performances incorporated therein;

(b) the performance took place-for performances not incorporated in phonograms;

(c) the broadcast took place-for broadcasts.

Article 15
[Permitted Exceptions: 1. Specific Limitations; 2. Equivalents with copyright]

1. Any Contracting State may, in its domestic laws and regulations, provide for exceptions to the protection guaranteed by this Convention as regards:

(a) private use;

(b) use of short excerpts in connexion with the reporting of current events;

(c) ephemeral fixation by a broadcasting organisation by means of its own facilities and for its own broadcasts;

(d) use solely for the purposes of teaching or scientific research.

2. Irrespective of paragraph 1 of this Article, any Contracting State may, in its domestic laws and regulations, provide for the same kinds of limitations with regard to the protection of performers, producers of phonograms and broadcasting organisations, as it provides for, in its domestic laws and regulations, in connexion with the protection of copyright in literary and artistic works. However, compulsory licences may be provided for only to the extent to which they are compatible with this Convention.

Article 16
[Reservations]

1. Any State, upon becoming party to this Convention, shall be bound by all the obligations and shall enjoy all the benefits thereof. However, a State may at any time, in a notification deposited with the Secretary-General of the United Nations, declare that:

(a) as regards Article 12:

(i)   it will not apply the provisions of that Article;

(ii)   it will not apply the provisions of that Article in respect of certain uses;

(iii)   as regards phonograms the producer of which is not a national of another Contracting State, it will not apply that Article;

(iv)   as regards phonograms the producer of which is a national of another Contracting State, it will limit the protection provided for by that Article to the extent to which, and to the term for which, the latter State grants protection to phonograms first fixed by a national of the State making the declaration; however, the fact that the Contracting State of which the producer is a national does not grant the protection to the same beneficiary or beneficiaries as the State making the declaration shall not be considered as a difference in the extent of the protection;

(b) as regards Article 13, it will not apply item 13(d); if a Contracting State makes such a declaration, the other Contracting States shall not be obliged to grant the right referred to in Article 13(d), to broadcasting organisations whose headquarters are in that State.

2. If the notification referred to in paragraph 1 of this Article is made after the date of the deposit of the instrument of ratification, acceptance or accession, the declaration will become effective six months after it has been deposited.

Article 17
[Certain countries applying only the "fixation" criterion]

Any State which, on October 26, 1961, grants protection to producers of phonograms solely on the basis of the criterion of fixation may, by a notification deposited with the Secretary-General of the United Nations at the time of ratification, acceptance or accession, declare that it will apply, for the purposes of Article 5, the criterion of fixation alone and, for the purposes of paragraph 16.1(a)(iii) and 16.1(a)(iv), the criterion of fixation instead of the criterion of nationality.

Article 18
[Withdrawal of reservations]

Any State which has deposited a notification under Article 5.3, Article 6.2, Article 16.1 or Article 17, may, by a further notification deposited with the Secretary-General of the United Nations, reduce its scope or withdraw it.

Article 19
[Performers' Rights in Films]

Notwithstanding anything in this Convention, once a performer has consented to the incorporation of his performance in a visual or audio-visual fixation, Article 7 shall have no further application.

Article 20
[Non-retroactivity]

1. This Convention shall not prejudice rights acquired in any Contracting State before the date of coming into force of this Convention for that State.

2. No Contracting State shall be bound to apply the provisions of this Convention to performances or broadcasts which took place, or to phonograms which were fixed, before the date of coming into force of this Convention for that State.

Article 21
[Protection by other means]

The protection provided for in this Convention shall not prejudice any protection otherwise secured to performers, producers of phonograms and broadcasting organisations.

Article 22
[Special agreements]

Contracting States reserve the right to enter into special agreements among themselves in so far as such agreements grant to performers, producers of phonograms or broadcasting organisations more extensive rights than those granted by this Convention or contain other provisions not contrary to this Convention.

Article 23
[Signature and deposit]

This Convention shall be deposited with the Secretary-General of the United Nations. It shall be open until June 30, 1962, for signature by any State invited to the Diplomatic Conference on the International Protection of Performers, Producers of Phonograms and Broadcasting Organisations which is a party to the Universal Copyright Convention or a member of the International Union for the Protection of Literary and Artistic Works.

Article 24
[Becoming Party to the Convention]

1. This Convention shall be subject to ratification or acceptance by the signatory States.

2. This Convention shall be open for accession by any State invited to the Conference referred to in Article 23, and by any State Member of the United Nations, provided that in either case such State is a party to the Universal Copyright Convention or a member of the International Union for the Protection of Literary and Artistic Works.

3. Ratification, acceptance or accession shall be effected by the deposit of an instrument to that effect with the Secretary-General of the United Nations.

Article 25
[Entry into force]

1. This Convention shall come into force three months after the date of deposit of the sixth instrument of ratification, acceptance or accession.

2. Subsequently, this Convention shall come into force in respect of each State three months after the date of deposit of its instrument of ratification, acceptance or accession.

Article 26
[Implementation of the Convention by the Provision of Domestic Law]

1. Each Contracting State undertakes to adopt, in accordance with its Constitution, the measures necessary to ensure the application of this Convention.

2. At the time of deposit of its instrument of ratification, acceptance or accession, each State must be in a position under its domestic law to give effect to the terms of this Convention.

Article 27
[Applicability of the Convention to Certain Territories]

1. Any State may, at the time of ratification, acceptance or accession, or

at any time thereafter, declare by notification addressed to the Secretary-General of the United Nations that this Convention shall extend to all or any of the territories for whose international relations it is responsible, provided that the Universal Copyright Convention or the International Convention for the Protection of Literary and Artistic Works applies to the territory or territories concerned. This notification shall take effect three months after the date of its receipt.

2. The notifications referred to in Article 5.3, Article 6.2, Article 16.1 and Articles 17 and 18, may be extended to cover all or any of the territories referred to in paragraph 1 of this Article.

Article 28
[Denunciation of the Convention]

1. Any Contracting State may denounce this Convention, on its own behalf or on behalf of all or any of the territories referred to in Article 27.

2. The denunciation shall be effected by a notification addressed to the Secretary-General of the United Nations and shall take effect twelve months after the date of receipt of the notification.

3. The right of denunciation shall not be exercised by a Contracting State before the expiry of a period of five years from the date on which the Convention came into force with respect to that State.

4. A Contracting State shall cease to be a party to this Convention from that time when it is neither a party to the Universal Copyright Convention nor a member of the International Union for the Protection of Literary and Artistic Works.

5. This Convention shall cease to apply to any territory referred to in Article 27 from that time when neither the Universal Copyright Convention nor the International Convention for the Protection of Literary and Artistic Works applies to that territory.

Article 29
[Revision of the Convention]

1. After this Convention has been in force for five years, any Contracting State may, by notification addressed to the Secretary-General of the United Nations, request that a conference be convened for the purpose of revising the Convention. The Secretary-General shall notify all Contracting States of this request. If, within a period of six months following the date of notification by the Secretary-General of the United Nations, not less than one half of the Contracting States notify him of their concurrence with the request, the Secretary-General shall inform the Director-General of the International Labour Office, the Director-General of the United Nations Educational, Scientific and Cultural Organization and the Director of the Bureau of the International Union for the Protection of Literary and Artistic Works, who shall convene a revision conference in co-operation with the Intergovernmental Committee provided for in Article 32.

2. The adoption of any revision of this Convention shall require an affirmative vote by two-thirds of the States attending the revision conference, provided that this majority includes two-thirds of the States which, at the time of the revision conference, are parties to the Convention.

3. In the event of adoption of a Convention revising this Convention in whole or in part, and unless the revising Convention provides otherwise:

(a) this Convention shall cease to be open to ratification, acceptance or accession as from the date of entry into force of the revising Convention;

(b) this Convention shall remain in force as regards relations between or with Contracting States which have not become parties to the revising Convention.

Article 30
[Settlement of disputes]

Any dispute which may arise between two or more Contracting States concerning the interpretation or application of this Convention and which is not settled by negotiation shall, at the request of any one of the parties to the dispute, be referred to the International Court of Justice for decision, unless they agree to another mode of settlement.

Article 31
[Limits on Reservations]

Without prejudice to the provisions of Article 5.3, Article 6.2, Article 16.1 and Article 17, no reservation may be made to this Convention.

Article 32
[Intergovernmental Committee]

1. An Intergovernmental Committee is hereby established with the following duties:

(a) to study questions concerning the application and operation of this Convention; and

(b) to collect proposals and to prepare documentation for possible revision of this Convention.

2. The Committee shall consist of representatives of the Contracting States, chosen with due regard to equitable geographical distribution. The number of members shall be six if there are twelve Contracting States or less, nine if there are thirteen to eighteen Contracting States and twelve if there are more than eighteen Contracting States.

3. The Committee shall be constituted twelve months after the Convention comes into force by an election organised among the Contracting States, each of which shall have one vote, by the Director-General of the International Labour Office, the Director-General of the United Nations Educational, Scientific and Cultural Organization and the Director of the Bureau of the International Union for the Protection of Literary and Artistic

Works, in accordance with rules previously approved by a majority of all Contracting States.

4. The Committee shall elect its Chairman and officers. It shall establish its own rules of procedure. These rules shall in particular provide for the future operation of the Committee and for a method of selecting its members for the future in such a way as to ensure rotation among the various Contracting States.

5. Officials of the International Labour Office, the United Nations Educational, Scientific and Cultural Organization and the Bureau of the International Union for the Protection of Literary and Artistic Works, designated by the Directors-General and the Director thereof, shall constitute the Secretariat of the Committee.

6. Meetings of the Committee, which shall be convened whenever a majority of its members deems it necessary, shall be held successively at the headquarters of the International Labour Office, the United Nations Educational, Scientific and Cultural Organization and the Bureau of the International Union for the Protection of Literary and Artistic Works.

7. Expenses of members of the Committee shall be borne by their respective Governments.

Article 33
[Languages]

1. The present Convention is drawn up in English, French and Spanish, the three texts being equally authentic.

2. In addition, official texts of the present Convention shall be drawn up in German, Italian and Portuguese.

Article 34
[Notifications]

1. The Secretary-General of the United Nations shall notify the States invited to the Conference referred to in Article 23 and every State Member of the United Nations, as well as the Director-General of the International Labour Office, the Director-General of the United Nations Educational, Scientific and Cultural Organization and the Director of the Bureau of the International Union for the Protection of Literary and Artistic Works:

(a) of the deposit of each instrument of ratification, acceptance or accession;

(b) of the date of entry into force of the Convention;

(c) of all notifications, declarations or communications provided for in this Convention;

(d) if any of the situations referred to in paragraphs 28.4 and 28.5 arise.

2. The Secretary-General of the United Nations shall also notify the Director-General of the International Labour Office, the Director-General of

the United Nations Educational, Scientific and Cultural Organization and the Director of the Bureau of the International Union for the Protection of Literary and Artistic Works of the requests communicated to him in accordance with Article 29, as well as of any communication received from the Contracting States concerning the revision of the Convention.

CONVENTION RELATING TO THE DISTRIBUTION OF PROGRAMME-CARRYING SIGNALS TRANSMITTED BY SATELLITE
Done at Brussels on May 21, 1974

The Contracting States,

Aware that the use of satellites for the distribution of programme-carrying signals is rapidly growing both in volume and geographical coverage;

Concerned that there is no world-wide system to prevent distributors from distributing programme-carrying signals transmitted by satellite which were not intended for those distributors, and that this lack is likely to hamper the use of satellite communications;

Recognizing, in this respect, the importance of the interests of authors, performers, producers of phonograms and broadcasting organizations;

Convinced that an international system should be established under which measures would be provided to prevent distributors from distributing programme-carrying signals transmitted by satellite which were not intended for those distributors;

Conscious of the need not to impair in any way international agreements already in force, including the International Telecommunication Convention and the Radio Regulations annexed to that Convention, and in particular in no way to prejudice wider acceptance of the Rome Convention of October 26, 1961, which affords protection to performers, producers of phonograms and broadcasting organizations,

Have agreed as follows:

Article 1

For the purposes of this Convention:

(i)   "signal" is an electronically-generated carrier capable of transmitting programmes;

(ii)   "programme" is a body of live or recorded material consisting of images, sounds or both, embodied in signals emitted for the purpose of ultimate distribution;

(iii)   "satellite" is any device in extraterrestrial space capable of transmitting signals;

(iv)   "emitted signal" or "signal emitted" is any programme-carrying signal that goes to or passes through a satellite;

(v)   "derived signal" is a signal obtained by modifying the technical characteristics of the emitted signal, whether or not there have been one or more intervening fixations;

(vi)   "originating organization" is the person or legal entity that decides what programme the emitted signals will carry;

(vii) "distributor" is the person or legal entity that decides that the transmission of the derived signals to the general public or any section thereof should take place;

(viii) "distribution" is the operation by which a distributor transmits derived signals to the general public or any section thereof.

Article 2

(1) Each Contracting State undertakes to take adequate measures to prevent the distribution on or from its territory of any programme-carrying signal by any distributor for whom the signal emitted to or passing through the satellite is not intended. This obligation shall apply where the originating organization is a national of another Contracting State and where the signal distributed is a derived signal.

(2) In any Contracting State in which the application of the measures referred to in paragraph (1) is limited in time, the duration thereof shall be fixed by its domestic law. The Secretary-General of the United Nations shall be notified in writing of such duration at the time of ratification, acceptance or accession, or if the domestic law comes into force or is changed thereafter, within six months of the coming into force of that law or of its modification.

(3) The obligation provided for in paragraph (1) shall not apply to the distribution of derived signals taken from signals which have already been distributed by a distributor for whom the emitted signals were intended.

Article 3

This Convention shall not apply where the signals emitted by or on behalf of the originating organization are intended for direct reception from the satellite by the general public.

Article 4

No Contracting State shall be required to apply the measures referred to in Article 2(1) where the signal distributed on its territory by a distributor for whom the emitted signal is not intended

(i) carries short excerpts of the programme carried by the emitted signal, consisting of reports of current events, but only to the extent justified by the informatory purpose of such excerpts, or

(ii) carries, as quotations, short excerpts of the programme carried by the emitted signal, provided that such quotations are compatible with fair practice and are justified by the informatory purpose of such quotations, or

(iii) carries, where the said territory is that of a Contracting State regarded as a developing country in conformity with the established practice of the General Assembly of the United Nations, a programme carried by the emitted signal, provided that the distribution is solely for the purpose of teaching, including teaching in the framework of adult education, or scientific research.

Article 5

No Contracting State shall be required to apply this Convention with respect to any signal emitted before this Convention entered into force for that State.

Article 6

This Convention shall in no way be interpreted to limit or prejudice the protection secured to authors, performers, producers of phonograms, or broadcasting organizations, under any domestic law or international agreement.

Article 7

This Convention shall in no way be interpreted as limiting the right of any Contracting State to apply its domestic law in order to prevent abuses of monopoly.

Article 8

(1) Subject to paragraph (2) and paragraph (3), no reservation to this Convention shall be permitted.

(2) Any Contracting State whose domestic law, on May 21, 1974, so provides may, by a written notification deposited with the Secretary-General of the United Nations, declare that, for its purposes, the words "where the originating organization is a national of another Contracting State" appearing in Article 2(1) shall be considered as if they were replaced by the words "where the signal is emitted from the territory of another Contracting State."

(3)

(a) Any Contracting State which, on May 21, 1974, limits or denies protection with respect to the distribution of programme-carrying signals by means of wires, cable or other similar communications channels to subscribing members of the public may, by a written notification deposited with the Secretary-General of the United Nations, declare that, to the extent that and as long as its domestic law limits or denies protection, it will not apply this Convention to such distributions.

(b) Any State that has deposited a notification in notify the States referred to in Article 9(1), as well as the accordance with subparagraph (a) shall notify the Secretary-General of the United Nations in writing, within six months of their coming into force, of any changes in its domestic law whereby the reservation under that subparagraph becomes inapplicable or more limited in scope.

Article 9

(1) This Convention shall be deposited with the Secretary-General of the United Nations. It shall be open until March 31, 1975, for signature by any State that is a member of the United Nations, any of the Specialized Agencies brought into relationship with the United Nations, or the International Atomic Energy Agency, or is a party to the Statute of the International Court of Justice.

(2) This Convention shall be subject to ratification or acceptance by the signatory States. It shall be open for accession by any State referred to in paragraph (1).

(3) Instruments of ratification, acceptance or accession shall be deposited with the Secretary-General of the United Nations.

(4) It is understood that, at the time a State becomes bound by this Convention, it will be in a position in accordance with its domestic law to give effect to the provisions of the Convention.

Article 10

(1) This Convention shall enter into force three months after the deposit of the fifth instrument of ratification, acceptance or accession.

(2) For each State ratifying, accepting or acceding to this Convention after the deposit of the fifth instrument of ratification, acceptance or accession, this Convention shall enter into force three months after the deposit of its instrument.

Article 11

(1) Any Contracting State may denounce this Convention by written notification deposited with the Secretary-General of the United Nations.

(2) Denunciation shall take effect twelve months after the date on which the notification referred to in paragraph (1) is received.

Article 12

(1) This Convention shall be signed in a single copy in English, French, Russian and Spanish, the four texts being equally authentic.

(2) Official texts shall be established by the Director-General of the United Nations Educational, Scientific and Cultural Organization and the Director General of the World Intellectual Property Organization, after consultation with the interested Governments, in the Arabic, Dutch, German, Italian and Portuguese languages.

(3) The Secretary-General of the United Nations shall notify the States referred to in Article 9(1), as well as the Director-General of the United Nations Educational, Scientific and Cultural Organization, the Director General of the World Intellectual Property Organization, the Director-

General of the International Labour Office and the Secretary-General of the International Telecommunication Union, of

    (i)   signatures to this Convention;

    (ii)   the deposit of instruments of ratification, acceptance or accession;

    (iii) the date of entry into force of this Convention under Article 10(1);

    (iv) the deposit of any notification relating to Article 2(2), Article 8(2) or Article 8(3), together with its text;

    (v)   the receipt of notifications of denunciation.

(4) The Secretary-General of the United Nations shall transmit two certified copies of this Convention to all States referred to in Article 9(1).

CONVENTION FOR THE PROTECTION OF PRODUCERS OF PHONOGRAMS AGAINST UNAUTHORIZED DUPLICATION OF THEIR PHONOGRAMS
Done at Geneva, October 29, 1971.

The Contracting States,

concerned at the widespread and increasing unauthorized duplication of phonograms and the damage this is occasioning to the interests of authors, performers and producers of phonograms;

convinced that the protection of producers of phonograms against such acts will also benefit the performers whose performances, and the authors whose works, are recorded on the said phonograms;

recognizing the value of the work undertaken in this field by the United Nations Educational, Scientific and Cultural Organization and the World Intellectual Property Organization;

anxious not to impair in any way international agreements already in force and in particular in no way to prejudice wider acceptance of the Rome Convention of October 26, 1961, which affords protection to performers and to broadcasting organizations as well as to producers of phonograms;

have agreed as follows:

Article 1

For the purposes of this convention:

(a) "phonogram" means any exclusively aural fixation of sounds of a performance or of other sounds;

(b) "producer of phonograms" means the person who, or the legal entity which, fist fixes the sounds of a performance or other sounds;

(c) "duplicate" means an article which contains sounds taken directly or indirectly from a phonogram and which embodies all or a substantial part of the sounds fixed in that phonogram;

(d) "distribution to the public" means any act by which duplicates of a phonogram are offered, directly or indirectly, to the general public or any section thereof.

Article 2

Each Contracting State shall protect producers of phonograms who are nationals of other Contracting States against the making of duplicates without the consent of the producer and against the importation of such duplicates, provided that any such making or importation is for the purpose of distribution to the public, and against the distribution of such duplicates to the public.

Article 3

The means by which this Convention is implemented shall be a matter for the domestic law of each Contracting State and shall include one or more of the following: protection by means of the grant of a copyright or other specific right; protection by means of the law relating to unfair competition; protection by means of penal sanctions.

Article 4

The duration of the protection given shall be a matter for the domestic law of each Contracting State. However, if the domestic law prescribes a specific duration for the protection, that duration shall not be less than 20 years from the end either of the year in which the sounds embodied in the phonogram were first fixed or the year in which the phonogram was first published.

Article 5

If, as a condition of protecting the producers of phonograms, a Contracting State, under its domestic law, requires compliance with formalities, these shall be considered as fulfilled if all the authorized duplicates of the phonogram distributed to the public or their containers bear a notice consisting of the symbol P, accompanied by the year date of the first publication, placed in such manner as to give reasonable notice of claim of protection; and, if the duplicates or their containers do not identify the producer, his successor in title or the exclusive licensee (by carrying his name, trademark or other appropriate designation), the notice shall also include the name of the producer, this successor in title or the exclusive licensee.

Article 6

Any Contracting State which affords protection by means of copyright or other specific right, or protection by means of penal sanction, may in its domestic law provide, with regard to the protection or producers of phonograms, the same kinds of limitations as are permitted with respect to the protection of authors of literary and artistic works. However, no compulsory licenses may be permitted unless all of the following conditions are met:

(a) The duplication is for use solely for the purpose of teaching or scientific research;

(b) The license shall be valid for duplication only withing the territory of the Contracting State whose competent authority has granted the license and shall not extent to the export of duplicates;

(c) the duplication made under license gives rise to an equitable remuneration fixed by the said authority taking into account, *inter alia* , the number of duplicates which will be made.

Article 7

(1) This Convention shall in no way be interpreted to limit or prejudice the protection otherwise secured to authors, to performers, to producers of phonograms or to broadcasting organizations under any domestic law or international agreement.

(2) It shall be a matter for the domestic law of each Contracting State to determine the extent, if any, to which performers whose performances are fixed in a phonogram are entitled to enjoy protection and the conditions for enjoying any such protection.

(3) No contracting State shall be required to apply the provisions of this Convention to any phonogram fixed before this Convention entered into force with respect to the State.

(4) Any contracting State which, on October 29, 1971, affords protection to producers of phonograms solely on the basis of the place of fist fixation may, by a notification deposited with the Director General of the World Intellectual Property Organization, declare that it will apply this criterion instead of the criterion of the nationality of the producer.

Article 8

(1) The International Bureau of the World Intellectual Property Organization shall assemble and publish information concerning the protection of phonograms. Each Contracting State shall promptly communicate the International Bureau all new laws and official texts on this subject.

(2) The International Bureau shall, on request, furnish information to any Contracting State on matters concerning this Convention, and shall conduct studies and provide services designed to facilitate the protection provided for therein.

(3) The International bureau shall exercise the functions enumerated in paragraphs (1) and (2) above in cooperation, for matters within their respective competence, with the United Nations Educational, Scientific and Cultural Organization and the International Labour Organizations.

Article 9

(1) This Convention shall be deposited with the Secretary-General of the United Nations. It shall be open until April 30, 1972, for signature by any State that is a member of the United Nations, any of the Specialized Agencies brought into relationship with the United Nations, or the International Atomic Energy Agency, or is a party to the Statute of the International Court of Justice.

(2) This Convention shall be subject to ratification of acceptance by the signatory States. It shall be open for accession by any State referred to in paragraph (1) of this Article.

(3) Instruments of ratification, acceptance of accession shall be deposited

with the Secretary-General of the United Nations.

(4) It is understood that, at the time a State becomes bound by the Convention, it will be in a position in accordance with its domestic law to give effect to the provisions of the Convention

Article 10

No reservations to this Convention are permitted.

Article 11

(1) This Convention shall enter into force three months after deposit of the fifth instrument of ratification, acceptance or accession.

(2) For each State ratifying, accepting or acceding to this Convention after the deposit of the fifth instrument of ratification, acceptance or accession, the Convention shall enter into force three months after the date on which the Director General of the World Intellectual Property Organization informs the States, in accordance with Article 13, paragraph (4), of the deposit of its instruments.

(3) Any State may, at the time of ratification, acceptance or accession or at any later date, declare by notification addressed to the Secretary-General of the United Nations that this Convention shall apply to all or any one of the territories for whose international affairs it is responsible. This notification will take effect three months after the date on which it is received.

(4) However, the preceding paragraph may in no way be understood as implying the recognition or tacit acceptance by a Contracting State of the factual situation concerning a territory to which this Convention is made applicable by another Contracting State by virtue of the said paragraph.

Article 12

(1) Any Contracting State may denounce this Convention, on its own behalf or on behalf of any of the territories referred to in Article 11, paragraph (3), by written notification addressed to the Secretary-General of the United Nations.

(2) Denunciation shall take effect twelve months after the date on which the Secretary-General of the United Nations has received the notification.

Article 13

(1) This Convention shall be signed in a single copy in English, French, Russian and Spanish, the four texts being equally authentic.

(2) Officials texts shall be established by the Director General of the World Intellectual Property Organization, after consultation with the interested Governments, in the Arabic, Dutch, German , Italian and Portuguese languages.

(3) The Secretary-General of the United Nations shall notify the Director

General of the World Intellectual Property Organization, the Director-General of the United Nations Educational, Scientific and Cultural Organization and the Director-General of the International Labour Office of:

(a) signatures to this Convention;

(b) the deposit of instruments of ratification, acceptance or accession;

(c) the date of entry into force of this Convention;

(d) any declaration notified pursuant to Article 11, paragraph (3);

(e) the receipt of notifications of denunciation.

(4) The Director General of the World Intellectual Property Organization shall inform the States referred to in Article 9, paragraph (1), of the notifications received pursuant to the preceding paragraph and of any declarations made under Article 7, paragraph (4). He shall also notify the Director-General of the United Nations Educational, Scientific and Cultural Organization and the Director-General of the International Labour Office of such declarations.

(5) The Secretary-General of the United Nations shall transmit two certified copies of this Convention to the Stated referred to in Article 9, paragraph (1).

EC TERM DIRECTIVE

Council Directive 93/98/EEC of 29 October 1993 harmonizing the term of protection of copyright and certain related rights

THE COUNCIL OF THE EUROPEAN COMMUNITIES,

Having regard to the Treaty establishing the European Economic Community, and in particular Articles 57(2), 66 and 100a thereof,

Having regard to the proposal from the Commission,

In cooperation with the European Parliament,

Having regard to the opinion of the Economic and Social Committee,

(1) Whereas the Berne Convention for the protection of literary and artistic works and the International Convention for the protection of performers, producers of phonograms and broadcasting organizations (Rome Convention) lay down only minimum terms of protection of the rights they refer to, leaving the Contracting States free to grant longer terms; whereas certain Member States have exercised this entitlement; whereas in addition certain Member States have not become party to the Rome Convention;

(2) Whereas there are consequently differences between the national laws governing the terms of protection of copyright and related rights, which are liable to impede the free movement of goods and freedom to provide services, and to distort competition in the common market; whereas therefore with a view to the smooth operation of the internal market, the laws of the Member States should be harmonized so as to make terms of protection identical throughout the Community;

(3) Whereas harmonization must cover not only the terms of protection as such, but also certain implementing arrangements such as the date from which each term of protection is calculated;

(4) Whereas the provisions of this Directive do not affect the application by the Member States of the provisions of Article 14a (2) (b), (c) and (d) and (3) of the Berne Convention;

(5) Whereas the minimum term of protection laid down by the Berne Convention, namely the life of the author and 50 years after his death, was intended to provide protection for the author and the first two generations of his descendants; whereas the average lifespan in the Community has grown longer, to the point where this term is no longer sufficient to cover two generations;

(6) Whereas certain Member States have granted a term longer than 50 years after the death of the author in order to offset the effects of the world wars on the exploitation of authors' works;

(7) Whereas for the protection of related rights certain Member States have introduced a term of 50 years after lawful publication or lawful communication to the public;

(8) Whereas under the Community position adopted for the Uruguay

Round negotiations under the General Agreement on Tariffs and Trade (GATT) the term of protection for producers of phonograms should be 50 years after first publication;

(9) Whereas due regard for established rights is one of the general principles of law protected by the Community legal order; whereas, therefore, a harmonization of the terms of protection of copyright and related rights cannot have the effect of reducing the protection currently enjoyed by rightholders in the Community; whereas in order to keep the effects of transitional measures to a minimum and to allow the internal market to operate in practice, the harmonization of the term of protection should take place on a long term basis;

(10) Whereas in its communication of 17 January 1991 'Follow-up to the Green Paper—Working programme of the Commission in the field of copyright and neighbouring rights' the Commission stresses the need to harmonize copyright and neighbouring rights at a high level of protection since these rights are fundamental to intellectual creation and stresses that their protection ensures the maintenance and development of creativity in the interest of authors, cultural industries, consumers and society as a whole;

(11) Whereas in order to establish a high level of protection which at the same time meets the requirements of the internal market and the need to establish a legal environment conducive to the harmonious development of literary and artistic creation in the Community, the term of protection for copyright should be harmonized at 70 years after the death of the author or 70 years after the work is lawfully made available to the public, and for related rights at 50 years after the event which sets the term running;

(12) Whereas collections are protected according to Article 2 (5) of the Berne Convention when, by reason of the selection and arrangement of their content, they constitute intellectual creations; whereas those works are protected as such, without prejudice to the copyright in each of the works forming part of such collections, whereas in consequence specific terms of protection may apply to works included in collections;

(13) Whereas in all cases where one or more physical persons are identified as authors the term of protection should be calculated after their death; whereas the question of authorship in the whole or a part of a work is a question of fact which the national courts may have to decide;

(14) Whereas terms of protection should be calculated from the first day of January of the year following the relevant event, as they are in the Berne and Rome Conventions;

(15) Whereas Article 1 of Council Directive 91/250/EEC of 14 May 1991 on the legal protection of computer programs provides that Member States are to protect computer programs, by copyright, as literary works within the meaning of the Berne Convention; whereas this

Directive harmonizes the term of protection of literary works in the Community; whereas Article 8 of Directive 91/250/EEC, which merely makes provisional arrangements governing the term of protection of computer programs, should accordingly be repealed;

(16) Whereas Articles 11 and 12 of Council Directive 92/100/EEC of 19 November 1992 on rental right and lending right and on certain rights related to copyright in the field of intellectual property make provision for minimum terms of protection only, subject to any further harmonization; whereas this Directive provides such further harmonization; whereas these Articles should accordingly be repealed;

(17) Whereas the protection of photographs in the Member States is the subject of varying regimes; whereas in order to achieve a sufficient harmonization of the term of protection of photographic works, in particular of those which, due to their artistic or professional character, are of importance within the internal market, it is necessary to define the level of originality required in this Directive; whereas a photographic work within the meaning of the Berne Convention is to be considered original if it is the author's own intellectual creation reflecting his personality, no other criteria such as merit or purpose being taken into account; whereas the protection of other photographs should be left to national law;

(18) Whereas, in order to avoid differences in the term of protection as regards related rights it is necessary to provide the same starting point for the calculation of the term throughout the Community; whereas the performance, fixation, transmission, lawful publication, and lawful communication to the public, that is to say the means of making a subject of a related right perceptible in all appropriate ways to persons in general, should be taken into account for the calculation of the term of protection regardless of the country where this performance, fixation, transmission, lawful publication, or lawful communication to the public takes place;

(19) Whereas the rights of broadcasting organizations in their broadcasts, whether these broadcasts are transmitted by wire or over the air, including by cable or satellite, should not be perpetual; whereas it is therefore necessary to have the term of protection running from the first transmission of a particular broadcast only; whereas this provision is understood to avoid a new term running in cases where a broadcast is identical to a previous one;

(20) Whereas the Member States should remain free to maintain or introduce other rights related to copyright in particular in relation to the protection of critical and scientific publications; whereas, in order to ensure transparency at Community level, it is however necessary for Member States which introduce new related rights to notify the Commission;

(21) Whereas it is useful to make clear that the harmonization brought about by this Directive does not apply to moral rights;

(22) Whereas, for works whose country of origin within the meaning of the Berne Convention is a third country and whose author is not a Community national, comparison of terms of protection should be applied, provided that the term accorded in the Community does not exceed the term laid down in this Directive;

(23) Whereas where a rightholder who is not a Community national qualifies for protection under an international agreement the term of protection of related rights should be the same as that laid down in this Directive, except that it should not exceed that fixed in the country of which the rightholder is a national;

(24) Whereas comparison of terms should not result in Member States being brought into conflict with their international obligations;

(25) Whereas, for the smooth functioning of the internal market this Directive should be applied as from 1 July 1995;

(26) Whereas Member States should remain free to adopt provisions on the interpretation, adaptation and further execution of contracts on the exploitation of protected works and other subject matter which were concluded before the extension of the term of protection resulting from this Directive;

(27) Whereas respect of acquired rights and legitimate expectations is part of the Community legal order; whereas Member States may provide in particular that in certain circumstances the copyright and related rights which are revived pursuant to this Directive may not give rise to payments by persons who undertook in good faith the exploitation of the works at the time when such works lay within the public domain,

HAS ADOPTED THIS DIRECTIVE:

Article 1
Duration of authors' rights

1. The rights of an author of a literary or artistic work within the meaning of Article 2 of the Berne Convention shall run for the life of the author and for 70 years after his death, irrespective of the date when the work is lawfully made available to the public.

2. In the case of a work of joint authorship the term referred to in paragraph 1 shall be calculated from the death of the last surviving author.

3. In the case of anonymous or pseudonymous works, the term of protection shall run for seventy years after the work is lawfully made available to the public. However, when the pseudonym adopted by the author leaves no doubt as to his identity, or if the author discloses his identity during the period referred to in the first sentence, the term of protection applicable shall be that laid down in paragraph 1.

4. Where a Member State provides for particular provisions on copyright

in respect of collective works or for a legal person to be designated as the rightholder, the term of protection shall be calculated according to the provisions of paragraph 3, except if the natural persons who have created the work as such are identified as such in the versions of the work which are made available to the public. This paragraph is without prejudice to the rights of identified authors whose identifiable contributions are included in such works, to which contributions paragraph 1 or 2 shall apply.

5. Where a work is published in volumes, parts, instalments, issues or episodes and the term of protection runs from the time when the work was lawfully made available to the public, the term of protection shall run for each such item separately.

6. In the case of works for which the term of protection is not calculated from the death of the author or authors and which have not been lawfully made available to the public within seventy years from their creation, the protection shall terminate.

Article 2
Cinematographic or audiovisual works

1. The principal director of a cinematographic or audiovisual work shall be considered as its author or one of its authors. Member States shall be free to designate other co-authors.

2. The term of protection of cinematographic or audiovisual works shall expire 70 years after the death of the last of the following persons to survive, whether or not these persons are designated as co-authors: the principal director, the author of the screenplay, the author of the dialogue and the composer of music specifically created for use in the cinematographic or audiovisual work.

Article 3
Duration of related rights

1. The rights of performers shall expire 50 years after the date of the performance. However, if a fixation of the performance is lawfully published or lawfully communicated to the public within this period, the rights shall expire 50 years from the date of the first such publication or the first such communication to the public, whichever is the earlier.

2. The rights of producers of phonograms shall expire 50 years after the fixation is made. However, if the phonogram is lawfully published or lawfully communicated to the public during this period, the rights shall expire 50 years from the date of the first such publication or the first such communication to the public, whichever is the earlier.

3. The rights of producers of the first fixation of a film shall expire 50 years after the fixation is made. However, if the film is lawfully published or lawfully communicated to the public during this period, the rights shall expire 50 years from the date of the first such publication or the first such communication to the public, whichever is the earlier. The term 'film' shall

designate a cinematographic or audiovisual work or moving images, whether or not accompanied by sound.

4. The rights of broadcasting organizations shall expire 50 years after the first transmission of a broadcast, whether this broadcast is transmitted by wire or over the air, including by cable or satellite.

Article 4
Protection of previously unpublished works

Any person who, after the expiry of copyright protection, for the first time lawfully publishes or lawfully communicates to the public a previously unpublished work, shall benefit from a protection equivalent to the economic rights of the author. The term of protection of such rights shall be 25 years from the time when the work was first lawfully published or lawfully communicated to the public.

Article 5
Critical and scientific publications

Member States may protect critical and scientific publications of works which have come into the public domain. The maximum term of protection of such rights shall be 30 years from the time when the publication was first lawfully published.

Article 6
Protection of photographs

Photographs which are original in the sense that they are the author's own intellectual creation shall be protected in accordance with Article 1. No other criteria shall be applied to determine their eligibility for protection. Member States may provide for the protection of other photographs.

Article 7
Protection vis-à-vis third countries

1. Where the country of origin of a work, within the meaning of the Berne Convention, is a third country, and the author of the work is not a Community national, the term of protection granted by the Member States shall expire on the date of expiry of the protection granted in the country of origin of the work, but may not exceed the term laid down in Article 1.

2. The terms of protection laid down in Article 3 shall also apply in the case of rightholders who are not Community nationals, provided Member States grant them protection. However, without prejudice to the international obligations of the Member States, the term of protection granted by Member States shall expire no later than the date of expiry of the protection granted in the country of which the rightholder is a national and may not exceed the term laid down in Article 3.

3. Member States which, at the date of adoption of this Directive, in particular pursuant to their international obligations, granted a longer term

of protection than that which would result from the provisions, referred to in paragraphs 1 and 2 may maintain this protection until the conclusion of international agreements on the term of protection by copyright or related rights.

Article 8
Calculation of terms

The terms laid down in this Directive are calculated from the first day of January of the year following the event which gives rise to them.

Article 9
Moral rights

This Directive shall be without prejudice to the provisions of the Member States regulating moral rights.

Article 10
Application in time

1. Where a term of protection, which is longer than the corresponding term provided for by this Directive, is already running in a Member State on the date referred to in Article 13(1), this Directive shall not have the effect of shortening that term of protection in that Member State.

2. The terms of protection provided for in this Directive shall apply to all works and subject matter which are protected in at least one Member State, on the date referred to in Article 13(1), pursuant to national provisions on copyright or related rights or which meet the criteria for protection under Directive 92/100/EEC.

3. This Directive shall be without prejudice to any acts of exploitation performed before the date referred to in Article 13(1). Member States shall adopt the necessary provisions to protect in particular acquired rights of third parties.

4. Member States need not apply the provisions of Article 2(1) to cinematographic or audiovisual works created before 1 July 1994.

5. Member States may determine the date as from which Article 2(1) shall apply, provided that date is no later than 1 July 1997.

Article 11
Technical adaptation

1. Article 8 of Directive 91/250/EEC is hereby repealed.

2. Articles 11 and 12 of Directive 92/100/EEC are hereby repealed.

Article 12
Notification procedure

Member States shall immediately notify the Commission of any governmental plan to grant new related rights, including the basic reasons for their introduction and the term of protection envisaged.

Article 13
General provisions

1. Member States shall bring into force the laws, regulations and administrative provisions necessary to comply with Articles 1 to 11 of this Directive before 1 July 1995.

When Member States adopt these provisions, they shall contain a reference to this Directive or shall be accompanied by such reference at the time of their official publication. The methods of making such a reference shall be laid down by the Member States.

Member States shall communicate to the Commission the texts of the provisions of national law which they adopt in the field governed by this Directive.

2. Member States shall apply Article 12 from the date of notification of this Directive.

Article 14

This Directive is addressed to the Member States.

Done at Brussels, 29 October 1993.

EC CABLE AND SATELLITE DIRECTIVE

Council Directive 93/83/EEC of 27 September 1993 on the coordination of certain rules concerning copyright and rights related to copyright applicable to satellite broadcasting and cable retransmission

THE COUNCIL OF THE EUROPEAN COMMUNITIES,

Having regard to the Treaty establishing the European Economic Community, and in particular Articles 57(2) and 66 thereof,

Having regard to the proposal from the Commission,

In cooperation with the European Parliament,

Having regard to the opinion of the Economic and Social Committee,

(1)   Whereas the objectives of the Community as laid down in the Treaty include establishing an ever closer union among the peoples of Europe, fostering closer relations between the States belonging to the Community and ensuring the economic and social progress of the Community countries by common action to eliminate the barriers which divide Europe;

(2)   Whereas, to that end, the Treaty provides for the establishment of a common market and an area without internal frontiers; whereas measures to achieve this include the abolition of obstacles to the free movement of services and the institution of a system ensuring that competition in the common market is not distorted; whereas, to that end, the Council may adopt directives for the coordination of the provisions laid down by law, regulation or administrative action in Member States concerning the taking up and pursuit of activities as self-employed persons;

(3)   Whereas broadcasts transmitted across frontiers within the Community, in particular by satellite and cable, are one of the most important ways of pursuing these Community objectives, which are at the same time political, economic, social, cultural and legal;

(4)   Whereas the Council has already adopted Directive 89/552/EEC of 3 October 1989 on the coordination of certain provisions laid down by law, regulation or administrative action in Member States concerning the pursuit of television broadcasting activities, which makes provision for the promotion of the distribution and production of European television programmes and for advertising and sponsorship, the protection of minors and the right of reply;

(5)   Whereas, however, the achievement of these objectives in respect of cross-border satellite broadcasting and the cable retransmission of programmes from other Member States is currently still obstructed by a series of differences between national rules of copyright and some degree of legal uncertainty; whereas this means that holders of rights are exposed to the threat of seeing their works exploited without payment of remuneration or that the individual holders of exclusive

rights in various Member States block the exploitation of their rights; whereas the legal uncertainty in particular constitutes a direct obstacle in the free circulation of programmes within the Community;

(6) Whereas a distinction is currently drawn for copyright purposes between communication to the public by direct satellite and communication to the public by communications satellite; whereas, since individual reception is possible and affordable nowadays with both types of satellite, there is no longer any justification for this differing legal treatment;

(7) Whereas the free broadcasting of programmes is further impeded by the current legal uncertainty over whether broadcasting by a satellite whose signals can be received directly affects the rights in the country of transmission only or in all countries of reception together; whereas, since communications satellites and direct satellites are treated alike for copyright purposes, this legal uncertainty now affects almost all programmes broadcast in the Community by satellite;

(8) Whereas, furthermore, legal certainty, which is a prerequisite for the free movement of broadcasts within the Community, is missing where programmes transmitted across frontiers are fed into and retransmitted through cable networks;

(9) Whereas the development of the acquisition of rights on a contractual basis by authorization is already making a vigorous contribution to the creation of the desired European audiovisual area; whereas the continuation of such contractual agreements should be ensured and their smooth application in practice should be promoted wherever possible;

(10) Whereas at present cable operators in particular cannot be sure that they have actually acquired all the programme rights covered by such an agreement;

(11) Whereas, lastly, parties in different Member States are not all similarly bound by obligations which prevent them from refusing without valid reason to negotiate on the acquisition of the rights necessary for cable distribution or allowing such negotiations to fail;

(12) Whereas the legal framework for the creation of a single audiovisual area laid down in Directive 89/552/EEC must, therefore, be supplemented with reference to copyright;

(13) Whereas, therefore, an end should be put to the differences of treatment of the transmission of programmes by communications satellite which exist in the Member States, so that the vital distinction throughout the Community becomes whether works and other protected subject matter are communicated to the public; whereas this will also ensure equal treatment of the suppliers of cross-border broadcasts, regardless of whether they use a direct broadcasting satellite or a communications satellite;

(14) Whereas the legal uncertainty regarding the rights to be acquired

which impedes cross-border satellite broadcasting should be overcome by defining the notion of communication to the public by satellite at a Community level; whereas this definition should at the same time specify where the act of communication takes place; whereas such a definition is necessary to avoid the cumulative application of several national laws to one single act of broadcasting; whereas communication to the public by satellite occurs only when, and in the Member State where, the programme-carrying signals are introduced under the control and responsibility of the broadcasting organization into an uninterrupted chain of communication leading to the satellite and down towards the earth; whereas normal technical procedures relating to the programme-carrying signals should not be considered as interruptions to the chain of broadcasting;

(15) Whereas the acquisition on a contractual basis of exclusive broadcasting rights should comply with any legislation on copyright and rights related to copyright in the Member State in which communication to the public by satellite occurs;

(16) Whereas the principle of contractual freedom on which this Directive is based will make it possible to continue limiting the exploitation of these rights, especially as far as certain technical means of transmission or certain language versions are concerned;

(17) Whereas, in arriving at the amount of the payment to be made for the rights acquired, the parties should take account of all aspects of the broadcast, such as the actual audience, the potential audience and the language version;

(18) Whereas the application of the country-of-origin principle contained in this Directive could pose a problem with regard to existing contracts; whereas this Directive should provide for a period of five years for existing contracts to be adapted, where necessary, in the light of the Directive; whereas the said country-of-origin principle should not, therefore, apply to existing contracts which expire before 1 January 2000; whereas if by that date parties still have an interest in the contract, the same parties should be entitled to renegotiate the conditions of the contract;

(19) Whereas existing international co-production agreements must be interpreted in the light of the economic purpose and scope envisaged by the parties upon signature; whereas in the past international co-production agreements have often not expressly and specifically addressed communication to the public by satellite within the meaning of this Directive a particular form of exploitation; whereas the underlying philosophy of many existing international co-production agreements is that the rights in the co-production are exercised separately and independently by each co-producer, by dividing the exploitation rights between them along territorial lines; whereas, as a general rule, in the situation where a communication to the public by satellite authorized by one co-producer would

prejudice the value of the exploitation rights of another co-producer, the interpretation of such an existing agreement would normally suggest that the latter co-producer would have to give his consent to the authorization, by the former co-producer, of the communication to the public by satellite; whereas the language exclusivity of the latter co-producer will be prejudiced where the language version or versions of the communication to the public, including where the version is dubbed or subtitled, coincide(s) with the language or the languages widely understood in the territory allotted by the agreement to the latter co-producer; whereas the notion of exclusivity should be understood in a wider sense where the communication to the public by satellite concerns a work which consists merely of images and contains no dialogue or subtitles; whereas a clear rule is necessary in cases where the international co-production agreement does not expressly regulate the division of rights in the specific case of communication to the public by satellite within the meaning of this Directive;

(20) Whereas communications to the public by satellite from non-member countries will under certain conditions be deemed to occur within a Member State of the Community;

(21) Whereas it is necessary to ensure that protection for authors, performers, producers of phonograms and broadcasting organizations is accorded in all Member States and that this protection is not subject to a statutory licence system; whereas only in this way is it possible to ensure that any difference in the level of protection within the common market will not create distortions of competition;

(22) Whereas the advent of new technologies is likely to have an impact on both the quality and the quantity of the exploitation of works and other subject matter;

(23) Whereas in the light of these developments the level of protection granted pursuant to this Directive to all rightholders in the areas covered by this Directive should remain under consideration;

(24) Whereas the harmonization of legislation envisaged in this Directive entails the harmonization of the provisions ensuring a high level of protection of authors, performers, phonogram producers and broadcasting organizations; whereas this harmonization should not allow a broadcasting organization to take advantage of differences in levels of protection by relocating activities, to the detriment of audiovisual productions;

(25) Whereas the protection provided for rights related to copyright should be aligned on that contained in Council Directive 92/100/EEC of 19 November 1992 on rental right and lending right and on certain rights related to copyright in the field of intellectual property for the purposes of communication to the public by satellite; whereas, in particular, this will ensure that performers and phonogram producers are guaranteed an appropriate remuneration for the communication

to the public by satellite of their performances or phonograms;

(26) Whereas the provisions of Article 4 do not prevent Member States from extending the presumption set out in Article 2 (5) of Directive 92/100/EEC to the exclusive rights referred to in Article 4; whereas, furthermore, the provisions of Article 4 do not prevent Member States from providing for a rebuttable presumption of the authorization of exploitation in respect of the exclusive rights of performers referred to in that Article, in so far as such presumption is compatible with the International Convention for the Protection of Performers, Producers of Phonograms and Broadcasting Organizations;

(27) Whereas the cable retransmission of programmes from other Member States is an act subject to copyright and, as the case may be, rights related to copyright; whereas the cable operator must, therefore, obtain the authorization from every holder of rights in each part of the programme retransmitted; whereas, pursuant to this Directive, the authorizations should be granted contractually unless a temporary exception is provided for in the case of existing legal licence schemes;

(28) Whereas, in order to ensure that the smooth operation of contractual arrangements is not called into question by the intervention of outsiders holding rights in individual parts of the programme, provision should be made, through the obligation to have recourse to a collecting society, for the exclusive collective exercise of the authorization right to the extent that this is required by the special features of cable retransmission; whereas the authorization right as such remains intact and only the exercise of this right is regulated to some extent, so that the right to authorize a cable retransmission can still be assigned; whereas this Directive does not affect the exercise of moral rights;

(29) Whereas the exemption provided for in Article 10 should not limit the choice of holders of rights to transfer their rights to a collecting society and thereby have a direct share in the remuneration paid by the cable distributor for cable retransmission;

(30) Whereas contractual arrangements regarding the authorization of cable retransmission should be promoted by additional measures; whereas a party seeking the conclusion of a general contract should, for its part, be obliged to submit collective proposals for an agreement; whereas, furthermore, any party shall be entitled, at any moment, to call upon the assistance of impartial mediators whose task is to assist negotiations and who may submit proposals; whereas any such proposals and any opposition thereto should be served on the parties concerned in accordance with the applicable rules concerning the service of legal documents, in particular as set out in existing international conventions; whereas, finally, it is necessary to ensure that the negotiations are not blocked without valid justification or that individual holders are not prevented without valid justification from taking part in the negotiations; whereas none of these measures

for the promotion of the acquisition of rights calls into question the contractual nature of the acquisition of cable retransmission rights;

(31) Whereas for a transitional period Member States should be allowed to retain existing bodies with jurisdiction in their territory over cases where the right to retransmit a programme by cable to the public has been unreasonably refused or offered on unreasonable terms by a broadcasting organization; whereas it is understood that the right of parties concerned to be heard by the body should be guaranteed and that the existence of the body should not prevent the parties concerned from having normal access to the courts;

(32) Whereas, however, Community rules are not needed to deal with all of those matters, the effects of which perhaps with some commercially insignificant exceptions, are felt only inside the borders of a single Member State;

(33) Whereas minimum rules should be laid down in order to establish and guarantee free and uninterrupted cross-border broadcasting by satellite and simultaneous, unaltered cable retransmission of programmes broadcast from other Member States, on an essentially contractual basis;

(34) Whereas this Directive should not prejudice further harmonization in the field of copyright and rights related to copyright and the collective administration of such rights; whereas the possibility for Member States to regulate the activities of collecting societies should not prejudice the freedom of contractual negotiation of the rights provided for in this Directive, on the understanding that such negotiation takes place within the framework of general or specific national rules with regard to competition law or the prevention of abuse of monopolies;

(35) Whereas it should, therefore, be for the Member States to supplement the general provisions needed to achieve the objectives of this Directive by taking legislative and administrative measures in their domestic law, provided that these do not run counter to the objectives of this Directive and are compatible with Community law;

(36) Whereas this Directive does not affect the applicability of the competition rules in Articles 85 and 86 of the Treaty,

HAS ADOPTED THIS DIRECTIVE:

CHAPTER I
DEFINITIONS

Article 1
Definitions

1. For the purpose of this Directive, 'satellite' means any satellite operating on frequency bands which, under telecommunications law, are reserved for the broadcast of signals for reception by the public or which are reserved for closed, point-to-point communication. In the latter case, however, the

circumstances in which individual reception of the signals takes place must be comparable to those which apply in the first case.

2. (a) For the purpose of this Directive, 'communication to the public by satellite' means the act of introducing, under the control and responsibility of the broadcasting organization, the programme-carrying signals intended for reception by the public into an uninterrupted chain of communication leading to the satellite and down towards the earth.

(b) The act of communication to the public by satellite occurs solely in the Member State where, under the control and responsibility of the broadcasting organization, the programme-carrying signals are introduced into an uninterrupted chain of communication leading to the satellite and down towards the earth.

(c) If the programme-carrying signals are encrypted, then there is communication to the public by satellite on condition that the means for decrypting the broadcast are provided to the public by the broadcasting organization or with its consent.

(d) Where an act of communication to the public by satellite occurs in a non-Community State which does not provide the level of protection provided for under Chapter II,

(i) if the programme-carrying signals are transmitted to the satellite from an uplink situation situated in a Member State, that act of communication to the public by satellite shall be deemed to have occurred in that Member State and the rights provided for under Chapter II shall be exercisable against the person operating the uplink station; or

(ii) if there is no use of an uplink station situated in a Member State but a broadcasting organization established in a Member State has commissioned the act of communication to the public by satellite, that act shall be deemed to have occurred in the Member State in which the broadcasting organization has its principal establishment in the Community and the rights provided for under Chapter II shall be exercisable against the broadcasting organization.

3. For the purposes of this Directive, 'cable retransmission' means the simultaneous, unaltered and unabridged retransmission by a cable or microwave system for reception by the public of an initial transmission from another Member State, by wire or over the air, including that by satellite, of television or radio programmes intended for reception by the public.

4. For the purposes of this Directive 'collecting society' means any organization which manages or administers copyright or rights related to copyright as its sole purpose or as one of its main purposes.

5. For the purposes of this Directive, the principal director of a cinematographic or audiovisual work shall be considered as its author or one of its authors. Member States may provide for others to be considered as its

co-authors.

CHAPTER II
BROADCASTING OF PROGRAMMES BY SATELLITE

Article 2
Broadcasting right

Member States shall provide an exclusive right for the author to authorize the communication to the public by satellite of copyright works, subject to the provisions set out in this chapter.

Article 3
Acquisition of broadcasting rights

1. Member States shall ensure that the authorization referred to in Article 2 may be acquired only be agreement.

2. A Member State may provide that a collective agreement between a collecting society and a broadcasting organization concerning a given category of works may be extended to rightholders of the same category who are not represented by the collecting society, provided that:

– the communication to the public by satellite simulcasts a terrestrial broadcast by the same broadcaster, and

– the unrepresented rightholder shall, at any time, have the possibility of excluding the extension of the collective agreement to his works and of exercising his rights either individually or collectively.

3. Paragraph 2 shall not apply to cinematographic works, including works created by a process analogous to cinematography.

4. Where the law of a Member State provides for the extension of a collective agreement in accordance with the provisions of paragraph 2, that Member States shall inform the Commission which broadcasting organizations are entitled to avail themselves of that law. The Commission shall publish this information in the *Official Journal of the European Communities* C series).

Article 4
Rights of performers, phonogram producers and
broadcasting organizations

1. For the purposes of communication to the public by satellite, the rights of performers, phonogram producers and broadcasting organizations shall be protected in accordance with the provisions of Articles 6, 7, 8 and 10 of Directive 92/100/EEC.

2. For the purposes of paragraph 1, 'broadcasting by wireless means' in Directive 92/100/EEC shall be understood as including communication to the public by satellite.

3. With regard to the exercise of the rights referred to in paragraph 1,

Articles 2(7) and 12 of Directive 92/100/EEC shall apply.

Article 5
Relation between copyright and related rights

Protection of copyright-related rights under this Directive shall leave intact and shall in no way affect the protection of copyright.

Article 6
Minimum protection

1. Member States may provide for more far-reaching protection for holders of rights related to copyright than that required by Article 8 of Directive 92/100/EEC.

2. In applying paragraph 1 Member States shall observe the definitions contained in Article 1 (1) and (2).

Article 7
Transitional provisions

1. With regard to the application in time of the rights referred to in Article 4(1) of this Directive, Article 13 (1), (2), (6) and (7) of Directive 92/100/EEC shall apply. Article 13(4) and (5) of Directive 92/100/EEC shall apply *mutatis mutandis.*

2. Agreements concerning the exploitation of works and other protected subject matter which are in force on the date mentioned in Article 14(1) shall be subject to the provisions of Articles 1(2), 2 and 3 as from 1 January 2000 if they expire after that date.

3. When an international co-production agreement concluded before the date mentioned in Article 14(1) between a co-producer from a Member State and one or more co-producers from other Member States or third countries expressly provides for a system of division of exploitation rights between the co-producers by geographical areas for all means of communication to the public, without distinguishing the arrangement applicable to communication to the public by satellite from the provisions applicable to the other means of communication, and where communication to the public by satellite of the co-production would prejudice the exclusivity, in particular the language exclusivity, of one of the co-producers or his assignees in a given territory, the authorization by one of the co-producers or his assignees for a communication to the public by satellite shall require the prior consent of the holder of that exclusivity, whether co-producer or assignee.

CHAPTER III
CABLE RETRANSMISSION

Article 8
Cable retransmission right

1. Member States shall ensure that when programmes from other Member States are retransmitted by cable in their territory the applicable copyright and related rights are observed and that such retransmission takes place on the basis of individual or collective contractual agreements between copyright owners, holders of related rights and cable operators.

2. Notwithstanding paragraph 1, Member States may retain until 31 December 1997 such statutory licence systems which are in operation or expressly provided for by national law on 31 July 1991.

Article 9
Exercise of the cable retransmission right

1. Member States shall ensure that the right of copyright owners and holders or related rights to grant or refuse authorization to a cable operator for a cable retransmission may be exercised only through a collecting society.

2. Where a rightholder has not transferred the management of his rights to a collecting society, the collecting society which manages rights of the same category shall be deemed to be mandated to manage his rights. Where more than one collecting society manages rights of that category, the rightholder shall be free to choose which of those collecting societies is deemed to be mandated to manage his rights. A rightholder referred to in this paragraph shall have the same rights and obligations resulting from the agreement between the cable operator and the collecting society which is deemed to be mandated to manage his rights as the rightholders who have mandated that collecting society and he shall be able to claim those rights within a period, to be fixed by the Member State concerned, which shall not be shorter than three years from the date of the cable retransmission which includes his work or other protected subject matter.

3. A Member State may provide that, when a rightholder authorizes the initial transmission within its territory of a work or other protected subject matter, he shall be deemed to have agreed not to exercise his cable retransmission rights on an individual basis but to exercise them in accordance with the provisions of this Directive.

Article 10
Exercise of the cable retransmission right by broadcasting organizations

Member States shall ensure that Article 9 does not apply to the rights exercised by a broadcasting organization in respect of its own transmission, irrespective of whether the rights concerned are its own or have been transferred to it by other copyright owners and/or holders of related rights.

Article 11
Mediators

1. Where no agreement is concluded regarding authorization of the cable retransmission of a broadcast. Member States shall ensure that either party may call upon the assistance of one or more mediators.

2. The task of the mediators shall be to provide assistance with negotiation. They may also submit proposals to the parties.

3. It shall be assumed that all the parties accept a proposal as referred to in paragraph 2 if none of them expresses its opposition within a period of three months. Notice of the proposal and of any opposition thereto shall be served on the parties concerned in accordance with the applicable rules concerning the service of legal documents.

4. The mediators shall be so selected that their independence and impartiality are beyond reasonable doubt.

Article 12
Prevention of the abuse of negotiating positions

1. Member States shall ensure by means of civil or administrative law, as appropriate, that the parties enter and conduct negotiations regarding authorization for cable retransmission in good faith and do not prevent or hinder negotiation without valid justification.

2. A Member State which, on the date mentioned in Article 14 (1), has a body with jurisdiction in its territory over cases where the right to retransmit a programme by cable to the public in that Member State has been unreasonably refused or offered on unreasonable terms by a broadcasting organization may retain that body.

3. Paragraph 2 shall apply for a transitional period of eight years from the date mentioned in Article 14 (1).

CHAPTER IV
GENERAL PROVISIONS
Article 13
Collective administration of rights

This Directive shall be without prejudice to the regulation of the activities of collecting societies by the Member States.

Article 14
Final provisions

1. Member States shall bring into force the laws, regulations and administrative provisions necessary to comply with this Directive before 1 January 1995. They shall immediately inform the Commission thereof.

When Member States adopt these measures, the latter shall contain a reference to this Directive or shall be accompanied by such reference at the time of their official publication. The methods of making such a reference shall be laid down by the Member States.

2. Member States shall communicate to the Commission the provisions of national law which they adopt in the field covered by this Directive.

3. Not later than 1 January 2000, the Commission shall submit to the European Parliament, the Council and the Economic and Social Committee a report on the application of this Directive and, if necessary, make further proposals to adapt it to developments in the audio and audiovisual sector.

Article 15

This Directive is addressed to the Member States.

Done at Brussels, 27 September 1993.

EC RENTAL RIGHTS DIRECTIVE

Council Directive 92/100/EEC of 19 November 1992 on rental right and lending right and on certain rights related to copyright in the field of intellectual property

THE COUNCIL OF THE EUROPEAN COMMUNITIES,

Having regard to the Treaty establishing the European Economic Community, and in particular Articles 57(2), 66 and 100a thereof,

Having regard to the proposal from the Commission,

In cooperation with the European Parliament,

Having regard to the opinion of the Economic and Social Committee,

Whereas differences exist in the legal protection provided by the laws and practices of the Member States for copyright works and subject matter of related rights protection as regards rental and lending; whereas such differences are sources of barriers to trade and distortions of competition which impede the achievement and proper functioning of the internal market;

Whereas such differences in legal protection could well become greater as Member States adopt new and different legislation or as national case-law interpreting such legislation develops differently;

Whereas such differences should therefore be eliminated in accordance with the objective of introducing an area without internal frontiers as set out in Article 8a of the Treaty so as to institute, pursuant to Article 3(f) of the Treaty, a system ensuring that competition in the common market is not distorted;

Whereas rental and lending of copyright works and the subject matter of related rights protection is playing an increasingly important role in particular for authors, performers and producers of phonograms and films; whereas piracy is becoming an increasing threat;

Whereas the adequate protection of copyright works and subject matter of related rights protection by rental and lending rights as well as the protection of the subject matter of related rights protection by the fixation right, reproduction right, distribution right, right to broadcast and communication to the public can accordingly be considered as being of fundamental importance for the Community's economic and cultural development;

Whereas copyright and related rights protection must adapt to new economic developments such as new forms of exploitation;

Whereas the creative and artistic work of authors and performers necessitates an adequate income as a basis for further creative and artistic work, and the investments required particularly for the production of phonograms and films are especially high and risky; whereas the possibility for securing that income and recouping that investment can only effectively be guaranteed through adequate legal protection of the rightholders concerned;

Whereas these creative, artistic and entrepreneurial activities are, to a large extent, activities of self-employed persons; whereas the pursuit of such activities must be made easier by providing a harmonized legal protection within the Community;

Whereas, to the extent that these activities principally constitute services, their provision must equally be facilitated by the establishment in the Community of a harmonized legal framework;

Whereas the legislation of the Member States should be approximated in such a way so as not to conflict with the international conventions on which many Member States' copyright and related rights laws are based;

Whereas the Community's legal framework on the rental right and lending right and on certain rights related to copyright can be limited to establishing that Member States provide rights with respect to rental and lending for certain groups of rightholders and further to establishing the rights of fixation, reproduction, distribution, broadcasting and communication to the public for certain groups of rightholders in the field of related rights protection;

Whereas it is necessary to define the concepts of rental and lending for the purposes of this Directive;

Whereas it is desirable, with a view to clarity, to exclude from rental and lending within the meaning of this Directive certain forms of making available, as for instance making available phonograms or films (cinematographic or audiovisual works or moving images, whether or not accompanied by sound) for the purpose of public performance or broadcasting, making available for the purpose of exhibition, or making available for on-the-spot reference use; whereas lending within the meaning of this Directive does not include making available between establishments which are accessible to the public;

Whereas, where lending by an establishment accessible to the public gives rise to a payment the amount of which does not go beyond what is necessary to cover the operating costs of the establishment, there is no direct or indirect economic or commercial advantage within the meaning of this Directive;

Whereas it is necessary to introduce arrangements ensuring that an unwaivable equitable remuneration is obtained by authors and performers who must retain the possibility to entrust the administration of this right to collecting societies representing them;

Whereas the equitable remuneration may be paid on the basis of one or several payments an any time on or after the conclusion of the contract;

Whereas the equitable remuneration must take account of the importance of the contribution of the authors and performers concerned to the phonogram or film;

Whereas it is also necessary to protect the rights at least of authors as regards public lending by providing for specific arrangements; whereas, however, any measures based on Article 5 of this Directive have to comply with Community law, in particular with Article 7 of the Treaty;

Whereas the provisions of Chapter II do not prevent Member States from extending the presumption set out in Article 2 (5) to the exclusive rights included in that chapter; whereas furthermore the provisions of Chapter II do not prevent Member States from providing for a rebuttable presumption of the authorization of exploitation in respect of the exclusive rights of performers provided for in those articles, in so far as such presumption is compatible with the International Convention for the Protection of Performers, Producers of Phonograms and Broadcasting Organizations (hereinafter referred to as the Rome Convention);

Whereas Member States may provide for more far-reaching protection for owners of rights related to copyright than that required by Article 8 of this Directive;

Whereas the harmonized rental and lending rights and the harmonized protection in the field of rights related to copyright should not be exercised in a way which constitutes a disguised restriction on trade between Member States or in a way which is contrary to the rule of media exploitation chronology, as recognized in the Judgment handed down in Société Cinéthèque v. FNCF,

HAS ADOPTED THIS DIRECTIVE:

CHAPTER I
RENTAL AND LENDING RIGHT

Article 1
Object of harmonization

1. In accordance with the provisions of this Chapter, Member States shall provide, subject to Article 5, a right to authorize or prohibit the rental and lending of originals and copies of copyright works, and other subject matter as set out in Article 2(1).

2. For the purposes of this Directive, 'rental' means making available for use, for a limited period of time and for direct or indirect economic or commercial advantage.

3. For the purposes of this Directive, 'lending' means making available for use, for a limited period of time and not for direct or indirect economic or commercial advantage, when it is made through establishments which are accessible to the public.

4. The rights referred to in paragraph 1 shall not be exhausted by any sale or other act of distribution of originals and copies of copyright works and other subject matter as set out in Article 2(1).

Article 2
Rightholders and subject matter of rental and lending right

1. The exclusive right to authorize or prohibit rental and lending shall belong:

— to the author in respect of the original and copies of his work,

— to the performer in respect of fixations of his performance,

— to the phonogram producer in respect of his phonograms, and

— to the producer of the first fixation of a film in respect of the original and copies of his film. For the purposes of this Directive, the term 'film' shall designate a cinematographic or audiovisual work or moving images, whether or not accompanied by sound.

2. For the purposes of this Directive the principal director of a cinematographic or audiovisual work shall be considered as its author or one of its authors. Member States may provide for others to be considered as its co-authors.

3. This Directive does not cover rental and lending rights in relation to buildings and to works of applied art.

4. The rights referred to in paragraph 1 may be transferred, assigned or subject to the granting of contractual licences.

5. Without prejudice to paragraph 7, when a contract concerning film production is concluded, individually or collectively, by performers with a film producer, the performer covered by this contract shall be presumed, subject to contractual clauses to the contrary, to have transferred his rental right, subject to Article 4.

6. Member States may provide for a similar presumption as set out in paragraph 5 with respect to authors.

7. Member States may provide that the signing of a contract concluded between a performer and a film producer concerning the production of a film has the effect of authorizing rental, provided that such contract provides for an equitable remuneration within the meaning of Article 4. Member States may also provide that this paragraph shall apply *mutatis mutandis* to the rights included in Chapter II.

Article 3
Rental of computer programs

This Directive shall be without prejudice to Article 4 (c) of Council Directive 91/250/EEC of 14 May 1991 on the legal protection of computer programs.

Article 4
Unwaivable right to equitable remuneration

1. Where an author or performer has transferred or assigned his rental right concerning a phonogram or an original or copy of a film to a phonogram or film producer, that author or performer shall retain the right to obtain an

equitable remuneration for the rental.

2. The right to obtain an equitable remuneration for rental cannot be waived by authors or performers.

3. The administration of this right to obtain an equitable remuneration may be entrusted to collecting societies representing authors or performers.

4. Member States may regulate whether and to what extent administration by collecting societies of the right to obtain an equitable remuneration may be imposed, as well as the question from whom this remuneration may be claimed or collected.

Article 5
Derogation from the exclusive public lending right

1. Member States may derogate from the exclusive right provided for in Article 1 in respect of public lending, provided that at least authors obtain a remuneration for such lending. Member States shall be free to determine this remuneration taking account of their cultural promotion objectives.

2. When Member States do not apply the exclusive lending right provided for in Article 1 as regards phonograms, films and computer programs, they shall introduce, at least for authors, a remuneration.

3. Member States may exempt certain categories of establishments from the payment of the remuneration referred to in paragraphs 1 and 2.

4. The Commission, in cooperation with the Member States, shall draw up before 1 July 1997 a report on public lending in the Community. It shall forward this report to the European Parliament and to the Council.

CHAPTER II
RIGHTS RELATED TO COPYRIGHT

Article 6
Fixation right

1. Member States shall provide for performers the exclusive right to authorize or prohibit the fixation of their performances.

2. Member States shall provide for broadcasting organizations the exclusive right to authorize or prohibit the fixation of their broadcasts, whether these broadcasts are transmitted by wire or over the air, including by cable or satellite.

3. A cable distributor shall not have the right provided for in paragraph 2 where it merely retransmits by cable the broadcasts of broadcasting organizations.

Article 7
Reproduction right

1. Member States shall provide the exclusive right to authorize or prohibit the direct or indirect reproduction:

- for performers, of fixations of their performances,
- for phonogram producers, of their phonograms,
- for producers of the first fixations of films, in respect of the original and copies of their films, and
- for broadcasting organizations, of fixations of their broadcasts, as set out in Article 6(2).

2. The reproduction right referred to in paragraph 1 may be transferred, assigned or subject to the granting of contractual licences.

Article 8
Broadcasting and communication to the public

1. Member States shall provide for performers the exclusive right to authorize or prohibit the broadcasting by wireless means and the communication to the public of their performances, except where the performance is itself already a broadcast performance or is made from a fixation.

2. Member States shall provide a right in order to ensure that a single equitable remuneration is paid by the user, if a phonogram published for commercial purposes, or a reproduction of such phonogram, is used for broadcasting by wireless means or for any communication to the public, and to ensure that this remuneration is shared between the relevant performers and phonogram producers. Member States may, in the absence of agreement between the performers and phonogram producers, lay down the conditions as to the sharing of this remuneration between them.

3. Member States shall provide for broadcasting organizations the exclusive right to authorize or prohibit the rebroadcasting of their broadcasts by wireless means, as well as the communication to the public of their broadcasts if such communication is made in places accessible to the public against payment of an entrance fee.

Article 9
Distribution right

1. Member States shall provide
- for performers, in respect of fixations of their performances,
- for phonogram producers, in respect of their phonograms,
- for producers of the first fixations of films, in respect of the original and copies of their films,
- for broadcasting organizations, in respect of fixations of their broadcast as set out in Article 6(2),

the exclusive right to make available these objects, including copies thereof, to the public by sale or otherwise, hereafter referred to as the 'distribution right'.

2. The distribution right shall not be exhausted within the Community in respect of an object as referred to in paragraph 1, except where the first sale

in the Community of that object is made by the rightholder or with his consent.

3. The distribution right shall be without prejudice to the specific provisions of Chapter I, in particular Article 1 (4).

4. The distribution right may be transferred, assigned or subject to the granting of contractual licences.

Article 10
Limitations to rights

1. Member States may provide for limitations to the rights referred to in Chapter II in respect of:

(a) private use;

(b) use of short excerpts in connection with the reporting of current events;

(c) ephemeral fixation by a broadcasting organization by means of its own facilities and for its own broadcasts;

(d) use solely for the purposes of teaching or scientific research.

2. Irrespective of paragraph 1, any Member State may provide for the same kinds of limitations with regard to the protection of performers, producers of phonograms, broadcasting organizations and of producers of the first fixations of films, as it provides for in connection with the protection of copyright in literary and artistic works. However, compulsory licences may be provided for only to the extent to which they are compatible with the Rome Convention.

3. Paragraph 1 (a) shall be without prejudice to any existing or future legislation on remuneration for reproduction for private use.

CHAPTER III
DURATION

Article 11
Duration of authors' rights

Without prejudice to further harmonization, the authors' rights referred to in this Directive shall not expire before the end of the term provided by the Berne Convention for the Protection of Literary and Artistic Works.

Article 12
Duration of related rights

Without prejudice to further harmonization, the rights referred to in this Directive of performers, phonogram producers and broadcasting organizations shall not expire before the end of the respective terms provided by the Rome Convention. The rights referred to in this Directive for producers of the first fixations of films shall not expire before the end of a period of 20 years computed from the end of the year in which the fixation was made.

CHAPTER IV
COMMON PROVISIONS

Article 13
Application in time

1. This Directive shall apply in respect of all copyright works, performances, phonograms, broadcasts and first fixations of films referred to in this Directive which are, on 1 July 1994, still protected by the legislation of the Member States in the field of copyright and related rights or meet the criteria for protection under the provisions of this Directive on that date.

2. This Directive shall apply without prejudice to any acts of exploitation performed before 1 July 1994.

3. Member States may provide that the rightholders are deemed to have given their authorization to the rental or lending of an object referred to in Article 2 (1) which is proven to have been made available to third parties for this purpose or to have been acquired before 1 July 1994. However, in particular where such an object is a digital recording, Member States may provide that rightholders shall have a right to obtain an adequate remuneration for the rental or lending of that object.

4. Member States need not apply the provisions of Article 2(2) to cinematographic or audiovisual works created before 1 July 1994.

5. Member States may determine the date as from which the Article 2(2) shall apply, provided that that date is no later than 1 July 1997.

6. This Directive shall, without prejudice to paragraph 3 and subject to paragraphs 8 and 9, not affect any contracts concluded before the date of its adoption.

7. Member States may provide, subject to the provisions of paragraphs 8 and 9, that when rightholders who acquire new rights under the national provisions adopted in implementation of this Directive have, before 1 July 1994, given their consent for exploitation, they shall be presumed to have transferred the new exclusive rights.

8. Member States may determine the date as from which the unwaivable right to an equitable remuneration referred to in Article 4 exists, provided that that date is no later than 1 July 1997.

9. For contracts concluded before 1 July 1994, the unwaivable right to an equitable remuneration provided for in Article 4 shall apply only where authors or performers or those representing them have submitted a request to that effect before 1 January 1997. In the absence of agreement between rightholders concerning the level of remuneration, Member States may fix the level of equitable remuneration.

Article 14
Relation between copyright and related rights

Protection of copyright-related rights under this Directive shall leave intact and shall in no way affect the protection of copyright.

Article 15
Final provisions

1. Member States shall bring into force the laws, regulations and administrative provisions necessary to comply with this Directive not later than 1 July 1994. They shall forthwith inform the Commission thereof.

When Member States adopt these measures, they shall contain a reference to this Directive or shall be accompanied by such reference at the time of their official publication. The methods of making such a reference shall be laid down by the Member States.

2. Member States shall communicate to the Commission the main provisions of domestic law which they adopt in the field covered by this Directive.

Article 16

This Directive is addressed to the Member States.

Done at Brussels, 19 November 1992

EC SOFTWARE DIRECTIVE
Council Directive 91/250/EEC of 14 May 1991 on the legal protection of computer programs

THE COUNCIL OF THE EUROPEAN COMMUNITIES,

Having regard to the Treaty establishing the European Economic Community and in particular Article 100a thereof,

Having regard to the proposal from the Commission,

In cooperation with the European Parliament,

Having regard to the opinion of the Economic and Social Committee,

Whereas computer programs are at present not clearly protected in all Member States by existing legislation and such protection, where it exists, has different attributes;

Whereas the development of computer programs requires the investment of considerable human, technical and financial resources while computer programs can be copied at a fraction of the cost needed to develop them independently;

Whereas computer programs are playing an increasingly important role in a broad range of industries and computer program technology can accordingly be considered as being of fundamental importance for the Community's industrial development;

Whereas certain differences in the legal protection of computer programs offered by the laws of the Member States have direct and negative effects on the functioning of the common market as regards computer programs and such differences could well become greater as Member States introduce new legislation on this subject;

Whereas existing differences having such effects need to be removed and new ones prevented from arising, while differences not adversely affecting the functioning of the common market to a substantial degree need not be removed or prevented from arising;

Whereas the Community's legal framework on the protection of computer programs can accordingly in the first instance be limited to establishing that Member States should accord protection to computer programs under copyright law as literary works and, further, to establishing who and what should be protected, the exclusive rights on which protected persons should be able to rely in order to authorize or prohibit certain acts and for how long the protection should apply;

Whereas, for the purpose of this Directive, the term 'computer program` shall include programs in any form, including those which are incorporated into hardware; whereas this term also includes preparatory design work leading to the development of a computer program provided that the nature of the preparatory work is such that a computer program can result from it at a later stage;

Whereas, in respect of the criteria to be applied in determining whether or not a computer program is an original work, no tests as to the qualitative or aesthetic merits of the program should be applied;

Whereas the Community is fully committed to the promotion of international standardization;

Whereas the function of a computer program is to communicate and work together with other components of a computer system and with users and, for this purpose, a logical and, where appropriate, physical interconnection and interaction is required to permit all elements of software and hardware to work with other software and hardware and with users in all the ways in which they are intended to function;

Whereas the parts of the program which provide for such interconnection and interaction between elements of software and hardware are generally known as 'interfaces';

Whereas this functional interconnection and interaction is generally known as 'interoperability'; whereas such interoperability can be defined as the ability to exchange information and mutually to use the information which has been exchanged;

Whereas, for the avoidance of doubt, it has to be made clear that only the expression of a computer program is protected and that ideas and principles which underlie any element of a program, including those which underlie its interfaces, are not protected by copyright under this Directive;

Whereas, in accordance with this principle of copyright, to the extent that logic, algorithms and programming languages comprise ideas and principles, those ideas and principles are not protected under this Directive;

Whereas, in accordance with the legislation and jurisprudence of the Member States and the international copyright conventions, the expression of those ideas and principles is to be protected by copyright;

Whereas, for the purposes of this Directive, the term 'rental` means the making available for use, for a limited period of time and for profit-making purposes, of a computer program or a copy thereof; whereas this term does not include public lending, which, accordingly, remains outside the scope of this Directive;

Whereas the exclusive rights of the author to prevent the unauthorized reproduction of his work have to be subject to a limited exception in the case of a computer program to allow the reproduction technically necessary for the use of that program by the lawful acquirer;

Whereas this means that the acts of loading and running necessary for the use of a copy of a program which has been lawfully acquired, and the act of correction of its errors, may not be prohibited by contract; whereas, in the absence of specific contractual provisions, including when a copy of the program has been sold, any other act necessary for the use of the copy of a program may be performed in accordance with its intended purpose by a lawful acquirer of that copy;

Whereas a person having a right to use a computer program should not be prevented from performing acts necessary to observe, study or test the functioning of the program, provided that these acts do not infringe the copyright in the program;

Whereas the unauthorized reproduction, translation, adaptation or transformation of the form of the code in which a copy of a computer program has been made available constitutes an infringement of the exclusive rights of the author;

Whereas, nevertheless, circumstances may exist when such a reproduction of the code and translation of its form within the meaning of Article 4 (a) and (b) are indispensable to obtain the necessary information to achieve the interoperability of an independently created program with other programs;

Whereas it has therefore to be considered that in these limited circumstances only, performance of the acts of reproduction and translation by or on behalf of a person having a right to use a copy of the program is legitimate and compatible with fair practice and must therefore be deemed not to require the authorization of the rightholder;

Whereas an objective of this exception is to make it possible to connect all components of a computer system, including those of different manufacturers, so that they can work together;

Whereas such an exception to the author's exclusive rights may not be used in a way which prejudices the legitimate interests of the rightholder or which conflicts with a normal exploitation of the program;

Whereas, in order to remain in accordance with the provisions of the Berne Convention for the Protection of Literary and Artistic Works, the term of protection should be the life of the author and fifty years from the first of January of the year following the year of his death or, in the case of an anonymous or pseudonymous work, 50 years from the first of January of the year following the year in which the work is first published;

Whereas protection of computer programs under copyright laws should be without prejudice to the application, in appropriate cases, of other forms of protection; whereas, however, any contractual provisions contrary to Article 6 or to the exceptions provided for in Article 5 (2) and (3) should be null and void;

Whereas the provisions of this Directive are without prejudice to the application of the competition rules under Articles 85 and 86 of the Treaty if a dominant supplier refuses to make information available which is necessary for interoperability as defined in this Directive;

Whereas the provisions of this Directive should be without prejudice to specific requirements of Community law already enacted in respect of the publication of interfaces in the telecommunications sector or Council Decisions relating to standardization in the field of information technology and telecommunication;

Whereas this Directive does not affect derogations provided for under national legislation in accordance with the Berne Convention on points not covered by this Directive,

HAS ADOPTED THIS DIRECTIVE:

Article 1
Object of protection

1. In accordance with the provisions of this Directive, Member States shall protect computer programs, by copyright, as literary works within the meaning of the Berne Convention for the Protection of Literary and Artistic Works. For the purposes of this Directive, the term 'computer programs' shall include their preparatory design material.

2. Protection in accordance with this Directive shall apply to the expression in any form of a computer program. Ideas and principles which underlie any element of a computer program, including those which underlie its interfaces, are not protected by copyright under this Directive.

3. A computer program shall be protected if it is original in the sense that it is the author's own intellectual creation. No other criteria shall be applied to determine its eligibility for protection.

Article 2
Authorship of computer programs

1. The author of a computer program shall be the natural person or group of natural persons who has created the program or, where the legislation of the Member State permits, the legal person designated as the rightholder by that legislation. Where collective works are recognized by the legislation of a Member State, the person considered by the legislation of the Member State to have created the work shall be deemed to be its author.

2. In respect of a computer program created by a group of natural persons jointly, the exclusive rights shall be owned jointly.

3. Where a computer program is created by an employee in the execution of his duties or following the instructions given by his employer, the employer exclusively shall be entitled to exercise all economic rights in the program so created, unless otherwise provided by contract.

Article 3
Beneficiaries of protection

Protection shall be granted to all natural or legal persons eligible under national copyright legislation as applied to literary works.

Article 4
Restricted Acts

Subject to the provisions of Articles 5 and 6, the exclusive rights of the rightholder within the meaning of Article 2, shall include the right to do or to authorize:

(a) the permanent or temporary reproduction of a computer program by any means and in any form, in part or in whole. Insofar as loading, displaying, running, transmission or storage of the computer program necessitate such reproduction, such acts shall be subject to authorization by the rightholder;

(b) the translation, adaptation, arrangement and any other alteration of a computer program and the reproduction of the results thereof, without prejudice to the rights of the person who alters the program;

(c) any form of distribution to the public, including the rental, of the original computer program or of copies thereof. The first sale in the Community of a copy of a program by the rightholder or with his consent shall exhaust the distribution right within the Community of that copy, with the exception of the right to control further rental of the program or a copy thereof.

Article 5
Exceptions to the restricted acts

1. In the absence of specific contractual provisions, the acts referred to in Article 4 (a) and (b) shall not require authorization by the rightholder where they are necessary for the use of the computer program by the lawful acquirer in accordance with its intended purpose, including for error correction.

2. The making of a back-up copy by a person having a right to use the computer program may not be prevented by contract insofar as it is necessary for that use.

3. The person having a right to use a copy of a computer program shall be entitled, without the authorization of the rightholder, to observe, study or test the functioning of the program in order to determine the ideas and principles which underlie any element of the program if he does so while performing any of the acts of loading, displaying, running, transmitting or storing the program which he is entitled to do.

Article 6
Decompilation

1. The authorization of the rightholder shall not be required where reproduction of the code and translation of its form within the meaning of Article 4 (a) and (b) are indispensable to obtain the information necessary to achieve the interoperability of an independently created computer program with other programs, provided that the following conditions are met:

(a) these acts are performed by the licensee or by another person having a right to use a copy of a program, or on their behalf by a person authorized to do so;

(b) the information necessary to achieve interoperability has not previously been readily available to the persons referred to in subparagraph (a); and

(c) these acts are confined to the parts of the original program which are necessary to achieve interoperability.

2. The provisions of paragraph 1 shall not permit the information obtained through its application:

(a) to be used for goals other than to achieve the interoperability of the independently created computer program;

(b) to be given to others, except when necessary for the interoperability of the independently created computer program; or

(c) to be used for the development, production or marketing of a computer program substantially similar in its expression, or for any other act which infringes copyright.

3. In accordance with the provisions of the Berne Convention for the protection of Literary and Artistic Works, the provisions of this Article may not be interpreted in such a way as to allow its application to be used in a manner which unreasonably prejudices the right holder's legitimate interests or conflicts with a normal exploitation of the computer program.

Article 7
Special measures of protection

1. Without prejudice to the provisions of Articles 4, 5 and 6, Member States shall provide, in accordance with their national legislation, appropriate remedies against a person committing any of the acts listed in subparagraphs (a), (b) and (c) below:

(a) any act of putting into circulation a copy of a computer program knowing, or having reason to believe, that it is an infringing copy;

(b) the possession, for commercial purposes, of a copy of a computer program knowing, or having reason to believe, that it is an infringing copy;

(c) any act of putting into circulation, or the possession for commercial purposes of, any means the sole intended purpose of which is to facilitate the unauthorized removal or circumvention of any technical device which may have been applied to protect a computer program.

2. Any infringing copy of a computer program shall be liable to seizure in accordance with the legislation of the Member State concerned.

3. Member States may provide for the seizure of any means referred to in paragraph 1(c).

Article 8
Term of protection

1. Protection shall be granted for the life of the author and for fifty years after his death or after the death of the last surviving author; where the computer program is an anonymous or pseudonymous work, or where a legal person is designated as the author by national legislation in accordance with Article 2(1), the term of protection shall be fifty years from the time that the computer program is first lawfully made available to the public. The term of protection shall be deemed to begin on the first of January of the year

following the abovementioned events.

2. Member States which already have a term of protection longer than that provided for in paragraph 1 are allowed to maintain their present term until such time as the term of protection for copyright works is harmonized by Community law in a more general way.

Article 9
Continued application of other legal provisions

1. The provisions of this Directive shall be without prejudice to any other legal provisions such as those concerning patent rights, trade-marks, unfair competition, trade secrets, protection of semi-conductor products or the law of contract. Any contractual provisions contrary to Article 6 or to the exceptions provided for in Article 5 (2) and (3) shall be null and void.

2. The provisions of this Directive shall apply also to programs created before 1 January 1993 without prejudice to any acts concluded and rights acquired before that date.

Article 10
Final provisions

1. Member States shall bring into force the laws, regulations and administrative provisions necessary to comply with this Directive before 1 January 1993.

When Member States adopt these measures, the latter shall contain a reference to this Directive or shall be accompanied by such reference on the occasion of their official publication. The methods of making such a reference shall be laid down by the Member States.

2. Member States shall communicate to the Commission the provisions of national law which they adopt in the field governed by this Directive.

Article 11

This Directive is addressed to the Member States.

Done at Brussels, 14 May 1991.

EC DATABASE DIRECTIVE

Directive 96/9/EC of the European Parliament and of the Council of 11 March 1996 on the legal protection of databases

THE EUROPEAN PARLIAMENT AND THE COUNCIL OF THE EUROPEAN UNION,

Having regard to the Treaty establishing the European Community, and in particular Article 57(2), 66 and 100a thereof,

Having regard to the proposal from the Commission,

Having regard to the opinion of the Economic and Social Committee,

Acting in accordance with the procedure laid down in Article 189b of the Treaty,

(1) Whereas databases are at present not sufficiently protected in all Member States by existing legislation; whereas such protection, where it exists, has different attributes;

(2) Whereas such differences in the legal protection of databases offered by the legislation of the Member States have direct negative effects on the functioning of the internal market as regards databases and in particular on the freedom of natural and legal persons to provide on-line database goods and services on the basis of harmonized legal arrangements throughout the Community; whereas such differences could well become more pronounced as Member States introduce new legislation in this field, which is now taking on an increasingly international dimension;

(3) Whereas existing differences distorting the functioning of the internal market need to be removed and new ones prevented from arising, while differences not adversely affecting the functioning of the internal market or the development of an information market within the Community need not be removed or prevented from arising;

(4) Whereas copyright protection for databases exists in varying forms in the Member States according to legislation or case-law, and whereas, if differences in legislation in the scope and conditions of protection remain between the Member States, such unharmonized intellectual property rights can have the effect of preventing the free movement of goods or services within the Community;

(5) Whereas copyright remains an appropriate form of exclusive right for authors who have created databases;

(6) Whereas, nevertheless, in the absence of a harmonized system of unfair-competition legislation or of case-law, other measures are required in addition to prevent the unauthorized extraction and/or re-utilization of the contents of a database;

(7) Whereas the making of databases requires the investment of considerable human, technical and financial resources while such databases can be copied or accessed at a fraction of the cost needed to

design them independently;

(8) Whereas the unauthorized extraction and/or re-utilization of the contents of a database constitute acts which can have serious economic and technical consequences;

(9) Whereas databases are a vital tool in the development of an information market within the Community; whereas this tool will also be of use in many other fields;

(10) Whereas the exponential growth, in the Community and worldwide, in the amount of information generated and processed annually in all sectors of commerce and industry calls for investment in all the Member States in advanced information processing systems;

(11) Whereas there is at present a very great imbalance in the level of investment in the database sector both as between the Member States and between the Community and the world's largest database-producing third countries;

(12) Whereas such an investment in modern information storage and processing systems will not take place within the Community unless a stable and uniform legal protection regime is introduced for the protection of the rights of makers of databases;

(13) Whereas this Directive protects collections, sometimes called 'compilations', of works, data or other materials which are arranged, stored and accessed by means which include electronic, electromagnetic or electro-optical processes or analogous processes;

(14) Whereas protection under this Directive should be extended to cover non-electronic databases;

(15) Whereas the criteria used to determine whether a database should be protected by copyright should be defined to the fact that the selection or the arrangement of the contents of the database is the author's own intellectual creation; whereas such protection should cover the structure of the database;

(16) Whereas no criterion other than originality in the sense of the author's intellectual creation should be applied to determine the eligibility of the database for copyright protection, and in particular no aesthetic or qualitative criteria should be applied;

(17) Whereas the term 'database` should be understood to include literary, artistic, musical or other collections of works or collections of other material such as texts, sound, images, numbers, facts, and data; whereas it should cover collections of independent works, data or other materials which are systematically or methodically arranged and can be individually accessed; whereas this means that a recording or an audiovisual, cinematographic, literary or musical work as such does not fall within the scope of this Directive;

(18) Whereas this Directive is without prejudice to the freedom of authors to decide whether, or in what manner, they will allow their works to be included in a database, in particular whether or not the

authorization given is exclusive; whereas the protection of databases by the sui generis right is without prejudice to existing rights over their contents, and whereas in particular where an author or the holder of a related right permits some of his works or subject matter to be included in a database pursuant to a non-exclusive agreement, a third party may make use of those works or subject matter subject to the required consent of the author or of the holder of the related right without the sui generis right of the maker of the database being invoked to prevent him doing so, on condition that those works or subject matter are neither extracted from the database nor re-utilized on the basis thereof;

(19) Whereas, as a rule, the compilation of several recordings of musical performances on a CD does not come within the scope of this Directive, both because, as a compilation, it does not meet the conditions for copyright protection and because it does not represent a substantial enough investment to be eligible under the sui generis right;

(20) Whereas protection under this Directive may also apply to the materials necessary for the operation or consultation of certain databases such as thesaurus and indexation systems;

(21) Whereas the protection provided for in this Directive relates to databases in which works, data or other materials have been arranged systematically or methodically; whereas it is not necessary for those materials to have been physically stored in an organized manner;

(22) Whereas electronic databases within the meaning of this Directive may also include devices such as CD-ROM and CD-i;

(23) Whereas the term 'database' should not be taken to extend to computer programs used in the making or operation of a database, which are protected by Council Directive 91/250/EEC of 14 May 1991 on the legal protection of computer programs;

(24) Whereas the rental and lending of databases in the field of copyright and related rights are governed exclusively by Council Directive 92/100/EEC of 19 November 1992 on rental right and lending right and on certain rights related to copyright in the field of intellectual property;

(25) Whereas the term of copyright is already governed by Council Directive 93/98/EEC of 29 October 1993 harmonizing the term of protection of copyright and certain related rights;

(26) Whereas works protected by copyright and subject matter protected by related rights, which are incorporated into a database, remain nevertheless protected by the respective exclusive rights and may not be incorporated into, or extracted from, the database without the permission of the rightholder or his successors in title;

(27) Whereas copyright in such works and related rights in subject matter

thus incorporated into a database are in no way affected by the existence of a separate right in the selection or arrangement of these works and subject matter in a database;

(28) Whereas the moral rights of the natural person who created the database belong to the author and should be exercised according to the legislation of the Member States and the provisions of the Berne Convention for the Protection of Literary and Artistic Works; whereas such moral rights remain outside the scope of this Directive;

(29) Whereas the arrangements applicable to databases created by employees are left to the discretion of the Member States; whereas, therefore nothing in this Directive prevents Member States from stipulating in their legislation that where a database is created by an employee in the execution of his duties or following the instructions given by his employer, the employer exclusively shall be entitled to exercise all economic rights in the database so created, unless otherwise provided by contract;

(30) Whereas the author's exclusive rights should include the right to determine the way in which his work is exploited and by whom, and in particular to control the distribution of his work to unauthorized persons;

(31) Whereas the copyright protection of databases includes making databases available by means other than the distribution of copies;

(32) Whereas Member States are required to ensure that their national provisions are at least materially equivalent in the case of such acts subject to restrictions as are provided for by this Directive;

(33) Whereas the question of exhaustion of the right of distribution does not arise in the case of on-line databases, which come within the field of provision of services; whereas this also applies with regard to a material copy of such a database made by the user of such a service with the consent of the rightholder; whereas, unlike CD-ROM or CD-i, where the intellectual property is incorporated in a material medium, namely an item of goods, every on-line service is in fact an act which will have to be subject to authorization where the copyright so provides;

(34) Whereas, nevertheless, once the rightholder has chosen to make available a copy of the database to a user, whether by an on-line service or by other means of distribution, that lawful user must be able to access and use the database for the purposes and in the way set out in the agreement with the rightholder, even if such access and use necessitate performance of otherwise restricted acts;

(35) Whereas a list should be drawn up of exceptions to restricted acts, taking into account the fact that copyright as covered by this Directive applies only to the selection or arrangements of the contents of a database; whereas Member States should be given the option of providing for such exceptions in certain cases; whereas, however, this option should be exercised in accordance with the Berne Convention

and to the extent that the exceptions relate to the structure of the database; whereas a distinction should be drawn between exceptions for private use and exceptions for reproduction for private purposes, which concerns provisions under national legislation of some Member States on levies on blank media or recording equipment;

(36) Whereas the term 'scientific research' within the meaning of this Directive covers both the natural sciences and the human sciences;

(37) Whereas Article 10(1) of the Berne Convention is not affected by this Directive;

(38) Whereas the increasing use of digital recording technology exposes the database maker to the risk that the contents of his database may be copied and rearranged electronically, without his authorization, to produce a database of identical content which, however, does not infringe any copyright in the arrangement of his database;

(39) Whereas, in addition to aiming to protect the copyright in the original selection or arrangement of the contents of a database, this Directive seeks to safeguard the position of makers of databases against misappropriation of the results of the financial and professional investment made in obtaining and collection the contents by protecting the whole or substantial parts of a database against certain acts by a user or competitor;

(40) Whereas the object of this sui generis right is to ensure protection of any investment in obtaining, verifying or presenting the contents of a database for the limited duration of the right; whereas such investment may consist in the deployment of financial resources and/or the expending of time, effort and energy;

(41) Whereas the objective of the sui generis right is to give the maker of a database the option of preventing the unauthorized extraction and/or re-utilization of all or a substantial part of the contents of that database; whereas the maker of a database is the person who takes the initiative and the risk of investing; whereas this excludes subcontractors in particular from the definition of maker;

(42) Whereas the special right to prevent unauthorized extraction and/or re-utilization relates to acts by the user which go beyond his legitimate rights and thereby harm the investment; whereas the right to prohibit extraction and/or re-utilization of all or a substantial part of the contents relates not only to the manufacture of a parasitical competing product but also to any user who, through his acts, causes significant detriment, evaluated qualitatively or quantitatively, to the investment;

(43) Whereas, in the case of on-line transmission, the right to prohibit re-utilization is not exhausted either as regards the database or as regards a material copy of the database or of part thereof made by the addressee of the transmission with the consent of the rightholder;

(44) Whereas, when on-screen display of the contents of a database

necessitates the permanent or temporary transfer of all or a substantial part of such contents to another medium, that act should be subject to authorization by the rightholder;

(45) Whereas the right to prevent unauthorized extraction and/or re-utilization does not in any way constitute an extension of copyright protection to mere facts or data;

(46) Whereas the existence of a right to prevent the unauthorized extraction and/or re-utilization of the whole or a substantial part of works, data or materials from a database should not give rise to the creation of a new right in the works, data or materials themselves;

(47) Whereas, in the interests of competition between suppliers of information products and services, protection by the sui generis right must not be afforded in such a way as to facilitate abuses of a dominant position, in particular as regards the creation and distribution of new products and services which have an intellectual, documentary, technical, economic or commercial added value; whereas, therefore, the provisions of this Directive are without prejudice to the application of Community or national competition rules;

(48) Whereas the objective of this Directive, which is to afford an appropriate and uniform level of protection of databases as a means to secure the remuneration of the maker of the database, is different from the aim of Directive 95/46/EC of the European Parliament and of the Council of 24 October 1995 on the protection of individuals with regard to the processing of personal data and on the free movement of such data, which is to guarantee free circulation of personal data on the basis of harmonized rules designed to protect fundamental rights, notably the right to privacy which is recognized in Article 8 of the European Convention for the Protection of Human Rights and Fundamental Freedoms; whereas the provisions of this Directive are without prejudice to data protection legislation;

(49) Whereas, notwithstanding the right to prevent extraction and/or re-utilization of all or a substantial part of a database, it should be laid down that the maker of a database or rightholder may not prevent a lawful user of the database from extracting and re-utilizing insubstantial parts; whereas, however, that user may not unreasonably prejudice either the legitimate interests of the holder of the sui generis right or the holder of copyright or a related right in respect of the works or subject matter contained in the database;

(50) Whereas the Member States should be given the option of providing for exceptions to the right to prevent the unauthorized extraction and/or re-utilization of a substantial part of the contents of a database in the case of extraction for private purposes, for the purposes of illustration for teaching or scientific research, or where extraction and/or re-utilization are/is carried out in the interests of public security or for the purposes of an administrative or judicial procedure;

whereas such operations must not prejudice the exclusive rights of the maker to exploit the database and their purpose must not be commercial;

(51) Whereas the Member States, where they avail themselves of the option to permit a lawful user of a database to extract a substantial part of the contents for the purposes of illustration for teaching or scientific research, may limit that permission to certain categories of teaching or scientific research institution;

(52) Whereas those Member States which have specific rules providing for a right comparable to the sui generis right provided for in this Directive should be permitted to retain, as far as the new right is concerned, the exceptions traditionally specified by such rules;

(53) Whereas the burden of proof regarding the date of completion of the making of a database lies with the maker of the database;

(54) Whereas the burden of proof that the criteria exist for concluding that a substantial modification of the contents of a database is to be regarded as a substantial new investment lies with the maker of the database resulting from such investment;

(55) Whereas a substantial new investment involving a new term of protection may include a substantial verification of the contents of the database;

(56) Whereas the right to prevent unauthorized extraction and/or re-utilization in respect of a database should apply to databases whose makers are nationals or habitual residents of third countries or to those produced by legal persons not established in a Member State, within the meaning of the Treaty, only if such third countries offer comparable protection to databases produced by nationals of a Member State or persons who have their habitual residence in the territory of the Community;

(57) Whereas, in addition to remedies provided under the legislation of the Member States for infringements of copyright or other rights, Member States should provide for appropriate remedies against unauthorized extraction and/or re-utilization of the contents of a database;

(58) Whereas, in addition to the protection given under this Directive to the structure of the database by copyright, and to its contents against unauthorized extraction and/or re-utilization under the sui generis right, other legal provisions in the Member States relevant to the supply of database goods and services continue to apply;

(59) Whereas this Directive is without prejudice to the application to databases composed of audiovisual works of any rules recognized by a Member State's legislation concerning the broadcasting of audiovisual programmes;

(60) Whereas some Member States currently protect under copyright arrangements databases which do not meet the criteria for eligibility for copyright protection laid down in this Directive; whereas, even if

the databases concerned are eligible for protection under the right laid down in this Directive to prevent unauthorized extraction and/or re-utilization of their contents, the term of protection under that right is considerably shorter than that which they enjoy under the national arrangements currently in force; whereas harmonization of the criteria for determining whether a database is to be protected by copyright may not have the effect of reducing the term of protection currently enjoyed by the rightholders concerned; whereas a derogation should be laid down to that effect; whereas the effects of such derogation must be confined to the territories of the Member States concerned,

HAVE ADOPTED THIS DIRECTIVE:

CHAPTER I
SCOPE

Article 1
Scope

1. This Directive concerns the legal protection of databases in any form.

2. For the purposes of this Directive, 'database' shall mean a collection of independent works, data or other materials arranged in a systematic or methodical way and individually accessible by electronic or other means.

3. Protection under this Directive shall not apply to computer programs used in the making or operation of databases accessible by electronic means.

Article 2
Limitations on the scope

This Directive shall apply without prejudice to Community provisions relating to:

(a) the legal protection of computer programs;

(b) rental right, lending right and certain rights related to copyright in the field of intellectual property;

(c) the term of protection of copyright and certain related rights.

CHAPTER II
COPYRIGHT

Article 3
Object of protection

1. In accordance with this Directive, databases which, by reason of the selection or arrangement of their contents, constitute the author's own intellectual creation shall be protected as such by copyright. No other criteria

shall be applied to determine their eligibility for that protection.

2. The copyright protection of databases provided for by this Directive shall not extend to their contents and shall be without prejudice to any rights subsisting in those contents themselves.

Article 4
Database authorship

1. The author of a database shall be the natural person or group of natural persons who created the base or, where the legislation of the Member States so permits, the legal person designated as the rightholder by that legislation.

2. Where collective works are recognized by the legislation of a Member State, the economic rights shall be owned by the person holding the copyright.

3. In respect of a database created by a group of natural persons jointly, the exclusive rights shall be owned jointly.

Article 5
Restricted acts

In respect of the expression of the database which is protectable by copyright, the author of a database shall have the exclusive right to carry out or to authorize:

(a) temporary or permanent reproduction by any means and in any form, in whole or in part;

(b) translation, adaptation, arrangement and any other alteration;

(c) any form of distribution to the public of the database or of copies thereof. The first sale in the Community of a copy of the database by the rightholder or with his consent shall exhaust the right to control resale of that copy within the Community;

(d) any communication, display or performance to the public;

(e) any reproduction, distribution, communication, display or performance to the public of the results of the acts referred to in (b).

Article 6
Exceptions to restricted acts

1. The performance by the lawful user of a database or of a copy thereof of any of the acts listed in Article 5 which is necessary for the purposes of access to the contents of the databases and normal use of the contents by the lawful user shall not require the authorization of the author of the database. Where the lawful user is authorized to use only part of the database, this provision shall apply only to that part.

2. Member States shall have the option of providing for limitations on the rights set out in Article 5 in the following cases:

(a) in the case of reproduction for private purposes of a non-electronic database;

(b) where there is use for the sole purpose of illustration for teaching or scientific research, as long as the source is indicated and to the extent justified by the non-commercial purpose to be achieved;

(c) where there is use for the purposes of public security of for the purposes of an administrative or judicial procedure;

(d) where other exceptions to copyright which are traditionally authorized under national law are involved, without prejudice to points (a), (b) and (c).

3. In accordance with the Berne Convention for the protection of Literary and Artistic Works, this Article may not be interpreted in such a way as to allow its application to be used in a manner which unreasonably prejudices the rightholder's legitimate interests or conflicts with normal exploitation of the database.

CHAPTER III
SUI GENERIS RIGHT

Article 7
Object of protection

1. Member States shall provide for a right for the maker of a database which shows that there has been qualitatively and/or quantitatively a substantial investment in either the obtaining, verification or presentation of the contents to prevent extraction and/or re-utilization of the whole or of a substantial part, evaluated qualitatively and/or quantitatively, of the contents of that database.

2. For the purposes of this Chapter:

(a) 'extraction' shall mean the permanent or temporary transfer of all or a substantial part of the contents of a database to another medium by any means or in any form;

(b) 're-utilization' shall mean any form of making available to the public all or a substantial part of the contents of a database by the distribution of copies, by renting, by on-line or other forms of transmission. The first sale of a copy of a database within the Community by the rightholder or with his consent shall exhaust the right to control resale of that copy within the Community;

Public lending is not an act of extraction or re-utilization.

3. The right referred to in paragraph 1 may be transferred, assigned or granted under contractual licence.

4. The right provided for in paragraph 1 shall apply irrespective of the eligibility of that database for protection by copyright or by other rights. Moreover, it shall apply irrespective of eligibility of the contents of that database for protection by copyright or by other rights. Protection of databases under the right provided for in paragraph 1 shall be without prejudice to rights existing in respect of their contents.

5. The repeated and systematic extraction and/or re-utilization of insubstantial parts of the contents of the database implying acts which conflict with a normal exploitation of that database or which unreasonably prejudice the legitimate interests of the maker of the database shall not be permitted.

Article 8
Rights and obligations of lawful users

1. The maker of a database which is made available to the public in whatever manner may not prevent a lawful user of the database from extracting and/or re-utilizing insubstantial parts of its contents, evaluated qualitatively and/or quantitatively, for any purposes whatsoever. Where the lawful user is authorized to extract and/or re-utilize only part of the database, this paragraph shall apply only to that part.

2. A lawful user of a database which is made available to the public in whatever manner may not perform acts which conflict with normal exploitation of the database or unreasonably prejudice the legitimate interests of the maker of the database.

3. A lawful user of a database which is made available to the public in any manner may not cause prejudice to the holder of a copyright or related right in respect of the works or subject matter contained in the database.

Article 9
Exceptions to the sui generis right

Member States may stipulate that lawful users of a database which is made available to the public in whatever manner may, without the authorization of its maker, extract or re-utilize a substantial part of its contents:

(a) in the case of extraction for private purposes of the contents of a non-electronic database;

(b) in the case of extraction for the purposes of illustration for teaching or scientific research, as long as the source is indicated and to the extent justified by the non-commercial purpose to be achieved;

(c) in the case of extraction and/or re-utilization for the purposes of public security or an administrative or judicial procedure.

Article 10
Term of protection

1. The right provided for in Article 7 shall run from the date of completion of the making of the database. It shall expire fifteen years from the first of January of the year following the date of completion.

2. In the case of a database which is made available to the public in whatever manner before expiry of the period provided for in paragraph 1, the term of protection by that right shall expire fifteen years from the first of January of the year following the date when the database was first made

available to the public.

3. Any substantial change, evaluated qualitatively or quantitatively, to the contents of a database, including any substantial change resulting from the accumulation of successive additions, deletions or alterations, which would result in the database being considered to be a substantial new investment, evaluated qualitatively or quantitatively, shall qualify the database resulting from that investment for its own term of protection.

Article 11
Beneficiaries of protection under the sui generis right

1. The right provided for in Article 7 shall apply to database whose makers or rightholders are nationals of a Member State or who have their habitual residence in the territory of the Community.

2. Paragraph 1 shall also apply to companies and firms formed in accordance with the law of a Member State and having their registered office, central administration or principal place of business within the Community; however, where such a company or firm has only its registered office in the territory of the Community, its operations must be genuinely linked on an ongoing basis with the economy of a Member State.

3. Agreements extending the right provided for in Article 7 to databases made in third countries and falling outside the provisions of paragraphs 1 and 2 shall be concluded by the Council acting on a proposal from the Commission. The term of any protection extended to databases by virtue of that procedure shall not exceed that available pursuant to Article 10.

CHAPTER IV
COMMON PROVISIONS

Article 12
Remedies

Member States shall provide appropriate remedies in respect of infringements of the rights provided for in this Directive.

Article 13
Continued application of other legal provisions

This Directive shall be without prejudice to provisions concerning in particular copyright, rights related to copyright or any other rights or obligations subsisting in the data, works or other materials incorporated into a database, patent rights, trade marks, design rights, the protection of national treasures, laws on restrictive practices and unfair competition, trade secrets, security, confidentiality, data protection and privacy, access to public documents, and the law of contract.

Article 14
Application over time

1. Protection pursuant to this Directive as regards copyright shall also be available in respect of databases created prior to the date referred to Article 16 (1) which on that date fulfil the requirements laid down in this Directive as regards copyright protection of databases.

2. Notwithstanding paragraph 1, where a database protected under copyright arrangements in a Member State on the date of publication of this Directive does not fulfil the eligibility criteria for copyright protection laid down in Article 3(1), this Directive shall not result in any curtailing in that Member State of the remaining term of protection afforded under those arrangements.

3. Protection pursuant to the provisions of this Directive as regards the right provided for in Article 7 shall also be available in respect of databases the making of which was completed not more than fifteen years prior to the date referred to in Article 16(1) and which on that date fulfil the requirements laid down in Article 7.

4. The protection provided for in paragraphs 1 and 3 shall be without prejudice to any acts concluded and rights acquired before the date referred to in those paragraphs.

5. In the case of a database the making of which was completed not more than fifteen years prior to the date referred to in Article 16 (1), the term of protection by the right provided for in Article 7 shall expire fifteen years from the first of January following that date.

Article 15
Binding nature of certain provisions

Any contractual provision contrary to Articles 6 (1) and 8 shall be null and void.

Article 16
Final provisions

1. Member States shall bring into force the laws, regulations and administrative provisions necessary to comply with this Directive before 1 January 1998.

When Member States adopt these provisions, they shall contain a reference to this Directive or shall be accompanied by such reference on the occasion of their official publication. The methods of making such reference shall be laid down by Member States.

2. Member States shall communicate to the Commission the text of the provisions of domestic law which they adopt in the field governed by this Directive.

3. Not later than at the end of the third year after the date referred to in paragraph 1, and every three years thereafter, the Commission shall submit to the European Parliament, the Council and the Economic and Social

Committee a report on the application of this Directive, in which, inter alia, on the basis of specific information supplied by the Member States, it shall examine in particular the application of the sui generis right, including Articles 8 and 9, and shall verify especially whether the application of this right has led to abuse of a dominant position or other interference with free competition which would justify appropriate measures being taken, including the establishment of non-voluntary licensing arrangements. Where necessary, it shall submit proposals for adjustment of this Directive in line with developments in the area of databases.

Article 17

This Directive is addressed to the Member States.

Done at Strasbourg, 11 March 1996.

EC E-COMMERCE DIRECTIVE

Directive 2000/31/EC of the European Parliament and of the Council of 8 June 2000 on certain legal aspects of information society services, in particular electronic commerce, in the Internal Market

THE EUROPEAN PARLIAMENT AND THE COUNCIL OF THE EUROPEAN UNION,

Having regard to the Treaty establishing the European Community, and in particular Articles 47(2), 55 and 95 thereof,

Having regard to the proposal from the Commission,

Having regard to the opinion of the Economic and Social Committee,

Acting in accordance with the procedure laid down in Article 251 of the Treaty,

Whereas:

(1)   The European Union is seeking to forge ever closer links between the States and peoples of Europe, to ensure economic and social progress; in accordance with Article 14(2) of the Treaty, the internal market comprises an area without internal frontiers in which the free movements of goods, services and the freedom of establishment are ensured; the development of information society services within the area without internal frontiers is vital to eliminating the barriers which divide the European peoples.

(2)   The development of electronic commerce within the information society offers significant employment opportunities in the Community, particularly in small and medium-sized enterprises, and will stimulate economic growth and investment in innovation by European companies, and can also enhance the competitiveness of European industry, provided that everyone has access to the Internet.

(3)   Community law and the characteristics of the Community legal order are a vital asset to enable European citizens and operators to take full advantage, without consideration of borders, of the opportunities afforded by electronic commerce; this Directive therefore has the purpose of ensuring a high level of Community legal integration in order to establish a real area without internal borders for information society services.

(4)   It is important to ensure that electronic commerce could fully benefit from the internal market and therefore that, as with Council Directive 89/552/EEC of 3 October 1989 on the coordination of certain provisions laid down by law, regulation or administrative action in Member States concerning the pursuit of television broadcasting activities, a high level of Community integration is achieved.

(5)   The development of information society services within the Community is hampered by a number of legal obstacles to the proper functioning of the internal market which make less attractive the

exercise of the freedom of establishment and the freedom to provide services; these obstacles arise from divergences in legislation and from the legal uncertainty as to which national rules apply to such services; in the absence of coordination and adjustment of legislation in the relevant areas, obstacles might be justified in the light of the case-law of the Court of Justice of the European Communities; legal uncertainty exists with regard to the extent to which Member States may control services originating from another Member State.

(6) In the light of Community objectives, of Articles 43 and 49 of the Treaty and of secondary Community law, these obstacles should be eliminated by coordinating certain national laws and by clarifying certain legal concepts at Community level to the extent necessary for the proper functioning of the internal market; by dealing only with certain specific matters which give rise to problems for the internal market, this Directive is fully consistent with the need to respect the principle of subsidiarity as set out in Article 5 of the Treaty.

(7) In order to ensure legal certainty and consumer confidence, this Directive must lay down a clear and general framework to cover certain legal aspects of electronic commerce in the internal market.

(8) The objective of this Directive is to create a legal framework to ensure the free movement of information society services between Member States and not to harmonise the field of criminal law as such.

(9) The free movement of information society services can in many cases be a specific reflection in Community law of a more general principle, namely freedom of expression as enshrined in Article 10(1) of the Convention for the Protection of Human Rights and Fundamental Freedoms, which has been ratified by all the Member States; for this reason, directives covering the supply of information society services must ensure that this activity may be engaged in freely in the light of that Article, subject only to the restrictions laid down in paragraph 2 of that Article and in Article 46(1) of the Treaty; this Directive is not intended to affect national fundamental rules and principles relating to freedom of expression.

(10) In accordance with the principle of proportionality, the measures provided for in this Directive are strictly limited to the minimum needed to achieve the objective of the proper functioning of the internal market; where action at Community level is necessary, and in order to guarantee an area which is truly without internal frontiers as far as electronic commerce is concerned, the Directive must ensure a high level of protection of objectives of general interest, in particular the protection of minors and human dignity, consumer protection and the protection of public health; according to Article 152 of the Treaty, the protection of public health is an essential component of other Community policies.

(11) This Directive is without prejudice to the level of protection for, in particular, public health and consumer interests, as established by

Community acts; amongst others, Council Directive 93/13/EEC of 5 April 1993 on unfair terms in consumer contracts and Directive 97/7/EC of the European Parliament and of the Council of 20 May 1997 on the protection of consumers in respect of distance contracts form a vital element for protecting consumers in contractual matters; those Directives also apply in their entirety to information society services; that same Community acquis, which is fully applicable to information society services, also embraces in particular Council Directive 84/450/EEC of 10 September 1984 concerning misleading and comparative advertising, Council Directive 87/102/EEC of 22 December 1986 for the approximation of the laws, regulations and administrative provisions of the Member States concerning consumer credit, Council Directive 93/22/EEC of 10 May 1993 on investment services in the securities field, Council Directive 90/314/EEC of 13 June 1990 on package travel, package holidays and package tours, Directive 98/6/EC of the European Parliament and of the Council of 16 February 1998 on consumer production in the indication of prices of products offered to consumers, Council Directive 92/59/EEC of 29 June 1992 on general product safety, Directive 94/47/EC of the European Parliament and of the Council of 26 October 1994 on the protection of purchasers in respect of certain aspects on contracts relating to the purchase of the right to use immovable properties on a timeshare basis, Directive 98/27/EC of the European Parliament and of the Council of 19 May 1998 on injunctions for the protection of consumers' interests, Council Directive 85/374/EEC of 25 July 1985 on the approximation of the laws, regulations and administrative provisions concerning liability for defective products, Directive 1999/44/EC of the European Parliament and of the Council of 25 May 1999 on certain aspects of the sale of consumer goods and associated guarantees, the future Directive of the European Parliament and of the Council concerning the distance marketing of consumer financial services and Council Directive 92/28/EEC of 31 March 1992 on the advertising of medicinal products; this Directive should be without prejudice to Directive 98/43/EC of the European Parliament and of the Council of 6 July 1998 on the approximation of the laws, regulations and administrative provisions of the Member States relating to the advertising and sponsorship of tobacco products adopted within the framework of the internal market, or to directives on the protection of public health; this Directive complements information requirements established by the abovementioned Directives and in particular Directive 97/7/EC.

(12) It is necessary to exclude certain activities from the scope of this Directive, on the grounds that the freedom to provide services in these fields cannot, at this stage, be guaranteed under the Treaty or existing secondary legislation; excluding these activities does not preclude any instruments which might prove necessary for the proper functioning of the internal market; taxation, particularly value added

tax imposed on a large number of the services covered by this Directive, must be excluded [from] the scope of this Directive.

(13) This Directive does not aim to establish rules on fiscal obligations nor does it pre-empt the drawing up of Community instruments concerning fiscal aspects of electronic commerce.

(14) The protection of individuals with regard to the processing of personal data is solely governed by Directive 95/46/EC of the European Parliament and of the Council of 24 October 1995 on the protection of individuals with regard to the processing of personal data and on the free movement of such data and Directive 97/66/EC of the European Parliament and of the Council of 15 December 1997 concerning the processing of personal data and the protection of privacy in the telecommunications sector which are fully applicable to information society services; these Directives already establish a Community legal framework in the field of personal data and therefore it is not necessary to cover this issue in this Directive in order to ensure the smooth functioning of the internal market, in particular the free movement of personal data between Member States; the implementation and application of this Directive should be made in full compliance with the principles relating to the protection of personal data, in particular as regards unsolicited commercial communication and the liability of intermediaries; this Directive cannot prevent the anonymous use of open networks such as the Internet.

(15) The confidentiality of communications is guaranteed by Article 5 Directive 97/66/EC; in accordance with that Directive, Member States must prohibit any kind of interception or surveillance of such communications by others than the senders and receivers, except when legally authorised.

(16) The exclusion of gambling activities from the scope of application of this Directive covers only games of chance, lotteries and betting transactions, which involve wagering a stake with monetary value; this does not cover promotional competitions or games where the purpose is to encourage the sale of goods or services and where payments, if they arise, serve only to acquire the promoted goods or services.

(17) The definition of information society services already exists in Community law in Directive 98/34/EC of the European Parliament and of the Council of 22 June 1998 laying down a procedure for the provision of information in the field of technical standards and regulations and of rules on information society services and in Directive 98/84/EC of the European Parliament and of the Council of 20 November 1998 on the legal protection of services based on, or consisting of, conditional access; this definition covers any service normally provided for remuneration, at a distance, by means of electronic equipment for the processing (including digital

compression) and storage of data, and at the individual request of a recipient of a service; those services referred to in the indicative list in Annex V to Directive 98/34/EC which do not imply data processing and storage are not covered by this definition.

(18) Information society services span a wide range of economic activities which take place on-line; these activities can, in particular, consist of selling goods on-line; activities such as the delivery of goods as such or the provision of services off-line are not covered; information society services are not solely restricted to services giving rise to on-line contracting but also, in so far as they represent an economic activity, extend to services which are not remunerated by those who receive them, such as those offering on-line information or commercial communications, or those providing tools allowing for search, access and retrieval of data; information society services also include services consisting of the transmission of information via a communication network, in providing access to a communication network or in hosting information provided by a recipient of the service; television broadcasting within the meaning of Directive EEC/89/552 and radio broadcasting are not information society services because they are not provided at individual request; by contrast, services which are transmitted point to point, such as video-on-demand or the provision of commercial communications by electronic mail are information society services; the use of electronic mail or equivalent individual communications for instance by natural persons acting outside their trade, business or profession including their use for the conclusion of contracts between such persons is not an information society service; the contractual relationship between an employee and his employer is not an information society service; activities which by their very nature cannot be carried out at a distance and by electronic means, such as the statutory auditing of company accounts or medical advice requiring the physical examination of a patient are not information society services.

(19) The place at which a service provider is established should be determined in conformity with the case-law of the Court of Justice according to which the concept of establishment involves the actual pursuit of an economic activity through a fixed establishment for an indefinite period; this requirement is also fulfilled where a company is constituted for a given period; the place of establishment of a company providing services via an Internet website is not the place at which the technology supporting its website is located or the place at which its website is accessible but the place where it pursues its economic activity; in cases where a provider has several places of establishment it is important to determine from which place of establishment the service concerned is provided; in cases where it is difficult to determine from which of several places of establishment a given service is provided, this is the place where the provider has the centre of his activities relating to this particular service.

(20) The definition of "recipient of a service" covers all types of usage of information society services, both by persons who provide information on open networks such as the Internet and by persons who seek information on the Internet for private or professional reasons.

(21) The scope of the coordinated field is without prejudice to future Community harmonisation relating to information society services and to future legislation adopted at national level in accordance with Community law; the coordinated field covers only requirements relating to on-line activities such as on-line information, on-line advertising, on-line shopping, on-line contracting and does not concern Member States' legal requirements relating to goods such as safety standards, labelling obligations, or liability for goods, or Member States' requirements relating to the delivery or the transport of goods, including the distribution of medicinal products; the coordinated field does not cover the exercise of rights of pre-emption by public authorities concerning certain goods such as works of art.

(22) Information society services should be supervised at the source of the activity, in order to ensure an effective protection of public interest objectives; to that end, it is necessary to ensure that the competent authority provides such protection not only for the citizens of its own country but for all Community citizens; in order to improve mutual trust between Member States, it is essential to state clearly this responsibility on the part of the Member State where the services originate; moreover, in order to effectively guarantee freedom to provide services and legal certainty for suppliers and recipients of services, such information society services should in principle be subject to the law of the Member State in which the service provider is established.

(23) This Directive neither aims to establish additional rules on private international law relating to conflicts of law nor does it deal with the jurisdiction of Courts; provisions of the applicable law designated by rules of private international law must not restrict the freedom to provide information society services as established in this Directive.

(24) In the context of this Directive, notwithstanding the rule on the control at source of information society services, it is legitimate under the conditions established in this Directive for Member States to take measures to restrict the free movement of information society services.

(25) National courts, including civil courts, dealing with private law disputes can take measures to derogate from the freedom to provide information society services in conformity with conditions established in this Directive.

(26) Member States, in conformity with conditions established in this Directive, may apply their national rules on criminal law and criminal proceedings with a view to taking all investigative and other measures necessary for the detection and prosecution of criminal

offences, without there being a need to notify such measures to the Commission.

(27) This Directive, together with the future Directive of the European Parliament and of the Council concerning the distance marketing of consumer financial services, contributes to the creating of a legal framework for the on-line provision of financial services; this Directive does not pre-empt future initiatives in the area of financial services in particular with regard to the harmonisation of rules of conduct in this field; the possibility for Member States, established in this Directive, under certain circumstances of restricting the freedom to provide information society services in order to protect consumers also covers measures in the area of financial services in particular measures aiming at protecting investors.

(28) The Member States' obligation not to subject access to the activity of an information society service provider to prior authorisation does not concern postal services covered by Directive 97/67/EC of the European Parliament and of the Council of 15 December 1997 on common rules for the development of the internal market of Community postal services and the improvement of quality of service consisting of the physical delivery of a printed electronic mail message and does not affect voluntary accreditation systems, in particular for providers of electronic signature certification service.

(29) Commercial communications are essential for the financing of information society services and for developing a wide variety of new, charge-free services; in the interests of consumer protection and fair trading, commercial communications, including discounts, promotional offers and promotional competitions or games, must meet a number of transparency requirements; these requirements are without prejudice to Directive 97/7/EC; this Directive should not affect existing Directives on commercial communications, in particular Directive 98/43/EC.

(30) The sending of unsolicited commercial communications by electronic mail may be undesirable for consumers and information society service providers and may disrupt the smooth functioning of interactive networks; the question of consent by recipient of certain forms of unsolicited commercial communications is not addressed by this Directive, but has already been addressed, in particular, by Directive 97/7/EC and by Directive 97/66/EC; in Member States which authorise unsolicited commercial communications by electronic mail, the setting up of appropriate industry filtering initiatives should be encouraged and facilitated; in addition it is necessary that in any event unsolicited commercial communities are clearly identifiable as such in order to improve transparency and to facilitate the functioning of such industry initiatives; unsolicited commercial communications by electronic mail should not result in additional communication costs for the recipient.

(31) Member States which allow the sending of unsolicited commercial communications by electronic mail without prior consent of the recipient by service providers established in their territory have to ensure that the service providers consult regularly and respect the opt-out registers in which natural persons not wishing to receive such commercial communications can register themselves.

(32) In order to remove barriers to the development of cross-border services within the Community which members of the regulated professions might offer on the Internet, it is necessary that compliance be guaranteed at Community level with professional rules aiming, in particular, to protect consumers or public health; codes of conduct at Community level would be the best means of determining the rules on professional ethics applicable to commercial communication; the drawing-up or, where appropriate, the adaptation of such rules should be encouraged without prejudice to the autonomy of professional bodies and associations.

(33) This Directive complements Community law and national law relating to regulated professions maintaining a coherent set of applicable rules in this field.

(34) Each Member State is to amend its legislation containing requirements, and in particular requirements as to form, which are likely to curb the use of contracts by electronic means; the examination of the legislation requiring such adjustment should be systematic and should cover all the necessary stages and acts of the contractual process, including the filing of the contract; the result of this amendment should be to make contracts concluded electronically workable; the legal effect of electronic signatures is dealt with by Directive 1999/93/EC of the European Parliament and of the Council of 13 December 1999 on a Community framework for electronic signatures; the acknowledgement of receipt by a service provider may take the form of the on-line provision of the service paid for.

(35) This Directive does not affect Member States' possibility of maintaining or establishing general or specific legal requirements for contracts which can be fulfilled by electronic means, in particular requirements concerning secure electronic signatures.

(36) Member States may maintain restrictions for the use of electronic contracts with regard to contracts requiring by law the involvement of courts, public authorities, or professions exercising public authority; this possibility also covers contracts which require the involvement of courts, public authorities, or professions exercising public authority in order to have an effect with regard to third parties as well as contracts requiring by law certification or attestation by a notary.

(37) Member States' obligation to remove obstacles to the use of electronic contracts concerns only obstacles resulting from legal requirements and not practical obstacles resulting from the impossibility of using electronic means in certain cases.

(38) Member States' obligation to remove obstacles to the use of electronic contracts is to be implemented in conformity with legal requirements for contracts enshrined in Community law.

(39) The exceptions to the provisions concerning the contracts concluded exclusively by electronic mail or by equivalent individual communications provided for by this Directive, in relation to information to be provided and the placing of orders, should not enable, as a result, the by-passing of those provisions by providers of information society services.

(40) Both existing and emerging disparities in Member States' legislation and case-law concerning liability of service providers acting as intermediaries prevent the smooth functioning of the internal market, in particular by impairing the development of cross-border services and producing distortions of competition; service providers have a duty to act, under certain circumstances, with a view to preventing or stopping illegal activities; this Directive should constitute the appropriate basis for the development of rapid and reliable procedures for removing and disabling access to illegal information; such mechanisms could be developed on the basis of voluntary agreements between all parties concerned and should be encouraged by Member States; it is in the interest of all parties involved in the provision of information society services to adopt and implement such procedures; the provisions of this Directive relating to liability should not preclude the development and effective operation, by the different interested parties, of technical systems of protection and identification and of technical surveillance instruments made possible by digital technology within the limits laid down by Directives 95/46/EC and 97/66/EC.

(41) This Directive strikes a balance between the different interests at stake and establishes principles upon which industry agreements and standards can be based.

(42) The exemptions from liability established in this Directive cover only cases where the activity of the information society service provider is limited to the technical process of operating and giving access to a communication network over which information made available by third parties is transmitted or temporarily stored, for the sole purpose of making the transmission more efficient; this activity is of a mere technical, automatic and passive nature, which implies that the information society service provider has neither knowledge of nor control over the information which is transmitted or stored.

(43) A service provider can benefit from the exemptions for "mere conduit" and for "caching" when he is in no way involved with the information transmitted; this requires among other things that he does not modify the information that he transmits; this requirement does not cover manipulations of a technical nature which take place in the course of the transmission as they do not alter the integrity of the information

contained in the transmission.

(44) A service provider who deliberately collaborates with one of the recipients of his service in order to undertake illegal acts goes beyond the activities of "mere conduit" or "caching" and as a result cannot benefit from the liability exemptions established for these activities.

(45) The limitations of the liability of intermediary service providers established in this Directive do not affect the possibility of injunctions of different kinds; such injunctions can in particular consist of orders by courts or administrative authorities requiring the termination or prevention of any infringement, including the removal of illegal information or the disabling of access to it.

(46) In order to benefit from a limitation of liability, the provider of an information society service, consisting of the storage of information, upon obtaining actual knowledge or awareness of illegal activities has to act expeditiously to remove or to disable access to the information concerned; the removal or disabling of access has to be undertaken in the observance of the principle of freedom of expression and of procedures established for this purpose at national level; this Directive does not affect Member States' possibility of establishing specific requirements which must be fulfilled expeditiously prior to the removal or disabling of information.

(47) Member States are prevented from imposing a monitoring obligation on service providers only with respect to obligations of a general nature; this does not concern monitoring obligations in a specific case and, in particular, does not affect orders by national authorities in accordance with national legislation.

(48) This Directive does not affect the possibility for Member States of requiring service providers, who host information provided by recipients of their service, to apply duties of care, which can reasonably be expected from them and which are specified by national law, in order to detect and prevent certain types of illegal activities.

(49) Member States and the Commission are to encourage the drawing-up of codes of conduct; this is not to impair the voluntary nature of such codes and the possibility for interested parties of deciding freely whether to adhere to such codes.

(50) It is important that the proposed directive on the harmonisation of certain aspects of copyright and related rights in the information society and this Directive come into force within a similar time scale with a view to establishing a clear framework of rules relevant to the issue of liability of intermediaries for copyright and relating rights infringements at Community level.

(51) Each Member State should be required, where necessary, to amend any legislation which is liable to hamper the use of schemes for the out-of-court settlement of disputes through electronic channels; the result of this amendment must be to make the functioning of such schemes genuinely and effectively possible in law and in practice,

even across borders.

(52) The effective exercise of the freedoms of the internal market makes it necessary to guarantee victims effective access to means of settling disputes; damage which may arise in connection with information society services is characterised both by its rapidity and by its geographical extent; in view of this specific character and the need to ensure that national authorities do not endanger the mutual confidence which they should have in one another, this Directive requests Member States to ensure that appropriate court actions are available; Member States should examine the need to provide access to judicial procedures by appropriate electronic means.

(53) Directive 98/27/EC, which is applicable to information society services, provides a mechanism relating to actions for an injunction aimed at the protection of the collective interests of consumers; this mechanism will contribute to the free movement of information society services by ensuring a high level of consumer protection.

(54) The sanctions provided for under this Directive are without prejudice to any other sanction or remedy provided under national law; Member States are not obliged to provide criminal sanctions for infringement of national provisions adopted pursuant to this Directive.

(55) This Directive does not affect the law applicable to contractual obligations relating to consumer contracts; accordingly, this Directive cannot have the result of depriving the consumer of the protection afforded to him by the mandatory rules relating to contractual obligations of the law of the Member State in which he has his habitual residence.

(56) As regards the derogation contained in this Directive regarding contractual obligations concerning contracts concluded by consumers, those obligations should be interpreted as including information on the essential elements of the content of the contract, including consumer rights, which have a determining influence on the decision to contract.

(57) The Court of Justice has consistently held that a Member State retains the right to take measures against a service provider that is established in another Member State but directs all or most of his activity to the territory of the first Member State if the choice of establishment was made with a view to evading the legislation that would have applied to the provider had he been established on the territory of the first Member State.

(58) This Directive should not apply to services supplied by service providers established in a third country; in view of the global dimension of electronic commerce, it is, however, appropriate to ensure that the Community rules are consistent with international rules; this Directive is without prejudice to the results of discussions within international organisations (amongst others WTO, OECD, Uncitral) on legal issues.

(59) Despite the global nature of electronic communications, coordination of national regulatory measures at European Union level is necessary in order to avoid fragmentation of the internal market, and for the establishment of an appropriate European regulatory framework; such coordination should also contribute to the establishment of a common and strong negotiating position in international forums.

(60) In order to allow the unhampered development of electronic commerce, the legal framework must be clear and simple, predictable and consistent with the rules applicable at international level so that it does not adversely affect the competitiveness of European industry or impede innovation in that sector.

(61) If the market is actually to operate by electronic means in the context of globalisation, the European Union and the major non-European areas need to consult each other with a view to making laws and procedures compatible.

(62) Cooperation with third countries should be strengthened in the area of electronic commerce, in particular with applicant countries, the developing countries and the European Union's other trading partners.

(63) The adoption of this Directive will not prevent the Member States from taking into account the various social, societal and cultural implications which are inherent in the advent of the information society; in particular it should not hinder measures which Member States might adopt in conformity with Community law to achieve social, cultural and democratic goals taking into account their linguistic diversity, national and regional specificities as well as their cultural heritage, and to ensure and maintain public access to the widest possible range of information society services; in any case, the development of the information society is to ensure that Community citizens can have access to the cultural European heritage provided in the digital environment.

(64) Electronic communication offers the Member States an excellent means of providing public services in the cultural, educational and linguistic fields.

(65) The Council, in its resolution of 19 January 1999 on the consumer dimension of the information society, stressed that the protection of consumers deserved special attention in this field; the Commission will examine the degree to which existing consumer protection rules provide insufficient protection in the context of the information society and will identify, where necessary, the deficiencies of this legislation and those issues which could require additional measures; if need be, the Commission should make specific additional proposals to resolve such deficiencies that will thereby have been identified,

HAVE ADOPTED THIS DIRECTIVE:

CHAPTER I
GENERAL PROVISIONS

Article 1
Objective and scope

1. This Directive seeks to contribute to the proper functioning of the internal market by ensuring the free movement of information society services between the Member States.

2. This Directive approximates, to the extent necessary for the achievement of the objective set out in paragraph 1, certain national provisions on information society services relating to the internal market, the establishment of service providers, commercial communications, electronic contracts, the liability of intermediaries, codes of conduct, out-of-court dispute settlements, court actions and cooperation between Member States.

3. This Directive complements Community law applicable to information society services without prejudice to the level of protection for, in particular, public health and consumer interests, as established by Community acts and national legislation implementing them in so far as this does not restrict the freedom to provide information society services.

4. This Directive does not establish additional rules on private international law nor does it deal with the jurisdiction of Courts.

5. This Directive shall not apply to:

(a) the field of taxation;

(b) questions relating to information society services covered by Directives 95/46/EC and 97/66/EC;

(c) questions relating to agreements or practices governed by cartel law;

(d) the following activities of information society services:

 – the activities of notaries or equivalent professions to the extent that they involve a direct and specific connection with the exercise of public authority,

 – the representation of a client and defence of his interests before the courts,

 – gambling activities which involve wagering a stake with monetary value in games of chance, including lotteries and betting transactions.

6. This Directive does not affect measures taken at Community or national level, in the respect of Community law, in order to promote cultural and linguistic diversity and to ensure the defence of pluralism.

Article 2
Definitions

For the purpose of this Directive, the following terms shall bear the following meanings:

(a) "information society services": services within the meaning of Article 1(2) of Directive 98/34/EC as amended by Directive 98/48/EC;

(b) "service provider": any natural or legal person providing an information society service;

(c) "established service provider": a service provider who effectively pursues an economic activity using a fixed establishment for an indefinite period. The presence and use of the technical means and technologies required to provide the service do not, in themselves, constitute an establishment of the provider;

(d) "recipient of the service": any natural or legal person who, for professional ends or otherwise, uses an information society service, in particular for the purposes of seeking information or making it accessible;

(e) "consumer": any natural person who is acting for purposes which are outside his or her trade, business or profession;

(f) "commercial communication": any form of communication designed to promote, directly or indirectly, the goods, services or image of a company, organisation or person pursuing a commercial, industrial or craft activity or exercising a regulated profession. The following do not in themselves constitute commercial communications:

— information allowing direct access to the activity of the company, organisation or person, in particular a domain name or an electronic-mail address,

— communications relating to the goods, services or image of the company, organisation or person compiled in an independent manner, particularly when this is without financial consideration;

(g) "regulated profession": any profession within the meaning of either Article 1(d) of Council Directive 89/48/EEC of 21 December 1988 on a general system for the recognition of higher-education diplomas awarded on completion of professional education and training of at least three-years' duration or of Article 1(f) of Council Directive 92/51/EEC of 18 June 1992 on a second general system for the recognition of professional education and training to supplement Directive 89/48/EEC;

(h) "coordinated field": requirements laid down in Member States' legal systems applicable to information society service providers or information society services, regardless of whether they are of a general nature or specifically designed for them.

(i) The coordinated field concerns requirements with which the service provider has to comply in respect of:

— the taking up of the activity of an information society service, such as requirements concerning qualifications, authorisation or notification,

— the pursuit of the activity of an information society service, such as requirements concerning the behaviour of the service provider, requirements regarding the quality or content of the service including those applicable to advertising and contracts, or requirements concerning the liability of the service provider;

  (ii) The coordinated field does not cover requirements such as:

     – requirements applicable to goods as such,

     – requirements applicable to the delivery of goods,

     – requirements applicable to services not provided by electronic means.

Article 3
Internal market

1. Each Member State shall ensure that the information society services provided by a service provider established on its territory comply with the national provisions applicable in the Member State in question which fall within the coordinated field.

2. Member States may not, for reasons falling within the coordinated field, restrict the freedom to provide information society services from another Member State.

3. Paragraphs 1 and 2 shall not apply to the fields referred to in the Annex.

4. Member States may take measures to derogate from paragraph 2 in respect of a given information society service if the following conditions are fulfilled:

(a) the measures shall be:

  (i) necessary for one of the following reasons:

     – public policy, in particular the prevention, investigation, detection and prosecution of criminal offences, including the protection of minors and the fight against any incitement to hatred on grounds of race, sex, religion or nationality, and violations of human dignity concerning individual persons,

     – the protection of public health,

     – public security, including the safeguarding of national security and defence,

     – the protection of consumers, including investors;

  (ii) taken against a given information society service which prejudices the objectives referred to in point (i) or which presents a serious and grave risk of prejudice to those objectives;

  (iii) proportionate to those objectives;

(b) before taking the measures in question and without prejudice to court proceedings, including preliminary proceedings and acts carried out in the framework of a criminal investigation, the Member State has:

     – asked the Member State referred to in paragraph 1 to take measures and the latter did not take such measures, or they were inadequate,

     – notified the Commission and the Member State referred to in paragraph 1 of its intention to take such measures.

5. Member States may, in the case of urgency, derogate from the conditions stipulated in paragraph 4(b). Where this is the case, the measures shall be notified in the shortest possible time to the Commission and to the Member State referred to in paragraph 1, indicating the reasons for which the Member State considers that there is urgency.

6. Without prejudice to the Member State's possibility of proceeding with the measures in question, the Commission shall examine the compatibility of the notified measures with Community law in the shortest possible time; where it comes to the conclusion that the measure is incompatible with Community law, the Commission shall ask the Member State in question to refrain from taking any proposed measures or urgently to put an end to the measures in question.

CHAPTER II
PRINCIPLES

Section 1: Establishment and information requirements

Article 4
Principle excluding prior authorisation

1. Member States shall ensure that the taking up and pursuit of the activity of an information society service provider may not be made subject to prior authorisation or any other requirement having equivalent effect.

2. Paragraph 1 shall be without prejudice to authorisation schemes which are not specifically and exclusively targeted at information society services, or which are covered by Directive 97/13/EC of the European Parliament and of the Council of 10 April 1997 on a common framework for general authorisations and individual licences in the field of telecommunications services.

Article 5
General information to be provided

1. In addition to other information requirements established by Community law, Member States shall ensure that the service provider shall render easily, directly and permanently accessible to the recipients of the service and competent authorities, at least the following information:

(a) the name of the service provider;

(b) the geographic address at which the service provider is established;

(c) the details of the service provider, including his electronic mail address, which allow him to be contacted rapidly and communicated with in a direct and effective manner;

(d) where the service provider is registered in a trade or similar public register, the trade register in which the service provider is entered and his registration number, or equivalent means of identification in that register;

(e) where the activity is subject to an authorisation scheme, the particulars of the relevant supervisory authority;

(f) as concerns the regulated professions:

- any professional body or similar institution with which the service provider is registered,

- the professional title and the Member State where it has been granted,

- a reference to the applicable professional rules in the Member State of establishment and the means to access them;

(g) where the service provider undertakes an activity that is subject to VAT, the identification number referred to in Article 22(1) of the sixth Council Directive 77/388/EEC of 17 May 1977 on the harmonisation of the laws of the Member States relating to turnover taxes—Common system of value added tax: uniform basis of assessment.

2. In addition to other information requirements established by Community law, Member States shall at least ensure that, where information society services refer to prices, these are to be indicated clearly and unambiguously and, in particular, must indicate whether they are inclusive of tax and delivery costs.

Section 2: Commercial communications

Article 6
Information to be provided

In addition to other information requirements established by Community law, Member States shall ensure that commercial communications which are part of, or constitute, an information society service comply at least with the following conditions:

(a) the commercial communication shall be clearly identifiable as such;

(b) the natural or legal person on whose behalf the commercial communication is made shall be clearly identifiable;

(c) promotional offers, such as discounts, premiums and gifts, where permitted in the Member State where the service provider is established, shall be clearly identifiable as such, and the conditions which are to be met to qualify for them shall be easily accessible and be presented clearly and unambiguously;

(d) promotional competitions or games, where permitted in the Member State where the service provider is established, shall be clearly identifiable as such, and the conditions for participation shall be easily accessible and be presented clearly and unambiguously.

Article 7
Unsolicited commercial communication

1. In addition to other requirements established by Community law, Member States which permit unsolicited commercial communication by electronic mail shall ensure that such commercial communication by a service provider established in their territory shall be identifiable clearly and unambiguously as such as soon as it is received by the recipient.

2. Without prejudice to Directive 97/7/EC and Directive 97/66/EC, Member States shall take measures to ensure that service providers undertaking unsolicited commercial communications by electronic mail consult regularly and respect the opt-out registers in which natural persons not wishing to receive such commercial communications can register themselves.

Article 8
Regulated professions

1. Member States shall ensure that the use of commercial communications which are part of, or constitute, an information society service provided by a member of a regulated profession is permitted subject to compliance with the professional rules regarding, in particular, the independence, dignity and honour of the profession, professional secrecy and fairness towards clients and other members of the profession.

2. Without prejudice to the autonomy of professional bodies and associations, Member States and the Commission shall encourage professional associations and bodies to establish codes of conduct at Community level in order to determine the types of information that can be given for the purposes of commercial communication in conformity with the rules referred to in paragraph 1.

3. When drawing up proposals for Community initiatives which may become necessary to ensure the proper functioning of the Internal Market with regard to the information referred to in paragraph 2, the Commission shall take due account of codes of conduct applicable at Community level and shall act in close cooperation with the relevant professional associations and bodies.

4. This Directive shall apply in addition to Community Directives concerning access to, and the exercise of, activities of the regulated professions.

Section 3: Contracts concluded by electronic means

Article 9
Treatment of contracts

1. Member States shall ensure that their legal system allows contracts to be concluded by electronic means. Member States shall in particular ensure that the legal requirements applicable to the contractual process neither create obstacles for the use of electronic contracts nor result in such contracts

being deprived of legal effectiveness and validity on account of their having been made by electronic means.

2. Member States may lay down that paragraph 1 shall not apply to all or certain contracts falling into one of the following categories:

(a) contracts that create or transfer rights in real estate, except for rental rights;

(b) contracts requiring by law the involvement of courts, public authorities or professions exercising public authority;

(c) contracts of suretyship granted and on collateral securities furnished by persons acting for purposes outside their trade, business or profession;

(d) contracts governed by family law or by the law of succession.

3. Member States shall indicate to the Commission the categories referred to in paragraph 2 to which they do not apply paragraph 1. Member States shall submit to the Commission every five years a report on the application of paragraph 2 explaining the reasons why they consider it necessary to maintain the category referred to in paragraph 2(b) to which they do not apply paragraph 1.

Article 10
Information to be provided

1. In addition to other information requirements established by Community law, Member States shall ensure, except when otherwise agreed by parties who are not consumers, that at least the following information is given by the service provider clearly, comprehensibly and unambiguously and prior to the order being placed by the recipient of the service:

(a) the different technical steps to follow to conclude the contract;

(b) whether or not the concluded contract will be filed by the service provider and whether it will be accessible;

(c) the technical means for identifying and correcting input errors prior to the placing of the order;

(d) the languages offered for the conclusion of the contract.

2. Member States shall ensure that, except when otherwise agreed by parties who are not consumers, the service provider indicates any relevant codes of conduct to which he subscribes and information on how those codes can be consulted electronically.

3. Contract terms and general conditions provided to the recipient must be made available in a way that allows him to store and reproduce them.

4. Paragraphs 1 and 2 shall not apply to contracts concluded exclusively by exchange of electronic mail or by equivalent individual communications.

Article 11
Placing of the order

1. Member States shall ensure, except when otherwise agreed by parties who are not consumers, that in cases where the recipient of the service places his order through technological means, the following principles apply:

- the service provider has to acknowledge the receipt of the recipient's order without undue delay and by electronic means,

- the order and the acknowledgement of receipt are deemed to be received when the parties to whom they are addressed are able to access them.

2. Member States shall ensure that, except when otherwise agreed by parties who are not consumers, the service provider makes available to the recipient of the service appropriate, effective and accessible technical means allowing him to identify and correct input errors, prior to the placing of the order.

3. Paragraph 1, first indent, and paragraph 2 shall not apply to contracts concluded exclusively by exchange of electronic mail or by equivalent individual communications.

Section 4: Liability of intermediary service providers

Article 12
"Mere conduit"

1. Where an information society service is provided that consists of the transmission in a communication network of information provided by a recipient of the service, or the provision of access to a communication network, Member States shall ensure that the service provider is not liable for the information transmitted, on condition that the provider:

(a) does not initiate the transmission;

(b) does not select the receiver of the transmission; and

(c) does not select or modify the information contained in the transmission.

2. The acts of transmission and of provision of access referred to in paragraph 1 include the automatic, intermediate and transient storage of the information transmitted in so far as this takes place for the sole purpose of carrying out the transmission in the communication network, and provided that the information is not stored for any period longer than is reasonably necessary for the transmission.

3. This Article shall not affect the possibility for a court or administrative authority, in accordance with Member States' legal systems, of requiring the service provider to terminate or prevent an infringement.

Article 13
"Caching"

1. Where an information society service is provided that consists of the transmission in a communication network of information provided by a

recipient of the service, Member States shall ensure that the service provider is not liable for the automatic, intermediate and temporary storage of that information, performed for the sole purpose of making more efficient the information's onward transmission to other recipients of the service upon their request, on condition that:

(a) the provider does not modify the information;

(b) the provider complies with conditions on access to the information;

(c) the provider complies with rules regarding the updating of the information, specified in a manner widely recognised and used by industry;

(d) the provider does not interfere with the lawful use of technology, widely recognised and used by industry, to obtain data on the use of the information; and

(e) the provider acts expeditiously to remove or to disable access to the information it has stored upon obtaining actual knowledge of the fact that the information at the initial source of the transmission has been removed from the network, or access to it has been disabled, or that a court or an administrative authority has ordered such removal or disablement.

2. This Article shall not affect the possibility for a court or administrative authority, in accordance with Member States' legal systems, of requiring the service provider to terminate or prevent an infringement.

Article 14
Hosting

1. Where an information society service is provided that consists of the storage of information provided by a recipient of the service, Member States shall ensure that the service provider is not liable for the information stored at the request of a recipient of the service, on condition that:

(a) the provider does not have actual knowledge of illegal activity or information and, as regards claims for damages, is not aware of facts or circumstances from which the illegal activity or information is apparent; or

(b) the provider, upon obtaining such knowledge or awareness, acts expeditiously to remove or to disable access to the information.

2. Paragraph 1 shall not apply when the recipient of the service is acting under the authority or the control of the provider.

3. This Article shall not affect the possibility for a court or administrative authority, in accordance with Member States' legal systems, of requiring the service provider to terminate or prevent an infringement, nor does it affect the possibility for Member States of establishing procedures governing the removal or disabling of access to information.

Article 15

No general obligation to monitor

1. Member States shall not impose a general obligation on providers, when providing the services covered by Articles 12, 13 and 14, to monitor the information which they transmit or store, nor a general obligation actively to seek facts or circumstances indicating illegal activity.

2. Member States may establish obligations for information society service providers promptly to inform the competent public authorities of alleged illegal activities undertaken or information provided by recipients of their service or obligations to communicate to the competent authorities, at their request, information enabling the identification of recipients of their service with whom they have storage agreements.

CHAPTER III
IMPLEMENTATION

Article 16
Codes of conduct

1. Member States and the Commission shall encourage:

(a) the drawing up of codes of conduct at Community level, by trade, professional and consumer associations or organisations, designed to contribute to the proper implementation of Articles 5 to 15;

(b) the voluntary transmission of draft codes of conduct at national or Community level to the Commission;

(c) the accessibility of these codes of conduct in the Community languages by electronic means;

(d) the communication to the Member States and the Commission, by trade, professional and consumer associations or organisations, of their assessment of the application of their codes of conduct and their impact upon practices, habits or customs relating to electronic commerce;

(e) the drawing up of codes of conduct regarding the protection of minors and human dignity.

2. Member States and the Commission shall encourage the involvement of associations or organisations representing consumers in the drafting and implementation of codes of conduct affecting their interests and drawn up in accordance with paragraph 1(a). Where appropriate, to take account of their specific needs, associations representing the visually impaired and disabled should be consulted.

Article 17
Out-of-court dispute settlement

1. Member States shall ensure that, in the event of disagreement between an information society service provider and the recipient of the service, their legislation does not hamper the use of out-of-court schemes, available under national law, for dispute settlement, including appropriate electronic means.

2. Member States shall encourage bodies responsible for the out-of-court settlement of, in particular, consumer disputes to operate in a way which provides adequate procedural guarantees for the parties concerned.

3. Member States shall encourage bodies responsible for out-of-court dispute settlement to inform the Commission of the significant decisions they take regarding information society services and to transmit any other information on the practices, usages or customs relating to electronic commerce.

Article 18
Court actions

1. Member States shall ensure that court actions available under national law concerning information society services' activities allow for the rapid adoption of measures, including interim measures, designed to terminate any alleged infringement and to prevent any further impairment of the interests involved.

2. The Annex to Directive 98/27/EC shall be supplemented as follows:

"11. Directive 2000/31/EC of the European Parliament and of the Council of 8 June 2000 on certain legal aspects on information society services, in particular electronic commerce, in the internal market (Directive on electronic commerce) (OJ L 178, 17.7.2000, p. 1)."

Article 19
Cooperation

1. Member States shall have adequate means of supervision and investigation necessary to implement this Directive effectively and shall ensure that service providers supply them with the requisite information.

2. Member States shall cooperate with other Member States; they shall, to that end, appoint one or several contact points, whose details they shall communicate to the other Member States and to the Commission.

3. Member States shall, as quickly as possible, and in conformity with national law, provide the assistance and information requested by other Member States or by the Commission, including by appropriate electronic means.

4. Member States shall establish contact points which shall be accessible at least by electronic means and from which recipients and service providers may:

(a) obtain general information on contractual rights and obligations as well as on the complaint and redress mechanisms available in the event of disputes, including practical aspects involved in the use of such mechanisms;

(b) obtain the details of authorities, associations or organisations from which they may obtain further information or practical assistance.

5. Member States shall encourage the communication to the Commission

of any significant administrative or judicial decisions taken in their territory regarding disputes relating to information society services and practices, usages and customs relating to electronic commerce. The Commission shall communicate these decisions to the other Member States.

Article 20
Sanctions

Member States shall determine the sanctions applicable to infringements of national provisions adopted pursuant to this Directive and shall take all measures necessary to ensure that they are enforced. The sanctions they provide for shall be effective, proportionate and dissuasive.

CHAPTER IV
FINAL PROVISIONS

Article 21
Re-examination

1. Before 17 July 2003, and thereafter every two years, the Commission shall submit to the European Parliament, the Council and the Economic and Social Committee a report on the application of this Directive, accompanied, where necessary, by proposals for adapting it to legal, technical and economic developments in the field of information society services, in particular with respect to crime prevention, the protection of minors, consumer protection and to the proper functioning of the internal market.

2. In examining the need for an adaptation of this Directive, the report shall in particular analyse the need for proposals concerning the liability of providers of hyperlinks and location tool services, "notice and take down" procedures and the attribution of liability following the taking down of content. The report shall also analyse the need for additional conditions for the exemption from liability, provided for in Articles 12 and 13, in the light of technical developments, and the possibility of applying the internal market principles to unsolicited commercial communications by electronic mail.

Article 22
Transposition

1. Member States shall bring into force the laws, regulations and administrative provisions necessary to comply with this Directive before 17 January 2002. They shall forthwith inform the Commission thereof.

2. When Member States adopt the measures referred to in paragraph 1, these shall contain a reference to this Directive or shall be accompanied by such reference at the time of their official publication. The methods of making such reference shall be laid down by Member States.

Article 23
Entry into force

This Directive shall enter into force on the day of its publication in the Official Journal of the European Communities.

Article 24
Addressees

This Directive is addressed to the Member States.

Done at Luxemburg, 8 June 2000.

ANNEX
DEROGATIONS FROM ARTICLE 3

As provided for in Article 3(3), Article 3(1) and (2) do not apply to:

- copyright, neighbouring rights, rights referred to in Directive 87/54/EEC and Directive 96/9/EC as well as industrial property rights,

- the emission of electronic money by institutions in respect of which Member States have applied one of the derogations provided for in Article 8(1) of Directive 2000/46/EC,

- Article 44(2) of Directive 85/611/EEC,

- Article 30 and Title IV of Directive 92/49/EEC, Title IV of Directive 92/96/EEC, Articles 7 and 8 of Directive 88/357/EEC and Article 4 of Directive 90/619/EEC,

- the freedom of the parties to choose the law applicable to their contract,

- contractual obligations concerning consumer contacts,

- formal validity of contracts creating or transferring rights in real estate where such contracts are subject to mandatory formal requirements of the law of the Member State where the real estate is situated,

- the permissibility of unsolicited commercial communications by electronic mail.

EC INFORMATION SOCIETY DIRECTIVE

Directive 2001/29/EC of the European Parliament and of the Council of 22 May 2001 on the harmonisation of certain aspects of copyright and related rights in the information society

THE EUROPEAN PARLIAMENT AND THE COUNCIL OF THE EUROPEAN UNION,

Having regard to the Treaty establishing the European Community, and in particular Articles 47(2), 55 and 95 thereof,

Having regard to the proposal from the Commission,

Having regard to the opinion of the Economic and Social Committee,

Acting in accordance with the procedure laid down in Article 251 of the Treaty,

Whereas:

(1)   The Treaty provides for the establishment of an internal market and the institution of a system ensuring that competition in the internal market is not distorted. Harmonisation of the laws of the Member States on copyright and related rights contributes to the achievement of these objectives.

(2)   The European Council, meeting at Corfu on 24 and 25 June 1994, stressed the need to create a general and flexible legal framework at Community level in order to foster the development of the information society in Europe. This requires, inter alia, the existence of an internal market for new products and services. Important Community legislation to ensure such a regulatory framework is already in place or its adoption is well under way. Copyright and related rights play an important role in this context as they protect and stimulate the development and marketing of new products and services and the creation and exploitation of their creative content.

(3)   The proposed harmonisation will help to implement the four freedoms of the internal market and relates to compliance with the fundamental principles of law and especially of property, including intellectual property, and freedom of expression and the public interest.

(4)   A harmonised legal framework on copyright and related rights, through increased legal certainty and while providing for a high level of protection of intellectual property, will foster substantial investment in creativity and innovation, including network infrastructure, and lead in turn to growth and increased competitiveness of European industry, both in the area of content provision and information technology and more generally across a wide range of industrial and cultural sectors. This will safeguard employment and encourage new job creation.

(5)   Technological development has multiplied and diversified the vectors

for creation, production and exploitation. While no new concepts for the protection of intellectual property are needed, the current law on copy right and related rights should be adapted and supplemented to respond adequately to economic realities such as new forms of exploitation.

(6) Without harmonisation at Community level, legislative activities at national level which have already been initiated in a number of Member States in order to respond to the technological challenges might result in significant differences in protection and thereby in restrictions on the free movement of services and products incorporating, or based on, intellectual property, leading to a refragmentation of the internal market and legislative inconsistency. The impact of such legislative differences and uncertainties will become more significant with the further development of the information society, which has already greatly increased transborder exploitation of intellectual property. This development will and should further increase. Significant legal differences and uncertainties in protection may hinder economics of scale for new products and services containing copyright and related rights.

(7) The Community legal framework for the protection of copyright and related rights must, therefore, also be adapted and supplemented as far as is necessary for the smooth functioning of the internal market. To that end, those national provisions on copyright and related rights which vary considerably from one Member State to another or which cause legal uncertainties hindering the smooth functioning of the internal market and the proper development of the information society in Europe should be adjusted, and inconsistent national responses to the technological developments should be avoided, whilst differences not adversely affecting the functioning of the internal market need not be removed or prevented.

(8) The various social, societal and cultural implications of the information society require that account be taken of the specific features of the content of products and services.

(9) Any harmonisation of copyright and related rights must take as a basis a high level of protection, since such rights are crucial to intellectual creation. Their protection helps to ensure the maintenance and development of creativity in the interests of authors, performers, producers, consumers, culture, industry and the public at large. Intellectual property has therefore been recognised as an integral part of property.

(10) If authors or performers are to continue their creative and artistic work, they have to receive an appropriate reward for the use of their work, as must producers in order to be able to finance this work. The investment required to produce products such as phonograms, films or multimedia products, and services such as 'on-demand' services, is considerable. Adequate legal protection of intellectual property rights

is necessary in order to guarantee the availability of such a reward and provide the opportunity for satisfactory returns on this investment.

(11) A rigorous, effective system for the protection of copyright and related rights is one of the main ways of ensuring that European cultural creativity and production receive the necessary resources and of safeguarding the independence and dignity of artistic creators and performers.

(12) Adequate protection of copyright works and subject-matter of related rights is also of great importance from a cultural standpoint. Article 151 of the Treaty requires the Community to take cultural aspects into account in its action.

(13) A common search for, and consistent application at European level of, technical measures to protect works and other subject-matter and to provide the necessary information on rights are essential insofar as the ultimate aim of these measures is to give effect to the principles and guarantees laid down in law.

(14) This Directive should seek to promote learning and culture by protecting works and other subject-matter while permitting exceptions or limitations in the public interest for the purpose of education and teaching.

(15) The Diplomatic Conference held under the auspices of the World Intellectual Property Organisation (WIPO) in December 1996 led to the adoption of two new Treaties, the 'WIPO Copyright Treaty' and the 'WIPO Performances and Phonograms Treaty', dealing respectively with the protection of authors and the protection of performers and phonogram producers. Those Treaties update the international protection for copyright and related rights significantly, not least with regard to the so-called 'digital agenda', and improve the means to fight piracy world-wide. The Community and a majority of Member States have already signed the Treaties and the process of making arrangements for the ratification of the Treaties by the Community and the Member States is under way. This Directive also serves to implement a number of the new international obligations.

(16) Liability for activities in the network environment concerns not only copyright and related rights but also other areas, such as defamation, misleading advertising, or infringement of trademarks, and is addressed horizontally in Directive 2000/31/EC of the European Parliament and of the Council of 8 June 2000 on certain legal aspects of information society services, in particular electronic commerce, in the internal market ('Directive on electronic commerce'), which clarifies and harmonises various legal issues relating to information society services including electronic commerce. This Directive should be implemented within a timescale similar to that for the implementation of the Directive on electronic commerce, since that Directive provides a harmonised framework of principles and

provisions relevant inter alia to important parts of this Directive. This Directive is without prejudice to provisions relating to liability in that Directive.

(17) It is necessary, especially in the light of the requirements arising out of the digital environment, to ensure that collecting societies achieve a higher level of rationalisation and transparency with regard to compliance with competition rules.

(18) This Directive is without prejudice to the arrangements in the Member States concerning the management of rights such as extended collective licences.

(19) The moral rights of rightholders should be exercised according to the legislation of the Member States and the provisions of the Berne Convention for the Protection of Literary and Artistic Works, of the WIPO Copyright Treaty and of the WIPO Performances and Phonograms Treaty. Such moral rights remain outside the scope of this Directive.

(20) This Directive is based on principles and rules already laid down in the Directives currently in force in this area, in particular [the Software, Rental Right, Cable and Satellite, Term and Database Directives], and it develops those principles and rules and places them in the context of the information society. The provisions of this Directive should be without prejudice to the provisions of those Directives, unless otherwise provided in this Directive.

(21) This Directive should define the scope of the acts covered by the reproduction right with regard to the different beneficiaries. This should be done in conformity with the *acquis communautaire*. A broad definition of these acts is needed to ensure legal certainty within the internal market.

(22) The objective of proper support for the dissemination of culture must not be achieved by sacrificing strict protection of rights or by tolerating illegal forms of distribution of counterfeited or pirated works.

(23) This Directive should harmonise further the author's right of communication to the public. This right should be understood in a broad sense covering all communication to the public not present at the place where the communication originates. This right should cover any such transmission or retransmission of a work to the public by wire or wireless means, including broad-casting. This right should not cover any other acts.

(24) The right to make available to the public subject-matter referred to in Article 3(2) should be understood as covering all acts of making available such subject-matter to members of the public not present at the place where the act of making available originates, and as not covering any other acts.

(25) The legal uncertainty regarding the nature and the level of protection

of acts of on-demand transmission of copyright works and subject-matter protected by related rights over networks should be overcome by providing for harmonised protection at Community level. It should be made clear that all rightholders recognised by this Directive should have an exclusive right to make available to the public copyright works or any other subject-matter by way of interactive on-demand transmissions. Such interactive on-demand transmissions are characterised by the fact that members of the public may access them from a place and at a time individually chosen by them.

(26) With regard to the making available in on-demand services by broadcasters of their radio or television productions incorporating music from commercial phonograms as an integral part thereof, collective licensing arrangements are to be encouraged in order to facilitate the clearance of the rights concerned.

(27) The mere provision of physical facilities for enabling or making a communication does not in itself amount to communication within the meaning of this Directive.

(28) Copyright protection under this Directive includes the exclusive right to control distribution of the work incorporated in a tangible article. The first sale in the Community of the original of a work or copies thereof by the rightholder or with his consent exhausts the right to control resale of that object in the Community. This right should not be exhausted in respect of the original or of copies thereof sold by the rightholder or with his consent outside the Community. Rental and lending rights for authors have been established in Directive 92/100/EEC. The distribution right provided for in this Directive is without prejudice to the provisions relating to the rental and lending rights contained in Chapter I of that Directive.

(29) The question of exhaustion does not arise in the case of services and on-line services in particular. This also applies with regard to a material copy of a work or other subject-matter made by a user of such a service with the consent of the rightholder. Therefore, the same applies to rental and lending of the original and copies of works or other subject-matter which are services by nature. Unlike CD-ROM or CD-I, where the intellectual property is incorporated in a material medium, namely an item of goods, every on-line service is in fact an act which should be subject to authorisation where the copyright or related right so provides.

(30) The rights referred to in this Directive may be transferred, assigned or subject to the granting of contractual licences, without prejudice to the relevant national legislation on copyright and related rights.

(31) A fair balance of rights and interests between the different categories of rightholders, as well as between the different categories of rightholders and users of protected subject-matter must be safeguarded. The existing exceptions and limitations to the rights as set out by the Member States have to be reassessed in the light of the

new electronic environment. Existing differences in the exceptions and limitations to certain restricted acts have direct negative effects on the functioning of the internal market of copyright and related rights. Such differences could well become more pronounced in view of the further development of transborder exploitation of works and cross-border activities. In order to ensure the proper functioning of the internal market, such exceptions and limitations should be defined more harmoniously. The degree of their harmonisation should be based on their impact on the smooth functioning of the internal market.

(32) This Directive provides for an exhaustive enumeration of exceptions and limitations to the reproduction right and the right of communication to the public. Some exceptions or limitations only apply to the reproduction right, where appropriate. This list takes due account of the different legal traditions in Member States, while, at the same time, aiming to ensure a functioning internal market. Member States should arrive at a coherent application of these exceptions and limitations, which will be assessed when reviewing implementing legislation in the future.

(33) The exclusive right of reproduction should be subject to an exception to allow certain acts of temporary reproduction, which are transient or incidental reproductions, forming an integral and essential part of a technological process and carried out for the sole purpose of enabling either efficient transmission in a network between third parties by an intermediary, or a lawful use of a work or other subject-matter to be made. The acts of reproduction concerned should have no separate economic value on their own. To the extent that they meet these conditions, this exception should include acts which enable browsing as well as acts of caching to take place, including those which enable transmission systems to function efficiently, provided that the intermediary does not modify the information and does not interfere with the lawful use of technology, widely recognised and used by industry, to obtain data on the use of the information. A use should be considered lawful where it is authorised by the rightholder or not restricted by law.

(34) Member States should be given the option of providing for certain exceptions or limitations for cases such as educational and scientific purposes, for the benefit of public institutions such as libraries and archives, for purposes of news reporting, for quotations, for use by people with disabilities, for public security uses and for uses in administrative and judicial proceedings.

(35) In certain cases of exceptions or limitations, rightholders should receive fair compensation to compensate them adequately for the use made of their protected works or other subject-matter. When determining the form, detailed arrangements and possible level of such fair compensation, account should be taken of the particular circumstances of each case. When evaluating these circumstances, a

valuable criterion would be the possible harm to the rightholders resulting from the act in question. In cases where rightholders have already received payment in some other form, for instance as part of a licence fee, no specific or separate payment may be due. The level of fair compensation should take full account of the degree of use of technological protection measures referred to in this Directive. In certain situations. where the prejudice to the rightholder would be minimal, no obligation for payment may arise.

(36) The Member States may provide for fair compensation for rightholders also when applying the optional provisions on exceptions or limitations which do not require such compensation.

(37) Existing national schemes on reprography, where they exist, do not create major barriers to the internal market. Member States should be allowed to provide for an exception or limitation in respect of reprography.

(38) Member States should be allowed to provide for an exception or limitation to the reproduction right for certain types of reproduction of audio, visual and audio visual material for private use, accompanied by fair compensation. This may include the introduction or continuation of remuneration schemes to compensate for the prejudice to rightholders. Although differences between those remuneration schemes affect the functioning of the internal market, those differences, with respect to analogue private reproduction, should not have a significant impact on the development of the information society. Digital private copying is likely to be more widespread and have a greater economic impact. Due account should therefore be taken of the differences between digital and analogue private copying and a distinction should be made in certain respects between them.

(39) When applying the exception or limitation on private copying, Member States should take due account of technological and economic developments, in particular with respect to digital private copying and remuneration schemes, when effective technological protection measures are available. Such exceptions or limitations should not inhibit the use of technological measures or their enforcement against circumvention.

(40) Member States may provide for an exception or limitation for the benefit of certain non-profit making establishments, such as publicly accessible libraries and equivalent institutions, as well as archives. However, this should be limited to certain special cases covered by the reproduction right. Such an exception or limitation should not cover uses made in the context of on-line delivery of protected works or other subject-matter. This Directive should be without prejudice to the Member States' option to derogate from the exclusive public lending right in accordance with Article 5 of Directive 92/100/EEC. Therefore, specific contracts or licences should be promoted which,

without creating imbalances, favour such establishments and the disseminative purposes they serve.

(41) When applying the exception or limitation in respect of ephemeral recordings made by broadcasting organisations it is understood that a broadcaster's own facilities include those of a person acting on behalf of and under the responsibility of the broadcasting organisation.

(42) When applying the exception or limitation for non-commercial educational and scientific research purposes, including distance learning, the non-commercial nature of the activity in question should be determined by that activity as such. The organisational structure and the means of funding of the establishment concerned are not the decisive factors in this respect.

(43) It is in any case important for the Member States to adopt all necessary measures to facilitate access to works by persons suffering from a disability which constitutes an obstacle to the use of the works themselves, and to pay particular attention to accessible formats.

(44) When applying the exceptions and limitations provided for in this Directive, they should be exercised in accordance with international obligations. Such exceptions and imitations may not be applied in a way which prejudices the legitimate interests of the rightholder or which conflicts with the normal exploitation of his work or other subject-matter. The provision of such exceptions or limitations by Member States should, in particular, duly reflect the increased economic impact that such exceptions or limitations may have in the context of the new electronic environment. Therefore, the scope of certain exceptions or limitations may have to be even more limited when it comes to certain new uses of copyright works and other subject-matter.

(45) The exceptions and limitations referred to in Article 5(2), (3) and (4) should not, however, prevent the definition of contractual relations designed to ensure fair compensation for the rightholders insofar as permitted by national law.

(46) Recourse to mediation could help users and rightholders to settle disputes. The Commission, in cooperation with the Member States within the Contact Committee, should undertake a study to consider new legal ways of settling disputes concerning copyright and related rights.

(47) Technological development will allow rightholders to make use of technological measures designed to prevent or restrict acts not authorised by the rightholders of any copyright, rights related to copyright or the sui *generis* right in databases. The danger, however, exists that illegal activities might be carried out in order to enable or facilitate the circumvention of the technical protection provided by these measures. In order to avoid fragmented legal approaches that could potentially hinder the functioning of the internal market, there

is a need to provide for harmonised legal protection against circumvention of effective technological measures and against provision of devices and products or services to this effect.

(48) Such legal protection should be provided in respect of technological measures that effectively restrict acts not authorised by the rightholders of any copyright, rights related to copyright or the sui *generis* right in databases without, however, preventing the normal operation of electronic equipment and its technological development. Such legal protection implies no obligation to design devices, products, components or services to correspond to technological measures, so long as such device, product, component or service does not otherwise fall under the prohibition of Article 6. Such legal protection should respect proportionality and should not prohibit those devices or activities which have a commercially significant purpose or use other than to circumvent the technical protection. In particular, this protection should not hinder research into cryptography.

(49) The legal protection of technological measures is without prejudice to the application of any national provisions which may prohibit the private possession of devices, products or components for the circumvention of technological measures.

(50) Such a harmonised legal protection does not affect the specific provisions on protection provided for by Directive 91/250/EEC. In particular, it should not apply to the protection of technological measures used in connection with computer programs, which is exclusively addressed in that Directive. It should neither inhibit nor prevent the development or use of any means of circumventing a technological measure that is necessary to enable acts to be undertaken in accordance with the terms of Article 5(3) or Article 6 of Directive 91/250/EEC. Articles 5 and 6 of that Directive exclusively determine exceptions to the exclusive rights applicable to computer programs.

(51) The legal protection of technological measures applies without prejudice to public policy, as reflected in Article 5, or public security. Member States should promote voluntary measures taken by rightholders, including the conclusion and implementation of agreements between rightholders and other parties concerned, to accommodate achieving the objectives of certain exceptions or limitations provided for in national law in accordance with this Directive. In the absence of such voluntary measures or agreements within a reasonable period of time, Member States should take appropriate measures to ensure that rightholders provide beneficiaries of such exceptions or limitations with appropriate means of benefiting from them, by modifying an implemented technological measure or by other means. However, in order to prevent abuse of such measures taken by right holders, including within the framework of agreements, or taken by a Member State, any technological measures applied in implementation of such measures

should enjoy legal protection.

(52) When implementing an exception or limitation for private copying in accordance with Article 5(2)(b), Member States should likewise promote the use of voluntary measures to accommodate achieving the objectives of such exception or limitation. If, within a reasonable period of time, no such voluntary measures to make reproduction for private use possible have been taken, Member States may take measures to enable beneficiaries of the exception or limitation concerned to benefit from it. Voluntary measures taken by rightholders, including agreements between rightholders and other parties concerned, as well as measures taken by Member States, do not prevent rightholders from using technological measures which are consistent with the exceptions or limitations on private copying in national law in accordance with Article 5(2)(b), taking account of the condition of fair compensation under that provision and the possible differentiation between various conditions of use in accordance with Article 5(5), such as controlling the number of reproductions. In order to prevent abuse of such measures, any technological measures applied in their implementation should enjoy legal protection.

(53) The protection of technological measures should ensure a secure environment for the provision of interactive on-demand services, in such a way that members of the public may access works or other subject-matter from a place and at a time individually chosen by them. Where such services are governed by contractual arrangements, the first and second subparagraphs of Article 6(4) should not apply. Non-interactive forms of online use should remain subject to those provisions.

(54) Important progress has been made in the international standardisation of technical systems of identification of works and protected subject-matter in digital format. In an increasingly networked environment, differences between technological measures could lead to an incompatibility of systems within the Community. Compatibility and interoperability of the different systems should be encouraged. It would be highly desirable to encourage the development of global systems.

(55) Technological development will facilitate the distribution of works, notably on networks, and this will entail the need for rightholders to identify better the work or other subject-matter, the author or any other rightholder, and to provide information about the terms and conditions of use of the work or other subject-matter in order to render easier the management of rights attached to them. Rightholders should be encouraged to use markings indicating, in addition to the information referred to above, inter alia their authorisation when putting works or other subject-matter on networks.

(56) There is, however, the danger that illegal activities might be carried

out in order to remove or alter the electronic copyright-management information attached to it, or otherwise to distribute, import for distribution, broadcast, communicate to the public or make available to the public works or other protected subject-matter from which such information has been removed without authority. In order to avoid fragmented legal approaches that could potentially hinder the functioning of the internal market, there is a need to provide for harmonised legal protection against any of these activities.

(57) Any such rights-management information systems referred to above may, depending on their design, at the same time process personal data about the consumption patterns of protected subject-matter by individuals and allow for tracing of on-line behaviour. These technical means, in their technical functions, should incorporate privacy safeguards in accordance with Directive 95/46/EC of the European Parliament and of the Council of 24 October 1995 on the protection of individuals with movement of such data.

(58) Member States should provide for effective sanctions and remedies for infringements of rights and obligations as set out in this Directive. They should take all the measures necessary to ensure that those sanctions and remedies are applied. The sanctions thus provided for should be effective, proportionate and dissuasive and should include the possibility of seeking damages and/or injunctive relief and, where appropriate, of applying for seizure of infringing material.

(59) In the digital environment, in particular, the services of intermediaries may increasingly be used by third parties for infringing activities. In many cases such intermediaries are best placed to bring such infringing activities to an end. Therefore, without prejudice to any other sanctions and remedies available, rightholders should have the possibility of applying for an injunction against an intermediary who carries a third party's infringement of a protected work or other subject-matter in a network. This possibility should be available even where the acts carried out by the intermediary are exempted under Article 5. The conditions and modalities relating to such injunctions should be left to the national law of the Member States.

(60) The protection provided under this Directive should be without prejudice to national or Community legal provisions in other areas, such as industrial property, data protection, conditional access, access to public documents, and the rule of media exploitation chronology, which may affect the protection of copyright or related rights.

(61) In order to comply with the WIPO Performances and Phonograms Treaty, Directives 92/100/EEC and 93/98/EEC should be amended,

HAVE ADOPTED THIS DIRECTIVE:

CHAPTER I
OBJECTIVE AND SCOPE

Article 1
Scope

1. This Directive concerns the legal protection of copyright and related rights in the framework of the internal market, with particular emphasis on the information society.

2. Except in the cases referred to in Article 11, this Directive shall leave intact and shall in no way affect existing Community provisions relating to:

(a) the legal protection of computer programs;

(b) rental right, lending right and certain rights related to copyright in the field of intellectual property;

(c) copyright and related rights applicable to broadcasting of programmes by satellite and cable retransmission;

(d) the term of protection of copyright and certain related rights;

(e) the legal protection of databases.

CHAPTER II
RIGHTS AND EXCEPTIONS

Article 2
Reproduction right

Member States shall provide for the exclusive right to authorise or prohibit direct or indirect, temporary or permanent reproduction by any means and in any form, in whole or in part:

(a) for authors, of their works;

(b) for performers, of fixations of their performances;

(c) for phonogram producers, of their phonograms;

(d) for the producers of the first fixations of films, in respect of the original and copies of their films;

(e) for broadcasting organisations, of fixations of their broadcasts, whether those broadcasts are transmitted by wire or over the air, including by cable or satellite.

Article 3
Right of communication to the public of works and right of making available to the public other subject-matter

1. Member States shall provide authors with the exclusive right to authorise or prohibit any communication to the public of their works, by wire or wireless means, including the making available to the public of their works in such a way that members of the public may access them from a place and at a time individually chosen by them.

2.   Member States shall provide for the exclusive right to authorise or prohibit the making available to the public, by wire or wireless means, in such a way that members of the public may access them from a place and at a time individually chosen by them:

(a)   for performers, of fixations of their performances;

(b)   for phonogram producers, of their phonograms;

(c)   for the producers of the first fixations of films, of the original and copies of their films;

(d)   for broadcasting organisations, of fixations of their broadcasts, whether these broadcasts are transmitted by wire or over the air, including by cable or satellite.

3.   The rights referred to in paragraphs 1 and 2 shall not be exhausted by any act of communication to the public or making available to the public as set out in this Article.

Article 4
Distribution right

1.   Member States shall provide for authors, in respect of the original of their works or of copies thereof, the exclusive right to authorise or prohibit any form of distribution to the public by sale or otherwise.

2.   The distribution right shall not be exhausted within the Community in respect of the original or copies of the work, except where the first sale or other transfer of ownership in the Community of that object is made by the rightholder or with his consent.

Article 5
Exceptions and limitations

1.   Temporary acts of reproduction referred to in Article 2, which are transient or incidental [and] an integral and essential part of a technological process and whose sole purpose is to enable:

(a)   a transmission in a network between third parties by an intermediary, or

(b)   a lawful use

of a work or other subject-matter to be made, and which have no independent economic significance, shall be exempted from the reproduction right provided for in Article 2.

2.   Member States may provide for exceptions or limitations to the reproduction right provided for in Article 2 in the following cases:

(a)   in respect of reproductions on paper or any similar medium, effected by the use of any kind of photographic technique or by some other process having similar effects, with the exception of sheet music, provided that the right holders receive fair compensation;

(b)   in respect of reproductions on any medium made by a natural person for private use and for ends that are neither directly nor indirectly commercial, on condition that the rightholders receive fair compensation which takes account of the application or non-application of technological measures referred to in Article 6 to the work or subject matter concerned;

(c) in respect of specific acts of reproduction made by publicly accessible libraries, educational establishments or museums, or by archives, which are not for direct or indirect economic or commercial advantage;

(d) in respect of ephemeral recordings of works made by broadcasting organisations by means of their own facilities and for their own broadcasts; the preservation of these recordings in official archives may, on the grounds of their exceptional documentary character, be permitted;

(e) in respect of reproductions of broadcasts made by social institutions pursuing non-commercial purposes, such as hospitals or prisons, on condition that the rightholders.

3. Member States may provide for exceptions or limitations to the rights provided for in Articles 2 and 3 in the following cases:

(a) use for the sole purpose of illustration for teaching or scientific research, as long as the source, including the author's name, is indicated, unless this turns out to be impossible and to the extent justified by the non-commercial purpose to be achieved;

(b) uses, for the benefit of people with a disability, which are directly related to the disability and of a non-commercial nature, to the extent required by the specific disability;

(c) reproduction by the press, communication to the public or making available of published articles on current economic, political or religious topics or of broadcast works or other subject-matter of the same character, in cases where such use is not expressly reserved, and as long as the source, including the author's name, is indicated, or use of works or other subject-matter in connection with the reporting of current events to the extent justified by the informatory purpose and as long as the source, including the author's name, is indicated, unless this turns out to be impossible;

(d) quotation for purposes such as criticism or review, provided that they relate to a work or other subject-matter which has already been lawfully made available to the public, that, unless this turns out to be impossible, the source, including the author's name, is indicated, and that their use is in accordance with fair practice, and to the extent required by the specific purpose;

(e) use for the purpose of public security or to ensure the proper performance or reporting of administrative, parliamentary or judicial proceedings;

(f) use of political speeches as well as extracts of public lectures or similar works or subject-matter to the extent justified by the informatory purpose and provided that the source, including the author's name, is indicated, except where this turns out to be impossible;

(g) use during religious celebrations or official celebrations organised by a public authority;

(h) use of works, such as works of architecture or sculpture, made to be located permanently in public places;

(i) incidental inclusion of a work or other subject-matter in other material;

(j) use for the purpose of advertising the public exhibition or sale of artistic works, to the extent necessary to promote the event, excluding any other commercial use;

(k) use for the purpose of caricature, parody or pastiche;

(l) use in connection with the demonstration or repair of equipment;

(m) use of an artistic work in the form of a building or a drawing or plan of a building for the purpose of reconstructing the building;

(n) use by communication or making available, for the purpose of research or private study, to individual members of the public by dedicated terminals on the premises of establishments referred to in paragraph 2(c) of works and other subject-matter not subject to purchase or licensing terms which are contained in their collections;

(o) use in certain other cases of minor importance where exceptions or limitations already exist under national law, provided that they only concern analogue uses and do not affect the free circulation of goods and services within the Community, without prejudice to the other exceptions and limitations contained in this Article.

4. Where the Member States may provide for an exception or limitation to the right of reproduction pursuant to paragraphs 2 and 3, they may provide similarly for an exception or limitation to the right of distribution as referred to in Article 4 to the extent justified by the purpose of the authorised act of reproduction.

5. The exception and limitations provided for in paragraphs 1, 2, 3 and 4 shall only be applied in certain special cases which do not conflict with a normal exploitation of the work or other subject-matter and do not unreasonably prejudice the legitimate interests of the rightholder.

CHAPTER III
PROTECTION OF TECHNOLOGICAL MEASURES AND RIGHTS MANAGEMENT INFORMATION

Article 6
Obligations as to technological measures

1. Member states shall provide adequate legal protection against the circumvention of any effective technological measures, which the person concerned carries out in the knowledge, or with reasonable grounds to know,

that he or she is pursuing that objective.

2. Member states shall provide adequate legal protection against the manufacture, import, distribution, sale, rental, advertisement for sale or rental, or possession for commercial purposes of devices, products or components or the provision of services which:

(a) are promoted, advertised or marketed for the purpose of circumvention of, or

(b) have only a limited commercially significant purpose or use other than to circumvent, or

(c) are primarily designed, produced, adapted or performed for the purpose of enabling or facilitating the circumvention of,

any effective technological measures.

3. For the purpose of this Directive, the expression 'technological measures' means any technology, device or component that, in the normal course of its operation, is designed to prevent or restrict acts, in respect of works or other subject-matter, which are not authorised by the rightholder of any copyright or any right related to copyright as provided for by law or the *sui generis* right provided for in Chapter III of Directive 96/9/EC. Technological measures shall be deemed 'effective' where the use of a protected work or other subject-matter is controlled by the rightholders through application of an access control or protection process, such as encryption, scrambling or other transformation of the work or other subject-matter or a copy control mechanism, which achieves the protection objective.

4. Notwithstanding the legal protection provided for in paragraph 1, in the absence of voluntary measure taken by rightholders, including agreements between rightholders and other parties concerned, Member States shall take appropriate measures to ensure that rightholders make available to the beneficiary of an exception or limitation provided for in national law in accordance with Article 5(2)(a), (2)(c), (2)(d), (2)(e), (3)(a), (3)(b) or (3)(e) the means of benefiting from that exception or limitation, to the extent necessary to benefit from that exception or limitation and were that beneficiary has legal access to the protected work or subject-matter concerned.

A Member State may also take such measures in respect of a beneficiary of an exception or limitation provided for in accordance with Article 5(2)(b), unless reproduction for private use has already been made possible by rightholders to the extent necessary to benefit from the exception or limitation concerned and in accordance with provisions of Article 5(2)(b) and (5), without preventing rightholders from adopting adequate measures regarding the number of reproductions in accordance with these provisions.

The technological measures applied voluntarily by rightholders, including those applied in implementation of voluntary agreements, and technological measures applied in implementation of the measures taken by Member States, shall enjoy the legal protection provided for in paragraph 1.

The provisions of the first and second subparagraphs shall not apply to works or other subject-matter available to the public on agreed contractual terms in such a way that members of the public may access them from a place and at a time individually chosen by them.

When this Article is applied in the context of Directive 92/100/EEC and 96/9/EC, this paragraph shall apply *mutatis mutandis*.

Article 7
Obligations concerning rights-management information

1.   Member States shall provide for adequate legal protection against any person knowingly performing without authority any of the following acts:

(a)   the removal or alteration of any electronic rights-management information;

(b)   the distribution, importation for distribution, broadcasting, communication or making available to the public of works or other subject-matter protected under the Directive or under Chapter III of Directive 96/9/EC from which electronic rights-management information has been removed or altered without authority,

if such person knows, or has reasonable grounds to know, that by so doing he is inducing, enabling, facilitating, or concealing an infringement of any copyright or any rights related to copyright as provided by law, or of the *sui generis* right provided for in Chapter III of Directive 96/9/EC.

2.   For the purposes of this Directive, the expression 'rights-management information' means any information provided by rightholders which identifies the work or other subject-matter referred to in this Directive or covered by the sui generis right provided for in Chapter III of Directive 96/9/EC, the author or any other rightholder, or information about the terms and condition of use of the work or other subject-matter, and any numbers or codes that represent such information.

The first subparagraph shall apply when any of these items of information is associated with a copy of, or appears in connection with the communication to the public of, a work or other subject-matter referred to in this Directive or covered by the *sui generis* right provided for in the Chapter III of Directive 96/9/EC.

CHAPTER IV
COMMON PROVISIONS

Article 8
Sanctions and remedies

1.   Member States shall provide appropriate sanctions and remedies in respect of infringements of the rights and obligations set out in this Directive and shall take all the measures necessary to ensure that those sanctions and remedies are applied. The sanctions thus provided for shall be effective, proportionate and dissuasive.

2.   Each Member State shall take the measures necessary to ensure that rightholders whose interests are affected by an infringing activity carried out

on its territory can bring an action for damages and/or apply for an injunction and, where appropriate, for the seizure of infringing material as well as of devices, products or components referred to in Article 6(2).

3. Member States shall ensure that rightholders are in a position to apply for an injunction against intermediaries whose services are used by a third party to infringe a copyright or related right.

Article 9
Continued application of other legal provisions

This Directive shall be without prejudice to provisions concerning in particular patent rights, trade marks, design rights, utility models, topographies of semi-conductor products, type faces, conditional access, access to cable of broadcasting services, protection of national treasures, legal deposit requirements, laws on restrictive practices and unfair competition, trade secrets, security, confidentiality, data protection and privacy, access to public documents, the law of contract.

Article 10
Application over time

1. The provisions of this Directive shall apply in respect of all works and other subject-matter referred to in this Directive which are, on 22 December 2002, protected by the Member States' legislation in the field of copyright and related rights, or which meet the criteria for protection under the provisions of this Directive or the provisions referred to in Article 1(2).

2. This Directive shall apply without prejudice to any acts concluded and rights acquired before 22 December 2002.

Article 11
Technical adaptions

1. Directive 92/100/EC is hereby amended as follows:

(a) Article 7 shall be deleted;

(b) Article 10(3) shall be replaced by the following:

'3. The limitations shall only be applied in certain special cases which do not conflict with a normal exploitation of the subject-matter and do not unreasonably prejudice the legitimate interests of the rightholder.'

2. Article 3(2) of Directive 93/98/EEC shall be replaced by the following:

'2. The rights of producers of phonograms shall expire 50 years after the fixation is made. However, if the phonogram has been lawfully published within this period, the said right shall expire 50 years from the date of the first lawful publication. If no lawful publication has taken place within the period mentioned in the first sentence, and if the phonogram has been lawfully communicated to the public within this period, the said rights shall expire 50 years from the date of the first lawful communication to the public.

However, where through the expiry of the term of protection granted pursuant to this paragraph in its version before amendment by Directive 20001/29/EC of the European Parliament and of the Council of 22 May 2001 on the harmonisation of certain aspects of copyright and related rights in the information society the rights of producers of phonograms are no longer protected on 22 December 2002, this paragraph shall not have the effect of protecting those rights anew.

Article 12
Final provisions

1. Not later than 22 December 2004 and every three years thereafter, the Commission shall submit to the European Parliament, the Council and the Economic and Social Committee a report on the application of this Directive, in which, inter alia, on the basis of specific information supplied by the Member States, it shall examine in particular the application of Articles 5, 6 and 8 in the light of the development of the digital market. In the case of Article 6, it shall examine in particular whether that Article confers a sufficient level of protection and whether acts which are permitted by law are being adversely affected by the use of effective technological measures. Where necessary, in particular to ensure the functioning of the internal market pursuant to Article 14 of the Treaty, it shall submit proposals for amendments to this Directive.

2. Protection of rights related to copyright under this Directive shall leave intact and shall in no way affect the protection of copyright.

3. A contact committee is hereby established. It shall be composed of representatives of the competent authorities of the Member States. It shall be chaired by a representative of the Commission and shall meet either on the initiative of the chairman or at the request of the delegation of a Member State.

4. The tasks of the committee shall be as follows:

(a) to examine the impact of this Directive on the functioning of the internal market, and to highlight any difficulties;

(b) to organise consultations on all questions deriving from the application of this Directive;

(c) to facilitate the exchange of information on relevant developments in legislation and case-law, as well as relevant economic, social, cultural and technological developments;

(d) to act as a forum for the assessment of the digital market in works and other items, including private copying and the use of technological measures.

Article 13
Implementation

1. Member States shall bring into force the laws, regulations and administrative provisions necessary to comply with this Directive before 22

December 2002. They shall forthwith inform the Commission thereof.

When Member States adopt these measures, they shall contain a reference to this Directive or shall be accompanied by such reference on the occasion of their official publication. The methods of making such reference shall be laid down by Member States.

2. Member States shall communicate to the commission the text of the provisions of domestic law which they adopt in the field governed by this Directive.

Article 14
Entry into force

This Directive shall enter into force on the day of its publication in the Official Journal of the European Communities.

Article 15
Addressees

This Directive is addressed to the Member States.

Done at Brussels, 22 May 2001.